The Institutes' Handbook of Insurance Policies

10th Edition

The Institutes
720 Providence Road, Suite 100
Malvern, PA 19355-3433

10th Edition • 1st Printing • September 2011

978-0-89463-500-7

Foreword

The Institutes are the trusted leader in delivering proven knowledge solutions that drive powerful business results for the risk management and property-casualty insurance industry. For more than 100 years, The Institutes have been meeting the industry's changing professional development needs with customer-driven products and services.

In conjunction with industry experts and members of the academic community, our Knowledge Resources Department develops our course and program content, including Institutes study materials. Practical and technical knowledge gained from Institutes courses enhances qualifications, improves performance, and contributes to professional growth—all of which drive results.

The Institutes' proven knowledge helps individuals and organizations achieve powerful results with a variety of flexible, customer-focused options:

Recognized Credentials—The Institutes offer an unmatched range of widely recognized and industry-respected specialty credentials. The Institutes' Chartered Property Casualty Underwriter (CPCU) professional designation is designed to provide a broad understanding of the property-casualty insurance industry. Depending on professional needs, CPCU students may select either a commercial insurance focus or a personal risk management and insurance focus and may choose from a variety of electives.

In addition, The Institutes offer certificate or designation programs in a variety of disciplines, including these:

Claims

Commercial underwriting

Fidelity and surety bonding

General insurance

Insurance accounting and finance

Insurance information technology

Insurance production and agency
   management

Insurance regulation and compliance

Management

Marine insurance

Personal insurance

Premium auditing

Quality insurance services

Reinsurance

Risk management

Surplus lines

Ethics—Ethical behavior is crucial to preserving not only the trust on which insurance transactions are based, but also the public's trust in our industry as a whole. All Institutes designations now have an ethics requirement, which is delivered online and free of charge. The ethics requirement content is designed specifically for insurance practitioners and uses insurance-based case studies to outline an ethical framework. More information is available in the Programs section of our Web site, www.TheInstitutes.org.

Flexible Online Learning—The Institutes have an unmatched variety of technical insurance content covering topics from accounting to underwriting, which we now deliver through hundreds of online courses. These cost-effective self-study courses are a convenient way to fill gaps in technical knowledge in a matter of hours without ever leaving the office.

Continuing Education—A majority of The Institutes' courses are filed for CE credit in most states. We also deliver quality, affordable, online CE courses quickly and conveniently through our newest business unit, CEU.com. Visit www.CEU.com to learn more.

College Credits—Most Institutes courses carry college credit recommendations from the American Council on Education. A variety of courses also qualify for credits toward certain associate, bachelor's, and master's degrees at several prestigious colleges and universities. More information is available in the Student Services section of our Web site, www.TheInstitutes.org.

Custom Applications—The Institutes collaborate with corporate customers to utilize our trusted course content and flexible delivery options in developing customized solutions that help them achieve their unique organizational goals.

Insightful Analysis—Our Insurance Research Council (IRC) division conducts public policy research on important contemporary issues in property-casualty insurance and risk management. Visit www.ircweb.org to learn more or purchase its most recent studies.

The Institutes look forward to serving the risk management and property-casualty insurance industry for another 100 years. We welcome comments from our students and course leaders; your feedback helps us continue to improve the quality of our study materials.

Peter L. Miller, CPCU
President and CEO
The Institutes

Introduction

The Institutes' Handbook of Insurance Policies is assigned or recommended for various courses offered by The Institutes. In addition, the *Handbook* is designed for any insurance student or professional in need of a guide to representative property and liability insurance policies.

For students, the primary purpose of the *Handbook* is to provide samples of insurance policies discussed in Institutes textbooks. Developing the ability to read and interpret insurance policies is a central objective of CPCU studies and of several other Institutes courses. Proficiency in reading and interpreting insurance policies cannot be developed without studying actual insurance policies. Using the *Handbook* will increase your understanding of the policy provisions discussed in the textbook for the course you are taking, and it will provide the basis for answering questions in the course guide.

The policy forms reprinted in the *Handbook* are organized by line of business, such as Homeowners, Personal Auto, Commercial Property, and so forth. Each grouping of forms in a particular line is preceded by a concise overview of that line.

The *Handbook* contains two features to help you find particular policies: the Table of Contents (pages vii to x) and the Alphabetical Listing of Forms (pages xi to xii).

For more information about The Institutes' programs, please call our Customer Service Department at (800) 644-2101, e-mail us at customerservice@TheInstitutes.org, or visit our Web site at www.TheInstitutes.org.

Table of Contents

Commercial Inland Marine

Ocean Marine

Commercial Crime

Equipment Breakdown

Businessowners

Farm

Commercial General Liability

Commercial Auto

Workers Compensation and Employers Liability

Miscellaneous Commercial Insurance Policies

Surety Bonds

Alphabetical Listing of Forms

Acknowledgments

The Institutes is grateful to the following organizations, which provided sample insurance forms for inclusion in *The CPCU Handbook of Insurance Policies*:

American Association of Insurance Services

American Institute of Marine Underwriters

Associated Aviation Underwriters

Chubb Group of Insurance Companies

Federal Emergency Management Agency

Global Aerospace, Inc.

Insurance Services Office, Inc.

International Marine Underwriters/OneBeacon Insurance Group

Markel Corporation

National Council on Compensation Insurance, Inc.

Shand Morahan & Company, Inc.

United States General Services Administration

XL America, Inc.

Homeowners Insurance

Homeowners insurance covers an individual or a family against many significant residential property and nonbusiness liability loss exposures. Although various homeowners forms are in use, most follow a format similar to that of the homeowners program of Insurance Services Office, Inc. (ISO).

Please note forms corresponding to the 2000 Homeowners Program and the 2011 Homeowners Program are included here for reference purposes.

Available Forms

The ISO homeowners program includes six policy forms and many endorsements for meeting particular coverage needs:

Homeowners 2—Broad Form

Homeowners 3—Special Form

Homeowners 4—Contents Broad Form

Homeowners 5—Comprehensive Form

Homeowners 6—Unit-Owners Form

Homeowners 8—Modified Coverage Form

Forms 2, 3, 5, and 8 are designed for owner-occupants; form 4 is designed for tenants living in apartments; and form 6 is designed for condominium unit owners. The homeowners form reproduced in this section of the *Handbook* is form 3, which is commonly used.

Coverages Included

All of the ISO homeowners forms provide the same liability and medical payments coverage, expressed in Section II of the policy. However, the property coverages, expressed in Section I of the policy, differ among the various forms. The owner-occupant forms—2, 3, 5, and 8—provide the property coverages listed below:

1. *Coverage A–Dwelling.* Covers physical loss of or damage to the dwelling.
2. *Coverage B–Other Structures.* Covers physical loss of or damage to other structures, such as a detached garage or shed.
3. *Coverage C–Personal Property.* Covers physical loss of or damage to personal property.
4. *Coverage D–Loss of Use.* Covers additional living expenses or loss of fair rental value when the property is uninhabitable because of a covered loss.

Form 4 provides only Coverage C and Coverage D because an apartment tenant normally only needs to cover his or her personal property and loss of use. Form 6 provides a modified version of Coverage A to insure building elements for which the unit owner may be responsible, such as alterations, appliances, and fixtures. Form 6 also covers personal property and loss of use.

Covered Causes of Loss

The causes of property loss covered by homeowners policies can be classified according to three levels of coverage: basic, broad, and special.

- The basic causes of loss consist of the following perils specifically named in the policy: fire, lightning, windstorm, hail, explosion, riot or civil commotion, aircraft, vehicles, smoke, vandalism or malicious mischief, theft, and volcanic eruption. Form 8 covers the basic causes of loss only.
- The broad causes of loss consist of the basic causes of loss plus six others. Forms 2, 4, and 6 cover the broad causes of loss.
- The special causes of loss include any "risk of direct physical loss" that is not specifically excluded. This approach, also called "open perils" coverage, covers even more causes of loss than the broad form.

Form 3 covers the special causes of loss with respect to the dwelling, other structures, and resulting loss of use. However, with respect to personal property (Coverage C), form 3 covers the broad causes of loss. Form 5 covers the special causes of loss for all covered property, including personal property.

All homeowners forms contain various exclusions relating to causes of loss. For example, all standard homeowners forms exclude flood and earthquake. Earthquake coverage can be added by endorsement. Flood can usually only be covered through a separate flood policy.

Valuation Provisions

Homeowners forms 2, 3, 4, 5, and 6 provide replacement cost coverage on most property losses involving buildings and other structures. Personal property losses are covered on an actual cash value basis unless the policy is modified by endorsement to provide personal property replacement cost coverage.

Form 8 is called the Modified Coverage Form mainly because of its valuation provisions. Instead of covering buildings and other structures on a replacement cost basis, it covers them on the basis of what it would cost to repair or replace the property "using common construction materials and methods where functionally equivalent to and less costly than obsolete, antique or custom construction materials and methods." Like the other homeowners forms, it covers personal property on an actual cash value basis.

Section II Coverages

Section II of the homeowners policy provides two coverages:

Coverage E—Personal Liability

Coverage F—Medical Payments to Others

Coverage E protects the homeowner and other insured persons against claims or suits made by others for bodily injury or property damage resulting from the insured's use of the residence premises or the insured's nonbusiness activities. The insurer agrees both to defend the insured against claims or suits alleging damages that would be covered by the policy and to pay damages to the claimant if the insured is liable for such damages. Several exclusions apply. Most notably, perhaps, auto liability is not covered.

Coverage F provides for medical payments to persons other than the insured or residents of the insured's household who are injured on the insured's premises or in connection with the insured's activities. Medical payments coverage is a form of accident insurance, rather than liability insurance, and therefore does not require that the insured be legally obligated to pay damages to the injured person. The coverage is usually limited to a small amount, such as $1,000 per person.

Homeowners Endorsements

Many endorsements are available for modifying homeowners policies to meet particular needs. Two commonly used endorsements are reproduced in the *Handbook*:

1. The Personal Property Replacement Cost Loss Settlement Endorsement, which amends the policy to cover personal property on a replacement cost basis.
2. The Scheduled Personal Property Endorsement, which covers certain classes of valuable property on a scheduled (specifically described), special-form basis, without any deductible.

POLICY NUMBER: **HOMEOWNERS**
HO DS 01 05 11

HOMEOWNERS POLICY DECLARATIONS

Company Name: Businesstown Insurance	

Producer Name: A.M. Abel

Named Insured: David M. and Joan G. Smith

Mailing Address:

216 Brookside Drive
Anytown, USA 40000

The Residence Premises Is Located At The Above Address Unless Otherwise Stated:

Policy Period Year(s)	
Number Of Year(s): 1	
From: March 30, 20X1	12:01 AM standard time at the residence premises
To: March 30, 20X2	12:01 AM standard time at the residence premises

We will provide the insurance described in this policy in return for the premium and compliance with all applicable policy provisions.

Coverage is provided where a premium or limit of liability is shown for the coverage.

Section I – Coverages	Limit Of Liability	
A. **Dwelling**	$ 220,000	
B. **Other Structures**	$ 22,000	
C. **Personal Property**	$ 110,000	
D. **Loss Of Use**	$ 66,000	
Section II – Coverages		
E. **Personal Liability**	$ 300,000	Each Occurrence
F. **Medical Payments To Others**	$ 1,000	Each Person
	Premium	
Basic Policy Premium	$ 550.00	
Additional Premium Charges Or Credits Related To Other Coverages Or Endorsements:		
Scheduled Personal Property Endorsement HO 04 61	$ 40.00	
	$	
	$	
Total Premium	$ 590.00	

Homeowners

Forms And Endorsements Made Part Of This Policy (Number(s) And Edition Date(s))
HO 00 03 10 00, HO 04 61 10 00

Deductible: Section I: $ 500   Other: $

Section II – Other Insured Locations (Address):

Mortgagee(s)/Lienholder(s)		
Name	**Address**	**Loan Number**
1. Argot Mortgage Assn. C/O Mortgagee, Inc.	P.O. Box 5000 Businesstown, USA 55000	
2.		
3.		

Loss Payee(s) – Personal Property (Name and Address of Loss Payee and Personal Property Involved)		
Name	**Address**	**Personal Property**
1.		
2.		
3.		

 HO DS 01 05 11

Countersignature Of Authorized Representative
Name:
Title:
Signature:
Date:

Homeowners

2000 EDITION

HOMEOWNERS
HO 00 03 10 00

HOMEOWNERS 3 – SPECIAL FORM

AGREEMENT

We will provide the insurance described in this policy in return for the premium and compliance with all applicable provisions of this policy.

DEFINITIONS

A. In this policy, "you" and "your" refer to the "named insured" shown in the Declarations and the spouse if a resident of the same household. "We", "us" and "our" refer to the Company providing this insurance.

B. In addition, certain words and phrases are defined as follows:

1. "Aircraft Liability", "Hovercraft Liability", "Motor Vehicle Liability" and "Watercraft Liability", subject to the provisions in **b.** below, mean the following:

a. Liability for "bodily injury" or "property damage" arising out of the:

(1) Ownership of such vehicle or craft by an "insured";

(2) Maintenance, occupancy, operation, use, loading or unloading of such vehicle or craft by any person;

(3) Entrustment of such vehicle or craft by an "insured" to any person;

(4) Failure to supervise or negligent supervision of any person involving such vehicle or craft by an "insured"; or

(5) Vicarious liability, whether or not imposed by law, for the actions of a child or minor involving such vehicle or craft.

b. For the purpose of this definition:

(1) Aircraft means any contrivance used or designed for flight except model or hobby aircraft not used or designed to carry people or cargo;

(2) Hovercraft means a self-propelled motorized ground effect vehicle and includes, but is not limited to, flarecraft and air cushion vehicles;

(3) Watercraft means a craft principally designed to be propelled on or in water by wind, engine power or electric motor; and

(4) Motor vehicle means a "motor vehicle" as defined in **7.** below.

2. "Bodily injury" means bodily harm, sickness or disease, including required care, loss of services and death that results.

3. "Business" means:

a. A trade, profession or occupation engaged in on a full-time, part-time or occasional basis; or

b. Any other activity engaged in for money or other compensation, except the following:

(1) One or more activities, not described in **(2)** through **(4)** below, for which no "insured" receives more than $2,000 in total compensation for the 12 months before the beginning of the policy period;

(2) Volunteer activities for which no money is received other than payment for expenses incurred to perform the activity;

(3) Providing home day care services for which no compensation is received, other than the mutual exchange of such services; or

(4) The rendering of home day care services to a relative of an "insured".

4. "Employee" means an employee of an "insured", or an employee leased to an "insured" by a labor leasing firm under an agreement between an "insured" and the labor leasing firm, whose duties are other than those performed by a "residence employee".

5. "Insured" means:

a. You and residents of your household who are:

(1) Your relatives; or

(2) Other persons under the age of 21 and in the care of any person named above;

b. A student enrolled in school full time, as defined by the school, who was a resident of your household before moving out to attend school, provided the student is under the age of:

(1) 24 and your relative; or

(2) 21 and in your care or the care of a person described in **a.(1)** above; or

c. Under Section **II:**

(1) With respect to animals or watercraft to which this policy applies, any person or organization legally responsible for these animals or watercraft which are owned by you or any person included in **a.** or **b.** above. "Insured" does not mean a person or organization using or having custody of these animals or watercraft in the course of any "business" or without consent of the owner; or

(2) With respect to a "motor vehicle" to which this policy applies:

(a) Persons while engaged in your employ or that of any person included in **a.** or **b.** above; or

(b) Other persons using the vehicle on an "insured location" with your consent.

Under both Sections **I** and **II,** when the word an immediately precedes the word "insured", the words an "insured" together mean one or more "insureds".

6. "Insured location" means:

a. The "residence premises";

b. The part of other premises, other structures and grounds used by you as a residence; and

(1) Which is shown in the Declarations; or

(2) Which is acquired by you during the policy period for your use as a residence;

c. Any premises used by you in connection with a premises described in **a.** and **b.** above;

d. Any part of a premises:

(1) Not owned by an "insured"; and

(2) Where an "insured" is temporarily residing;

e. Vacant land, other than farm land, owned by or rented to an "insured";

f. Land owned by or rented to an "insured" on which a one, two, three or four family dwelling is being built as a residence for an "insured";

g. Individual or family cemetery plots or burial vaults of an "insured"; or

h. Any part of a premises occasionally rented to an "insured" for other than "business" use.

7. "Motor vehicle" means:

a. A self-propelled land or amphibious vehicle; or

b. Any trailer or semitrailer which is being carried on, towed by or hitched for towing by a vehicle described in **a.** above.

8. "Occurrence" means an accident, including continuous or repeated exposure to substantially the same general harmful conditions, which results, during the policy period, in:

a. "Bodily injury"; or

b. "Property damage".

9. "Property damage" means physical injury to, destruction of, or loss of use of tangible property.

10. "Residence employee" means:

a. An employee of an "insured", or an employee leased to an "insured" by a labor leasing firm, under an agreement between an "insured" and the labor leasing firm, whose duties are related to the maintenance or use of the "residence premises", including household or domestic services; or

b. One who performs similar duties elsewhere not related to the "business" of an "insured".

A "residence employee" does not include a temporary employee who is furnished to an "insured" to substitute for a permanent "residence employee" on leave or to meet seasonal or short-term workload conditions.

11. "Residence premises" means:

a. The one family dwelling where you reside;

b. The two, three or four family dwelling where you reside in at least one of the family units; or

c. That part of any other building where you reside;

and which is shown as the "residence premises" in the Declarations.

"Residence premises" also includes other structures and grounds at that location.

DEDUCTIBLE

Unless otherwise noted in this policy, the following deductible provision applies:

Subject to the policy limits that apply, we will pay only that part of the total of all loss payable under Section **I** that exceeds the deductible amount shown in the Declarations.

SECTION I – PROPERTY COVERAGES

A. Coverage A – Dwelling

  1. We cover:

   a. The dwelling on the "residence premises" shown in the Declarations, including structures attached to the dwelling; and

   b. Materials and supplies located on or next to the "residence premises" used to construct, alter or repair the dwelling or other structures on the "residence premises".

  2. We do not cover land, including land on which the dwelling is located.

B. Coverage B – Other Structures

  1. We cover other structures on the "residence premises" set apart from the dwelling by clear space. This includes structures connected to the dwelling by only a fence, utility line, or similar connection.

  2. We do not cover:

   a. Land, including land on which the other structures are located;

   b. Other structures rented or held for rental to any person not a tenant of the dwelling, unless used solely as a private garage;

   c. Other structures from which any "business" is conducted; or

   d. Other structures used to store "business" property. However, we do cover a structure that contains "business" property solely owned by an "insured" or a tenant of the dwelling provided that "business" property does not include gaseous or liquid fuel, other than fuel in a permanently installed fuel tank of a vehicle or craft parked or stored in the structure.

  3. The limit of liability for this coverage will not be more than 10% of the limit of liability that applies to Coverage **A**. Use of this coverage does not reduce the Coverage **A** limit of liability.

C. Coverage C – Personal Property

  1. Covered Property

   We cover personal property owned or used by an "insured" while it is anywhere in the world. After a loss and at your request, we will cover personal property owned by:

   a. Others while the property is on the part of the "residence premises" occupied by an "insured"; or

   b. A guest or a "residence employee", while the property is in any residence occupied by an "insured".

  2. Limit For Property At Other Residences

   Our limit of liability for personal property usually located at an "insured's" residence, other than the "residence premises", is 10% of the limit of liability for Coverage **C**, or $1,000, whichever is greater. However, this limitation does not apply to personal property:

   a. Moved from the "residence premises" because it is being repaired, renovated or rebuilt and is not fit to live in or store property in; or

   b. In a newly acquired principal residence for 30 days from the time you begin to move the property there.

  3. Special Limits Of Liability

   The special limit for each category shown below is the total limit for each loss for all property in that category. These special limits do not increase the Coverage **C** limit of liability.

   a. $200 on money, bank notes, bullion, gold other than goldware, silver other than silverware, platinum other than platinumware, coins, medals, scrip, stored value cards and smart cards.

   b. $1,500 on securities, accounts, deeds, evidences of debt, letters of credit, notes other than bank notes, manuscripts, personal records, passports, tickets and stamps. This dollar limit applies to these categories regardless of the medium (such as paper or computer software) on which the material exists.

   This limit includes the cost to research, replace or restore the information from the lost or damaged material.

c. $1,500 on watercraft of all types, including their trailers, furnishings, equipment and outboard engines or motors.

d. $1,500 on trailers or semitrailers not used with watercraft of all types.

e. $1,500 for loss by theft of jewelry, watches, furs, precious and semiprecious stones.

f. $2,500 for loss by theft of firearms and related equipment.

g. $2,500 for loss by theft of silverware, silver-plated ware, goldware, gold-plated ware, platinumware, platinum-plated ware and pewterware. This includes flatware, hollow-ware, tea sets, trays and trophies made of or including silver, gold or pewter.

h. $2,500 on property, on the "residence premises", used primarily for "business" purposes.

i. $500 on property, away from the "residence premises", used primarily for "business" purposes. However, this limit does not apply to loss to electronic apparatus and other property described in Categories **j.** and **k.** below.

j. $1,500 on electronic apparatus and accessories, while in or upon a "motor vehicle", but only if the apparatus is equipped to be operated by power from the "motor vehicle's" electrical system while still capable of being operated by other power sources.

Accessories include antennas, tapes, wires, records, discs or other media that can be used with any apparatus described in this Category **j.**

k. $1,500 on electronic apparatus and accessories used primarily for "business" while away from the "residence premises" and not in or upon a "motor vehicle". The apparatus must be equipped to be operated by power from the "motor vehicle's" electrical system while still capable of being operated by other power sources.

Accessories include antennas, tapes, wires, records, discs or other media that can be used with any apparatus described in this Category **k.**

4. Property Not Covered

We do not cover:

a. Articles separately described and specifically insured, regardless of the limit for which they are insured, in this or other insurance;

b. Animals, birds or fish;

c. "Motor vehicles".

(1) This includes:

(a) Their accessories, equipment and parts; or

(b) Electronic apparatus and accessories designed to be operated solely by power from the electrical system of the "motor vehicle". Accessories include antennas, tapes, wires, records, discs or other media that can be used with any apparatus described above.

The exclusion of property described in **(a)** and **(b)** above applies only while such property is in or upon the "motor vehicle".

(2) We do cover "motor vehicles" not required to be registered for use on public roads or property which are:

(a) Used solely to service an "insured's" residence; or

(b) Designed to assist the handicapped;

d. Aircraft meaning any contrivance used or designed for flight including any parts whether or not attached to the aircraft.

We do cover model or hobby aircraft not used or designed to carry people or cargo;

e. Hovercraft and parts. Hovercraft means a self-propelled motorized ground effect vehicle and includes, but is not limited to, flare-craft and air cushion vehicles;

f. Property of roomers, boarders and other tenants, except property of roomers and boarders related to an "insured";

g. Property in an apartment regularly rented or held for rental to others by an "insured", except as provided in **E.10.** Landlord's Furnishings under Section I – Property Coverages;

h. Property rented or held for rental to others off the "residence premises";

i. "Business" data, including such data stored in:

(1) Books of account, drawings or other paper records; or

(2) Computers and related equipment.

We do cover the cost of blank recording or storage media, and of prerecorded computer programs available on the retail market;

         HO 00 03 10 00

j. Credit cards, electronic fund transfer cards or access devices used solely for deposit, withdrawal or transfer of funds except as provided in **E.6.** Credit Card, Electronic Fund Transfer Card Or Access Device, Forgery And Counterfeit Money under Section I – Property Coverages; or

k. Water or steam.

D. Coverage D – Loss Of Use

The limit of liability for Coverage **D** is the total limit for the coverages in **1.** Additional Living Expense, **2.** Fair Rental Value and **3.** Civil Authority Prohibits Use below.

1. Additional Living Expense

If a loss covered under Section I makes that part of the "residence premises" where you reside not fit to live in, we cover any necessary increase in living expenses incurred by you so that your household can maintain its normal standard of living.

Payment will be for the shortest time required to repair or replace the damage or, if you permanently relocate, the shortest time required for your household to settle elsewhere.

2. Fair Rental Value

If a loss covered under Section I makes that part of the "residence premises" rented to others or held for rental by you not fit to live in, we cover the fair rental value of such premises less any expenses that do not continue while it is not fit to live in.

Payment will be for the shortest time required to repair or replace such premises.

3. Civil Authority Prohibits Use

If a civil authority prohibits you from use of the "residence premises" as a result of direct damage to neighboring premises by a Peril Insured Against, we cover the loss as provided in **1.** Additional Living Expense and **2.** Fair Rental Value above for no more than two weeks.

4. Loss Or Expense Not Covered

We do not cover loss or expense due to cancellation of a lease or agreement.

The periods of time under **1.** Additional Living Expense, **2.** Fair Rental Value and **3.** Civil Authority Prohibits Use above are not limited by expiration of this policy.

E. Additional Coverages

1. Debris Removal

a. We will pay your reasonable expense for the removal of:

(1) Debris of covered property if a Peril Insured Against that applies to the damaged property causes the loss; or

(2) Ash, dust or particles from a volcanic eruption that has caused direct loss to a building or property contained in a building.

This expense is included in the limit of liability that applies to the damaged property. If the amount to be paid for the actual damage to the property plus the debris removal expense is more than the limit of liability for the damaged property, an additional 5% of that limit is available for such expense.

b. We will also pay your reasonable expense, up to $1,000, for the removal from the "residence premises" of:

(1) Your tree(s) felled by the peril of Windstorm or Hail or Weight of Ice, Snow or Sleet; or

(2) A neighbor's tree(s) felled by a Peril Insured Against under Coverage **C**;

provided the tree(s):

(3) Damage(s) a covered structure; or

(4) Does not damage a covered structure, but:

(a) Block(s) a driveway on the "residence premises" which prevent(s) a "motor vehicle", that is registered for use on public roads or property, from entering or leaving the "residence premises"; or

(b) Block(s) a ramp or other fixture designed to assist a handicapped person to enter or leave the dwelling building.

The $1,000 limit is the most we will pay in any one loss regardless of the number of fallen trees. No more than $500 of this limit will be paid for the removal of any one tree.

This coverage is additional insurance.

2. Reasonable Repairs

a. We will pay the reasonable cost incurred by you for the necessary measures taken solely to protect covered property that is damaged by a Peril Insured Against from further damage.

b. If the measures taken involve repair to other damaged property, we will only pay if that property is covered under this policy and the damage is caused by a Peril Insured Against. This coverage does not:

(1) Increase the limit of liability that applies to the covered property; or

(2) Relieve you of your duties, in case of a loss to covered property, described in **B.4.** under Section I – Conditions.

3. Trees, Shrubs And Other Plants

We cover trees, shrubs, plants or lawns, on the "residence premises", for loss caused by the following Perils Insured Against:

a. Fire or Lightning;

b. Explosion;

c. Riot or Civil Commotion;

d. Aircraft;

e. Vehicles not owned or operated by a resident of the "residence premises";

f. Vandalism or Malicious Mischief; or

g. Theft.

We will pay up to 5% of the limit of liability that applies to the dwelling for all trees, shrubs, plants or lawns. No more than $500 of this limit will be paid for any one tree, shrub or plant. We do not cover property grown for "business" purposes.

This coverage is additional insurance.

4. Fire Department Service Charge

We will pay up to $500 for your liability assumed by contract or agreement for fire department charges incurred when the fire department is called to save or protect covered property from a Peril Insured Against. We do not cover fire department service charges if the property is located within the limits of the city, municipality or protection district furnishing the fire department response.

This coverage is additional insurance. No deductible applies to this coverage.

5. Property Removed

We insure covered property against direct loss from any cause while being removed from a premises endangered by a Peril Insured Against and for no more than 30 days while removed.

This coverage does not change the limit of liability that applies to the property being removed.

6. Credit Card, Electronic Fund Transfer Card Or Access Device, Forgery And Counterfeit Money

a. We will pay up to $500 for:

(1) The legal obligation of an "insured" to pay because of the theft or unauthorized use of credit cards issued to or registered in an "insured's" name;

(2) Loss resulting from theft or unauthorized use of an electronic fund transfer card or access device used for deposit, withdrawal or transfer of funds, issued to or registered in an "insured's" name;

(3) Loss to an "insured" caused by forgery or alteration of any check or negotiable instrument; and

(4) Loss to an "insured" through acceptance in good faith of counterfeit United States or Canadian paper currency.

All loss resulting from a series of acts committed by any one person or in which any one person is concerned or implicated is considered to be one loss.

This coverage is additional insurance. No deductible applies to this coverage.

b. We do not cover:

(1) Use of a credit card, electronic fund transfer card or access device:

(a) By a resident of your household;

(b) By a person who has been entrusted with either type of card or access device; or

(c) If an "insured" has not complied with all terms and conditions under which the cards are issued or the devices accessed; or

(2) Loss arising out of "business" use or dishonesty of an "insured".

c. If the coverage in **a.** above applies, the following defense provisions also apply:

(1) We may investigate and settle any claim or suit that we decide is appropriate. Our duty to defend a claim or suit ends when the amount we pay for the loss equals our limit of liability.

(2) If a suit is brought against an "insured" for liability under **a.(1)** or **(2)** above, we will provide a defense at our expense by counsel of our choice.

(3) We have the option to defend at our expense an "insured" or an "insured's" bank against any suit for the enforcement of payment under **a.(3)** above.

 HO 00 03 10 00

7. Loss Assessment

  a. We will pay up to $1,000 for your share of loss assessment charged during the policy period against you, as owner or tenant of the "residence premises", by a corporation or association of property owners. The assessment must be made as a result of direct loss to property, owned by all members collectively, of the type that would be covered by this policy if owned by you, caused by a Peril Insured Against under Coverage **A,** other than:

   (1) Earthquake; or

   (2) Land shock waves or tremors before, during or after a volcanic eruption.

   The limit of $1,000 is the most we will pay with respect to any one loss, regardless of the number of assessments. We will only apply one deductible, per unit, to the total amount of any one loss to the property described above, regardless of the number of assessments.

  b. We do not cover assessments charged against you or a corporation or association of property owners by any governmental body.

  c. Paragraph **P.** Policy Period under Section **I** – Conditions does not apply to this coverage.

  This coverage is additional insurance.

8. Collapse

  a. With respect to this Additional Coverage:

   (1) Collapse means an abrupt falling down or caving in of a building or any part of a building with the result that the building or part of the building cannot be occupied for its current intended purpose.

   (2) A building or any part of a building that is in danger of falling down or caving in is not considered to be in a state of collapse.

   (3) A part of a building that is standing is not considered to be in a state of collapse even if it has separated from another part of the building.

   (4) A building or any part of a building that is standing is not considered to be in a state of collapse even if it shows evidence of cracking, bulging, sagging, bending, leaning, settling, shrinkage or expansion.

  b. We insure for direct physical loss to covered property involving collapse of a building or any part of a building if the collapse was caused by one or more of the following:

   (1) The Perils Insured Against named under Coverage **C;**

   (2) Decay that is hidden from view, unless the presence of such decay is known to an "insured" prior to collapse;

   (3) Insect or vermin damage that is hidden from view, unless the presence of such damage is known to an "insured" prior to collapse;

   (4) Weight of contents, equipment, animals or people;

   (5) Weight of rain which collects on a roof; or

   (6) Use of defective material or methods in construction, remodeling or renovation if the collapse occurs during the course of the construction, remodeling or renovation.

  c. Loss to an awning, fence, patio, deck, pavement, swimming pool, underground pipe, flue, drain, cesspool, septic tank, foundation, retaining wall, bulkhead, pier, wharf or dock is not included under **b.(2)** through **(6)** above, unless the loss is a direct result of the collapse of a building or any part of a building.

  d. This coverage does not increase the limit of liability that applies to the damaged covered property.

9. Glass Or Safety Glazing Material

  a. We cover:

   (1) The breakage of glass or safety glazing material which is part of a covered building, storm door or storm window;

   (2) The breakage of glass or safety glazing material which is part of a covered building, storm door or storm window when caused directly by earth movement; and

   (3) The direct physical loss to covered property caused solely by the pieces, fragments or splinters of broken glass or safety glazing material which is part of a building, storm door or storm window.

b. This coverage does not include loss:

(1) To covered property which results because the glass or safety glazing material has been broken, except as provided in **a.(3)** above; or

(2) On the "residence premises" if the dwelling has been vacant for more than 60 consecutive days immediately before the loss, except when the breakage results directly from earth movement as provided in **a.(2)** above. A dwelling being constructed is not considered vacant.

c. This coverage does not increase the limit of liability that applies to the damaged property.

10. Landlord's Furnishings

We will pay up to $2,500 for your appliances, carpeting and other household furnishings, in each apartment on the "residence premises" regularly rented or held for rental to others by an "insured", for loss caused by a Peril Insured Against in Coverage **C**, other than Theft.

This limit is the most we will pay in any one loss regardless of the number of appliances, carpeting or other household furnishings involved in the loss.

This coverage does not increase the limit of liability applying to the damaged property.

11. Ordinance Or Law

a. You may use up to 10% of the limit of liability that applies to Coverage **A** for the increased costs you incur due to the enforcement of any ordinance or law which requires or regulates:

(1) The construction, demolition, remodeling, renovation or repair of that part of a covered building or other structure damaged by a Peril Insured Against;

(2) The demolition and reconstruction of the undamaged part of a covered building or other structure, when that building or other structure must be totally demolished because of damage by a Peril Insured Against to another part of that covered building or other structure; or

(3) The remodeling, removal or replacement of the portion of the undamaged part of a covered building or other structure necessary to complete the remodeling, repair or replacement of that part of the covered building or other structure damaged by a Peril Insured Against.

b. You may use all or part of this ordinance or law coverage to pay for the increased costs you incur to remove debris resulting from the construction, demolition, remodeling, renovation, repair or replacement of property as stated in **a.** above.

c. We do not cover:

(1) The loss in value to any covered building or other structure due to the requirements of any ordinance or law; or

(2) The costs to comply with any ordinance or law which requires any "insured" or others to test for, monitor, clean up, remove, contain, treat, detoxify or neutralize, or in any way respond to, or assess the effects of, pollutants in or on any covered building or other structure.

Pollutants means any solid, liquid, gaseous or thermal irritant or contaminant, including smoke, vapor, soot, fumes, acids, alkalis, chemicals and waste. Waste includes materials to be recycled, reconditioned or reclaimed.

This coverage is additional insurance.

12. Grave Markers

We will pay up to $5,000 for grave markers, including mausoleums, on or away from the "residence premises" for loss caused by a Peril Insured Against under Coverage **C**.

This coverage does not increase the limits of liability that apply to the damaged covered property.

SECTION I – PERILS INSURED AGAINST

A. Coverage A – Dwelling And Coverage B – Other Structures

1. We insure against risk of direct physical loss to property described in Coverages **A** and **B**.

2. We do not insure, however, for loss:

a. Excluded under Section **I** – Exclusions;

b. Involving collapse, except as provided in **E.8.** Collapse under Section **I** – Property Coverages; or

c. Caused by:

(1) Freezing of a plumbing, heating, air conditioning or automatic fire protective sprinkler system or of a household appliance, or by discharge, leakage or overflow from within the system or appliance caused by freezing. This provision does not apply if you have used reasonable care to:

(a) Maintain heat in the building; or

(b) Shut off the water supply and drain all systems and appliances of water.

However, if the building is protected by an automatic fire protective sprinkler system, you must use reasonable care to continue the water supply and maintain heat in the building for coverage to apply.

For purposes of this provision a plumbing system or household appliance does not include a sump, sump pump or related equipment or a roof drain, gutter, downspout or similar fixtures or equipment;

(2) Freezing, thawing, pressure or weight of water or ice, whether driven by wind or not, to a:

(a) Fence, pavement, patio or swimming pool;

(b) Footing, foundation, bulkhead, wall, or any other structure or device that supports all or part of a building, or other structure;

(c) Retaining wall or bulkhead that does not support all or part of a building or other structure; or

(d) Pier, wharf or dock;

(3) Theft in or to a dwelling under construction, or of materials and supplies for use in the construction until the dwelling is finished and occupied;

(4) Vandalism and malicious mischief, and any ensuing loss caused by any intentional and wrongful act committed in the course of the vandalism or malicious mischief, if the dwelling has been vacant for more than 60 consecutive days immediately before the loss. A dwelling being constructed is not considered vacant;

(5) Mold, fungus or wet rot. However, we do insure for loss caused by mold, fungus or wet rot that is hidden within the walls or ceilings or beneath the floors or above the ceilings of a structure if such loss results from the accidental discharge or overflow of water or steam from within:

(a) A plumbing, heating, air conditioning or automatic fire protective sprinkler system, or a household appliance, on the "residence premises"; or

(b) A storm drain, or water, steam or sewer pipes, off the "residence premises".

For purposes of this provision, a plumbing system or household appliance does not include a sump, sump pump or related equipment or a roof drain, gutter, downspout or similar fixtures or equipment; or

(6) Any of the following:

(a) Wear and tear, marring, deterioration;

(b) Mechanical breakdown, latent defect, inherent vice, or any quality in property that causes it to damage or destroy itself;

(c) Smog, rust or other corrosion, or dry rot;

(d) Smoke from agricultural smudging or industrial operations;

(e) Discharge, dispersal, seepage, migration, release or escape of pollutants unless the discharge, dispersal, seepage, migration, release or escape is itself caused by a Peril Insured Against named under Coverage **C.**

Pollutants means any solid, liquid, gaseous or thermal irritant or contaminant, including smoke, vapor, soot, fumes, acids, alkalis, chemicals and waste. Waste includes materials to be recycled, reconditioned or reclaimed;

(f) Settling, shrinking, bulging or expansion, including resultant cracking, of bulkheads, pavements, patios, footings, foundations, walls, floors, roofs or ceilings;

(g) Birds, vermin, rodents, or insects; or

(h) Animals owned or kept by an "insured".

Exception To c.(6)

Unless the loss is otherwise excluded, we cover loss to property covered under Coverage **A** or **B** resulting from an accidental discharge or overflow of water or steam from within a:

(i) Storm drain, or water, steam or sewer pipe, off the "residence premises"; or

(ii) Plumbing, heating, air conditioning or automatic fire protective sprinkler system or household appliance on the "residence premises". This includes the cost to tear out and replace any part of a building, or other structure, on the "residence premises", but only when necessary to repair the system or appliance. However, such tear out and replacement coverage only applies to other structures if the water or steam causes actual damage to a building on the "residence premises".

We do not cover loss to the system or appliance from which this water or steam escaped.

For purposes of this provision, a plumbing system or household appliance does not include a sump, sump pump or related equipment or a roof drain, gutter, down spout or similar fixtures or equipment.

Section I – Exclusion **A.3.** Water Damage, Paragraphs **a.** and **c.** that apply to surface water and water below the surface of the ground do not apply to loss by water covered under **c.(5)** and **(6)** above.

Under **2.b.** and **c.** above, any ensuing loss to property described in Coverages **A** and **B** not precluded by any other provision in this policy is covered.

B. Coverage C – Personal Property

We insure for direct physical loss to the property described in Coverage **C** caused by any of the following perils unless the loss is excluded in Section I – Exclusions.

1. Fire Or Lightning

2. Windstorm Or Hail

This peril includes loss to watercraft of all types and their trailers, furnishings, equipment, and outboard engines or motors, only while inside a fully enclosed building.

This peril does not include loss to the property contained in a building caused by rain, snow, sleet, sand or dust unless the direct force of wind or hail damages the building causing an opening in a roof or wall and the rain, snow, sleet, sand or dust enters through this opening.

3. Explosion

4. Riot Or Civil Commotion

5. Aircraft

This peril includes self-propelled missiles and spacecraft.

6. Vehicles

7. Smoke

This peril means sudden and accidental damage from smoke, including the emission or puffback of smoke, soot, fumes or vapors from a boiler, furnace or related equipment.

This peril does not include loss caused by smoke from agricultural smudging or industrial operations.

8. Vandalism Or Malicious Mischief

9. Theft

a. This peril includes attempted theft and loss of property from a known place when it is likely that the property has been stolen.

b. This peril does not include loss caused by theft:

(1) Committed by an "insured";

(2) In or to a dwelling under construction, or of materials and supplies for use in the construction until the dwelling is finished and occupied;

(3) From that part of a "residence premises" rented by an "insured" to someone other than another "insured"; or

(4) That occurs off the "residence premises" of:

(a) Trailers, semitrailers and campers;

(b) Watercraft of all types, and their furnishings, equipment and outboard engines or motors; or

(c) Property while at any other residence owned by, rented to, or occupied by an "insured", except while an "insured" is temporarily living there. Property of an "insured" who is a student is covered while at the residence the student occupies to attend school as long as the student has been there at any time during the 60 days immediately before the loss.

10. Falling Objects

This peril does not include loss to property contained in a building unless the roof or an outside wall of the building is first damaged by a falling object. Damage to the falling object itself is not included.

11. Weight Of Ice, Snow Or Sleet

This peril means weight of ice, snow or sleet which causes damage to property contained in a building.

       HO 00 03 10 00

12. Accidental Discharge Or Overflow Of Water Or Steam

a. This peril means accidental discharge or overflow of water or steam from within a plumbing, heating, air conditioning or automatic fire protective sprinkler system or from within a household appliance.

b. This peril does not include loss:

(1) To the system or appliance from which the water or steam escaped;

(2) Caused by or resulting from freezing except as provided in Peril Insured Against **14.** Freezing;

(3) On the "residence premises" caused by accidental discharge or overflow which occurs off the "residence premises"; or

(4) Caused by mold, fungus or wet rot unless hidden within the walls or ceilings or beneath the floors or above the ceilings of a structure.

c. In this peril, a plumbing system or household appliance does not include a sump, sump pump or related equipment or a roof drain, gutter, downspout or similar fixtures or equipment.

d. Section I – Exclusion **A.3.** Water Damage, Paragraphs **a.** and **c.** that apply to surface water and water below the surface of the ground do not apply to loss by water covered under this peril.

13. Sudden And Accidental Tearing Apart, Cracking, Burning Or Bulging

This peril means sudden and accidental tearing apart, cracking, burning or bulging of a steam or hot water heating system, an air conditioning or automatic fire protective sprinkler system, or an appliance for heating water.

We do not cover loss caused by or resulting from freezing under this peril.

14. Freezing

a. This peril means freezing of a plumbing, heating, air conditioning or automatic fire protective sprinkler system or of a household appliance but only if you have used reasonable care to:

(1) Maintain heat in the building; or

(2) Shut off the water supply and drain all systems and appliances of water.

However, if the building is protected by an automatic fire protective sprinkler system, you must use reasonable care to continue the water supply and maintain heat in the building for coverage to apply.

b. In this peril, a plumbing system or household appliance does not include a sump, sump pump or related equipment or a roof drain, gutter, downspout or similar fixtures or equipment.

15. Sudden And Accidental Damage From Artificially Generated Electrical Current

This peril does not include loss to tubes, transistors, electronic components or circuitry that are a part of appliances, fixtures, computers, home entertainment units or other types of electronic apparatus.

16. Volcanic Eruption

This peril does not include loss caused by earthquake, land shock waves or tremors.

SECTION I – EXCLUSIONS

A. We do not insure for loss caused directly or indirectly by any of the following. Such loss is excluded regardless of any other cause or event contributing concurrently or in any sequence to the loss. These exclusions apply whether or not the loss event results in widespread damage or affects a substantial area.

1. Ordinance Or Law

Ordinance Or Law means any ordinance or law:

a. Requiring or regulating the construction, demolition, remodeling, renovation or repair of property, including removal of any resulting debris. This Exclusion **A.1.a.** does not apply to the amount of coverage that may be provided for in **E.11.** Ordinance Or Law under Section I – Property Coverages;

b. The requirements of which result in a loss in value to property; or

c. Requiring any "insured" or others to test for, monitor, clean up, remove, contain, treat, detoxify or neutralize, or in any way respond to, or assess the effects of, pollutants.

Pollutants means any solid, liquid, gaseous or thermal irritant or contaminant, including smoke, vapor, soot, fumes, acids, alkalis, chemicals and waste. Waste includes materials to be recycled, reconditioned or reclaimed.

This Exclusion **A.1.** applies whether or not the property has been physically damaged.

2. Earth Movement

Earth Movement means:

a. Earthquake, including land shock waves or tremors before, during or after a volcanic eruption;

b. Landslide, mudslide or mudflow;

c. Subsidence or sinkhole; or

d. Any other earth movement including earth sinking, rising or shifting;

caused by or resulting from human or animal forces or any act of nature unless direct loss by fire or explosion ensues and then we will pay only for the ensuing loss.

This Exclusion **A.2.** does not apply to loss by theft.

3. Water Damage

Water Damage means:

a. Flood, surface water, waves, tidal water, overflow of a body of water, or spray from any of these, whether or not driven by wind;

b. Water or water-borne material which backs up through sewers or drains or which overflows or is discharged from a sump, sump pump or related equipment; or

c. Water or water-borne material below the surface of the ground, including water which exerts pressure on or seeps or leaks through a building, sidewalk, driveway, foundation, swimming pool or other structure;

caused by or resulting from human or animal forces or any act of nature.

Direct loss by fire, explosion or theft resulting from water damage is covered.

4. Power Failure

Power Failure means the failure of power or other utility service if the failure takes place off the "residence premises". But if the failure results in a loss, from a Peril Insured Against on the "residence premises", we will pay for the loss caused by that peril.

5. Neglect

Neglect means neglect of an "insured" to use all reasonable means to save and preserve property at and after the time of a loss.

6. War

War includes the following and any consequence of any of the following:

a. Undeclared war, civil war, insurrection, rebellion or revolution;

b. Warlike act by a military force or military personnel; or

c. Destruction, seizure or use for a military purpose.

Discharge of a nuclear weapon will be deemed a warlike act even if accidental.

7. Nuclear Hazard

This Exclusion **A.7.** pertains to Nuclear Hazard to the extent set forth in **M.** Nuclear Hazard Clause under Section **I** – Conditions.

8. Intentional Loss

Intentional Loss means any loss arising out of any act an "insured" commits or conspires to commit with the intent to cause a loss.

In the event of such loss, no "insured" is entitled to coverage, even "insureds" who did not commit or conspire to commit the act causing the loss.

9. Governmental Action

Governmental Action means the destruction, confiscation or seizure of property described in Coverage **A, B** or **C** by order of any governmental or public authority.

This exclusion does not apply to such acts ordered by any governmental or public authority that are taken at the time of a fire to prevent its spread, if the loss caused by fire would be covered under this policy.

B. We do not insure for loss to property described in Coverages **A** and **B** caused by any of the following. However, any ensuing loss to property described in Coverages **A** and **B** not precluded by any other provision in this policy is covered.

1. Weather conditions. However, this exclusion only applies if weather conditions contribute in any way with a cause or event excluded in **A.** above to produce the loss.

2. Acts or decisions, including the failure to act or decide, of any person, group, organization or governmental body.

3. Faulty, inadequate or defective:

a. Planning, zoning, development, surveying, siting;

b. Design, specifications, workmanship, repair, construction, renovation, remodeling, grading, compaction;

c. Materials used in repair, construction, renovation or remodeling; or

d. Maintenance;

of part or all of any property whether on or off the "residence premises".

SECTION I – CONDITIONS

A. Insurable Interest And Limit Of Liability

Even if more than one person has an insurable interest in the property covered, we will not be liable in any one loss:

1. To an "insured" for more than the amount of such "insured's" interest at the time of loss; or

2. For more than the applicable limit of liability.

B. Duties After Loss

In case of a loss to covered property, we have no duty to provide coverage under this policy if the failure to comply with the following duties is prejudicial to us. These duties must be performed either by you, an "insured" seeking coverage, or a representative of either:

1. Give prompt notice to us or our agent;

2. Notify the police in case of loss by theft;

3. Notify the credit card or electronic fund transfer card or access device company in case of loss as provided for in **E.6.** Credit Card, Electronic Fund Transfer Card Or Access Device, Forgery And Counterfeit Money under Section I – Property Coverages;

4. Protect the property from further damage. If repairs to the property are required, you must:

    a. Make reasonable and necessary repairs to protect the property; and

    b. Keep an accurate record of repair expenses;

5. Cooperate with us in the investigation of a claim;

6. Prepare an inventory of damaged personal property showing the quantity, description, actual cash value and amount of loss. Attach all bills, receipts and related documents that justify the figures in the inventory;

7. As often as we reasonably require:

    a. Show the damaged property;

    b. Provide us with records and documents we request and permit us to make copies; and

    c. Submit to examination under oath, while not in the presence of another "insured", and sign the same;

8. Send to us, within 60 days after our request, your signed, sworn proof of loss which sets forth, to the best of your knowledge and belief:

    a. The time and cause of loss;

    b. The interests of all "insureds" and all others in the property involved and all liens on the property;

    c. Other insurance which may cover the loss;

    d. Changes in title or occupancy of the property during the term of the policy;

    e. Specifications of damaged buildings and detailed repair estimates;

    f. The inventory of damaged personal property described in **6.** above;

    g. Receipts for additional living expenses incurred and records that support the fair rental value loss; and

    h. Evidence or affidavit that supports a claim under **E.6.** Credit Card, Electronic Fund Transfer Card Or Access Device, Forgery And Counterfeit Money under Section I – Property Coverages, stating the amount and cause of loss.

C. Loss Settlement

In this Condition **C.**, the terms "cost to repair or replace" and "replacement cost" do not include the increased costs incurred to comply with the enforcement of any ordinance or law, except to the extent that coverage for these increased costs is provided in **E.11.** Ordinance Or Law under Section I – Property Coverages. Covered property losses are settled as follows:

1. Property of the following types:

    a. Personal property;

    b. Awnings, carpeting, household appliances, outdoor antennas and outdoor equipment, whether or not attached to buildings;

    c. Structures that are not buildings; and

    d. Grave markers, including mausoleums;

    at actual cash value at the time of loss but not more than the amount required to repair or replace.

2. Buildings covered under Coverage **A** or **B** at replacement cost without deduction for depreciation, subject to the following:

    a. If, at the time of loss, the amount of insurance in this policy on the damaged building is 80% or more of the full replacement cost of the building immediately before the loss, we will pay the cost to repair or replace, after application of any deductible and without deduction for depreciation, but not more than the least of the following amounts:

        (1) The limit of liability under this policy that applies to the building;

        (2) The replacement cost of that part of the building damaged with material of like kind and quality and for like use; or

        (3) The necessary amount actually spent to repair or replace the damaged building.

If the building is rebuilt at a new premises, the cost described in **(2)** above is limited to the cost which would have been incurred if the building had been built at the original premises.

b. If, at the time of loss, the amount of insurance in this policy on the damaged building is less than 80% of the full replacement cost of the building immediately before the loss, we will pay the greater of the following amounts, but not more than the limit of liability under this policy that applies to the building:

(1) The actual cash value of that part of the building damaged; or

(2) That proportion of the cost to repair or replace, after application of any deductible and without deduction for depreciation, that part of the building damaged, which the total amount of insurance in this policy on the damaged building bears to 80% of the replacement cost of the building.

c. To determine the amount of insurance required to equal 80% of the full replacement cost of the building immediately before the loss, do not include the value of:

(1) Excavations, footings, foundations, piers, or any other structures or devices that support all or part of the building, which are below the undersurface of the lowest basement floor;

(2) Those supports described in **(1)** above which are below the surface of the ground inside the foundation walls, if there is no basement; and

(3) Underground flues, pipes, wiring and drains.

d. We will pay no more than the actual cash value of the damage until actual repair or replacement is complete. Once actual repair or replacement is complete, we will settle the loss as noted in **2.a.** and **b.** above.

However, if the cost to repair or replace the damage is both:

(1) Less than 5% of the amount of insurance in this policy on the building; and

(2) Less than $2,500;

we will settle the loss as noted in **2.a.** and **b.** above whether or not actual repair or replacement is complete.

e. You may disregard the replacement cost loss settlement provisions and make claim under this policy for loss to buildings on an actual cash value basis. You may then make claim for any additional liability according to the provisions of this Condition **C. Loss Settlement**, provided you notify us of your intent to do so within 180 days after the date of loss.

D. Loss To A Pair Or Set

In case of loss to a pair or set we may elect to:

1. Repair or replace any part to restore the pair or set to its value before the loss; or

2. Pay the difference between actual cash value of the property before and after the loss.

E. Appraisal

If you and we fail to agree on the amount of loss, either may demand an appraisal of the loss. In this event, each party will choose a competent and impartial appraiser within 20 days after receiving a written request from the other. The two appraisers will choose an umpire. If they cannot agree upon an umpire within 15 days, you or we may request that the choice be made by a judge of a court of record in the state where the "residence premises" is located. The appraisers will separately set the amount of loss. If the appraisers submit a written report of an agreement to us, the amount agreed upon will be the amount of loss. If they fail to agree, they will submit their differences to the umpire. A decision agreed to by any two will set the amount of loss.

Each party will:

1. Pay its own appraiser; and

2. Bear the other expenses of the appraisal and umpire equally.

F. Other Insurance And Service Agreement

If a loss covered by this policy is also covered by:

1. Other insurance, we will pay only the proportion of the loss that the limit of liability that applies under this policy bears to the total amount of insurance covering the loss; or

2. A service agreement, this insurance is excess over any amounts payable under any such agreement. Service agreement means a service plan, property restoration plan, home warranty or other similar service warranty agreement, even if it is characterized as insurance.

G. Suit Against Us

No action can be brought against us unless there has been full compliance with all of the terms under Section **I** of this policy and the action is started within two years after the date of loss.

H. Our Option

If we give you written notice within 30 days after we receive your signed, sworn proof of loss, we may repair or replace any part of the damaged property with material or property of like kind and quality.

I. Loss Payment

We will adjust all losses with you. We will pay you unless some other person is named in the policy or is legally entitled to receive payment. Loss will be payable 60 days after we receive your proof of loss and:

1. Reach an agreement with you;

2. There is an entry of a final judgment; or

3. There is a filing of an appraisal award with us.

J. Abandonment Of Property

We need not accept any property abandoned by an "insured".

K. Mortgage Clause

1. If a mortgagee is named in this policy, any loss payable under Coverage **A** or **B** will be paid to the mortgagee and you, as interests appear. If more than one mortgagee is named, the order of payment will be the same as the order of precedence of the mortgages.

2. If we deny your claim, that denial will not apply to a valid claim of the mortgagee, if the mortgagee:

   a. Notifies us of any change in ownership, occupancy or substantial change in risk of which the mortgagee is aware;

   b. Pays any premium due under this policy on demand if you have neglected to pay the premium; and

   c. Submits a signed, sworn statement of loss within 60 days after receiving notice from us of your failure to do so. Paragraphs **E.** Appraisal, **G.** Suit Against Us and **I.** Loss Payment under Section **I** – Conditions also apply to the mortgagee.

3. If we decide to cancel or not to renew this policy, the mortgagee will be notified at least 10 days before the date cancellation or nonrenewal takes effect.

4. If we pay the mortgagee for any loss and deny payment to you:

   a. We are subrogated to all the rights of the mortgagee granted under the mortgage on the property; or

   b. At our option, we may pay to the mortgagee the whole principal on the mortgage plus any accrued interest. In this event, we will receive a full assignment and transfer of the mortgage and all securities held as collateral to the mortgage debt.

5. Subrogation will not impair the right of the mortgagee to recover the full amount of the mortgagee's claim.

L. No Benefit To Bailee

We will not recognize any assignment or grant any coverage that benefits a person or organization holding, storing or moving property for a fee regardless of any other provision of this policy.

M. Nuclear Hazard Clause

1. "Nuclear Hazard" means any nuclear reaction, radiation, or radioactive contamination, all whether controlled or uncontrolled or however caused, or any consequence of any of these.

2. Loss caused by the nuclear hazard will not be considered loss caused by fire, explosion, or smoke, whether these perils are specifically named in or otherwise included within the Perils Insured Against.

3. This policy does not apply under Section **I** to loss caused directly or indirectly by nuclear hazard, except that direct loss by fire resulting from the nuclear hazard is covered.

N. Recovered Property

If you or we recover any property for which we have made payment under this policy, you or we will notify the other of the recovery. At your option, the property will be returned to or retained by you or it will become our property. If the recovered property is returned to or retained by you, the loss payment will be adjusted based on the amount you received for the recovered property.

O. Volcanic Eruption Period

One or more volcanic eruptions that occur within a 72 hour period will be considered as one volcanic eruption.

P. Policy Period

This policy applies only to loss which occurs during the policy period.

Q. Concealment Or Fraud

We provide coverage to no "insureds" under this policy if, whether before or after a loss, an "insured" has:

1. Intentionally concealed or misrepresented any material fact or circumstance;

2. Engaged in fraudulent conduct; or

3. Made false statements;

relating to this insurance.

R. Loss Payable Clause

If the Declarations show a loss payee for certain listed insured personal property, the definition of "insured" is changed to include that loss payee with respect to that property.

If we decide to cancel or not renew this policy, that loss payee will be notified in writing.

SECTION II – LIABILITY COVERAGES

A. Coverage E – Personal Liability

If a claim is made or a suit is brought against an "insured" for damages because of "bodily injury" or "property damage" caused by an "occurrence" to which this coverage applies, we will:

1. Pay up to our limit of liability for the damages for which an "insured" is legally liable. Damages include prejudgment interest awarded against an "insured"; and

2. Provide a defense at our expense by counsel of our choice, even if the suit is groundless, false or fraudulent. We may investigate and settle any claim or suit that we decide is appropriate. Our duty to settle or defend ends when our limit of liability for the "occurrence" has been exhausted by payment of a judgment or settlement.

B. Coverage F – Medical Payments To Others

We will pay the necessary medical expenses that are incurred or medically ascertained within three years from the date of an accident causing "bodily injury". Medical expenses means reasonable charges for medical, surgical, x-ray, dental, ambulance, hospital, professional nursing, prosthetic devices and funeral services. This coverage does not apply to you or regular residents of your household except "residence employees". As to others, this coverage applies only:

1. To a person on the "insured location" with the permission of an "insured"; or

2. To a person off the "insured location", if the "bodily injury":

a. Arises out of a condition on the "insured location" or the ways immediately adjoining;

b. Is caused by the activities of an "insured";

c. Is caused by a "residence employee" in the course of the "residence employee's" employment by an "insured"; or

d. Is caused by an animal owned by or in the care of an "insured".

SECTION II – EXCLUSIONS

A. "Motor Vehicle Liability"

1. Coverages **E** and **F** do not apply to any "motor vehicle liability" if, at the time and place of an "occurrence", the involved "motor vehicle":

a. Is registered for use on public roads or property;

b. Is not registered for use on public roads or property, but such registration is required by a law, or regulation issued by a government agency, for it to be used at the place of the "occurrence"; or

c. Is being:

(1) Operated in, or practicing for, any prearranged or organized race, speed contest or other competition;

(2) Rented to others;

(3) Used to carry persons or cargo for a charge; or

(4) Used for any "business" purpose except for a motorized golf cart while on a golfing facility.

2. If Exclusion **A.1.** does not apply, there is still no coverage for "motor vehicle liability" unless the "motor vehicle" is:

a. In dead storage on an "insured location";

b. Used solely to service an "insured's" residence;

c. Designed to assist the handicapped and, at the time of an "occurrence", it is:

(1) Being used to assist a handicapped person; or

(2) Parked on an "insured location";

d. Designed for recreational use off public roads and:

(1) Not owned by an "insured"; or

(2) Owned by an "insured" provided the "occurrence" takes place on an "insured location" as defined in Definitions **B. 6.a., b., d., e.** or **h.**; or

e. A motorized golf cart that is owned by an "insured", designed to carry up to 4 persons, not built or modified after manufacture to exceed a speed of 25 miles per hour on level ground and, at the time of an "occurrence", is within the legal boundaries of:

(1) A golfing facility and is parked or stored there, or being used by an "insured" to:

(a) Play the game of golf or for other recreational or leisure activity allowed by the facility;

(b) Travel to or from an area where "motor vehicles" or golf carts are parked or stored; or

(c) Cross public roads at designated points to access other parts of the golfing facility; or

(2) A private residential community, including its public roads upon which a motorized golf cart can legally travel, which is subject to the authority of a property owners association and contains an "insured's" residence.

B. "Watercraft Liability"

1. Coverages **E** and **F** do not apply to any "watercraft liability" if, at the time of an "occurrence", the involved watercraft is being:

a. Operated in, or practicing for, any prearranged or organized race, speed contest or other competition. This exclusion does not apply to a sailing vessel or a predicted log cruise;

b. Rented to others;

c. Used to carry persons or cargo for a charge; or

d. Used for any "business" purpose.

2. If Exclusion **B.1.** does not apply, there is still no coverage for "watercraft liability" unless, at the time of the "occurrence", the watercraft:

a. Is stored;

b. Is a sailing vessel, with or without auxiliary power, that is:

(1) Less than 26 feet in overall length; or

(2) 26 feet or more in overall length and not owned by or rented to an "insured"; or

c. Is not a sailing vessel and is powered by:

(1) An inboard or inboard-outdrive engine or motor, including those that power a water jet pump, of:

(a) 50 horsepower or less and not owned by an "insured"; or

(b) More than 50 horsepower and not owned by or rented to an "insured"; or

(2) One or more outboard engines or motors with:

(a) 25 total horsepower or less;

(b) More than 25 horsepower if the outboard engine or motor is not owned by an "insured";

(c) More than 25 horsepower if the outboard engine or motor is owned by an "insured" who acquired it during the policy period; or

(d) More than 25 horsepower if the outboard engine or motor is owned by an "insured" who acquired it before the policy period, but only if:

(i) You declare them at policy inception; or

(ii) Your intent to insure them is reported to us in writing within 45 days after you acquire them.

The coverages in **(c)** and **(d)** above apply for the policy period.

Horsepower means the maximum power rating assigned to the engine or motor by the manufacturer.

C. "Aircraft Liability"

This policy does not cover "aircraft liability".

D. "Hovercraft Liability"

This policy does not cover "hovercraft liability".

E. Coverage E – Personal Liability And Coverage F – Medical Payments To Others

Coverages **E** and **F** do not apply to the following:

1. Expected Or Intended Injury

"Bodily injury" or "property damage" which is expected or intended by an "insured" even if the resulting "bodily injury" or "property damage":

a. Is of a different kind, quality or degree than initially expected or intended; or

b. Is sustained by a different person, entity, real or personal property, than initially expected or intended.

However, this Exclusion **E.1.** does not apply to "bodily injury" resulting from the use of reasonable force by an "insured" to protect persons or property;

2. "Business"

a. "Bodily injury" or "property damage" arising out of or in connection with a "business" conducted from an "insured location" or engaged in by an "insured", whether or not the "business" is owned or operated by an "insured" or employs an "insured".

This Exclusion **E.2.** applies but is not limited to an act or omission, regardless of its nature or circumstance, involving a service or duty rendered, promised, owed, or implied to be provided because of the nature of the "business".

b. This Exclusion **E.2.** does not apply to:

(1) The rental or holding for rental of an "insured location";

(a) On an occasional basis if used only as a residence;

(b) In part for use only as a residence, unless a single family unit is intended for use by the occupying family to lodge more than two roomers or boarders; or

(c) In part, as an office, school, studio or private garage; and

(2) An "insured" under the age of 21 years involved in a part-time or occasional, self-employed "business" with no employees;

3. Professional Services

"Bodily injury" or "property damage" arising out of the rendering of or failure to render professional services;

4. "Insured's" Premises Not An "Insured Location"

"Bodily injury" or "property damage" arising out of a premises:

a. Owned by an "insured";

b. Rented to an "insured"; or

c. Rented to others by an "insured";

that is not an "insured location";

5. War

"Bodily injury" or "property damage" caused directly or indirectly by war, including the following and any consequence of any of the following:

a. Undeclared war, civil war, insurrection, rebellion or revolution;

b. Warlike act by a military force or military personnel; or

c. Destruction, seizure or use for a military purpose.

Discharge of a nuclear weapon will be deemed a warlike act even if accidental;

6. Communicable Disease

"Bodily injury" or "property damage" which arises out of the transmission of a communicable disease by an "insured";

7. Sexual Molestation, Corporal Punishment Or Physical Or Mental Abuse

"Bodily injury" or "property damage" arising out of sexual molestation, corporal punishment or physical or mental abuse; or

8. Controlled Substance

"Bodily injury" or "property damage" arising out of the use, sale, manufacture, delivery, transfer or possession by any person of a Controlled Substance as defined by the Federal Food and Drug Law at 21 U.S.C.A. Sections 811 and 812. Controlled Substances include but are not limited to cocaine, LSD, marijuana and all narcotic drugs. However, this exclusion does not apply to the legitimate use of prescription drugs by a person following the orders of a licensed physician.

Exclusions **A.** "Motor Vehicle Liability", **B.** "Watercraft Liability", **C.** "Aircraft Liability", **D.** "Hovercraft Liability" and **E.4.** "Insured's" Premises Not An "Insured Location" do not apply to "bodily injury" to a "residence employee" arising out of and in the course of the "residence employee's" employment by an "insured".

F. Coverage E – Personal Liability

Coverage **E** does not apply to:

1. Liability:

a. For any loss assessment charged against you as a member of an association, corporation or community of property owners, except as provided in **D.** Loss Assessment under Section **II** – Additional Coverages;

b. Under any contract or agreement entered into by an "insured". However, this exclusion does not apply to written contracts:

(1) That directly relate to the ownership, maintenance or use of an "insured location"; or

(2) Where the liability of others is assumed by you prior to an "occurrence";

unless excluded in **a.** above or elsewhere in this policy;

2. "Property damage" to property owned by an "insured". This includes costs or expenses incurred by an "insured" or others to repair, replace, enhance, restore or maintain such property to prevent injury to a person or damage to property of others, whether on or away from an "insured location";

3. "Property damage" to property rented to, occupied or used by or in the care of an "insured". This exclusion does not apply to "property damage" caused by fire, smoke or explosion;

4. "Bodily injury" to any person eligible to receive any benefits voluntarily provided or required to be provided by an "insured" under any:

a. Workers' compensation law;

b. Non-occupational disability law; or

c. Occupational disease law;

5. "Bodily injury" or "property damage" for which an "insured" under this policy:

a. Is also an insured under a nuclear energy liability policy issued by the:

(1) Nuclear Energy Liability Insurance Association;

(2) Mutual Atomic Energy Liability Underwriters;

(3) Nuclear Insurance Association of Canada;

or any of their successors; or

b. Would be an insured under such a policy but for the exhaustion of its limit of liability; or

6. "Bodily injury" to you or an "insured" as defined under Definitions **5.a.** or **b.**

This exclusion also applies to any claim made or suit brought against you or an "insured":

a. To repay; or

b. Share damages with;

another person who may be obligated to pay damages because of "bodily injury" to an "insured".

G. Coverage F – Medical Payments To Others

Coverage **F** does not apply to "bodily injury":

1. To a "residence employee" if the "bodily injury":

a. Occurs off the "insured location"; and

b. Does not arise out of or in the course of the "residence employee's" employment by an "insured";

2. To any person eligible to receive benefits voluntarily provided or required to be provided under any:

a. Workers' compensation law;

b. Non-occupational disability law; or

c. Occupational disease law;

3. From any:

a. Nuclear reaction;

b. Nuclear radiation; or

c. Radioactive contamination;

all whether controlled or uncontrolled or however caused; or

d. Any consequence of any of these; or

4. To any person, other than a "residence employee" of an "insured", regularly residing on any part of the "insured location".

SECTION II – ADDITIONAL COVERAGES

We cover the following in addition to the limits of liability:

A. Claim Expenses

We pay:

1. Expenses we incur and costs taxed against an "insured" in any suit we defend;

2. Premiums on bonds required in a suit we defend, but not for bond amounts more than the Coverage **E** limit of liability. We need not apply for or furnish any bond;

3. Reasonable expenses incurred by an "insured" at our request, including actual loss of earnings (but not loss of other income) up to $250 per day, for assisting us in the investigation or defense of a claim or suit; and

4. Interest on the entire judgment which accrues after entry of the judgment and before we pay or tender, or deposit in court that part of the judgment which does not exceed the limit of liability that applies.

B. First Aid Expenses

We will pay expenses for first aid to others incurred by an "insured" for "bodily injury" covered under this policy. We will not pay for first aid to an "insured".

C. Damage To Property Of Others

1. We will pay, at replacement cost, up to $1,000 per "occurrence" for "property damage" to property of others caused by an "insured".

2. We will not pay for "property damage":

a. To the extent of any amount recoverable under Section **I**;

b. Caused intentionally by an "insured" who is 13 years of age or older;

c. To property owned by an "insured";

d. To property owned by or rented to a tenant of an "insured" or a resident in your household; or

e. Arising out of:

(1) A "business" engaged in by an "insured";

(2) Any act or omission in connection with a premises owned, rented or controlled by an "insured", other than the "insured location"; or

(3) The ownership, maintenance, occupancy, operation, use, loading or unloading of aircraft, hovercraft, watercraft or "motor vehicles".

This exclusion **e.(3)** does not apply to a "motor vehicle" that:

(a) Is designed for recreational use off public roads;

(b) Is not owned by an "insured"; and

(c) At the time of the "occurrence", is not required by law, or regulation issued by a government agency, to have been registered for it to be used on public roads or property.

D. Loss Assessment

1. We will pay up to $1,000 for your share of loss assessment charged against you, as owner or tenant of the "residence premises", during the policy period by a corporation or association of property owners, when the assessment is made as a result of:

   a. "Bodily injury" or "property damage" not excluded from coverage under Section **II** – Exclusions; or

   b. Liability for an act of a director, officer or trustee in the capacity as a director, officer or trustee, provided such person:

      (1) Is elected by the members of a corporation or association of property owners; and

      (2) Serves without deriving any income from the exercise of duties which are solely on behalf of a corporation or association of property owners.

2. Paragraph **I.** Policy Period under Section **II** – Conditions does not apply to this Loss Assessment Coverage.

3. Regardless of the number of assessments, the limit of $1,000 is the most we will pay for loss arising out of:

   a. One accident, including continuous or repeated exposure to substantially the same general harmful condition; or

   b. A covered act of a director, officer or trustee. An act involving more than one director, officer or trustee is considered to be a single act.

4. We do not cover assessments charged against you or a corporation or association of property owners by any governmental body.

SECTION II – CONDITIONS

A. Limit Of Liability

Our total liability under Coverage **E** for all damages resulting from any one "occurrence" will not be more than the Coverage **E** limit of liability shown in the Declarations. This limit is the same regardless of the number of "insureds", claims made or persons injured. All "bodily injury" and "property damage" resulting from any one accident or from continuous or repeated exposure to substantially the same general harmful conditions shall be considered to be the result of one "occurrence".

Our total liability under Coverage **F** for all medical expense payable for "bodily injury" to one person as the result of one accident will not be more than the Coverage **F** limit of liability shown in the Declarations.

B. Severability Of Insurance

This insurance applies separately to each "insured". This condition will not increase our limit of liability for any one "occurrence".

C. Duties After "Occurrence"

In case of an "occurrence", you or another "insured" will perform the following duties that apply. We have no duty to provide coverage under this policy if your failure to comply with the following duties is prejudicial to us. You will help us by seeing that these duties are performed:

1. Give written notice to us or our agent as soon as is practical, which sets forth:

   a. The identity of the policy and the "named insured" shown in the Declarations;

   b. Reasonably available information on the time, place and circumstances of the "occurrence"; and

   c. Names and addresses of any claimants and witnesses;

2. Cooperate with us in the investigation, settlement or defense of any claim or suit;

3. Promptly forward to us every notice, demand, summons or other process relating to the "occurrence";

4. At our request, help us:

   a. To make settlement;

   b. To enforce any right of contribution or indemnity against any person or organization who may be liable to an "insured";

c. With the conduct of suits and attend hearings and trials; and

d. To secure and give evidence and obtain the attendance of witnesses;

5. With respect to **C.** Damage To Property Of Others under Section **II** – Additional Coverages, submit to us within 60 days after the loss, a sworn statement of loss and show the damaged property, if in an "insured's" control;

6. No "insured" shall, except at such "insured's" own cost, voluntarily make payment, assume obligation or incur expense other than for first aid to others at the time of the "bodily injury".

D. Duties Of An Injured Person – Coverage F – Medical Payments To Others

1. The injured person or someone acting for the injured person will:

   a. Give us written proof of claim, under oath if required, as soon as is practical; and

   b. Authorize us to obtain copies of medical reports and records.

2. The injured person will submit to a physical exam by a doctor of our choice when and as often as we reasonably require.

E. Payment Of Claim – Coverage F – Medical Payments To Others

Payment under this coverage is not an admission of liability by an "insured" or us.

F. Suit Against Us

1. No action can be brought against us unless there has been full compliance with all of the terms under this Section **II**.

2. No one will have the right to join us as a party to any action against an "insured".

3. Also, no action with respect to Coverage **E** can be brought against us until the obligation of such "insured" has been determined by final judgment or agreement signed by us.

G. Bankruptcy Of An "Insured"

Bankruptcy or insolvency of an "insured" will not relieve us of our obligations under this policy.

H. Other Insurance

This insurance is excess over other valid and collectible insurance except insurance written specifically to cover as excess over the limits of liability that apply in this policy.

I. Policy Period

This policy applies only to "bodily injury" or "property damage" which occurs during the policy period.

J. Concealment Or Fraud

We do not provide coverage to an "insured" who, whether before or after a loss, has:

1. Intentionally concealed or misrepresented any material fact or circumstance;

2. Engaged in fraudulent conduct; or

3. Made false statements;

relating to this insurance.

SECTIONS I AND II – CONDITIONS

A. Liberalization Clause

If we make a change which broadens coverage under this edition of our policy without additional premium charge, that change will automatically apply to your insurance as of the date we implement the change in your state, provided that this implementation date falls within 60 days prior to or during the policy period stated in the Declarations.

This Liberalization Clause does not apply to changes implemented with a general program revision that includes both broadenings and restrictions in coverage, whether that general program revision is implemented through introduction of:

1. A subsequent edition of this policy; or

2. An amendatory endorsement.

B. Waiver Or Change Of Policy Provisions

A waiver or change of a provision of this policy must be in writing by us to be valid. Our request for an appraisal or examination will not waive any of our rights.

C. Cancellation

1. You may cancel this policy at any time by returning it to us or by letting us know in writing of the date cancellation is to take effect.

2. We may cancel this policy only for the reasons stated below by letting you know in writing of the date cancellation takes effect. This cancellation notice may be delivered to you, or mailed to you at your mailing address shown in the Declarations. Proof of mailing will be sufficient proof of notice.

   a. When you have not paid the premium, we may cancel at any time by letting you know at least 10 days before the date cancellation takes effect.

   b. When this policy has been in effect for less than 60 days and is not a renewal with us, we may cancel for any reason by letting you know at least 10 days before the date cancellation takes effect.

c. When this policy has been in effect for 60 days or more, or at any time if it is a renewal with us, we may cancel:

   (1) If there has been a material misrepresentation of fact which if known to us would have caused us not to issue the policy; or

   (2) If the risk has changed substantially since the policy was issued.

   This can be done by letting you know at least 30 days before the date cancellation takes effect.

d. When this policy is written for a period of more than one year, we may cancel for any reason at anniversary by letting you know at least 30 days before the date cancellation takes effect.

3. When this policy is canceled, the premium for the period from the date of cancellation to the expiration date will be refunded pro rata.

4. If the return premium is not refunded with the notice of cancellation or when this policy is returned to us, we will refund it within a reasonable time after the date cancellation takes effect.

D. Nonrenewal

We may elect not to renew this policy. We may do so by delivering to you, or mailing to you at your mailing address shown in the Declarations, written notice at least 30 days before the expiration date of this policy. Proof of mailing will be sufficient proof of notice.

E. Assignment

Assignment of this policy will not be valid unless we give our written consent.

F. Subrogation

An "insured" may waive in writing before a loss all rights of recovery against any person. If not waived, we may require an assignment of rights of recovery for a loss to the extent that payment is made by us.

If an assignment is sought, an "insured" must sign and deliver all related papers and cooperate with us.

Subrogation does not apply to Coverage **F** or Paragraph **C.** Damage To Property Of Others under Section **II** – Additional Coverages.

G. Death

If any person named in the Declarations or the spouse, if a resident of the same household, dies, the following apply:

1. We insure the legal representative of the deceased but only with respect to the premises and property of the deceased covered under the policy at the time of death; and

2. "Insured" includes:

   a. An "insured" who is a member of your household at the time of your death, but only while a resident of the "residence premises"; and

   b. With respect to your property, the person having proper temporary custody of the property until appointment and qualification of a legal representative.

HO 00 03 10 00

2010 EDITION

HOMEOWNERS
HO 00 03 05 11

HOMEOWNERS 3 – SPECIAL FORM

Homeowners

AGREEMENT

We will provide the insurance described in this policy in return for the premium and compliance with all applicable provisions of this policy.

DEFINITIONS

A. In this policy, "you" and "your" refer to the "named insured" shown in the Declarations and the spouse if a resident of the same household. "We", "us" and "our" refer to the Company providing this insurance.

B. In addition, certain words and phrases are defined as follows:

1. "Aircraft Liability", "Hovercraft Liability", "Motor Vehicle Liability" and "Watercraft Liability", subject to the provisions in **b.** below, mean the following:

  a. Liability for "bodily injury" or "property damage" arising out of the:

    (1) Ownership of such vehicle or craft by an "insured";

    (2) Maintenance, occupancy, operation, use, loading or unloading of such vehicle or craft by any person;

    (3) Entrustment of such vehicle or craft by an "insured" to any person;

    (4) Failure to supervise or negligent supervision of any person involving such vehicle or craft by an "insured"; or

    (5) Vicarious liability, whether or not imposed by law, for the actions of a child or minor involving such vehicle or craft.

  b. For the purpose of this definition:

    (1) Aircraft means any contrivance used or designed for flight except model or hobby aircraft not used or designed to carry people or cargo;

    (2) Hovercraft means a self-propelled motorized ground effect vehicle and includes, but is not limited to, flarecraft and air cushion vehicles;

    (3) Watercraft means a craft principally designed to be propelled on or in water by wind, engine power or electric motor; and

    (4) Motor vehicle means a "motor vehicle" as defined in **7.** below.

2. "Bodily injury" means bodily harm, sickness or disease, including required care, loss of services and death that results.

3. "Business" means:

  a. A trade, profession or occupation engaged in on a full-time, part-time or occasional basis; or

  b. Any other activity engaged in for money or other compensation, except the following:

    (1) One or more activities, not described in **(2)** through **(4)** below, for which no "insured" receives more than $2,000 in total compensation for the 12 months before the beginning of the policy period;

    (2) Volunteer activities for which no money is received other than payment for expenses incurred to perform the activity;

    (3) Providing home day care services for which no compensation is received, other than the mutual exchange of such services; or

    (4) The rendering of home day care services to a relative of an "insured".

4. "Employee" means an employee of an "insured", or an employee leased to an "insured" by a labor leasing firm under an agreement between an "insured" and the labor leasing firm, whose duties are other than those performed by a "residence employee".

5. "Insured" means:

  a. You and residents of your household who are:

    (1) Your relatives; or

    (2) Other persons under the age of 21 and in your care or the care of a resident of your household who is your relative;

  b. A student enrolled in school full-time, as defined by the school, who was a resident of your household before moving out to attend school, provided the student is under the age of:

    (1) 24 and your relative; or

(2) 21 and in your care or the care of a resident of your household who is your relative; or

c. Under Section **II:**

   (1) With respect to animals or watercraft to which this policy applies, any person or organization legally responsible for these animals or watercraft which are owned by you or any person described in **5.a.** or **b.** "Insured" does not mean a person or organization using or having custody of these animals or watercraft in the course of any "business" or without consent of the owner; or

   (2) With respect to a "motor vehicle" to which this policy applies:

      (a) Persons while engaged in your employ or that of any person described in **5.a.** or **b.;** or

      (b) Other persons using the vehicle on an "insured location" with your consent.

Under both Sections **I** and **II,** when the word an immediately precedes the word "insured", the words an "insured" together mean one or more "insureds".

6. "Insured location" means:

   a. The "residence premises";

   b. The part of other premises, other structures and grounds used by you as a residence; and

      (1) Which is shown in the Declarations; or

      (2) Which is acquired by you during the policy period for your use as a residence;

   c. Any premises used by you in connection with a premises described in **a.** and **b.** above;

   d. Any part of a premises:

      (1) Not owned by an "insured"; and

      (2) Where an "insured" is temporarily residing;

   e. Vacant land, other than farm land, owned by or rented to an "insured";

   f. Land owned by or rented to an "insured" on which a one-, two-, three- or four-family dwelling is being built as a residence for an "insured";

g. Individual or family cemetery plots or burial vaults of an "insured"; or

h. Any part of a premises occasionally rented to an "insured" for other than "business" use.

7. "Motor vehicle" means:

   a. A self-propelled land or amphibious vehicle; or

   b. Any trailer or semitrailer which is being carried on, towed by or hitched for towing by a vehicle described in **a.** above.

8. "Occurrence" means an accident, including continuous or repeated exposure to substantially the same general harmful conditions, which results, during the policy period, in:

   a. "Bodily injury"; or

   b. "Property damage".

9. "Property damage" means physical injury to, destruction of, or loss of use of tangible property.

10. "Residence employee" means:

   a. An employee of an "insured", or an employee leased to an "insured" by a labor leasing firm, under an agreement between an "insured" and the labor leasing firm, whose duties are related to the maintenance or use of the "residence premises", including household or domestic services; or

   b. One who performs similar duties elsewhere not related to the "business" of an "insured".

A "residence employee" does not include a temporary employee who is furnished to an "insured" to substitute for a permanent "residence employee" on leave or to meet seasonal or short-term workload conditions.

11. "Residence premises" means:

   a. The one-family dwelling where you reside;

   b. The two-, three- or four-family dwelling where you reside in at least one of the family units; or

   c. That part of any other building where you reside;

and which is shown as the "residence premises" in the Declarations.

"Residence premises" also includes other structures and grounds at that location.

       HO 00 03 05 11

SECTION I – PROPERTY COVERAGES

A. Coverage A – Dwelling

1. We cover:

   a. The dwelling on the "residence premises" shown in the Declarations, including structures attached to the dwelling; and

   b. Materials and supplies located on or next to the "residence premises" used to construct, alter or repair the dwelling or other structures on the "residence premises".

2. We do not cover land, including land on which the dwelling is located.

B. Coverage B – Other Structures

1. We cover other structures on the "residence premises" set apart from the dwelling by clear space. This includes structures connected to the dwelling by only a fence, utility line, or similar connection.

2. We do not cover:

   a. Land, including land on which the other structures are located;

   b. Other structures rented or held for rental to any person not a tenant of the dwelling, unless used solely as a private garage;

   c. Other structures from which any "business" is conducted; or

   d. Other structures used to store "business" property. However, we do cover a structure that contains "business" property solely owned by an "insured" or a tenant of the dwelling, provided that "business" property does not include gaseous or liquid fuel, other than fuel in a permanently installed fuel tank of a vehicle or craft parked or stored in the structure.

3. The limit of liability for this coverage will not be more than 10% of the limit of liability that applies to Coverage **A**. Use of this coverage does not reduce the Coverage **A** limit of liability.

C. Coverage C – Personal Property

1. **Covered Property**

   We cover personal property owned or used by an "insured" while it is anywhere in the world. After a loss and at your request, we will cover personal property owned by:

   a. Others while the property is on the part of the "residence premises" occupied by an "insured"; or

   b. A guest or a "residence employee", while the property is in any residence occupied by an "insured".

2. **Limit For Property At Other Locations**

   a. **Other Residences**

   Our limit of liability for personal property usually located at an "insured's" residence, other than the "residence premises", is 10% of the limit of liability for Coverage **C**, or $1,000, whichever is greater. However, this limitation does not apply to personal property:

   (1) Moved from the "residence premises" because it is:

   (a) Being repaired, renovated or rebuilt; and

   (b) Not fit to live in or store property in; or

   (2) In a newly acquired principal residence for 30 days from the time you begin to move the property there.

   b. **Self-storage Facilities**

   Our limit of liability for personal property owned or used by an "insured" and located in a self-storage facility is 10% of the limit of liability for Coverage **C**, or $1,000, whichever is greater. However, this limitation does not apply to personal property:

   (1) Moved from the "residence premises" because it is:

   (a) Being repaired, renovated or rebuilt; and

   (b) Not fit to live in or store property in; or

   (2) Usually located in an "insured's" residence, other than the "residence premises".

3. **Special Limits Of Liability**

The special limit for each category shown below is the total limit for each loss for all property in that category. These special limits do not increase the Coverage **C** limit of liability.

a. $200 on money, bank notes, bullion, gold other than goldware, silver other than silverware, platinum other than platinumware, coins, medals, scrip, stored value cards and smart cards.

b. $1,500 on securities, accounts, deeds, evidences of debt, letters of credit, notes other than bank notes, manuscripts, personal records, passports, tickets and stamps. This dollar limit applies to these categories regardless of the medium (such as paper or computer software) on which the material exists.

This limit includes the cost to research, replace or restore the information from the lost or damaged material.

c. $1,500 on watercraft of all types, including their trailers, furnishings, equipment and outboard engines or motors.

d. $1,500 on trailers or semitrailers not used with watercraft of all types.

e. $1,500 for loss by theft of jewelry, watches, furs, precious and semiprecious stones.

f. $2,500 for loss by theft of firearms and related equipment.

g. $2,500 for loss by theft of silverware, silver-plated ware, goldware, gold-plated ware, platinumware, platinum-plated ware and pewterware. This includes flatware, hollowware, tea sets, trays and trophies made of or including silver, gold or pewter.

h. $2,500 on property, on the "residence premises", used primarily for "business" purposes.

i. $1,500 on property, away from the "residence premises", used primarily for "business" purposes. However, this limit does not apply to antennas, tapes, wires, records, disks or other media that are:

   (1) Used with electronic equipment that reproduces, receives or transmits audio, visual or data signals; and

   (2) In or upon a "motor vehicle".

j. $1,500 on portable electronic equipment that:

   (1) Reproduces, receives or transmits audio, visual or data signals;

   (2) Is designed to be operated by more than one power source, one of which is a "motor vehicle's" electrical system; and

   (3) Is in or upon a "motor vehicle".

k. $250 for antennas, tapes, wires, records, disks or other media that are:

   (1) Used with electronic equipment that reproduces, receives or transmits audio, visual or data signals; and

   (2) In or upon a "motor vehicle".

4. **Property Not Covered**

We do not cover:

a. Articles separately described and specifically insured, regardless of the limit for which they are insured, in this or other insurance;

b. Animals, birds or fish;

c. "Motor vehicles".

This includes a "motor vehicle's" equipment and parts. However, this Paragraph **4.c.** does not apply to:

   (1) Portable electronic equipment that:

      (a) Reproduces, receives or transmits audio, visual or data signals; and

      (b) Is designed so that it may be operated from a power source other than a "motor vehicle's" electrical system.

   (2) "Motor vehicles" not required to be registered for use on public roads or property which are:

      (a) Used solely to service a residence; or

      (b) Designed to assist the handicapped;

d. Aircraft, meaning any contrivance used or designed for flight, including any parts whether or not attached to the aircraft.

We do cover model or hobby aircraft not used or designed to carry people or cargo;

e. Hovercraft and parts. Hovercraft means a self-propelled motorized ground effect vehicle and includes, but is not limited to, flarecraft and air cushion vehicles;

f. Property of roomers, boarders and other tenants, except property of roomers and boarders related to an "insured";

g. Property in an apartment regularly rented or held for rental to others by an "insured", except as provided in **E.10.** Landlord's Furnishings under Section I – Property Coverages;

h. Property rented or held for rental to others off the "residence premises";

i. "Business" data, including such data stored in:

   (1) Books of account, drawings or other paper records; or

   (2) Computers and related equipment.

   We do cover the cost of blank recording or storage media and of prerecorded computer programs available on the retail market;

j. Credit cards, electronic fund transfer cards or access devices used solely for deposit, withdrawal or transfer of funds except as provided in **E.6.** Credit Card, Electronic Fund Transfer Card Or Access Device, Forgery And Counterfeit Money under Section I – Property Coverages; or

k. Water or steam.

D. Coverage D – Loss Of Use

The limit of liability for Coverage **D** is the total limit for the coverages in **1.** Additional Living Expense, **2.** Fair Rental Value and **3.** Civil Authority Prohibits Use below.

1. Additional Living Expense

If a loss covered under Section I makes that part of the "residence premises" where you reside not fit to live in, we cover any necessary increase in living expenses incurred by you so that your household can maintain its normal standard of living.

Payment will be for the shortest time required to repair or replace the damage or, if you permanently relocate, the shortest time required for your household to settle elsewhere.

2. Fair Rental Value

If a loss covered under Section I makes that part of the "residence premises" rented to others or held for rental by you not fit to live in, we cover the fair rental value of such premises less any expenses that do not continue while it is not fit to live in.

Payment will be for the shortest time required to repair or replace such premises.

3. Civil Authority Prohibits Use

If a civil authority prohibits you from use of the "residence premises" as a result of direct damage to neighboring premises by a Peril Insured Against, we cover the loss as provided in **1.** Additional Living Expense and **2.** Fair Rental Value above for no more than two weeks.

4. Loss Or Expense Not Covered

We do not cover loss or expense due to cancellation of a lease or agreement.

The periods of time under **1.** Additional Living Expense, **2.** Fair Rental Value and **3.** Civil Authority Prohibits Use above are not limited by expiration of this policy.

E. Additional Coverages

1. Debris Removal

a. We will pay your reasonable expense for the removal of:

   (1) Debris of covered property if a Peril Insured Against that applies to the damaged property causes the loss; or

   (2) Ash, dust or particles from a volcanic eruption that has caused direct loss to a building or property contained in a building.

   This expense is included in the limit of liability that applies to the damaged property. If the amount to be paid for the actual damage to the property plus the debris removal expense is more than the limit of liability for the damaged property, an additional 5% of that limit is available for such expense.

b. We will also pay your reasonable expense, up to $1,000, for the removal from the "residence premises" of:

   (1) Your trees felled by the peril of Windstorm or Hail or Weight of Ice, Snow or Sleet; or

   (2) A neighbor's trees felled by a Peril Insured Against under Coverage **C;**

   provided the trees:

   (3) Damage a covered structure; or

   (4) Do not damage a covered structure, but:

      (a) Block a driveway on the "residence premises" which prevents a "motor vehicle", that is registered for use on public roads or property, from entering or leaving the "residence premises"; or

(b) Block a ramp or other fixture designed to assist a handicapped person to enter or leave the dwelling building.

The $1,000 limit is the most we will pay in any one loss, regardless of the number of fallen trees. No more than $500 of this limit will be paid for the removal of any one tree.

This coverage is additional insurance.

2. Reasonable Repairs

a. We will pay the reasonable cost incurred by you for the necessary measures taken solely to protect covered property that is damaged by a Peril Insured Against from further damage.

b. If the measures taken involve repair to other damaged property, we will only pay if that property is covered under this policy and the damage is caused by a Peril Insured Against. This coverage does not:

(1) Increase the limit of liability that applies to the covered property; or

(2) Relieve you of your duties, in case of a loss to covered property, described in **C.4.** under Section **I** – Conditions.

3. Trees, Shrubs And Other Plants

We cover trees, shrubs, plants or lawns, on the "residence premises", for loss caused by the following Perils Insured Against:

a. Fire or Lightning;

b. Explosion;

c. Riot or Civil Commotion;

d. Aircraft;

e. Vehicles not owned or operated by a resident of the "residence premises";

f. Vandalism or Malicious Mischief; or

g. Theft.

We will pay up to 5% of the limit of liability that applies to the dwelling for all trees, shrubs, plants or lawns. No more than $500 of this limit will be paid for any one tree, shrub or plant. We do not cover property grown for "business" purposes.

This coverage is additional insurance.

4. Fire Department Service Charge

We will pay up to $500 for your liability assumed by contract or agreement for fire department charges incurred when the fire department is called to save or protect covered property from a Peril Insured Against. We do not cover fire department service charges if the property is located within the limits of the city, municipality or protection district furnishing the fire department response.

This coverage is additional insurance. No deductible applies to this coverage.

5. Property Removed

We insure covered property against direct loss from any cause while being removed from a premises endangered by a Peril Insured Against and for no more than 30 days while removed.

This coverage does not change the limit of liability that applies to the property being removed.

6. Credit Card, Electronic Fund Transfer Card Or Access Device, Forgery And Counterfeit Money

a. We will pay up to $500 for:

(1) The legal obligation of an "insured" to pay because of the theft or unauthorized use of credit cards issued to or registered in an "insured's" name;

(2) Loss resulting from theft or unauthorized use of an electronic fund transfer card or access device used for deposit, withdrawal or transfer of funds, issued to or registered in an "insured's" name;

(3) Loss to an "insured" caused by forgery or alteration of any check or negotiable instrument; and

(4) Loss to an "insured" through acceptance in good faith of counterfeit United States or Canadian paper currency.

All loss resulting from a series of acts committed by any one person or in which any one person is concerned or implicated is considered to be one loss.

This coverage is additional insurance. No deductible applies to this coverage.

b. We do not cover:

(1) Use of a credit card, electronic fund transfer card or access device:

  (a) By a resident of your household;

  (b) By a person who has been entrusted with either type of card or access device; or

  (c) If an "insured" has not complied with all terms and conditions under which the cards are issued or the devices accessed; or

(2) Loss arising out of "business" use or dishonesty of an "insured".

c. If the coverage in **a.** above applies, the following defense provisions also apply:

(1) We may investigate and settle any claim or suit that we decide is appropriate. Our duty to defend a claim or suit ends when the amount we pay for the loss equals our limit of liability.

(2) If a suit is brought against an "insured" for liability under **a.(1)** or **(2)** above, we will provide a defense at our expense by counsel of our choice.

(3) We have the option to defend at our expense an "insured" or an "insured's" bank against any suit for the enforcement of payment under **a.(3)** above.

7. Loss Assessment

a. We will pay up to $1,000 for your share of loss assessment charged during the policy period against you, as owner or tenant of the "residence premises", by a corporation or association of property owners. The assessment must be made as a result of direct loss to property, owned by all members collectively, of the type that would be covered by this policy if owned by you, caused by a Peril Insured Against under Coverage **A,** other than:

(1) Earthquake; or

(2) Land shock waves or tremors before, during or after a volcanic eruption.

The limit of $1,000 is the most we will pay with respect to any one loss, regardless of the number of assessments. We will only apply one deductible, per unit, to the total amount of any one loss to the property described above, regardless of the number of assessments.

b. We do not cover assessments charged against you or a corporation or association of property owners by any governmental body.

c. Paragraph **Q.** Policy Period under Section **I** – Conditions does not apply to this coverage.

This coverage is additional insurance.

8. Collapse

a. The coverage provided under this Additional Coverage – Collapse applies only to an abrupt collapse.

b. For the purpose of this Additional Coverage – Collapse, abrupt collapse means an abrupt falling down or caving in of a building or any part of a building with the result that the building or part of the building cannot be occupied for its intended purpose.

c. This Additional Coverage – Collapse does not apply to:

(1) A building or any part of a building that is in danger of falling down or caving in;

(2) A part of a building that is standing, even if it has separated from another part of the building; or

(3) A building or any part of a building that is standing, even if it shows evidence of cracking, bulging, sagging, bending, leaning, settling, shrinkage or expansion.

d. We insure for direct physical loss to covered property involving abrupt collapse of a building or any part of a building if such collapse was caused by one or more of the following:

(1) The Perils Insured Against named under Coverage **C**;

(2) Decay, of a building or any part of a building, that is hidden from view, unless the presence of such decay is known to an "insured" prior to collapse;

(3) Insect or vermin damage, to a building or any part of a building, that is hidden from view, unless the presence of such damage is known to an "insured" prior to collapse;

(4) Weight of contents, equipment, animals or people;

(5) Weight of rain which collects on a roof; or

(6) Use of defective material or methods in construction, remodeling or renovation if the collapse occurs during the course of the construction, remodeling or renovation.

e. Loss to an awning, fence, patio, deck, pavement, swimming pool, underground pipe, flue, drain, cesspool, septic tank, foundation, retaining wall, bulkhead, pier, wharf or dock is not included under **d.(2)** through **(6)** above, unless the loss is a direct result of the collapse of a building or any part of a building.

f. This coverage does not increase the limit of liability that applies to the damaged covered property.

9. Glass Or Safety Glazing Material

a. We cover:

(1) The breakage of glass or safety glazing material which is part of a covered building, storm door or storm window;

(2) The breakage of glass or safety glazing material which is part of a covered building, storm door or storm window when caused directly by earth movement; and

(3) The direct physical loss to covered property caused solely by the pieces, fragments or splinters of broken glass or safety glazing material which is part of a building, storm door or storm window.

b. This coverage does not include loss:

(1) To covered property which results because the glass or safety glazing material has been broken, except as provided in **a.(3)** above; or

(2) On the "residence premises" if the dwelling has been vacant for more than 60 consecutive days immediately before the loss, except when the breakage results directly from earth movement as provided in **a.(2)** above. A dwelling being constructed is not considered vacant.

c. This coverage does not increase the limit of liability that applies to the damaged property.

10. Landlord's Furnishings

We will pay up to $2,500 for your appliances, carpeting and other household furnishings, in each apartment on the "residence premises" regularly rented or held for rental to others by an "insured", for loss caused by a Peril Insured Against in Coverage **C,** other than Theft.

This limit is the most we will pay in any one loss regardless of the number of appliances, carpeting or other household furnishings involved in the loss.

This coverage does not increase the limit of liability applying to the damaged property.

11. Ordinance Or Law

a. You may use up to 10% of the limit of liability that applies to Coverage **A** for the increased costs you incur due to the enforcement of any ordinance or law which requires or regulates:

(1) The construction, demolition, remodeling, renovation or repair of that part of a covered building or other structure damaged by a Peril Insured Against;

(2) The demolition and reconstruction of the undamaged part of a covered building or other structure, when that building or other structure must be totally demolished because of damage by a Peril Insured Against to another part of that covered building or other structure; or

(3) The remodeling, removal or replacement of the portion of the undamaged part of a covered building or other structure necessary to complete the remodeling, repair or replacement of that part of the covered building or other structure damaged by a Peril Insured Against.

b. You may use all or part of this ordinance or law coverage to pay for the increased costs you incur to remove debris resulting from the construction, demolition, remodeling, renovation, repair or replacement of property as stated in **a.** above.

c. We do not cover:

(1) The loss in value to any covered building or other structure due to the requirements of any ordinance or law; or

(2) The costs to comply with any ordinance or law which requires any "insured" or others to test for, monitor, clean up, remove, contain, treat, detoxify or neutralize, or in any way respond to, or assess the effects of, pollutants in or on any covered building or other structure.

Pollutants means any solid, liquid, gaseous or thermal irritant or contaminant, including smoke, vapor, soot, fumes, acids, alkalis, chemicals and waste. Waste includes materials to be recycled, reconditioned or reclaimed.

This coverage is additional insurance.

12. Grave Markers

We will pay up to $5,000 for grave markers, including mausoleums, on or away from the "residence premises" for loss caused by a Peril Insured Against under Coverage **C.**

This coverage does not increase the limits of liability that apply to the damaged covered property.

SECTION I – PERILS INSURED AGAINST

A. Coverage A – Dwelling And Coverage B – Other Structures

1. We insure against direct physical loss to property described in Coverages **A** and **B.**

2. We do not insure, however, for loss:

   a. Excluded under Section **I** – Exclusions;

   b. Involving collapse, including any of the following conditions of property or any part of the property:

      (1) An abrupt falling down or caving in;

      (2) Loss of structural integrity, including separation of parts of the property or property in danger of falling down or caving in; or

      (3) Any cracking, bulging, sagging, bending, leaning, settling, shrinkage or expansion as such condition relates to **(1)** or **(2)** above;

      except as provided in **E.8.** Collapse under Section **I** – Property Coverages; or

   c. Caused by:

      (1) Freezing of a plumbing, heating, air conditioning or automatic fire protective sprinkler system or of a household appliance, or by discharge, leakage or overflow from within the system or appliance caused by freezing. This provision does not apply if you have used reasonable care to:

         (a) Maintain heat in the building; or

         (b) Shut off the water supply and drain all systems and appliances of water.

However, if the building is protected by an automatic fire protective sprinkler system, you must use reasonable care to continue the water supply and maintain heat in the building for coverage to apply.

For purposes of this provision, a plumbing system or household appliance does not include a sump, sump pump or related equipment or a roof drain, gutter, downspout or similar fixtures or equipment;

      (2) Freezing, thawing, pressure or weight of water or ice, whether driven by wind or not, to a:

         (a) Fence, pavement, patio or swimming pool;

         (b) Footing, foundation, bulkhead, wall, or any other structure or device that supports all or part of a building, or other structure;

         (c) Retaining wall or bulkhead that does not support all or part of a building or other structure; or

         (d) Pier, wharf or dock;

      (3) Theft in or to a dwelling under construction, or of materials and supplies for use in the construction until the dwelling is finished and occupied;

      (4) Vandalism and malicious mischief, and any ensuing loss caused by any intentional and wrongful act committed in the course of the vandalism or malicious mischief, if the dwelling has been vacant for more than 60 consecutive days immediately before the loss. A dwelling being constructed is not considered vacant;

      (5) Mold, fungus or wet rot. However, we do insure for loss caused by mold, fungus or wet rot that is hidden within the walls or ceilings or beneath the floors or above the ceilings of a structure if such loss results from the accidental discharge or overflow of water or steam from within:

         (a) A plumbing, heating, air conditioning or automatic fire protective sprinkler system, or a household appliance, on the "residence premises"; or

         (b) A storm drain, or water, steam or sewer pipes, off the "residence premises".

For purposes of this provision, a plumbing system or household appliance does not include a sump, sump pump or related equipment or a roof drain, gutter, downspout or similar fixtures or equipment; or

(6) Any of the following:

(a) Wear and tear, marring, deterioration;

(b) Mechanical breakdown, latent defect, inherent vice or any quality in property that causes it to damage or destroy itself;

(c) Smog, rust or other corrosion, or dry rot;

(d) Smoke from agricultural smudging or industrial operations;

(e) Discharge, dispersal, seepage, migration, release or escape of pollutants unless the discharge, dispersal, seepage, migration, release or escape is itself caused by a Peril Insured Against named under Coverage **C**.

Pollutants means any solid, liquid, gaseous or thermal irritant or contaminant, including smoke, vapor, soot, fumes, acids, alkalis, chemicals and waste. Waste includes materials to be recycled, reconditioned or reclaimed;

(f) Settling, shrinking, bulging or expansion, including resultant cracking, of bulkheads, pavements, patios, footings, foundations, walls, floors, roofs or ceilings;

(g) Birds, rodents or insects;

(h) Nesting or infestation, or discharge or release of waste products or secretions, by any animals; or

(i) Animals owned or kept by an "insured".

Exception To c.(6)

Unless the loss is otherwise excluded, we cover loss to property covered under Coverage **A** or **B** resulting from an accidental discharge or overflow of water or steam from within a:

(i) Storm drain, or water, steam or sewer pipe, off the "residence premises"; or

(ii) Plumbing, heating, air conditioning or automatic fire protective sprinkler system or household appliance on the "residence premises". This includes the cost to tear out and replace any part of a building, or other structure, on the "residence premises", but only when necessary to repair the system or appliance. However, such tear out and replacement coverage only applies to other structures if the water or steam causes actual damage to a building on the "residence premises".

We do not cover loss to the system or appliance from which this water or steam escaped.

For purposes of this provision, a plumbing system or household appliance does not include a sump, sump pump or related equipment or a roof drain, gutter, downspout or similar fixtures or equipment.

Section **I** – Exclusion **A.3.** Water, Paragraphs **a.** and **c.** that apply to surface water and water below the surface of the ground do not apply to loss by water covered under **c.(5)** and **(6)** above.

Under **2.b.** and **c.** above, any ensuing loss to property described in Coverages **A** and **B** not precluded by any other provision in this policy is covered.

B. Coverage C – Personal Property

We insure for direct physical loss to the property described in Coverage **C** caused by any of the following perils unless the loss is excluded in Section **I** – Exclusions.

1. Fire Or Lightning

2. Windstorm Or Hail

This peril includes loss to watercraft of all types and their trailers, furnishings, equipment, and outboard engines or motors, only while inside a fully enclosed building.

This peril does not include loss to the property contained in a building caused by rain, snow, sleet, sand or dust unless the direct force of wind or hail damages the building causing an opening in a roof or wall and the rain, snow, sleet, sand or dust enters through this opening.

3. **Explosion**

4. **Riot Or Civil Commotion**

5. **Aircraft**

This peril includes self-propelled missiles and spacecraft.

6. **Vehicles**

7. **Smoke**

This peril means sudden and accidental damage from smoke, including the emission or puffback of smoke, soot, fumes or vapors from a boiler, furnace or related equipment.

This peril does not include loss caused by smoke from agricultural smudging or industrial operations.

8. **Vandalism Or Malicious Mischief**

9. **Theft**

a. This peril includes attempted theft and loss of property from a known place when it is likely that the property has been stolen.

b. This peril does not include loss caused by theft:

(1) Committed by an "insured";

(2) In or to a dwelling under construction, or of materials and supplies for use in the construction until the dwelling is finished and occupied;

(3) From that part of a "residence premises" rented by an "insured" to someone other than another "insured"; or

(4) That occurs off the "residence premises" of:

(a) Trailers, semitrailers and campers;

(b) Watercraft of all types, and their furnishings, equipment and outboard engines or motors; or

(c) Property while at any other residence owned by, rented to, or occupied by an "insured", except while an "insured" is temporarily living there. Property of an "insured" who is a student is covered while at the residence the student occupies to attend school as long as the student has been there at any time during the 90 days immediately before the loss.

10. **Falling Objects**

This peril does not include loss to property contained in a building unless the roof or an outside wall of the building is first damaged by a falling object. Damage to the falling object itself is not included.

11. **Weight Of Ice, Snow Or Sleet**

This peril means weight of ice, snow or sleet which causes damage to property contained in a building.

12. **Accidental Discharge Or Overflow Of Water Or Steam**

a. This peril means accidental discharge or overflow of water or steam from within a plumbing, heating, air conditioning or automatic fire protective sprinkler system or from within a household appliance.

b. This peril does not include loss:

(1) To the system or appliance from which the water or steam escaped;

(2) Caused by or resulting from freezing except as provided in Peril Insured Against **14.** Freezing;

(3) On the "residence premises" caused by accidental discharge or overflow which occurs off the "residence premises"; or

(4) Caused by mold, fungus or wet rot unless hidden within the walls or ceilings or beneath the floors or above the ceilings of a structure.

c. In this peril, a plumbing system or household appliance does not include a sump, sump pump or related equipment or a roof drain, gutter, downspout or similar fixtures or equipment.

d. Section **I** – Exclusion **A.3.** Water, Paragraphs **a.** and **c.** that apply to surface water and water below the surface of the ground do not apply to loss by water covered under this peril.

13. **Sudden And Accidental Tearing Apart, Cracking, Burning Or Bulging**

This peril means sudden and accidental tearing apart, cracking, burning or bulging of a steam or hot water heating system, an air conditioning or automatic fire protective sprinkler system, or an appliance for heating water.

We do not cover loss caused by or resulting from freezing under this peril.

14. Freezing

a. This peril means freezing of a plumbing, heating, air conditioning or automatic fire protective sprinkler system or of a household appliance, but only if you have used reasonable care to:

   (1) Maintain heat in the building; or

   (2) Shut off the water supply and drain all systems and appliances of water.

   However, if the building is protected by an automatic fire protective sprinkler system, you must use reasonable care to continue the water supply and maintain heat in the building for coverage to apply.

b. In this peril, a plumbing system or household appliance does not include a sump, sump pump or related equipment or a roof drain, gutter, downspout or similar fixtures or equipment.

15. Sudden And Accidental Damage From Artificially Generated Electrical Current

This peril does not include loss to tubes, transistors, electronic components or circuitry that is a part of appliances, fixtures, computers, home entertainment units or other types of electronic apparatus.

16. Volcanic Eruption

This peril does not include loss caused by earthquake, land shock waves or tremors.

SECTION I – EXCLUSIONS

A. We do not insure for loss caused directly or indirectly by any of the following. Such loss is excluded regardless of any other cause or event contributing concurrently or in any sequence to the loss. These exclusions apply whether or not the loss event results in widespread damage or affects a substantial area.

1. Ordinance Or Law

Ordinance Or Law means any ordinance or law:

a. Requiring or regulating the construction, demolition, remodeling, renovation or repair of property, including removal of any resulting debris. This Exclusion **A.1.a.** does not apply to the amount of coverage that may be provided for in **E.11.** Ordinance Or Law under Section **I** – Property Coverages;

b. The requirements of which result in a loss in value to property; or

c. Requiring any "insured" or others to test for, monitor, clean up, remove, contain, treat, detoxify or neutralize, or in any way respond to, or assess the effects of, pollutants.

   Pollutants means any solid, liquid, gaseous or thermal irritant or contaminant, including smoke, vapor, soot, fumes, acids, alkalis, chemicals and waste. Waste includes materials to be recycled, reconditioned or reclaimed.

This Exclusion **A.1.** applies whether or not the property has been physically damaged.

2. Earth Movement

Earth Movement means:

a. Earthquake, including land shock waves or tremors before, during or after a volcanic eruption;

b. Landslide, mudslide or mudflow;

c. Subsidence or sinkhole; or

d. Any other earth movement including earth sinking, rising or shifting.

This Exclusion **A.2.** applies regardless of whether any of the above, in **A.2.a.** through **A.2.d.**, is caused by an act of nature or is otherwise caused.

However, direct loss by fire, explosion or theft resulting from any of the above, in **A.2.a.** through **A.2.d.**, is covered.

3. Water

This means:

a. Flood, surface water, waves, including tidal wave and tsunami, tides, tidal water, overflow of any body of water, or spray from any of these, all whether or not driven by wind, including storm surge;

b. Water which:

   (1) Backs up through sewers or drains; or

   (2) Overflows or is otherwise discharged from a sump, sump pump or related equipment;

c. Water below the surface of the ground, including water which exerts pressure on, or seeps, leaks or flows through a building, sidewalk, driveway, patio, foundation, swimming pool or other structure; or

d. Waterborne material carried or otherwise moved by any of the water referred to in **A.3.a.** through **A.3.c.** of this exclusion.

This Exclusion **A.3.** applies regardless of whether any of the above, in **A.3.a.** through **A.3.d.,** is caused by an act of nature or is otherwise caused.

This Exclusion **A.3.** applies to, but is not limited to, escape, overflow or discharge, for any reason, of water or waterborne material from a dam, levee, seawall or any other boundary or containment system.

However, direct loss by fire, explosion or theft resulting from any of the above, in **A.3.a.** through **A.3.d.,** is covered.

4. Power Failure

Power Failure means the failure of power or other utility service if the failure takes place off the "residence premises". But if the failure results in a loss, from a Peril Insured Against on the "residence premises", we will pay for the loss caused by that peril.

5. Neglect

Neglect means neglect of an "insured" to use all reasonable means to save and preserve property at and after the time of a loss.

6. War

War includes the following and any consequence of any of the following:

a. Undeclared war, civil war, insurrection, rebellion or revolution;

b. Warlike act by a military force or military personnel; or

c. Destruction, seizure or use for a military purpose.

Discharge of a nuclear weapon will be deemed a warlike act even if accidental.

7. Nuclear Hazard

This Exclusion **A.7.** pertains to Nuclear Hazard to the extent set forth in **N.** Nuclear Hazard Clause under Section **I** – Conditions.

8. Intentional Loss

Intentional Loss means any loss arising out of any act an "insured" commits or conspires to commit with the intent to cause a loss.

In the event of such loss, no "insured" is entitled to coverage, even "insureds" who did not commit or conspire to commit the act causing the loss.

9. Governmental Action

Governmental Action means the destruction, confiscation or seizure of property described in Coverage **A, B** or **C** by order of any governmental or public authority.

This exclusion does not apply to such acts ordered by any governmental or public authority that are taken at the time of a fire to prevent its spread, if the loss caused by fire would be covered under this policy.

B. We do not insure for loss to property described in Coverages **A** and **B** caused by any of the following. However, any ensuing loss to property described in Coverages **A** and **B** not precluded by any other provision in this policy is covered.

1. Weather conditions. However, this exclusion only applies if weather conditions contribute in any way with a cause or event excluded in **A.** above to produce the loss.

2. Acts or decisions, including the failure to act or decide, of any person, group, organization or governmental body.

3. Faulty, inadequate or defective:

a. Planning, zoning, development, surveying, siting;

b. Design, specifications, workmanship, repair, construction, renovation, remodeling, grading, compaction;

c. Materials used in repair, construction, renovation or remodeling; or

d. Maintenance;

of part or all of any property whether on or off the "residence premises".

SECTION I – CONDITIONS

A. Insurable Interest And Limit Of Liability

Even if more than one person has an insurable interest in the property covered, we will not be liable in any one loss:

1. To an "insured" for more than the amount of such "insured's" interest at the time of loss; or

2. For more than the applicable limit of liability.

B. Deductible

Unless otherwise noted in this policy, the following deductible provision applies:

With respect to any one loss:

1. Subject to the applicable limit of liability, we will pay only that part of the total of all loss payable that exceeds the deductible amount shown in the Declarations.

2. If two or more deductibles under this policy apply to the loss, only the highest deductible amount will apply.

C. Duties After Loss

In case of a loss to covered property, we have no duty to provide coverage under this policy if the failure to comply with the following duties is prejudicial to us. These duties must be performed either by you, an "insured" seeking coverage, or a representative of either:

1. Give prompt notice to us or our agent;

2. Notify the police in case of loss by theft;

3. Notify the credit card or electronic fund transfer card or access device company in case of loss as provided for in **E.6.** Credit Card, Electronic Fund Transfer Card Or Access Device, Forgery And Counterfeit Money under Section I – Property Coverages;

4. Protect the property from further damage. If repairs to the property are required, you must:

   a. Make reasonable and necessary repairs to protect the property; and

   b. Keep an accurate record of repair expenses;

5. Cooperate with us in the investigation of a claim;

6. Prepare an inventory of damaged personal property showing the quantity, description, actual cash value and amount of loss. Attach all bills, receipts and related documents that justify the figures in the inventory;

7. As often as we reasonably require:

   a. Show the damaged property;

   b. Provide us with records and documents we request and permit us to make copies; and

   c. Submit to examination under oath, while not in the presence of another "insured", and sign the same;

8. Send to us, within 60 days after our request, your signed, sworn proof of loss which sets forth, to the best of your knowledge and belief:

   a. The time and cause of loss;

   b. The interests of all "insureds" and all others in the property involved and all liens on the property;

   c. Other insurance which may cover the loss;

   d. Changes in title or occupancy of the property during the term of the policy;

   e. Specifications of damaged buildings and detailed repair estimates;

   f. The inventory of damaged personal property described in **6.** above;

   g. Receipts for additional living expenses incurred and records that support the fair rental value loss; and

   h. Evidence or affidavit that supports a claim under **E.6.** Credit Card, Electronic Fund Transfer Card Or Access Device, Forgery And Counterfeit Money under Section I – Property Coverages, stating the amount and cause of loss.

D. Loss Settlement

In this Condition **D.**, the terms "cost to repair or replace" and "replacement cost" do not include the increased costs incurred to comply with the enforcement of any ordinance or law, except to the extent that coverage for these increased costs is provided in **E.11.** Ordinance Or Law under Section I – Property Coverages. Covered property losses are settled as follows:

1. Property of the following types:

   a. Personal property;

   b. Awnings, carpeting, household appliances, outdoor antennas and outdoor equipment, whether or not attached to buildings;

   c. Structures that are not buildings; and

   d. Grave markers, including mausoleums;

   at actual cash value at the time of loss but not more than the amount required to repair or replace.

2. Buildings covered under Coverage **A** or **B** at replacement cost without deduction for depreciation, subject to the following:

   a. If, at the time of loss, the amount of insurance in this policy on the damaged building is 80% or more of the full replacement cost of the building immediately before the loss, we will pay the cost to repair or replace, without deduction for depreciation, but not more than the least of the following amounts:

      (1) The limit of liability under this policy that applies to the building;

      (2) The replacement cost of that part of the building damaged with material of like kind and quality and for like use; or

      (3) The necessary amount actually spent to repair or replace the damaged building.

      If the building is rebuilt at a new premises, the cost described in **(2)** above is limited to the cost which would have been incurred if the building had been built at the original premises.

b. If, at the time of loss, the amount of insurance in this policy on the damaged building is less than 80% of the full replacement cost of the building immediately before the loss, we will pay the greater of the following amounts, but not more than the limit of liability under this policy that applies to the building:

(1) The actual cash value of that part of the building damaged; or

(2) That proportion of the cost to repair or replace, without deduction for depreciation, that part of the building damaged, which the total amount of insurance in this policy on the damaged building bears to 80% of the replacement cost of the building.

c. To determine the amount of insurance required to equal 80% of the full replacement cost of the building immediately before the loss, do not include the value of:

(1) Excavations, footings, foundations, piers, or any other structures or devices that support all or part of the building, which are below the undersurface of the lowest basement floor;

(2) Those supports described in **(1)** above which are below the surface of the ground inside the foundation walls, if there is no basement; and

(3) Underground flues, pipes, wiring and drains.

d. We will pay no more than the actual cash value of the damage until actual repair or replacement is complete. Once actual repair or replacement is complete, we will settle the loss as noted in **2.a.** and **b.** above.

However, if the cost to repair or replace the damage is both:

(1) Less than 5% of the amount of insurance in this policy on the building; and

(2) Less than $2,500;

we will settle the loss as noted in **2.a.** and **b.** above whether or not actual repair or replacement is complete.

e. You may disregard the replacement cost loss settlement provisions and make claim under this policy for loss to buildings on an actual cash value basis. You may then make claim for any additional liability according to the provisions of this Condition **D. Loss Settlement**, provided you notify us, within 180 days after the date of loss, of your intent to repair or replace the damaged building.

E. Loss To A Pair Or Set

In case of loss to a pair or set we may elect to:

1. Repair or replace any part to restore the pair or set to its value before the loss; or

2. Pay the difference between actual cash value of the property before and after the loss.

F. Appraisal

If you and we fail to agree on the amount of loss, either may demand an appraisal of the loss. In this event, each party will choose a competent and impartial appraiser within 20 days after receiving a written request from the other. The two appraisers will choose an umpire. If they cannot agree upon an umpire within 15 days, you or we may request that the choice be made by a judge of a court of record in the state where the "residence premises" is located. The appraisers will separately set the amount of loss. If the appraisers submit a written report of an agreement to us, the amount agreed upon will be the amount of loss. If they fail to agree, they will submit their differences to the umpire. A decision agreed to by any two will set the amount of loss.

Each party will:

1. Pay its own appraiser; and

2. Bear the other expenses of the appraisal and umpire equally.

G. Other Insurance And Service Agreement

If a loss covered by this policy is also covered by:

1. Other insurance, we will pay only the proportion of the loss that the limit of liability that applies under this policy bears to the total amount of insurance covering the loss; or

2. A service agreement, this insurance is excess over any amounts payable under any such agreement. Service agreement means a service plan, property restoration plan, home warranty or other similar service warranty agreement, even if it is characterized as insurance.

H. Suit Against Us

No action can be brought against us unless there has been full compliance with all of the terms under Section I of this policy and the action is started within two years after the date of loss.

I. Our Option

If we give you written notice within 30 days after we receive your signed, sworn proof of loss, we may repair or replace any part of the damaged property with material or property of like kind and quality.

J. Loss Payment

We will adjust all losses with you. We will pay you unless some other person is named in the policy or is legally entitled to receive payment. Loss will be payable 60 days after we receive your proof of loss and:

1. Reach an agreement with you;

2. There is an entry of a final judgment; or

3. There is a filing of an appraisal award with us.

K. Abandonment Of Property

We need not accept any property abandoned by an "insured".

L. Mortgage Clause

1. If a mortgagee is named in this policy, any loss payable under Coverage **A** or **B** will be paid to the mortgagee and you, as interests appear. If more than one mortgagee is named, the order of payment will be the same as the order of precedence of the mortgages.

2. If we deny your claim, that denial will not apply to a valid claim of the mortgagee, if the mortgagee:

   a. Notifies us of any change in ownership, occupancy or substantial change in risk of which the mortgagee is aware;

   b. Pays any premium due under this policy on demand if you have neglected to pay the premium; and

   c. Submits a signed, sworn statement of loss within 60 days after receiving notice from us of your failure to do so. Paragraphs **F.** Appraisal, **H.** Suit Against Us and **J.** Loss Payment under Section I – Conditions also apply to the mortgagee.

3. If we decide to cancel or not to renew this policy, the mortgagee will be notified at least 10 days before the date cancellation or nonrenewal takes effect.

4. If we pay the mortgagee for any loss and deny payment to you:

   a. We are subrogated to all the rights of the mortgagee granted under the mortgage on the property; or

   b. At our option, we may pay to the mortgagee the whole principal on the mortgage plus any accrued interest. In this event, we will receive a full assignment and transfer of the mortgage and all securities held as collateral to the mortgage debt.

5. Subrogation will not impair the right of the mortgagee to recover the full amount of the mortgagee's claim.

M. No Benefit To Bailee

We will not recognize any assignment or grant any coverage that benefits a person or organization holding, storing or moving property for a fee regardless of any other provision of this policy.

N. Nuclear Hazard Clause

1. "Nuclear Hazard" means any nuclear reaction, radiation, or radioactive contamination, all whether controlled or uncontrolled or however caused, or any consequence of any of these.

2. Loss caused by the nuclear hazard will not be considered loss caused by fire, explosion, or smoke, whether these perils are specifically named in or otherwise included within the Perils Insured Against.

3. This policy does not apply under Section I to loss caused directly or indirectly by nuclear hazard, except that direct loss by fire resulting from the nuclear hazard is covered.

O. Recovered Property

If you or we recover any property for which we have made payment under this policy, you or we will notify the other of the recovery. At your option, the property will be returned to or retained by you or it will become our property. If the recovered property is returned to or retained by you, the loss payment will be adjusted based on the amount you received for the recovered property.

P. Volcanic Eruption Period

One or more volcanic eruptions that occur within a 72-hour period will be considered as one volcanic eruption.

Q. Policy Period

This policy applies only to loss which occurs during the policy period.

R. Concealment Or Fraud

We provide coverage to no "insureds" under this policy if, whether before or after a loss, an "insured" has:

1. Intentionally concealed or misrepresented any material fact or circumstance;

2. Engaged in fraudulent conduct; or

3. Made false statements;

relating to this insurance.

S. Loss Payable Clause

If the Declarations shows a loss payee for certain listed insured personal property, the definition of "insured" is changed to include that loss payee with respect to that property.

If we decide to cancel or not renew this policy, that loss payee will be notified in writing.

SECTION II – LIABILITY COVERAGES

A. Coverage E – Personal Liability

If a claim is made or a suit is brought against an "insured" for damages because of "bodily injury" or "property damage" caused by an "occurrence" to which this coverage applies, we will:

1. Pay up to our limit of liability for the damages for which an "insured" is legally liable. Damages include prejudgment interest awarded against an "insured"; and

2. Provide a defense at our expense by counsel of our choice, even if the suit is groundless, false or fraudulent. We may investigate and settle any claim or suit that we decide is appropriate. Our duty to settle or defend ends when our limit of liability for the "occurrence" has been exhausted by payment of a judgment or settlement.

B. Coverage F – Medical Payments To Others

We will pay the necessary medical expenses that are incurred or medically ascertained within three years from the date of an accident causing "bodily injury". Medical expenses means reasonable charges for medical, surgical, x-ray, dental, ambulance, hospital, professional nursing, prosthetic devices and funeral services. This coverage does not apply to you or regular residents of your household except "residence employees". As to others, this coverage applies only:

1. To a person on the "insured location" with the permission of an "insured"; or

2. To a person off the "insured location", if the "bodily injury":

   a. Arises out of a condition on the "insured location" or the ways immediately adjoining;

   b. Is caused by the activities of an "insured";

   c. Is caused by a "residence employee" in the course of the "residence employee's" employment by an "insured"; or

   d. Is caused by an animal owned by or in the care of an "insured".

SECTION II – EXCLUSIONS

A. "Motor Vehicle Liability"

1. Coverages **E** and **F** do not apply to any "motor vehicle liability" if, at the time and place of an "occurrence", the involved "motor vehicle":

   a. Is registered for use on public roads or property;

   b. Is not registered for use on public roads or property, but such registration is required by a law, or regulation issued by a government agency, for it to be used at the place of the "occurrence"; or

   c. Is being:

      (1) Operated in, or practicing for, any prearranged or organized race, speed contest or other competition;

      (2) Rented to others;

      (3) Used to carry persons or cargo for a charge; or

      (4) Used for any "business" purpose except for a motorized golf cart while on a golfing facility.

2. If Exclusion **A.1.** does not apply, there is still no coverage for "motor vehicle liability", unless the "motor vehicle" is:

   a. In dead storage on an "insured location";

   b. Used solely to service a residence;

   c. Designed to assist the handicapped and, at the time of an "occurrence", it is:

      (1) Being used to assist a handicapped person; or

      (2) Parked on an "insured location";

   d. Designed for recreational use off public roads and:

      (1) Not owned by an "insured"; or

(2) Owned by an "insured" provided the "occurrence" takes place:

(a) On an "insured location" as defined in Definition **B.6.a., b., d., e.** or **h.;** or

(b) Off an "insured location" and the "motor vehicle" is:

(i) Designed as a toy vehicle for use by children under seven years of age;

(ii) Powered by one or more batteries; and

(iii) Not built or modified after manufacture to exceed a speed of five miles per hour on level ground;

e. A motorized golf cart that is owned by an "insured", designed to carry up to four persons, not built or modified after manufacture to exceed a speed of 25 miles per hour on level ground and, at the time of an "occurrence", is within the legal boundaries of:

(1) A golfing facility and is parked or stored there, or being used by an "insured" to:

(a) Play the game of golf or for other recreational or leisure activity allowed by the facility;

(b) Travel to or from an area where "motor vehicles" or golf carts are parked or stored; or

(c) Cross public roads at designated points to access other parts of the golfing facility; or

(2) A private residential community, including its public roads upon which a motorized golf cart can legally travel, which is subject to the authority of a property owners association and contains an "insured's" residence.

B. "Watercraft Liability"

1. Coverages **E** and **F** do not apply to any "watercraft liability" if, at the time of an "occurrence", the involved watercraft is being:

a. Operated in, or practicing for, any prearranged or organized race, speed contest or other competition. This exclusion does not apply to a sailing vessel or a predicted log cruise;

b. Rented to others;

c. Used to carry persons or cargo for a charge; or

d. Used for any "business" purpose.

2. If Exclusion **B.1.** does not apply, there is still no coverage for "watercraft liability" unless, at the time of the "occurrence", the watercraft:

a. Is stored;

b. Is a sailing vessel, with or without auxiliary power, that is:

(1) Less than 26 feet in overall length; or

(2) 26 feet or more in overall length and not owned by or rented to an "insured"; or

c. Is not a sailing vessel and is powered by:

(1) An inboard or inboard-outdrive engine or motor, including those that power a water jet pump, of:

(a) 50 horsepower or less and not owned by an "insured"; or

(b) More than 50 horsepower and not owned by or rented to an "insured"; or

(2) One or more outboard engines or motors with:

(a) 25 total horsepower or less;

(b) More than 25 horsepower if the outboard engine or motor is not owned by an "insured";

(c) More than 25 horsepower if the outboard engine or motor is owned by an "insured" who acquired it during the policy period; or

(d) More than 25 horsepower if the outboard engine or motor is owned by an "insured" who acquired it before the policy period, but only if:

(i) You declare them at policy inception; or

(ii) Your intent to insure them is reported to us in writing within 45 days after you acquire them.

The coverages in **(c)** and **(d)** above apply for the policy period.

Horsepower means the maximum power rating assigned to the engine or motor by the manufacturer.

C. "Aircraft Liability"

This policy does not cover "aircraft liability".

D. "Hovercraft Liability"

This policy does not cover "hovercraft liability".

E. Coverage E – Personal Liability And Coverage F – Medical Payments To Others

Coverages **E** and **F** do not apply to the following:

1. Expected Or Intended Injury

"Bodily injury" or "property damage" which is expected or intended by an "insured", even if the resulting "bodily injury" or "property damage":

a. Is of a different kind, quality or degree than initially expected or intended; or

b. Is sustained by a different person, entity or property than initially expected or intended.

However, this Exclusion **E.1.** does not apply to "bodily injury" or "property damage" resulting from the use of reasonable force by an "insured" to protect persons or property;

2. "Business"

a. "Bodily injury" or "property damage" arising out of or in connection with a "business" conducted from an "insured location" or engaged in by an "insured", whether or not the "business" is owned or operated by an "insured" or employs an "insured".

This Exclusion **E.2.** applies but is not limited to an act or omission, regardless of its nature or circumstance, involving a service or duty rendered, promised, owed, or implied to be provided because of the nature of the "business".

b. This Exclusion **E.2.** does not apply to:

(1) The rental or holding for rental of an "insured location";

(a) On an occasional basis if used only as a residence;

(b) In part for use only as a residence, unless a single-family unit is intended for use by the occupying family to lodge more than two roomers or boarders; or

(c) In part, as an office, school, studio or private garage; and

(2) An "insured" under the age of 21 years involved in a part-time or occasional, self-employed "business" with no employees;

3. Professional Services

"Bodily injury" or "property damage" arising out of the rendering of or failure to render professional services;

4. "Insured's" Premises Not An "Insured Location"

"Bodily injury" or "property damage" arising out of a premises:

a. Owned by an "insured";

b. Rented to an "insured"; or

c. Rented to others by an "insured";

that is not an "insured location";

5. War

"Bodily injury" or "property damage" caused directly or indirectly by war, including the following and any consequence of any of the following:

a. Undeclared war, civil war, insurrection, rebellion or revolution;

b. Warlike act by a military force or military personnel; or

c. Destruction, seizure or use for a military purpose.

Discharge of a nuclear weapon will be deemed a warlike act even if accidental;

6. Communicable Disease

"Bodily injury" or "property damage" which arises out of the transmission of a communicable disease by an "insured";

7. Sexual Molestation, Corporal Punishment Or Physical Or Mental Abuse

"Bodily injury" or "property damage" arising out of sexual molestation, corporal punishment or physical or mental abuse; or

8. Controlled Substance

"Bodily injury" or "property damage" arising out of the use, sale, manufacture, delivery, transfer or possession by any person of a Controlled Substance as defined by the Federal Food and Drug Law at 21 U.S.C.A. Sections 811 and 812. Controlled Substances include but are not limited to cocaine, LSD, marijuana and all narcotic drugs. However, this exclusion does not apply to the legitimate use of prescription drugs by a person following the lawful orders of a licensed health care professional.

Exclusions **A.** "Motor Vehicle Liability", **B.** "Watercraft Liability", **C.** "Aircraft Liability", **D.** "Hovercraft Liability" and **E.4.** "Insured's" Premises Not An "Insured Location" do not apply to "bodily injury" to a "residence employee" arising out of and in the course of the "residence employee's" employment by an "insured".

F. Coverage E – Personal Liability

Coverage **E** does not apply to:

1. Liability:

    a. For any loss assessment charged against you as a member of an association, corporation or community of property owners, except as provided in **D.** Loss Assessment under Section **II** – Additional Coverages;

    b. Under any contract or agreement entered into by an "insured". However, this exclusion does not apply to written contracts:

        (1) That directly relate to the ownership, maintenance or use of an "insured location"; or

        (2) Where the liability of others is assumed by you prior to an "occurrence";

        unless excluded in **a.** above or elsewhere in this policy;

2. "Property damage" to property owned by an "insured". This includes costs or expenses incurred by an "insured" or others to repair, replace, enhance, restore or maintain such property to prevent injury to a person or damage to property of others, whether on or away from an "insured location";

3. "Property damage" to property rented to, occupied or used by or in the care of an "insured". This exclusion does not apply to "property damage" caused by fire, smoke or explosion;

4. "Bodily injury" to any person eligible to receive any benefits voluntarily provided or required to be provided by an "insured" under any:

    a. Workers' compensation law;

    b. Non-occupational disability law; or

    c. Occupational disease law;

5. "Bodily injury" or "property damage" for which an "insured" under this policy:

    a. Is also an insured under a nuclear energy liability policy issued by the:

        (1) Nuclear Energy Liability Insurance Association;

        (2) Mutual Atomic Energy Liability Underwriters;

        (3) Nuclear Insurance Association of Canada;

        or any of their successors; or

    b. Would be an insured under such a policy but for the exhaustion of its limit of liability; or

6. "Bodily injury" to you or an "insured" as defined under Definition **5.a.** or **b.**

    This exclusion also applies to any claim made or suit brought against you or an "insured" to:

    a. Repay; or

    b. Share damages with;

    another person who may be obligated to pay damages because of "bodily injury" to an "insured".

G. Coverage F – Medical Payments To Others

Coverage **F** does not apply to "bodily injury":

1. To a "residence employee" if the "bodily injury":

    a. Occurs off the "insured location"; and

    b. Does not arise out of or in the course of the "residence employee's" employment by an "insured";

2. To any person eligible to receive benefits voluntarily provided or required to be provided under any:

    a. Workers' compensation law;

    b. Non-occupational disability law; or

    c. Occupational disease law;

3. From any:

    a. Nuclear reaction;

    b. Nuclear radiation; or

    c. Radioactive contamination;

    all whether controlled or uncontrolled or however caused; or

    d. Any consequence of any of these; or

4. To any person, other than a "residence employee" of an "insured", regularly residing on any part of the "insured location".

SECTION II – ADDITIONAL COVERAGES

We cover the following in addition to the limits of liability:

A. Claim Expenses

We pay:

1. Expenses we incur and costs taxed against an "insured" in any suit we defend;

2. Premiums on bonds required in a suit we defend, but not for bond amounts more than the Coverage **E** limit of liability. We need not apply for or furnish any bond;

3. Reasonable expenses incurred by an "insured" at our request, including actual loss of earnings (but not loss of other income) up to $250 per day, for assisting us in the investigation or defense of a claim or suit; and

4. Interest on the entire judgment which accrues after entry of the judgment and before we pay or tender, or deposit in court that part of the judgment which does not exceed the limit of liability that applies.

B. First Aid Expenses

We will pay expenses for first aid to others incurred by an "insured" for "bodily injury" covered under this policy. We will not pay for first aid to an "insured".

C. Damage To Property Of Others

1. We will pay, at replacement cost, up to $1,000 per "occurrence" for "property damage" to property of others caused by an "insured".

2. We will not pay for "property damage":

   a. To the extent of any amount recoverable under Section I;

   b. Caused intentionally by an "insured" who is 13 years of age or older;

   c. To property owned by an "insured";

   d. To property owned by or rented to a tenant of an "insured" or a resident in your household; or

   e. Arising out of:

      (1) A "business" engaged in by an "insured";

      (2) Any act or omission in connection with a premises owned, rented or controlled by an "insured", other than the "insured location"; or

      (3) The ownership, maintenance, occupancy, operation, use, loading or unloading of aircraft, hovercraft, watercraft or "motor vehicles".

      This Exclusion e.(3) does not apply to a "motor vehicle" that:

      (a) Is designed for recreational use off public roads;

      (b) Is not owned by an "insured"; and

      (c) At the time of the "occurrence", is not required by law, or regulation issued by a government agency, to have been registered for it to be used on public roads or property.

D. Loss Assessment

1. We will pay up to $1,000 for your share of loss assessment charged against you, as owner or tenant of the "residence premises", during the policy period by a corporation or association of property owners, when the assessment is made as a result of:

   a. "Bodily injury" or "property damage" not excluded from coverage under Section II – Exclusions; or

   b. Liability for an act of a director, officer or trustee in the capacity as a director, officer or trustee, provided such person:

      (1) Is elected by the members of a corporation or association of property owners; and

      (2) Serves without deriving any income from the exercise of duties which are solely on behalf of a corporation or association of property owners.

2. Paragraph I. Policy Period under Section II – Conditions does not apply to this Loss Assessment Coverage.

3. Regardless of the number of assessments, the limit of $1,000 is the most we will pay for loss arising out of:

   a. One accident, including continuous or repeated exposure to substantially the same general harmful condition; or

   b. A covered act of a director, officer or trustee. An act involving more than one director, officer or trustee is considered to be a single act.

4. We do not cover assessments charged against you or a corporation or association of property owners by any governmental body.

SECTION II – CONDITIONS

A. Limit Of Liability

Our total liability under Coverage **E** for all damages resulting from any one "occurrence" will not be more than the Coverage **E** Limit Of Liability shown in the Declarations. This limit is the same regardless of the number of "insureds", claims made or persons injured. All "bodily injury" and "property damage" resulting from any one accident or from continuous or repeated exposure to substantially the same general harmful conditions shall be considered to be the result of one "occurrence".

Our total liability under Coverage **F** for all medical expense payable for "bodily injury" to one person as the result of one accident will not be more than the Coverage **F** Limit Of Liability shown in the Declarations.

B. Severability Of Insurance

This insurance applies separately to each "insured". This condition will not increase our limit of liability for any one "occurrence".

C. Duties After "Occurrence"

In case of an "occurrence", you or another "insured" will perform the following duties that apply. We have no duty to provide coverage under this policy if your failure to comply with the following duties is prejudicial to us. You will help us by seeing that these duties are performed:

1. Give written notice to us or our agent as soon as is practical, which sets forth:

    a. The identity of the policy and the "named insured" shown in the Declarations;

    b. Reasonably available information on the time, place and circumstances of the "occurrence"; and

    c. Names and addresses of any claimants and witnesses;

2. Cooperate with us in the investigation, settlement or defense of any claim or suit;

3. Promptly forward to us every notice, demand, summons or other process relating to the "occurrence";

4. At our request, help us:

    a. To make settlement;

    b. To enforce any right of contribution or indemnity against any person or organization who may be liable to an "insured";

    c. With the conduct of suits and attend hearings and trials; and

    d. To secure and give evidence and obtain the attendance of witnesses;

5. With respect to **C.** Damage To Property Of Others under Section **II** – Additional Coverages, submit to us within 60 days after the loss a sworn statement of loss and show the damaged property, if in an "insured's" control;

6. No "insured" shall, except at such "insured's" own cost, voluntarily make payment, assume obligation or incur expense other than for first aid to others at the time of the "bodily injury".

D. Duties Of An Injured Person – Coverage F – Medical Payments To Others

1. The injured person or someone acting for the injured person will:

    a. Give us written proof of claim, under oath if required, as soon as is practical; and

    b. Authorize us to obtain copies of medical reports and records.

2. The injured person will submit to a physical exam by a doctor of our choice when and as often as we reasonably require.

E. Payment Of Claim – Coverage F – Medical Payments To Others

Payment under this coverage is not an admission of liability by an "insured" or us.

F. Suit Against Us

1. No action can be brought against us unless there has been full compliance with all of the terms under this Section **II**.

2. No one will have the right to join us as a party to any action against an "insured".

3. Also, no action with respect to Coverage **E** can be brought against us until the obligation of such "insured" has been determined by final judgment or agreement signed by us.

G. Bankruptcy Of An "Insured"

Bankruptcy or insolvency of an "insured" will not relieve us of our obligations under this policy.

H. Other Insurance

This insurance is excess over other valid and collectible insurance except insurance written specifically to cover as excess over the limits of liability that apply in this policy.

I. Policy Period

This policy applies only to "bodily injury" or "property damage" which occurs during the policy period.

J. Concealment Or Fraud

We do not provide coverage to an "insured" who, whether before or after a loss, has:

1. Intentionally concealed or misrepresented any material fact or circumstance;

2. Engaged in fraudulent conduct; or

3. Made false statements;

relating to this insurance.

SECTIONS I AND II – CONDITIONS

A. Liberalization Clause

If we make a change which broadens coverage under this edition of our policy without additional premium charge, that change will automatically apply to your insurance as of the date we implement the change in your state, provided that this implementation date falls within 60 days prior to or during the policy period stated in the Declarations.

This Liberalization Clause does not apply to changes implemented with a general program revision that includes both broadenings and restrictions in coverage, whether that general program revision is implemented through introduction of:

1. A subsequent edition of this policy; or

2. An amendatory endorsement.

B. Waiver Or Change Of Policy Provisions

A waiver or change of a provision of this policy must be in writing by us to be valid. Our request for an appraisal or examination will not waive any of our rights.

C. Cancellation

1. You may cancel this policy at any time by returning it to us or by letting us know in writing of the date cancellation is to take effect.

2. We may cancel this policy only for the reasons stated below by letting you know in writing of the date cancellation takes effect. This cancellation notice may be delivered to you, or mailed to you at your mailing address shown in the Declarations. Proof of mailing will be sufficient proof of notice.

   a. When you have not paid the premium, we may cancel at any time by letting you know at least 10 days before the date cancellation takes effect.

   b. When this policy has been in effect for less than 60 days and is not a renewal with us, we may cancel for any reason by letting you know at least 10 days before the date cancellation takes effect.

   c. When this policy has been in effect for 60 days or more, or at any time if it is a renewal with us, we may cancel:

      (1) If there has been a material misrepresentation of fact which if known to us would have caused us not to issue the policy; or

      (2) If the risk has changed substantially since the policy was issued.

      This can be done by letting you know at least 30 days before the date cancellation takes effect.

   d. When this policy is written for a period of more than one year, we may cancel for any reason at anniversary by letting you know at least 30 days before the date cancellation takes effect.

3. When this policy is canceled, the premium for the period from the date of cancellation to the expiration date will be refunded pro rata.

4. If the return premium is not refunded with the notice of cancellation or when this policy is returned to us, we will refund it within a reasonable time after the date cancellation takes effect.

D. Nonrenewal

We may elect not to renew this policy. We may do so by delivering to you, or mailing to you at your mailing address shown in the Declarations, written notice at least 30 days before the expiration date of this policy. Proof of mailing will be sufficient proof of notice.

E. Assignment

Assignment of this policy will not be valid unless we give our written consent.

F. Subrogation

An "insured" may waive in writing before a loss all rights of recovery against any person. If not waived, we may require an assignment of rights of recovery for a loss to the extent that payment is made by us.

If an assignment is sought, an "insured" must sign and deliver all related papers and cooperate with us.

Subrogation does not apply to Coverage **F** or Paragraph **C.** Damage To Property Of Others under Section **II** – Additional Coverages.

G. Death

If any person named in the Declarations or the spouse, if a resident of the same household, dies, the following apply:

1. We insure the legal representative of the deceased but only with respect to the premises and property of the deceased covered under the policy at the time of death; and

2. "Insured" includes:

a. An "insured" who is a member of your household at the time of your death, but only while a resident of the "residence premises"; and

b. With respect to your property, the person having proper temporary custody of the property until appointment and qualification of a legal representative.

2000 EDITION

HOMEOWNERS
HO 04 90 10 00

THIS ENDORSEMENT CHANGES THE POLICY. PLEASE READ IT CAREFULLY.

PERSONAL PROPERTY REPLACEMENT COST LOSS SETTLEMENT

A. Eligible Property

1. Covered losses to the following property are settled at replacement cost at the time of the loss:

   a. Coverage **C**; and

   b. If covered in this policy:

      (1) Awnings, outdoor antennas and outdoor equipment; and

      (2) Carpeting and household appliances;

   whether or not attached to buildings.

2. This method of loss settlement will also apply to the following articles or classes of property if they are separately described and specifically insured in this policy and not subject to agreed value loss settlement:

   a. Jewelry;

   b. Furs and garments:

      (1) Trimmed with fur; or

      (2) Consisting principally of fur;

   c. Cameras, projection machines, films and related articles of equipment;

   d. Musical equipment and related articles of equipment;

   e. Silverware, silver-plated ware, goldware, gold-plated ware and pewterware, but excluding:

      (1) Pens or pencils;

      (2) Flasks;

      (2) Smoking implements; or

      (3) Jewelry; and

   f. Golfer's equipment meaning golf clubs, golf clothing and golf equipment.

Personal Property Replacement Cost loss settlement will not apply to other classes of property separately described and specifically insured.

B. Ineligible Property

Property listed below is not eligible for replacement cost loss settlement. Any loss will be settled at actual cash value at the time of loss but not more than the amount required to repair or replace.

1. Antiques, fine arts, paintings and similar articles of rarity or antiquity which cannot be replaced.

2. Memorabilia, souvenirs, collectors items and similar articles whose age or history contribute to their value.

3. Articles not maintained in good or workable condition.

4. Articles that are outdated or obsolete and are stored or not being used.

C. Replacement Cost Loss Settlement Condition

The following loss settlement condition applies to all property described in **A.** above:

1. We will pay no more than the least of the following amounts:

   a. Replacement cost at the time of loss without deduction for depreciation;

   b. The full cost of repair at the time of loss;

   c. The limit of liability that applies to Coverage **C,** if applicable;

   d. Any applicable special limits of liability stated in this policy; or

   e. For loss to any item described in **A.2.a. - f.** above, the limit of liability that applies to the item.

2. If the cost to repair or replace the property described in **A.** above is more than $500, we will pay no more than the actual cash value for the loss until the actual repair or replacement is complete.

3. You may make a claim for loss on an actual cash value basis and then make claim for any additional liability in accordance with this endorsement provided you notify us of your intent to do so within 180 days after the date of loss.

All other provisions of this policy apply.

2010 EDITION

HOMEOWNERS
HO 04 90 05 11

THIS ENDORSEMENT CHANGES THE POLICY. PLEASE READ IT CAREFULLY.

PERSONAL PROPERTY REPLACEMENT COST LOSS SETTLEMENT

A. Eligible Property

1. Covered losses to the following property are settled at replacement cost at the time of the loss:

   a. Coverage **C;** and

   b. If covered in this policy:

      (1) Awnings, outdoor antennas and outdoor equipment; and

      (2) Carpeting and household appliances;

      whether or not attached to buildings.

2. This method of loss settlement will also apply to the following articles or classes of property if they are separately described and specifically insured in this policy and not subject to agreed value loss settlement:

   a. Jewelry;

   b. Furs and garments:

      (1) Trimmed with fur; or

      (2) Consisting principally of fur;

   c. Cameras, projection machines, films and related articles of equipment;

   d. Musical equipment and related articles of equipment;

   e. Silverware, silver-plated ware, goldware, gold-plated ware and pewterware, but excluding:

      (1) Pens or pencils;

      (2) Flasks;

      (3) Smoking implements; or

      (4) Jewelry; and

   f. Golfer's equipment meaning golf clubs, golf clothing and golf equipment.

   Personal Property Replacement Cost loss settlement will not apply to other classes of property separately described and specifically insured.

B. Ineligible Property

Property listed below is not eligible for replacement cost loss settlement. Any loss will be settled at actual cash value at the time of loss but not more than the amount required to repair or replace.

1. Antiques, fine arts, paintings and similar articles of rarity or antiquity, which cannot be replaced.

2. Memorabilia, souvenirs, collectors items and similar articles, whose age or history contribute to their value.

3. Articles not maintained in good or workable condition.

4. Articles that are outdated or obsolete and are stored or not being used.

C. Replacement Cost Loss Settlement Condition

The following loss settlement condition applies to all property described in **A.** above:

1. We will pay no more than the least of the following amounts:

   a. Replacement cost at the time of loss without deduction for depreciation;

   b. The full cost of repair at the time of loss;

   c. The limit of liability that applies to Coverage **C,** if applicable;

   d. Any applicable special limits of liability stated in this policy; or

   e. For loss to any item described in **A.2.a. – f.** above, the limit of liability that applies to the item.

2. If the cost to repair or replace the property described in **A.** above is more than $500, we will pay no more than the actual cash value for the loss until the actual repair or replacement is complete.

3. You may make a claim for loss on an actual cash value basis and then make claim for any additional liability in accordance with this endorsement provided you notify us, within 180 days after the date of the loss, of your intent to repair or replace the damaged property.

All other provisions of this policy apply.

2000 EDITION

POLICY NUMBER:

HOMEOWNERS
HO 04 61 10 00

THIS ENDORSEMENT CHANGES THE POLICY. PLEASE READ IT CAREFULLY.

SCHEDULED PERSONAL PROPERTY ENDORSEMENT

SCHEDULE*

	Class Of Personal Property	Amount Of Insurance	Premium
1.	**Jewelry,** as scheduled below.	$	$
2.	**Furs** and garments trimmed with fur or consisting principally of fur, as scheduled below.		
3.	**Cameras,** projection machines, films and related articles of equipment, as listed below.		
4.	**Musical instruments** and related articles of equipment, as listed below. You agree not to perform with these instruments for pay unless specifically provided under this policy.		
5.	**Silverware,** silver-plated ware, goldware, gold-plated ware and pewterware, but excluding pens, pencils, flasks, smoking implements or jewelry.		
6.	**Golfer's equipment** meaning golf clubs, golf clothing and golf equipment.		
7.a.	**Fine Arts,** as scheduled below. This premium is based on your statement that the property insured is located at the following address: at at	Total Fine Arts Amount $	
7.b.	For an additional premium, Paragraph **5.b.** under **C.** Perils Insured Against is deleted only for the articles marked with a double asterisk (**) in the schedule below.	Amount of **7.b.** only $	
8.	**Postage Stamps**		
9.	**Rare and Current Coins**		

Article Or Property	Description	Amount Of Insurance

THE AMOUNTS SHOWN FOR EACH ITEM IN THIS SCHEDULE ARE LIMITED BY THE LOSS SETTLEMENT CONDITION IN PARAGRAPH F.2.

*Entries may be left blank if shown elsewhere in this policy for this coverage.

We cover the classes of personal property which are indicated in the Schedule above by an amount of insurance.

This coverage is subject to the:

1. Definitions;

2. Section I – Conditions; and

3. Sections I and II – Conditions;

in the policy and all provisions of this endorsement.

Any deductible stated in this policy does not apply to this coverage.

A. Newly Acquired Property – Jewelry, Furs, Cameras And Musical Instruments Only

1. We cover newly acquired property of a class of property already insured. The lesser of the following limits applies:

    a. 25% of the amount of insurance for that class of property; or

    b. $10,000.

2. When you acquire new property you must:

    a. Report these objects to us within 30 days; and

    b. Pay the additional premium from the date acquired.

B. Newly Acquired Fine Arts

When Fine Arts are scheduled, we cover objects of art acquired during the policy period for their actual cash value. However, we will pay no more than 25% of the amount of insurance for fine arts scheduled. For coverage to apply for newly acquired fine arts you must:

1. Report these objects to us within 90 days; and

2. Pay the additional premium from the date acquired.

C. Perils Insured Against

We insure against risks of direct loss to property described only if that loss is a physical loss to property; however, we do not insure loss caused by any of the following:

1. Wear and tear, gradual deterioration or inherent vice.

2. Insects or vermin.

3. War, including the following and any consequence of any of the following:

    a. Undeclared war, civil war, insurrection, rebellion or revolution;

    b. Warlike act by a military force or military personnel; or

    c. Destruction, seizure or use for a military purpose.

    Discharge of a nuclear weapon will be deemed a warlike act even if accidental.

4. Nuclear Hazard, to the extent set forth in the Nuclear Hazard Clause of Section I – Conditions.

5. If Fine Arts are covered:

    a. Repairing, restoration or retouching process;

    b. Breakage of art glass windows, glassware, statuary, marble, bric-a-brac, porcelains and similar fragile articles. We cover loss by breakage if caused by:

    (1) Fire or lightning;

    (2) Explosion, aircraft or collision;

    (3) Windstorm, earthquake or flood;

    (4) Malicious damage or theft;

    (5) Derailment or overturn of a conveyance.

    We do not insure loss, from any cause, to property on exhibition at fair grounds or premises of national or international expositions unless the premises are covered by this policy.

6. If Postage Stamps or Rare and Current Coins collections are covered:

    a. Fading, creasing, denting, scratching, tearing or thinning;

    b. Transfer of colors, inherent defect, dampness, extremes of temperature, or depreciation;

    c. Being handled or worked on;

    d. The disappearance of individual stamps, coins or other articles unless the item is:

    (1) Described and scheduled with a specific amount of insurance; or

    (2) Mounted in a volume and the page it is attached to is also lost; or

    e. Shipping by mail other than registered mail.

    However, we do not insure loss, from any cause, to property in the custody of transportation companies or not part of a stamp or coin collection.

D. Territorial Limits

We cover the property described worldwide.

E. Special Provisions

1. Fine Arts: You agree that the covered property will be handled by competent packers.

2. Golfer's Equipment includes your other clothing while contained in a locker when you are playing golf. We cover golf balls for loss by fire or burglary provided there are visible marks of forcible entry into the building, room or locker.

3. Postage Stamps includes the following owned by or in the custody or control of the "insured":

   a. Due, envelope, official, revenue, match and medicine stamps;

   b. Covers, locals, reprints, essays, proofs and other philatelic property; or

   c. Books, pages and mounting of items in **a.** and **b.**

4. Rare and Current Coins includes the following owned by or in custody or control of the "insured":

   a. Medals, paper money, bank notes;

   b. Tokens of money and other numismatic property; or

   c. Coin albums, containers, frames, cards and display cabinets in use with such collection.

F. Conditions

1. Loss Clause

The amount of insurance under this endorsement will not be reduced except for a total loss of a scheduled article. We will refund the unearned premium applicable to such article after the loss or you may apply it to the premium due for the replacement of the scheduled article.

2. Loss Settlement

Covered property losses are settled as follows:

   a. **Fine Arts**

   (1) We will pay, for each article designated in the Schedule, the full amount shown in the Schedule which is agreed to be the value of that article or property. At our request, you will surrender that article or property to us if not lost or stolen.

   (2) If the scheduled article or property is a pair or set, or consists of several parts when complete, we will pay the full amount shown in the Schedule for that pair, set or complete article. At our request, you will surrender that article or property to us if not lost or stolen.

   (3) In the event lost or stolen property is recovered and we have paid you the full amount shown in the Schedule for that property, you will surrender that property to us.

   (4) We will, at your request, sell back to you, at a price you and we agree upon, any class of property or scheduled article you surrendered to us to comply with the terms in **(1)**, **(2)** or **(3)** above.

   b. **POSTAGE STAMPS OR RARE AND CURRENT COIN COLLECTION**

   IN CASE OF LOSS TO ANY SCHEDULED ITEM, THE AMOUNT TO BE PAID WILL BE DETERMINED IN ACCORDANCE WITH PARAGRAPH 2.c. OTHER PROPERTY.

   WHEN COINS OR STAMPS ARE COVERED ON A BLANKET BASIS, WE WILL PAY THE CASH MARKET VALUE AT TIME OF LOSS BUT NOT MORE THAN $1,000 ON ANY UNSCHEDULED COIN COLLECTION NOR MORE THAN $250 FOR ANY ONE STAMP, COIN OR INDIVIDUAL ARTICLE OR ANY ONE PAIR, STRIP, BLOCK, SERIES SHEET, COVER, FRAME OR CARD.

   WE WILL NOT PAY A GREATER PROPORTION OF ANY LOSS ON BLANKET PROPERTY THAN THE AMOUNT INSURED ON BLANKET PROPERTY BEARS TO THE CASH MARKET VALUE AT TIME OF LOSS.

   c. **OTHER PROPERTY**

   (1) THE VALUE OF THE PROPERTY INSURED IS NOT AGREED UPON BUT WILL BE ASCERTAINED AT THE TIME OF LOSS OR DAMAGE. WE WILL NOT PAY MORE THAN THE LEAST OF THE FOLLOWING AMOUNTS:

   (a) THE ACTUAL CASH VALUE OF THE PROPERTY AT THE TIME OF LOSS OR DAMAGE;

   (b) THE AMOUNT FOR WHICH THE PROPERTY COULD REASONABLY BE EXPECTED TO BE REPAIRED TO ITS CONDITION IMMEDIATELY PRIOR TO LOSS;

   (c) THE AMOUNT FOR WHICH THE ARTICLE COULD REASONABLY BE EXPECTED TO BE REPLACED WITH ONE SUBSTANTIALLY IDENTICAL TO THE ARTICLE LOST OR DAMAGED; OR

   (d) THE AMOUNT OF INSURANCE.

(2) THE ACTUAL CASH VALUE CONDITION IN PARAGRAPH (1)(a) ABOVE DOES NOT APPLY IF, AT THE TIME OF LOSS, COVERAGE C – PERSONAL PROPERTY COVERED IN THE POLICY TO WHICH THIS ENDORSEMENT IS ATTACHED IS SUBJECT TO REPLACEMENT COST LOSS SETTLEMENT.

3. PAIR, SET OR PARTS OTHER THAN FINE ARTS

a. LOSS TO A PAIR OR SET

IN CASE OF A LOSS TO A PAIR OR SET WE MAY ELECT TO:

(1) REPAIR OR REPLACE ANY PART TO RESTORE THE PAIR OR SET TO ITS VALUE BEFORE THE LOSS; OR

(2) PAY THE DIFFERENCE BETWEEN ACTUAL CASH VALUE OF THE PROPERTY BEFORE AND AFTER THE LOSS.

b. PARTS

IN CASE OF A LOSS TO ANY PART OF COVERED PROPERTY, CONSISTING OF SEVERAL PARTS WHEN COMPLETE, WE WILL PAY FOR THE VALUE OF THE PART LOST OR DAMAGED.

HO 04 61 10 00

POLICY NUMBER: **2010 EDITION**   HOMEOWNERS
                                                                        HO 04 61 05 11

THIS ENDORSEMENT CHANGES THE POLICY. PLEASE READ IT CAREFULLY.

SCHEDULED PERSONAL PROPERTY ENDORSEMENT

SCHEDULE

Class Of Personal Property	Amount Of Insurance	Premium
1. **Jewelry,** as scheduled below.	$	$
2. **Furs** and garments trimmed with fur or consisting principally of fur, as scheduled below.	$	$
3. **Cameras,** projection machines, films and related articles of equipment, as listed below.	$	$
4. **Musical Instruments** and related articles of equipment, as listed below. You agree not to perform with these instruments for pay unless specifically provided under this policy.	$	$
5. **Silverware,** silver-plated ware, goldware, gold-plated ware and pewterware, but excluding pens, pencils, flasks, smoking implements or jewelry.	$	$
6. **Golfer's Equipment,** meaning golf clubs, golf clothing and golf equipment.	$	$
7.a. **Fine Arts,** as scheduled below. This premium is based on your statement that the property insured is located at the following address: at at	**Total Fine Arts Amount** $	$
7.b. For an additional premium, Paragraph **5.b.** under **C. Perils Insured Against** is deleted only for the articles marked with a double asterisk (**) in the Schedule below.	**Amount of 7.b. only** $	$
8. **Postage Stamps**	$	$
9. **Rare And Current Coins**	$	$

Article Or Property	Description	Amount Of Insurance
		$

THE AMOUNTS SHOWN FOR EACH ITEM IN THIS SCHEDULE ARE LIMITED BY THE LOSS SETTLEMENT CONDITION IN PARAGRAPH F.2.

Information required to complete this Schedule, if not shown above, will be shown in the Declarations.

We cover the classes of personal property which are indicated in the Schedule above by an amount of insurance.

This coverage is subject to the:

1. Definitions;

2. Section I – Conditions; and

3. Sections I and II – Conditions;

in the policy and all provisions of this endorsement.

Any deductible stated in this policy does not apply to this coverage.

A. Newly Acquired Property – Jewelry, Furs, Cameras And Musical Instruments Only

1. We cover newly acquired property of a class of property already insured. The lesser of the following limits applies:

   a. 25% of the amount of insurance for that class of property; or

   b. $10,000.

2. When you acquire new property, you must:

   a. Report these objects to us within 30 days; and

   b. Pay the additional premium from the date acquired.

B. Newly Acquired Fine Arts

When Fine Arts are scheduled, we cover objects of art acquired during the policy period for their actual cash value. However, we will pay no more than 25% of the amount of insurance for fine arts scheduled. For coverage to apply for newly acquired fine arts, you must:

1. Report these objects to us within 90 days; and

2. Pay the additional premium from the date acquired.

C. Perils Insured Against

We insure against direct loss to property described only if that loss is a physical loss to property; however, we do not insure loss caused by any of the following:

1. Wear and tear, gradual deterioration or inherent vice.

2. Insects or vermin.

3. War, including the following and any consequence of any of the following:

   a. Undeclared war, civil war, insurrection, rebellion or revolution;

   b. Warlike act by a military force or military personnel; or

   c. Destruction, seizure or use for a military purpose.

   Discharge of a nuclear weapon will be deemed a warlike act even if accidental.

4. Nuclear Hazard, to the extent set forth in the Nuclear Hazard Clause of Section I – Conditions.

5. If Fine Arts are covered:

   a. Repairing, restoration or retouching process;

   b. Breakage of art glass windows, glassware, statuary, marble, bric-a-brac, porcelains and similar fragile articles. We cover loss by breakage if caused by:

      (1) Fire or lightning;

      (2) Explosion, aircraft or collision;

      (3) Windstorm, earthquake or flood;

      (4) Malicious damage or theft;

      (5) Derailment or overturn of a conveyance.

   We do not insure loss, from any cause, to property on exhibition at fairgrounds or premises of national or international expositions unless the premises are covered by this policy.

6. If Postage Stamps or Rare And Current Coins collections are covered:

   a. Fading, creasing, denting, scratching, tearing or thinning;

   b. Transfer of colors, inherent defect, dampness, extremes of temperature, or depreciation;

   c. Being handled or worked on;

   d. The disappearance of individual stamps, coins or other articles unless the item is:

      (1) Described and scheduled with a specific amount of insurance; or

      (2) Mounted in a volume and the page it is attached to is also lost; or

   e. Shipping by mail other than registered mail.

   However, we do not insure loss, from any cause, to property in the custody of transportation companies or not part of a stamp or coin collection.

D. Territorial Limits

We cover the property described worldwide.

E. Special Provisions

1. Fine Arts: You agree that the covered property will be handled by competent packers.

2. Golfer's Equipment includes your other clothing while contained in a locker when you are playing golf. We cover golf balls for loss by fire or burglary, provided there are visible marks of forcible entry into the building, room or locker.

3. Postage Stamps includes the following owned by or in the custody or control of the "insured":

   a. Due, envelope, official, revenue, match and medicine stamps;

   b. Covers, locals, reprints, essays, proofs and other philatelic property; or

   c. Books, pages and mounting of items in **a.** and **b.**

4. Rare And Current Coins includes the following owned by or in custody or control of the "insured":

   a. Medals, paper money, bank notes;

   b. Tokens of money and other numismatic property; or

   c. Coin albums, containers, frames, cards and display cabinets in use with such collection.

F. Conditions

1. Loss Clause

The amount of insurance under this endorsement will not be reduced except for a total loss of a scheduled article. We will refund the unearned premium applicable to such article after the loss or you may apply it to the premium due for the replacement of the scheduled article.

2. Loss Settlement

Covered property losses are settled as follows:

   a. Fine Arts

   (1) We will pay, for each article designated in the Schedule, the full amount shown in the Schedule which is agreed to be the value of that article or property. At our request, you will surrender that article or property to us if not lost or stolen.

   (2) If the scheduled article or property is a pair or set, or consists of several parts when complete, we will pay the full amount shown in the Schedule for that pair, set or complete article. At our request, you will surrender that article or property to us if not lost or stolen.

(3) In the event lost or stolen property is recovered and we have paid you the full amount shown in the Schedule for that property, you will surrender that property to us.

(4) We will, at your request, sell back to you, at a price you and we agree upon, any class of property or scheduled article you surrendered to us to comply with the terms in **(1)**, **(2)** or **(3)** above.

b. POSTAGE STAMPS OR RARE AND CURRENT COIN COLLECTION

IN CASE OF LOSS TO ANY SCHEDULED ITEM, THE AMOUNT TO BE PAID WILL BE DETERMINED IN ACCORDANCE WITH PARAGRAPH **2.c.** OTHER PROPERTY.

WHEN COINS OR STAMPS ARE COVERED ON A BLANKET BASIS, WE WILL PAY THE CASH MARKET VALUE AT TIME OF LOSS BUT NOT MORE THAN $1,000 ON ANY UNSCHEDULED COIN COLLECTION NOR MORE THAN $250 FOR ANY ONE STAMP, COIN OR INDIVIDUAL ARTICLE OR ANY ONE PAIR, STRIP, BLOCK, SERIES SHEET, COVER, FRAME OR CARD.

WE WILL NOT PAY A GREATER PROPORTION OF ANY LOSS ON BLANKET PROPERTY THAN THE AMOUNT INSURED ON BLANKET PROPERTY BEARS TO THE CASH MARKET VALUE AT TIME OF LOSS.

c. OTHER PROPERTY

(1) THE VALUE OF THE PROPERTY INSURED IS NOT AGREED UPON BUT WILL BE ASCERTAINED AT THE TIME OF LOSS OR DAMAGE. WE WILL NOT PAY MORE THAN THE LEAST OF THE FOLLOWING AMOUNTS:

   (a) THE ACTUAL CASH VALUE OF THE PROPERTY AT THE TIME OF LOSS OR DAMAGE;

   (b) THE AMOUNT FOR WHICH THE PROPERTY COULD REASONABLY BE EXPECTED TO BE REPAIRED TO ITS CONDITION IMMEDIATELY PRIOR TO LOSS;

(c) **THE AMOUNT FOR WHICH THE ARTICLE COULD REASONABLY BE EXPECTED TO BE REPLACED WITH ONE SUBSTANTIALLY IDENTICAL TO THE ARTICLE LOST OR DAMAGED; OR**

(d) **THE AMOUNT OF INSURANCE.**

(2) **THE ACTUAL CASH VALUE CONDITION IN PARAGRAPH (1)(a) ABOVE DOES NOT APPLY IF, AT THE TIME OF LOSS, COVERAGE C – PERSONAL PROPERTY COVERED IN THE POLICY TO WHICH THIS ENDORSEMENT IS ATTACHED IS SUBJECT TO REPLACEMENT COST LOSS SETTLEMENT.**

3. **PAIR, SET OR PARTS OTHER THAN FINE ARTS**

a. **LOSS TO A PAIR OR SET**

IN CASE OF A LOSS TO A PAIR OR SET WE MAY ELECT TO:

(1) **REPAIR OR REPLACE ANY PART TO RESTORE THE PAIR OR SET TO ITS VALUE BEFORE THE LOSS; OR**

(2) **PAY THE DIFFERENCE BETWEEN ACTUAL CASH VALUE OF THE PROPERTY BEFORE AND AFTER THE LOSS.**

b. **PARTS**

IN CASE OF A LOSS TO ANY PART OF COVERED PROPERTY, CONSISTING OF SEVERAL PARTS WHEN COMPLETE, WE WILL PAY FOR THE VALUE OF THE PART LOST OR DAMAGED.

HO 04 61 05 11

Personal Auto Insurance

The Personal Auto Policy (PAP) of Insurance Services Office, Inc., is typical of the policies used to insure the property and liability loss exposures associated with automobiles owned or used by individuals or families. The PAP provides four basic coverages.

Part A—Liability Coverage. Insures covered persons against liability to others for bodily injury or property damage arising out of the ownership, maintenance, or use of a "covered auto."

Part B—Medical Payments Coverage. Provides reimbursement for medical expenses when insureds or other persons are injured while occupying a covered auto or when the named insured or a family member is injured as a pedestrian.

Part C—Uninsured Motorists Coverage. Provides a source of recovery for insureds who are injured in an auto accident caused either by a hit-and-run motorist or by an identified motorist who is "uninsured" as defined in the PAP. An underinsured motorists coverage endorsement can be added to the PAP to cover accidents caused by a motorist who has some liability insurance but less than the uninsured/underinsured motorists coverage limit carried by the insured. An example of an underinsured motorists coverage endorsement is included in the sample forms that follow.

Part D—Coverage for Damage to Your Auto. Covers physical damage to a covered auto. Covered causes of loss are in two categories: collision and other than collision.

- Collision coverage applies only to loss resulting from "collision," defined as the upset of an auto or its impact with another vehicle or object.
- Other-than-collision coverage applies to all nonexcluded perils other than collision that cause accidental loss to an auto.

The amount payable under Part D is limited to the actual cash value of the stolen or damaged property or the amount required to repair or replace it—whichever is less.

Part E of the PAP describes the duties that any person seeking coverage must perform. Part F expresses the general provisions.

In states that have an automobile no-fault statute, medical payments coverage may be replaced or supplemented with personal injury protection coverage, which provides broader coverage. The benefits may include medical benefits, disability benefits (wage-loss replacement), payment for substitute services (such as a babysitter to substitute for an injured parent), funeral benefits, and other specified benefits, which vary from state to state. An example of a personal injury protection endorsement is included in the sample forms that follow.

Personal Auto Policy Declarations

POLICYHOLDER:
(Named Insured)

David M. and Joan G. Smith
216 Brookside Drive
Anytown, USA 40000

POLICY NUMBER: 296 S 468211

POLICY PERIOD: **FROM:** June 25, 20X1
TO: December 25, 20X1

But only if the required premium for this period has been paid, and for six-month renewal periods if renewal premiums are paid as required. Each period begins and ends at 12:01 A.M. standard time at the address of the policyholder.

**INSURED VEHICLES AND
SCHEDULE OF COVERAGES**

VEHICLE	COVERAGES	LIMITS OF INSURANCE	PREMIUM
1	20XX Toyota Camry	VIN XXX	
	Coverage A—Liability	$ 300,000 **Each Occurrence**	**$ 223.00**
	Coverage B—Medical Payments	$ 5,000 **Each Person**	**$ 36.00**
	Coverage C—Uninsured Motorists	$ 300,000 **Each Occurrence**	**$ 61.80**
			TOTAL $ 320.80
2	20XX Ford Focus	VIN XXX	
	Coverage A—Liability	$ 300,000 **Each Occurrence**	**$ 203.00**
	Coverage B—Medical Payments	$ 5,000 **Each Person**	**$ 36.00**
	Coverage C—Uninsured Motorists	$ 300,000 **Each Occurrence**	**$ 61.80**
	Coverage D—Other Than Collision	**Actual Cash Value Less $** 250	**$ 141.60**
	—Collision	**Actual Cash Value Less $** 500	**$ 231.00**
			TOTAL $ 673.40

POLICY FORM AND ENDORSEMENTS: PP 00 01

COUNTERSIGNATURE DATE: June 1, 20X1

AGENT: A.M. Abel

PERSONAL AUTO
PP 00 01 01 05

PERSONAL AUTO POLICY

AGREEMENT

In return for payment of the premium and subject to all the terms of this policy, we agree with you as follows:

DEFINITIONS

A. Throughout this policy, "you" and "your" refer to:

1. The "named insured" shown in the Declarations; and

2. The spouse if a resident of the same household.

If the spouse ceases to be a resident of the same household during the policy period or prior to the inception of this policy, the spouse will be considered "you" and "your" under this policy but only until the earlier of:

1. The end of 90 days following the spouse's change of residency;

2. The effective date of another policy listing the spouse as a named insured; or

3. The end of the policy period.

B. "We", "us" and "our" refer to the Company providing this insurance.

C. For purposes of this policy, a private passenger type auto, pickup or van shall be deemed to be owned by a person if leased:

1. Under a written agreement to that person; and

2. For a continuous period of at least 6 months.

Other words and phrases are defined. They are in quotation marks when used.

D. "Bodily injury" means bodily harm, sickness or disease, including death that results.

E. "Business" includes trade, profession or occupation.

F. "Family member" means a person related to you by blood, marriage or adoption who is a resident of your household. This includes a ward or foster child.

G. "Occupying" means:

1. In;

2. Upon; or

3. Getting in, on, out or off.

H. "Property damage" means physical injury to, destruction of or loss of use of tangible property.

I. "Trailer" means a vehicle designed to be pulled by a:

1. Private passenger auto; or

2. Pickup or van.

It also means a farm wagon or farm implement while towed by a vehicle listed in **1.** or **2.** above.

J. "Your covered auto" means:

1. Any vehicle shown in the Declarations.

2. A "newly acquired auto".

3. Any "trailer" you own.

4. Any auto or "trailer" you do not own while used as a temporary substitute for any other vehicle described in this definition which is out of normal use because of its:

   a. Breakdown;

   b. Repair;

   c. Servicing;

   d. Loss; or

   e. Destruction.

   This Provision (**J.4.**) does not apply to Coverage For Damage To Your Auto.

K. "Newly acquired auto":

1. "Newly acquired auto" means any of the following types of vehicles you become the owner of during the policy period:

   a. A private passenger auto; or

   b. A pickup or van, for which no other insurance policy provides coverage, that:

      (1) Has a Gross Vehicle Weight Rating of 10,000 lbs. or less; and

      (2) Is not used for the delivery or transportation of goods and materials unless such use is:

         (a) Incidental to your "business" of installing, maintaining or repairing furnishings or equipment; or

         (b) For farming or ranching.

2. Coverage for a "newly acquired auto" is provided as described below. If you ask us to insure a "newly acquired auto" after a specified time period described below has elapsed, any coverage we provide for a "newly acquired auto" will begin at the time you request the coverage.

a. For any coverage provided in this policy except Coverage For Damage To Your Auto, a "newly acquired auto" will have the broadest coverage we now provide for any vehicle shown in the Declarations. Coverage begins on the date you become the owner. However, for this coverage to apply to a "newly acquired auto" which is in addition to any vehicle shown in the Declarations, you must ask us to insure it within 14 days after you become the owner.

If a "newly acquired auto" replaces a vehicle shown in the Declarations, coverage is provided for this vehicle without your having to ask us to insure it.

b. Collision Coverage for a "newly acquired auto" begins on the date you become the owner. However, for this coverage to apply, you must ask us to insure it within:

(1) 14 days after you become the owner if the Declarations indicate that Collision Coverage applies to at least one auto. In this case, the "newly acquired auto" will have the broadest coverage we now provide for any auto shown in the Declarations.

(2) Four days after you become the owner if the Declarations do not indicate that Collision Coverage applies to at least one auto. If you comply with the 4 day requirement and a loss occurred before you asked us to insure the "newly acquired auto", a Collision deductible of $500 will apply.

c. Other Than Collision Coverage for a "newly acquired auto" begins on the date you become the owner. However, for this coverage to apply, you must ask us to insure it within:

(1) 14 days after you become the owner if the Declarations indicate that Other Than Collision Coverage applies to at least one auto. In this case, the "newly acquired auto" will have the broadest coverage we now provide for any auto shown in the Declarations.

(2) Four days after you become the owner if the Declarations do not indicate that Other Than Collision Coverage applies to at least one auto. If you comply with the 4 day requirement and a loss occurred before you asked us to insure the "newly acquired auto", an Other Than Collision deductible of $500 will apply.

PART A – LIABILITY COVERAGE

INSURING AGREEMENT

A. We will pay damages for "bodily injury" or "property damage" for which any "insured" becomes legally responsible because of an auto accident. Damages include prejudgment interest awarded against the "insured". We will settle or defend, as we consider appropriate, any claim or suit asking for these damages. In addition to our limit of liability, we will pay all defense costs we incur. Our duty to settle or defend ends when our limit of liability for this coverage has been exhausted by payment of judgments or settlements. We have no duty to defend any suit or settle any claim for "bodily injury" or "property damage" not covered under this policy.

B. "Insured" as used in this Part means:

1. You or any "family member" for the ownership, maintenance or use of any auto or "trailer".

2. Any person using "your covered auto".

3. For "your covered auto", any person or organization but only with respect to legal responsibility for acts or omissions of a person for whom coverage is afforded under this Part.

4. For any auto or "trailer", other than "your covered auto", any other person or organization but only with respect to legal responsibility for acts or omissions of you or any "family member" for whom coverage is afforded under this Part. This Provision **(B.4.)** applies only if the person or organization does not own or hire the auto or "trailer".

SUPPLEMENTARY PAYMENTS

We will pay on behalf of an "insured":

1. Up to $250 for the cost of bail bonds required because of an accident, including related traffic law violations. The accident must result in "bodily injury" or "property damage" covered under this policy.

2. Premiums on appeal bonds and bonds to release attachments in any suit we defend.

3. Interest accruing after a judgment is entered in any suit we defend. Our duty to pay interest ends when we offer to pay that part of the judgment which does not exceed our limit of liability for this coverage.

 PP 00 01 01 05

4. Up to $200 a day for loss of earnings, but not other income, because of attendance at hearings or trials at our request.

5. Other reasonable expenses incurred at our request.

These payments will not reduce the limit of liability.

EXCLUSIONS

A. We do not provide Liability Coverage for any "insured":

1. Who intentionally causes "bodily injury" or "property damage".

2. For "property damage" to property owned or being transported by that "insured".

3. For "property damage" to property:

   a. Rented to;

   b. Used by; or

   c. In the care of;

   that "insured".

   This Exclusion (A.3.) does not apply to "property damage" to a residence or private garage.

4. For "bodily injury" to an employee of that "insured" during the course of employment. This Exclusion (A.4.) does not apply to "bodily injury" to a domestic employee unless workers' compensation benefits are required or available for that domestic employee.

5. For that "insured's" liability arising out of the ownership or operation of a vehicle while it is being used as a public or livery conveyance. This Exclusion (A.5.) does not apply to a share-the-expense car pool.

6. While employed or otherwise engaged in the "business" of:

   a. Selling;

   b. Repairing;

   c. Servicing;

   d. Storing; or

   e. Parking;

   vehicles designed for use mainly on public highways. This includes road testing and delivery. This Exclusion (A.6.) does not apply to the ownership, maintenance or use of "your covered auto" by:

   a. You;

   b. Any "family member"; or

   c. Any partner, agent or employee of you or any "family member".

7. Maintaining or using any vehicle while that "insured" is employed or otherwise engaged in any "business" (other than farming or ranching) not described in Exclusion A.6.

   This Exclusion (A.7.) does not apply to the maintenance or use of a:

   a. Private passenger auto;

   b. Pickup or van; or

   c. "Trailer" used with a vehicle described in a. or b. above.

8. Using a vehicle without a reasonable belief that that "insured" is entitled to do so. This Exclusion (A.8.) does not apply to a "family member" using "your covered auto" which is owned by you.

9. For "bodily injury" or "property damage" for which that "insured":

   a. Is an insured under a nuclear energy liability policy; or

   b. Would be an insured under a nuclear energy liability policy but for its termination upon exhaustion of its limit of liability.

   A nuclear energy liability policy is a policy issued by any of the following or their successors:

   a. Nuclear Energy Liability Insurance Association;

   b. Mutual Atomic Energy Liability Underwriters; or

   c. Nuclear Insurance Association of Canada.

B. We do not provide Liability Coverage for the ownership, maintenance or use of:

1. Any vehicle which:

   a. Has fewer than four wheels; or

   b. Is designed mainly for use off public roads.

   This Exclusion (B.1.) does not apply:

   a. While such vehicle is being used by an "insured" in a medical emergency;

   b. To any "trailer"; or

   c. To any non-owned golf cart.

2. Any vehicle, other than "your covered auto", which is:

   a. Owned by you; or

   b. Furnished or available for your regular use.

3. Any vehicle, other than "your covered auto", which is:

   a. Owned by any "family member"; or

   b. Furnished or available for the regular use of any "family member".

However, this Exclusion (**B.3.**) does not apply to you while you are maintaining or "occupying" any vehicle which is:

   a. Owned by a "family member"; or

   b. Furnished or available for the regular use of a "family member".

4. Any vehicle, located inside a facility designed for racing, for the purpose of:

   a. Competing in; or

   b. Practicing or preparing for;

any prearranged or organized racing or speed contest.

LIMIT OF LIABILITY

A. The limit of liability shown in the Declarations for each person for Bodily Injury Liability is our maximum limit of liability for all damages, including damages for care, loss of services or death, arising out of "bodily injury" sustained by any one person in any one auto accident. Subject to this limit for each person, the limit of liability shown in the Declarations for each accident for Bodily Injury Liability is our maximum limit of liability for all damages for "bodily injury" resulting from any one auto accident.

The limit of liability shown in the Declarations for each accident for Property Damage Liability is our maximum limit of liability for all "property damage" resulting from any one auto accident.

This is the most we will pay regardless of the number of:

1. "Insureds";

2. Claims made;

3. Vehicles or premiums shown in the Declarations; or

4. Vehicles involved in the auto accident.

B. No one will be entitled to receive duplicate payments for the same elements of loss under this coverage and:

   1. Part **B** or Part **C** of this policy; or

2. Any Underinsured Motorists Coverage provided by this policy.

OUT OF STATE COVERAGE

If an auto accident to which this policy applies occurs in any state or province other than the one in which "your covered auto" is principally garaged, we will interpret your policy for that accident as follows:

A. If the state or province has:

   1. A financial responsibility or similar law specifying limits of liability for "bodily injury" or "property damage" higher than the limit shown in the Declarations, your policy will provide the higher specified limit.

   2. A compulsory insurance or similar law requiring a nonresident to maintain insurance whenever the nonresident uses a vehicle in that state or province, your policy will provide at least the required minimum amounts and types of coverage.

B. No one will be entitled to duplicate payments for the same elements of loss.

FINANCIAL RESPONSIBILITY

When this policy is certified as future proof of financial responsibility, this policy shall comply with the law to the extent required.

OTHER INSURANCE

If there is other applicable liability insurance we will pay only our share of the loss. Our share is the proportion that our limit of liability bears to the total of all applicable limits. However, any insurance we provide for a vehicle you do not own, including any vehicle while used as a temporary substitute for "your covered auto", shall be excess over any other collectible insurance.

PART B – MEDICAL PAYMENTS COVERAGE

INSURING AGREEMENT

A. We will pay reasonable expenses incurred for necessary medical and funeral services because of "bodily injury":

   1. Caused by accident; and

   2. Sustained by an "insured".

We will pay only those expenses incurred for services rendered within 3 years from the date of the accident.

B. "Insured" as used in this Part means:

   1. You or any "family member":

     a. While "occupying"; or

     b. As a pedestrian when struck by;

   a motor vehicle designed for use mainly on public roads or a trailer of any type.

   2. Any other person while "occupying" "your covered auto".

EXCLUSIONS

We do not provide Medical Payments Coverage for any "insured" for "bodily injury":

1. Sustained while "occupying" any motorized vehicle having fewer than four wheels.

2. Sustained while "occupying" "your covered auto" when it is being used as a public or livery conveyance. This Exclusion (2.) does not apply to a share-the-expense car pool.

3. Sustained while "occupying" any vehicle located for use as a residence or premises.

4. Occurring during the course of employment if workers' compensation benefits are required or available for the "bodily injury".

5. Sustained while "occupying", or when struck by, any vehicle (other than "your covered auto") which is:

   a. Owned by you; or

   b. Furnished or available for your regular use.

6. Sustained while "occupying", or when struck by, any vehicle (other than "your covered auto") which is:

   a. Owned by any "family member"; or

   b. Furnished or available for the regular use of any "family member".

   However, this Exclusion (6.) does not apply to you.

7. Sustained while "occupying" a vehicle without a reasonable belief that that "insured" is entitled to do so. This Exclusion (7.) does not apply to a "family member" using "your covered auto" which is owned by you.

8. Sustained while "occupying" a vehicle when it is being used in the "business" of an "insured". This Exclusion (8.) does not apply to "bodily injury" sustained while "occupying" a:

   a. Private passenger auto;

   b. Pickup or van; or

   c. "Trailer" used with a vehicle described in a. or b. above.

9. Caused by or as a consequence of:

   a. Discharge of a nuclear weapon (even if accidental);

   b. War (declared or undeclared);

   c. Civil war;

   d. Insurrection; or

   e. Rebellion or revolution.

10. From or as a consequence of the following, whether controlled or uncontrolled or however caused:

    a. Nuclear reaction;

    b. Radiation; or

    c. Radioactive contamination.

11. Sustained while "occupying" any vehicle located inside a facility designed for racing, for the purpose of:

    a. Competing in; or

    b. Practicing or preparing for;

    any prearranged or organized racing or speed contest.

LIMIT OF LIABILITY

A. The limit of liability shown in the Declarations for this coverage is our maximum limit of liability for each person injured in any one accident. This is the most we will pay regardless of the number of:

   1. "Insureds";

   2. Claims made;

   3. Vehicles or premiums shown in the Declarations; or

   4. Vehicles involved in the accident.

B. No one will be entitled to receive duplicate payments for the same elements of loss under this coverage and:

   1. Part A or Part C of this policy; or

   2. Any Underinsured Motorists Coverage provided by this policy.

OTHER INSURANCE

If there is other applicable auto medical payments insurance we will pay only our share of the loss. Our share is the proportion that our limit of liability bears to the total of all applicable limits. However, any insurance we provide with respect to a vehicle you do not own, including any vehicle while used as a temporary substitute for "your covered auto", shall be excess over any other collectible auto insurance providing payments for medical or funeral expenses.

PART C – UNINSURED MOTORISTS COVERAGE

INSURING AGREEMENT

A. We will pay compensatory damages which an "insured" is legally entitled to recover from the owner or operator of an "uninsured motor vehicle" because of "bodily injury":

   1. Sustained by an "insured"; and

   2. Caused by an accident.

The owner's or operator's liability for these damages must arise out of the ownership, maintenance or use of the "uninsured motor vehicle".

Any judgment for damages arising out of a suit brought without our written consent is not binding on us.

B. "Insured" as used in this Part means:

   1. You or any "family member".

   2. Any other person "occupying" "your covered auto".

   3. Any person for damages that person is entitled to recover because of "bodily injury" to which this coverage applies sustained by a person described in **1.** or **2.** above.

C. "Uninsured motor vehicle" means a land motor vehicle or trailer of any type:

   1. To which no bodily injury liability bond or policy applies at the time of the accident.

   2. To which a bodily injury liability bond or policy applies at the time of the accident. In this case its limit for bodily injury liability must be less than the minimum limit for bodily injury liability specified by the financial responsibility law of the state in which "your covered auto" is principally garaged.

   3. Which is a hit-and-run vehicle whose operator or owner cannot be identified and which hits:

   a. You or any "family member";

   b. A vehicle which you or any "family member" are "occupying"; or

   c. "Your covered auto".

   4. To which a bodily injury liability bond or policy applies at the time of the accident but the bonding or insuring company:

   a. Denies coverage; or

   b. Is or becomes insolvent.

However, "uninsured motor vehicle" does not include any vehicle or equipment:

   1. Owned by or furnished or available for the regular use of you or any "family member".

   2. Owned or operated by a self-insurer under any applicable motor vehicle law, except a self-insurer which is or becomes insolvent.

   3. Owned by any governmental unit or agency.

   4. Operated on rails or crawler treads.

   5. Designed mainly for use off public roads while not on public roads.

   6. While located for use as a residence or premises.

EXCLUSIONS

A. We do not provide Uninsured Motorists Coverage for "bodily injury" sustained:

   1. By an "insured" while "occupying", or when struck by, any motor vehicle owned by that "insured" which is not insured for this coverage under this policy. This includes a trailer of any type used with that vehicle.

   2. By any "family member" while "occupying", or when struck by, any motor vehicle you own which is insured for this coverage on a primary basis under any other policy.

B. We do not provide Uninsured Motorists Coverage for "bodily injury" sustained by any "insured":

   1. If that "insured" or the legal representative settles the "bodily injury" claim and such settlement prejudices our right to recover payment.

   2. While "occupying" "your covered auto" when it is being used as a public or livery conveyance. This Exclusion (**B.2.**) does not apply to a share-the-expense car pool.

   3. Using a vehicle without a reasonable belief that that "insured" is entitled to do so. This Exclusion (**B.3.**) does not apply to a "family member" using "your covered auto" which is owned by you.

C. This coverage shall not apply directly or indirectly to benefit any insurer or self-insurer under any of the following or similar law:

   1. Workers' compensation law; or

   2. Disability benefits law.

D. We do not provide Uninsured Motorists Coverage for punitive or exemplary damages.

LIMIT OF LIABILITY

A. The limit of liability shown in the Declarations for each person for Uninsured Motorists Coverage is our maximum limit of liability for all damages, including damages for care, loss of services or death, arising out of "bodily injury" sustained by any one person in any one accident. Subject to this limit for each person, the limit of liability shown in the Declarations for each accident for Uninsured Motorists Coverage is our maximum limit of liability for all damages for "bodily injury" resulting from any one accident.

This is the most we will pay regardless of the number of:

1. "Insureds";

2. Claims made;

3. Vehicles or premiums shown in the Declarations; or

4. Vehicles involved in the accident.

B. No one will be entitled to receive duplicate payments for the same elements of loss under this coverage and:

1. Part **A** or Part **B** of this policy; or

2. Any Underinsured Motorists Coverage provided by this policy.

C. We will not make a duplicate payment under this coverage for any element of loss for which payment has been made by or on behalf of persons or organizations who may be legally responsible.

D. We will not pay for any element of loss if a person is entitled to receive payment for the same element of loss under any of the following or similar law:

1. Workers' compensation law; or

2. Disability benefits law.

OTHER INSURANCE

If there is other applicable insurance available under one or more policies or provisions of coverage that is similar to the insurance provided under this Part of the policy:

1. Any recovery for damages under all such policies or provisions of coverage may equal but not exceed the highest applicable limit for any one vehicle under any insurance providing coverage on either a primary or excess basis.

2. Any insurance we provide with respect to a vehicle you do not own, including any vehicle while used as a temporary substitute for "your covered auto", shall be excess over any collectible insurance providing such coverage on a primary basis.

3. If the coverage under this policy is provided:

   a. On a primary basis, we will pay only our share of the loss that must be paid under insurance providing coverage on a primary basis. Our share is the proportion that our limit of liability bears to the total of all applicable limits of liability for coverage provided on a primary basis.

   b. On an excess basis, we will pay only our share of the loss that must be paid under insurance providing coverage on an excess basis. Our share is the proportion that our limit of liability bears to the total of all applicable limits of liability for coverage provided on an excess basis.

ARBITRATION

A. If we and an "insured" do not agree:

1. Whether that "insured" is legally entitled to recover damages; or

2. As to the amount of damages which are recoverable by that "insured";

from the owner or operator of an "uninsured motor vehicle", then the matter may be arbitrated. However, disputes concerning coverage under this Part may not be arbitrated.

Both parties must agree to arbitration. If so agreed, each party will select an arbitrator. The two arbitrators will select a third. If they cannot agree within 30 days, either may request that selection be made by a judge of a court having jurisdiction.

B. Each party will:

1. Pay the expenses it incurs; and

2. Bear the expenses of the third arbitrator equally.

C. Unless both parties agree otherwise, arbitration will take place in the county in which the "insured" lives. Local rules of law as to procedure and evidence will apply. A decision agreed to by at least two of the arbitrators will be binding as to:

1. Whether the "insured" is legally entitled to recover damages; and

2. The amount of damages. This applies only if the amount does not exceed the minimum limit for bodily injury liability specified by the financial responsibility law of the state in which "your covered auto" is principally garaged. If the amount exceeds that limit, either party may demand the right to a trial. This demand must be made within 60 days of the arbitrators' decision. If this demand is not made, the amount of damages agreed to by the arbitrators will be binding.

PART D – COVERAGE FOR DAMAGE TO YOUR AUTO

INSURING AGREEMENT

A. We will pay for direct and accidental loss to "your covered auto" or any "non-owned auto", including their equipment, minus any applicable deductible shown in the Declarations. If loss to more than one "your covered auto" or "non-owned auto" results from the same "collision", only the highest applicable deductible will apply. We will pay for loss to "your covered auto" caused by:

    1. Other than "collision" only if the Declarations indicate that Other Than Collision Coverage is provided for that auto.

    2. "Collision" only if the Declarations indicate that Collision Coverage is provided for that auto.

    If there is a loss to a "non-owned auto", we will provide the broadest coverage applicable to any "your covered auto" shown in the Declarations.

B. "Collision" means the upset of "your covered auto" or a "non-owned auto" or their impact with another vehicle or object.

    Loss caused by the following is considered other than "collision":

    1. Missiles or falling objects;

    2. Fire;

    3. Theft or larceny;

    4. Explosion or earthquake;

    5. Windstorm;

    6. Hail, water or flood;

    7. Malicious mischief or vandalism;

    8. Riot or civil commotion;

    9. Contact with bird or animal; or

    10. Breakage of glass.

    If breakage of glass is caused by a "collision", you may elect to have it considered a loss caused by "collision".

C. "Non-owned auto" means:

    1. Any private passenger auto, pickup, van or "trailer" not owned by or furnished or available for the regular use of you or any "family member" while in the custody of or being operated by you or any "family member"; or

    2. Any auto or "trailer" you do not own while used as a temporary substitute for "your covered auto" which is out of normal use because of its:

        a. Breakdown;

        b. Repair;

        c. Servicing;

        d. Loss; or

        e. Destruction.

TRANSPORTATION EXPENSES

A. In addition, we will pay, without application of a deductible, up to a maximum of $600 for:

    1. Temporary transportation expenses not exceeding $20 per day incurred by you in the event of a loss to "your covered auto". We will pay for such expenses if the loss is caused by:

        a. Other than "collision" only if the Declarations indicate that Other Than Collision Coverage is provided for that auto.

        b. "Collision" only if the Declarations indicate that Collision Coverage is provided for that auto.

    2. Expenses for which you become legally responsible in the event of loss to a "non-owned auto". We will pay for such expenses if the loss is caused by:

        a. Other than "collision" only if the Declarations indicate that Other Than Collision Coverage is provided for any "your covered auto".

        b. "Collision" only if the Declarations indicate that Collision Coverage is provided for any "your covered auto".

    However, the most we will pay for any expenses for loss of use is $20 per day.

B. Subject to the provisions of Paragraph **A.**, if the loss is caused by:

    1. A total theft of "your covered auto" or a "non-owned auto", we will pay only expenses incurred during the period:

        a. Beginning 48 hours after the theft; and

        b. Ending when "your covered auto" or the "non-owned auto" is returned to use or we pay for its loss.

    2. Other than theft of a "your covered auto" or a "non-owned auto", we will pay only expenses beginning when the auto is withdrawn from use for more than 24 hours.

    Our payment will be limited to that period of time reasonably required to repair or replace the "your covered auto" or the "non-owned auto".

EXCLUSIONS

We will not pay for:

1. Loss to "your covered auto" or any "non-owned auto" which occurs while it is being used as a public or livery conveyance. This Exclusion (1.) does not apply to a share-the-expense car pool.

2. Damage due and confined to:

   a. Wear and tear;

   b. Freezing;

   c. Mechanical or electrical breakdown or failure; or

   d. Road damage to tires.

   This Exclusion (2.) does not apply if the damage results from the total theft of "your covered auto" or any "non-owned auto".

3. Loss due to or as a consequence of:

   a. Radioactive contamination;

   b. Discharge of any nuclear weapon (even if accidental);

   c. War (declared or undeclared);

   d. Civil war;

   e. Insurrection; or

   f. Rebellion or revolution.

4. Loss to any electronic equipment that reproduces, receives or transmits audio, visual or data signals. This includes but is not limited to:

   a. Radios and stereos;

   b. Tape decks;

   c. Compact disk systems;

   d. Navigation systems;

   e. Internet access systems;

   f. Personal computers;

   g. Video entertainment systems;

   h. Telephones;

   i. Televisions;

   j. Two-way mobile radios;

   k. Scanners; or

   l. Citizens band radios.

   This Exclusion (4.) does not apply to electronic equipment that is permanently installed in "your covered auto" or any "non-owned auto".

5. Loss to tapes, records, disks or other media used with equipment described in Exclusion 4.

6. A total loss to "your covered auto" or any "non-owned auto" due to destruction or confiscation by governmental or civil authorities.

   This Exclusion (6.) does not apply to the interests of Loss Payees in "your covered auto".

7. Loss to:

   a. A "trailer", camper body, or motor home, which is not shown in the Declarations; or

   b. Facilities or equipment used with such "trailer", camper body or motor home. Facilities or equipment include but are not limited to:

      (1) Cooking, dining, plumbing or refrigeration facilities;

      (2) Awnings or cabanas; or

      (3) Any other facilities or equipment used with a "trailer", camper body, or motor home.

   This Exclusion (7.) does not apply to a:

   a. "Trailer", and its facilities or equipment, which you do not own; or

   b. "Trailer", camper body, or the facilities or equipment in or attached to the "trailer" or camper body, which you:

      (1) Acquire during the policy period; and

      (2) Ask us to insure within 14 days after you become the owner.

8. Loss to any "non-owned auto" when used by you or any "family member" without a reasonable belief that you or that "family member" are entitled to do so.

9. Loss to equipment designed or used for the detection or location of radar or laser.

10. Loss to any custom furnishings or equipment in or upon any pickup or van. Custom furnishings or equipment include but are not limited to:

    a. Special carpeting or insulation;

    b. Furniture or bars;

    c. Height-extending roofs; or

    d. Custom murals, paintings or other decals or graphics.

    This Exclusion (10.) does not apply to a cap, cover or bedliner in or upon any "your covered auto" which is a pickup.

11. Loss to any "non-owned auto" being maintained or used by any person while employed or otherwise engaged in the "business" of:

    a. Selling;

    b. Repairing;

   c. Servicing;

   d. Storing; or

   e. Parking;

vehicles designed for use on public highways. This includes road testing and delivery.

12. Loss to "your covered auto" or any "non-owned auto", located inside a facility designed for racing, for the purpose of:

   a. Competing in; or

   b. Practicing or preparing for;

any prearranged or organized racing or speed contest.

13. Loss to, or loss of use of, a "non-owned auto" rented by:

   a. You; or

   b. Any "family member";

if a rental vehicle company is precluded from recovering such loss or loss of use, from you or that "family member", pursuant to the provisions of any applicable rental agreement or state law.

LIMIT OF LIABILITY

A. Our limit of liability for loss will be the lesser of the:

   1. Actual cash value of the stolen or damaged property; or

   2. Amount necessary to repair or replace the property with other property of like kind and quality.

However, the most we will pay for loss to:

   1. Any "non-owned auto" which is a trailer is $1500.

   2. Electronic equipment that reproduces, receives or transmits audio, visual or data signals, which is permanently installed in the auto in locations not used by the auto manufacturer for installation of such equipment, is $1,000.

B. An adjustment for depreciation and physical condition will be made in determining actual cash value in the event of a total loss.

C. If a repair or replacement results in better than like kind or quality, we will not pay for the amount of the betterment.

PAYMENT OF LOSS

We may pay for loss in money or repair or replace the damaged or stolen property. We may, at our expense, return any stolen property to:

   1. You; or

   2. The address shown in this policy.

If we return stolen property we will pay for any damage resulting from the theft. We may keep all or part of the property at an agreed or appraised value.

If we pay for loss in money, our payment will include the applicable sales tax for the damaged or stolen property.

NO BENEFIT TO BAILEE

This insurance shall not directly or indirectly benefit any carrier or other bailee for hire.

OTHER SOURCES OF RECOVERY

If other sources of recovery also cover the loss, we will pay only our share of the loss. Our share is the proportion that our limit of liability bears to the total of all applicable limits. However, any insurance we provide with respect to a "non-owned auto" shall be excess over any other collectible source of recovery including, but not limited to:

   1. Any coverage provided by the owner of the "non-owned auto";

   2. Any other applicable physical damage insurance;

   3. Any other source of recovery applicable to the loss.

APPRAISAL

A. If we and you do not agree on the amount of loss, either may demand an appraisal of the loss. In this event, each party will select a competent and impartial appraiser. The two appraisers will select an umpire. The appraisers will state separately the actual cash value and the amount of loss. If they fail to agree, they will submit their differences to the umpire. A decision agreed to by any two will be binding. Each party will:

   1. Pay its chosen appraiser; and

   2. Bear the expenses of the appraisal and umpire equally.

B. We do not waive any of our rights under this policy by agreeing to an appraisal.

PART E – DUTIES AFTER AN ACCIDENT OR LOSS

We have no duty to provide coverage under this policy if the failure to comply with the following duties is prejudicial to us:

A. We must be notified promptly of how, when and where the accident or loss happened. Notice should also include the names and addresses of any injured persons and of any witnesses.

B. A person seeking any coverage must:

  1. Cooperate with us in the investigation, settlement or defense of any claim or suit.

  2. Promptly send us copies of any notices or legal papers received in connection with the accident or loss.

  3. Submit, as often as we reasonably require:

     a. To physical exams by physicians we select. We will pay for these exams.

     b. To examination under oath and subscribe the same.

  4. Authorize us to obtain:

     a. Medical reports; and

     b. Other pertinent records.

  5. Submit a proof of loss when required by us.

C. A person seeking Uninsured Motorists Coverage must also:

  1. Promptly notify the police if a hit-and-run driver is involved.

  2. Promptly send us copies of the legal papers if a suit is brought.

D. A person seeking Coverage For Damage To Your Auto must also:

  1. Take reasonable steps after loss to protect "your covered auto" or any "non-owned auto" and their equipment from further loss. We will pay reasonable expenses incurred to do this.

  2. Promptly notify the police if "your covered auto" or any "non-owned auto" is stolen.

  3. Permit us to inspect and appraise the damaged property before its repair or disposal.

PART F – GENERAL PROVISIONS

BANKRUPTCY

Bankruptcy or insolvency of the "insured" shall not relieve us of any obligations under this policy.

CHANGES

A. This policy contains all the agreements between you and us. Its terms may not be changed or waived except by endorsement issued by us.

B. If there is a change to the information used to develop the policy premium, we may adjust your premium. Changes during the policy term that may result in a premium increase or decrease include, but are not limited to, changes in:

  1. The number, type or use classification of insured vehicles;

  2. Operators using insured vehicles;

  3. The place of principal garaging of insured vehicles;

  4. Coverage, deductible or limits.

If a change resulting from **A.** or **B.** requires a premium adjustment, we will make the premium adjustment in accordance with our manual rules.

C. If we make a change which broadens coverage under this edition of your policy without additional premium charge, that change will automatically apply to your policy as of the date we implement the change in your state. This Paragraph **(C.)** does not apply to changes implemented with a general program revision that includes both broadenings and restrictions in coverage, whether that general program revision is implemented through introduction of:

  1. A subsequent edition of your policy; or

  2. An Amendatory Endorsement.

FRAUD

We do not provide coverage for any "insured" who has made fraudulent statements or engaged in fraudulent conduct in connection with any accident or loss for which coverage is sought under this policy.

LEGAL ACTION AGAINST US

A. No legal action may be brought against us until there has been full compliance with all the terms of this policy. In addition, under Part **A**, no legal action may be brought against us until:

  1. We agree in writing that the "insured" has an obligation to pay; or

  2. The amount of that obligation has been finally determined by judgment after trial.

B. No person or organization has any right under this policy to bring us into any action to determine the liability of an "insured".

OUR RIGHT TO RECOVER PAYMENT

A. If we make a payment under this policy and the person to or for whom payment was made has a right to recover damages from another we shall be subrogated to that right. That person shall do:

  1. Whatever is necessary to enable us to exercise our rights; and

  2. Nothing after loss to prejudice them.

  However, our rights in this Paragraph **(A.)** do not apply under Part **D**, against any person using "your covered auto" with a reasonable belief that that person is entitled to do so.

B. If we make a payment under this policy and the person to or for whom payment is made recovers damages from another, that person shall:

  1. Hold in trust for us the proceeds of the recovery; and

  2. Reimburse us to the extent of our payment.

POLICY PERIOD AND TERRITORY

A. This policy applies only to accidents and losses which occur:

  1. During the policy period as shown in the Declarations; and

  2. Within the policy territory.

B. The policy territory is:

  1. The United States of America, its territories or possessions;

  2. Puerto Rico; or

  3. Canada.

  This policy also applies to loss to, or accidents involving, "your covered auto" while being transported between their ports.

TERMINATION

A. Cancellation

  This policy may be cancelled during the policy period as follows:

  1. The named insured shown in the Declarations may cancel by:

    a. Returning this policy to us; or

    b. Giving us advance written notice of the date cancellation is to take effect.

  2. We may cancel by mailing to the named insured shown in the Declarations at the address shown in this policy:

    a. At least 10 days notice:

      (1) If cancellation is for nonpayment of premium; or

      (2) If notice is mailed during the first 60 days this policy is in effect and this is not a renewal or continuation policy; or

    b. At least 20 days notice in all other cases.

  3. After this policy is in effect for 60 days, or if this is a renewal or continuation policy, we will cancel only:

    a. For nonpayment of premium; or

    b. If your driver's license or that of:

      (1) Any driver who lives with you; or

      (2) Any driver who customarily uses "your covered auto";

      has been suspended or revoked. This must have occurred:

      (1) During the policy period; or

      (2) Since the last anniversary of the original effective date if the policy period is other than 1 year; or

    c. If the policy was obtained through material misrepresentation.

B. Nonrenewal

  If we decide not to renew or continue this policy, we will mail notice to the named insured shown in the Declarations at the address shown in this policy. Notice will be mailed at least 20 days before the end of the policy period. Subject to this notice requirement, if the policy period is:

  1. Less than 6 months, we will have the right not to renew or continue this policy every 6 months, beginning 6 months after its original effective date.

  2. 6 months or longer, but less than one year, we will have the right not to renew or continue this policy at the end of the policy period.

  3. 1 year or longer, we will have the right not to renew or continue this policy at each anniversary of its original effective date.

C. Automatic Termination

  If we offer to renew or continue and you or your representative do not accept, this policy will automatically terminate at the end of the current policy period. Failure to pay the required renewal or continuation premium when due shall mean that you have not accepted our offer.

  If you obtain other insurance on "your covered auto", any similar insurance provided by this policy will terminate as to that auto on the effective date of the other insurance.

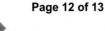

D. Other Termination Provisions

1. We may deliver any notice instead of mailing it. Proof of mailing of any notice shall be sufficient proof of notice.

2. If this policy is cancelled, you may be entitled to a premium refund. If so, we will send you the refund. The premium refund, if any, will be computed according to our manuals. However, making or offering to make the refund is not a condition of cancellation.

3. The effective date of cancellation stated in the notice shall become the end of the policy period.

TRANSFER OF YOUR INTEREST IN THIS POLICY

A. Your rights and duties under this policy may not be assigned without our written consent. However, if a named insured shown in the Declarations dies, coverage will be provided for:

1. The surviving spouse if resident in the same household at the time of death. Coverage applies to the spouse as if a named insured shown in the Declarations; and

2. The legal representative of the deceased person as if a named insured shown in the Declarations. This applies only with respect to the representative's legal responsibility to maintain or use "your covered auto".

B. Coverage will only be provided until the end of the policy period.

TWO OR MORE AUTO POLICIES

If this policy and any other auto insurance policy issued to you by us apply to the same accident, the maximum limit of our liability under all the policies shall not exceed the highest applicable limit of liability under any one policy.

Personal Auto

POLICY NUMBER:

PERSONAL AUTO
PP 05 90 05 10

THIS ENDORSEMENT CHANGES THE POLICY. PLEASE READ IT CAREFULLY.

PERSONAL INJURY PROTECTION COVERAGE – MICHIGAN

With respect to the coverage provided by this endorsement, the provisions of the policy apply unless modified by the endorsement.

SCHEDULE

Benefits	Limit Of Liability
Medical Expenses	No maximum dollar amount
Funeral Expenses	Up to $1,750 per person
Work Loss	Up to $4,878* for any 30-day period
Replacement Services	$20 per day maximum
Survivor's Loss Consisting Of Income Loss And Replacement Services	Up to $4,878* for any 30-day period subject to a $20 per day maximum for replacement services
*Or whatever amount is established under the Michigan Insurance Code for accidents occurring on or after the date of the change in the maximum.	

The following options apply as indicated in the Declarations or by an X in the box below:

COORDINATION OF BENEFITS

☐ Coordination of medical expenses (excluding Medicare benefits provided by the Federal Government) applies to you or any "family member".

☐ Coordination of work loss applies to you or any "family member".

REJECTION OF WORK LOSS

☐ Work loss does not apply to an "insured" age 60 or older who has signed a form rejecting the work loss benefit.

DEDUCTIBLE

☐ A deductible of **$**   applies to you or any "family member".

I. Definitions

The **Definitions** Section is amended as follows:

A. The definition of "your covered auto" is replaced by the following:

"Your covered auto" means an "auto":

1. For which you are required to maintain security under the Michigan Insurance Code; and

2. To which the bodily injury liability coverage of this policy applies.

B. The following definitions are added:

1. "Auto" means a motor vehicle or trailer operated or designed for use on public roads. It does not include:

   a. A motorcycle or moped;

   b. A farm tractor or other implement of husbandry which is not subject to the registration requirements of the Michigan Vehicle Code; or

   c. A vehicle operated by muscular power or with fewer than three wheels.

2. "Auto accident" means a loss involving the ownership, operation, maintenance or use of an "auto" as an "auto" regardless of whether the accident also involves the ownership, operation, maintenance or use of a motorcycle as a motorcycle.

C. "Insured" as used in this endorsement means:

1. You or any "family member" injured in an "auto accident";

2. Anyone else injured in an "auto accident":

   a. While "occupying" "your covered auto"; or

   b. If the accident involves any other "auto":

      (1) Which is operated by you or any "family member"; and

      (2) To which Part **A** of this policy applies;

   c. While not "occupying" any "auto" if the accident involves "your covered auto".

II. Personal Injury Protection Coverage

INSURING AGREEMENT

A. We will pay personal injury protection benefits to or for an "insured" who sustains "bodily injury". The "bodily injury" must:

1. Be caused by accident; and

2. Result from the ownership, maintenance or use of an "auto" as an "auto".

B. These benefits are subject to the provisions of the Michigan Insurance Code. Subject to the limits shown in the Schedule or Declarations, personal injury protection benefits consist of the following:

1. **Medical Expenses**

   Reasonable and necessary medical expenses incurred for an "insured's":

   a. Care;

   b. Recovery; or

   c. Rehabilitation.

   Only semiprivate room charges will be paid unless special or intensive care is required.

2. **Funeral Expenses**

   Reasonable funeral and burial expenses incurred.

3. **Work Loss**

   Up to 85% of an "insured's" actual loss of income from work. We will pay a higher percentage if the "insured" gives us reasonable proof that net income is more than 85% of gross income. The most we will pay in any 30-day period for this benefit is the amount shown in the Schedule or Declarations unless another amount is established by law. Any income an "insured" earns during the 30-day period is included in determining the income benefit we will pay. This benefit is payable for loss sustained during the three years after the accident. It does not apply after an "insured" dies. We will prorate this benefit for any period less than 30 days.

4. **Replacement Services**

   Reasonable expenses for obtaining services to replace those an "insured" would have done:

   a. Without pay; and

   b. For the benefit of that "insured" or that "insured's" dependents.

   This benefit is payable for loss sustained during the three years after the accident. It does not apply after an "insured" dies.

5. **Survivor's Loss**

   a. Income Loss

   The contributions a deceased "insured's" spouse and dependents would have received as dependents, if the "insured" had not died. The contributions must be tangible things of economic value, not including services.

   b. Replacement Services

   Reasonable expenses incurred for obtaining services to replace those a deceased "insured" would have done for that "insured's" spouse and dependents.

   The most we will pay in any 30-day period for the total of these benefits is the amount shown in the Schedule or Declarations unless another amount is established by law. These benefits are payable for loss sustained during the three years after the accident. A deceased "insured's" spouse must have either:

   a. Resided with; or

   b. Been dependent on;

   the "insured" at the time of death. The benefits end for a spouse at remarriage or death.

© Insurance Services Office, Inc., 2009   **PP 05 90 05 10**

Any other person who was dependent upon the deceased "insured" at the time of death qualifies for benefits if, and as long as that dependent is:

a. Under age 18; or

b. Physically or mentally unable to earn a living; or

c. In a full-time formal program of academic or vocational education or training.

EXCLUSIONS

A. We do not provide Personal Injury Protection Coverage for "bodily injury":

1. To any "insured" who intentionally caused the "bodily injury".

2. Sustained by any "insured" using an "auto" which that "insured" had taken unlawfully. This Exclusion (**A.2.**) does not apply if the "insured" had a reasonable belief that he or she was entitled to use the "auto".

3. Sustained by any "insured" while not "occupying" an "auto" if the accident takes place outside Michigan. However, this Exclusion (**A.3.**) does not apply to:

a. You; or

b. Any "family member".

4. To you while "occupying", or struck by while not "occupying", any "auto":

a. Owned or registered by you; and

b. Which is not "your covered auto".

5. Sustained by the owner or registrant of an "auto" involved in the accident and for which the security required under the Michigan Insurance Code is not in effect.

6. Sustained by anyone entitled to Michigan no-fault benefits as a family member under another policy except while an operator or passenger of a motorcycle involved in the accident. This Exclusion (**A.6.**) does not apply to:

a. You; or

b. Any "family member".

7. Sustained by anyone entitled to Michigan no-fault benefits as a named insured under another policy except while an operator or passenger of a motorcycle involved in the accident. This Exclusion (**A.7.**) does not apply to you.

8. Sustained while "occupying", or struck by while not "occupying", an "auto" (other than "your covered auto") if:

a. Operated by you or any "family member"; and

b. The owner or registrant has the security required under the Michigan Insurance Code.

This Exclusion (**A.8.**) does not apply to:

a. You; or

b. Any "family member".

9. Sustained while "occupying" an "auto" located for use as a residence or premises.

10. Sustained while "occupying" a public auto for which the security required under the Michigan Insurance Code is in effect. This Exclusion (**A.10.**) does not apply to "bodily injury" to you or a "family member" while a passenger in a:

a. School bus;

b. Certified common carrier;

c. Bus operated under government sponsored transportation program;

d. Bus operated by or servicing a non-profit organization;

e. Bus operated by a watercraft, bicycle or horse livery used only to transport passengers to or from a destination point; or

f. Taxicab.

11. Sustained by you or any "family member" while "occupying" an "auto" which is owned or registered by:

a. Your employer; or

b. Any "family member's" employer; and

for which the security required under the Michigan Insurance Code is in effect.

12. Sustained while "occupying" an "auto" other than "your covered auto":

a. For which the owner or registrant is not required to provide security under the Michigan Insurance Code; and

b. Which is being operated by you or a "family member" outside Michigan.

This Exclusion (**A.12.**) does not apply to:

a. You or any "family member"; or

b. Medical or funeral expense benefits.

13. Arising out of the ownership, operation, maintenance or use of a parked "auto". This Exclusion **(A.13.)** does not apply if:

   a. The "auto" was parked in such a way as to cause unreasonable risk of the "bodily injury"; or

   b. The "bodily injury" resulted from physical contact with:

     (1) Equipment permanently mounted on the "auto" while the equipment was being used; or

     (2) Property being lifted onto or lowered from the "auto"; or

   c. The "bodily injury" was sustained while "occupying" the "auto".

   However, Exceptions **b.** and **c.** to this Exclusion **(A.13.)** do not apply to any employee that has Michigan workers' disability compensation benefits available and who sustains "bodily injury" in the course of employment while loading, unloading or doing mechanical work on an auto, unless the injury arises from the use or operation of another vehicle.

14. Sustained in an "auto accident" by you or any "family member" while an operator or passenger of a motorcycle, if the owner, registrant or operator of the "auto" has provided security for that "auto" as required under the Michigan Insurance Code.

B. We do not provide Personal Injury Protection Coverage for:

1. Medical expenses for you or any "family member":

   a. To the extent that similar benefits are paid or payable under any other insurance, service, benefit or reimbursement plan (excluding Medicare benefits provided by the Federal Government); and

   b. If Coordination of Benefits for medical expenses is indicated in the Schedule or Declarations.

2. Work loss for you or any "family member":

   a. To the extent that similar benefits are paid or payable under any other insurance, service, benefit or reimbursement plan; and

   b. If Coordination of Benefits for work loss is indicated in the Schedule or Declarations.

3. Work loss for an "insured" age 60 or older if:

   a. Rejection of Work Loss is indicated in the Schedule or Declarations; and

   b. That "insured" has signed a form rejecting the work loss benefit.

LIMIT OF LIABILITY

The Limits Of Liability shown in the Schedule or Declarations for Personal Injury Protection Coverage are the most we will pay for each "insured" injured in any one accident, regardless of the number of:

1. "Insureds";

2. Claims made;

3. Vehicles or premiums shown in the Declarations;

4. Vehicles involved in the accident; or

5. Insurers providing no-fault benefits.

Any amount payable under this insurance shall be reduced by:

1. Any amounts paid, payable or required to be provided by state or federal law except any amounts paid, payable or required to be provided by Medicare, provided that the benefits:

   a. Serve the same purpose as personal injury protection benefits paid or payable to an "insured" under this policy; and

   b. Are provided or required to be provided as a result of the same accident for which this insurance is payable. However, this insurance shall not be reduced by any amount of workers' compensation benefits, if workers' compensation benefits that are required to be provided are not available to an "insured".

2. Any deductible you elect. However, the deductible applies only to you and any "family member".

III. Part E – Duties After An Accident Or Loss

Part **E** is amended as follows:

A. Duties **B.1.** and **B.5.** are replaced by the following:

A person seeking coverage must:

1. Cooperate with us in the investigation or settlement of any claim.

2. Submit a written proof of claim when required by us.

© Insurance Services Office, Inc., 2009   **PP 05 90 05 10**

B. Duty **B.2.** does not apply.

C. The following duty is added:

A person seeking coverage must promptly send us copies of the legal papers if a suit is brought.

D. Paragraph **B.3.b.** does not apply.

IV. Part F – General Provisions

Part **F** is amended as follows:

A. The **Legal Action Against Us** Provision is replaced by the following:

Legal Action Against Us

No legal action may be brought against us until there has been full compliance with the terms of this coverage. In addition, no legal action may be brought against us after one year from the date of accident causing the injury unless:

1. Written notice of the injury has been given to us within one year from the date of the accident; or

2. We have already paid any personal injury protection benefits for the injury.

If either **1.** or **2.** applies, you may bring action against us. Action must be brought within one year from the date the most recent medical or funeral expense or work or survivor's loss was incurred. No one may recover benefits for any portion of the loss incurred more than one year before the date on which the action was begun.

B. The **Our Right To Recover Payment** Provision is amended as follows:

Our Right To Recover Payment

1. Paragraph **A.** of the provision is replaced by the following:

If we make a payment under this coverage and the person to or for whom payment was made has a right to recover damages from the owner or operator of a motor vehicle, and that owner or operator is an uninsured motorist, we shall be subrogated to that right. That person shall do:

1. Whatever is necessary to enable us to exercise our rights; and

2. Nothing after loss to prejudice them.

2. The following is added to Paragraph **B.** of the provision:

Our right is subject to any applicable limitations stated in the Michigan Insurance Code.

C. The following provisions are added:

Duplication Of Benefits

No one will be entitled to duplicate payments for the same elements of loss under this coverage regardless of the number of:

1. Vehicles covered; or

2. Insurers (including self-insurers) providing security in accordance with the Michigan Insurance Code or any other similar law.

An "insured" who sustains "bodily injury" resulting from an "auto accident" which shows evidence of the involvement of an "auto" while an operator or passenger of a motorcycle shall claim insurance benefits in the following order of priority:

1. The insurer of the owner or registrant of the "auto" involved in the accident.

2. The insurer of the operator of the "auto" involved in the accident.

3. The "auto" insurer of the operator of the motorcycle involved in the accident.

4. The "auto" insurer of the owner or registrant of the motorcycle involved in the accident.

Premium Recomputation

The Michigan Insurance Code places certain limitations on a person's right to sue for damages. The premium for this policy reflects these limitations. A court from which there is no appeal can declare any of these limitations unenforceable. If this occurs, we will have the right to recompute the premium. You can choose to delete any coverage as the result of the court's decision. If you do, we will compute any refund of premium on a pro rata basis.

This endorsement must be attached to the Change Endorsement when issued after the policy is written.

POLICY NUMBER:

PERSONAL AUTO
PP 04 47 04 09

THIS ENDORSEMENT CHANGES THE POLICY. PLEASE READ IT CAREFULLY.

UNDERINSURED MOTORISTS COVERAGE – ILLINOIS

SCHEDULE

Limit Of Liability		Premium		
		Auto 1	Auto 2	Auto 3
$ Each Person		$	$	$
$ Each Accident				

With respect to the coverage provided by this endorsement, the provisions of the policy apply unless modified by the endorsement.

INSURING AGREEMENT

A. We will pay compensatory damages which an "insured" is legally entitled to recover from the owner or operator of an "underinsured motor vehicle" because of "bodily injury":

1. Sustained by an "insured"; and

2. Caused by an accident.

The owner's or operator's liability for these damages must arise out of the ownership, maintenance or use of the "underinsured motor vehicle".

We will pay under this coverage only after the limits of liability under any bodily injury liability bonds or policies applicable to the "underinsured motor vehicle" have been exhausted by payment of judgments or settlements, unless:

1. We have been given written notice of a "tentative settlement" and decide to advance payment to the "insured" in an amount equal to that settlement; or

2. We and an "insured" have reached a "settlement agreement".

B. "Insured" as used in this endorsement means:

1. You or any "family member".

2. Any other person "occupying":

   a. "Your covered auto"; or

   b. Any other auto operated by you.

3. Any person for damages that person is entitled to recover because of "bodily injury" to which this coverage applies sustained by a person described in **1.** or **2.** above.

C. "Underinsured motor vehicle" means a land motor vehicle or trailer of any type to which a bodily injury liability bond or policy applies at the time of the accident but its limit for bodily injury liability is either:

1. Less than the limit of liability for this coverage; or

2. Reduced by payments to others injured in the accident to an amount which is less than the limit of liability for this coverage.

However, "underinsured motor vehicle" does not include any vehicle or equipment:

1. To which a bodily injury liability bond or policy applies at the time of the accident but its limit for bodily injury liability is less than the minimum limit for bodily injury liability specified by the financial responsibility law of Illinois.

2. Owned by or furnished or available for the regular use of you or any "family member".

3. Owned by any governmental unit or agency.

4. Operated on rails or crawler treads.

5. Designed mainly for use off public roads while not upon public roads.

6. While located for use as a residence or premises.

7. Owned or operated by a person qualifying as a self-insurer under any applicable motor vehicle law.

8. To which a bodily injury liability bond or policy applies at the time of the accident but the bonding or insuring company:

   a. Denies coverage; or

   b. Is or becomes insolvent.

PP 04 47 04 09   **Page 1 of 4**

D. "Tentative settlement" means an offer from the owner or operator of the "underinsured motor vehicle" to compensate an "insured" for damages incurred because of "bodily injury" sustained in an accident involving the "underinsured motor vehicle".

E. "Settlement agreement" means we and an "insured" agree that the "insured" is legally entitled to recover, from the owner or operator of the "underinsured motor vehicle", damages for "bodily injury" and, without arbitration, agree also as to the amount of damages. Such agreement shall be final and binding regardless of any subsequent judgment or settlement reached by the "insured" with the owner or operator of the "underinsured motor vehicle".

EXCLUSIONS

A. We do not provide Underinsured Motorists Coverage for "bodily injury" sustained:

  1. By an "insured" while "occupying", or when struck by, any motor vehicle owned by that "insured" which is not insured for this coverage under this policy. This includes a trailer of any type used with that vehicle.

  2. By any "family member" while "occupying", or when struck by, any motor vehicle you own which is insured for this coverage on a primary basis under any other policy.

B. We do not provide Underinsured Motorists Coverage for "bodily injury" sustained by any "insured":

  1. While "occupying" "your covered auto" when it is being used as a public or livery conveyance. This Exclusion **(B.1.)** does not apply to a share-the-expense car pool.

  2. Using a vehicle without a reasonable belief that that "insured" is entitled to do so. This Exclusion **(B.2.)** does not apply to a "family member" using "your covered auto" which is owned by you.

  3. While "occupying" any auto not owned by, or furnished or available for the regular use of, you or any "family member" when it is being used as a public or livery conveyance. However, this Exclusion **(B.3.)** does not apply to:

    a. A share-the-expense car pool; or

    b. You or any "family member".

C. This coverage shall not apply directly or indirectly to benefit any insurer or self-insurer under any of the following or similar law:

  1. Workers' compensation law; or

  2. Disability benefits law.

D. We do not provide Underinsured Motorists Coverage for punitive or exemplary damages.

LIMIT OF LIABILITY

A. The limit of liability shown in the Schedule or in the Declarations for each person for Underinsured Motorists Coverage is our maximum limit of liability for all damages, including damages for care, loss of services or death, arising out of "bodily injury" sustained by any one person in any one accident. Subject to this limit for each person, the limit of liability shown in the Schedule or in the Declarations for each accident for Underinsured Motorists Coverage is our maximum limit of liability for all damages for "bodily injury" resulting from any one accident.

This is the most we will pay regardless of the number of:

  1. "Insureds;"

  2. Claims made;

  3. Vehicles or premiums shown in the Schedule or Declarations; or

  4. Vehicles involved in the accident.

B. Except in the event of a "settlement agreement", the limit of liability for this coverage shall be reduced by all sums paid because of the "bodily injury" by or on behalf of persons or organizations who may be legally responsible. This includes all sums paid under Part **A** of this policy.

C. In the event of a "settlement agreement", the maximum limit of liability for this coverage shall be the amount by which the limit of liability for this coverage exceeds the limits of bodily injury liability bonds or policies applicable to the owner or operator of the "underinsured motor vehicle".

D. The limit of liability for this coverage shall be reduced by all sums:

  1. Paid or payable because of the "bodily injury" under any automobile medical payments coverage. This includes all sums paid under Part **B** of this policy.

  2. Paid or payable because of the "bodily injury" under any of the following or similar law:

    a. Workers' compensation law; or

    b. Disability benefits law.

    However, this Paragraph **(D.2.)** shall not apply to disability benefits received under the federal Social Security Act.

E. No one will be entitled to receive duplicate payments for the same elements of loss under this coverage and Part **A**, Part **B** or Part **C** of this policy.

F. We will not make a duplicate payment under this coverage for any element of loss for which payment has been made by or on behalf of persons or organizations who may be legally responsible.

G. We will not pay for any element of loss if a person is entitled to receive payment for the same element of loss under any of the following or similar law:

1. Workers' compensation law; or

2. Disability benefits law.

However, this Paragraph **(G.)** shall not apply to disability benefits received under the federal Social Security Act.

OTHER INSURANCE

If there is other applicable insurance available under one or more policies or provisions of coverage that is similar to the insurance provided by this endorsement:

1. Any recovery for damages under all such policies or provisions of coverage may equal but not exceed the highest applicable limit for any one vehicle under any insurance providing coverage on either a primary or excess basis.

2. Any insurance we provide with respect to a vehicle you do not own, including any vehicle while used as a temporary substitute for "your covered auto", shall be excess over any collectible insurance providing such coverage on a primary basis.

3. If the coverage under this policy is provided:

a. On a primary basis, we will pay only our share of the loss that must be paid under insurance providing coverage on a primary basis. Our share is the proportion that our limit of liability bears to the total of all applicable limits of liability for coverage provided on a primary basis.

b. On an excess basis, we will pay only our share of the loss that must be paid under insurance providing coverage on an excess basis. Our share is the proportion that our limit of liability bears to the total of all applicable limits of liability for coverage provided on an excess basis.

ARBITRATION

A. If we and an "insured" do not agree:

1. Whether that person is legally entitled to recover damages under this endorsement; or

2. As to the amount of damages;

either party may make a written demand for arbitration. In this event, each party will select an arbitrator. The two arbitrators will select a third. If such arbitrators are not selected within 45 days, either party may request that the arbitration be submitted to the American Arbitration Association.

B. We will bear all the expenses of the arbitration except when the "insured's" recovery exceeds the minimum limit specified in the Illinois Safety Responsibility Law. If this occurs, the "insured" will be responsible up to the amount by which the "insured's" recovery exceeds the statutory minimum for:

1. Payment of his or her expenses; and

2. An equal share of the third arbitrator's expenses.

C. Unless both parties agree otherwise, arbitration will take place in the county in which the "insured" lives. Local rules of law as to procedure and evidence will apply. A decision agreed to by at least two of the arbitrators will be binding as to:

1. Whether the "insured" is legally entitled to recover damages; and

2. The amount of damages.

ADDITIONAL DUTIES

Any person seeking coverage under this endorsement must also:

1. Give us written notice of a "tentative settlement" and allow us 30 days to advance payment in an amount equal to that settlement to preserve our rights against the owner or operator of the "underinsured motor vehicle".

2. File suit against the owner or operator of the "underinsured motor vehicle" prior to the conclusion of a "settlement agreement". Such suit cannot be abandoned or settled without giving us written notice of a "tentative settlement" and allowing us 30 days to advance payment in an amount equal to that settlement to preserve our rights against the owner or operator of the "underinsured motor vehicle".

3. Promptly send us copies of the legal papers if a suit is brought.

PART F – GENERAL PROVISIONS

The **Our Right To Recover Payment** Provision of Part **F** is replaced by the following with respect to Underinsured Motorists Coverage:

OUR RIGHT TO RECOVER PAYMENT

A. If we make a payment under this policy and the person to or for whom payment was made has a right to recover damages from another we shall be subrogated to that right. That person shall do:

   1. Whatever is necessary to enable us to exercise our rights; and

   2. Nothing after loss to prejudice them.

However, our rights in this Paragraph **(A.)** do not apply if we:

   1. Have been given written notice of a "tentative settlement"; and

   2. Fail to advance payment to the "insured" in an amount equal to the "tentative settlement" within 30 days after receipt of notification.

If we advance payment to the "insured" in an amount equal to the "tentative settlement" within 30 days after receipt of notification:

   1. That payment will be separate from any amount the "insured" is entitled to recover under the provisions of Underinsured Motorists Coverage.

   2. We also have a right to recover the advanced payment.

B. If we make a payment under this policy and the person to or for whom payment is made recovers damages from another, that person shall:

   1. Hold in trust for us the proceeds of the recovery; and

   2. Reimburse us to the extent of our payment.

However, in the event of a "settlement agreement", we shall be entitled to a recovery under Paragraphs **A.** and **B.** only for amounts which exceed the limit of bodily injury liability bonds or policies applicable to the owner or operator of the "underinsured motor vehicle".

This endorsement must be attached to the Change Endorsement when issued after the policy is written.

Miscellaneous Personal Insurance Policies

Although a homeowners policy and a personal auto policy cover most of the property and liability loss exposures of an individual or a family, additional policies are often needed. This section of the *Handbook* contains samples of three such policies: a yacht policy, a flood insurance policy, and a personal umbrella liability policy.

Boatowner/Yacht Policy

Because homeowners policies contain several restrictions on watercraft coverage, many boatowners obtain broader coverage under separate boatowner, or yacht, policies. A boatowner policy resembles a personal auto policy, because it provides liability and physical damage insurance and may even provide medical payments and "uninsured boaters" coverage. However, the coverages are specially suited to the needs of boatowners. For example, the physical damage coverage applies to certain perils that can occur only on water, and the liability coverage covers certain exposures unique to maritime law, such as liability under the U.S. Longshore and Harbor Workers' Compensation Act.

Flood Insurance Policy

Most homeowners policies exclude loss caused by flood. Often, the National Flood Insurance Program (NFIP) is the only source of flood insurance for individuals and families. The Standard Flood Insurance Policy—Dwelling Form is the form that the NFIP uses to provide flood insurance on dwellings and their contents. The NFIP uses a separate, but similar, form to insure business properties.

Personal Umbrella Liability Policy

A personal umbrella liability policy serves two basic purposes:

1. It adds additional amounts of liability insurance above the limits in the insured's homeowners, personal auto, and perhaps other underlying liability policies.
2. It covers some exposures that would not be covered at all by the insured's underlying policies.

Historically, there was no standard form for personal umbrella liability insurance, so each insurer that wished to write personal umbrella policies developed its own form. However, both Insurance Services Office, Inc., (ISO) and the American Association of Insurance Services (AAIS) now offer standard personal umbrella liability policies for their member companies' use. The ISO Personal Umbrella Liability Policy is reproduced in the *Handbook*.

YACHT POLICY

AGREEMENT

This marine insurance policy is a legal contract between "you" and "us". In return for "your" payment of premium and in reliance upon the information "you" give "us" or "our" authorized representative, "we" will provide "you" with the insurance described in this policy.

Various provisions in this policy restrict coverage. Read the entire policy carefully to determine rights, duties and what is and what is not covered.

PRIVATE PLEASURE USE ONLY

Coverage under this policy applies only while the covered "yacht" is used for private pleasure purposes. This includes recreational boating and leisure time activities. There is no coverage while the covered "yacht" is used for charter, hire, to carry persons or property for a fee or for any other commercial use unless prior written consent has been obtained from "us". Commercial use includes use in any trade, occupation or profession. Business entertainment for which there is no direct remuneration is private pleasure use.

"We" cover the "yacht" while:

a. Afloat within the navigational limits described on the Declaration Page;

b. Ashore within the continental United States or Canada. **However, while being transported by a common, contract or any other carrier for hire, coverage applies only within a two hundred fifty (250) mile radius from the home port or storage location unless prior written consent has been obtained from "us".**

DEFINITIONS

Throughout this policy the words **"you" "your"** and **"yours"** mean the **"insured person"**. The words **"we"**, **"our"** and **"us"** mean the insurance company providing this insurance. Also throughout this policy the word **"yacht"** means the hull; machinery; furniture; electronic and other equipment including "navigation equipment" normally necessary to be on board for safe operation and routine maintenance; spars; sails; masts; rigging; fittings; "tenders" or "dinghies". "Yacht" does not include "personal effects," or any "trailer" (except a trailer for the "tender" or "dinghy"). Other words and phrases that appear in quotation marks have special meaning as shown below.

"Insured Person" means the person named on the Declaration Page and any of his or her "family members." It shall also include any person, firm, corporation or legal entity whom "you" permit to operate the covered "yacht" without charge and for private pleasure use only. It does not mean any person or organization or employee thereof operating a boatyard, marina, yacht chartering or sales agency, or similar organization.

"Family Members" means persons related by blood, marriage or adoption (including a ward or foster child).

"Tender" or **"Dinghy"** means a launch or small boat (including its outboard engine and trailer) not exceeding 16 feet in length and 35 hp, unless otherwise scheduled, used primarily to travel to and from the covered "yacht" and usually carried on or towed behind the covered "yacht".

"Trailer" or **"Boat Trailer"** means the trailer described on the Declaration Page.

"Personal Effects" means wearing apparel; sports equipment; fishing equipment including fish finders and other personal property not otherwise excluded. Furniture; radios; stereos; "navigation equipment"; television sets and similar electronic equipment are not "personal effects".

"Latent Defect" means a hidden flaw in the material existing at the time of manufacture of the covered "yacht" or its machinery that is not discoverable by ordinary methods of testing.

"Deductible" means the portion of the loss that "you" have to bear.

"Navigation Equipment" means equipment used in the navigation of the "yacht" which is either permanently attached to the vessel, or which can be removed and which is not otherwise excluded under this policy. This includes handheld devices such as GPS units, and portable marine radios, sextants, radars, lorans.

"Uninsured or Underinsured Boater", **"Uninsured or Underinsured Owner"** and **"Uninsured or Underinsured Operator"** mean an owner or operator of a watercraft other than the covered "yacht" described in this policy who is wholly or partially responsible for the accident; AND to whom no legal liability insurance policy applies at the time of the accident; OR for whom the sum of the limits of liability under all bodily injury liability bonds or policies applicable at the time of the accident is not enough to pay the full amount the injured person is legally entitled to recover as damages; OR who cannot be identified.

"Total Loss" means that the covered "yacht" was completely lost or destroyed, or the cost to recover and/or repair the covered "yacht" is greater than the applicable amount of insurance.

"Pollution" means property damage and assessments, clean up costs or containment expenses incurred or imposed by any Federal, State or Local Statutes or Regulations; arising out of the sudden and accidental discharge, spillage, leakage or emission of oil, fuel, petroleum products or "Other Pollutants".

"Other Pollutants" means any solid, liquid or gaseous thermal irritant or contaminant, including smoke, vapor, soot, fumes, acids, chemicals and waste. "Other Pollutants" does not include radioactive material or substance.

"Punitive Damages" means damages that are awarded to punish or deter wrongful conduct; to set an example; to fine, penalize or impose a statutory penalty; and damages that are awarded for any purpose other than as compensatory damages.

Form No   G53171   04 07
Page No.   2 OF 10

SECTION A – PROPERTY INSURANCE

PROPERTY COVERED

"We" insure:

1. The "yacht" described on the Declaration Page.
2. Any "yacht" not over 15 years old and similar in length and type "you" acquire by ownership during the policy period provided:
   a. "You" notify "us" within 15 days of acquisition;
   b. It is an acceptable risk to "us"; and
   c. "You" pay an additional premium as required.

   Unless otherwise agreed, "we" will not pay more than the cost to "you" or $100,000, whichever is lesser. The "yacht" deductible described on the Declaration Page shall apply to a newly acquired "yacht".
3. The "boat trailer".
4. "Personal effects" while on board the covered "yacht" or being carried onto or off the covered "yacht".

PROPERTY NOT COVERED

"We" do not cover:

1. Personal watercraft such as hydrocycles, jetskis, wave runners, windsurfers or similar types of vessels;
2. Boat houses, boat sheds, moorings, cradles, boat lifts or similar apparatus used for the mooring or storage of the covered "yacht";
3. Fuel, stores, provisions, food, beverages or liquor;
4. Accounts, bills, money, travelers checks or other valuable papers or documents;
5. Jewelry, gems, precious metals, furs, fine arts, watches, cameras, cellular or portable phones, portable computers (unless they are specifically used as "navigation equipment") or animals;
6. Firearms.

LOSSES COVERED

Subject to all terms, conditions and exclusions set forth elsewhere in this policy and to limitations as to the amount set forth below and on the Declaration Page, SECTION A, "we" will pay for the following that occurs during the policy period:

1. Accidental, direct physical loss of or damage to the insured property;
2. Physical loss or damage to the covered "yacht" caused by a "latent defect" in the hull or machinery, excluding the cost of repairing or replacing the defective part.

PROTECTION AND RECOVERY EXPENSES

"We" will pay the reasonable costs "you" incur to protect or recover the covered "yacht" from further loss or damage following an insured loss. However, the amount "we" pay will not exceed the amount of insurance under SECTION A on the Declaration Page. The first $500.00 of expenses under this clause will not be subject to the policy "deductible."

If the National Weather Service or the National Hurricane Service issues a hurricane watch or warning for the area where the covered "yacht" is located, "we" will share equally in the reasonable costs "you" incur to move, prepare and protect the "yacht" from the impending storm.

Costs incurred within forty-eight (48) hours prior to the watch or warning being issued are included; provided the watch or warning is issued. The most "we" will pay for any one hurricane is $500.00. These payments will not be subject to the policy "deductible."

LOSSES NOT COVERED (EXCLUSIONS)

"We" will not pay any loss, damage or expense caused by or resulting from:

1. Wear and tear; gradual deterioration; weathering; bubbling; osmosis; blistering; delamination of fiberglass or plywood; corrosion; rusting; electrolysis; mold; rot; inherent vice; vermin; insects or marine life;
2. "Your" failure to maintain the covered "yacht" in good condition and repair;
3. Marring, scratching, chipping or denting, unless caused by sudden and accidental impact with another object;
4. Freezing or extremes of temperature; except "we" will pay for loss, damage or expense caused by or resulting from improper winterizing if such winterizing was performed by a competent marina or similar facility;
5. Ice, except this exclusion shall apply only while the vessel is moored or laid up afloat, and it shall not apply in any event to loss, damage, or expense caused by or resulting from contact with floating or falling ice;
6. Delay or loss of use;
7. Error in or improper design;
8. Claims not reported to "us" within one year of the happening of the physical event giving rise to the loss.

DEDUCTIBLE

"We" will not pay for loss, damage or expense for any one covered occurrence unless the total amount of the loss, damage or expense exceeds the "deductible" shown on the Declaration Page. "We" agree, however, the "deductible" applicable to any loss, damage, or expense to a "tender" or "dinghy" not exceeding 16 feet in length and 35 hp shall be $100.00. "We" will pay the amount of loss, damage or expense in excess of the "deductible" up to the applicable limit of insurance. All loss, damage or expense resulting from the same occurrence will be considered to be one loss, and only the highest "deductible" shall apply to the loss.

If the covered "yacht" is a "total loss", the "deductible" will not apply. However, this provision does not apply to a "total loss" to a portion of the covered "yacht", such as its "tender", machinery or equipment, sails or spars.

Windstorm Deductible

If a percentage is shown on the declarations page for the windstorm deductible, such deductible will apply as respects all loss, damage, or expense, inclusive of all partial, total, or constructive total losses caused by or resulting from wind, storm surge, rain, wave, or hail when those losses are the result of either "Tropical Depression", "Tropical Storm", or "Hurricane". The deductible applied shall be the greater of (a) that percentage multiplied by the amount of insurance under Section A - Property Insurance: yacht or (b) the deductible amount shown under Section A – Property Insurance: yacht.

The above stated storm deductible is not applicable to the $500 expense coverage available under the Protection and

Form No.   G53171   04 07
Page No.   3 OF 10

Misc. Personal

Recovery Expenses section of this policy, nor does it reduce or impact the hurricane haul expense provision of that clause.

Definitions:
Tropical Depressions, Tropical Storms and Hurricanes are defined as those so designated either by name or number, by the National Weather Service and /or the National Hurricane Center.

All other terms and conditions of this policy remain unchanged.

WHAT "WE" WILL PAY

Subject to the conditions set forth in the policy:

1. In the event of a covered loss "we" will pay as follows:

   (a) "Total Loss": If the covered "yacht" is completely lost or destroyed "we" will pay the amount of insurance shown in the Declaration Page. If the covered "yacht" is stolen and not recovered within 30 days after "you" present "your" claim to "us" or "our" agent, the covered "yacht" shall be considered a "total loss."

   (b) If part of the covered "yacht" or other property covered is lost, damaged or destroyed "we" will pay the cost to repair or replace the part without deduction for depreciation. However, with regard to:

      1. Bottom paint over 1 year of age;
      2. Sails, protective covers, carpeting, upholstery, cushions or fabrics;
      3. Inboard machinery over 10 years of age;
      4. Outdrive units and all other external propulsion machinery over 2 years of age;
      5. "Tenders" or "dinghies", and outboard engines over 1 year of age;
      6. Batteries or tires;
      7. "Trailers" over 1 year of age;
      8. "Personal effects";

   "We" will pay the least of:

      1. The actual cash value of that property at the time of the loss;
      2. The cost of reasonably restoring that property to its condition immediately prior to the loss;
      3. The cost of replacing that property with substantially identical property; or
      4. The cost of an equivalent remanufactured or rebuilt engine or outdrive unit.

   The cost of repairs or replacement shall be determined by repair yards, or equipment repairers, and agreed to by surveyors approved by "us".

2. "We" have the option of paying for repairs:

   (a) According to customary boatyard repair practices, including the reasonable cost of suitable patches to the damaged area, or using reconditioned or rebuilt parts or components; or

   (b) According to repair procedures recommended by the builder or manufacturer of the insured property.

3. If any covered damage is not repaired, "we" will pay "you" the estimated cost of repairs in accordance with the preceding clauses less the applicable "deductible." If "we" subsequently pay "you" for a "total loss," "we" will first deduct any prior unrepaired damage payments and not make any additional payments for unrepaired damage.

4. If "we" pay "you" for a "total loss" of the covered "yacht" "we" reserve the right to take possession of the remains or its proceeds if "we" so elect. "You" will, if "we" ask, transfer title of that property to "us" or to a salvage buyer designated by "us." "We" are not obligated to accept any property that "you" abandon.

5. Equipment temporarily removed from the covered "yacht" for storage or repair ashore is limited to 50% of the amount of insurance on the covered "yacht". During such removal, the amount of insurance on the covered "yacht" will be reduced by the value of the equipment stored ashore,

COMMERCIAL TOWING AND ASSISTANCE

"We" will reimburse "you" up to $500.00 for any one occurrence, and up to $1,000.00 in any one policy year, for the reasonable expenses "you" incur for the following emergency services:

1. Towing to the nearest place where necessary repairs can be made; or
2. Delivering gas, oil or repair parts (but excluding the cost of these items themselves); or
3. Labor for emergency repairs at the site of disablement; or
4. "Boat trailer" roadside repair if the "trailer" is covered by this policy.

This coverage applies only if the covered "yacht" becomes disabled for any reason other than a covered loss while away from a safe harbor (or while on a "trailer" away from a safe parking place).

Claims under this clause will not be subject to the policy "deductible."

SECTION B-1 – LIABILITY INSURANCE

LOSSES COVERED

"We" will pay those sums "you" become legally obligated to pay as damages arising out of "your" ownership, operation or maintenance of the covered "yacht" as respects to:

1. Loss of life or bodily injury;
2. Property damage; except this section B-1 does not apply to liability covered under section B-2.

"Our" payment will include:

(a) The costs or expenses incurred for the attempted or actual raising, removal or destruction of the wreck of the covered "yacht" if compulsory by law.

(b) The cost of any bond necessary to obtain the release of the covered "yacht" if a legal authority has arrested, confiscated or detained the covered "yacht" as a result of an occurrence covered by SECTION B.

(c) The costs or expenses incurred with "our" approval to represent "your" interest in investigation of, and legal

Reprinted with permission from International Marine Underwriters/OneBeacon Insurance Group.

proceedings related to, any claims against "you" arising out of liability or alleged liability covered by SECTION B.

"We" have the right to select an attorney to represent "you."

(d) The cost of any bond required in any civil suit "we" defend, but not the cost of a bond for an amount exceeding the limit of liability under SECTION B-1 on the Declaration Page.

(e) The interest on "our" portion of a judgment which accrues after entry of the judgment and before "we" have paid, offered to pay or deposited in court the part of the judgment that is within the limit of liability under SECTION B-1 on the Declaration Page.

The allocation of insurance benefits among these classes of expenses may be directed by "you". In the event "you" fail or refuse to settle any claim "we" authorize, "our" liability will be limited to the amount for which settlement could have been made.

LIMIT OF LIABILITY

"We" will pay no more than the amount of insurance for SECTION B-1, LIABILITY INSURANCE, shown on the Declaration Page, regardless of the type of expense, number of persons, claims made or property involved in any one accident or series of accidents arising out of the same event, and regardless of the number of insured persons against whom claims are asserted.

"Our" payment UNDER SECTION B-1 will be reduced by any amounts that "we" pay to or on behalf of the injured person under any other section of this policy EXCEPT SECTION B-2.

SECTION B-2 – POLLUTION LIABILITY INSURANCE

LOSSES COVERED

"We" will pay those sums "you" become legally obligated to pay on account of "pollution" arising out of "your" ownership, operation or maintenance of the covered "yacht".

"Our" payment will include:

(a) The cost of any bond necessary to obtain the release of the covered "yacht" if a legal authority has arrested, confiscated or detained the covered "yacht" as a result of "pollution".

(b) The costs or expenses incurred with "our" approval to represent "your" interest in investigation of, and legal proceedings related to, any claims against "you" arising out of liability or alleged liability covered by SECTION B-2.

"We" have the right to select an attorney to represent "you."

(c) The cost of any bond required in any civil suit "we" defend, but not the cost of a bond for an amount exceeding the limit of liability under SECTION B-2 on the Declaration Page.

(d) The interest on "our" portion of a judgment which accrues after entry of the judgment and before "we" have paid, offered to pay or deposited in court the part of the judgment that is within the limit of liability under SECTION B-2 on the Declaration Page.

The allocation of insurance benefits among these classes of expenses may be directed by "you". In the event "you" fail or refuse to settle any claim "we" authorize, "our" liability will be limited to the amount for which settlement could have been made.

LIMIT OF LIABILITY

We" will pay no more than the amount of insurance for SECTION B-2, LIABILITY INSURANCE, shown on the Declaration Page, regardless of the type of expense, number of persons, claims made or property involved in any one accident or series of accidents arising out of the same event, and regardless of the number of insured persons against whom claims are asserted.

LOSSES NOT COVERED (EXCLUSIONS) Section B-1 Liability and Section B -2 Pollution Liability

"We" will not pay:

1. For loss of life, bodily injury or property damage which occurs while the insured property is being transported on land;

2. For any liability assumed by "you" under any contract or agreement. However this exclusion will not apply to liabilities "you" assume by signing hold harmless agreements that are in registration forms for sailboat races or in storage or slip rental contracts, prior to any loss or damage;

3. For any liability between or among "family members";

4. For any loss or damage to any property owned by, rented to, used by or in the care of an "insured person";

5. For loss of life of or bodily injury to any person to or for whom benefits are required to be provided or are available under any state or federal compensation law or act or any similar law or act;

6. For any liability for loss of life or bodily injury to any paid captain or crew of the covered "yacht" under the Federal Jones Act, Death on the High Seas Act or General Maritime law;

7. For any liability "you" may have to any of "your" directors, officers, shareholders, partners or charterers or any such liability which any of them have to "you";

8. For any fine or penalty imposed by any governmental unit;

9. For any exemplary or "punitive damages," even if caused by someone for whom "you" are only vicariously liable;

10. For any loss, damage or liability willfully or intentionally caused or incurred by an "insured person";

11. For any loss of life, bodily injury or property damage sustained while a person is being towed from the covered "yacht" in or on a device designed for flight such as parasailing or kiteskiing;

12. For any loss of life or bodily injury arising out of the transmission of a communicable disease by an "insured person";

13. For any liability arising from the discharge, spillage, or emission of any radioactive material or substance;

14. For loss of life, bodily injury or property damage arising out of the use of any property not covered by this policy.

Form No.   G53171   04 07
Page No.   5 OF 10

NON-OWNED "YACHT"

This section shall also cover "your" legal liability for loss of life, bodily injury or property damage or "pollution liability" arising from "your" operation or maintenance of any "yacht" similar in length and type to the one described on the Declaration Page, provided:

1. Such "yacht" is not used by "you" on a regular basis;
2. Such "yacht" is not owned in whole or in part by "you";
3. "Your" use is free, for private pleasure only and with the permission of the owner; and
4. That loss or damage to such "yacht" shall be subject to the deductible shown on the Declaration Page under SECTION A, PROPERTY INSURANCE.

For purposes of this Section, similar in length and type means a "yacht" which is not more than 10 feet shorter or longer, and (if applicable) with horsepower not more than 20% greater, than the "yacht" described on the Declaration Page.

SECTION C – LONGSHORE AND HARBOR WORKERS' COMPENSATION INSURANCE

This section is applicable only if coverage under SECTION B, LIABILITY INSURANCE, is provided. "We" will cover the liability which "you" as owner of the covered "yacht" incur during the term of the policy under the Federal Longshore and Harbor Workers' Compensation Act.

SECTION D – MEDICAL PAYMENTS INSURANCE

This section is applicable only if coverage under SECTION B, LIABILITY INSURANCE, is provided.

This coverage is provided only for persons (including "insured person(s))" injured while on, boarding or leaving the covered "yacht"; or while engaged in water-skiing, aquaplaning or similar activities from the covered "yacht", unless otherwise excluded.

LOSSES COVERED

"We" will pay the reasonable medical, dental, ambulance, hospital, professional nursing and funeral expenses that become necessary due to a covered accidental bodily injury.

LOSSES NOT COVERED (EXCLUSIONS)

"We" do not cover any person:

1. Who is covered under any federal or state workers compensation law or act;
2. Who is an employee of "yours" injured while in the course of employment;
3. Who is a trespasser;
4. Whose injury resulted from or was connected with being towed in or on a device designed for flight such as parasailing or kiteskiing.

"We" will pay for only those costs incurred within one year of the date of the accident.

A person presenting a claim under this Section must also:

1. Submit to physical examination by physicians of "our" choice as often as "we" require;

2. Provide to "us" or permit "us" to obtain copies of medical reports and other necessary medical records;
3. Provide copies of any other insurance policies or other evidence of health coverage that may cover the claim;
4. Furnish full obtainable information pertaining to the accident.

LIMIT OF LIABILITY

"We" will pay each injured person up to, but not more than, the amount of insurance shown on the Declaration Page, SECTION D, MEDICAL PAYMENTS, as a result of any one accident or series of accidents arising out of the same event.

"Our" payment will be reduced by any amounts paid or recoverable from the injured person's health plan or medical insurance. "Our" payment will also be reduced by any amounts that "we" pay to or on behalf of the injured person under any other section of this policy.

ADMISSION OF LIABILITY

Any payment made under this section is not an admission of liability by "you" or "us".

SECTION E – UNINSURED OR UNDERINSURED BOATER INSURANCE

This section is applicable only if coverage under SECTION B, LIABILITY INSURANCE, is provided.

This coverage is provided only for persons who are injured while on, boarding or leaving the covered "yacht" or while engaged in water-skiing, aquaplaning or similar activities from the covered "yacht", unless otherwise excluded.

LOSSES COVERED

"We" will pay the damages that an injured person is legally entitled to recover from an "uninsured or underinsured owner" or "uninsured or underinsured operator" of another boat, because of bodily injury sustained by the injured person arising out of the operation, maintenance or use of the other boat. For the purpose of this coverage, determination as to whether the injured person is legally entitled to recover such damages, and if so, the amount thereof, shall be determined by agreement between the injured person and "us"; or if "we" fail to agree, by arbitration as described in SECTION G, GENERAL CONDITIONS.

LOSSES NOT COVERED (EXCLUSIONS)

"We" will not pay any loss under this Section:

1. For claims settled without "our" consent;
2. If the uninsured boat is owned by a governmental agency or unit;
3. Where no evidence of physical contact exists between the covered "yacht" or the injured person and the boat owned or operated by the "uninsured or underinsured boater" or unidentified boat;
4. If the boat operated by the "uninsured or underinsured boater" is owned by, or furnished for the regular use of an insured person";
5. For any injured person:
   a. Who is covered under any federal or state workers compensation law or act;
   b. Who is an employee of "yours";

Form No   G53171   04 07
Page No.   6 OF 10

c. Who is a trespasser;

d. Who makes a claim after one year from the date of the accident;

6. For injuries sustained while being towed in or on a device designed for flight such as parasailing or kiteskiing;

7. For "punitive damages" awarded to the injured person.

This coverage will not apply directly or indirectly to the benefit of any insurer under any state or federal workers compensation law or act.

A person presenting a claim under this Section must also:

1. Submit to physical examination by physicians of "our" choice as often as "we" require;

2. Provide to "us" or permit "us" to obtain copies of medical reports and other necessary medical records;

3. Provide copies of any other insurance policies or other evidence of health coverage that may cover the claim;

4. Furnish full obtainable information pertaining to the accident.

Payment made to or on behalf of an injured person will be reduced by any amounts covered by the injured person's health plan or medical insurance. "Our" payment will also be reduced by any amounts "we" pay to or on behalf of the injured person under any other section of this policy.

LIMIT OF LIABILITY

The amount shown for "Uninsured or Underinsured Boater" coverage on the Declaration Page is the most "we" will pay under SECTION E, regardless of the type of expense, number of injured persons claims made or number of "yachts" involved in any one accident or series of accidents arising out of the same occurrence.

SECTION F – DUTIES AFTER AN ACCIDENT OR LOSS

If there is a loss or a claim that may be covered under this policy, "you" must:

1. Take all reasonable steps to protect the insured property from further loss and make every reasonable effort to recover it. Any steps "you" take will not mean "you" are waiving any rights "you" have to abandon the property. "We" will pay the reasonable expenses so incurred as provided in SECTION A, PROPERTY INSURANCE.

2. Give "us" immediate notice with details such as:

   (a) When and where the occurrence took place;

   (b) What property was involved and where it may be seen;

   (c) The names and addresses of any injured persons;

   (d) The names and addresses of witnesses;

   (e) All other information that may assist "us" in determining the rights and liabilities of persons involved.

3. Allow "us" to inspect the insured property before it is repaired or disposed of.

4. Give prompt notice to the appropriate law enforcement agencies and/or United States Coast Guard in the event of theft, vandalism, collision, property damage, loss of life or bodily injury.

5. Advise anyone else responsible for the loss or damage, as soon as possible, in writing, that "you" are holding them liable.

6. Cooperate with "us" in the investigation, defense or settlement of any loss, including permitting "us" to conduct non-destructive testing of the insured property at "our" expense.

7. Obtain repair specifications, bids and estimates from alternative sources if requested.

8. Permit "us" to examine any records "we" require to verify the loss or its amount,

9. Immediately notify "us" and send "us" every demand, notice, summons or other legal papers received by "you" or "your" representative if a claim is made or a suit is brought against "you". "We" will have the option of naming an attorney(s) to represent "you".

10. Not assume any obligation or admit any liability without "our" written permission.

11. Provide "us" with copies of other insurance policies that may cover the loss.

12. Submit to an examination under oath if "we" so request.

13. Submit a detailed written proof of loss signed and sworn by "you" and evidence of an insured interest, if "we" so request.

14. As respects "pollution":

    (a) Report the incident creating "your" legal obligation as required by law if "you" know or have reason to know of the incident;

    (b) Provide all reasonable cooperation and assistance requested by responsible authorities in connection with clean up activities.

If "you" fail or refuse to comply with any of these duties there will be no coverage under this policy unless "you" prove that "we" have not been prejudiced by "your" failure or refusal.

SECTION G – GENERAL CONDITIONS

This section contains conditions that apply to all SECTIONS of the policy.

POLICY PERIOD, TERRITORY

This policy applies only to accidents or losses which occur:

1. During the policy period; and

2. Within the navigation or transportation limits specified.

CHANGES

This policy contains all the agreements between "you" and "us" concerning the insurance afforded. The first named insured shown in the declarations is authorized to make changes in the terms of this policy with "our" consent. This policy's terms can be amended or waived only by endorsement issued by "us" and made part of this policy.

PREMIUMS

The first named insured shown in the declarations:

1. Is responsible for the payment of all premiums; and

2. Will be the payee for any return premiums "we" pay.

Misc. Personal

Form No.   G53171   04 07
Page No.   7 OF 10

LAY-UP

If the covered "yacht" is to be laid up and out of commission for the period shown on the Declaration Page:

1. It must be in a safe berth for storage ashore or afloat, as indicated on the Declaration Page;

2. It must not be used for any purpose whatsoever (but repairs, repainting, dismantling and fitting out can be carried on), and must not be equipped and ready for immediate use;

3. It must not be used for living on board or overnight accommodation;

4. It must not be operated.

EXTENSION OF COVERAGE

If the Navigational Limits or Lay Up Warranty shown on the Declaration Page are breached due to matters beyond "your" control, the policy will remain in effect if "you" give "us" written notice of the breach within ten (10) days after the breach. "You" agree to pay any additional premiums due "us" for this extension of coverage. If the Navigational Limits or Lay Up Warranty is breached voluntarily, there shall be no coverage under this policy during the breach without both prior notice to and approval by "us".

TRANSFER OF INTEREST

All coverage provided by "us" will terminate upon the sale, assignment, transfer or pledge of the insured property or of this contract unless prior written consent has been obtained from "us".

"OUR" RIGHT TO RECOVERY OR IMPAIRMENT OF RECOVERY

If "we" make a payment under this policy and the person to or for whom payment was made has the right to recover from others for the covered loss, "we" will be entitled to that right. That person will do whatever is necessary to enable "us" to exercise "our" rights and will do nothing after the loss to prejudice "our" rights.

If "we" make a payment under this policy and the person to or for whom payment is made, recovers damages from others on account of the matters giving rise to "our" payment, that person will hold the proceeds of the recovery for "us" and will reimburse "us" to the extent of "our" payment.

If, whether before or after a loss, "you" give up "your" rights to recover damages from any third party or organization who may be liable to "you" for the injury or damage giving rise to "your" claim under this policy, "you" give up "your" right to recover the loss or any part of it from "us". This paragraph does not apply to written waivers contained in registration forms for sailboat races, or storage or slip rental contracts; provided they are signed by "you" before any loss or damage.

PAYMENT OF LOSS

"We" will pay for losses covered under this policy within 30 days after:

1. "We" reach an agreement with "you"; or

2. An arbitration award is rendered.

ARBITRATION

If "you" make a claim under this policy and "we" disagree about whether the claim is payable or about the amount due to "you" under the policy, the disagreement must be resolved by binding arbitration according to the following procedure:

1. "You" and "we" will agree on a single arbitrator to decide the dispute. The arbitrator's fee and arbitration costs will be shared equally by "you" and "us", unless that is prohibited by the law of the state where this policy is issued, in which case "we" will pay the fees and costs of arbitration.

2. If "you" and "we" are unable to agree on a single arbitrator, then at "your" election either:

    a. "You" and "we" will each appoint an arbitrator and those two arbitrators will appoint a third arbitrator. The three arbitrators will decide the dispute by a majority vote. "You" will pay the fee of the arbitrator "you" appoint. "We" will pay the fee of the arbitrator "we" appoint. The third arbitrator's fee and arbitration costs will be shared equally by "you" and "us".

        or

    b. "We" will petition an appropriate court in the jurisdiction where this policy was issued to appoint an arbitrator. The arbitrator's fee and arbitration costs will be shared equally by "you" and "us", unless that is prohibited by the law of the state where this policy is issued, in which case "we" will pay the fees and costs of arbitration.

3. The arbitrator(s) need not be a member(s) of any particular association of arbitrators, and may be commercial persons with relevant experience in the marine industry. The arbitrator(s) shall have the same powers as arbitrators under the Federal Arbitration Act (9 U.S.C. Section 1, et. seq.).

The demand for arbitration must be made within one (1) year of the date of the loss or damage.

GOVERNING LAW

The rights and obligations of the parties under this policy shall be governed by the general maritime law of the United States.

LEGAL ACTION AGAINST US

"You" may not bring a suit against "us" unless "you" have complied with all terms of this policy, including arbitration. In addition:

1. With respect to any claim for loss or damage to insured property, any suit against "us" must be commenced within one (1) year of the date of loss or damage.

2. With respect to any other claim, no suit may be brought against "us" until the amount of the "insured person's" obligation to pay has been determined by final judgment after trial or by written agreement signed by "you", "us" and the claimant. Any such legal action against "us" must be commenced within one year of the date of judgment or written agreement.

WAR, CONFISCATION, NUCLEAR EXCLUSION

"We" will not pay under any section for any loss, damage, liability, or expense caused in any way by, or resulting directly or indirectly from:

1. War or warlike operations (whether or not war is declared), civil war, insurrection, rebellion, revolution, destruction or seizure for a military purpose, or any consequences of any of these;

Reprinted with permission from International Marine Underwriters/OneBeacon Insurance Group.

2. Lawful or unlawful capture, seizure, arrest, requisition, confiscation or detainment by order of any civil or military authority, or an attempt at any of these;

3. Any nuclear, chemical, biological, bio-chemical or electromagnetic weapon or device;

4. Harmful properties of any radioactive matter (except radioactive isotopes being prepared, carried, stored, or used for peaceful purpose).

EXTENDED RADIOACTIVE CONTAMINATION EXCLUSION CLAUSE WITH U.S.A. ENDORSEMENT

This clause shall be paramount and shall override anything contained in this insurance inconsistent therewith.

1. In no case shall this insurance cover loss, damage, liability or expense directly or indirectly caused by or contributed to by or arising from:

   1.1 Ionizing radiations from or contamination by radioactivity from any nuclear fuel or from any nuclear waste or from the combustion of nuclear fuel;

   1.2 The radioactive, toxic, explosive or other hazardous or contaminating properties of any nuclear installation, reactor or other nuclear assembly or nuclear component thereof;

   1.3 Any weapon or device employing atomic or nuclear fission and/or fusion or other like reaction or radioactive force or matter;

   1.4 The radioactive, toxic, explosive or other hazardous or contaminating properties of any radioactive matter. The exclusion in this sub-clause does not extend to radioactive isotopes, other than nuclear fuel, when such isotopes are being prepared, carried, stored, or used for commercial, agricultural, medical, scientific or other similar peaceful purposes.

This insurance is subject to the Extended Radioactive Contamination Exclusion Clause provided that if fire is an insured peril, and, where the subject matter insured is within the U.S.A., its islands, onshore territories or possessions, and a fire arises directly or indirectly from one or more of the causes detailed in Sub-Clauses 1.1, 1.2, and 1.4 of the Extended Radioactive Contamination Exclusion Clause, any loss or damage arising directly from that fire, shall, subject to the provisions of this insurance, be covered, EXCLUDING, however, any loss, damage, liability or expense caused by nuclear reaction, nuclear radiation, or radioactive contamination arising directly or indirectly from that fire.

UNITED STATES ECONOMIC AND TRADE SANCTIONS CLAUSE

Whenever coverage provided by this policy would be in violation of any United States economic or trade sanctions such as, but not limited to, those sanctions administered and enforced by the United States Treasury Department's Office of Foreign Assets Control ("OFAC"), such coverage shall be null and void.

Similarly, any coverage relating to or referred to in any certificates or other evidences of insurance or any claim that would be in violation of United States economic or trade sanctions as described above shall also be null and void.

RACING

"We" will not pay any loss, injury, damage or expense occurring while the "yacht" is being operated in any official race or speed test. This limitation does not apply to sailboats or predicted log events.

CONCEALMENT, FRAUD, MISREPRESENTATION

This policy shall be void if "you" conceal, misrepresent or fail to disclose any material information regarding this insurance.

ILLEGAL PURPOSE

"We" will not pay any loss, injury, damage or expense arising out of or during any illegal purpose on "your" part or on the part of anyone using the insured property with "your" permission.

OTHER INSURANCE

If at the time of loss there is any other insurance that would cover the loss in the absence of this policy, the amount "we" pay will be determined as follows:

1. SECTION A, Property insurance: "we" will pay only the proportion of the loss that "our" amount of insurance bears to the total of all applicable amounts of insurance covering the loss.

2. All other SECTIONS: any insurance provided by this policy shall apply only as excess over any other valid and collectible insurance.

BANKRUPTCY

Bankruptcy of any person insured under this policy does not relieve "us" of any of "our" obligations under this policy.

NON-WAIVER PROVISION

No action on "our" part after a loss to recover or save the property from further loss, nor any action which "we" take in connection with the investigation of any claim or loss shall be considered as a waiver of any of "our" rights under this policy.

BROADENING COVERAGE

If "we" adopt any change during the term of this policy, applicable to all policyholders, which broadens coverage without additional premium, the broader coverage will automatically apply to "your" policy.

CANCELLATION

The first named insured shown in the declarations may cancel this policy by returning it to "us" or "our" authorized agent; or by written notice to "us" or "our" authorized agent advising the date of cancellation. "We" may cancel by delivering or mailing written notice to the first named insured at the last address shown in "our" records. "Our" notice will state when, not less than 10 days after mailing, the policy will be canceled. Proof of mailing will be sufficient proof of notice. The date of the cancellation stated in the notice shall become the end of the policy period.

If "we" pay "you" for a "total loss" of the covered "yacht", the entire policy is terminated as of the date "we" make such payment without further notice to "you".

Misc. Personal

RETURN PREMIUMS

If this policy is cancelled "you" may be entitled to a premium refund. If "we" cancel, return premium will be computed on a pro rata basis. If "you" cancel, return premium will be computed 90% of pro-rata. Cancellation will be effective whether or not return premium is tendered with notice of cancellation. If not so tendered, "we" will refund it within a reasonable time after the effective date of cancellation.

No premium will be returned if "we" have paid "you" for a "total loss" of the covered "yacht". In the event "we" pay a "total loss" of the covered "yacht", full annual premium is due and payable.

CONFORMITY TO STATE LAW

If any provision of this policy conflicts with any applicable state law, the policy shall automatically conform to the minimum requirements of the state law.

Our Secretary and President have signed this policy. It is valid when countersigned by "our" authorized representative on the Declaration Page.

Dennis R. Smith

Dennis R Smith, Secretary

Mike Miller

T. Michael Miller, President & CEO

NOTICE OF INFORMATION PRACTICES

When you applied to International Marine Underwriters, you gave us some personal information about yourself. In many cases, the application you complete gives us all the information we need to evaluate your request for insurance. Sometimes we need additional information or want to verify information you have given us. It is common for an insurance company to do this by contacting an independent source, commonly called a "consumer reporting agency." Consumer reporting agencies are companies which are in the business of supplying such information to insurance companies. If we do retain a consumer reporting agency to gather information for us, we will choose one which is discreet and impartial.

The information which we receive about you may be disclosed to others without your authorization to the extent allowed by law in certain specified circumstances. Information about you may be kept in our policy records. We may refer to and use that information for purposes related to issuing and servicing insurance policies and settling claims.

You have the right to obtain access to and review of certain items of the personal information about you which is contained in our files. You have the further right to request correction, amendment, or deletion of information you feel to be inaccurate.

If you wish a more detailed description of our information practices, please contact us at the address shown on the Declarations Page attached to this policy.

Form No.   G53171   04 07
Page No.   10 OF 10

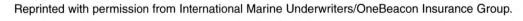

Reprinted with permission from International Marine Underwriters/OneBeacon Insurance Group.

FEDERAL EMERGENCY MANAGEMENT AGENCY
NATIONAL FLOOD INSURANCE PROGRAM

STANDARD FLOOD INSURANCE POLICY

DWELLING FORM

PLEASE READ THE POLICY CAREFULLY. THE FLOOD INSURANCE PROVIDED IS SUBJECT TO LIMITATIONS, RESTRICTIONS, AND EXCLUSIONS.

THIS POLICY COVERS ONLY:

1. A NON-CONDOMINIUM RESIDENTIAL BUILDING DESIGNED FOR PRINCIPAL USE AS A DWELLING PLACE FOR ONE TO FOUR FAMILIES, OR

2. A SINGLE-FAMILY DWELLING UNIT IN A CONDOMINIUM BUILDING.

I. AGREEMENT

The Federal Emergency Management Agency (FEMA) provides flood insurance under the terms of the National Flood Insurance Act of 1968 and its amendments, and Title 44 of the Code of Federal Regulations (CFR).

We will pay you for **direct physical loss by or from flood** to your insured property if you:

1. Have paid the correct premium;

2. Comply with all terms and conditions of this **policy**; and

3. Have furnished accurate information and statements.

We have the right to review the information you give us at any time and to revise your **policy** based on our review.

II. DEFINITIONS

A. In this **policy**, "you" and "your" refer to the insured(s) shown on the **Declarations Page** of this **policy** and your spouse, if a resident of the same household. "Insured(s)" includes: Any mortgagee and loss payee named in the **Application** and **Declarations Page**, as well as any other mortgagee or loss payee determined to exist at the time of loss in the order of precedence. "We," "us," and "our" refer to the insurer.

Some definitions are complex because they are provided as they appear in the law or regulations, or result from court cases. The precise definitions are intended to protect you.

Flood, as used in this flood insurance **policy**, means:

1. A general and temporary condition of partial or complete inundation of two or more acres of normally dry land area or of two or more properties (at least one of which is your property) from:

    a. Overflow of inland or tidal waters;

    b. Unusual and rapid accumulation or runoff of surface waters from any source;

    c. **Mudflow**.

2. Collapse or subsidence of land along the shore of a lake or similar body of water as a result of erosion or undermining caused by waves or currents of water exceeding anticipated cyclical levels that result in a **flood** as defined in **A.1.a.** above.

B. The following are the other key definitions that we use in this **policy**:

1. **Act.** The National Flood Insurance Act of 1968 and any amendments to it.

2. **Actual Cash Value.** The cost to replace an insured item of property at the time of loss, less the value of its physical depreciation.

3. **Application.** The statement made and signed by you or your agent in applying for this **policy**. The **application** gives information we use to determine the eligibility of the risk, the kind of **policy** to be issued, and the correct premium payment. The **application** is part of this flood insurance **policy**. For us to issue you a **policy**, the correct premium payment must accompany the **application**.

4. **Base Flood.** A **flood** having a one percent chance of being equaled or exceeded in any given year.

Page 1 of 19

5. **Basement.** Any area of the **building**, including any sunken room or sunken portion of a room, having its floor below ground level (subgrade) on all sides.

6. **Building**.

   a. A structure with two or more outside rigid walls and a fully secured roof, that is affixed to a permanent site;

   b. A manufactured home (a "manufactured home," also known as a mobile home, is a structure: built on a permanent chassis, transported to its site in one or more sections, and affixed to a permanent foundation); or

   c. A travel trailer without wheels, built on a chassis and affixed to a permanent foundation, that is regulated under the community's floodplain management and building ordinances or laws.

   Building does not mean a gas or liquid storage tank or a recreational vehicle, park trailer, or other similar vehicle, except as described in **B.6.c.** above.

7. **Cancellation.** The ending of the insurance coverage provided by this **policy** before the expiration date.

8. **Condominium.** That form of ownership of real property in which each **unit** owner has an undivided interest in common elements.

9. **Condominium Association**. The entity made up of the **unit** owners responsible for the maintenance and operation of:

   a. Common elements owned in undivided shares by **unit** owners; and

   b. Other real property in which the **unit** owners have use rights;

   where membership in the entity is a required condition of **unit** ownership.

10. **Declarations Page.** A computer-generated summary of information you provided in the **application** for insurance. The **Declarations Page** also describes the term of the **policy**, limits of coverage, and displays the premium and our name. The **Declarations Page** is a part of this flood insurance **policy.**

11. **Described Location.** The location where the insured **building**(s) or personal property are found. The **described location** is shown on the **Declarations Page.**

12. **Direct Physical Loss By or From Flood.** Loss or damage to insured property, directly caused by a **flood**. There must be evidence of physical changes to the property.

13. **Dwelling.** A **building** designed for use as a residence for no more than four families or a single-family **unit**

in a **building** under a **condominium** form of ownership.

14. **Elevated Building.** A **building** that has no **basement** and that has its lowest elevated floor raised above ground level by foundation walls, shear walls, posts, piers, pilings, or columns.

15. **Emergency Program.** The initial phase of a community's participation in the **National Flood Insurance Program.** During this phase, only limited amounts of insurance are available under the **Act**.

16. **Expense Constant.** A flat charge you must pay on each new or renewal **policy** to defray the expenses of the Federal Government related to flood insurance.

17. **Federal Policy Fee.** A flat charge you must pay on each new or renewal **policy** to defray certain administrative expenses incurred in carrying out the **National Flood Insurance Program.** This fee covers expenses not covered by the **expense constant.**

18. **Improvements.** Fixtures, alterations, installations, or additions comprising a part of the insured **dwelling** or the apartment in which you reside.

19. **Mudflow.** A river of liquid and flowing mud on the surfaces of normally dry land areas, as when earth is carried by a current of water. Other earth movements, such as landslide, slope failure, or a saturated soil mass moving by liquidity down a slope, are not **mudflows**.

20. **National Flood Insurance Program (NFIP).** The program of flood insurance coverage and floodplain management administered under the **Act** and applicable Federal regulations in Title 44 of the Code of Federal Regulations, Subchapter B.

21. **Policy.** The entire written contract between you and us. It includes:

    a. This printed form;

    b. The **application** and **Declarations Page**;

    c. Any endorsement(s) that may be issued; and

    d. Any renewal certificate indicating that coverage has been instituted for a new **policy** and new **policy** term.

    Only one **dwelling,** which you specifically described in the **application,** may be insured under this **policy**.

22. **Pollutants.** Substances that include, but are not limited to, any solid, liquid, gaseous, or thermal irritant or contaminant, including smoke, vapor, soot, fumes, acids, alkalis, chemicals, and waste. "Waste" includes, but is not limited to, materials to be recycled, reconditioned, or reclaimed.

23. **Post-FIRM Building.** A **building** for which construction or substantial improvement occurred after December 31, 1974, or on or after the effective date of an initial Flood Insurance Rate Map (FIRM), whichever is later.

24. **Probation Premium.** A flat charge you must pay on each new or renewal **policy** issued covering property in a community that the NFIP has placed on probation under the provisions of 44 CFR 59.24.

25. **Regular Program.** The final phase of a community's participation in the **National Flood Insurance Program.** In this phase, a Flood Insurance Rate Map is in effect and full limits of coverage are available under the **Act.**

26. **Special Flood Hazard Area.** An area having special **flood,** or **mudflow,** and/or **flood**-related erosion hazards, and shown on a Flood Hazard Boundary Map or Flood Insurance Rate Map as Zone A, AO, A1-A30, AE, A99, AH, AR, AR/A, AR/AE, AR/AH, AR/AO, AR/A1-A30, V1-V30, VE, or V.

27. **Unit.** A single-family **unit** you own in a **condominium building.**

28. **Valued Policy.** A **policy** in which the insured and the insurer agree on the value of the property insured, that value being payable in the event of a total loss. The Standard Flood Insurance Policy is not a **valued policy.**

III. PROPERTY COVERED

A. COVERAGE A - BUILDING PROPERTY

We insure against **direct physical loss by or from flood** to:

1. The **dwelling** at the **described location**, or for a period of 45 days at another location as set forth in **III.C.2.b.**, Property Removed to Safety.

2. Additions and extensions attached to and in contact with the **dwelling** by means of a rigid exterior wall, a solid load-bearing interior wall, a stairway, an elevated walkway, or a roof. At your option, additions and extensions connected by any of these methods may be separately insured. Additions and extensions attached to and in contact with the **building** by means of a common interior wall that is not a solid load-bearing wall are always considered part of the **dwelling** and cannot be separately insured.

3. A detached garage at the **described location.** Coverage is limited to no more than 10 percent of the limit of liability on the **dwelling.** Use of this insurance is at your option but reduces the **building** limit of liability. We do not cover any detached garage used or held for use for residential (i.e., **dwelling**), business, or farming purposes.

4. Materials and supplies to be used for construction, alteration, or repair of the **dwelling** or a detached garage while the materials and supplies are stored in a fully enclosed **building** at the **described location** or on an adjacent property.

5. A **building** under construction, alteration, or repair at the **described location.**

   a. If the structure is not yet walled or roofed as described in the definition for **building** (see **II.B. 6.a.**) then coverage applies:

   (1) Only while such work is in progress; or

   (2) If such work is halted, only for a period of up to 90 continuous days thereafter.

   b. However, coverage does not apply until the **building** is walled and roofed if the lowest floor, including the **basement** floor, of a non-**elevated building** or the lowest elevated floor of an **elevated building** is:

   (1) Below the **base flood** elevation in Zones AH, AE, A1-A30, AR, AR/AE, AR/AH, AR/A1-A30, AR/A, AR/AO; or

   (2) Below the **base flood** elevation adjusted to include the effect of wave action in Zones VE or V1-V30.

   The lowest floor levels are based on the bottom of the lowest horizontal structural member of the floor in Zones VE or V1-V30 and the top of the floor in Zones AH, AE, A1-A30, AR, AR/AE, AR/AH, AR/A1-A30, AR/A, AR/AO.

6. A manufactured home or a travel trailer as described in the Definitions section (see **II.B.6.b.** and **II.B.6.c.**).

   If the manufactured home or travel trailer is in a **special flood hazard area**, it must be anchored in the following manner at the time of the loss:

   a. By over-the-top or frame ties to ground anchors; or

   b. In accordance with the manufacturer's specifications; or

   c. In compliance with the community's floodplain management requirements;

Page 3 of 19

unless it has been continuously insured by the **NFIP** at the same **described location** since September 30, 1982.

7. The following items of property which are covered under Coverage **A** only:

   a. Awnings and canopies;
   b. Blinds;
   c. Built-in dishwashers;
   d. Built-in microwave ovens;
   e. Carpet permanently installed over unfinished flooring;
   f. Central air conditioners;
   g. Elevator equipment;
   h. Fire sprinkler systems;
   i. Walk-in freezers;
   j. Furnaces and radiators;
   k. Garbage disposal units;
   l. Hot water heaters, including solar water heaters;
   m. Light fixtures;
   n. Outdoor antennas and aerials fastened to **buildings**;
   o. Permanently installed cupboards, bookcases, cabinets, paneling, and wallpaper;
   p. Plumbing fixtures;
   q. Pumps and machinery for operating pumps;
   r. Ranges, cooking stoves, and ovens;
   s. Refrigerators; and
   t. Wall mirrors, permanently installed.

8. Items of property in a **building** enclosure below the lowest elevated floor of an **elevated post-FIRM building** located in Zones A1-A30, AE, AH, AR, AR/A, AR/AE, AR/AH, AR/A1-A30, V1-V30, or VE, or in a **basement**, regardless of the zone. Coverage is limited to the following:

   a. Any of the following items, if installed in their functioning locations and, if necessary for operation, connected to a power source:

      (1) Central air conditioners;
      (2) Cisterns and the water in them;
      (3) Drywall for walls and ceilings in a **basement** and the cost of labor to nail it, unfinished and unfloated and not taped, to the framing;
      (4) Electrical junction and circuit breaker boxes;
      (5) Electrical outlets and switches;
      (6) Elevators, dumbwaiters, and related equipment, except for related equipment installed below the **base flood** elevation after September 30, 1987;
      (7) Fuel tanks and the fuel in them;
      (8) Furnaces and hot water heaters;
      (9) Heat pumps;
      (10) Nonflammable insulation in a **basement**;
      (11) Pumps and tanks used in solar energy systems;
      (12) Stairways and staircases attached to the **building**, not separated from it by elevated walkways;
      (13) Sump pumps;

   (14) Water softeners and the chemicals in them, water filters, and faucets installed as an integral part of the plumbing system;
   (15) Well water tanks and pumps;
   (16) Required utility connections for any item in this list; and
   (17) Footings, foundations, posts, pilings, piers, or other foundation walls and anchorage systems required to support a **building.**

   b. Clean-up.

B. COVERAGE B - PERSONAL PROPERTY

1. If you have purchased personal property coverage, we insure against **direct physical loss by or from flood** to personal property inside a **building** at the **described location**, if:

   a. The property is owned by you or your household family members; and

   b. At your option, the property is owned by guests or servants.

   Personal property is also covered for a period of 45 days at another location as set forth in **III.C.2.b.**, Property Removed to Safety.

   Personal property in a **building** that is not fully enclosed must be secured to prevent flotation out of the **building**. If the personal property does float out during a **flood**, it will be conclusively presumed that it was not reasonably secured. In that case there is no coverage for such property.

2. Coverage for personal property includes the following property, subject to **B.1.** above, which is covered under Coverage **B** only:

   a. Air conditioning units, portable or window type;
   b. Carpets, not permanently installed, over unfinished flooring;
   c. Carpets over finished flooring;
   d. Clothes washers and dryers;
   e. "Cook-out" grills;
   f. Food freezers, other than walk-in, and food in any freezer; and
   g. Portable microwave ovens and portable dishwashers.

3. Coverage for items of property in a **building** enclosure below the lowest elevated floor of an **elevated post-FIRM building** located in Zones A1-A30, AE, AH, AR, AR/A, AR/AE, AR/AH, AR/A1-A30, V1-V30, or VE, or in a **basement,** regardless of the zone, is limited to the following items, if installed in their functioning locations and, if necessary for operation, connected to a power source:

   a. Air conditioning units, portable or window type;
   b. Clothes washers and dryers; and
   c. Food freezers, other than walk-in, and food in any freezer.

Page 4 of 19

4. If you are a tenant and have insured personal property under Coverage **B** in this **policy**, we will cover such property, including your cooking stove or range and refrigerator. The **policy** will also cover **improvements** made or acquired solely at your expense in the **dwelling** or apartment in which you reside, but for not more than 10 percent of the limit of liability shown for personal property on the **Declarations Page**. Use of this insurance is at your option but reduces the personal property limit of liability.

5. If you are the owner of a **unit** and have insured personal property under Coverage **B** in this **policy**, we will also cover your interior walls, floor, and ceiling (not otherwise covered under a flood insurance **policy** purchased by your **condominium association**) for not more than 10 percent of the limit of liability shown for personal property on the **Declarations Page**. Use of this insurance is at your option but reduces the personal property limit of liability.

6. **Special Limits.** We will pay no more than $2,500 for any one loss to one or more of the following kinds of personal property:

    a. Artwork, photographs, collectibles, or memorabilia, including but not limited to, porcelain or other figures, and sports cards;

    b. Rare books or autographed items;

    c. Jewelry, watches, precious and semiprecious stones, or articles of gold, silver, or platinum;

    d. Furs or any article containing fur which represents its principal value; or

    e. Personal property used in any business.

7. We will pay only for the functional value of antiques.

C. **COVERAGE C - OTHER COVERAGES**

1. **Debris Removal**

    a. We will pay the expense to remove non-owned debris on or in insured property and owned debris anywhere.

    b. If you or a member of your household perform the removal work, the value of your work will be based on the Federal minimum wage.

    c. This coverage does not increase the Coverage **A** or Coverage **B** limit of liability.

2. **Loss Avoidance Measures**

    a. **Sandbags, Supplies, and Labor**

        (1) We will pay up to $1,000 for costs you incur to protect the insured **building** from a **flood** or imminent danger of **flood**, for the following:

            (a) Your reasonable expenses to buy:

                (i) Sandbags, including sand to fill them;

                (ii) Fill for temporary levees;

                (iii) Pumps; and

                (iv) Plastic sheeting and lumber used in connection with these items.

            (b) The value of work, at the Federal minimum wage, that you or a member of your household perform.

        (2) This coverage for Sandbags, Supplies, and Labor applies only if damage to insured property by or from **flood** is imminent, and the threat of **flood** damage is apparent enough to lead a person of common prudence to anticipate **flood** damage. One of the following must also occur:

            (a) A general and temporary condition of flooding in the area near the **described location** must occur, even if the **flood** does not reach the insured **building**; or

            (b) A legally authorized official must issue an evacuation order or other civil order for the community in which the insured **building** is located calling for measures to preserve life and property from the peril of **flood**.

    This coverage does not increase the Coverage **A** or Coverage **B** limit of liability.

    b. **Property Removed to Safety**

        (1) We will pay up to $1,000 for the reasonable expenses you incur to move insured property to a place other than the **described location** that contains the property in order to protect it from **flood** or the imminent danger of **flood**.

Page 5 of 19

Reasonable expenses include the value of work, at the Federal minimum wage, that you or a member of your household perform.

(2) If you move insured property to a location other than the **described location** that contains the property, in order to protect it from **flood** or the imminent danger of **flood**, we will cover such property while at that location for a period of 45 consecutive days from the date you begin to move it there. The personal property that is moved must be placed in a fully enclosed **building** or otherwise reasonably protected from the elements.

Any property removed, including a moveable home described in **II.B.6.b.** and **c.**, must be placed above ground level or outside of the **special flood hazard area**.

This coverage does not increase the Coverage **A** or Coverage **B** limit of liability.

3.   Condominium Loss Assessments

a.   If this **policy** insures a **unit**, we will pay, up to the Coverage **A** limit of liability, your share of loss assessments charged against you by the **condominium association** in accordance with the **condominium association's** articles of association, declarations and your deed.

The assessment must be made as a result of **direct physical loss by or from flood** during the **policy** term, to the **building's** common elements.

b.   We will not pay any loss assessment charged against you:

(1) And the **condominium association** by any governmental body;

(2) That results from a deductible under the insurance purchased by the **condominium association** insuring common elements;

(3) That results from a loss to personal property, including contents of a **condominium building**;

(4) That results from a loss sustained by the **condominium association** that was not reimbursed under a flood insurance **policy** written in the name of the association under the **Act** because the **building** was not, at the time of loss, insured for an amount equal to the lesser of:

(a) 80 percent or more of its full replacement cost; or

(b) The maximum amount of insurance permitted under the **Act**;

(5) To the extent that payment under this **policy** for a **condominium building** loss, in combination with payments under any other **NFIP policies** for the same **building** loss, exceeds the maximum amount of insurance permitted under the **Act** for that kind of **building**; or

(6) To the extent that payment under this **policy** for a **condominium building** loss, in combination with any recovery available to you as a tenant in common under any **NFIP condominium association policies** for the same **building** loss, exceeds the amount of insurance permitted under the **Act** for a single-family dwelling.

Loss assessment coverage does not increase the Coverage A limit of liability.

D.   COVERAGE D - INCREASED COST OF COMPLIANCE

1.   General

This **policy** pays you to comply with a State or local floodplain management law or ordinance affecting repair or reconstruction of a structure suffering **flood** damage. Compliance activities eligible for payment are: elevation, floodproofing, relocation, or demolition (or any combination of these activities) of your structure. Eligible floodproofing activities are limited to:

a.   Nonresidential structures.

b.   Residential structures with **basements** that satisfy FEMA's standards published in the Code of Federal Regulations [44 CFR 60.6 (b) or (c)].

2.   Limit of Liability

We will pay you up to $30,000 under this Coverage **D** - Increased Cost of Compliance, which only applies to **policies** with **building** coverage (Coverage **A**). Our payment of claims under Coverage **D** is in addition to the amount of coverage which you selected on the **application** and which appears on the **Declarations Page**. But the maximum you can collect under this **policy** for both Coverage **A** - Building Property and Coverage **D** - Increased Cost of Compliance cannot exceed the maximum permitted under the **Act**. We do not charge a separate deductible for a claim under Coverage **D**.

3. **Eligibility**

   a. A structure covered under Coverage **A** - Building Property sustaining a loss caused by a **flood** as defined by this **policy** must:

      (1) Be a "repetitive loss structure." A repetitive loss structure is one that meets the following conditions:

         (a) The structure is covered by a contract of flood insurance issued under the **NFIP**.

         (b) The structure has suffered **flood** damage on two occasions during a 10-year period which ends on the date of the second loss.

         (c) The cost to repair the **flood** damage, on average, equaled or exceeded 25 percent of the market value of the structure at the time of each flood loss.

         (d) In addition to the current claim, the **NFIP** must have paid the previous qualifying claim, and the State or community must have a cumulative, substantial damage provision or repetitive loss provision in its floodplain management law or ordinance being enforced against the structure; or

      (2) Be a structure that has had **flood** damage in which the cost to repair equals or exceeds 50 percent of the market value of the structure at the time of the **flood**. The State or community must have a substantial damage provision in its floodplain management law or ordinance being enforced against the structure.

   b. This Coverage **D** pays you to comply with State or local floodplain management laws or ordinances that meet the minimum standards of the **National Flood Insurance Program** found in the Code of Federal Regulations at 44 CFR 60.3. We pay for compliance activities that exceed those standards under these conditions:

      (1) 3.a.(1) above.

      (2) Elevation or floodproofing in any risk zone to preliminary or advisory **base flood** elevations provided by FEMA which the State or local government has adopted and is enforcing for **flood**-damaged structures in such areas. (This includes compliance activities in B, C, X, or D zones which are being changed to zones with **base flood** elevations. This also includes compliance activities in zones where **base flood**

elevations are being increased, and a **flood**-damaged structure must comply with the higher advisory **base flood** elevation.) Increased Cost of Compliance coverage does not apply to situations in B, C, X, or D zones where the community has derived its own elevations and is enforcing elevation or floodproofing requirements for **flood**-damaged structures to elevations derived solely by the community.

      (3) Elevation or floodproofing above the **base flood** elevation to meet State or local "freeboard" requirements, i.e., that a structure must be elevated above the **base flood** elevation.

   c. Under the minimum **NFIP** criteria at 44 CFR 60.3 (b)(4), States and communities must require the elevation or floodproofing of structures in unnumbered A zones to the **base flood** elevation where elevation data is obtained from a Federal, State, or other source. Such compliance activities are also eligible for Coverage **D**.

   d. This coverage will also pay for the incremental cost, after demolition or relocation, of elevating or floodproofing a structure during its rebuilding at the same or another site to meet State or local floodplain management laws or ordinances, subject to Exclusion **D.5.g.** below.

   e. This coverage will also pay to bring a **flood**-damaged structure into compliance with State or local floodplain management laws or ordinances even if the structure had received a variance before the present loss from the applicable floodplain management requirements.

4. **Conditions**

   a. When a structure covered under Coverage **A** - Building Property sustains a loss caused by a **flood**, our payment for the loss under this Coverage **D** will be for the increased cost to elevate, floodproof, relocate, or demolish (or any combination of these activities) caused by the enforcement of current State or local floodplain management ordinances or laws. Our payment for eligible demolition activities will be for the cost to demolish and clear the site of the **building** debris or a portion thereof caused by the enforcement of current State or local floodplain management ordinances or laws. Eligible activities for the cost of clearing the site will include those necessary to discontinue utility service to the site and ensure proper abandonment of on-site utilities.

   b. When the **building** is repaired or rebuilt, it must be intended for the same occupancy as the present **building** unless otherwise required by current floodplain management ordinances or laws.

Page 7 of 19

5. **Exclusions**

Under this Coverage **D** - Increased Cost of Compliance, we will not pay for:

a. The cost to comply with any floodplain management law or ordinance in communities participating in the **Emergency Program**.

b. The cost associated with enforcement of any ordinance or law that requires any insured or others to test for, monitor, clean up, remove, contain, treat, detoxify or neutralize, or in any way respond to, or assess the effects of **pollutants**.

c. The loss in value to any insured **building** or other structure due to the requirements of any ordinance or law.

d. The loss in residual value of the undamaged portion of a **building** demolished as a consequence of enforcement of any State or local floodplain management law or ordinance.

e. Any Increased Cost of Compliance under this Coverage **D**:

  (1) Until the **building** is elevated, floodproofed, demolished, or relocated on the same or to another premises; and

  (2) Unless the **building** is elevated, floodproofed, demolished, or relocated as soon as reasonably possible after the loss, not to exceed 2 years (see **3.b.**).

f. Any code upgrade requirements, e.g., plumbing or electrical wiring, not specifically related to the State or local floodplain management law or ordinance.

g. Any compliance activities needed to bring additions or **improvements** made after the loss occurred into compliance with State or local floodplain management laws or ordinances.

h. Loss due to any ordinance or law that you were required to comply with before the current loss.

i. Any rebuilding activity to standards that do not meet the **NFIP's** minimum requirements. This includes any situation where you have received from the State or community a variance in connection with the current **flood** loss to rebuild the property to an elevation below the **base flood** elevation.

j. Increased Cost of Compliance for a garage or carport.

k. Any structure insured under an **NFIP** Group Flood Insurance Policy.

l. Assessments made by a **condominium association** on individual **condominium unit** owners to pay increased costs of repairing commonly owned **buildings** after a **flood** in compliance with State or local floodplain management ordinances or laws.

6. **Other Provisions**

a. Increased Cost of Compliance coverage will not be included in the calculation to determine whether coverage meets the 80 percent insurance-to-value requirement for replacement cost coverage as set forth in **VII.** General Conditions, **V.** Loss Settlement.

b. All other conditions and provisions of this **policy** apply.

IV. PROPERTY NOT COVERED

We do not cover any of the following property:

1. Personal property not inside the fully enclosed **building**;

2. A **building**, and personal property in it, located entirely in, on, or over water or seaward of mean high tide if it was constructed or substantially improved after September 30, 1982;

3. Open structures, including a **building** used as a boathouse or any structure or **building** into which boats are floated, and personal property located in, on, or over water;

4. Recreational vehicles other than travel trailers described in **II.B.6.c.**, whether affixed to a permanent foundation or on wheels;

5. Self-propelled vehicles or machines, including their parts and equipment. However, we do cover self-propelled vehicles or machines not licensed for use on public roads that are:

a. Used mainly to service the **described location**, or

b. Designed and used to assist handicapped persons,

while the vehicles or machines are inside a **building** at the **described location**;

6. Land, land values, lawns, trees, shrubs, plants, growing crops, or animals;

7. Accounts, bills, coins, currency, deeds, evidences of debt, medals, money, scrip, stored value cards, postage stamps, securities, bullion, manuscripts, or other valuable papers;

8. Underground structures and equipment, including wells, septic tanks, and septic systems;

9. Those portions of walks, walkways, decks, driveways, patios, and other surfaces, all whether protected by a roof or not, located outside the perimeter, exterior walls of the insured **building** or the **building** in which the insured **unit** is located;

10. Containers, including related equipment, such as, but not limited to, tanks containing gases or liquids;

11. **Buildings** or **units** and all their contents if more than 49 percent of the **actual cash value** of the **building** or **unit** is below ground, unless the lowest level is at or above the **base flood** elevation and is below ground by reason of earth having been used as insulation material in conjunction with energy efficient building techniques;

12. Fences, retaining walls, seawalls, bulkheads, wharves, piers, bridges, and docks;

13. Aircraft or watercraft, or their furnishings and equipment;

14. Hot tubs and spas that are not bathroom fixtures, and swimming pools, and their equipment such as, but not limited to, heaters, filters, pumps, and pipes, wherever located;

15. Property not eligible for flood insurance pursuant to the provisions of the Coastal Barrier Resources Act and the Coastal Barrier Improvement Act and amendments to these acts;

16. Personal property you own in common with other **unit** owners comprising the membership of a **condominium association**.

V. EXCLUSIONS

A. We only provide coverage for **direct physical loss by or from flood**, which means that we do not pay you for:

1. Loss of revenue or profits;

2. Loss of access to the insured property or **described location**;

3. Loss of use of the insured property or **described location**;

4. Loss from interruption of business or production;

5. Any additional living expenses incurred while the insured **building** is being repaired or is unable to be occupied for any reason;

6. The cost of complying with any ordinance or law requiring or regulating the construction, demolition, remodeling, renovation, or repair of property, including removal of any resulting debris. This exclusion does not apply to any eligible activities that we describe in Coverage **D** - Increased Cost of Compliance; or

7. Any other economic loss.

B. We do not insure a loss directly or indirectly caused by a **flood** that is already in progress at the time and date:

1. The **policy** term begins; or

2. Coverage is added at your request.

C. We do not insure for loss to property caused directly by earth movement even if the earth movement is caused by **flood**. Some examples of earth movement that we do not cover are:

1. Earthquake;

2. Landslide;

3. Land subsidence;

4. Sinkholes;

5. Destabilization or movement of land that results from accumulation of water in subsurface land area; or

6. Gradual erosion.

We do, however, pay for losses from **mudflow** and land subsidence as a result of erosion that are specifically covered under our definition of **flood** (see **II.A.1.c.** and **II.A.2.**).

D. We do not insure for direct physical loss caused directly or indirectly by any of the following:

1. The pressure or weight of ice;

2. Freezing or thawing;

3. Rain, snow, sleet, hail, or water spray;

4. Water, moisture, mildew, or mold damage that results primarily from any condition:

a. Substantially confined to the **dwelling**; or

b. That is within your control, including but not limited to:

(1) Design, structural, or mechanical defects;

Page 9 of 19

(2) Failure, stoppage, or breakage of water or sewer lines, drains, pumps, fixtures, or equipment; or

(3) Failure to inspect and maintain the property after a **flood** recedes;

5. Water or waterborne material that:

a. Backs up through sewers or drains;

b. Discharges or overflows from a sump, sump pump, or related equipment; or

c. Seeps or leaks on or through the covered property;

unless there is a **flood** in the area and the **flood** is the proximate cause of the sewer or drain backup, sump pump discharge or overflow, or seepage of water;

6. The pressure or weight of water unless there is a **flood** in the area and the **flood** is the proximate cause of the damage from the pressure or weight of water;

7. Power, heating, or cooling failure unless the failure results from **direct physical loss by or from flood** to power, heating, or cooling equipment on the **described location**;

8. Theft, fire, explosion, wind, or windstorm;

9. Anything you or any member of your household do or conspire to do to cause loss by **flood** deliberately; or

10. Alteration of the insured property that significantly increases the risk of flooding.

E. We do not insure for loss to any **building** or personal property located on land leased from the Federal Government, arising from or incident to the flooding of the land by the Federal Government, where the lease expressly holds the Federal Government harmless under flood insurance issued under any Federal Government program.

F. We do not pay for the testing for or monitoring of **pollutants** unless required by law or ordinance.

VI. DEDUCTIBLES

A. When a loss is covered under this **policy**, we will pay only that part of the loss that exceeds your deductible amount, subject to the limit of liability that applies. The deductible amount is shown on the **Declarations Page**.

However, when a **building** under construction, alteration, or repair does not have at least two rigid exterior walls and a fully secured roof at the time of loss, your deductible amount will be two times the deductible that would otherwise apply to a completed **building**.

B. In each loss from **flood**, separate deductibles apply to the **building** and personal property insured by this **policy**.

C. The deductible does not apply to:

1. **III.C.2.** Loss Avoidance Measures;

2. **III.C.3.** Condominium Loss Assessments; or

3. **III.D.** Increased Cost of Compliance.

VII. GENERAL CONDITIONS

A. Pairs and Sets

In case of loss to an article that is part of a pair or set, we will have the option of paying you:

1. An amount equal to the cost of replacing the lost, damaged, or destroyed article, minus its depreciation; or

2. The amount that represents the fair proportion of the total value of the pair or set that the lost, damaged, or destroyed article bears to the pair or set.

B. Concealment or Fraud and Policy Voidance

1. With respect to all insureds under this **policy**, this **policy**:

a. Is void;

b. Has no legal force or effect;

c. Cannot be renewed; and

d. Cannot be replaced by a new **NFIP policy**;

if, before or after a loss, you or any other insured or your agent have at any time:

    (1) Intentionally concealed or misrepresented any material fact or circumstance;

    (2) Engaged in fraudulent conduct; or

    (3) Made false statements;

    relating to this **policy** or any other **NFIP** insurance.

2. This **policy** will be void as of the date the wrongful acts described in **B.1.** above were committed.

3. Fines, civil penalties, and imprisonment under applicable Federal laws may also apply to the acts of fraud or concealment described above.

4. This **policy** is also void for reasons other than fraud, misrepresentation, or wrongful act. This **policy** is void from its inception and has no legal force under the following conditions:

    a. If the property is located in a community that was not participating in the **NFIP** on the **policy's** inception date and did not join or reenter the program during the **policy** term and before the loss occurred; or

    b. If the property listed on the **application** is otherwise not eligible for coverage under the **NFIP**.

C. Other Insurance

1. If a loss covered by this **policy** is also covered by other insurance that includes **flood** coverage not issued under the **Act**, we will not pay more than the amount of insurance that you are entitled to for lost, damaged, or destroyed property insured under this **policy** subject to the following:

    a. We will pay only the proportion of the loss that the amount of insurance that applies under this **policy** bears to the total amount of insurance covering the loss, unless **C.1.b.** or **c.** immediately below applies.

    b. If the other policy has a provision stating that it is excess insurance, this **policy** will be primary.

    c. This **policy** will be primary (but subject to its own deductible) up to the deductible in the other **flood** policy (except another policy as described in **C.1.b.** above). When the other deductible amount is reached, this **policy** will participate in the same proportion that the amount of insurance under this **policy** bears to the total amount of both policies, for the remainder of the loss.

2. If there is other insurance in the name of your **condominium association** covering the same property covered by this **policy**, then this **policy** will be in excess over the other insurance.

D. Amendments, Waivers, Assignment

This **policy** cannot be changed nor can any of its provisions be waived without the express written consent of the Federal Insurance Administrator. No action that we take under the terms of this **policy** constitutes a waiver of any of our rights. You may assign this **policy** in writing when you transfer title of your property to someone else, except under these conditions:

1. When this **policy** covers only personal property; or

2. When this **policy** covers a structure during the course of construction.

E. Cancellation of Policy by You

1. You may cancel this **policy** in accordance with the applicable rules and regulations of the **NFIP**.

2. If you cancel this **policy**, you may be entitled to a full or partial refund of premium also under the applicable rules and regulations of the **NFIP**.

F. Nonrenewal of the Policy by Us

Your **policy** will not be renewed:

1. If the community where your covered property is located stops participating in the **NFIP**; or

2. If your **building** has been declared ineligible under Section 1316 of the **Act**.

G. Reduction and Reformation of Coverage

1. If the premium we received from you was not enough to buy the kind and amount of coverage you requested, we will provide only the amount of coverage that can be purchased for the premium payment we received.

2. The **policy** can be reformed to increase the amount of coverage resulting from the reduction described in **G.1.** above to the amount you requested as follows:

    a. Discovery of insufficient premium or incomplete rating information before a loss.

    (1) If we discover before you have a **flood** loss that your premium payment was not enough to buy the requested amount of coverage, we will send you and any mortgagee or trustee known to us a bill for the required additional premium for the current **policy** term (or that portion of the current **policy** term following any endorsement changing the amount of coverage). If you or the mortgagee or trustee pay the additional premium within 30 days from the date of our bill, we will reform the **policy** to increase the amount of coverage to the originally requested amount effective to the beginning of the current **policy** term (or subsequent date of any endorsement changing the amount of coverage).

(2) If we determine before you have a **flood** loss that the rating information we have is incomplete and prevents us from calculating the additional premium, we will ask you to send the required information. You must submit the information within 60 days of our request. Once we determine the amount of additional premium for the current **policy** term, we will follow the procedure in **G.2.a.(1)** above.

(3) If we do not receive the additional premium (or additional information) by the date it is due, the amount of coverage can only be increased by endorsement subject to any appropriate waiting period.

b. Discovery of insufficient premium or incomplete rating information after a loss.

(1) If we discover after you have a **flood** loss that your premium payment was not enough to buy the requested amount of coverage, we will send you and any mortgagee or trustee known to us a bill for the required additional premium for the current and the prior **policy** terms. If you or the mortgagee or trustee pay the additional premium within 30 days from the date of our bill, we will reform the **policy** to increase the amount of coverage to the originally requested amount effective to the beginning of the prior **policy** term.

(2) If we discover after you have a **flood** loss that the rating information we have is incomplete and prevents us from calculating the additional premium, we will ask you to send the required information. You must submit the information before your claim can be paid. Once we determine the amount of additional premium for the current and prior **policy** terms, we will follow the procedure in **G.2.b.(1)** above.

(3) If we do not receive the additional premium by the date it is due, your flood insurance claim will be settled based on the reduced amount of coverage. The amount of coverage can only be increased by endorsement subject to any appropriate waiting period.

3. However, if we find that you or your agent intentionally did not tell us, or falsified, any important fact or circumstance or did anything fraudulent relating to this insurance, the provisions of Condition **B.** Concealment or Fraud and Policy Voidance apply.

H.   Policy Renewal

1. This **policy** will expire at 12:01 a.m. on the last day of the **policy** term.

2. We must receive the payment of the appropriate renewal premium within 30 days of the expiration date.

3. If we find, however, that we did not place your renewal notice into the U.S. Postal Service, or if we did mail it, we made a mistake, e.g., we used an incorrect, incomplete, or illegible address, which delayed its delivery to you before the due date for the renewal premium, then we will follow these procedures:

a. If you or your agent notified us, not later than 1 year after the date on which the payment of the renewal premium was due, of nonreceipt of a renewal notice before the due date for the renewal premium, and we determine that the circumstances in the preceding paragraph apply, we will mail a second bill providing a revised due date, which will be 30 days after the date on which the bill is mailed.

b. If we do not receive the premium requested in the second bill by the revised due date, then we will not renew the **policy**. In that case, the **policy** will remain an expired **policy** as of the expiration date shown on the **Declarations Page**.

4. In connection with the renewal of this **policy**, we may ask you during the **policy** term to recertify, on a Recertification Questionnaire we will provide to you, the rating information used to rate your most recent **application** for or renewal of insurance.

I.   Conditions Suspending or Restricting Insurance

We are not liable for loss that occurs while there is a hazard that is increased by any means within your control or knowledge.

J.   Requirements in Case of Loss

In case of a **flood** loss to insured property, you must:

1. Give prompt written notice to us;

2. As soon as reasonably possible, separate the damaged and undamaged property, putting it in the best possible order so that we may examine it;

3. Prepare an inventory of damaged property showing the quantity, description, **actual cash value,** and amount of loss. Attach all bills, receipts, and related documents;

4. Within 60 days after the loss, send us a proof of loss, which is your statement of the amount you are claiming under the **policy** signed and sworn to by you, and which furnishes us with the following information:

   a. The date and time of loss;

   b. A brief explanation of how the loss happened;

   c. Your interest (for example, "owner") and the interest, if any, of others in the damaged property;

   d. Details of any other insurance that may cover the loss;

   e. Changes in title or occupancy of the covered property during the term of the **policy**;

   f. Specifications of damaged **buildings** and detailed repair estimates;

   g. Names of mortgagees or anyone else having a lien, charge, or claim against the covered property;

   h. Details about who occupied any insured **building** at the time of loss and for what purpose; and

   i. The inventory of damaged personal property described in **J.3.** above.

5. In completing the proof of loss, you must use your own judgment concerning the amount of loss and justify that amount.

6. You must cooperate with the adjuster or representative in the investigation of the claim.

7. The insurance adjuster whom we hire to investigate your claim may furnish you with a proof of loss form, and she or he may help you complete it. However, this is a matter of courtesy only, and you must still send us a proof of loss within 60 days after the loss even if the adjuster does not furnish the form or help you complete it.

8. We have not authorized the adjuster to approve or disapprove claims or to tell you whether we will approve your claim.

9. At our option, we may accept the adjuster's report of the loss instead of your proof of loss. The adjuster's report will include information about your loss and the damages you sustained. You must sign the adjuster's report. At our option, we may require you to swear to the report.

K. Our Options After a Loss

Options we may, in our sole discretion, exercise after loss include the following:

1. At such reasonable times and places that we may designate, you must:

   a. Show us or our representative the damaged property;

   b. Submit to examination under oath, while not in the presence of another insured, and sign the same; and

   c. Permit us to examine and make extracts and copies of:

      (1) Any policies of property insurance insuring you against loss and the deed establishing your ownership of the insured real property;

      (2) **Condominium association** documents including the Declarations of the **condominium**, its Articles of Association or Incorporation, Bylaws, rules and regulations, and other relevant documents if you are a **unit** owner in a **condominium building**; and

      (3) All books of accounts, bills, invoices and other vouchers, or certified copies pertaining to the damaged property if the originals are lost.

2. We may request, in writing, that you furnish us with a complete inventory of the lost, damaged, or destroyed property, including:

   a. Quantities and costs;

   b. **Actual cash values** or replacement cost (whichever is appropriate);

   c. Amounts of loss claimed;

   d. Any written plans and specifications for repair of the damaged property that you can reasonably make available to us; and

   e. Evidence that prior **flood** damage has been repaired.

3. If we give you written notice within 30 days after we receive your signed, sworn proof of loss, we may:

   a. Repair, rebuild, or replace any part of the lost, damaged, or destroyed property with material or property of like kind and quality or its functional equivalent; and

   b. Take all or any part of the damaged property at the value we agree upon or its appraised value.

L. No Benefit to Bailee

No person or organization, other than you, having custody of covered property will benefit from this insurance.

Misc. Personal

Page 13 of 19

M. Loss Payment

1. We will adjust all losses with you. We will pay you unless some other person or entity is named in the **policy** or is legally entitled to receive payment. Loss will be payable 60 days after we receive your proof of loss (or within 90 days after the insurance adjuster files an adjuster's report signed and sworn to by you in lieu of a proof of loss) and:

    a. We reach an agreement with you;

    b. There is an entry of a final judgment; or

    c. There is a filing of an appraisal award with us, as provided in **VII.P**.

2. If we reject your proof of loss in whole or in part you may:

    a. Accept our denial of your claim;

    b. Exercise your rights under this **policy**; or

    c. File an amended proof of loss, as long as it is filed within 60 days of the date of the loss.

N. Abandonment

You may not abandon to us damaged or undamaged property insured under this **policy**.

O. Salvage

We may permit you to keep damaged insured property after a loss, and we will reduce the amount of the loss proceeds payable to you under the **policy** by the value of the salvage.

P. Appraisal

If you and we fail to agree on the **actual cash value** or, if applicable, replacement cost of your damaged property to settle upon the amount of loss, then either may demand an appraisal of the loss. In this event, you and we will each choose a competent and impartial appraiser within 20 days after receiving a written request from the other. The two appraisers will choose an umpire. If they cannot agree upon an umpire within 15 days, you or we may request that the choice be made by a judge of a court of record in the State where the covered property is located. The appraisers will separately state the **actual cash value,** the replacement cost, and the amount of loss to each item. If the appraisers submit a written report of an agreement to us, the amount agreed upon will be the amount of loss. If they fail to agree, they will submit their differences to the umpire. A decision agreed to by any two will set the amount of **actual cash value** and loss, or if it applies, the replacement cost and loss.

Each party will:

1. Pay its own appraiser; and

2. Bear the other expenses of the appraisal and umpire equally.

Q. Mortgage Clause

The word "mortgagee" includes trustee.

Any loss payable under Coverage **A** - Building Property will be paid to any mortgagee of whom we have actual notice as well as any other mortgagee or loss payee determined to exist at the time of loss, and you, as interests appear. If more than one mortgagee is named, the order of payment will be the same as the order of precedence of the mortgages.

If we deny your claim, that denial will not apply to a valid claim of the mortgagee, if the mortgagee:

1. Notifies us of any change in the ownership or occupancy, or substantial change in risk of which the mortgagee is aware;

2. Pays any premium due under this **policy** on demand if you have neglected to pay the premium; and

3. Submits a signed, sworn proof of loss within 60 days after receiving notice from us of your failure to do so.

All of the terms of this **policy** apply to the mortgagee.

The mortgagee has the right to receive loss payment even if the mortgagee has started foreclosure or similar action on the **building**.

If we decide to cancel or not renew this **policy,** it will continue in effect for the benefit of the mortgagee only for 30 days after we notify the mortgagee of the cancellation or nonrenewal.

If we pay the mortgagee for any loss and deny payment to you, we are subrogated to all the rights of the mortgagee granted under the mortgage on the property. Subrogation will not impair the right of the mortgagee to recover the full amount of the mortgagee's claim.

R. Suit Against Us

You may not sue us to recover money under this **policy** unless you have complied with all the requirements of the **policy**. If you do sue, you must start the suit within 1 year after the date of the written denial of all or part of the claim, and you must file the suit in the United States District Court of the district in which the insured property was located at the time of loss. This requirement applies to any claim that you may have under this **policy** and to any dispute that you may have arising out of the handling of any claim under the **policy**.

S. Subrogation

Whenever we make a payment for a loss under this **policy**, we are subrogated to your right to recover for that loss from any other person. That means that your right to recover for a loss that was partly or totally caused by someone else is automatically transferred to us, to the extent that we have paid you for the loss. We may require you to acknowledge this transfer in writing. After the loss, you may not give up our right to recover this money or do anything that would prevent us from recovering it. If you make any claim against any person who caused your loss and recover any money, you must pay us back first before you may keep any of that money.

T. Continuous Lake Flooding

1. If your insured **building** has been flooded by rising lake waters continuously for 90 days or more and it appears reasonably certain that a continuation of this flooding will result in a covered loss to the insured **building** equal to or greater than the **building policy** limits plus the deductible or the maximum payable under the **policy** for any one **building** loss, we will pay you the lesser of these two amounts without waiting for the further damage to occur if you sign a release agreeing:

   a. To make no further claim under this **policy**;

   b. Not to seek renewal of this **policy**;

   c. Not to apply for any flood insurance under the **Act** for property at the **described location**; and

   d. Not to seek a premium refund for current or prior terms.

   If the **policy** term ends before the insured **building** has been flooded continuously for 90 days, the provisions of this paragraph **T.1.** will apply when the insured **building** suffers a covered loss before the **policy** term ends.

2. If your insured **building** is subject to continuous lake flooding from a closed basin lake, you may elect to file a claim under either paragraph **T.1.** above or paragraph **T.2.** (A "closed basin lake" is a natural lake from which water leaves primarily through evaporation and whose surface area now exceeds or has exceeded 1 square mile at any time in the recorded past. Most of the nation's closed basin lakes are in the western half of the United States, where annual evaporation exceeds annual precipitation and where lake levels and surface areas are subject to considerable fluctuation due to wide variations in the climate. These lakes may overtop their basins on rare occasions.) Under this paragraph **T.2.** we will pay your claim as if the **building** is a total loss even though it has not been continuously inundated for 90 days, subject to the following conditions:

   a. Lake **flood** waters must damage or imminently threaten to damage your **building**.

   b. Before approval of your claim, you must:

(1) Agree to a claim payment that reflects your buying back the salvage on a negotiated basis; and

(2) Grant the conservation easement described in FEMA's "Policy Guidance for Closed Basin Lakes," to be recorded in the office of the local recorder of deeds. FEMA, in consultation with the community in which the property is located, will identify on a map an area or areas of special consideration (ASC) in which there is a potential for **flood** damage from continuous lake flooding. FEMA will give the community the agreed-upon map showing the ASC. This easement will only apply to that portion of the property in the ASC. It will allow certain agricultural and recreational uses of the land. The only structures that it will allow on any portion of the property within the ASC are certain simple agricultural and recreational structures. If any of these allowable structures are insurable buildings under the **NFIP** and are insured under the **NFIP**, they will not be eligible for the benefits of this paragraph **T.2.** If a U.S. Army Corps of Engineers certified **flood** control project or otherwise certified **flood** control project later protects the property, FEMA will, upon request, amend the ASC to remove areas protected by those projects. The restrictions of the easement will then no longer apply to any portion of the property removed from the ASC; and

(3) Comply with paragraphs **T.1.a.** through **T.1.d.** above.

   c. Within 90 days of approval of your claim, you must move your **building** to a new location outside the ASC. FEMA will give you an additional 30 days to move if you show that there is sufficient reason to extend the time.

   d. Before the final payment of your claim, you must acquire an elevation certificate and a floodplain development permit from the local floodplain administrator for the new location of your **building**.

   e. Before the approval of your claim, the community having jurisdiction over your **building** must:

(1) Adopt a permanent land use ordinance, or a temporary moratorium for a period not to exceed 6 months to be followed immediately by a permanent land use ordinance, that is consistent with the provisions specified in the easement required in paragraph **T.2.b.** above.

(2) Agree to declare and report any violations of this ordinance to FEMA so that under Section 1316 of the National Flood Insurance Act of 1968, as amended, flood insurance to the **building** can be denied; and

(3) Agree to maintain as deed-restricted, for purposes compatible with open space or agricultural or recreational use only, any affected property the community acquires an interest in. These deed restrictions must be consistent with the provisions of paragraph **T.2.b.** above, except that, even if a certified project protects the property, the land use restrictions continue to apply if the property was acquired under the Hazard Mitigation Grant Program or the Flood Mitigation Assistance Program. If a nonprofit land trust organization receives the property as a donation, that organization must maintain the property as deed-restricted, consistent with the provisions of paragraph **T.2.b.** above.

f. Before the approval of your claim, the affected State must take all action set forth in FEMA's "Policy Guidance for Closed Basin Lakes."

g. You must have **NFIP** flood insurance coverage continuously in effect from a date established by FEMA until you file a claim under paragraph **T.2.** If a subsequent owner buys **NFIP** insurance that goes into effect within 60 days of the date of transfer of title, any gap in coverage during that 60-day period will not be a violation of this continuous coverage requirement. For the purpose of honoring a claim under this paragraph **T.2.**, we will not consider to be in effect any increased coverage that became effective after the date established by FEMA. The exception to this is any increased coverage in the amount suggested by your insurer as an inflation adjustment.

h. This paragraph **T.2.** will be in effect for a community when the FEMA Regional Director for the affected region provides to the community, in writing, the following:

(1) Confirmation that the community and the State are in compliance with the conditions in paragraphs **T.2.e.** and **T.2.f.** above; and

(2) The date by which you must have flood insurance in effect.

U. Duplicate Policies Not Allowed

1. We will not insure your property under more than one **NFIP policy**.

If we find that the duplication was not knowingly created, we will give you written notice. The notice will advise you that you may choose one of several options under the following procedures:

a. If you choose to keep in effect the **policy** with the earlier effective date, you may also choose to add the coverage limits of the later **policy** to the limits of the earlier **policy**. The change will become effective as of the effective date of the later **policy**.

b. If you choose to keep in effect the **policy** with the later effective date, you may also choose to add the coverage limits of the earlier **policy** to the limits of the later **policy**. The change will be effective as of the effective date of the later **policy**.

In either case, you must pay the pro rata premium for the increased coverage limits within 30 days of the written notice. In no event will the resulting coverage limits exceed the permissible limits of coverage under the **Act** or your insurable interest, whichever is less.

We will make a refund to you, according to applicable **NFIP** rules, of the premium for the **policy** not being kept in effect.

2. Your option under Condition **U.** Duplicate Policies Not Allowed to elect which **NFIP policy** to keep in effect does not apply when duplicates have been knowingly created. Losses occurring under such circumstances will be adjusted according to the terms and conditions of the earlier **policy**. The **policy** with the later effective date will be canceled.

V. Loss Settlement

1. Introduction

This **policy** provides three methods of settling losses: Replacement Cost, Special Loss Settlement, and **Actual Cash Value**. Each method is used after a different type of property, as explained in **a.-c.** below.

a. Replacement Cost loss settlement, described in **V.2.** below, applies to a single-family **dwelling** provided:

(1) It is your principal residence, which means that, at the time of loss, you or your spouse lived there for at least 80 percent of:

(a) The 365 days immediately preceding the loss; or

(b) The period of your ownership, if you owned the **dwelling** for less than 365 days; and

(2) At the time of loss, the amount of insurance in this **policy** that applies to the **dwelling** is 80 percent or more of its full replacement cost immediately before the loss, or is the maximum amount of insurance available under the **NFIP**.

b. Special loss settlement, described in **V.3.** below, applies to a single-family **dwelling** that is a manufactured or mobile home or a travel trailer.

c. **Actual Cash Value** loss settlement applies to a single-family **dwelling** not subject to replacement cost or special loss settlement, and to the property listed in **V.4.** below.

2. Replacement Cost Loss Settlement

The following loss settlement conditions apply to a single-family **dwelling** described in **V.1.a.** above:

a. We will pay to repair or replace the damaged **dwelling** after application of the deductible and without deduction for depreciation, but not more than the least of the following amounts:

    (1) The **building** limit of liability shown on your **Declarations Page;**

    (2) The replacement cost of that part of the **dwelling** damaged, with materials of like kind and quality, and for like use; or

    (3) The necessary amount actually spent to repair or replace the damaged part of the **dwelling** for like use.

b. If the **dwelling** is rebuilt at a new location, the cost described above is limited to the cost that would have been incurred if the **dwelling** had been rebuilt at its former location.

c. When the full cost of repair or replacement is more than $1,000 or more than 5 percent of the whole amount of insurance that applies to the **dwelling**, we will not be liable for any loss under **V.2.a.** above or **V.4.a.(2)** below unless and until actual repair or replacement is completed.

d. You may disregard the replacement cost conditions above and make claim under this **policy** for loss to **dwellings** on an **actual cash value** basis. You may then make claim for any additional liability according to **V.2.a., b.,** and **c.** above, provided you notify us of your intent to do so within 180 days after the date of loss.

e. If the community in which your **dwelling** is located has been converted from the **Emergency Program** to the **Regular Program** during the current **policy** term, then we will consider the maximum amount of available **NFIP** insurance to be the amount that was available at the beginning of the current **policy** term.

3. Special Loss Settlement

a. The following loss settlement conditions apply to a single-family **dwelling** that:

    (1) Is a manufactured or mobile home or a travel trailer, as defined in **II.B.6.b.** and **II.B.6.c.**;

    (2) Is at least 16 feet wide when fully assembled and has an area of at least 600 square feet within its perimeter walls when fully assembled; and

    (3) Is your principal residence, as specified in **V.1.a.(1)** above.

b. If such a **dwelling** is totally destroyed or damaged to such an extent that, in our judgment, it is not economically feasible to repair, at least to its predamage condition, we will, at our discretion, pay the least of the following amounts:

    (1) The lesser of the replacement cost of the **dwelling** or 1.5 times the **actual cash value,** or

    (2) The **building** limit of liability shown on your **Declarations Page.**

c. If such a **dwelling** is partially damaged and, in our judgment, it is economically feasible to repair it to its predamage condition, we will settle the loss according to the Replacement Cost conditions in paragraph **V.2.** above.

4. Actual Cash Value Loss Settlement

The types of property noted below are subject to **actual cash value** [or in the case of **V.4.a.(2)** below, proportional] loss settlement.

a. A **dwelling**, at the time of loss, when the amount of insurance on the **dwelling** is both less than 80 percent of its full replacement cost immediately before the loss and less than the maximum amount of insurance available under the **NFIP**. In that case, we will pay the greater of the following amounts, but not more than the amount of insurance that applies to that **dwelling**:

    (1) The **actual cash value**, as defined in **II.B.2.**, of the damaged part of the **dwelling**; or

    (2) A proportion of the cost to repair or replace the damaged part of the **dwelling**, without deduction for physical depreciation and after application of the deductible.

    This proportion is determined as follows: If 80 percent of the full replacement cost of the **dwelling** is less than the maximum amount of insurance available under the **NFIP**, then the proportion is determined by dividing the actual amount of insurance on the **dwelling** by the amount of insurance that represents 80 percent of its full replacement cost. But if 80 percent of the full replacement cost of the **dwelling** is greater than the maximum amount of insurance available under the **NFIP**, then the proportion is determined by dividing the actual amount of insurance on the **dwelling** by the maximum amount of insurance available under the **NFIP**.

b. A two-, three-, or four-family **dwelling.**

c. A **unit** that is not used exclusively for single-family **dwelling** purposes.

Page 17 of 19

d.   Detached garages.

e.   Personal property.

f.   Appliances, carpets, and carpet pads.

g.   Outdoor awnings, outdoor antennas or aerials of any type, and other outdoor equipment.

h.   Any property covered under this **policy** that is abandoned after a loss and remains as debris anywhere on the **described location**.

i.   A **dwelling** that is not your principal residence.

5.   **Amount of Insurance Required**

To determine the amount of insurance required for a **dwelling** immediately before the loss, do not include the value of:

a.   Footings, foundations, piers, or any other structures or devices that are below the undersurface of the lowest basement floor and support all or part of the **dwelling;**

b.   Those supports listed in **V.5.a.** above that are below the surface of the ground inside the foundation walls if there is no basement; and

c.   Excavations and underground flues, pipes, wiring, and drains.

The Coverage **D** - Increased Cost of Compliance limit of liability is not included in the determination of the amount of insurance required.

VIII. LIBERALIZATION CLAUSE

If we make a change that broadens your coverage under this edition of our **policy,** but does not require any additional premium, then that change will automatically apply to your insurance as of the date we implement the change, provided that this implementation date falls within 60 days before, or during, the **policy** term stated on the **Declarations Page**.

IX. WHAT LAW GOVERNS

This **policy** and all disputes arising from the handling of any claim under the **policy** are governed exclusively by the flood insurance regulations issued by FEMA, the National Flood Insurance Act of 1968, as amended (42 U.S.C. 4001, et seq.), and Federal common law.

IN WITNESS WHEREOF, we have signed this **policy** below and hereby enter into this Insurance Agreement.

Edward L. Connor

Edward L. Connor
Acting Administrator, National Flood Insurance Program
Federal Emergency Management Agency

CLAIM GUIDELINES IN CASE OF A FLOOD

For the protection of you and your family, the following claim guidelines are provided by the National Flood Insurance Program (NFIP). If you are ever in doubt as to what action is needed, consult your insurance representative or call the NFIP toll-free at 1-800-638-6620 or on the TDD line at 1-800-447-9487.

Know your insurance representative's name and telephone number. List them here for fast reference:

Insurance Representative _____

Representative's Phone Number _____

- Notify us or your insurance representative, in writing, as soon as possible after the flood.

- If you report to your insurance representative, remind him or her to assign the claim to an NFIP-approved claims adjuster. The NFIP pays for the services of the independent claims adjuster assigned to your claim.

- Determine the independent claims adjuster assigned to your claim and contact him or her if you have not been contacted within 24 hours after you reported the claim to your insurance representative.

- As soon as possible, separate damaged property from undamaged property so that damage can be inspected and evaluated.

- Discuss with the claims adjuster any need you may have for an advance or partial payment for your loss.

- To help the claims adjuster, try to take photographs of the outside of the premises showing the flooding and the damage and photographs of the inside of the premises showing the height of the water and the damaged property.

- Place all account books, financial records, receipts, and other loss verification material in a safe place for examination and evaluation by the claims adjuster.

- Work cooperatively and promptly with the claims adjuster to determine and document all claim items. Be prepared to advise the claims adjuster of the cause and responsible party(ies), if the flooding resulted from other than natural cause.

- Make sure that the claims adjuster fully explains, and that you fully understand, all allowances and procedures for processing claim payments on the basis of your proof of loss. This policy requires you to send us detailed proof of loss within 60 days after the loss.

- Any and all coverage problems and claim allowance restrictions must be communicated directly from the NFIP. Claims adjusters are not authorized to approve or deny claims; their job is to report to the NFIP on the elements of flood cause and damage.

At our option, we may accept an adjuster's report of the loss instead of your proof of loss. The adjuster's report will include information about your loss and the damages to your insured property. You must sign the adjuster's report. At our option, we may require you to swear to the report.

FEMA Form 81-34 (5/03)   F-122 (8/09)

PERSONAL LIABILITY
DL 98 01 10 06

PERSONAL UMBRELLA LIABILITY POLICY

AGREEMENT

In return for payment of the premium and subject to all the terms of this policy, we agree with you as follows:

I. Definitions

A. Throughout this policy, "you" and "your" refer to:

1. The "named insured" shown in the Declarations; and

2. The spouse if a resident of the same household.

B. "We", "us" and "our" refer to the Company providing this insurance.

C. For purposes of this policy, a private passenger type auto, pickup or van shall be deemed to be owned by a person if leased:

1. Under a written agreement to that person; and

2. For a continuous period of at least 6 months.

Other words and phrases are defined. They are in quotation marks when used.

D. "Aircraft Liability", "Hovercraft Liability", "Recreational Motor Vehicle Liability" and "Watercraft Liability", subject to the provisions in **2.** below, mean the following:

1. Liability for "bodily injury" or "property damage" arising out of:

a. The ownership of such vehicle or craft by an "insured";

b. The maintenance, occupancy, operation, use, loading or unloading of such vehicle or craft by any person;

c. The entrustment of such vehicle or craft by an "insured" to any person;

d. The failure to supervise or negligent supervision of any person involving such vehicle or craft by an "insured"; or

e. Vicarious liability, whether or not imposed by law, for the actions of a child or minor involving such vehicle or craft.

2. For the purpose of this definition:

a. Aircraft means any contrivance used or designed for flight, except model or hobby aircraft not used or designed to carry people or cargo;

b. Hovercraft means a self-propelled motorized ground effect vehicle and includes, but is not limited to, flarecraft and air cushion vehicles;

c. Watercraft means a craft principally designed to be propelled on or in water by wind, engine power or electric motor; and

d. Recreational Motor Vehicle means a "recreational motor vehicle" as defined in Paragraph **N.**

E. "Auto" means:

1. A private passenger motor vehicle, motorcycle, moped or motor home;

2. A vehicle designed to be pulled by a private passenger motor vehicle or motor home; or

3. A farm wagon or farm implement while towed by a private passenger motor vehicle or motor home.

F. "Bodily injury" means bodily harm, sickness or disease, including required care, loss of services and death that results.

G. "Business" means:

1. A trade, profession or occupation engaged in on a full-time, part-time or occasional basis; or

2. Any other activity engaged in for money or other compensation, except the following:

a. One or more activities, not described in **b.** through **d.** below, for which no "insured" receives more than $2000 in total compensation for the 12 months before the beginning of the policy period;

b. Volunteer activities for which no money is received other than payment for expenses incurred to perform the activity;

c. Providing home day care services for which no compensation is received, other than the mutual exchange of such services; or

d. The rendering of home day care services to a relative of an "insured".

H. "Family member" means a resident of your household who is:

1. Your relative, including a ward or foster child; or

2. Under the age of 21 and in the care of you or an "insured" who is age 21 or over.

I. "Fuel System" means:

1. One or more containers, tanks or vessels which have a total combined storage capacity of 100 or more U.S. gallons of liquid fuel; and:

    a. Are, or were, located on any single location covered by "underlying insurance"; and

    b. Are, or were, used to hold liquid fuel that is intended to be used solely for one or more of the following:

        (1) To heat or cool a building;

        (2) To heat water;

        (3) To cook food; or

        (4) To power motor vehicles, other motorized land conveyances or watercraft owned by an "insured";

2. Any pumping apparatus, which includes the motor, gauge, nozzle, hose or pipes that are, or were, connected to one or more containers, tanks or vessels described in Paragraph **I.1.**;

3. Filler pipes and flues connected to one or more containers, tanks or vessels described in Paragraph **I.1.**;

4. A boiler, furnace or a water heater, the liquid fuel for which is stored in a container, tank or vessel described in Paragraph **I.1.**;

5. Fittings and pipes connecting the boiler, furnace or water heater to one or more containers, tanks or vessels described in Paragraph **I.1.**;

6. A structure that is specifically designed and built to hold the liquid fuel that escapes from one or more containers, tanks or vessels described in Paragraph **I.1.**

J. "Insured" means:

1. You.

2. A "family member".

3. Any person using an "auto", "recreational motor vehicle", or watercraft, which is owned by you and covered under this policy. Any person using a temporary substitute for such "auto" or "recreational motor vehicle" is also an "insured".

4. Any other person or organization but only with respect to the legal responsibility for acts or omissions of you or any "family member" while you or any "family member" is using an "auto" or "recreational motor vehicle" covered under this policy. However, the owner or lessor of an "auto" or "recreational motor vehicle" loaned to or hired for use by an "insured" or on an "insured's" behalf, is not an "insured".

5. With respect to animals owned by you or any "family member", any person or organization legally responsible for such animals. However, a person or organization using or having custody of such animals in the course of any "business" or without the consent of the owner is not an "insured".

K. "Occurrence" means an accident, including continuous or repeated exposure to substantially the same general harmful conditions, which results, during the policy period, in:

1. "Bodily injury"; or

2. "Property damage".

L. "Personal injury" means injury arising out of one or more of the following offenses, but only if the offense was committed during the policy period:

1. False arrest, detention or imprisonment;

2. Malicious prosecution;

3. The wrongful eviction from, wrongful entry into, or invasion of the right of private occupancy of a room, dwelling or premises that a person occupies, committed by or on behalf of its owner, landlord or lessor;

4. Oral or written publication of material that slanders or libels a person or organization or disparages a person's or organization's goods, products or services; or

5. Oral or written publication of material that violates a person's right of privacy.

M. "Property damage" means physical injury to, destruction of, or loss of use of tangible property.

N. "Recreational motor vehicle" means:

1. All-terrain vehicle;

2. Dune buggy;

3. Golf cart;

4. Snowmobile; or

5. Any other motorized land vehicle which is designed for recreational use off public roads.

 DL 98 01 10 06

O. "Retained limit" means:

1. The total limits of any "underlying insurance" and any other insurance that applies to an "occurrence" or offense which:

   a. Are available to an "insured"; or

   b. Would have been available except for the bankruptcy or insolvency of an insurer providing "underlying insurance"; or

2. The deductible, if any, as stated in the Declarations, if the "occurrence" or offense:

   a. Is covered by this policy; and

   b. Is not covered by "underlying insurance" or any other insurance.

P. "Underlying insurance" means any policy providing the "insured" with primary liability insurance covering one or more of the types of liability listed in the Declarations and at limits no less than the retained policy limits shown for those types of liability listed in the Declarations.

II. Coverages

A. Insuring Agreement

We will pay damages, in excess of the "retained limit", for:

1. "Bodily injury" or "property damage" for which an "insured" becomes legally liable due to an "occurrence" to which this insurance applies; and

2. "Personal injury" for which an "insured" becomes legally liable due to one or more offenses listed under the definition of "personal injury" to which this insurance applies.

Damages include prejudgment interest awarded against an "insured".

B. Defense Coverage

1. If a claim is made or a suit is brought against an "insured" for damages because of "bodily injury" or "property damage" caused by an "occurrence" or "personal injury" caused by an offense to which this policy applies, we:

   a. Will provide a defense at our expense by counsel of our choice, even if the suit is groundless, false or fraudulent. However, we are not obligated to defend any suit or settle any claim if:

   (1) The "occurrence" or offense is covered by other "underlying insurance" available to the "insured"; or

   (2) There is no applicable "underlying insurance" in effect at the time of the "occurrence" or offense and the amount of damages claimed or incurred is less than the applicable deductible amount shown in the Declarations.

   b. May join, at our expense, with the "insured" or any insurer providing "underlying insurance" in the investigation, defense or settlement of any claim or suit which we believe may require payment under this policy.

   However, we will not contribute to the costs and expenses incurred by any insurer providing "underlying insurance"; and

   c. Will pay any expense incurred for the "insured's" defense, with our written consent, in any country where we are prevented from defending an "insured" because of laws or other reasons.

2. We may investigate and settle any claim or suit that we decide is appropriate. Our duty to settle or defend ends when our limit of liability for the "occurrence" or offense has been exhausted by payment of judgments or settlements.

C. Additional Coverages

We will pay:

1. Expenses we incur and costs taxed against an "insured" in any suit we defend;

2. Premiums on bonds required in a suit we defend, but not for bond amounts to the extent they exceed our limit of liability. We need not apply for or furnish any bond; and

3. Reasonable expenses incurred by an "insured" at our request, including actual loss of earnings (but not loss of other income) up to $250 per day, for assisting us in the investigation or defense of a claim or suit; and

4. Interest on our share of the judgment which accrues after entry of the judgment and before we pay or tender, or deposit in court, that part of the judgment which does not exceed the limit of liability that applies.

These payments will not reduce the limit of liability.

D. Limit Of Liability

Our total liability under this policy for all damages resulting from any one "occurrence" or offense will not be more than the limit of liability as shown in the Declarations of this policy. This limit is the most we will pay regardless of the number of "insureds", claims made, persons injured, or vehicles involved in an accident.

III. Exclusions

A. The coverages provided by this policy do not apply to:

1. "Bodily injury" or "property damage" which is expected or intended by an "insured" even if the resulting "bodily injury" or "property damage":

   a. Is of a different kind, quality or degree than initially expected or intended; or

   b. Is sustained by a different person, entity, real or personal property, than initially expected or intended.

However, this Exclusion **(A.1.)** does not apply to:

   a. "Bodily injury" resulting from the use of reasonable force by an "insured" to protect persons or property; or

   b. "Bodily injury" or "property damage" resulting from the use of reasonable force by an "insured" to prevent or eliminate danger in the operation of "autos", "recreational motor vehicles" or watercraft;

2. "Personal injury":

   a. Caused by or at the direction of an "insured" with the knowledge that the act would violate the rights of another and would inflict "personal injury";

   b. Arising out of oral or written publication of material, if done by or at the direction of an "insured" with knowledge of its falsity;

   c. Arising out of oral or written publication of material whose first publication took place before the beginning of the policy period;

   d. Arising out of a criminal act committed by or at the direction of an "insured"; or

   e. Sustained by any person as a result of an offense directly or indirectly related to the employment of this person by an "insured";

3. "Bodily injury", "personal injury" or "property damage" arising out of or in connection with a "business":

   a. Engaged in by an "insured"; or

   b. Conducted from:

     (1) Any part of a premises owned by or rented to an "insured"; or

     (2) Vacant land owned by or rented to an "insured".

This Exclusion **(A.3.)** applies but is not limited to an act or omission, regardless of its nature or circumstance, involving a service or duty rendered, promised, owed, or implied to be provided because of the nature of the "business".

However, this Exclusion **(A.3.)** does not apply to:

   a. The rental or holding for rental of:

     (1) The residence premises shown in the Declarations:

       (a) On an occasional basis if used only as a residence;

       (b) In part, for use only as a residence, unless a single family unit is intended for use by the occupying family to lodge more than two roomers or boarders; or

       (c) In part, as an office, school, studio or private garage;

     (2) Any part of a one to four family dwelling other than the residence premises to the extent that personal liability coverage is provided by "underlying insurance";

     (3) A condominium, cooperative, or apartment unit other than the residence premises to the extent that personal liability coverage is provided by "underlying insurance";

   b. Civic or public activities performed by an "insured" without compensation other than reimbursement of expenses;

   c. An insured minor involved in self-employed "business" pursuits, which are occasional or part-time and customarily undertaken on that basis by minors. A minor means a person who has not attained his or her:

     (1) 18th birthday; or

     (2) 21st birthday if a full-time student;

Misc. Personal

d. The use of an "auto" you own, or a temporary substitute for such "auto", by you, a "family member" or a partner, agent or employee of you or a "family member" while employed or otherwise engaged in the "business" of:

   (1) Selling;

   (2) Repairing;

   (3) Servicing;

   (4) Storing; or

   (5) Parking;

   vehicles designed for use mainly on public highways;

e. The use of an "auto" for "business" purposes, other than an auto business, by an "insured";

4. "Bodily injury" or "property damage" arising out of the ownership or operation of an "auto" while it is being used as a public or livery conveyance. This Exclusion **(A.4.)** does not apply to a share-the-expense car pool;

5. "Bodily injury", "personal injury" or "property damage" arising out of the rendering of or failure to render professional services;

6. "Aircraft Liability";

7. "Hovercraft Liability";

8. "Watercraft Liability".

   However, this Exclusion **(A.8)** does not apply to the extent that watercraft coverage is provided by "underlying insurance" at the time of the "occurrence";

9. "Recreational Motor Vehicle Liability".

   However, this Exclusion **(A.9.)** does not apply with respect to any "recreational motor vehicle":

   a. Owned by you or a "family member" to the extent that "recreational motor vehicle" coverage is provided by "underlying insurance" at the time of the "occurrence"; or

   b. That you or a "family member" do not own;

10. "Bodily injury" or "property damage" caused directly or indirectly by war, including the following and any consequence of any of the following:

   a. Undeclared war, civil war, insurrection, rebellion or revolution;

b. Warlike act by a military force or military personnel; or

c. Destruction, seizure or use for a military purpose.

   Discharge of a nuclear weapon will be deemed a warlike act even if accidental;

11. A person using an "auto", "recreational motor vehicle" or watercraft without a reasonable belief that that person is entitled to do so. This Exclusion **(A.11.)** does not apply to a "family member" using an "auto", "recreational motor vehicle" or watercraft you own;

12. The use of "autos", "recreational motor vehicles" or watercraft while they are being operated in, or practicing for, any prearranged or organized race, speed contest or other similar competition. However, this Exclusion **(A.12.)** does not apply to:

   a. Sailboats; or

   b. Watercraft involved in predicted log cruises;

13. "Bodily injury" or "personal injury" to you or a "family member".

   This exclusion also applies to any claim made or suit brought:

   a. To repay; or

   b. Share damages with;

   another person who may be obligated to pay damages because of "bodily injury" or "personal injury" to you or a "family member";

14. "Bodily injury" or "personal injury" arising out of:

   a. The transmission of a communicable disease by an "insured";

   b. Sexual molestation, corporal punishment or physical or mental abuse; or

   c. The use, sale, manufacture, delivery, transfer or possession by any person of a Controlled Substance(s) as defined by the Federal Food and Drug Law at 21 U.S.C.A. Sections 811 and 812. Controlled Substances include but are not limited to cocaine, LSD, marijuana and all narcotic drugs. However, this Exclusion **(A.14.)** does not apply to the legitimate use of prescription drugs by a person following the orders of a licensed physician;

15. "Bodily injury", "personal injury" or "property damage" arising out of an act or omission of an "insured" as an officer or member of a board of directors of a corporation or organization. However, this Exclusion **(A.15.)** does not apply if the corporation or organization is not-for-profit and the "insured" receives no compensation other than reimbursement of expenses;

16. "Property damage" to property owned by an "insured". This includes costs or expenses incurred by an "insured" or others to repair, replace, enhance, restore or maintain such property to prevent injury to a person or damage to property of others, whether on or away from the residence premises shown in the Declarations;

17. "Property damage" to property rented to, occupied or used by, or in the care, custody or control of, an "insured" to the extent that the "insured" is obligated by contract to provide insurance for such property. However, this Exclusion **(A.17.)** does not apply to "property damage" caused by fire, smoke or explosion;

18. "Bodily injury" to any person eligible to receive any benefits:

    a. Voluntarily provided; or

    b. Required to be provided;

    by an "insured" under any:

    a. Workers' compensation law;

    b. Non-occupational disability law; or

    c. Occupational disease law;

19. "Bodily injury" or "property damage" for which an "insured" under this policy:

    a. Is also an insured under a nuclear energy liability policy issued by the:

    (1) Nuclear Energy Liability Insurance Association;

    (2) Mutual Atomic Energy Liability Underwriters; or

    (3) Nuclear Insurance Association of Canada;

    or any of their successors; or

    b. Would be an insured under that policy but for the exhaustion of its limit of liability;

20. "Bodily injury", "personal injury" or "property damage" caused by an "occurrence" or offense involving the escape of fuel from a "fuel system";

21. "Bodily injury" or "personal injury" caused by an "occurrence" or offense involving the absorption, ingestion or inhalation of lead;

22. "Personal injury" or "property damage" caused by an "occurrence" or offense of lead contamination.

B. Liability coverage does not apply to any assessment charged against you as a member of an association, corporation or community of property owners.

C. We do not provide:

    1. Automobile no-fault or any similar coverage under this policy; or

    2. Uninsured Motorists Coverage, Underinsured Motorists Coverage, or any similar coverage unless this policy is endorsed to provide such coverage.

IV. Maintenance Of Underlying Insurance

You must maintain the "underlying insurance" at the full limits stated in the Declarations and with no change to more restrictive conditions during the term of this policy. If any "underlying insurance" is canceled or not renewed and not replaced, you must notify us at once.

If you fail to maintain "underlying insurance", we will not be liable under this policy for more than we would have been liable if that "underlying insurance" was in effect.

V. Duties After Loss

In case of an "occurrence" or offense likely to involve the insurance under this policy, you or another "insured" will perform the following duties that apply. We have no duty to provide coverage under this policy if your failure to comply with the following duties is prejudicial to us. You will help us by seeing that these duties are performed:

A. Give written notice to us or our agent as soon as is practical. Such notice shall set forth:

    1. The identity of the policy and named insured shown in the Declarations;

    2. Reasonably available information about the time, place and circumstances of the "occurrence" or offense; and

    3. The names and addresses of any claimants and witnesses.

B. If a claim is made or a suit is brought against an "insured", the "insured" must:

    1. Notify us immediately in writing;

    2. Cooperate with us in the investigation, settlement or defense of any claim or suit;

3. Promptly forward to us every notice, demand, summons or other process relating to the "occurrence" or offense;

4. At our request, help us:

   a. To make settlement;

   b. To enforce any right of contribution or indemnity against any person or organization who may be liable to an "insured";

   c. With the conduct of suits and attend hearings and trials; and

   d. To secure and give evidence and obtain the attendance of witnesses.

C. The "insured" will not, except at the "insured's" own cost, voluntarily make payment, assume obligation or incur expense to others.

VI. General Provisions

A. Appeals

If an "insured" or any insurer providing "underlying insurance" elects not to appeal a judgment which exceeds the "retained limit", we may do so at our own expense. We will pay all costs, taxes, expenses and interest related to our appeal. The amounts we pay will be in addition to our limit of liability.

B. Bankruptcy Of An Insured

Bankruptcy or insolvency of an "insured" will neither:

1. Relieve us of our obligations under this policy; nor

2. Operate to cause this policy to become primary in the event the "insured" is unable to satisfy the "retained limit" either because of insufficient "underlying insurance" or insufficient personal assets.

C. Bankruptcy Of An Underlying Insurer

In the event of bankruptcy or insolvency of any "underlying insurer", the insurance afforded by this policy shall not replace such "underlying insurance", but shall apply as if the "underlying insurance" was valid and collectible.

D. Fraud

We do not provide coverage for any "insured" who has made fraudulent statements or engaged in fraudulent conduct in connection with any "occurrence" or offense for which coverage is sought under this policy.

E. Liberalization Clause

If we make a change which broadens coverage under this edition of our policy without additional premium charge, that change will automatically apply to your insurance as of the date we implement the change in your state, provided that this implementation date falls within 60 days prior to or during the policy period stated in the Declarations.

This Liberalization Clause does not apply to changes implemented with a general program revision that includes both broadenings and restrictions in coverage, whether that general program revision is implemented through introduction of:

1. A subsequent edition of this policy; or

2. An amendatory endorsement.

F. Other Insurance

The coverage afforded by this policy is excess over any other insurance available to an "insured", except insurance written specifically to be excess over this policy.

G. Our Right To Recover Payment

If we make a payment under this policy, we are entitled to exercise the "insured's" rights of recovery against any person liable for the loss. The "insured" must do nothing after loss to prejudice those rights.

H. Policy Period And Territory

The policy period is stated in the Declarations. This policy applies to an "occurrence" or offense which takes place anywhere in the world.

I. Severability Of Insurance

This insurance applies separately to each "insured". However, this provision will not increase our limit of liability for any one "occurrence" or offense.

J. Suit Against Us

1. No legal action can be brought against us:

   a. Unless there has been full compliance with all of the terms of this policy; and

   b. Until the obligation of the "insured" has been determined by final judgment or by agreement signed by us.

2. No person or organization has any right under this policy to join us as a party to any legal action against an "insured".

K. Termination

1. Cancellation By You

You may cancel this policy by:

a. Returning it to us; or

b. Giving us advance written notice of the date cancellation is to take effect.

2. Cancellation By Us

We may cancel this policy as stated below by letting you know in writing of the date cancellation takes effect. This cancellation notice may be delivered to you, or mailed to you at your mailing address shown in the Declarations.

Proof of mailing will be sufficient proof of notice.

a. When you have not paid the premium, we may cancel at any time by letting you know at least 10 days before the date cancellation takes effect.

b. When this policy has been in effect for less than 60 days and is not a renewal with us, we may cancel for any reason by letting you know at least 10 days before the date cancellation takes effect.

c. When this policy has been in effect for 60 days or more, or at any time if it is a renewal with us, we may cancel by letting you know at least 30 days before the date cancellation takes effect.

3. Nonrenewal

We may elect not to renew this policy. We may do so by delivering to you, or mailing to you at your mailing address shown in the Declarations, written notice at least 30 days before the expiration date of this policy. Proof of mailing will be sufficient proof of notice.

4. Other Termination Provisions

a. When this policy is canceled, the premium for the period from the date of cancellation to the expiration date will be refunded pro rata.

b. If the return premium is not refunded with the notice of cancellation or when this policy is returned to us, we will refund it within a reasonable time after the date cancellation takes effect.

L. Transfer Of Your Interest In This Policy

1. Your rights and duties under this policy may not be assigned without our written consent. However, if you die, coverage will be provided for:

a. The surviving spouse if resident in the same household at the time of death. Coverage applies to the spouse as if a named insured shown in the Declarations;

b. Any member of your household who is an "insured" at the time of your death, but only while a resident of the residence premises; or

c. The legal representative of the deceased person as if a named insured shown in the Declarations. This applies only with respect to the representative's legal responsibility to maintain or use your "autos" or the residence premises shown in the Declarations.

2. Coverage will only be provided until the end of the policy period.

M. Waiver Or Change Of Policy Provisions

This policy contains all the agreements between you and us. Its terms may not be changed or waived except by endorsement issued by us. If a change requires a premium adjustment, we will adjust the premium as of the effective date of the change.

Misc. Personal

Commercial Property Insurance

In a general sense, commercial property insurance includes any kind of commercial insurance that covers loss of or damage to property. However, insurers often use the term "commercial property" in a more specific sense to describe insurance on commercial buildings and personal property in such buildings or on (or within 100 feet of) the insured location. The commercial property forms reprinted in the *Handbook* correspond to the more specific meaning of the term and are part of the commercial lines insurance program of Insurance Services Office, Inc. (ISO).

The ISO commercial lines program uses various *coverage parts* (such as commercial property, commercial general liability, and commercial auto) to make up modular policies. A commercial property coverage part consists of the following components.

Commercial Property Coverage Part Declarations Page. This form is filled in by the insurer with information about the policyholder and the coverage provided by the policy. The *Handbook* reprints this form, with filled-in information showing how it was completed for a fictitious insured.

Commercial Property Conditions. This form, also reprinted in the *Handbook*, contains several conditions that apply to any commercial property coverage form included in the coverage part (unless the coverage form says otherwise).

One or more commercial property coverage forms. A coverage form contains insuring agreements, exclusions, and other applicable policy provisions. The *Handbook* reprints three common examples of commercial property coverage forms: the Building and Personal Property Coverage Form, the Condominium Association Coverage Form, and the Business Income (and Extra Expense) Coverage Form.

One or more causes of loss forms. Any of the commercial property coverage forms must be supplemented with a causes of loss form to state the covered causes of loss. Three causes of loss forms are available: the Causes of Loss— Basic Form, the Causes of Loss—Broad Form, and the Causes of Loss— Special Form. The *Handbook* reprints the Broad Form and the Special Form.

Any applicable endorsements. Many endorsements are available for modifying commercial property forms to meet the policyholder's or insurer's needs. The *Handbook* reprints representative endorsements for adding flood coverage, adding earthquake and volcanic eruption coverage, adding ordinance or law coverage, and addressing losses caused by terrorism.

A commercial property coverage part can be combined with other coverage parts in a commercial package policy (CPP) or issued by itself as a monoline policy. In either case, an additional form, called the Common Policy Conditions, must be attached to the policy. The Common Policy Conditions form is also reprinted in this section, even though it is not exclusively a commercial property form.

COMMERCIAL PROPERTY
CP DS 00 10 00

COMMERCIAL PROPERTY COVERAGE PART
DECLARATIONS PAGE

POLICY NO. SP 0001   **EFFECTIVE DATE** 10 / 1 / 20X1   ☒ **"X" If Supplemental**
                                                                         Declarations Is Attached

NAMED INSURED

Barnley Corporation

DESCRIPTION OF PREMISES

Prem. No.	Bldg. No.	Location, Construction And Occupancy
001	001	2000 Industrial Highway, Workingtown, PA 19000
		Joisted Masonry
		Storm Door Manufacturing

COVERAGES PROVIDED   **Insurance At The Described Premises Applies Only For Coverages For Which A Limit Of Insurance Is Shown**

Prem. No.	Bldg. No.	Coverage	Limit Of Insurance	Covered Causes Of Loss	Coinsurance*	Rates
001	001	Building	2,000,000	Special	80%	(See Sched.)
		Your Business Personal Prop.	1,120,000	Broad	80%	
		Personal Prop. of Others	50,000	Broad	80%	
		Business Income & Extra Expense	680,000	Special	80%	

***If Extra Expense Coverage, Limits On Loss Payment**

OPTIONAL COVERAGES   **Applicable Only When Entries Are Made In The Schedule Below**

Prem. No.	Bldg. No.	Agreed Value			Replacement Cost (X)		
		Expiration Date	Cov.	Amount	Building	Pers. Prop.	Including "Stock"
001	001	10/1/20X2	Building	$2,000,000	X		

Inflation Guard (%)		*Monthly Limit Of	Maximum Period	*Extended Period
Bldg.	Pers. Prop.	Indemnity (Fraction)	Of Indemnity (X)	Of Indemnity (Days)
3%	3%			

***Applies to Business Income Only**

MORTGAGEHOLDERS

Prem. No.	Bldg. No.	Mortgageholder Name And Mailing Address
001	001	Workingtown Savings and Loan Assn.
		400 Main Street
		Workingtown, PA 19001

DEDUCTIBLE

$1,000.   **Exceptions:**

FORMS APPLICABLE

To All Coverages: CP 00 10, CP 00 30, CP 00 90, CP 10 30

CP DS 00 10 00   Copyright, Insurance Services Office, Inc., 1999   **Page 1 of 1**   ▢

IL 00 17 11 98

COMMON POLICY CONDITIONS

All Coverage Parts included in this policy are subject to the following conditions.

A. Cancellation

1. The first Named Insured shown in the Declarations may cancel this policy by mailing or delivering to us advance written notice of cancellation.

2. We may cancel this policy by mailing or delivering to the first Named Insured written notice of cancellation at least:

   a. 10 days before the effective date of cancellation if we cancel for nonpayment of premium; or

   b. 30 days before the effective date of cancellation if we cancel for any other reason.

3. We will mail or deliver our notice to the first Named Insured's last mailing address known to us.

4. Notice of cancellation will state the effective date of cancellation. The policy period will end on that date.

5. If this policy is cancelled, we will send the first Named Insured any premium refund due. If we cancel, the refund will be pro rata. If the first Named Insured cancels, the refund may be less than pro rata. The cancellation will be effective even if we have not made or offered a refund.

6. If notice is mailed, proof of mailing will be sufficient proof of notice.

B. Changes

This policy contains all the agreements between you and us concerning the insurance afforded. The first Named Insured shown in the Declarations is authorized to make changes in the terms of this policy with our consent. This policy's terms can be amended or waived only by endorsement issued by us and made a part of this policy.

C. Examination Of Your Books And Records

We may examine and audit your books and records as they relate to this policy at any time during the policy period and up to three years afterward.

D. Inspections And Surveys

1. We have the right to:

   a. Make inspections and surveys at any time;

   b. Give you reports on the conditions we find; and

   c. Recommend changes.

2. We are not obligated to make any inspections, surveys, reports or recommendations and any such actions we do undertake relate only to insurability and the premiums to be charged. We do not make safety inspections. We do not undertake to perform the duty of any person or organization to provide for the health or safety of workers or the public. And we do not warrant that conditions:

   a. Are safe or healthful; or

   b. Comply with laws, regulations, codes or standards.

3. Paragraphs **1.** and **2.** of this condition apply not only to us, but also to any rating, advisory, rate service or similar organization which makes insurance inspections, surveys, reports or recommendations.

4. Paragraph **2.** of this condition does not apply to any inspections, surveys, reports or recommendations we may make relative to certification, under state or municipal statutes, ordinances or regulations, of boilers, pressure vessels or elevators.

E. Premiums

The first Named Insured shown in the Declarations:

1. Is responsible for the payment of all premiums; and

2. Will be the payee for any return premiums we pay.

F. Transfer Of Your Rights And Duties Under This Policy

Your rights and duties under this policy may not be transferred without our written consent except in the case of death of an individual named insured.

If you die, your rights and duties will be transferred to your legal representative but only while acting within the scope of duties as your legal representative. Until your legal representative is appointed, anyone having proper temporary custody of your property will have your rights and duties but only with respect to that property.

COMMERCIAL PROPERTY CONDITIONS

This Coverage Part is subject to the following conditions, the Common Policy Conditions and applicable Loss Conditions and Additional Conditions in Commercial Property Coverage Forms.

A. CONCEALMENT, MISREPRESENTATION OR FRAUD

This Coverage Part is void in any case of fraud by you as it relates to this Coverage Part at any time. It is also void if you or any other insured, at any time, intentionally conceal or misrepresent a material fact concerning:

1. This Coverage Part;
2. The Covered Property;
3. Your interest in the Covered Property; or
4. A claim under this Coverage Part.

B. CONTROL OF PROPERTY

Any act or neglect of any person other than you beyond your direction or control will not affect this insurance.

The breach of any condition of this Coverage Part at any one or more locations will not affect coverage at any location where, at the time of loss or damage, the breach of condition does not exist.

C. INSURANCE UNDER TWO OR MORE COVERAGES

If two or more of this policy's coverages apply to the same loss or damage, we will not pay more than the actual amount of the loss or damage.

D. LEGAL ACTION AGAINST US

No one may bring a legal action against us under this Coverage Part unless:

1. There has been full compliance with all of the terms of this Coverage Part; and
2. The action is brought within 2 years after the date on which the direct physical loss or damage occurred.

E. LIBERALIZATION

If we adopt any revision that would broaden the coverage under this Coverage Part without additional premium within 45 days prior to or during the policy period, the broadened coverage will immediately apply to this Coverage Part.

F. NO BENEFIT TO BAILEE

No person or organization, other than you, having custody of Covered Property will benefit from this insurance.

G. OTHER INSURANCE

1. You may have other insurance subject to the same plan, terms, conditions and provisions as the insurance under this Coverage Part. If you do, we will pay our share of the covered loss or damage. Our share is the proportion that the applicable Limit of Insurance under this Coverage Part bears to the Limits of Insurance of all insurance covering on the same basis.
2. If there is other insurance covering the same loss or damage, other than that described in 1. above, we will pay only for the amount of covered loss or damage in excess of the amount due from that other insurance, whether you can collect on it or not. But we will not pay more than the applicable Limit of Insurance.

H. POLICY PERIOD, COVERAGE TERRITORY

Under this Coverage Part:

1. We cover loss or damage commencing:
   a. During the policy period shown in the Declarations; and
   b. Within the coverage territory.
2. The coverage territory is:
   a. The United States of America (including its territories and possessions);
   b. Puerto Rico; and
   c. Canada.

▶▶

I. TRANSFER OF RIGHTS OF RECOVERY AGAINST OTHERS TO US

If any person or organization to or for whom we make payment under this Coverage Part has rights to recover damages from another, those rights are transferred to us to the extent of our payment. That person or organization must do everything necessary to secure our rights and must do nothing after loss to impair them. But you may waive your rights against another party in writing:

1. Prior to a loss to your Covered Property or Covered Income.

2. After a loss to your Covered Property or Covered Income only if, at time of loss, that party is one of the following:

   a. Someone insured by this insurance;

   b. A business firm:

      (1) Owned or controlled by you; or

      (2) That owns or controls you; or

   c. Your tenant.

This will not restrict your insurance.

Copyright, ISO Commercial Risk Services, Inc., 1983, 1987   **CP 00 90 07 88**   □

Commercial Property

BUILDING AND PERSONAL PROPERTY COVERAGE FORM

Various provisions in this policy restrict coverage. Read the entire policy carefully to determine rights, duties and what is and is not covered.

Throughout this policy the words "you" and "your" refer to the Named Insured shown in the Declarations. The words "we", "us" and "our" refer to the Company providing this insurance.

Other words and phrases that appear in quotation marks have special meaning. Refer to Section **H.**, Definitions.

A. Coverage

We will pay for direct physical loss of or damage to Covered Property at the premises described in the Declarations caused by or resulting from any Covered Cause of Loss.

1. Covered Property

Covered Property, as used in this Coverage Part, means the type of property described in this section, **A.1.**, and limited in **A.2.**, Property Not Covered, if a Limit of Insurance is shown in the Declarations for that type of property.

a. Building, meaning the building or structure described in the Declarations, including:

(1) Completed additions;

(2) Fixtures, including outdoor fixtures;

(3) Permanently installed:

(a) Machinery and

(b) Equipment;

(4) Personal property owned by you that is used to maintain or service the building or structure or its premises, including:

(a) Fire-extinguishing equipment;

(b) Outdoor furniture;

(c) Floor coverings; and

(d) Appliances used for refrigerating, ventilating, cooking, dishwashing or laundering;

(5) If not covered by other insurance:

(a) Additions under construction, alterations and repairs to the building or structure;

(b) Materials, equipment, supplies and temporary structures, on or within 100 feet of the described premises, used for making additions, alterations or repairs to the building or structure.

b. Your Business Personal Property located in or on the building described in the Declarations or in the open (or in a vehicle) within 100 feet of the described premises, consisting of the following unless otherwise specified in the Declarations or on the Your Business Personal Property – Separation Of Coverage form:

(1) Furniture and fixtures;

(2) Machinery and equipment;

(3) "Stock";

(4) All other personal property owned by you and used in your business;

(5) Labor, materials or services furnished or arranged by you on personal property of others;

(6) Your use interest as tenant in improvements and betterments. Improvements and betterments are fixtures, alterations, installations or additions:

(a) Made a part of the building or structure you occupy but do not own; and

(b) You acquired or made at your expense but cannot legally remove;

(7) Leased personal property for which you have a contractual responsibility to insure, unless otherwise provided for under Personal Property Of Others.

          ☐

c. Personal Property Of Others that is:

(1) In your care, custody or control; and

(2) Located in or on the building described in the Declarations or in the open (or in a vehicle) within 100 feet of the described premises.

However, our payment for loss of or damage to personal property of others will only be for the account of the owner of the property.

2. Property Not Covered

Covered Property does not include:

a. Accounts, bills, currency, food stamps or other evidences of debt, money, notes or securities. Lottery tickets held for sale are not securities;

b. Animals, unless owned by others and boarded by you, or if owned by you, only as "stock" while inside of buildings;

c. Automobiles held for sale;

d. Bridges, roadways, walks, patios or other paved surfaces;

e. Contraband, or property in the course of illegal transportation or trade;

f. The cost of excavations, grading, backfilling or filling;

g. Foundations of buildings, structures, machinery or boilers if their foundations are below:

(1) The lowest basement floor; or

(2) The surface of the ground, if there is no basement;

h. Land (including land on which the property is located), water, growing crops or lawns;

i. Personal property while airborne or waterborne;

j. Bulkheads, pilings, piers, wharves or docks;

k. Property that is covered under another coverage form of this or any other policy in which it is more specifically described, except for the excess of the amount due (whether you can collect on it or not) from that other insurance;

l. Retaining walls that are not part of a building;

m. Underground pipes, flues or drains;

n. Electronic data, except as provided under the Additional Coverage, Electronic Data. Electronic data means information, facts or computer programs stored as or on, created or used on, or transmitted to or from computer software (including systems and applications software), on hard or floppy disks, CD-ROMs, tapes, drives, cells, data processing devices or any other repositories of computer software which are used with electronically controlled equipment. The term computer programs, referred to in the foregoing description of electronic data, means a set of related electronic instructions which direct the operations and functions of a computer or device connected to it, which enable the computer or device to receive, process, store, retrieve or send data. This paragraph, **n.,** does not apply to your "stock" of prepackaged software;

o. The cost to replace or restore the information on valuable papers and records, including those which exist as electronic data. Valuable papers and records include but are not limited to proprietary information, books of account, deeds, manuscripts, abstracts, drawings and card index systems. Refer to the Coverage Extension for Valuable Papers And Records (Other Than Electronic Data) for limited coverage for valuable papers and records other than those which exist as electronic data;

p. Vehicles or self-propelled machines (including aircraft or watercraft) that:

(1) Are licensed for use on public roads; or

(2) Are operated principally away from the described premises.

This paragraph does not apply to:

(a) Vehicles or self-propelled machines or autos you manufacture, process or warehouse;

(b) Vehicles or self-propelled machines, other than autos, you hold for sale;

(c) Rowboats or canoes out of water at the described premises; or

(d) Trailers, but only to the extent provided for in the Coverage Extension for Non-owned Detached Trailers;

q. The following property while outside of buildings:

(1) Grain, hay, straw or other crops;

(2) Fences, radio or television antennas (including satellite dishes) and their lead-in wiring, masts or towers, trees, shrubs or plants (other than "stock" of trees, shrubs or plants), all except as provided in the Coverage Extensions.

3. Covered Causes Of Loss

See applicable Causes Of Loss Form as shown in the Declarations.

4. Additional Coverages

a. Debris Removal

(1) Subject to Paragraphs **(3)** and **(4)**, we will pay your expense to remove debris of Covered Property caused by or resulting from a Covered Cause of Loss that occurs during the policy period. The expenses will be paid only if they are reported to us in writing within 180 days of the date of direct physical loss or damage.

(2) Debris Removal does not apply to costs to:

(a) Extract "pollutants" from land or water; or

(b) Remove, restore or replace polluted land or water.

(3) Subject to the exceptions in Paragraph **(4)**, the following provisions apply:

(a) The most we will pay for the total of direct physical loss or damage plus debris removal expense is the Limit of Insurance applicable to the Covered Property that has sustained loss or damage.

(b) Subject to **(a)** above, the amount we will pay for debris removal expense is limited to 25% of the sum of the deductible plus the amount that we pay for direct physical loss or damage to the Covered Property that has sustained loss or damage.

(4) We will pay up to an additional $10,000 for debris removal expense, for each location, in any one occurrence of physical loss or damage to Covered Property, if one or both of the following circumstances apply:

(a) The total of the actual debris removal expense plus the amount we pay for direct physical loss or damage exceeds the Limit of Insurance on the Covered Property that has sustained loss or damage.

(b) The actual debris removal expense exceeds 25% of the sum of the deductible plus the amount that we pay for direct physical loss or damage to the Covered Property that has sustained loss or damage.

Therefore, if **(4)(a)** and/or **(4)(b)** apply, our total payment for direct physical loss or damage and debris removal expense may reach but will never exceed the Limit of Insurance on the Covered Property that has sustained loss or damage, plus $10,000.

(5) **Examples**

The following examples assume that there is no Coinsurance penalty.

EXAMPLE #1

Limit of Insurance:	$ 90,000
Amount of Deductible:	$ 500
Amount of Loss:	$ 50,000
Amount of Loss Payable:	$ 49,500
	($50,000 – $500)
Debris Removal Expense:	$ 10,000
Debris Removal Expense Payable:	$ 10,000

($10,000 is 20% of $50,000.)

The debris removal expense is less than 25% of the sum of the loss payable plus the deductible. The sum of the loss payable and the debris removal expense ($49,500 + $10,000 = $59,500) is less than the Limit of Insurance. Therefore the full amount of debris removal expense is payable in accordance with the terms of Paragraph **(3)**.

EXAMPLE #2

Limit of Insurance:		$ 90,000
Amount of Deductible:		$ 500
Amount of Loss:		$ 80,000
Amount of Loss Payable:		$ 79,500
		($80,000 – $500)
Debris Removal Expense:		$ 30,000
Debris Removal Expense Payable		
	Basic Amount:	$ 10,500
	Additional Amount:	$ 10,000

The basic amount payable for debris removal expense under the terms of Paragraph **(3)** is calculated as follows: $80,000 ($79,500 + $500) x .25 = $20,000; capped at $10,500. The cap applies because the sum of the loss payable ($79,500) and the basic amount payable for debris removal expense ($10,500) cannot exceed the Limit of Insurance ($90,000).

The additional amount payable for debris removal expense is provided in accordance with the terms of Paragraph **(4),** because the debris removal expense ($30,000) exceeds 25% of the loss payable plus the deductible ($30,000 is 37.5% of $80,000), and because the sum of the loss payable and debris removal expense ($79,500 + $30,000 = $109,500) would exceed the Limit of Insurance ($90,000). The additional amount of covered debris removal expense is $10,000, the maximum payable under Paragraph **(4).** Thus the total payable for debris removal expense in this example is $20,500; $9,500 of the debris removal expense is not covered.

b. Preservation Of Property

If it is necessary to move Covered Property from the described premises to preserve it from loss or damage by a Covered Cause of Loss, we will pay for any direct physical loss or damage to that property:

(1) While it is being moved or while temporarily stored at another location; and

(2) Only if the loss or damage occurs within 30 days after the property is first moved.

c. Fire Department Service Charge

When the fire department is called to save or protect Covered Property from a Covered Cause of Loss, we will pay up to $1,000, unless a higher limit is shown in the Declarations, for your liability for fire department service charges:

(1) Assumed by contract or agreement prior to loss; or

(2) Required by local ordinance.

No Deductible applies to this Additional Coverage.

d. Pollutant Clean-up And Removal

We will pay your expense to extract "pollutants" from land or water at the described premises if the discharge, dispersal, seepage, migration, release or escape of the "pollutants" is caused by or results from a Covered Cause of Loss that occurs during the policy period. The expenses will be paid only if they are reported to us in writing within 180 days of the date on which the Covered Cause of Loss occurs.

This Additional Coverage does not apply to costs to test for, monitor or assess the existence, concentration or effects of "pollutants". But we will pay for testing which is performed in the course of extracting the "pollutants" from the land or water.

The most we will pay under this Additional Coverage for each described premises is $10,000 for the sum of all covered expenses arising out of Covered Causes of Loss occurring during each separate 12-month period of this policy.

e. Increased Cost Of Construction

(1) This Additional Coverage applies only to buildings to which the Replacement Cost Optional Coverage applies.

(2) In the event of damage by a Covered Cause of Loss to a building that is Covered Property, we will pay the increased costs incurred to comply with enforcement of an ordinance or law in the course of repair, rebuilding or replacement of damaged parts of that property, subject to the limitations stated in **e.(3)** through **e.(9)** of this Additional Coverage.

(3) The ordinance or law referred to in **e.(2)** of this Additional Coverage is an ordinance or law that regulates the construction or repair of buildings or establishes zoning or land use requirements at the described premises, and is in force at the time of loss.

Commercial Property

(4) Under this Additional Coverage, we will not pay any costs due to an ordinance or law that:

(a) You were required to comply with before the loss, even when the building was undamaged; and

(b) You failed to comply with.

(5) Under this Additional Coverage, we will not pay for:

(a) The enforcement of any ordinance or law which requires demolition, repair, replacement, reconstruction, remodeling or remediation of property due to contamination by "pollutants" or due to the presence, growth, proliferation, spread or any activity of "fungus", wet or dry rot or bacteria; or

(b) Any costs associated with the enforcement of an ordinance or law which requires any insured or others to test for, monitor, clean up, remove, contain, treat, detoxify or neutralize, or in any way respond to, or assess the effects of "pollutants", "fungus", wet or dry rot or bacteria.

(6) The most we will pay under this Additional Coverage, for each described building insured under this Coverage Form, is $10,000 or 5% of the Limit of Insurance applicable to that building, whichever is less. If a damaged building is covered under a blanket Limit of Insurance which applies to more than one building or item of property, then the most we will pay under this Additional Coverage, for that damaged building, is the lesser of: $10,000 or 5% times the value of the damaged building as of the time of loss times the applicable Coinsurance percentage.

The amount payable under this Additional Coverage is additional insurance.

(7) With respect to this Additional Coverage:

(a) We will not pay for the Increased Cost of Construction:

(i) Until the property is actually repaired or replaced, at the same or another premises; and

(ii) Unless the repairs or replacement are made as soon as reasonably possible after the loss or damage, not to exceed two years. We may extend this period in writing during the two years.

(b) If the building is repaired or replaced at the same premises, or if you elect to rebuild at another premises, the most we will pay for the Increased Cost of Construction, subject to the provisions of **e.(6)** of this Additional Coverage, is the increased cost of construction at the same premises.

(c) If the ordinance or law requires relocation to another premises, the most we will pay for the Increased Cost of Construction, subject to the provisions of **e.(6)** of this Additional Coverage, is the increased cost of construction at the new premises.

(8) This Additional Coverage is not subject to the terms of the Ordinance Or Law Exclusion, to the extent that such Exclusion would conflict with the provisions of this Additional Coverage.

(9) The costs addressed in the Loss Payment and Valuation Conditions, and the Replacement Cost Optional Coverage, in this Coverage Form, do not include the increased cost attributable to enforcement of an ordinance or law. The amount payable under this Additional Coverage, as stated in **e.(6)** of this Additional Coverage, is not subject to such limitation.

f. Electronic Data

(1) Under this Additional Coverage, electronic data has the meaning described under Property Not Covered, Electronic Data.

(2) Subject to the provisions of this Additional Coverage, we will pay for the cost to replace or restore electronic data which has been destroyed or corrupted by a Covered Cause of Loss. To the extent that electronic data is not replaced or restored, the loss will be valued at the cost of replacement of the media on which the electronic data was stored, with blank media of substantially identical type.

(3) The Covered Causes of Loss applicable to Your Business Personal Property apply to this Additional Coverage, Electronic Data, subject to the following:

(a) If the Causes Of Loss – Special Form applies, coverage under this Additional Coverage, Electronic Data, is limited to the "specified causes of loss" as defined in that form, and Collapse as set forth in that form.

(b) If the Causes Of Loss – Broad Form applies, coverage under this Additional Coverage, Electronic Data, includes Collapse as set forth in that form.

(c) If the Causes Of Loss Form is endorsed to add a Covered Cause of Loss, the additional Covered Cause of Loss does not apply to the coverage provided under this Additional Coverage, Electronic Data.

(d) The Covered Causes of Loss include a virus, harmful code or similar instruction introduced into or enacted on a computer system (including electronic data) or a network to which it is connected, designed to damage or destroy any part of the system or disrupt its normal operation. But there is no coverage for loss or damage caused by or resulting from manipulation of a computer system (including electronic data) by any employee, including a temporary or leased employee, or by an entity retained by you or for you to inspect, design, install, modify, maintain, repair or replace that system.

(4) The most we will pay under this Additional Coverage, Electronic Data, is $2,500 for all loss or damage sustained in any one policy year, regardless of the number of occurrences of loss or damage or the number of premises, locations or computer systems involved. If loss payment on the first occurrence does not exhaust this amount, then the balance is available for subsequent loss or damage sustained in but not after that policy year. With respect to an occurrence which begins in one policy year and continues or results in additional loss or damage in a subsequent policy year(s), all loss or damage is deemed to be sustained in the policy year in which the occurrence began.

5. Coverage Extensions

Except as otherwise provided, the following Extensions apply to property located in or on the building described in the Declarations or in the open (or in a vehicle) within 100 feet of the described premises.

If a Coinsurance percentage of 80% or more, or a Value Reporting period symbol, is shown in the Declarations, you may extend the insurance provided by this Coverage Part as follows:

a. Newly Acquired Or Constructed Property

(1) Buildings

If this policy covers Building, you may extend that insurance to apply to:

(a) Your new buildings while being built on the described premises; and

(b) Buildings you acquire at locations, other than the described premises, intended for:

(i) Similar use as the building described in the Declarations; or

(ii) Use as a warehouse.

The most we will pay for loss or damage under this Extension is $250,000 at each building.

(2) Your Business Personal Property

(a) If this policy covers Your Business Personal Property, you may extend that insurance to apply to:

(i) Business personal property, including such property that you newly acquire, at any location you acquire other than at fairs, trade shows or exhibitions;

(ii) Business personal property, including such property that you newly acquire, located at your newly constructed or acquired buildings at the location described in the Declarations; or

(iii) Business personal property that you newly acquire, located at the described premises.

The most we will pay for loss or damage under this Extension is $100,000 at each building.

(b) This Extension does not apply to:

(i) Personal property of others that is temporarily in your possession in the course of installing or performing work on such property; or

(ii) Personal property of others that is temporarily in your possession in the course of your manufacturing or wholesaling activities.

(3) Period Of Coverage

With respect to insurance on or at each newly acquired or constructed property, coverage will end when any of the following first occurs:

(a) This policy expires;

(b) 30 days expire after you acquire the property or begin construction of that part of the building that would qualify as covered property; or

(c) You report values to us.

We will charge you additional premium for values reported from the date you acquire the property or begin construction of that part of the building that would qualify as covered property.

b. Personal Effects And Property Of Others

You may extend the insurance that applies to Your Business Personal Property to apply to:

(1) Personal effects owned by you, your officers, your partners or members, your managers or your employees. This Extension does not apply to loss or damage by theft.

(2) Personal property of others in your care, custody or control.

The most we will pay for loss or damage under this Extension is $2,500 at each described premises. Our payment for loss of or damage to personal property of others will only be for the account of the owner of the property.

c. Valuable Papers And Records (Other Than Electronic Data)

(1) You may extend the insurance that applies to Your Business Personal Property to apply to the cost to replace or restore the lost information on valuable papers and records for which duplicates do not exist. But this Extension does not apply to valuable papers and records which exist as electronic data. Electronic data has the meaning described under Property Not Covered, Electronic Data.

(2) If the Causes Of Loss – Special Form applies, coverage under this Extension is limited to the "specified causes of loss" as defined in that form, and Collapse as set forth in that form.

(3) If the Causes Of Loss – Broad Form applies, coverage under this Extension includes Collapse as set forth in that form.

(4) Under this Extension, the most we will pay to replace or restore the lost information is $2,500 at each described premises, unless a higher limit is shown in the Declarations. Such amount is additional insurance. We will also pay for the cost of blank material for reproducing the records (whether or not duplicates exist), and (when there is a duplicate) for the cost of labor to transcribe or copy the records. The costs of blank material and labor are subject to the applicable Limit of Insurance on Your Business Personal Property and therefore coverage of such costs is not additional insurance.

d. Property Off-premises

(1) You may extend the insurance provided by this Coverage Form to apply to your Covered Property while it is away from the described premises, if it is:

(a) Temporarily at a location you do not own, lease or operate;

(b) In storage at a location you lease, provided the lease was executed after the beginning of the current policy term; or

(c) At any fair, trade show or exhibition.

(2) This Extension does not apply to property:

    (a) In or on a vehicle; or

    (b) In the care, custody or control of your salespersons, unless the property is in such care, custody or control at a fair, trade show or exhibition.

(3) The most we will pay for loss or damage under this Extension is $10,000.

e. Outdoor Property

You may extend the insurance provided by this Coverage Form to apply to your outdoor fences, radio and television antennas (including satellite dishes), trees, shrubs and plants (other than "stock" of trees, shrubs or plants), including debris removal expense, caused by or resulting from any of the following causes of loss if they are Covered Causes of Loss:

(1) Fire;

(2) Lightning;

(3) Explosion;

(4) Riot or Civil Commotion; or

(5) Aircraft.

The most we will pay for loss or damage under this Extension is $1,000, but not more than $250 for any one tree, shrub or plant. These limits apply to any one occurrence, regardless of the types or number of items lost or damaged in that occurrence.

f. Non-owned Detached Trailers

(1) You may extend the insurance that applies to Your Business Personal Property to apply to loss or damage to trailers that you do not own, provided that:

    (a) The trailer is used in your business;

    (b) The trailer is in your care, custody or control at the premises described in the Declarations; and

    (c) You have a contractual responsibility to pay for loss or damage to the trailer.

(2) We will not pay for any loss or damage that occurs:

    (a) While the trailer is attached to any motor vehicle or motorized conveyance, whether or not the motor vehicle or motorized conveyance is in motion;

    (b) During hitching or unhitching operations, or when a trailer becomes accidentally unhitched from a motor vehicle or motorized conveyance.

(3) The most we will pay for loss or damage under this Extension is $5,000, unless a higher limit is shown in the Declarations.

(4) This insurance is excess over the amount due (whether you can collect on it or not) from any other insurance covering such property.

Each of these Extensions is additional insurance unless otherwise indicated. The Additional Condition, Coinsurance, does not apply to these Extensions.

B. Exclusions And Limitations

See applicable Causes Of Loss Form as shown in the Declarations.

C. Limits Of Insurance

The most we will pay for loss or damage in any one occurrence is the applicable Limit of Insurance shown in the Declarations.

The most we will pay for loss or damage to outdoor signs, whether or not the sign is attached to a building, is $2,500 per sign in any one occurrence.

The amounts of insurance stated in the following Additional Coverages apply in accordance with the terms of such coverages and are separate from the Limit(s) of Insurance shown in the Declarations for any other coverage:

1. Fire Department Service Charge;

2. Pollutant Clean-up And Removal;

3. Increased Cost Of Construction; and

4. Electronic Data.

Payments under the Preservation Of Property Additional Coverage will not increase the applicable Limit of Insurance.

Commercial Property

CP 00 10 06 07

D. Deductible

In any one occurrence of loss or damage (hereinafter referred to as loss), we will first reduce the amount of loss if required by the Coinsurance Condition or the Agreed Value Optional Coverage. If the adjusted amount of loss is less than or equal to the Deductible, we will not pay for that loss. If the adjusted amount of loss exceeds the Deductible, we will then subtract the Deductible from the adjusted amount of loss, and will pay the resulting amount or the Limit of Insurance, whichever is less.

When the occurrence involves loss to more than one item of Covered Property and separate Limits of Insurance apply, the losses will not be combined in determining application of the Deductible. But the Deductible will be applied only once per occurrence.

EXAMPLE #1

(This example assumes there is no Coinsurance penalty.)

Deductible:	$ 250
Limit of Insurance – Building #1:	$ 60,000
Limit of Insurance – Building #2:	$ 80,000
Loss to Building #1:	$ 60,100
Loss to Building #2:	$ 90,000

The amount of loss to Building #1 ($60,100) is less than the sum ($60,250) of the Limit of Insurance applicable to Building #1 plus the Deductible.

The Deductible will be subtracted from the amount of loss in calculating the loss payable for Building #1:

$$\begin{array}{r} \$\ 60,100 \\ -\ \ \ \ 250 \\ \hline \$\ 59,850 \end{array}\ \text{Loss Payable – Building \#1}$$

The Deductible applies once per occurrence and therefore is not subtracted in determining the amount of loss payable for Building #2. Loss payable for Building #2 is the Limit of Insurance of $80,000.

Total amount of loss payable:

$59,850 + $80,000 = $139,850

EXAMPLE #2

(This example, too, assumes there is no Coinsurance penalty.)

The Deductible and Limits of Insurance are the same as those in Example #1.

Loss to Building #1:	$ 70,000
(Exceeds Limit of Insurance plus Deductible)	
Loss to Building #2:	$ 90,000
(Exceeds Limit of Insurance plus Deductible)	
Loss Payable – Building #1:	$ 60,000
(Limit of Insurance)	
Loss Payable – Building #2:	$ 80,000
(Limit of Insurance)	
Total amount of loss payable:	$ 140,000

E. Loss Conditions

The following conditions apply in addition to the Common Policy Conditions and the Commercial Property Conditions.

1. Abandonment

There can be no abandonment of any property to us.

2. Appraisal

If we and you disagree on the value of the property or the amount of loss, either may make written demand for an appraisal of the loss. In this event, each party will select a competent and impartial appraiser. The two appraisers will select an umpire. If they cannot agree, either may request that selection be made by a judge of a court having jurisdiction. The appraisers will state separately the value of the property and amount of loss. If they fail to agree, they will submit their differences to the umpire. A decision agreed to by any two will be binding. Each party will:

a. Pay its chosen appraiser; and

b. Bear the other expenses of the appraisal and umpire equally.

If there is an appraisal, we will still retain our right to deny the claim.

3. Duties In The Event Of Loss Or Damage

a. You must see that the following are done in the event of loss or damage to Covered Property:

(1) Notify the police if a law may have been broken.

(2) Give us prompt notice of the loss or damage. Include a description of the property involved.

(3) As soon as possible, give us a description of how, when and where the loss or damage occurred.

(4) Take all reasonable steps to protect the Covered Property from further damage, and keep a record of your expenses necessary to protect the Covered Property, for consideration in the settlement of the claim. This will not increase the Limit of Insurance. However, we will not pay for any subsequent loss or damage resulting from a cause of loss that is not a Covered Cause of Loss. Also, if feasible, set the damaged property aside and in the best possible order for examination.

(5) At our request, give us complete inventories of the damaged and undamaged property. Include quantities, costs, values and amount of loss claimed.

(6) As often as may be reasonably required, permit us to inspect the property proving the loss or damage and examine your books and records.

Also permit us to take samples of damaged and undamaged property for inspection, testing and analysis, and permit us to make copies from your books and records.

(7) Send us a signed, sworn proof of loss containing the information we request to investigate the claim. You must do this within 60 days after our request. We will supply you with the necessary forms.

(8) Cooperate with us in the investigation or settlement of the claim.

b. We may examine any insured under oath, while not in the presence of any other insured and at such times as may be reasonably required, about any matter relating to this insurance or the claim, including an insured's books and records. In the event of an examination, an insured's answers must be signed.

4. Loss Payment

a. In the event of loss or damage covered by this Coverage Form, at our option, we will either:

(1) Pay the value of lost or damaged property;

(2) Pay the cost of repairing or replacing the lost or damaged property, subject to **b.** below;

(3) Take all or any part of the property at an agreed or appraised value; or

(4) Repair, rebuild or replace the property with other property of like kind and quality, subject to **b.** below.

We will determine the value of lost or damaged property, or the cost of its repair or replacement, in accordance with the applicable terms of the Valuation Condition in this Coverage Form or any applicable provision which amends or supersedes the Valuation Condition.

b. The cost to repair, rebuild or replace does not include the increased cost attributable to enforcement of any ordinance or law regulating the construction, use or repair of any property.

c. We will give notice of our intentions within 30 days after we receive the sworn proof of loss.

d. We will not pay you more than your financial interest in the Covered Property.

e. We may adjust losses with the owners of lost or damaged property if other than you. If we pay the owners, such payments will satisfy your claims against us for the owners' property. We will not pay the owners more than their financial interest in the Covered Property.

f. We may elect to defend you against suits arising from claims of owners of property. We will do this at our expense.

g. We will pay for covered loss or damage within 30 days after we receive the sworn proof of loss, if you have complied with all of the terms of this Coverage Part and:

(1) We have reached agreement with you on the amount of loss; or

(2) An appraisal award has been made.

Commercial Property

CP 00 10 06 07   □

h. A party wall is a wall that separates and is common to adjoining buildings that are owned by different parties. In settling covered losses involving a party wall, we will pay a proportion of the loss to the party wall based on your interest in the wall in proportion to the interest of the owner of the adjoining building. However, if you elect to repair or replace your building and the owner of the adjoining building elects not to repair or replace that building, we will pay you the full value of the loss to the party wall, subject to all applicable policy provisions including Limits of Insurance, the Valuation and Coinsurance Conditions and all other provisions of this Loss Payment Condition. Our payment under the provisions of this paragraph does not alter any right of subrogation we may have against any entity, including the owner or insurer of the adjoining building, and does not alter the terms of the Transfer Of Rights Of Recovery Against Others To Us Condition in this policy.

5. Recovered Property

If either you or we recover any property after loss settlement, that party must give the other prompt notice. At your option, the property will be returned to you. You must then return to us the amount we paid to you for the property. We will pay recovery expenses and the expenses to repair the recovered property, subject to the Limit of Insurance.

6. Vacancy

a. Description Of Terms

(1) As used in this Vacancy Condition, the term building and the term vacant have the meanings set forth in **(1)(a)** and **(1)(b)** below:

(a) When this policy is issued to a tenant, and with respect to that tenant's interest in Covered Property, building means the unit or suite rented or leased to the tenant. Such building is vacant when it does not contain enough business personal property to conduct customary operations.

(b) When this policy is issued to the owner or general lessee of a building, building means the entire building. Such building is vacant unless at least 31% of its total square footage is:

(i) Rented to a lessee or sub-lessee and used by the lessee or sub-lessee to conduct its customary operations; and/or

(ii) Used by the building owner to conduct customary operations.

(2) Buildings under construction or renovation are not considered vacant.

b. Vacancy Provisions

If the building where loss or damage occurs has been vacant for more than 60 consecutive days before that loss or damage occurs:

(1) We will not pay for any loss or damage caused by any of the following even if they are Covered Causes of Loss:

(a) Vandalism;

(b) Sprinkler leakage, unless you have protected the system against freezing;

(c) Building glass breakage;

(d) Water damage;

(e) Theft; or

(f) Attempted theft.

(2) With respect to Covered Causes of Loss other than those listed in **b.(1)(a)** through **b.(1)(f)** above, we will reduce the amount we would otherwise pay for the loss or damage by 15%.

7. Valuation

We will determine the value of Covered Property in the event of loss or damage as follows:

a. At actual cash value as of the time of loss or damage, except as provided in **b., c., d.** and **e.** below.

b. If the Limit of Insurance for Building satisfies the Additional Condition, Coinsurance, and the cost to repair or replace the damaged building property is $2,500 or less, we will pay the cost of building repairs or replacement.

The cost of building repairs or replacement does not include the increased cost attributable to enforcement of any ordinance or law regulating the construction, use or repair of any property.

However, the following property will be valued at the actual cash value even when attached to the building:

(1) Awnings or floor coverings;

(2) Appliances for refrigerating, ventilating, cooking, dishwashing or laundering; or

(3) Outdoor equipment or furniture.

c. "Stock" you have sold but not delivered at the selling price less discounts and expenses you otherwise would have had.

d. Glass at the cost of replacement with safety-glazing material if required by law.

e. Tenants' Improvements and Betterments at:

(1) Actual cash value of the lost or damaged property if you make repairs promptly.

(2) A proportion of your original cost if you do not make repairs promptly. We will determine the proportionate value as follows:

(a) Multiply the original cost by the number of days from the loss or damage to the expiration of the lease; and

(b) Divide the amount determined in **(a)** above by the number of days from the installation of improvements to the expiration of the lease.

If your lease contains a renewal option, the expiration of the renewal option period will replace the expiration of the lease in this procedure.

(3) Nothing if others pay for repairs or replacement.

F. Additional Conditions

The following conditions apply in addition to the Common Policy Conditions and the Commercial Property Conditions.

1. Coinsurance

If a Coinsurance percentage is shown in the Declarations, the following condition applies.

a. We will not pay the full amount of any loss if the value of Covered Property at the time of loss times the Coinsurance percentage shown for it in the Declarations is greater than the Limit of Insurance for the property.

Instead, we will determine the most we will pay using the following steps:

(1) Multiply the value of Covered Property at the time of loss by the Coinsurance percentage;

(2) Divide the Limit of Insurance of the property by the figure determined in Step **(1)**;

(3) Multiply the total amount of loss, before the application of any deductible, by the figure determined in Step **(2)**; and

(4) Subtract the deductible from the figure determined in Step **(3)**.

We will pay the amount determined in Step **(4)** or the limit of insurance, whichever is less. For the remainder, you will either have to rely on other insurance or absorb the loss yourself.

EXAMPLE #1 (UNDERINSURANCE)

When:		
The value of the property is:	$ 250,000
The Coinsurance percentage for it is:	80%
The Limit of Insurance for it is:	$ 100,000
The Deductible is:	$ 250
The amount of loss is:	$ 40,000

Step **(1)**: $250,000 x 80% = $200,000

(the minimum amount of insurance to meet your Coinsurance requirements)

Step **(2)**: $100,000 ÷ $200,000 = .50

Step **(3)**: $40,000 x .50 = $20,000

Step **(4)**: $20,000 − $250 = $19,750

We will pay no more than $19,750. The remaining $20,250 is not covered.

Commercial Property

EXAMPLE #2 (ADEQUATE INSURANCE)

When:	The value of the property is:	$ 250,000
	The Coinsurance percentage for it is:	80%
	The Limit of Insurance for it is:	$ 200,000
	The Deductible is:	$ 250
	The amount of loss is:	$ 40,000

The minimum amount of insurance to meet your Coinsurance requirement is $200,000 ($250,000 x 80%). Therefore, the Limit of Insurance in this example is adequate and no penalty applies. We will pay no more than $39,750 ($40,000 amount of loss minus the deductible of $250).

b. If one Limit of Insurance applies to two or more separate items, this condition will apply to the total of all property to which the limit applies.

EXAMPLE #3

When:	The value of the property is:	
	Building at Location #1:	$ 75,000
	Building at Location #2:	$ 100,000
	Personal Property at Location #2:	$ 75,000
		$ 250,000
	The Coinsurance percentage for it is:	90%
	The Limit of Insurance for Buildings and Personal Property at Locations #1 and #2 is:	$ 180,000
	The Deductible is:	$ 1,000
	The amount of loss is:	
	Building at Location #2:	$ 30,000
	Personal Property at Location #2:	$ 20,000
		$ 50,000

Step **(1):** $250,000 x 90% = $225,000

(the minimum amount of insurance to meet your Coinsurance requirements and to avoid the penalty shown below)

Step **(2):** $180,000 ÷ $225,000 = .80

Step **(3):** $50,000 x .80 = $40,000

Step **(4):** $40,000 – $1,000 = $39,000

We will pay no more than $39,000. The remaining $11,000 is not covered.

2. Mortgageholders

a. The term mortgageholder includes trustee.

b. We will pay for covered loss of or damage to buildings or structures to each mortgageholder shown in the Declarations in their order of precedence, as interests may appear.

c. The mortgageholder has the right to receive loss payment even if the mortgageholder has started foreclosure or similar action on the building or structure.

d. If we deny your claim because of your acts or because you have failed to comply with the terms of this Coverage Part, the mortgageholder will still have the right to receive loss payment if the mortgageholder:

(1) Pays any premium due under this Coverage Part at our request if you have failed to do so;

(2) Submits a signed, sworn proof of loss within 60 days after receiving notice from us of your failure to do so; and

(3) Has notified us of any change in ownership, occupancy or substantial change in risk known to the mortgageholder.

All of the terms of this Coverage Part will then apply directly to the mortgageholder.

e. If we pay the mortgageholder for any loss or damage and deny payment to you because of your acts or because you have failed to comply with the terms of this Coverage Part:

(1) The mortgageholder's rights under the mortgage will be transferred to us to the extent of the amount we pay; and

(2) The mortgageholder's right to recover the full amount of the mortgageholder's claim will not be impaired.

At our option, we may pay to the mortgageholder the whole principal on the mortgage plus any accrued interest. In this event, your mortgage and note will be transferred to us and you will pay your remaining mortgage debt to us.

f. If we cancel this policy, we will give written notice to the mortgageholder at least:

(1) 10 days before the effective date of cancellation if we cancel for your nonpayment of premium; or

(2) 30 days before the effective date of cancellation if we cancel for any other reason.

g. If we elect not to renew this policy, we will give written notice to the mortgageholder at least 10 days before the expiration date of this policy.

G. Optional Coverages

If shown as applicable in the Declarations, the following Optional Coverages apply separately to each item.

1. Agreed Value

a. The Additional Condition, Coinsurance, does not apply to Covered Property to which this Optional Coverage applies. We will pay no more for loss of or damage to that property than the proportion that the Limit of Insurance under this Coverage Part for the property bears to the Agreed Value shown for it in the Declarations.

b. If the expiration date for this Optional Coverage shown in the Declarations is not extended, the Additional Condition, Coinsurance, is reinstated and this Optional Coverage expires.

c. The terms of this Optional Coverage apply only to loss or damage that occurs:

(1) On or after the effective date of this Optional Coverage; and

(2) Before the Agreed Value expiration date shown in the Declarations or the policy expiration date, whichever occurs first.

2. Inflation Guard

a. The Limit of Insurance for property to which this Optional Coverage applied will automatically increase by the annual percentage shown in the Declarations.

b. The amount of increase will be:

(1) The Limit of Insurance that applied on the most recent of the policy inception date, the policy anniversary date, or any other policy change amending the Limit of Insurance, times

(2) The percentage of annual increase shown in the Declarations, expressed as a decimal (example: 8% is .08), times

(3) The number of days since the beginning of the current policy year or the effective date of the most recent policy change amending the Limit of Insurance, divided by 365.

EXAMPLE

If: The applicable Limit of Insurance is: $ 100,000

The annual percentage increase is: 8%

The number of days since the beginning of the policy year (or last policy change) is: 146

The amount of increase is:
$100,000 x .08 x 146 ÷ 365 = $ 3,200

3. Replacement Cost

a. Replacement Cost (without deduction for depreciation) replaces Actual Cash Value in the Valuation Loss Condition of this Coverage Form.

b. This Optional Coverage does not apply to:

(1) Personal property of others;

(2) Contents of a residence;

(3) Works of art, antiques or rare articles, including etchings, pictures, statuary, marbles, bronzes, porcelains and bric-a-brac; or

(4) "Stock", unless the Including "Stock" option is shown in the Declarations.

Under the terms of this Replacement Cost Optional Coverage, tenants' improvements and betterments are not considered to be the personal property of others.

c. You may make a claim for loss or damage covered by this insurance on an actual cash value basis instead of on a replacement cost basis. In the event you elect to have loss or damage settled on an actual cash value basis, you may still make a claim for the additional coverage this Optional Coverage provides if you notify us of your intent to do so within 180 days after the loss or damage.

d. We will not pay on a replacement cost basis for any loss or damage:

(1) Until the lost or damaged property is actually repaired or replaced; and

(2) Unless the repairs or replacement are made as soon as reasonably possible after the loss or damage.

Commercial Property

With respect to tenants' improvements and betterments, the following also apply:

(3) If the conditions in **d.(1)** and **d.(2)** above are not met, the value of tenants' improvements and betterments will be determined as a proportion of your original cost, as set forth in the Valuation Loss Condition of this Coverage Form; and

(4) We will not pay for loss or damage to tenants' improvements and betterments if others pay for repairs or replacement.

e. We will not pay more for loss or damage on a replacement cost basis than the least of **(1)**, **(2)** or **(3)**, subject to **f.** below:

(1) The Limit of Insurance applicable to the lost or damaged property;

(2) The cost to replace the lost or damaged property with other property:

(a) Of comparable material and quality; and

(b) Used for the same purpose; or

(3) The amount actually spent that is necessary to repair or replace the lost or damaged property.

If a building is rebuilt at a new premises, the cost described in **e.(2)** above is limited to the cost which would have been incurred if the building had been rebuilt at the original premises.

f. The cost of repair or replacement does not include the increased cost attributable to enforcement of any ordinance or law regulating the construction, use or repair of any property.

4. Extension Of Replacement Cost To Personal Property Of Others

a. If the Replacement Cost Optional Coverage is shown as applicable in the Declarations, then this Extension may also be shown as applicable. If the Declarations show this Extension as applicable, then Paragraph **3.b.(1)** of the Replacement Cost Optional Coverage is deleted and all other provisions of the Replacement Cost Optional Coverage apply to replacement cost on personal property of others.

b. With respect to replacement cost on the personal property of others, the following limitation applies:

If an item(s) of personal property of others is subject to a written contract which governs your liability for loss or damage to that item(s), then valuation of that item(s) will be based on the amount for which you are liable under such contract, but not to exceed the lesser of the replacement cost of the property or the applicable Limit of Insurance.

H. Definitions

1. "Fungus" means any type or form of fungus, including mold or mildew, and any mycotoxins, spores, scents or by-products produced or released by fungi.

2. "Pollutants" means any solid, liquid, gaseous or thermal irritant or contaminant, including smoke, vapor, soot, fumes, acids, alkalis, chemicals and waste. Waste includes materials to be recycled, reconditioned or reclaimed.

3. "Stock" means merchandise held in storage or for sale, raw materials and in-process or finished goods, including supplies used in their packing or shipping.

POLICY NUMBER:

COMMERCIAL PROPERTY
CP 13 10 04 02

THIS ENDORSEMENT CHANGES THE POLICY. PLEASE READ IT CAREFULLY.

VALUE REPORTING FORM

This endorsement modifies insurance provided under the following:

BUILDING AND PERSONAL PROPERTY COVERAGE FORM
CONDOMINIUM COMMERCIAL UNIT-OWNERS COVERAGE FORM
STANDARD PROPERTY POLICY

One or more of the following symbols will be shown in the Declarations in place of a Coinsurance percentage: DR, WR, MR, QR, PR. For an explanation of these symbols, refer to "Reporting Period" under Section **D.** – Definitions.

A. Additional Covered Property

1. Covered Property is extended to include personal property at the following types of locations for which a Limit of Insurance is shown in the Declarations or on the Reported – Acquired – Incidental Locations Schedule:

   a. "Reported locations";

   b. "Acquired locations"; and

   c. "Incidental locations".

2. The following is added to Property Not Covered:

   Covered Property does not include property at fairs or exhibitions.

B. Reporting Provisions

For Covered Property to which this endorsement applies:

1. **Reports Of Values**

   a. You must file a report with us following each "reporting period" and at expiration, in accordance with **b.** or **c.** below, showing the values of Covered Property separately at each location. Each report must show the values that existed on the dates required by the "reporting period"; these dates are the report dates.

   b. If this policy is a renewal of a value reporting form policy we previously issued, you must file a report with us within 30 days of the end of each "reporting period" and at expiration.

   c. If coverage was not previously issued by us on a value reporting form basis and:

      (1) Reporting Period symbol DR (Daily), WR (Weekly) or MR (Monthly) is shown in the Declarations, you must:

      (a) File the first report with us within 60 days of the end of the first "reporting period"; and

      (b) File the second report with us within 30 days of the end of the second "reporting period", concurrent with submission of the first report; and

      (c) File each subsequent report with us within 30 days of the end of each subsequent "reporting period" and at expiration.

      (2) Reporting Period symbol QR (Quarterly) is shown in the Declarations and the inception date of the policy falls in March, June, September or December, you must:

      (a) File the first report with us within 60 days of the end of the first "reporting period"; and

      (b) File each subsequent report with us within 30 days of the end of each subsequent "reporting period" and at expiration.

      (3) Reporting Period symbol QR (Quarterly) is shown in the Declarations and the inception date of the policy does **not** fall in March, June, September or December, you must file a report with us within 30 days of the end of each "reporting period" and at expiration.

      (4) Reporting Period symbol PR (Policy Year) is shown in the Declarations, you must file a report with us within 30 days of the end of each "reporting period" and at expiration.

   d. For property at "incidental locations", your reports must show separately the entire values in each state.

e. You may not correct inaccurate reports after loss or damage.

2. Full Reporting

The **Coinsurance** Additional Condition is replaced by the following:

COINSURANCE

a. If your report of values for a location where loss or damage occurs, for the last "reporting period" before loss or damage, shows less than the full value of the Covered Property at that location on the report dates, we will pay only a proportion of the loss. The proportion of loss payable, prior to application of the deductible, will not be greater than the proportion determined by:

(1) The values you reported for the location where the loss or damage occurred, divided by

(2) The value of the Covered Property at that location on the report dates.

b. For locations you acquire after the last report of values, we will not pay a greater proportion of loss, prior to the application of the deductible, than the proportion determined by:

(1) The values you reported for all locations, divided by

(2) The value of the Covered Property at all locations on the report dates.

Example of Under Reporting:

If: The values reported are	$	90,000
The actual values on the report dates were	$	120,000
The deductible is	$	250
The amount of loss is	$	60,000

Step **a:** $90,000 ÷ $120,000 = .75

Step **b:** .75 x $60,000 = $45,000

Step **c:** $45,000 – $250 = $44,750

The most we will pay is $44,750. The remaining $15,250 is not covered.

3. Reports In Excess Of Limit Of Insurance

If the values you report exceed the Limit of Insurance:

a. We will determine final premium based on all the values you report, less "specific insurance";

b. In the event of loss or damage, we will not pay more than the Limit of Insurance applicable to the Covered Property.

4. Failure To Submit Reports

If at the time of loss or damage you have failed to submit:

a. The first required report of values:

(1) We will not pay more than 75% of the amount we would otherwise have paid; and

(2) We will only pay for loss or damage at locations shown in the Declarations.

b. Any required report of values after the first required report:

(1) We will not pay more for loss or damage at any location than the values you last reported for that location; and

(2) We will only pay for loss or damage at locations reported in your last report filed before the loss.

5. Treatment Of "Specific Insurance"

a. You must include the amount of all "specific insurance" in your reports of value.

b. We will subtract the value of "specific insurance" from your values when computing advance and final premium under this endorsement.

Example:

If: The value of the property is	$ 400,000
The amount of "specific insurance" is	$ 50,000
The Limit of Insurance under this form is	$ 300,000
Your report of values should show:	
Value of Property	$ 400,000
Amount of "Specific Insurance"	$ 50,000
Difference	$ 350,000

We will compute final premium based on the values in excess of reported "specific insurance" during the policy year.

c. Subject to all other applicable provisions of this policy, including the applicable Limit of Insurance, the most we will pay is that portion of the loss that exceeds the sum of **(1)** and **(2)** below:

(1) The amount due from "specific insurance", whether you can collect on it or not; plus

(2) The amount of any deductible applying to such "specific insurance".

       CP 13 10 04 02   ☐

Examples

The following examples assume that the Reporting Provisions applicable to this form have been complied with.

If: the amount of the "specific insurance" is $50,000;

the Limit of Insurance under this form is $300,000;

the Deductible applicable to the "specific insurance" is $5,000; and

the Deductible applicable to this insurance is $1,000;

we will determine the most we will pay as follows:

Example #1

("Specific insurance" **not** subject to a coinsurance requirement.)

Amount of loss		$300,000
Deductibles		
"Specific Insurance"	$ 5,000	
This insurance	$ 1,000	
Amount due from		
"Specific Insurance"	$50,000*	
	$56,000	– $ 56,000
The most this insurance will pay		$244,000

The most payable, combined, from the "specific insurance" and this insurance is $294,000 ($50,000 + $244,000). The remainder of the loss, $6,000, is not covered.

Example #2

("Specific insurance" subject to 100% coinsurance requirement. Value of property at time of loss is $350,000.)

Amount of loss		$300,000
Deductibles		
"Specific Insurance"	$ 5,000	
This insurance	$ 1,000	
Amount due from		
"Specific Insurance"	$37,900*	
	$43,900	– $ 43,900
The most this insurance will pay		$256,100

The most payable, combined, from the "specific insurance" and this insurance is $294,000 ($37,900 + $256,100). The remainder of the loss, $6,000, is not covered.

Example #3

("Specific insurance" subject to 100% coinsurance requirement. Value of property at time of loss is $370,000.)

Amount of loss		$360,000
Deductibles		
"Specific Insurance"	$ 5,000	
This insurance	$ 1,000	
Amount due from		
"Specific Insurance"	$43,600*	
	$49,600	– $ 49,600
		$310,400

The most this insurance will pay is $300,000 (the Limit of Insurance).

The most payable, combined, from the "specific insurance" and this insurance is $343,600 ($43,600 + $300,000). The remainder of the loss, $16,400, is not covered.

*The amount due from "specific insurance" will vary based on such factors as the amount of loss, the value of property at time of loss, and the coinsurance requirement, if any, applicable under the policy providing "specific insurance".

C. Premium Adjustment

For Covered Property to which this endorsement applies:

1. The premium charged at the inception of each policy year is an advance premium. We will determine the final premium for this insurance after the policy year, or expiration, based on the average of your reports of value.

2. Based on the difference between the advance premium and the final premium, for each policy year, we will:

   a. Charge additional premium; or

   b. Return excess premium.

   The due date for any additional premium is the date shown as the due date on the bill.

D. Definitions

1. **"Acquired Locations"** means any locations in the policy territory acquired after the inception of the coverage under this endorsement.

2. **"Incidental Locations"** means any locations not shown in the Declarations, other than "acquired locations" and "reported locations", with values of $25,000 or less.

3. **"Reported Locations"** means any locations, other than those shown in the Declarations, that have been reported to us at the inception of the coverage under this endorsement.

4. **"Reporting Period"** means the period of time for which new reports of value are due, as shown by a symbol in the Declarations. If the symbol is:

   a. DR (Daily), reports must show values as of each day; but the "reporting period" ends on the last day of the month.

   b. WR (Weekly), reports must show values as of the last day of each week; but the "reporting period" ends on the last day of the month.

   c. MR (Monthly), reports must show values as of the last day of the month; and the "reporting period" ends on the last day of each month.

   d. QR (Quarterly), reports must show values as of the last day of each month; but the "reporting period" ends on the last day of:

      (1) March;

      (2) June;

      (3) September; and

      (4) December.

   e. PR (Policy Year), reports must show values as of the last day of each month; but the "reporting period" ends on the policy anniversary date.

5. **"Specific Insurance"** means other insurance that:

   a. Covers the same Covered Property to which this endorsement applies; and

   b. Is not subject to the same plan, terms, conditions and provisions as this insurance, including this endorsement.

COMMERCIAL PROPERTY
CP 10 20 06 07

CAUSES OF LOSS – BROAD FORM

A. Covered Causes Of Loss

When Broad is shown in the Declarations, Covered Causes of Loss means the following:

1. Fire.

2. Lightning.

3. Explosion, including the explosion of gases or fuel within the furnace of any fired vessel or within the flues or passages through which the gases of combustion pass. This cause of loss does not include loss or damage by:

   a. Rupture, bursting or operation of pressure-relief devices; or

   b. Rupture or bursting due to expansion or swelling of the contents of any building or structure, caused by or resulting from water.

4. Windstorm or Hail, but not including:

   a. Frost or cold weather;

   b. Ice (other than hail), snow or sleet, whether driven by wind or not; or

   c. Loss or damage to the interior of any building or structure, or the property inside the building or structure, caused by rain, snow, sand or dust, whether driven by wind or not, unless the building or structure first sustains wind or hail damage to its roof or walls through which the rain, snow, sand or dust enters.

5. Smoke causing sudden and accidental loss or damage. This cause of loss does not include smoke from agricultural smudging or industrial operations.

6. Aircraft or Vehicles, meaning only physical contact of an aircraft, a spacecraft, a self-propelled missile, a vehicle or an object thrown up by a vehicle with the described property or with the building or structure containing the described property. This cause of loss includes loss or damage by objects falling from aircraft.

   We will not pay for loss or damage caused by or resulting from vehicles you own or which are operated in the course of your business.

7. Riot or Civil Commotion, including:

   a. Acts of striking employees while occupying the described premises; and

   b. Looting occurring at the time and place of a riot or civil commotion.

8. Vandalism, meaning willful and malicious damage to, or destruction of, the described property.

   We will not pay for loss or damage caused by or resulting from theft, except for building damage caused by the breaking in or exiting of burglars.

9. Sprinkler Leakage, meaning leakage or discharge of any substance from an Automatic Sprinkler System, including collapse of a tank that is part of the system.

   If the building or structure containing the Automatic Sprinkler System is Covered Property, we will also pay the cost to:

   a. Repair or replace damaged parts of the Automatic Sprinkler System if the damage:

      (1) Results in sprinkler leakage; or

      (2) Is directly caused by freezing.

   b. Tear out and replace any part of the building or structure to repair damage to the Automatic Sprinkler System that has resulted in sprinkler leakage.

   Automatic Sprinkler System means:

      (1) Any automatic fire-protective or extinguishing system, including connected:

         (a) Sprinklers and discharge nozzles;

         (b) Ducts, pipes, valves and fittings;

         (c) Tanks, their component parts and supports; and

         (d) Pumps and private fire protection mains.

      (2) When supplied from an automatic fire-protective system:

         (a) Non-automatic fire-protective systems; and

         (b) Hydrants, standpipes and outlets.

10. Sinkhole Collapse, meaning loss or damage caused by the sudden sinking or collapse of land into underground empty spaces created by the action of water on limestone or dolomite. This cause of loss does not include:

    a. The cost of filling sinkholes; or

    b. Sinking or collapse of land into man-made underground cavities.

11. Volcanic Action, meaning direct loss or damage resulting from the eruption of a volcano when the loss or damage is caused by:

  a. Airborne volcanic blast or airborne shock waves;

  b. Ash, dust or particulate matter; or

  c. Lava flow.

All volcanic eruptions that occur within any 168-hour period will constitute a single occurrence.

This cause of loss does not include the cost to remove ash, dust or particulate matter that does not cause direct physical loss or damage to the described property.

12. Falling Objects

But we will not pay for loss or damage to:

  a. Personal property in the open; or

  b. The interior of a building or structure, or property inside a building or structure, unless the roof or an outside wall of the building or structure is first damaged by a falling object.

13. Weight Of Snow, Ice Or Sleet

But we will not pay for loss or damage to personal property outside of buildings or structures.

14. Water Damage

  a. Water Damage, meaning accidental discharge or leakage of water or steam as the direct result of the breaking apart or cracking of a plumbing, heating, air conditioning or other system or appliance, that is located on the described premises and contains water or steam.

However, Water Damage does not include:

  (1) Discharge or leakage from:

    (a) An Automatic Sprinkler System;

    (b) A sump or related equipment and parts, including overflow due to sump pump failure or excessive volume of water; or

    (c) Roof drains, gutters, downspouts or similar fixtures or equipment;

  (2) The cost to repair any defect that caused the loss or damage;

  (3) Loss or damage caused by or resulting from continuous or repeated seepage or leakage of water, or the presence or condensation of humidity, moisture or vapor, that occurs over a period of 14 days or more; or

  (4) Loss or damage caused by or resulting from freezing, unless:

    (a) You do your best to maintain heat in the building or structure; or

    (b) You drain the equipment and shut off the water supply if the heat is not maintained.

  b. If coverage applies subject to **a.** above, and the building or structure containing the system or appliance is Covered Property, we will also pay the cost to tear out and replace any part of the building or structure to repair damage to the system or appliance from which the water or steam escapes. But we will not pay the cost to repair any defect that caused the loss or damage.

B. Exclusions

  1. We will not pay for loss or damage caused directly or indirectly by any of the following. Such loss or damage is excluded regardless of any other cause or event that contributes concurrently or in any sequence to the loss.

    a. Ordinance Or Law

    The enforcement of any ordinance or law:

    (1) Regulating the construction, use or repair of any property; or

    (2) Requiring the tearing down of any property including the cost of removing its debris.

    This exclusion, Ordinance Or Law, applies whether the loss results from:

    (a) An ordinance or law that is enforced even if the property has not been damaged; or

    (b) The increased costs incurred to comply with an ordinance or law in the course of construction, repair, renovation, remodeling or demolition of property, or removal of its debris, following a physical loss to that property.

    b. Earth Movement

    (1) Earthquake, including any earth sinking, rising or shifting related to such event;

    (2) Landslide, including any earth sinking, rising or shifting related to such event;

    (3) Mine subsidence, meaning subsidence of a man-made mine, whether or not mining activity has ceased;

(4) Earth sinking (other than sinkhole collapse), rising or shifting including soil conditions which cause settling, cracking or other disarrangement of foundations or other parts of realty. Soil conditions include contraction, expansion, freezing, thawing, erosion, improperly compacted soil and the action of water under the ground surface.

But if Earth Movement, as described in **b.(1)** through **(4)** above, results in fire or explosion, we will pay for the loss or damage caused by that fire or explosion.

(5) Volcanic eruption, explosion or effusion. But if volcanic eruption, explosion or effusion results in fire, building glass breakage or Volcanic Action, we will pay for the loss or damage caused by that fire, building glass breakage or Volcanic Action.

c. Governmental Action

Seizure or destruction of property by order of governmental authority.

But we will pay for loss or damage caused by or resulting from acts of destruction ordered by governmental authority and taken at the time of a fire to prevent its spread, if the fire would be covered under this Coverage Part.

d. Nuclear Hazard

Nuclear reaction or radiation, or radioactive contamination, however caused.

But if nuclear reaction or radiation, or radioactive contamination, results in fire, we will pay for the loss or damage caused by that fire.

e. Utility Services

The failure of power, communication, water or other utility service supplied to the described premises, however caused, if the failure:

(1) Originates away from the described premises; or

(2) Originates at the described premises, but only if such failure involves equipment used to supply the utility service to the described premises from a source away from the described premises.

Failure of any utility service includes lack of sufficient capacity and reduction in supply.

Loss or damage caused by a surge of power is also excluded, if the surge would not have occurred but for an event causing a failure of power.

But if the failure or surge of power, or the failure of communication, water or other utility service, results in a Covered Cause of Loss, we will pay for the loss or damage caused by that Covered Cause of Loss.

Communication services include but are not limited to service relating to Internet access or access to any electronic, cellular or satellite network.

f. War And Military Action

(1) War, including undeclared or civil war;

(2) Warlike action by a military force, including action in hindering or defending against an actual or expected attack, by any government, sovereign or other authority using military personnel or other agents; or

(3) Insurrection, rebellion, revolution, usurped power, or action taken by governmental authority in hindering or defending against any of these.

g. Water

(1) Flood, surface water, waves, tides, tidal waves, overflow of any body of water, or their spray, all whether driven by wind or not;

(2) Mudslide or mudflow;

(3) Water that backs up or overflows from a sewer, drain or sump; or

(4) Water under the ground surface pressing on, or flowing or seeping through:

(a) Foundations, walls, floors or paved surfaces;

(b) Basements, whether paved or not; or

(c) Doors, windows or other openings.

But if Water, as described in **g.(1)** through **g.(4)** above, results in fire, explosion or sprinkler leakage, we will pay for the loss or damage caused by that fire, explosion or sprinkler leakage.

h. "Fungus", Wet Rot, Dry Rot And Bacteria

Presence, growth, proliferation, spread or any activity of "fungus", wet or dry rot or bacteria.

But if "fungus", wet or dry rot or bacteria results in a Covered Cause of Loss, we will pay for the loss or damage caused by that Covered Cause of Loss.

Commercial Property

This exclusion does not apply:

1. When "fungus", wet or dry rot or bacteria results from fire or lightning; or

2. To the extent that coverage is provided in the Additional Coverage – Limited Coverage For "Fungus", Wet Rot, Dry Rot And Bacteria with respect to loss or damage by a cause of loss other than fire or lightning.

Exclusions **B.1.a.** through **B.1.h.** apply whether or not the loss event results in widespread damage or affects a substantial area.

2. We will not pay for loss or damage caused by or resulting from:

   a. Artificially generated electrical, magnetic or electromagnetic energy that damages, disturbs, disrupts or otherwise interferes with any:

      (1) Electrical or electronic wire, device, appliance, system or network; or

      (2) Device, appliance, system or network utilizing cellular or satellite technology.

      For the purpose of this exclusion, electrical, magnetic or electromagnetic energy includes but is not limited to:

      (a) Electrical current, including arcing;

      (b) Electrical charge produced or conducted by a magnetic or electromagnetic field;

      (c) Pulse of electromagnetic energy; or

      (d) Electromagnetic waves or microwaves.

      But if fire results, we will pay for the loss or damage caused by that fire.

   b. Explosion of steam boilers, steam pipes, steam engines or steam turbines owned or leased by you, or operated under your control.

      But if explosion of steam boilers, steam pipes, steam engines or steam turbines results in fire or combustion explosion, we will pay for the loss or damage caused by that fire or combustion explosion.

   c. Mechanical breakdown, including rupture or bursting caused by centrifugal force.

      But if mechanical breakdown results in a Covered Cause of Loss, we will pay for the loss or damage caused by that Covered Cause of Loss.

   d. Neglect of an insured to use all reasonable means to save and preserve property from further damage at and after the time of loss.

3. **Special Exclusions**

   The following provisions apply only to the specified Coverage Forms.

   a. **Business Income (And Extra Expense) Coverage Form, Business Income (Without Extra Expense) Coverage Form, Or Extra Expense Coverage Form**

      We will not pay for:

      (1) Any loss caused by or resulting from:

          (a) Damage or destruction of "finished stock"; or

          (b) The time required to reproduce "finished stock".

          This exclusion does not apply to Extra Expense.

      (2) Any loss caused by or resulting from direct physical loss or damage to radio or television antennas (including satellite dishes) and their lead-in wiring, masts or towers.

      (3) Any increase of loss caused by or resulting from:

          (a) Delay in rebuilding, repairing or replacing the property or resuming "operations", due to interference at the location of the rebuilding, repair or replacement by strikers or other persons; or

          (b) Suspension, lapse or cancellation of any license, lease or contract. But if the suspension, lapse or cancellation is directly caused by the "suspension" of "operations", we will cover such loss that affects your Business Income during the "period of restoration" and any extension of the "period of restoration" in accordance with the terms of the Extended Business Income Additional Coverage and the Extended Period Of Indemnity Optional Coverage or any variation of these.

      (4) Any Extra Expense caused by or resulting from suspension, lapse or cancellation of any license, lease or contract beyond the "period of restoration".

      (5) Any other consequential loss.

 CP 10 20 06 07 ☐

b. Leasehold Interest Coverage Form

(1) Paragraph **B.1.a.**, Ordinance Or Law, does not apply to insurance under this Coverage Form.

(2) We will not pay for any loss caused by:

(a) Your cancelling the lease;

(b) The suspension, lapse or cancellation of any license; or

(c) Any other consequential loss.

c. Legal Liability Coverage Form

(1) The following exclusions do not apply to insurance under this Coverage Form:

(a) Paragraph **B.1.a.**, Ordinance Or Law;

(b) Paragraph **B.1.c.**, Governmental Action;

(c) Paragraph **B.1.d.**, Nuclear Hazard;

(d) Paragraph **B.1.e.**, Utility Services; and

(e) Paragraph **B.1.f.**, War And Military Action.

(2) The following additional exclusions apply to insurance under this Coverage Form:

(a) **Contractual Liability**

We will not defend any claim or "suit", or pay damages that you are legally liable to pay, solely by reason of your assumption of liability in a contract or agreement. But this exclusion does not apply to a written lease agreement in which you have assumed liability for building damage resulting from an actual or attempted burglary or robbery, provided that:

(i) Your assumption of liability was executed prior to the accident; and

(ii) The building is Covered Property under this Coverage Form.

(b) **Nuclear Hazard**

We will not defend any claim or "suit", or pay any damages, loss, expense or obligation, resulting from nuclear reaction or radiation, or radioactive contamination, however caused.

C. Additional Coverage – Collapse

The coverage provided under this Additional Coverage – Collapse applies only to an abrupt collapse as described and limited in **C.1.** through **C.7.**

1. For the purpose of this Additional Coverage – Collapse, abrupt collapse means an abrupt falling down or caving in of a building or any part of a building with the result that the building or part of the building cannot be occupied for its intended purpose.

2. We will pay for direct physical loss or damage to Covered Property, caused by abrupt collapse of a building or any part of a building that is insured under this Coverage Form or that contains Covered Property insured under this Coverage Form, if such collapse is caused by one or more of the following:

a. Fire; lightning; explosion; windstorm or hail; smoke; aircraft or vehicles; riot or civil commotion; vandalism; leakage from fire-extinguishing equipment; sinkhole collapse; volcanic action; breakage of building glass; falling objects; weight of snow, ice or sleet; water damage, meaning accidental discharge or leakage of water or steam as the direct result of the breaking apart or cracking of a plumbing, heating, air conditioning or other system or appliance (other than a sump system including its related equipment and parts), that is located on the described premises and contains water or steam; all only as insured against in this Coverage Part;

b. Building decay that is hidden from view, unless the presence of such decay is known to an insured prior to collapse;

c. Insect or vermin damage that is hidden from view, unless the presence of such damage is known to an insured prior to collapse;

d. Weight of people or personal property;

e. Weight of rain that collects on a roof;

f. Use of defective material or methods in construction, remodeling or renovation if the abrupt collapse occurs during the course of the construction, remodeling or renovation. However, if such collapse occurs after construction, remodeling or renovation is complete and is caused in part by a cause of loss listed in **2.a.** through **2.e.**, we will pay for the loss or damage even if use of defective material or methods, in construction, remodeling or renovation, contributes to the collapse.

Commercial Property

This Additional Coverage – Collapse does not limit the coverage otherwise provided under this Causes of Loss Form for the causes of loss listed in **2.a.**

3. This **Additional Coverage – Collapse** does **not** apply to:

   a. A building or any part of a building that is in danger of falling down or caving in;

   b. A part of a building that is standing, even if it has separated from another part of the building; or

   c. A building that is standing or any part of a building that is standing, even if it shows evidence of cracking, bulging, sagging, bending, leaning, settling, shrinkage or expansion.

4. With respect to the following property:

   a. Outdoor radio or television antennas (including satellite dishes) and their lead-in wiring, masts or towers;

   b. Awnings, gutters and downspouts;

   c. Yard fixtures;

   d. Outdoor swimming pools;

   e. Fences;

   f. Piers, wharves and docks;

   g. Beach or diving platforms or appurtenances;

   h. Retaining walls; and

   i. Walks, roadways and other paved surfaces;

   if an abrupt collapse is caused by a cause of loss listed in **2.b.** through **2.f.** we will pay for loss or damage to that property only if:

   (1) Such loss or damage is a direct result of the abrupt collapse of a building insured under this Coverage Form; and

   (2) The property is Covered Property under this Coverage Form.

5. If personal property abruptly falls down or caves in and such collapse is **not** the result of abrupt collapse of a building, we will pay for loss or damage to Covered Property caused by such collapse of personal property only if:

   a. The collapse of personal property was caused by a cause of loss listed in **2.a.** through **2.f.** above;

   b. The personal property which collapses is inside a building; and

   c. The property which collapses is not of a kind listed in **4.**, regardless of whether that kind of property is considered to be personal property or real property.

The coverage stated in this Paragraph **5.** does not apply to personal property if marring and/or scratching is the only damage to that personal property caused by the collapse.

6. This Additional Coverage – Collapse does not apply to personal property that has not abruptly fallen down or caved in, even if the personal property shows evidence of cracking, bulging, sagging, bending, leaning, settling, shrinkage or expansion.

7. This Additional Coverage – Collapse will not increase the Limits of Insurance provided in this Coverage Part.

8. The term Covered Cause of Loss includes the Additional Coverage – Collapse as described and limited in **C.1.** through **C.7.**

D. **Additional Coverage – Limited Coverage For "Fungus", Wet Rot, Dry Rot And Bacteria**

1. The coverage described in **D.2.** and **D.6.** only applies when the "fungus", wet or dry rot or bacteria is the result of one or more of the following causes that occurs during the policy period and only if all reasonable means were used to save and preserve the property from further damage at the time of and after that occurrence.

   a. A Covered Cause of Loss other than fire or lightning; or

   b. Flood, if the Flood Coverage Endorsement applies to the affected premises.

2. We will pay for loss or damage by "fungus", wet or dry rot or bacteria. As used in this Limited Coverage, the term loss or damage means:

   a. Direct physical loss or damage to Covered Property caused by "fungus", wet or dry rot or bacteria, including the cost of removal of the "fungus", wet or dry rot or bacteria;

   b. The cost to tear out and replace any part of the building or other property as needed to gain access to the "fungus", wet or dry rot or bacteria; and

   c. The cost of testing performed after removal, repair, replacement or restoration of the damaged property is completed, provided there is a reason to believe that "fungus", wet or dry rot or bacteria are present.

3. The coverage described under **D.2.** of this Limited Coverage is limited to $15,000. Regardless of the number of claims, this limit is the most we will pay for the total of all loss or damage arising out of all occurrences of Covered Causes of Loss (other than fire or lightning) and Flood which take place in a 12-month period (starting with the beginning of the present annual policy period). With respect to a particular occurrence of loss which results in "fungus", wet or dry rot or bacteria, we will not pay more than a total of $15,000 even if the "fungus", wet or dry rot or bacteria continues to be present or active, or recurs, in a later policy period.

4. The coverage provided under this Limited Coverage does not increase the applicable Limit of Insurance on any Covered Property. If a particular occurrence results in loss or damage by "fungus", wet or dry rot or bacteria, and other loss or damage, we will not pay more, for the total of all loss or damage, than the applicable Limit of Insurance on the affected Covered Property.

   If there is covered loss or damage to Covered Property, not caused by "fungus", wet or dry rot or bacteria, loss payment will not be limited by the terms of this Limited Coverage, except to the extent that "fungus", wet or dry rot or bacteria causes an increase in the loss. Any such increase in the loss will be subject to the terms of this Limited Coverage.

5. The terms of this Limited Coverage do not increase or reduce the coverage provided under Paragraph **b.** of Covered Cause Of Loss **9.**, Sprinkler Leakage, or Paragraph **b.** of Covered Causes Of Loss **14.**, Water Damage, or under the Additional Coverage – Collapse.

6. The following, **6.a.** or **6.b.**, applies only if Business Income and/or Extra Expense Coverage applies to the described premises and only if the "suspension" of "operations" satisfies all terms and conditions of the applicable Business Income and/or Extra Expense Coverage Form.

   a. If the loss which resulted in "fungus", wet or dry rot or bacteria does not in itself necessitate a "suspension" of "operations", but such "suspension" is necessary due to loss or damage to property caused by "fungus", wet or dry rot or bacteria, then our payment under Business Income and/or Extra Expense is limited to the amount of loss and/or expense sustained in a period of not more than 30 days. The days need not be consecutive.

   b. If a covered "suspension" of "operations" was caused by loss or damage other than "fungus", wet or dry rot or bacteria but remediation of "fungus", wet or dry rot or bacteria prolongs the "period of restoration", we will pay for loss and/or expense sustained during the delay (regardless of when such a delay occurs during the "period of restoration"), but such coverage is limited to 30 days. The days need not be consecutive.

E. Limitation

We will pay for loss of animals only if they are killed or their destruction is made necessary.

F. Definitions

"Fungus" means any type or form of fungus, including mold or mildew, and any mycotoxins, spores, scents or by-products produced or released by fungi.

Commercial Property

COMMERCIAL PROPERTY
CP 10 30 06 07

CAUSES OF LOSS – SPECIAL FORM

Words and phrases that appear in quotation marks have special meaning. Refer to Section **G.**, Definitions.

A. Covered Causes Of Loss

When Special is shown in the Declarations, Covered Causes of Loss means Risks Of Direct Physical Loss unless the loss is:

1. Excluded in Section **B.**, Exclusions; or

2. Limited in Section **C.**, Limitations;

that follow.

B. Exclusions

1. We will not pay for loss or damage caused directly or indirectly by any of the following. Such loss or damage is excluded regardless of any other cause or event that contributes concurrently or in any sequence to the loss.

a. Ordinance Or Law

The enforcement of any ordinance or law:

(1) Regulating the construction, use or repair of any property; or

(2) Requiring the tearing down of any property, including the cost of removing its debris.

This exclusion, Ordinance Or Law, applies whether the loss results from:

(a) An ordinance or law that is enforced even if the property has not been damaged; or

(b) The increased costs incurred to comply with an ordinance or law in the course of construction, repair, renovation, remodeling or demolition of property, or removal of its debris, following a physical loss to that property.

b. Earth Movement

(1) Earthquake, including any earth sinking, rising or shifting related to such event;

(2) Landslide, including any earth sinking, rising or shifting related to such event;

(3) Mine subsidence, meaning subsidence of a man-made mine, whether or not mining activity has ceased;

(4) Earth sinking (other than sinkhole collapse), rising or shifting including soil conditions which cause settling, cracking or other disarrangement of foundations or other parts of realty. Soil conditions include contraction, expansion, freezing, thawing, erosion, improperly compacted soil and the action of water under the ground surface.

But if Earth Movement, as described in **b.(1)** through **(4)** above, results in fire or explosion, we will pay for the loss or damage caused by that fire or explosion.

(5) Volcanic eruption, explosion or effusion. But if volcanic eruption, explosion or effusion results in fire, building glass breakage or Volcanic Action, we will pay for the loss or damage caused by that fire, building glass breakage or Volcanic Action.

Volcanic Action means direct loss or damage resulting from the eruption of a volcano when the loss or damage is caused by:

(a) Airborne volcanic blast or airborne shock waves;

(b) Ash, dust or particulate matter; or

(c) Lava flow.

All volcanic eruptions that occur within any 168-hour period will constitute a single occurrence.

Volcanic Action does not include the cost to remove ash, dust or particulate matter that does not cause direct physical loss or damage to the described property.

c. Governmental Action

Seizure or destruction of property by order of governmental authority.

But we will pay for loss or damage caused by or resulting from acts of destruction ordered by governmental authority and taken at the time of a fire to prevent its spread, if the fire would be covered under this Coverage Part.

d. Nuclear Hazard

Nuclear reaction or radiation, or radioactive contamination, however caused.

But if nuclear reaction or radiation, or radioactive contamination, results in fire, we will pay for the loss or damage caused by that fire.

e. Utility Services

The failure of power, communication, water or other utility service supplied to the described premises, however caused, if the failure:

(1) Originates away from the described premises; or

(2) Originates at the described premises, but only if such failure involves equipment used to supply the utility service to the described premises from a source away from the described premises.

Failure of any utility service includes lack of sufficient capacity and reduction in supply.

Loss or damage caused by a surge of power is also excluded, if the surge would not have occurred but for an event causing a failure of power.

But if the failure or surge of power, or the failure of communication, water or other utility service, results in a Covered Cause of Loss, we will pay for the loss or damage caused by that Covered Cause of Loss.

Communication services include but are not limited to service relating to Internet access or access to any electronic, cellular or satellite network.

f. War And Military Action

(1) War, including undeclared or civil war;

(2) Warlike action by a military force, including action in hindering or defending against an actual or expected attack, by any government, sovereign or other authority using military personnel or other agents; or

(3) Insurrection, rebellion, revolution, usurped power, or action taken by governmental authority in hindering or defending against any of these.

g. Water

(1) Flood, surface water, waves, tides, tidal waves, overflow of any body of water, or their spray, all whether driven by wind or not;

(2) Mudslide or mudflow;

(3) Water that backs up or overflows from a sewer, drain or sump; or

(4) Water under the ground surface pressing on, or flowing or seeping through:

(a) Foundations, walls, floors or paved surfaces;

(b) Basements, whether paved or not; or

(c) Doors, windows or other openings.

But if Water, as described in **g.(1)** through **g.(4)** above, results in fire, explosion or sprinkler leakage, we will pay for the loss or damage caused by that fire, explosion or sprinkler leakage.

h. "Fungus", Wet Rot, Dry Rot And Bacteria

Presence, growth, proliferation, spread or any activity of "fungus", wet or dry rot or bacteria.

But if "fungus", wet or dry rot or bacteria results in a "specified cause of loss", we will pay for the loss or damage caused by that "specified cause of loss".

This exclusion does not apply:

1. When "fungus", wet or dry rot or bacteria results from fire or lightning; or

2. To the extent that coverage is provided in the Additional Coverage – Limited Coverage For "Fungus", Wet Rot, Dry Rot And Bacteria with respect to loss or damage by a cause of loss other than fire or lightning.

Exclusions **B.1.a.** through **B.1.h.** apply whether or not the loss event results in widespread damage or affects a substantial area.

2. We will not pay for loss or damage caused by or resulting from any of the following:

a. Artificially generated electrical, magnetic or electromagnetic energy that damages, disturbs, disrupts or otherwise interferes with any:

(1) Electrical or electronic wire, device, appliance, system or network; or

(2) Device, appliance, system or network utilizing cellular or satellite technology.

For the purpose of this exclusion, electrical, magnetic or electromagnetic energy includes but is not limited to:

(a) Electrical current, including arcing;

(b) Electrical charge produced or conducted by a magnetic or electromagnetic field;

(c) Pulse of electromagnetic energy; or

(d) Electromagnetic waves or microwaves.

But if fire results, we will pay for the loss or damage caused by that fire.

b. Delay, loss of use or loss of market.

c. Smoke, vapor or gas from agricultural smudging or industrial operations.

d. (1) Wear and tear;

(2) Rust or other corrosion, decay, deterioration, hidden or latent defect or any quality in property that causes it to damage or destroy itself;

(3) Smog;

(4) Settling, cracking, shrinking or expansion;

(5) Nesting or infestation, or discharge or release of waste products or secretions, by insects, birds, rodents or other animals.

(6) Mechanical breakdown, including rupture or bursting caused by centrifugal force. But if mechanical breakdown results in elevator collision, we will pay for the loss or damage caused by that elevator collision.

(7) The following causes of loss to personal property:

(a) Dampness or dryness of atmosphere;

(b) Changes in or extremes of temperature; or

(c) Marring or scratching.

But if an excluded cause of loss that is listed in **2.d.(1)** through **(7)** results in a "specified cause of loss" or building glass breakage, we will pay for the loss or damage caused by that "specified cause of loss" or building glass breakage.

e. Explosion of steam boilers, steam pipes, steam engines or steam turbines owned or leased by you, or operated under your control. But if explosion of steam boilers, steam pipes, steam engines or steam turbines results in fire or combustion explosion, we will pay for the loss or damage caused by that fire or combustion explosion. We will also pay for loss or damage caused by or resulting from the explosion of gases or fuel within the furnace of any fired vessel or within the flues or passages through which the gases of combustion pass.

f. Continuous or repeated seepage or leakage of water, or the presence or condensation of humidity, moisture or vapor, that occurs over a period of 14 days or more.

g. Water, other liquids, powder or molten material that leaks or flows from plumbing, heating, air conditioning or other equipment (except fire protective systems) caused by or resulting from freezing, unless:

(1) You do your best to maintain heat in the building or structure; or

(2) You drain the equipment and shut off the supply if the heat is not maintained.

h. Dishonest or criminal act by you, any of your partners, members, officers, managers, employees (including leased employees), directors, trustees, authorized representatives or anyone to whom you entrust the property for any purpose:

(1) Acting alone or in collusion with others; or

(2) Whether or not occurring during the hours of employment.

This exclusion does not apply to acts of destruction by your employees (including leased employees); but theft by employees (including leased employees) is not covered.

i. Voluntary parting with any property by you or anyone else to whom you have entrusted the property if induced to do so by any fraudulent scheme, trick, device or false pretense.

j. Rain, snow, ice or sleet to personal property in the open.

k. Collapse, including any of the following conditions of property or any part of the property:

(1) An abrupt falling down or caving in;

(2) Loss of structural integrity, including separation of parts of the property or property in danger of falling down or caving in; or

(3) Any cracking, bulging, sagging, bending, leaning, settling, shrinkage or expansion as such condition relates to **(1)** or **(2)** above.

But if collapse results in a Covered Cause of Loss at the described premises, we will pay for the loss or damage caused by that Covered Cause of Loss.

This exclusion, **k.**, does not apply:

(a) To the extent that coverage is provided under the Additional Coverage – Collapse; or

(b) To collapse caused by one or more of the following:

(i) The "specified causes of loss";

(ii) Breakage of building glass;

(iii) Weight of rain that collects on a roof; or

(iv) Weight of people or personal property.

l. Discharge, dispersal, seepage, migration, release or escape of "pollutants" unless the discharge, dispersal, seepage, migration, release or escape is itself caused by any of the "specified causes of loss". But if the discharge, dispersal, seepage, migration, release or escape of "pollutants" results in a "specified cause of loss", we will pay for the loss or damage caused by that "specified cause of loss".

This exclusion, **l.**, does not apply to damage to glass caused by chemicals applied to the glass.

m. Neglect of an insured to use all reasonable means to save and preserve property from further damage at and after the time of loss.

3. We will not pay for loss or damage caused by or resulting from any of the following, **3.a.** through **3.c.** But if an excluded cause of loss that is listed in **3.a.** through **3.c.** results in a Covered Cause of Loss, we will pay for the loss or damage caused by that Covered Cause of Loss.

a. Weather conditions. But this exclusion only applies if weather conditions contribute in any way with a cause or event excluded in Paragraph **1.** above to produce the loss or damage.

b. Acts or decisions, including the failure to act or decide, of any person, group, organization or governmental body.

c. Faulty, inadequate or defective:

(1) Planning, zoning, development, surveying, siting;

(2) Design, specifications, workmanship, repair, construction, renovation, remodeling, grading, compaction;

(3) Materials used in repair, construction, renovation or remodeling; or

(4) Maintenance;

of part or all of any property on or off the described premises.

4. Special Exclusions

The following provisions apply only to the specified Coverage Forms.

a. Business Income (And Extra Expense) Coverage Form, Business Income (Without Extra Expense) Coverage Form, Or Extra Expense Coverage Form

We will not pay for:

(1) Any loss caused by or resulting from:

(a) Damage or destruction of "finished stock"; or

(b) The time required to reproduce "finished stock".

This exclusion does not apply to Extra Expense.

(2) Any loss caused by or resulting from direct physical loss or damage to radio or television antennas (including satellite dishes) and their lead-in wiring, masts or towers.

(3) Any increase of loss caused by or resulting from:

(a) Delay in rebuilding, repairing or replacing the property or resuming "operations", due to interference at the location of the rebuilding, repair or replacement by strikers or other persons; or

Commercial Property

(b) Suspension, lapse or cancellation of any license, lease or contract. But if the suspension, lapse or cancellation is directly caused by the "suspension" of "operations", we will cover such loss that affects your Business Income during the "period of restoration" and any extension of the "period of restoration" in accordance with the terms of the Extended Business Income Additional Coverage and the Extended Period Of Indemnity Optional Coverage or any variation of these.

(4) Any Extra Expense caused by or resulting from suspension, lapse or cancellation of any license, lease or contract beyond the "period of restoration".

(5) Any other consequential loss.

b. Leasehold Interest Coverage Form

(1) Paragraph **B.1.a.**, Ordinance Or Law, does not apply to insurance under this Coverage Form.

(2) We will not pay for any loss caused by:

(a) Your cancelling the lease;

(b) The suspension, lapse or cancellation of any license; or

(c) Any other consequential loss.

c. Legal Liability Coverage Form

(1) The following exclusions do not apply to insurance under this Coverage Form:

(a) Paragraph **B.1.a.**, Ordinance Or Law;

(b) Paragraph **B.1.c.**, Governmental Action;

(c) Paragraph **B.1.d.**, Nuclear Hazard;

(d) Paragraph **B.1.e.**, Utility Services; and

(e) Paragraph **B.1.f.**, War And Military Action.

(2) The following additional exclusions apply to insurance under this Coverage Form:

(a) Contractual Liability

We will not defend any claim or "suit", or pay damages that you are legally liable to pay, solely by reason of your assumption of liability in a contract or agreement. But this exclusion does not apply to a written lease agreement in which you have assumed liability for building damage resulting from an actual or attempted burglary or robbery, provided that:

(i) Your assumption of liability was executed prior to the accident; and

(ii) The building is Covered Property under this Coverage Form.

(b) Nuclear Hazard

We will not defend any claim or "suit", or pay any damages, loss, expense or obligation, resulting from nuclear reaction or radiation, or radioactive contamination, however caused.

5. Additional Exclusion

The following provisions apply only to the specified property.

LOSS OR DAMAGE TO PRODUCTS

We will not pay for loss or damage to any merchandise, goods or other product caused by or resulting from error or omission by any person or entity (including those having possession under an arrangement where work or a portion of the work is outsourced) in any stage of the development, production or use of the product, including planning, testing, processing, packaging, installation, maintenance or repair. This exclusion applies to any effect that compromises the form, substance or quality of the product. But if such error or omission results in a Covered Cause of Loss, we will pay for the loss or damage caused by that Covered Cause of Loss.

C. Limitations

The following limitations apply to all policy forms and endorsements, unless otherwise stated.

1. We will not pay for loss of or damage to property, as described and limited in this section. In addition, we will not pay for any loss that is a consequence of loss or damage as described and limited in this section.

   a. Steam boilers, steam pipes, steam engines or steam turbines caused by or resulting from any condition or event inside such equipment. But we will pay for loss of or damage to such equipment caused by or resulting from an explosion of gases or fuel within the furnace of any fired vessel or within the flues or passages through which the gases of combustion pass.

   b. Hot water boilers or other water heating equipment caused by or resulting from any condition or event inside such boilers or equipment, other than an explosion.

   c. The interior of any building or structure, or to personal property in the building or structure, caused by or resulting from rain, snow, sleet, ice, sand or dust, whether driven by wind or not, unless:

      (1) The building or structure first sustains damage by a Covered Cause of Loss to its roof or walls through which the rain, snow, sleet, ice, sand or dust enters; or

      (2) The loss or damage is caused by or results from thawing of snow, sleet or ice on the building or structure.

   d. Building materials and supplies not attached as part of the building or structure, caused by or resulting from theft.

      However, this limitation does not apply to:

      (1) Building materials and supplies held for sale by you, unless they are insured under the Builders Risk Coverage Form; or

      (2) Business Income Coverage or Extra Expense Coverage.

   e. Property that is missing, where the only evidence of the loss or damage is a shortage disclosed on taking inventory, or other instances where there is no physical evidence to show what happened to the property.

   f. Property that has been transferred to a person or to a place outside the described premises on the basis of unauthorized instructions.

2. We will not pay for loss of or damage to the following types of property unless caused by the "specified causes of loss" or building glass breakage:

   a. Animals, and then only if they are killed or their destruction is made necessary.

   b. Fragile articles such as statuary, marbles, chinaware and porcelains, if broken. This restriction does not apply to:

      (1) Glass; or

      (2) Containers of property held for sale.

   c. Builders' machinery, tools and equipment owned by you or entrusted to you, provided such property is Covered Property.

      However, this limitation does not apply:

      (1) If the property is located on or within 100 feet of the described premises, unless the premises is insured under the Builders Risk Coverage Form; or

      (2) To Business Income Coverage or to Extra Expense Coverage.

3. The special limit shown for each category, **a.** through **d.,** is the total limit for loss of or damage to all property in that category. The special limit applies to any one occurrence of theft, regardless of the types or number of articles that are lost or damaged in that occurrence. The special limits are:

   a. $2,500 for furs, fur garments and garments trimmed with fur.

   b. $2,500 for jewelry, watches, watch movements, jewels, pearls, precious and semi-precious stones, bullion, gold, silver, platinum and other precious alloys or metals. This limit does not apply to jewelry and watches worth $100 or less per item.

   c. $2,500 for patterns, dies, molds and forms.

   d. $250 for stamps, tickets, including lottery tickets held for sale, and letters of credit.

   These special limits are part of, not in addition to, the Limit of Insurance applicable to the Covered Property.

   This limitation, **C.3.,** does not apply to Business Income Coverage or to Extra Expense Coverage.

4. We will not pay the cost to repair any defect to a system or appliance from which water, other liquid, powder or molten material escapes. But we will pay the cost to repair or replace damaged parts of fire-extinguishing equipment if the damage:

a. Results in discharge of any substance from an automatic fire protection system; or

b. Is directly caused by freezing.

However, this limitation does not apply to Business Income Coverage or to Extra Expense Coverage.

D. Additional Coverage – Collapse

The coverage provided under this Additional Coverage – Collapse applies only to an abrupt collapse as described and limited in **D.1.** through **D.7.**

1. For the purpose of this Additional Coverage – Collapse, abrupt collapse means an abrupt falling down or caving in of a building or any part of a building with the result that the building or part of the building cannot be occupied for its intended purpose.

2. We will pay for direct physical loss or damage to Covered Property, caused by abrupt collapse of a building or any part of a building that is insured under this Coverage Form or that contains Covered Property insured under this Coverage Form, if such collapse is caused by one or more of the following:

a. Building decay that is hidden from view, unless the presence of such decay is known to an insured prior to collapse;

b. Insect or vermin damage that is hidden from view, unless the presence of such damage is known to an insured prior to collapse;

c. Use of defective material or methods in construction, remodeling or renovation if the abrupt collapse occurs during the course of the construction, remodeling or renovation.

d. Use of defective material or methods in construction, remodeling or renovation if the abrupt collapse occurs after the construction, remodeling or renovation is complete, but only if the collapse is caused in part by:

(1) A cause of loss listed in **2.a.** or **2.b.**;

(2) One or more of the "specified causes of loss";

(3) Breakage of building glass;

(4) Weight of people or personal property; or

(5) Weight of rain that collects on a roof.

3. This **Additional Coverage – Collapse** does **not** apply to:

a. A building or any part of a building that is in danger of falling down or caving in;

b. A part of a building that is standing, even if it has separated from another part of the building; or

c. A building that is standing or any part of a building that is standing, even if it shows evidence of cracking, bulging, sagging, bending, leaning, settling, shrinkage or expansion.

4. With respect to the following property:

a. Outdoor radio or television antennas (including satellite dishes) and their lead-in wiring, masts or towers;

b. Awnings, gutters and downspouts;

c. Yard fixtures;

d. Outdoor swimming pools;

e. Fences;

f. Piers, wharves and docks;

g. Beach or diving platforms or appurtenances;

h. Retaining walls; and

i. Walks, roadways and other paved surfaces;

if an abrupt collapse is caused by a cause of loss listed in **2.a.** through **2.d.**, we will pay for loss or damage to that property only if:

(1) Such loss or damage is a direct result of the abrupt collapse of a building insured under this Coverage Form; and

(2) The property is Covered Property under this Coverage Form.

5. If personal property abruptly falls down or caves in and such collapse is **not** the result of abrupt collapse of a building, we will pay for loss or damage to Covered Property caused by such collapse of personal property only if:

a. The collapse of personal property was caused by a cause of loss listed in **2.a.** through **2.d.**;

b. The personal property which collapses is inside a building; and

c. The property which collapses is not of a kind listed in **4.**, regardless of whether that kind of property is considered to be personal property or real property.

The coverage stated in this Paragraph **5.** does not apply to personal property if marring and/or scratching is the only damage to that personal property caused by the collapse.

6. This Additional Coverage – Collapse does not apply to personal property that has not abruptly fallen down or caved in, even if the personal property shows evidence of cracking, bulging, sagging, bending, leaning, settling, shrinkage or expansion.

7. This Additional Coverage – Collapse will not increase the Limits of Insurance provided in this Coverage Part.

8. The term Covered Cause of Loss includes the Additional Coverage – Collapse as described and limited in **D.1.** through **D.7.**

E. **Additional Coverage – Limited Coverage For "Fungus", Wet Rot, Dry Rot And Bacteria**

1. The coverage described in **E.2.** and **E.6.** only applies when the "fungus", wet or dry rot or bacteria is the result of one or more of the following causes that occurs during the policy period and only if all reasonable means were used to save and preserve the property from further damage at the time of and after that occurrence.

   a. A "specified cause of loss" other than fire or lightning; or

   b. Flood, if the Flood Coverage Endorsement applies to the affected premises.

2. We will pay for loss or damage by "fungus", wet or dry rot or bacteria. As used in this Limited Coverage, the term loss or damage means:

   a. Direct physical loss or damage to Covered Property caused by "fungus", wet or dry rot or bacteria, including the cost of removal of the "fungus", wet or dry rot or bacteria;

   b. The cost to tear out and replace any part of the building or other property as needed to gain access to the "fungus", wet or dry rot or bacteria; and

   c. The cost of testing performed after removal, repair, replacement or restoration of the damaged property is completed, provided there is a reason to believe that "fungus", wet or dry rot or bacteria are present.

3. The coverage described under **E.2.** of this Limited Coverage is limited to $15,000. Regardless of the number of claims, this limit is the most we will pay for the total of all loss or damage arising out of all occurrences of "specified causes of loss" (other than fire or lightning) and Flood which take place in a 12-month period (starting with the beginning of the present annual policy period). With respect to a particular occurrence of loss which results in "fungus", wet or dry rot or bacteria, we will not pay more than a total of $15,000 even if the "fungus", wet or dry rot or bacteria continues to be present or active, or recurs, in a later policy period.

4. The coverage provided under this Limited Coverage does not increase the applicable Limit of Insurance on any Covered Property. If a particular occurrence results in loss or damage by "fungus", wet or dry rot or bacteria, and other loss or damage, we will not pay more, for the total of all loss or damage, than the applicable Limit of Insurance on the affected Covered Property.

   If there is covered loss or damage to Covered Property, not caused by "fungus", wet or dry rot or bacteria, loss payment will not be limited by the terms of this Limited Coverage, except to the extent that "fungus", wet or dry rot or bacteria causes an increase in the loss. Any such increase in the loss will be subject to the terms of this Limited Coverage.

5. The terms of this Limited Coverage do not increase or reduce the coverage provided under Paragraph **F.2.** (Water Damage, Other Liquids, Powder Or Molten Material Damage) of this Causes Of Loss Form or under the Additional Coverage – Collapse.

6. The following, **6.a.** or **6.b.**, applies only if Business Income and/or Extra Expense Coverage applies to the described premises and only if the "suspension" of "operations" satisfies all terms and conditions of the applicable Business Income and/or Extra Expense Coverage Form.

© ISO Properties, Inc., 2007

Commercial Property

a. If the loss which resulted in "fungus", wet or dry rot or bacteria does not in itself necessitate a "suspension" of "operations", but such "suspension" is necessary due to loss or damage to property caused by "fungus", wet or dry rot or bacteria, then our payment under Business Income and/or Extra Expense is limited to the amount of loss and/or expense sustained in a period of not more than 30 days. The days need not be consecutive.

b. If a covered "suspension" of "operations" was caused by loss or damage other than "fungus", wet or dry rot or bacteria but remediation of "fungus", wet or dry rot or bacteria prolongs the "period of restoration", we will pay for loss and/or expense sustained during the delay (regardless of when such a delay occurs during the "period of restoration"), but such coverage is limited to 30 days. The days need not be consecutive.

F. Additional Coverage Extensions

1. Property In Transit

This Extension applies only to your personal property to which this form applies.

a. You may extend the insurance provided by this Coverage Part to apply to your personal property (other than property in the care, custody or control of your salespersons) in transit more than 100 feet from the described premises. Property must be in or on a motor vehicle you own, lease or operate while between points in the coverage territory.

b. Loss or damage must be caused by or result from one of the following causes of loss:

(1) Fire, lightning, explosion, windstorm or hail, riot or civil commotion, or vandalism.

(2) Vehicle collision, upset or overturn. Collision means accidental contact of your vehicle with another vehicle or object. It does not mean your vehicle's contact with the roadbed.

(3) Theft of an entire bale, case or package by forced entry into a securely locked body or compartment of the vehicle. There must be visible marks of the forced entry.

c. The most we will pay for loss or damage under this Extension is $5,000.

This Coverage Extension is additional insurance. The Additional Condition, Coinsurance, does not apply to this Extension.

2. Water Damage, Other Liquids, Powder Or Molten Material Damage

If loss or damage caused by or resulting from covered water or other liquid, powder or molten material damage loss occurs, we will also pay the cost to tear out and replace any part of the building or structure to repair damage to the system or appliance from which the water or other substance escapes. This Coverage Extension does not increase the Limit of Insurance.

3. Glass

a. We will pay for expenses incurred to put up temporary plates or board up openings if repair or replacement of damaged glass is delayed.

b. We will pay for expenses incurred to remove or replace obstructions when repairing or replacing glass that is part of a building. This does not include removing or replacing window displays.

This Coverage Extension, **F.3.**, does not increase the Limit of Insurance.

G. Definitions

1. "Fungus" means any type or form of fungus, including mold or mildew, and any mycotoxins, spores, scents or by-products produced or released by fungi.

2. "Specified causes of loss" means the following: fire; lightning; explosion; windstorm or hail; smoke; aircraft or vehicles; riot or civil commotion; vandalism; leakage from fire-extinguishing equipment; sinkhole collapse; volcanic action; falling objects; weight of snow, ice or sleet; water damage.

a. Sinkhole collapse means the sudden sinking or collapse of land into underground empty spaces created by the action of water on limestone or dolomite. This cause of loss does not include:

(1) The cost of filling sinkholes; or

(2) Sinking or collapse of land into man-made underground cavities.

b. Falling objects does not include loss or damage to:

(1) Personal property in the open; or

(2) The interior of a building or structure, or property inside a building or structure, unless the roof or an outside wall of the building or structure is first damaged by a falling object.

c. Water damage means accidental discharge or leakage of water or steam as the direct result of the breaking apart or cracking of a plumbing, heating, air conditioning or other system or appliance (other than a sump system including its related equipment and parts), that is located on the described premises and contains water or steam.

Commercial Property

THIS ENDORSEMENT CHANGES THE POLICY. PLEASE READ IT CAREFULLY.

ORDINANCE OR LAW COVERAGE

This endorsement modifies insurance provided under the following:

BUILDING AND PERSONAL PROPERTY COVERAGE FORM
CONDOMINIUM ASSOCIATION COVERAGE FORM
STANDARD PROPERTY POLICY

SCHEDULE*

Bldg. No./ Prem. No.	Cov. A	Cov. B Limit Of Insur.	Cov. C Limit Of Insur.	Cov. B And C Combined Limit Of Insur.
/	☐	$	$	$ **
/	☐	$	$	$ **
/	☐	$	$	$ **

*Information required to complete the Schedule, if not shown on this endorsement, will be shown in the Declarations.

Do **not enter a Combined Limit of Insurance if individual Limits of Insurance are selected for Coverages **B** and **C,** or if one of these Coverages is not applicable.

A. Each Coverage – Coverage **A,** Coverage **B** and Coverage **C** – is provided under this endorsement only if that Coverage(s) is chosen by entry in the above Schedule and then only with respect to the building identified for that Coverage(s) in the Schedule.

B. Application Of Coverage(s)

The Coverage(s) provided by this endorsement apply only if both **B.1.** and **B.2.** are satisfied and are then subject to the qualifications set forth in **B.3.**

1. The ordinance or law:

   a. Regulates the demolition, construction or repair of buildings, or establishes zoning or land use requirements at the described premises; and

   b. Is in force at the time of loss.

   But coverage under this endorsement applies only in response to the minimum requirements of the ordinance or law. Losses and costs incurred in complying with recommended actions or standards that exceed actual requirements are not covered under this endorsement.

2.**a.** The building sustains direct physical damage that is covered under this policy and such damage results in enforcement of the ordinance or law; or

   b. The building sustains both direct physical damage that is covered under this policy and direct physical damage that is not covered under this policy, and the building damage in its entirety results in enforcement of the ordinance or law.

   c. But if the building sustains direct physical damage that is not covered under this policy, and such damage is the subject of the ordinance or law, then there is no coverage under this endorsement even if the building has also sustained covered direct physical damage.

3. In the situation described in **B.2.b.** above, we will not pay the full amount of loss otherwise payable under the terms of Coverages **A, B,** and/or **C** of this endorsement. Instead, we will pay a proportion of such loss; meaning the proportion that the covered direct physical damage bears to the total direct physical damage.

(Section **H.** of this endorsement provides an example of this procedure.)

However, if the covered direct physical damage, alone, would have resulted in enforcement of the ordinance or law, then we will pay the full amount of loss otherwise payable under the terms of Coverages **A, B** and/or **C** of this endorsement.

C. We will not pay under Coverage **A, B** or **C** of this endorsement for:

1. Enforcement of any ordinance or law which requires the demolition, repair, replacement, reconstruction, remodeling or remediation of property due to contamination by "pollutants" or due to the presence, growth, proliferation, spread or any activity of "fungus", wet or dry rot or bacteria; or

2. The costs associated with the enforcement of any ordinance or law which requires any insured or others to test for, monitor, clean up, remove, contain, treat, detoxify or neutralize, or in any way respond to, or assess the effects of "pollutants", "fungus", wet or dry rot or bacteria.

D. Coverage

1. **Coverage A – Coverage For Loss To The Undamaged Portion Of The Building**

   With respect to the building that has sustained covered direct physical damage, we will pay under Coverage **A** for the loss in value of the undamaged portion of the building as a consequence of enforcement of an ordinance or law that requires demolition of undamaged parts of the same building.

   Coverage **A** is included within the Limit of Insurance shown in the Declarations as applicable to the covered building. Coverage **A** does not increase the Limit of Insurance.

2. **Coverage B – Demolition Cost Coverage**

   With respect to the building that has sustained covered direct physical damage, we will pay the cost to demolish and clear the site of undamaged parts of the same building, as a consequence of enforcement of an ordinance or law that requires demolition of such undamaged property.

   The Coinsurance Additional Condition does not apply to Demolition Cost Coverage.

3. **Coverage C – Increased Cost Of Construction Coverage**

   a. With respect to the building that has sustained covered direct physical damage, we will pay the increased cost to:

   (1) Repair or reconstruct damaged portions of that building; and/or

   (2) Reconstruct or remodel undamaged portions of that building, whether or not demolition is required;

   when the increased cost is a consequence of enforcement of the minimum requirements of the ordinance or law.

   However:

   (1) This coverage applies only if the restored or remodeled property is intended for similar occupancy as the current property, unless such occupancy is not permitted by zoning or land use ordinance or law.

   (2) We will not pay for the increased cost of construction if the building is not repaired, reconstructed or remodeled.

   The Coinsurance Additional Condition does not apply to Increased Cost of Construction Coverage.

   b. When a building is damaged or destroyed and Coverage **C** applies to that building in accordance with **3.a.** above, coverage for the increased cost of construction also applies to repair or reconstruction of the following, subject to the same conditions stated in **3.a.**:

   (1) The cost of excavations, grading, backfilling and filling;

   (2) Foundation of the building;

   (3) Pilings; and

   (4) Underground pipes, flues and drains.

   The items listed in **b.(1)** through **b.(4)** above are deleted from Property Not Covered, but only with respect to the coverage described in this Provision, **3.b.**

E. Loss Payment

1. All following loss payment Provisions, **E.2.** through **E.5.**, are subject to the apportionment procedures set forth in Section **B.3.** of this endorsement.

2. When there is a loss in value of an undamaged portion of a building to which Coverage **A** applies, the loss payment for that building, including damaged and undamaged portions, will be determined as follows:

   a. If the Replacement Cost Coverage Option applies and the property is being repaired or replaced, on the same or another premises, we will not pay more than the lesser of:

      (1) The amount you would actually spend to repair, rebuild or reconstruct the building, but not for more than the amount it would cost to restore the building on the same premises and to the same height, floor area, style and comparable quality of the original property insured; or

      (2) The Limit of Insurance shown in the Declarations as applicable to the covered building.

   b. If the Replacement Cost Coverage Option applies and the property is **not** repaired or replaced, or if the Replacement Cost Coverage Option does **not** apply, we will not pay more than the lesser of:

      (1) The actual cash value of the building at the time of loss; or

      (2) The Limit of Insurance shown in the Declarations as applicable to the covered building.

3. Unless Paragraph **E.5.** applies, loss payment under Coverage **B** – Demolition Cost Coverage will be determined as follows:

   We will not pay more than the lesser of the following:

   a. The amount you actually spend to demolish and clear the site of the described premises; or

   b. The applicable Limit of Insurance shown for Coverage **B** in the Schedule above.

4. Unless Paragraph **E.5.** applies, loss payment under Coverage **C** – Increased Cost of Construction Coverage will be determined as follows:

   a. We will not pay under Coverage **C**:

      (1) Until the property is actually repaired or replaced, at the same or another premises; and

      (2) Unless the repairs or replacement are made as soon as reasonably possible after the loss or damage, not to exceed two years. We may extend this period in writing during the two years.

   b. If the building is repaired or replaced at the same premises, or if you elect to rebuild at another premises, the most we will pay under Coverage **C** is the lesser of:

      (1) The increased cost of construction at the same premises; or

      (2) The applicable Limit of Insurance shown for Coverage **C** in the Schedule above.

   c. If the ordinance or law requires relocation to another premises, the most we will pay under Coverage **C** is the lesser of:

      (1) The increased cost of construction at the new premises; or

      (2) The applicable Limit of Insurance shown for Coverage **C** in the Schedule above.

5. If a **Combined** Limit of Insurance is shown for Coverages **B** and **C** in the Schedule above, Paragraphs **E.3.** and **E.4.** of this endorsement do not apply with respect to the building that is subject to the Combined Limit, and the following loss payment provisions apply instead:

   The most we will pay, for the total of all covered losses for Demolition Cost and Increased Cost of Construction, is the Combined Limit of Insurance shown for Coverages **B** and **C** in the Schedule above. Subject to this Combined Limit of Insurance, the following loss payment provisions apply:

   a. For Demolition Cost, we will not pay more than the amount you actually spend to demolish and clear the site of the described premises.

   b. With respect to the Increased Cost of Construction:

      (1) We will not pay for the increased cost of construction:

         (a) Until the property is actually repaired or replaced, at the same or another premises; and

         (b) Unless the repairs or replacement are made as soon as reasonably possible after the loss or damage, not to exceed two years. We may extend this period in writing during the two years.

      (2) If the building is repaired or replaced at the same premises, or if you elect to rebuild at another premises, the most we will pay for the increased cost of construction is the increased cost of construction at the same premises.

(3) If the ordinance or law requires relocation to another premises, the most we will pay for the increased cost of construction is the increased cost of construction at the new premises.

F. The terms of this endorsement apply separately to each building to which this endorsement applies.

G. Under this endorsement we will not pay for loss due to any ordinance or law that:

1. You were required to comply with before the loss, even if the building was undamaged; and

2. You failed to comply with.

H. Example of Proportionate Loss Payment for Ordinance Or Law Coverage Losses (procedure as set forth in Section **B.3.** of this endorsement.)

Assume:

- Wind is a Covered Cause of Loss; Flood is an excluded Cause of Loss
- The building has a value of $200,000
- Total direct physical damage to building: $100,000
- The ordinance or law in this jurisdiction is enforced when building damage equals or exceeds 50% of the building's value
- Portion of direct physical damage that is covered (caused by wind): $30,000
- Portion of direct physical damage that is not covered (caused by flood): $70,000
- Loss under Ordinance Or Law Coverage **C** of this endorsement: $60,000

Step **1:**

Determine the proportion that the covered direct physical damage bears to the total direct physical damage.

$30,000 ÷ $100,000 = .30

Step **2:**

Apply that proportion to the Ordinance or Law loss.

$60,000 x .30 = $18,000

In this example, the most we will pay under this endorsement for the Coverage **C** loss is $18,000, subject to the applicable Limit of Insurance and any other applicable provisions.

Note: The same procedure applies to losses under Coverages **A** and **B** of this endorsement.

I. The following definition is added:

"Fungus" means any type or form of fungus, including mold or mildew, and any mycotoxins, spores, scents or by-products produced or released by fungi.

POLICY NUMBER:

IL 09 85 01 08

THIS ENDORSEMENT IS ATTACHED TO AND MADE PART OF YOUR POLICY IN RESPONSE TO THE DISCLOSURE REQUIREMENTS OF THE TERRORISM RISK INSURANCE ACT. THIS ENDORSEMENT DOES NOT GRANT ANY COVERAGE OR CHANGE THE TERMS AND CONDITIONS OF ANY COVERAGE UNDER THE POLICY.

DISCLOSURE PURSUANT TO TERRORISM RISK INSURANCE ACT

SCHEDULE

Terrorism Premium (Certified Acts) $ **This premium is the total Certified Acts premium attributable to the following Coverage Part(s), Coverage Form(s) and/or Policy(s):**   **Additional information, if any, concerning the terrorism premium:**
Information required to complete this Schedule, if not shown above, will be shown in the Declarations.

A. Disclosure Of Premium

In accordance with the federal Terrorism Risk Insurance Act, we are required to provide you with a notice disclosing the portion of your premium, if any, attributable to coverage for terrorist acts certified under the Terrorism Risk Insurance Act. The portion of your premium attributable to such coverage is shown in the Schedule of this endorsement or in the policy Declarations.

B. Disclosure Of Federal Participation In Payment Of Terrorism Losses

The United States Government, Department of the Treasury, will pay a share of terrorism losses insured under the federal program. The federal share equals 85% of that portion of the amount of such insured losses that exceeds the applicable insurer retention. However, if aggregate insured losses attributable to terrorist acts certified under the Terrorism Risk Insurance Act exceed $100 billion in a Program Year (January 1 through December 31), the Treasury shall not make any payment for any portion of the amount of such losses that exceeds $100 billion.

C. Cap On Insurer Participation In Payment Of Terrorism Losses

If aggregate insured losses attributable to terrorist acts certified under the Terrorism Risk Insurance Act exceed $100 billion in a Program Year (January 1 through December 31) and we have met our insurer deductible under the Terrorism Risk Insurance Act, we shall not be liable for the payment of any portion of the amount of such losses that exceeds $100 billion, and in such case insured losses up to that amount are subject to pro rata allocation in accordance with procedures established by the Secretary of the Treasury.

POLICY NUMBER: **IL 09 53 01 08**

THIS ENDORSEMENT CHANGES THE POLICY. PLEASE READ IT CAREFULLY.

EXCLUSION OF CERTIFIED ACTS OF TERRORISM

This endorsement modifies insurance provided under the following:

> BOILER AND MACHINERY COVERAGE PART
> COMMERCIAL INLAND MARINE COVERAGE PART
> COMMERCIAL PROPERTY COVERAGE PART
> CRIME AND FIDELITY COVERAGE PART
> EQUIPMENT BREAKDOWN COVERAGE PART
> FARM COVERAGE PART
> STANDARD PROPERTY POLICY

SCHEDULE

The **Exception Covering Certain Fire Losses** (Paragraph **C**) applies to property located in the following state(s), if covered under the indicated Coverage Form, Coverage Part or Policy:

State(s)	Coverage Form, Coverage Part Or Policy

Information required to complete this Schedule, if not shown above, will be shown in the Declarations.

A. The following definition is added with respect to the provisions of this endorsement:

"Certified act of terrorism" means an act that is certified by the Secretary of the Treasury, in concurrence with the Secretary of State and the Attorney General of the United States, to be an act of terrorism pursuant to the federal Terrorism Risk Insurance Act. The criteria contained in the Terrorism Risk Insurance Act for a "certified act of terrorism" include the following:

1. The act resulted in insured losses in excess of $5 million in the aggregate, attributable to all types of insurance subject to the Terrorism Risk Insurance Act; and

2. The act is a violent act or an act that is dangerous to human life, property or infrastructure and is committed by an individual or individuals as part of an effort to coerce the civilian population of the United States or to influence the policy or affect the conduct of the United States Government by coercion.

B. The following exclusion is added:

CERTIFIED ACT OF TERRORISM EXCLUSION

We will not pay for loss or damage caused directly or indirectly by a "certified act of terrorism". Such loss or damage is excluded regardless of any other cause or event that contributes concurrently or in any sequence to the loss.

C. Exception Covering Certain Fire Losses

The following exception to the exclusion in Paragraph **B.** applies only if indicated and as indicated in the Schedule of this endorsement.

If a "certified act of terrorism" results in fire, we will pay for the loss or damage caused by that fire. Such coverage for fire applies only to direct loss or damage by fire to Covered Property. Therefore, for example, the coverage does not apply to insurance provided under Business Income and/or Extra Expense coverage forms or endorsements which apply to those forms, or to the Legal Liability Coverage Form or the Leasehold Interest Coverage Form.

IL 09 53 01 08   © ISO Properties, Inc., 2007   **Page 1 of 2**   □

If aggregate insured losses attributable to terrorist acts certified under the Terrorism Risk Insurance Act exceed $100 billion in a Program Year (January 1 through December 31) and we have met our insurer deductible under the Terrorism Risk Insurance Act, we shall not be liable for the payment of any portion of the amount of such losses that exceeds $100 billion, and in such case insured losses up to that amount are subject to pro rata allocation in accordance with procedures established by the Secretary of the Treasury.

D. Application Of Other Exclusions

The terms and limitations of any terrorism exclusion, or the inapplicability or omission of a terrorism exclusion, do not serve to create coverage for any loss which would otherwise be excluded under this Coverage Part or Policy, such as losses excluded by the Nuclear Hazard Exclusion or the War And Military Action Exclusion.

COMMERCIAL PROPERTY
CP 00 17 06 07

CONDOMINIUM ASSOCIATION COVERAGE FORM

Various provisions in this policy restrict coverage. Read the entire policy carefully to determine rights, duties and what is and is not covered.

Throughout this policy the words "you" and "your" refer to the Named Insured shown in the Declarations. The words "we", "us" and "our" refer to the Company providing this insurance.

Other words and phrases that appear in quotation marks have special meaning. Refer to Section **H.**, Definitions.

A. Coverage

We will pay for direct physical loss of or damage to Covered Property at the premises described in the Declarations caused by or resulting from any Covered Cause of Loss.

1. Covered Property

Covered Property, as used in this Coverage Part, means the type of property described in this section, **A.1.**, and limited in **A.2.**, Property Not Covered, if a Limit of Insurance is shown in the Declarations for that type of property.

a. Building, meaning the building or structure described in the Declarations, including:

(1) Completed additions;

(2) Fixtures, outside of individual units, including outdoor fixtures;

(3) Permanently installed:

(a) Machinery; and

(b) Equipment;

(4) Personal property owned by you that is used to maintain or service the building or structure or its premises, including:

(a) Fire-extinguishing equipment;

(b) Outdoor furniture;

(c) Floor coverings; and

(d) Appliances used for refrigerating, ventilating, cooking, dishwashing or laundering that are not contained within individual units;

(5) If not covered by other insurance:

(a) Additions under construction, alterations and repairs to the building or structure;

(b) Materials, equipment, supplies, and temporary structures, on or within 100 feet of the described premises, used for making additions, alterations or repairs to the building or structure; and

(6) Any of the following types of property contained within a unit, regardless of ownership, if your Condominium Association Agreement requires you to insure it:

(a) Fixtures, improvements and alterations that are a part of the building or structure; and

(b) Appliances, such as those used for refrigerating, ventilating, cooking, dishwashing, laundering, security or housekeeping.

But Building does not include personal property owned by, used by or in the care, custody or control of a unit-owner except for personal property listed in Paragraph **A.1.a.(6)** above.

b. Your Business Personal Property located in or on the building described in the Declarations or in the open (or in a vehicle) within 100 feet of the described premises, consisting of the following:

(1) Personal property owned by you or owned indivisibly by all unit-owners;

(2) Your interest in the labor, materials or services furnished or arranged by you on personal property of others;

(3) Leased personal property for which you have a contractual responsibility to insure, unless otherwise provided for under Personal Property Of Others.

But Your Business Personal Property does not include personal property owned only by a unit-owner.

   c. Personal Property Of Others that is:

     (1) In your care, custody or control; and

     (2) Located in or on the building described in the Declarations or in the open (or in a vehicle) within 100 feet of the described premises.

     However, our payment for loss of or damage to personal property of others will only be for the account of the owner of the property.

2. Property Not Covered

Covered Property does not include:

  a. Accounts, bills, currency, food stamps or other evidences of debt, money, notes or securities. Lottery tickets held for sale are not securities;

  b. Animals, unless owned by others and boarded by you;

  c. Automobiles held for sale;

  d. Bridges, roadways, walks, patios or other paved surfaces;

  e. Contraband, or property in the course of illegal transportation or trade;

  f. The cost of excavations, grading, backfilling or filling;

  g. Foundations of buildings, structures, machinery or boilers if their foundations are below:

    (1) The lowest basement floor; or

    (2) The surface of the ground if there is no basement;

  h. Land (including land on which the property is located), water, growing crops or lawns;

  i. Personal property while airborne or waterborne;

  j. Bulkheads, pilings, piers, wharves or docks;

  k. Property that is covered under this or any other policy in which it is more specifically described, except for the excess of the amount due (whether you can collect on it or not) from that other insurance;

  l. Retaining walls that are not part of a building;

  m. Underground pipes, flues or drains;

  n. Electronic data, except as provided under the Additional Coverage, Electronic Data. Electronic data means information, facts or computer programs stored as or on, created or used on, or transmitted to or from computer software (including systems and applications software), on hard or floppy disks, CD-ROMs, tapes, drives, cells, data processing devices or any other repositories of computer software which are used with electronically controlled equipment. The term computer programs, referred to in the foregoing description of electronic data, means a set of related electronic instructions which direct the operations and functions of a computer or device connected to it, which enable the computer or device to receive, process, store, retrieve or send data;

  o. The cost to replace or restore the information on valuable papers and records, including those which exist as electronic data. Valuable papers and records include but are not limited to proprietary information, books of account, deeds, manuscripts, abstracts, drawings and card index systems. Refer to the Coverage Extension for Valuable Papers And Records (Other Than Electronic Data) for limited coverage for valuable papers and records other than those which exist as electronic data;

  p. Vehicles or self-propelled machines (including aircraft or watercraft) that:

    (1) Are licensed for use on public roads; or

    (2) Are operated principally away from the described premises.

    This paragraph does not apply to:

      (a) Vehicles or self-propelled machines or autos you manufacture or warehouse;

      (b) Vehicles or self-propelled machines, other than autos, you hold for sale;

      (c) Rowboats or canoes out of water at the described premises; or

      (d) Trailers, but only to the extent provided for in the Coverage Extension for Non-owned Detached Trailers;

q. The following property while outside of buildings:

(1) Grain, hay, straw or other crops; or

(2) Fences, radio or television antennas (including satellite dishes) and their lead-in wiring, masts or towers, trees, shrubs, or plants (other than "stock" of trees, shrubs or plants), all except as provided in the Coverage Extensions.

3. Covered Causes Of Loss

See applicable Causes Of Loss Form as shown in the Declarations.

4. Additional Coverages

a. Debris Removal

(1) Subject to Paragraphs (3) and (4), we will pay your expense to remove debris of Covered Property caused by or resulting from a Covered Cause of Loss that occurs during the policy period. The expenses will be paid only if they are reported to us in writing within 180 days of the date of direct physical loss or damage.

(2) Debris Removal does not apply to costs to:

(a) Extract "pollutants" from land or water; or

(b) Remove, restore or replace polluted land or water.

(3) Subject to the exceptions in Paragraph (4), the following provisions apply:

(a) The most we will pay for the total of direct physical loss or damage plus debris removal expense is the Limit of Insurance applicable to the Covered Property that has sustained loss or damage.

(b) Subject to (a) above, the amount we will pay for debris removal expense is limited to 25% of the sum of the deductible plus the amount that we pay for direct physical loss or damage to the Covered Property that has sustained loss or damage.

(4) We will pay up to an additional $10,000 for debris removal expense, for each location, in any one occurrence of physical loss or damage to Covered Property, if one or both of the following circumstances apply:

(a) The total of the actual debris removal expense plus the amount we pay for direct physical loss or damage exceeds the Limit of Insurance on the Covered Property that has sustained loss or damage.

(b) The actual debris removal expense exceeds 25% of the sum of the deductible plus the amount that we pay for direct physical loss or damage to the Covered Property that has sustained loss or damage.

Therefore, if (4)(a) and/or (4)(b) apply, our total payment for direct physical loss or damage and debris removal expense may reach but will never exceed the Limit of Insurance on the Covered Property that has sustained loss or damage, plus $10,000.

(5) Examples

The following examples assume that there is no Coinsurance penalty.

EXAMPLE #1

Limit of Insurance:	$ 90,000
Amount of Deductible:	$ 500
Amount of Loss:	$ 50,000
Amount of Loss Payable:	$ 49,500
	($50,000 – $500)
Debris Removal Expense:	$ 10,000
Debris Removal Expense Payable:	$ 10,000

($10,000 is 20% of $50,000.)

The debris removal expense is less than 25% of the sum of the loss payable plus the deductible. The sum of the loss payable and the debris removal expense ($49,500 + $10,000 = $59,500) is less than the Limit of Insurance. Therefore, the full amount of debris removal expense is payable in accordance with the terms of Paragraph (3).

Commercial Property

EXAMPLE #2

Limit of Insurance:	$	90,000
Amount of Deductible:	$	500
Amount of Loss:	$	80,000
Amount of Loss Payable:	$	79,500
	($80,000 – $500)	
Debris Removal Expense:	$	30,000
Debris Removal Expense Payable		
Basic Amount:	$	10,500
Additional Amount:	$	10,000

The basic amount payable for debris removal expense under the terms of Paragraph **(3)** is calculated as follows: $80,000 ($79,500 + $500) x .25 = $20,000; capped at $10,500. The cap applies because the sum of the loss payable ($79,500) and the basic amount payable for debris removal expense ($10,500) cannot exceed the Limit of Insurance ($90,000).

The additional amount payable for debris removal expense is provided in accordance with the terms of Paragraph **(4)**, because the debris removal expense ($30,000) exceeds 25% of the loss payable plus the deductible ($30,000 is 37.5% of $80,000), and because the sum of the loss payable and debris removal expense ($79,500 + $30,000 = $109,500) would exceed the Limit of Insurance ($90,000). The additional amount of covered debris removal expense is $10,000, the maximum payable under Paragraph **(4)**. Thus the total payable for debris removal expense in this example is $20,500; $9,500 of the debris removal expense is not covered.

b. Preservation Of Property

If it is necessary for you to move Covered Property from the described premises to preserve it from loss or damage by a Covered Cause of Loss, we will pay for any direct physical loss or damage to that property:

(1) While it is being moved or while temporarily stored at another location; and

(2) Only if the loss or damage occurs within 30 days after the property is first moved.

c. Fire Department Service Charge

When the fire department is called to save or protect Covered Property from a Covered Cause of Loss, we will pay up to $1,000, unless a higher limit is shown in the Declarations, for your liability for fire department service charges:

(1) Assumed by contract or agreement prior to loss; or

(2) Required by local ordinance.

No Deductible applies to this Additional Coverage.

d. Pollutant Clean-up And Removal

We will pay your expense to extract "pollutants" from land or water at the described premises if the discharge, dispersal, seepage, migration, release or escape of the "pollutants" is caused by or results from a Covered Cause of Loss that occurs during the policy period. The expenses will be paid only if they are reported to us in writing within 180 days of the date on which the Covered Cause of Loss occurs.

This Additional Coverage does not apply to costs to test for, monitor or assess the existence, concentration or effects of "pollutants". But we will pay for testing which is performed in the course of extracting the "pollutants" from the land or water.

The most we will pay under this Additional Coverage for each described premises is $10,000 for the sum of all covered expenses arising out of Covered Causes of Loss occurring during each separate 12-month period of this policy.

e. Increased Cost Of Construction

(1) This Additional Coverage applies only to buildings to which the Replacement Cost Optional Coverage applies.

(2) In the event of damage by a Covered Cause of Loss to a building that is Covered Property, we will pay the increased costs incurred to comply with enforcement of an ordinance or law in the course of repair, rebuilding or replacement of damaged parts of that property, subject to the limitations stated in **e.(3)** through **e.(9)** of this Additional Coverage.

(3) The ordinance or law referred to in **e.(2)** of this Additional Coverage is an ordinance or law that regulates the construction or repair of buildings or establishes zoning or land use requirements at the described premises, and is in force at the time of loss.

(4) Under this Additional Coverage, we will not pay any costs due to an ordinance or law that:

(a) You were required to comply with before the loss, even when the building was undamaged; and

(b) You failed to comply with.

(5) Under this Additional Coverage, we will not pay for:

(a) The enforcement of any ordinance or law which requires demolition, repair, replacement, reconstruction, remodeling or remediation of property due to contamination by "pollutants" or due to the presence, growth, proliferation, spread or any activity of "fungus", wet or dry rot or bacteria; or

(b) Any costs associated with the enforcement of an ordinance or law which requires any insured or others to test for, monitor, clean up, remove, contain, treat, detoxify or neutralize, or in any way respond to, or assess the effects of "pollutants", "fungus", wet or dry rot or bacteria.

(6) The most we will pay under this Additional Coverage, for each described building insured under this Coverage Form, is $10,000 or 5% of the Limit of Insurance applicable to that building, whichever is less. If a damaged building is covered under a blanket Limit of Insurance which applies to more than one building or item of property, then the most we will pay under this Additional Coverage, for that damaged building, is the lesser of: $10,000 or 5% times the value of the damaged building as of the time of loss times the applicable Coinsurance percentage.

The amount payable under this Additional Coverage is additional insurance.

(7) With respect to this Additional Coverage:

(a) We will not pay for the Increased Cost of Construction:

(i) Until the property is actually repaired or replaced, at the same or another premises; and

(ii) Unless the repairs or replacement are made as soon as reasonably possible after the loss or damage, not to exceed two years. We may extend this period in writing during the two years.

(b) If the building is repaired or replaced at the same premises, or if you elect to rebuild at another premises, the most we will pay for the Increased Cost of Construction, subject to the provisions of **e.(6)** of this Additional Coverage, is the increased cost of construction at the same premises.

(c) If the ordinance or law requires relocation to another premises, the most we will pay for the Increased Cost of Construction, subject to the provisions of **e.(6)** of this Additional Coverage, is the increased cost of construction at the new premises.

(8) This Additional Coverage is not subject to the terms of the Ordinance Or Law Exclusion, to the extent that such Exclusion would conflict with the provisions of this Additional Coverage.

(9) The costs addressed in the Loss Payment and Valuation Conditions, and the Replacement Cost Optional Coverage, in this Coverage Form, do not include the increased cost attributable to enforcement of an ordinance or law. The amount payable under this Additional Coverage, as stated in **e.(6)** of this Additional Coverage, is not subject to such limitation.

f. Electronic Data

(1) Under this Additional Coverage, electronic data has the meaning described under Property Not Covered, Electronic Data.

(2) Subject to the provisions of this Additional Coverage, we will pay for the cost to replace or restore electronic data which has been destroyed or corrupted by a Covered Cause of Loss. To the extent that electronic data is not replaced or restored, the loss will be valued at the cost of replacement of the media on which the electronic data was stored, with blank media of substantially identical type.

Commercial Property

(3) The Covered Causes of Loss applicable to Your Business Personal Property apply to this Additional Coverage, Electronic Data, subject to the following:

(a) If the Causes Of Loss – Special Form applies, coverage under this Additional Coverage, Electronic Data, is limited to the "specified causes of loss" as defined in that form, and Collapse as set forth in that form.

(b) If the Causes Of Loss – Broad Form applies, coverage under this Additional Coverage, Electronic Data, includes Collapse as set forth in that form.

(c) If the Causes Of Loss Form is endorsed to add a Covered Cause of Loss, the additional Covered Cause of Loss does not apply to the coverage provided under this Additional Coverage, Electronic Data.

(d) The Covered Causes of Loss include a virus, harmful code or similar instruction introduced into or enacted on a computer system (including electronic data) or a network to which it is connected, designed to damage or destroy any part of the system or disrupt its normal operation. But there is no coverage for loss or damage caused by or resulting from manipulation of a computer system (including electronic data) by any employee, including a temporary or leased employee, or by an entity retained by you or for you to inspect, design, install, modify, maintain, repair or replace that system.

(4) The most we will pay under this Additional Coverage, Electronic Data, is $2,500 for all loss or damage sustained in any one policy year, regardless of the number of occurrences of loss or damage or the number of premises, locations or computer systems involved. If loss payment on the first occurrence does not exhaust this amount, then the balance is available for subsequent loss or damage sustained in but not after that policy year. With respect to an occurrence which begins in one policy year and continues or results in additional loss or damage in a subsequent policy year(s), all loss or damage is deemed to be sustained in the policy year in which the occurrence began.

5. Coverage Extensions

Except as otherwise provided, the following Extensions apply to property located in or on the building described in the Declarations or in the open (or in a vehicle) within 100 feet of the described premises.

If a Coinsurance percentage of 80% or more is shown in the Declarations, you may extend the insurance provided by this Coverage Part as follows:

a. Newly Acquired Or Constructed Property

(1) Buildings

You may extend the insurance that applies to Building to apply to:

(a) Your new buildings while being built on the described premises; and

(b) Buildings you acquire at locations, other than the described premises, intended for:

(i) Similar use as the building described in the Declarations; or

(ii) Use as a warehouse.

The most we will pay for loss or damage under this Extension is $250,000 at each building.

(2) Your Business Personal Property

(a) If this policy covers Your Business Personal Property, you may extend that insurance to apply to:

(i) Business personal property, including such property that you newly acquire, at any location you acquire other than at fairs, trade shows or exhibitions;

(ii) Business personal property, including such property that you newly acquire, located at your newly constructed or acquired buildings at the location described in the Declarations; or

(iii) Business personal property that you newly acquire, located at the described premises.

The most we will pay for loss or damage under this Extension is $100,000 at each building.

(b) This Extension does not apply to:

(i) Personal property of others that is temporarily in your possession in the course of installing or performing work on such property; or

(ii) Personal property of others that is temporarily in your possession in the course of your manufacturing or wholesaling activities.

(3) Period Of Coverage

With respect to insurance on or at each newly acquired or constructed property, coverage will end when any of the following first occurs:

(a) This policy expires;

(b) 30 days expire after you acquire the property or begin construction of that part of the building that would qualify as covered property; or

(c) You report values to us.

We will charge you additional premium for values reported from the date you acquire the property or begin construction of that part of the building that would qualify as covered property.

b. Personal Effects And Property Of Others

You may extend the insurance that applies to Your Business Personal Property to apply to:

(1) Personal effects owned by you, your officers, your partners or members, your managers or your employees. This Extension does not apply to loss or damage by theft.

(2) Personal property of others in your care, custody or control.

The most we will pay for loss or damage under this Extension is $2,500 at each described premises. Our payment for loss of or damage to personal property of others will only be for the account of the owner of the property.

c. Valuable Papers And Records (Other Than Electronic Data)

(1) You may extend the insurance that applies to Your Business Personal Property to apply to the cost to replace or restore the lost information on valuable papers and records for which duplicates do not exist. But this Extension does not apply to valuable papers and records which exist as electronic data. Electronic data has the meaning described under Property Not Covered, Electronic Data.

(2) If the Causes Of Loss – Special Form applies, coverage under this Extension is limited to the "specified causes of loss" as defined in that form, and Collapse as set forth in that form.

(3) If the Causes Of Loss – Broad Form applies, coverage under this Extension includes Collapse as set forth in that form.

(4) Under this Extension, the most we will pay to replace or restore the lost information is $2,500 at each described premises, unless a higher limit is shown in the Declarations. Such amount is additional insurance. We will also pay for the cost of blank material for reproducing the records (whether or not duplicates exist), and (when there is a duplicate) for the cost of labor to transcribe or copy the records. The costs of blank material and labor are subject to the applicable Limit of Insurance on Your Business Personal Property and therefore coverage of such costs is not additional insurance.

d. Property Off-premises

(1) You may extend the insurance provided by this Coverage Form to apply to your Covered Property while it is away from the described premises, if it is:

(a) Temporarily at a location you do not own, lease or operate;

(b) In storage at a location you lease, provided the lease was executed after the beginning of the current policy term; or

(c) At any fair, trade show or exhibition.

(2) This Extension does not apply to property:

(a) In or on a vehicle; or

(b) In the care, custody or control of your salespersons, unless the property is in such care, custody or control at a fair, trade show or exhibition.

(3) The most we will pay for loss or damage under this Extension is $10,000.

Commercial Property

e. Outdoor Property

You may extend the insurance provided by this Coverage Form to apply to your outdoor fences, radio and television antennas (including satellite dishes), trees, shrubs and plants (other than "stock" of trees, shrubs or plants), including debris removal expense, caused by or resulting from any of the following causes of loss if they are Covered Causes of Loss:

(1) Fire;

(2) Lightning;

(3) Explosion;

(4) Riot or Civil Commotion; or

(5) Aircraft.

The most we will pay for loss or damage under this Extension is $1,000, but not more than $250 for any one tree, shrub or plant. These limits apply to any one occurrence, regardless of the types or number of items lost or damaged in that occurrence.

f. Non-owned Detached Trailers

(1) You may extend the insurance that applies to Your Business Personal Property to apply to loss or damage to trailers that you do not own, provided that:

(a) The trailer is used in your business;

(b) The trailer is in your care, custody or control at the premises described in the Declarations; and

(c) You have a contractual responsibility to pay for loss or damage to the trailer.

(2) We will not pay for any loss or damage that occurs:

(a) While the trailer is attached to any motor vehicle or motorized conveyance, whether or not the motor vehicle or motorized conveyance is in motion;

(b) During hitching or unhitching operations, or when a trailer becomes accidentally unhitched from a motor vehicle or motorized conveyance.

(3) The most we will pay for loss or damage under this Extension is $5,000, unless a higher limit is shown in the Declarations.

(4) This insurance is excess over the amount due (whether you can collect on it or not) from any other insurance covering such property.

Each of these Extensions is additional insurance unless otherwise indicated. The Additional Condition, Coinsurance, does not apply to these Extensions.

B. Exclusions And Limitations

See applicable Causes Of Loss Form as shown in the Declarations.

C. Limits Of Insurance

The most we will pay for loss or damage in any one occurrence is the applicable Limit of Insurance shown in the Declarations.

The most we will pay for loss or damage to outdoor signs, whether or not the sign is attached to a building, is $2,500 per sign in any one occurrence.

The amounts of insurance stated in the following Additional Coverages apply in accordance with the terms of such coverages and are separate from the Limit(s) of Insurance shown in the Declarations for any other coverage:

1. Fire Department Service Charge;

2. Pollutant Clean-up And Removal;

3. Increased Cost Of Construction; and

4. Electronic Data.

Payments under the Preservation Of Property Additional Coverage will not increase the applicable Limit of Insurance.

D. Deductible

In any one occurrence of loss or damage (hereinafter referred to as loss), we will first reduce the amount of loss if required by the Coinsurance Condition or the Agreed Value Optional Coverage. If the adjusted amount of loss is less than or equal to the Deductible, we will not pay for that loss. If the adjusted amount of loss exceeds the Deductible, we will then subtract the Deductible from the adjusted amount of loss, and will pay the resulting amount or the Limit of Insurance, whichever is less.

When the occurrence involves loss to more than one item of Covered Property and separate Limits of Insurance apply, the losses will not be combined in determining application of the Deductible. But the Deductible will be applied only once per occurrence.

EXAMPLE #1

(This example assumes there is no Coinsurance penalty.)

Deductible:	$ 250
Limit of Insurance – Building #1:	$ 60,000
Limit of Insurance – Building #2:	$ 80,000
Loss to Building #1:	$ 60,100
Loss to Building #2:	$ 90,000

The amount of loss to Building #1 ($60,100) is less than the sum ($60,250) of the Limit of Insurance applicable to Building #1 plus the Deductible.

The Deductible will be subtracted from the amount of loss in calculating the loss payable for Building #1:

$ 60,100
– 250
$ 59,850   Loss Payable – Building #1

The Deductible applies once per occurrence and therefore is not subtracted in determining the amount of loss payable for Building #2. Loss payable for Building #2 is the Limit of Insurance of $80,000.

Total amount of loss payable:

$59,850 + $80,000 = $139,850

EXAMPLE #2

(This example, too, assumes there is no Coinsurance penalty.)

The Deductible and Limits of Insurance are the same as those in Example #1.

Loss to Building #1:	$ 70,000
(Exceeds Limit of Insurance plus Deductible)	
Loss to Building #2:	$ 90,000
(Exceeds Limit of Insurance plus Deductible)	
Loss Payable – Building #1:	$ 60,000
(Limit of Insurance)	
Loss Payable – Building #2:	$ 80,000
(Limit of Insurance)	
Total amount of loss payable:	$ 140,000

E. Loss Conditions

The following conditions apply in addition to the Common Policy Conditions and the Commercial Property Conditions.

1. Abandonment

There can be no abandonment of any property to us.

2. Appraisal

If we and you disagree on the value of the property or the amount of loss, either may make written demand for an appraisal of the loss. In this event, each party will select a competent and impartial appraiser. The two appraisers will select an umpire. If they cannot agree, either may request that selection be made by a judge of a court having jurisdiction. The appraisers will state separately the value of the property and amount of loss. If they fail to agree, they will submit their differences to the umpire. A decision agreed to by any two will be binding. Each party will:

a. Pay its chosen appraiser; and

b. Bear the other expenses of the appraisal and umpire equally.

If there is an appraisal, we will still retain our right to deny the claim.

3. Duties In The Event Of Loss Or Damage

a. You must see that the following are done in the event of loss or damage to Covered Property:

(1) Notify the police if a law may have been broken.

(2) Give us prompt notice of the loss or damage. Include a description of the property involved.

(3) As soon as possible, give us a description of how, when and where the loss or damage occurred.

(4) Take all reasonable steps to protect the Covered Property from further damage, and keep a record of your expenses necessary to protect the Covered Property, for consideration in the settlement of the claim. This will not increase the Limit of Insurance. However, we will not pay for any subsequent loss or damage resulting from a cause of loss that is not a Covered Cause of Loss. Also, if feasible, set the damaged property aside and in the best possible order for examination.

Commercial Property

(5) At our request, give us complete inventories of the damaged and undamaged property. Include quantities, costs, values and amount of loss claimed.

(6) As often as may be reasonably required, permit us to inspect the property proving the loss or damage and examine your books and records.

Also permit us to take samples of damaged and undamaged property for inspection, testing and analysis, and permit us to make copies from your books and records.

(7) Send us a signed, sworn proof of loss containing the information we request to investigate the claim. You must do this within 60 days after our request. We will supply you with the necessary forms.

(8) Cooperate with us in the investigation or settlement of the claim.

b. We may examine any insured under oath, while not in the presence of any other insured and at such times as may be reasonably required, about any matter relating to this insurance or the claim, including an insured's books and records. In the event of an examination, an insured's answers must be signed.

4. Loss Payment

a. In the event of loss or damage covered by this Coverage Form, at our option, we will either:

(1) Pay the value of lost or damaged property;

(2) Pay the cost of repairing or replacing the lost or damaged property, subject to **b.** below;

(3) Take all or any part of the property at an agreed or appraised value; or

(4) Repair, rebuild or replace the property with other property of like kind and quality, subject to **b.** below.

We will determine the value of lost or damaged property, or the cost of its repair or replacement, in accordance with the applicable terms of the Valuation Condition in this Coverage Form or any applicable provision which amends or supersedes the Valuation Condition.

b. The cost to repair, rebuild or replace does not include the increased cost attributable to enforcement of any ordinance or law regulating the construction, use or repair of any property.

c. We will give notice of our intentions within 30 days after we receive the sworn proof of loss.

d. We will not pay you more than your financial interest in the Covered Property.

e. We may adjust losses with the owners of lost or damaged property if other than you. If we pay the owners, such payments will satisfy your claims against us for the owners' property. We will not pay the owners more than their financial interest in the Covered Property.

f. We may elect to defend you against suits arising from claims of owners of property. We will do this at our expense.

g. We will pay for covered loss or damage to Covered Property within 30 days after we receive the sworn proof of loss, if you have complied with all of the terms of this Coverage Part and:

(1) We have reached agreement with you on the amount of loss; or

(2) An appraisal award has been made.

If you name an insurance trustee, we will adjust losses with you, but we will pay the insurance trustee. If we pay the trustee, the payments will satisfy your claims against us.

h. A party wall is a wall that separates and is common to adjoining buildings that are owned by different parties. In settling covered losses involving a party wall, we will pay a proportion of the loss to the party wall based on your interest in the wall in proportion to the interest of the owner of the adjoining building. However, if you elect to repair or replace your building and the owner of the adjoining building elects not to repair or replace that building, we will pay you the full value of the loss to the party wall, subject to all applicable policy provisions including Limits of Insurance, the Valuation and Coinsurance Conditions and all other provisions of this Loss Payment Condition. Our payment under the provisions of this paragraph does not alter any right of subrogation we may have against any entity, including the owner or insurer of the adjoining building, and does not alter the terms of the Transfer Of Rights Of Recovery Against Others To Us Condition in this policy.

 CP 00 17 06 07 ☐

5. Recovered Property

If either you or we recover any property after loss settlement, that party must give the other prompt notice. At your option, the property will be returned to you. You must then return to us the amount we paid to you for the property. We will pay recovery expenses and the expenses to repair the recovered property, subject to the Limit of Insurance.

6. Unit-owner's Insurance

A unit-owner may have other insurance covering the same property as this insurance. This insurance is intended to be primary, and not to contribute with such other insurance.

7. Vacancy

a. Description Of Terms

(1) As used in this Vacancy Condition, the term building and the term vacant have the meanings set forth in **(1)(a)** and **(1)(b)** below:

(a) When this policy is issued to a tenant, and with respect to that tenant's interest in Covered Property, building means the unit or suite rented or leased to the tenant. Such building is vacant when it does not contain enough business personal property to conduct customary operations.

(b) When this policy is issued to the owner or general lessee of a building, building means the entire building. Such building is vacant unless at least 31% of its total square footage is:

(i) Rented to a lessee or sub-lessee and used by the lessee or sub-lessee to conduct its customary operations; and/or

(ii) Used by the building owner to conduct customary operations.

(2) Buildings under construction or renovation are not considered vacant.

b. Vacancy Provisions

If the building where loss or damage occurs has been vacant for more than 60 consecutive days before that loss or damage occurs:

(1) We will not pay for any loss or damage caused by any of the following even if they are Covered Causes of Loss:

(a) Vandalism;

(b) Sprinkler leakage, unless you have protected the system against freezing;

(c) Building glass breakage;

(d) Water damage;

(e) Theft; or

(f) Attempted theft.

(2) With respect to Covered Causes of Loss other than those listed in **b.(1)(a)** through **b.(1)(f)** above, we will reduce the amount we would otherwise pay for the loss or damage by 15%.

8. Valuation

We will determine the value of Covered Property in the event of loss or damage as follows:

a. At actual cash value as of the time of loss or damage, except as provided in **b.** and **c.** below.

b. If the Limit of Insurance for Building satisfies the Additional Condition, Coinsurance, and the cost to repair or replace the damaged building property is $2,500 or less, we will pay the cost of building repairs or replacement.

The cost of building repairs or replacement does not include the increased cost attributable to enforcement of any ordinance or law regulating the construction, use or repair of any property. However, the following property will be valued at the actual cash value even when attached to the building:

(1) Awnings or floor coverings;

(2) Appliances for refrigerating, ventilating, cooking, dishwashing or laundering; or

(3) Outdoor equipment or furniture.

c. Glass at the cost of replacement with safety-glazing material if required by law.

9. Waiver Of Rights Of Recovery

We waive our rights to recover payment from any unit-owner of the condominium that is shown in the Declarations.

F. Additional Conditions

The following conditions apply in addition to the Common Policy Conditions and the Commercial Property Conditions.

1. Coinsurance

If a Coinsurance percentage is shown in the Declarations, the following condition applies.

a. We will not pay the full amount of any loss if the value of Covered Property at the time of loss times the Coinsurance percentage shown for it in the Declarations is greater than the Limit of Insurance for the property.

Instead, we will determine the most we will pay using the following steps:

(1) Multiply the value of Covered Property at the time of loss by the Coinsurance percentage;

(2) Divide the Limit of Insurance of the property by the figure determined in Step **(1)**;

(3) Multiply the total amount of loss, before the application of any deductible, by the figure determined in Step **(2)**; and

(4) Subtract the deductible from the figure determined in Step **(3)**.

We will pay the amount determined in Step **(4)** or the Limit of Insurance, whichever is less. For the remainder, you will either have to rely on other insurance or absorb the loss yourself.

EXAMPLE #1 (UNDERINSURANCE)

When: The value of the property is: $ 250,000

The Coinsurance percentage for it is: 80%

The Limit of Insurance for it is: $ 100,000

The Deductible is: $ 250

The amount of loss is: $ 40,000

Step **(1)**: $250,000 x 80% = $200,000

(the minimum amount of insurance to meet your Coinsurance requirements)

Step **(2)**: $100,000 ÷ $200,000 = .50

Step **(3)**: $40,000 x .50 = $20,000

Step **(4)**: $20,000 – $250 = $19,750

We will pay no more than $19,750. The remaining $20,250 is not covered.

EXAMPLE #2 (ADEQUATE INSURANCE)

When: The value of the property is: $ 250,000

The Coinsurance percentage for it is: 80%

The Limit of Insurance for it is: $ 200,000

The Deductible is: $ 250

The amount of loss is: $ 40,000

The minimum amount of insurance to meet your Co-insurance requirement is $200,000 ($250,000 x 80%). Therefore, the Limit of Insurance in this example is adequate and no penalty applies. We will pay no more than $39,750 ($40,000 amount of loss minus the deductible of $250).

b. If one Limit of Insurance applies to two or more separate items, this condition will apply to the total of all property to which the limit applies.

EXAMPLE #3

When: The value of the property is:

Building at Location #1: $ 75,000

Building at Location #2: $ 100,000

Personal Property at Location #2: $ 75,000
                                                         $ 250,000

The Coinsurance percentage for it is: 90%

The Limit of Insurance for Buildings and Personal Property at Locations #1 and #2 is: $ 180,000

The Deductible is: $ 1,000

The amount of loss is:

Building at Location #2: $ 30,000

Personal Property at Location #2: $ 20,000
                                                         $ 50,000

Step **(1)**: $250,000 x 90% = $225,000

(the minimum amount of insurance to meet your Coinsurance requirements and to avoid the penalty shown below)

Step **(2)**: $180,000 ÷ $225,000 = .80

Step **(3)**: $50,000 x .80 = $40,000

Step **(4)**: $40,000 – $1,000 = $39,000

We will pay no more than $39,000. The remaining $11,000 is not covered.

2. Mortgageholders

a. The term mortgageholder includes trustee.

b. We will pay for covered loss of or damage to buildings or structures to each mortgageholder shown in the Declarations in their order of precedence, as interests may appear.

c. The mortgageholder has the right to receive loss payment even if the mortgageholder has started foreclosure or similar action on the building or structure.

d. If we deny your claim because of your acts or because you have failed to comply with the terms of this Coverage Part, the mortgageholder will still have the right to receive loss payment if the mortgageholder:

(1) Pays any premium due under this Coverage Part at our request if you have failed to do so;

(2) Submits a signed, sworn proof of loss within 60 days after receiving notice from us of your failure to do so; and

(3) Has notified us of any change in ownership, occupancy or substantial change in risk known to the mortgageholder.

All of the terms of this Coverage Part will then apply directly to the mortgageholder.

e. If we pay the mortgageholder for any loss or damage and deny payment to you because of your acts or because you have failed to comply with the terms of this Coverage Part:

(1) The mortgageholder's rights under the mortgage will be transferred to us to the extent of the amount we pay; and

(2) The mortgageholder's right to recover the full amount of the mortgageholder's claim will not be impaired.

At our option, we may pay to the mortgageholder the whole principal on the mortgage plus any accrued interest. In this event, your mortgage and note will be transferred to us and you will pay your remaining mortgage debt to us.

f. If we cancel this policy, we will give written notice to the mortgageholder at least:

(1) 10 days before the effective date of cancellation if we cancel for your nonpayment of premium; or

(2) 30 days before the effective date of cancellation if we cancel for any other reason.

g. If we elect not to renew this policy, we will give written notice to the mortgageholder at least 10 days before the expiration date of this policy.

G. Optional Coverages

If shown as applicable in the Declarations, the following Optional Coverages apply separately to each item.

1. Agreed Value

a. The Additional Condition, Coinsurance, does not apply to Covered Property to which this Optional Coverage applies. We will pay no more for loss of or damage to that property than the proportion that the Limit of Insurance under this Coverage Part for the property bears to the Agreed Value shown for it in the Declarations.

b. If the expiration date for this Optional Coverage shown in the Declarations is not extended, the Additional Condition, Coinsurance, is reinstated and this Optional Coverage expires.

c. The terms of this Optional Coverage apply only to loss or damage that occurs:

(1) On or after the effective date of this Optional Coverage; and

(2) Before the Agreed Value expiration date shown in the Declarations or the policy expiration date, whichever occurs first.

2. Inflation Guard

a. The Limit of Insurance for property to which this Optional Coverage applies will automatically increase by the annual percentage shown in the Declarations.

b. The amount of increase will be:

(1) The Limit of Insurance that applied on the most recent of the policy inception date, the policy anniversary date, or any other policy change amending the Limit of Insurance, times

(2) The percentage of annual increase shown in the Declarations, expressed as a decimal (example: 8% is .08), times

(3) The number of days since the beginning of the current policy year or the effective date of the most recent policy change amending the Limit of Insurance, divided by 365.

CP 00 17 06 07   © ISO Properties, Inc., 2007   **Page 13 of 14**   □

EXAMPLE

If:

The applicable Limit of Insurance is:	$ 100,000	
The annual percentage increase is:	8%	
The number of days since the beginning of the policy year (or last policy change) is:	146	
The amount of increase is: $100,000 x .08 x 146 ÷ 365 =	$	3,200

3. **Replacement Cost**

   a. Replacement Cost (without deduction for depreciation) replaces Actual Cash Value in the Loss Condition, Valuation, of this Coverage Form.

   b. This Optional Coverage does not apply to:

   (1) Personal property of others;

   (2) Contents of a residence; or

   (3) Works of art, antiques or rare articles, including etchings, pictures, statuary, marbles, bronzes, porcelains and bric-a-brac.

   Under the terms of this Replacement Cost Optional Coverage, personal property owned indivisibly by all unit-owners, and the property covered under Paragraph **A.1.a.(6)** of this Coverage Form, are not considered to be the personal property of others.

   c. You may make a claim for loss or damage covered by this insurance on an actual cash value basis instead of on a replacement cost basis. In the event you elect to have loss or damage settled on an actual cash value basis, you may still make a claim for the additional coverage this Optional Coverage provides if you notify us of your intent to do so within 180 days after the loss or damage.

   d. We will not pay on a replacement cost basis for any loss or damage:

   (1) Until the lost or damaged property is actually repaired or replaced; and

   (2) Unless the repairs or replacement are made as soon as reasonably possible after the loss or damage.

   e. We will not pay more for loss or damage on a replacement cost basis than the least of **(1)**, **(2)** or **(3)**, subject to **f.** below:

   (1) The Limit of Insurance applicable to the lost or damaged property;

   (2) The cost to replace the lost or damaged property with other property:

   (a) Of comparable material and quality; and

   (b) Used for the same purpose; or

   (3) The amount actually spent that is necessary to repair or replace the lost or damaged property.

   If a building is rebuilt at a new premises, the cost described in **e.(2)** above is limited to the cost which would have been incurred if the building had been rebuilt at the original premises.

   f. The cost of repair or replacement does not include the increased cost attributable to enforcement of any ordinance or law regulating the construction, use or repair of any property.

4. **Extension Of Replacement Cost To Personal Property Of Others**

   a. If the Replacement Cost Optional Coverage is shown as applicable in the Declarations, then this Extension may also be shown as applicable. If the Declarations show this Extension as applicable, then Paragraph **3.b.(1)** of the Replacement Cost Optional Coverage is deleted and all other provisions of the Replacement Cost Optional Coverage apply to replacement cost on personal property of others.

   b. With respect to replacement cost on the personal property of others, the following limitation applies:

   If an item(s) of personal property of others is subject to a written contract which governs your liability for loss or damage to that item(s), then valuation of that item(s) will be based on the amount for which you are liable under such contract, but not to exceed the lesser of the replacement cost of the property or the applicable Limit of Insurance.

H. Definitions

1. "Fungus" means any type or form of fungus, including mold or mildew, and any mycotoxins, spores, scents or by-products produced or released by fungi.

2. "Pollutants" means any solid, liquid, gaseous or thermal irritant or contaminant, including smoke, vapor, soot, fumes, acids, alkalis, chemicals and waste. Waste includes materials to be recycled, reconditioned or reclaimed.

COMMERCIAL PROPERTY
CP 10 65 06 07

THIS ENDORSEMENT CHANGES THE POLICY. PLEASE READ IT CAREFULLY.

FLOOD COVERAGE ENDORSEMENT

This endorsement modifies insurance provided under the following:

COMMERCIAL PROPERTY COVERAGE PART
STANDARD PROPERTY POLICY

A. When this endorsement is attached to the Standard Property Policy, the terms Coverage Part and Coverage Form in this endorsement are replaced by the term Policy.

B. This endorsement applies to the Covered Property and Coverages for which a Flood Limit of Insurance is shown in the Flood Coverage Schedule or in the Declarations.

C. Additional Covered Cause Of Loss

The following is added to the Covered Causes Of Loss:

Flood, meaning a general and temporary condition of partial or complete inundation of normally dry land areas due to:

1. The overflow of inland or tidal waters;

2. The unusual or rapid accumulation or runoff of surface waters from any source; or

3. Mudslides or mudflows which are caused by flooding as defined in **C.2.** above. For the purpose of this Covered Cause Of Loss, a mudslide or mudflow involves a river of liquid and flowing mud on the surface of normally dry land areas as when earth is carried by a current of water and deposited along the path of the current.

All flooding in a continuous or protracted event will constitute a single flood.

D. Exclusions, Limitations And Related Provisions

1. The Exclusions and Limitation(s) sections of the Causes Of Loss Form (and the Exclusions section of the Mortgageholders Errors And Omissions Coverage Form and the Standard Property Policy) apply to coverage provided under this endorsement except as provided in **D.2.** and **D.3.** below.

2. To the extent that a part of the Water Exclusion might conflict with coverage provided under this endorsement, that part of the Water Exclusion does not apply.

3. To the extent that a tsunami causes the overflow of tidal waters, the exclusion of earthquake, in the Earth Movement Exclusion, does not apply.

4. The **Ordinance Or Law** Exclusion in this Coverage Part continues to apply with respect to any loss under this Coverage Part including any loss under this endorsement, unless Ordinance Or Law Coverage is added by endorsement.

5. The following exclusions and limitations are added and apply to coverage under this endorsement:

a. We will not pay for any loss or damage caused by or resulting from any Flood that begins before or within 72 hours after the inception date of this endorsement. If you request and we provide an increase in the stated Limit of Insurance for Flood, the increase will not apply to loss or damage from any Flood that begins before or within 72 hours after your request was made.

If the Flood is due to the overflow of inland or tidal waters, then the Flood is considered to begin when the water first overflows its banks.

b. We will not pay for loss or damage caused by or resulting from destabilization of land arising from the accumulation of water in subsurface land areas.

Commercial Property

c. Under this Coverage Part, as set forth under Property Not Covered in the Coverage Form to which this endorsement is attached, land is not covered property, nor is the cost of excavations, grading, backfilling or filling. Therefore, coverage under this endorsement does not include the cost of restoring or remediating land due to the collapse or sinking of land caused by or resulting from Flood. However, coverage under this endorsement includes damage to the covered portions of the building and to covered personal property, caused by collapse or sinking of land along the shore of a body of water as the result of erosion or undermining caused by waves or currents of water which exceed the cyclical levels and cause Flood.

d. We do not cover loss or damage by Flood to personal property in the open except to the extent that such coverage, if any, is specified in the Flood Coverage Schedule or in the Declarations.

e. Property Not Covered, in the Coverage Form to which this endorsement is attached, is amended and supplemented as follows with respect to Flood Coverage:

(1) Property Not Covered includes any building or other property that is not eligible for flood insurance pursuant to the provisions of the Coastal Barrier Resources Act, 16 U.S.C. 3501 *et seq.* and the Coastal Barrier Improvement Act of 1990, Pub. L. 101-591, 16 U.S.C. 3501 *et seq.*

(2) Property Not Covered includes boat houses and open structures, and any property in or on the foregoing, if the structure is located on or over a body of water.

(3) If bulkheads, pilings, piers, wharves, docks, or retaining walls that are not part of a building, have been removed from Property Not Covered and added as Covered Property by separate endorsement, this Flood Coverage Endorsement does not apply to such property.

(4) The following are removed from Property Not Covered and are therefore Covered Property:

(a) Foundations below the lowest basement floor or the subsurface of the ground; and

(b) Underground pipes, flues and drains.

f. We will not pay for loss or damage caused by sewer back-up or overflow unless such back-up or overflow results from Flood and occurs within 72 hours after the flood recedes.

E. **Additional Coverages And Coverage Extensions**

1. With respect to Flood Coverage, the Debris Removal Additional Coverage (and any additional limit for Debris Removal under a Limit Of Insurance clause or an endorsement) is not applicable and is replaced by the following:

DEBRIS REMOVAL

a. We will pay your expense to remove debris of Covered Property and other debris that is on the described premises, when such debris is caused by or results from Flood. However, we will not pay to remove deposits of mud or earth from the grounds of the described premises.

b. We will also pay the expense to remove debris of Covered Property that has floated or been hurled off the described premises by Flood.

c. This coverage for Debris Removal, as set forth in **E.1.a.** and **E.1.b.** above, does not increase the applicable Limit of Insurance for Flood. Therefore, the most we will pay for the total of debris removal and loss or damage to Covered Property is the Limit of Insurance for Flood that applies to the Covered Property at the affected described premises covered under this endorsement.

2. With respect to Flood Coverage, the Coverage Extension for Newly Acquired or Constructed Property is amended by adding the following:

a. With respect to Flood Coverage, this Coverage Extension does not apply to any building or structure that is not fully enclosed by walls and roof.

b. With respect to a building or structure covered under this Coverage Extension, the amounts of coverage stated in the Coverage Extension do not apply to Flood Coverage. Instead, the most we will pay for all loss or damage to property covered under this Coverage Extension is 10% of the total of all Limits of Insurance for Flood Coverage as provided under this endorsement. Such coverage does not increase the Limit of Insurance for Flood.

 CP 10 65 06 07 ☐

3. With respect to any applicable Additional Coverages and Coverage Extensions in the Coverage Form to which this endorsement is attached, other than those addressed in **E.1.** and **E.2.** above, amounts payable under such other provisions, as set forth therein, do not increase the Limit of Insurance for Flood.

F. Coinsurance

1. The **Coinsurance** Condition, if any, in the applicable Coverage Form applies to the coverage provided under this endorsement, unless the No-Coinsurance Option, in the Flood Coverage Schedule or in the Declarations, is specified as being applicable.

2. Various Coverage Extensions, in the Coverage Form to which this endorsement is attached, require coinsurance. If the No-Coinsurance Option applies, then the coinsurance requirement for such Coverage Extensions is eliminated.

G. Limit Of Insurance

1. General Information

Flood Coverage may be written at a Limit of Insurance that is equal to or less than the Limit of Insurance which applies to other Covered Causes of Loss (e.g., Fire) under this Commercial Property Coverage Part.

The Limit of Insurance for Flood is shown in the Flood Coverage Schedule or in the Declarations. If such Limit is not shown, then the Limit applicable to Fire also applies to Flood.

2. Application Of Limit And Aggregate

The Limit of Insurance for Flood is the most we will pay in a single occurrence of Flood for loss or damage caused by the Flood. If there is more than one Flood in a 12-month period (starting with the beginning of the present annual policy period), the most we will pay for the total of all loss or damage sustained during that period of time and caused by Flood is the amount that is identified as the Annual Aggregate for Flood as shown in the Flood Coverage Schedule or the Declarations.

If the Limit of Insurance and the Annual Aggregate amount are the same, or if there is no amount stated as an Annual Aggregate, then the Limit of Insurance is the most we will pay for the total of all loss or damage that is caused by Flood in a 12-month period (starting with the beginning of the present annual policy period), even if there is more than one occurrence of Flood during that period of time. Thus, if the first Flood does not exhaust the applicable Limit of Insurance, then the balance of that Limit is available for a subsequent Flood(s).

If a single occurrence of Flood begins during one annual policy period and ends during the following annual policy period, any Limit of Insurance or Annual Aggregate applicable to the following annual policy period will **not** apply to that Flood.

3. Ensuing Loss

In the event of covered ensuing loss, for example, loss caused by Fire, Explosion and/or Sprinkler Leakage which results from the Flood, the most we will pay, for the total of all loss or damage caused by flood, fire, explosion and sprinkler leakage, is the Limit of Insurance applicable to Fire. We will **not** pay the sum of the Fire and Flood Limits.

EXAMPLES – ENSUING LOSS

Two examples follow, using these facts: The Commercial Property Coverage Part, in these examples, includes the Causes of Loss – Basic Form (which covers fire) and this Flood Coverage Endorsement. A building is damaged by Flood and by Fire which is caused by the Flood. The value of the damaged building is $1,000,000. The Limit of Insurance applicable to the building, for the Basic Causes of Loss, is $800,000. The Limit of Insurance for Flood is $400,000. The Flood Deductible amount is $5,000.

EXAMPLE #1

The damage due to Flood is $500,000. The damage due to Fire is $500,000.

Payment for Flood damage is $400,000 ($500,000 damage minus $5,000 Flood deductible = $495,000; Limit is $400,000).

Payment for Fire damage is $400,000 ($500,000 damage capped at the difference between the Basic Limit and the Flood Limit).

Total Loss Payment is $800,000.

EXAMPLE #2

The damage due to Flood is $800,000. The damage due to Fire is $100,000.

Payment for Flood damage is $400,000 ($800,000 damage minus $5,000 Flood deductible = $795,000; Limit is $400,000).

Payment for Fire damage is $100,000 (amount of damage).

Total Loss Payment is $500,000.

Note: These Examples are given only to illustrate the situation of flood and ensuing loss. Therefore, the loss payment stated for flood damage does not address the situation where another policy also covers the flood damage.

H. Deductible

1. The Deductible for coverage provided under this endorsement is the Deductible applicable to Flood as shown in the Flood Coverage Schedule or in the Declarations.

2. We will not pay that part of the loss that is attributable to any Deductible(s) in the National Flood Insurance Program policy.

3. If Flood results in another Covered Cause of Loss and if both Covered Causes of Loss cause loss or damage, then only the higher deductible applies (e.g., the Flood deductible or the Fire deductible).

I. Other Insurance

The **Other Insurance** Commercial Property Condition is replaced by the following with respect to the coverage provided under this endorsement:

1. If the loss is also covered under a National Flood Insurance Program (NFIP) policy, or if the property is eligible to be written under an NFIP policy but there is no such policy in effect, then we will pay only for the amount of loss in excess of the maximum limit that can be insured under that policy. This provision applies whether or not the maximum NFIP limit was obtained or maintained, and whether or not you can collect on the NFIP policy. We will not, under any circumstances, pay more than the applicable Limit of Insurance for Flood as stated in the Flood Coverage Schedule or the Declarations of this Coverage Part.

However, this Provision **I.1.** does not apply under the following circumstances:

a. At the time of loss, the property is eligible to be written under an NFIP policy but such policy is not in effect due solely to ineligibility of the property at the time this Flood Coverage Endorsement was written; or

b. An NFIP policy is not in effect because we have agreed to write this Flood Coverage Endorsement without underlying NFIP coverage. There is such an agreement only if the Flood Coverage Schedule or the Declarations indicate that the Underlying Insurance Waiver applies.

2. If there is other insurance covering the loss, other than that described in **I.1.** above, we will pay our share of the loss. Our share is the proportion that the applicable Limit of Insurance under this endorsement bears to the total of the applicable Limits of Insurance under all other such insurance. But we will not pay more than the applicable Limit of Insurance stated in the Flood Coverage Schedule or the Declarations of this Coverage Part.

COMMERCIAL PROPERTY
CP 10 45 08 99

THIS ENDORSEMENT CHANGES THE POLICY. PLEASE READ IT CAREFULLY.

EARTHQUAKE AND VOLCANIC ERUPTION ENDORSEMENT (SUB-LIMIT FORM)

This endorsement modifies insurance provided under the following:

COMMERCIAL PROPERTY COVERAGE PART
STANDARD PROPERTY POLICY

A. When this endorsement is attached to the Standard Property Policy, the terms Coverage Part and Coverage Form in this endorsement are replaced by the term Policy.

B. This endorsement applies to the Covered Property and Coverages for which an Earthquake – Volcanic Eruption Limit of Insurance is shown in the Earthquake – Volcanic Eruption Coverage Schedule or in the Declarations.

C. Additional Covered Causes Of Loss

   1. The following are added to the Covered Causes of Loss:

   a. Earthquake.

   b. Volcanic Eruption, meaning the eruption, explosion or effusion of a volcano.

   All Earthquake shocks or Volcanic Eruptions that occur within any 168-hour period will constitute a single Earthquake or Volcanic Eruption. The expiration of this policy will not reduce the 168-hour period.

   2. If the Earthquake – Volcanic Eruption Coverage Schedule or the Declarations indicate that this endorsement covers Earthquake-Sprinkler Leakage Only, then the Covered Causes of Loss in Paragraph **C.1.** of this endorsement do not apply, and the following apply instead:

   a. Sprinkler Leakage resulting from Earthquake.

   b. Sprinkler Leakage resulting from Volcanic Eruption. Volcanic Eruption means the eruption, explosion or effusion of a volcano.

All Earthquake shocks or Volcanic Eruptions that occur within any 168-hour period will constitute a single Earthquake or Volcanic Eruption. The expiration of this policy will not reduce the 168-hour period.

D. Exclusions, Limitations And Related Provisions

   1. The Exclusions and Limitation(s) sections of the Causes of Loss Form (and the Exclusions section of the Mortgageholders Errors and Omissions Coverage Form and the Standard Property Policy) apply to coverage provided under this endorsement, except as provided in **D.2.** and **D.3.** below.

   2. To the extent that the Earth Movement Exclusion might conflict with coverage provided under this endorsement, the Earth Movement Exclusion does not apply.

   3. The exclusion of collapse, in the Causes of Loss-Special Form and Mortgageholders Errors And Omissions Coverage Form, does not apply to collapse caused by Earthquake or Volcanic Eruption.

   4. The Additional Coverage – Collapse, in the Causes of Loss – Broad Form, Causes of Loss – Special Form and Mortgageholders Errors And Omissions Coverage Form, does not apply to the coverage provided under this endorsement. This endorsement includes coverage for collapse caused by Earthquake or Volcanic Eruption.

   5. We will not pay for loss or damage caused directly or indirectly by tidal wave or tsunami, even if attributable to an Earthquake or Volcanic Eruption.

Commercial Property

6. We will not pay for loss or damage caused by or resulting from any Earthquake or Volcanic Eruption that begins before the inception of this insurance.

7. The Ordinance Or Law Exclusion in this Coverage Part continues to apply with respect to any loss under this Coverage Part including any loss under this endorsement, unless Ordinance Or Law Coverage is added by endorsement.

8. We will not pay for loss of or damage to exterior masonry veneer (except stucco) on wood frame walls caused by or resulting from Earthquake or Volcanic Eruption. The value of such veneer will not be included in the value of Covered Property or the amount of loss when applying the Property Damage Deductible applicable to this endorsement.

   This limitation, **D.8.**, does not apply if:

   a. The Earthquake – Volcanic Eruption Coverage Schedule or the Declarations indicate that the "Including Masonry Veneer" option applies; or

   b. Less than 10% of the total outside wall area is faced with masonry veneer (excluding stucco).

9. Under this Coverage Part, as set forth under Property Not Covered in the Coverage Form to which this endorsement is attached, land is not covered property, nor is the cost of excavations, grading, backfilling or filling. Therefore, coverage under this endorsement does not include the cost of restoring or remediating land.

E. No Coinsurance

The Coinsurance Condition in this policy, if any, does not apply to the coverage provided under this endorsement.

Various Coverage Extensions, in the Coverage Form to which this endorsement is attached, require coinsurance. The coinsurance requirement for such Coverage Extensions is eliminated with respect to coverage provided under this endorsement.

F. Limit Of Insurance

1. General Information

The term Limit of Insurance means the Limit of Insurance applicable to Earthquake – Volcanic Eruption for the Covered Property or Coverage under which loss or damage is sustained.

The Earthquake – Volcanic Eruption Coverage Schedule or the Declarations provide information on the Limit of Insurance applicable to Covered Property and Coverages for Earthquake – Volcanic Eruption.

2. Annual Aggregate Limit

The Limit of Insurance for Earthquake – Volcanic Eruption is an annual aggregate limit and as such is the most we will pay for the total of all loss or damage that is caused by Earthquake or Volcanic Eruption in a 12-month period (starting with the beginning of the present annual policy period), even if there is more than one Earthquake or Volcanic Eruption during that period of time. Thus, if the first Earthquake or Volcanic Eruption does not exhaust the Limit of Insurance, then the balance of that Limit is available for a subsequent Earthquake(s) or Volcanic Eruption(s).

If a single Earthquake or Volcanic Eruption (as defined in Section **C.** of this endorsement) begins during one annual policy period and ends during the following annual policy period, any Limit of Insurance applicable to the following annual policy period will **not** apply to such Earthquake or Volcanic Eruption.

3. Increased Annual Aggregate Limit Option

If the Earthquake – Volcanic Eruption Coverage Schedule or the Declarations indicate that the Increased Annual Aggregate Limit Option applies, then the following applies instead of Paragraph **F.2.** above:

The Limit of Insurance for Earthquake – Volcanic Eruption is the most we will pay in a single Earthquake or Volcanic Eruption (as defined in Section **C.** of this endorsement) for loss or damage caused by the Earthquake or Volcanic Eruption. If there is more than one Earthquake or Volcanic Eruption in a 12-month period (starting with the beginning of the present annual policy period), the most we will pay for the total of all loss or damage sustained during that period of time and caused by Earthquake or Volcanic Eruption is two times the Limit of Insurance.

If a single Earthquake or Volcanic Eruption (as defined in Section **C.** of this endorsement) begins during one annual policy period and ends during the following annual policy period, any Limit of Insurance applicable to the following annual policy period will **not** apply to such Earthquake or Volcanic Eruption.

4. Additional Coverages And Coverage Extensions

Amounts payable under an Additional Coverage or Coverage Extension, as set forth in the applicable Coverage Form, do not increase the Limit of Insurance for Earthquake – Volcanic Eruption.

5. Limitation

For property or coverage that is subject to a Blanket Limit on Earthquake – Volcanic Eruption (as shown in the Earthquake – Volcanic Eruption Coverage Schedule or in the Declarations), we will not pay more than we would pay in the absence of such Blanket Limit. Therefore, the maximum amount payable for any such item of property or coverage is the Limit of Insurance or stated value (as shown in a Statement of Values on file with us) specific to that item of property or coverage for Covered Causes of Loss other than Earthquake – Volcanic Eruption.

6. Ensuing Loss

If a Cause of Loss (such as fire) is covered by means of an exception to the Earth Movement Exclusion, in the Causes of Loss Form, we will also pay for the loss or damage caused by that other Covered Cause of Loss. But the most we will pay, for the total of all loss or damage caused by the Earthquake, Volcanic Eruption and other Covered Cause of Loss, is the Limit of Insurance applicable to such other Covered Cause of Loss. We will **not** pay the sum of the two Limits.

EXAMPLES – ENSUING LOSS

Two examples follow, using these facts: The Commercial Property Coverage Part, in these examples, includes the Causes of Loss – Basic Form (which covers fire) and this Earthquake – Volcanic Eruption Endorsement. A building is damaged by Earthquake, and by Fire which is caused by the Earthquake. The value of the damaged building is $1,000,000. The Limit of Insurance applicable to the building, for the Basic Causes of Loss, is $800,000. The Limit of Insurance for Earthquake – Volcanic Eruption is $400,000. The Earthquake Deductible amount is $50,000.

Example #1

The damage due to Earthquake is $500,000.

The damage due to Fire is $500,000.

Payment for Earthquake damage is $400,000 ($500,000 damage minus $50,000 Earthquake deductible = $450,000; Limit is $400,000)

Payment for Fire damage is $400,000 ($500,000 damage capped at the difference between the Basic Limit and the Earthquake Limit)

Total Loss Payment is $800,000.

Example #2

The damage due to Earthquake is $800,000.

The damage due to Fire is $100,000.

Payment for Earthquake damage is $400,000 ($800,000 damage minus $50,000 Earthquake deductible = $750,000; Limit is $400,000)

Payment for Fire damage is $100,000 (amount of damage)

Total Loss Payment is $500,000.

G. Property Damage Deductible

1. The provisions of Section **G.2.** of this endorsement are applicable to all Coverage Forms except:

   a. Business Income (And Extra Expense) Coverage Form;

   b. Business Income (Without Extra Expense) Coverage Form;

   c. Extra Expense Coverage Form.

2. The Deductible, if any, in this Coverage Part is replaced by the following with respect to Earthquake and Volcanic Eruption:

   a. **All Policies**

      (1) The Deductible provisions apply to each Earthquake or Volcanic Eruption.

      (2) Separate Deductibles are calculated for, and apply to, each building, personal property at each building and personal property in the open. Deductibles are separately calculated and applied even if:

         (a) Two or more buildings sustain loss or damage;

         (b) Personal property at two or more buildings sustains loss or damage; and/or

         (c) A building and the personal property in that building sustain loss or damage.

      (3) We will not pay for loss or damage until the amount of loss or damage exceeds the applicable Deductible. We will then pay the amount of loss or damage in excess of that Deductible, up to the applicable Limit of Insurance.

Commercial Property

(4) When property is covered under the Coverage Extension for Newly Acquired or Constructed Property: In determining the amount, if any, that we will pay for loss or damage, we will deduct an amount equal to a percentage of the value of the property at time of loss. The applicable percentage for Newly Acquired or Constructed Property is the highest percentage shown in the Earthquake – Volcanic Eruption Coverage Schedule or in the Declarations for any described premises.

(5) If there is loss or damage caused by Earthquake or Volcanic Eruption, and loss or damage caused by a Cause of Loss (e.g., fire) that is covered by means of an exception to the Earth Movement Exclusion, then the only applicable Deductible provisions are those stated in this endorsement.

b. Calculation Of The Deductible – Specific Insurance Other Than Builders Risk

(1) Property Not Subject To Value Reporting Forms

In determining the amount, if any, that we will pay for loss or damage, we will deduct an amount equal to a percentage (as shown in the Earthquake – Volcanic Eruption Coverage Schedule or in the Declarations, concerning the Earthquake – Volcanic Eruption Deductible) of the value of the property that has sustained loss or damage. The value to be used is that shown in the most recent Statement of Values on file with us.

(2) Property Subject To Value Reporting Forms

In determining the amount, if any, that we will pay for loss or damage, we will deduct an amount equal to a percentage (as shown in the Earthquake – Volcanic Eruption Coverage Schedule or in the Declarations, concerning the Earthquake – Volcanic Eruption Deductible) of the value of the property that has sustained loss or damage. The value to be used is the latest value shown in the most recent Report of Values on file with us.

However:

(a) If the most recent Report of Values shows less than the full value of the property on the report dates, we will determine the deductible amount as a percentage of the full value as of the report dates.

(b) If the first Report of Values is not filed with us prior to loss or damage, we will determine the deductible amount as a percentage of the value shown in the most recent Statement of Values on file with us.

c. Calculation Of The Deductible – Blanket Insurance Other Than Builders Risk

(1) Property Not Subject To Value Reporting Forms

In determining the amount, if any, that we will pay for loss or damage, we will deduct an amount equal to a percentage (as shown in the Earthquake – Volcanic Eruption Coverage Schedule or in the Declarations, concerning the Earthquake – Volcanic Eruption Deductible) of the value of the property that has sustained loss or damage. The value to be used is that shown in the most recent Statement of Values on file with us.

(2) Property Subject To Value Reporting Forms

In determining the amount, if any, that we will pay for property that has sustained loss or damage, we will deduct an amount equal to a percentage (as shown in the Earthquake – Volcanic Eruption Coverage Schedule or in the Declarations, concerning the Earthquake – Volcanic Eruption Deductible) of the value of that property as of the time of loss or damage.

d. Calculation Of The Deductible – Builders Risk Insurance

(1) Builders Risk Other Than Reporting Form

In determining the amount, if any, that we will pay for property that has sustained loss or damage, we will deduct an amount equal to a percentage (as shown in the Earthquake – Volcanic Eruption Coverage Schedule or in the Declarations, concerning the Earthquake – Volcanic Eruption Deductible) of the actual cash value of that property as of the time of loss or damage.

 CP 10 45 08 99   □

(2) Builders Risk Reporting Form

In determining the amount, if any, that we will pay for loss or damage, we will deduct an amount equal to a percentage (as shown in the Earthquake – Volcanic Eruption Coverage Schedule or in the Declarations, concerning the Earthquake – Volcanic Eruption Deductible) of the value of the property that has sustained loss or damage. The value to be used is the actual cash value shown in the most recent Report of Values on file with us.

However:

(a) If the most recent Report of Values shows less than the actual cash value of the property on the report date, we will determine the deductible amount as a percentage of the actual cash value as of the report date.

(b) If the first Report of Values is not filed with us prior to loss or damage, we will determine the deductible amount as a percentage of the actual cash value of the property as of the time of loss or damage.

H. Example – Application Of Deductible In G.2.b.(1) And G.2.c.(1) – For Specific Or Blanket Insurance Other Than Builders Risk (Not Subject To Value Reporting Forms)

The values, as shown in the most recent Statement of Values on file with us, are:

Building #1 $500,000

Building #2 $500,000

Business Personal Property at Building #1 $250,000

Business Personal Property at Building #2 $250,000

For this example, assume that the amounts of loss do not exceed the applicable Limits of Insurance (for specific insurance). Also assume that the total amount of loss does not exceed the applicable blanket Limit of Insurance (for blanket insurance).

Building #1 and Business Personal Property at Building #1 have sustained damage; the amounts of loss are $95,000 (Building) and $5,000 (Business Personal Property).

The Deductible is 10%.

Building

Step **(1):** $500,000 x 10% = $50,000

Step **(2):** $95,000 - $50,000 = $45,000

Business Personal Property

Step **(1):** $250,000 x 10% = $25,000

The loss, $5,000, does not exceed the deductible.

The most we will pay is $45,000. The remainder of the building loss, $50,000, is not covered due to application of the Deductible. There is no loss payment for the business personal property.

I. Business Income And Extra Expense Period Of Restoration

This Section, **I.**, is applicable only to the Coverage Forms specified below:

1. Business Income (And Extra Expense) Coverage Form;

2. Business Income (Without Extra Expense) Coverage Form;

3. Extra Expense Coverage Form.

The "period of restoration" definition stated in the Coverage Form, or in any endorsement amending the beginning of the "period of restoration", applies to each Earthquake or Volcanic Eruption. A single Earthquake or Volcanic Eruption is defined in Section **C.** of this endorsement.

Commercial Property

COMMERCIAL PROPERTY
CP 00 30 06 07

BUSINESS INCOME (AND EXTRA EXPENSE) COVERAGE FORM

Various provisions in this policy restrict coverage. Read the entire policy carefully to determine rights, duties and what is and is not covered.

Throughout this policy the words "you" and "your" refer to the Named Insured shown in the Declarations. The words "we", "us" and "our" refer to the Company providing this insurance.

Other words and phrases that appear in quotation marks have special meaning. Refer to Section **F.**, Definitions.

A. Coverage

1. Business Income

Business Income means the:

a. Net Income (Net Profit or Loss before income taxes) that would have been earned or incurred; and

b. Continuing normal operating expenses incurred, including payroll.

For manufacturing risks, Net Income includes the net sales value of production.

Coverage is provided as described and limited below for one or more of the following options for which a Limit of Insurance is shown in the Declarations:

(1) Business Income Including "Rental Value".

(2) Business Income Other Than "Rental Value".

(3) "Rental Value".

If option **(1)** above is selected, the term Business Income will include "Rental Value". If option **(3)** above is selected, the term Business Income will mean "Rental Value" only.

If Limits of Insurance are shown under more than one of the above options, the provisions of this Coverage Part apply separately to each.

We will pay for the actual loss of Business Income you sustain due to the necessary "suspension" of your "operations" during the "period of restoration". The "suspension" must be caused by direct physical loss of or damage to property at premises which are described in the Declarations and for which a Business Income Limit of Insurance is shown in the Declarations. The loss or damage must be caused by or result from a Covered Cause of Loss. With respect to loss of or damage to personal property in the open or personal property in a vehicle, the described premises include the area within 100 feet of the site at which the described premises are located.

With respect to the requirements set forth in the preceding paragraph, if you occupy only part of the site at which the described premises are located, your premises means:

(a) The portion of the building which you rent, lease or occupy; and

(b) Any area within the building or on the site at which the described premises are located, if that area services, or is used to gain access to, the described premises.

2. Extra Expense

a. Extra Expense Coverage is provided at the premises described in the Declarations only if the Declarations show that Business Income Coverage applies at that premises.

b. Extra Expense means necessary expenses you incur during the "period of restoration" that you would not have incurred if there had been no direct physical loss or damage to property caused by or resulting from a Covered Cause of Loss.

We will pay Extra Expense (other than the expense to repair or replace property) to:

(1) Avoid or minimize the "suspension" of business and to continue operations at the described premises or at replacement premises or temporary locations, including relocation expenses and costs to equip and operate the replacement location or temporary location.

(2) Minimize the "suspension" of business if you cannot continue "operations".

We will also pay Extra Expense to repair or replace property, but only to the extent it reduces the amount of loss that otherwise would have been payable under this Coverage Form.

3. Covered Causes Of Loss, Exclusions And Limitations

See applicable Causes Of Loss Form as shown in the Declarations.

4. Additional Limitation – Interruption Of Computer Operations

a. Coverage for Business Income does not apply when a "suspension" of "operations" is caused by destruction or corruption of electronic data, or any loss or damage to electronic data, except as provided under the Additional Coverage – Interruption Of Computer Operations.

b. Coverage for Extra Expense does not apply when action is taken to avoid or minimize a "suspension" of "operations" caused by destruction or corruption of electronic data, or any loss or damage to electronic data, except as provided under the Additional Coverage – Interruption Of Computer Operations.

c. Electronic data means information, facts or computer programs stored as or on, created or used on, or transmitted to or from computer software (including systems and applications software), on hard or floppy disks, CD-ROMs, tapes, drives, cells, data processing devices or any other repositories of computer software which are used with electronically controlled equipment. The term computer programs, referred to in the foregoing description of electronic data, means a set of related electronic instructions which direct the operations and functions of a computer or device connected to it, which enable the computer or device to receive, process, store, retrieve or send data.

5. Additional Coverages

a. Civil Authority

In this Additional Coverage – Civil Authority, the described premises are premises to which this Coverage Form applies, as shown in the Declarations.

When a Covered Cause of Loss causes damage to property other than property at the described premises, we will pay for the actual loss of Business Income you sustain and necessary Extra Expense caused by action of civil authority that prohibits access to the described premises, provided that both of the following apply:

(1) Access to the area immediately surrounding the damaged property is prohibited by civil authority as a result of the damage, and the described premises are within that area but are not more than one mile from the damaged property; and

(2) The action of civil authority is taken in response to dangerous physical conditions resulting from the damage or continuation of the Covered Cause of Loss that caused the damage, or the action is taken to enable a civil authority to have unimpeded access to the damaged property.

Civil Authority Coverage for Business Income will begin 72 hours after the time of the first action of civil authority that prohibits access to the described premises and will apply for a period of up to four consecutive weeks from the date on which such coverage began.

Civil Authority Coverage for Extra Expense will begin immediately after the time of the first action of civil authority that prohibits access to the described premises and will end:

(1) Four consecutive weeks after the date of that action; or

(2) When your Civil Authority Coverage for Business Income ends;

whichever is later.

b. Alterations And New Buildings

We will pay for the actual loss of Business Income you sustain and necessary Extra Expense you incur due to direct physical loss or damage at the described premises caused by or resulting from any Covered Cause of Loss to:

(1) New buildings or structures, whether complete or under construction;

(2) Alterations or additions to existing buildings or structures; and

© ISO Properties, Inc., 2007 □

Commercial Property

(3) Machinery, equipment, supplies or building materials located on or within 100 feet of the described premises and:

(a) Used in the construction, alterations or additions; or

(b) Incidental to the occupancy of new buildings.

If such direct physical loss or damage delays the start of "operations", the "period of restoration" for Business Income Coverage will begin on the date "operations" would have begun if the direct physical loss or damage had not occurred.

c. Extended Business Income

(1) Business Income Other Than "Rental Value"

If the necessary "suspension" of your "operations" produces a Business Income loss payable under this policy, we will pay for the actual loss of Business Income you incur during the period that:

(a) Begins on the date property (except "finished stock") is actually repaired, rebuilt or replaced and "operations" are resumed; and

(b) Ends on the earlier of:

(i) The date you could restore your "operations", with reasonable speed, to the level which would generate the business income amount that would have existed if no direct physical loss or damage had occurred; or

(ii) 30 consecutive days after the date determined in **(1)(a)** above.

However, Extended Business Income does not apply to loss of Business Income incurred as a result of unfavorable business conditions caused by the impact of the Covered Cause of Loss in the area where the described premises are located.

Loss of Business Income must be caused by direct physical loss or damage at the described premises caused by or resulting from any Covered Cause of Loss.

(2) "Rental Value"

If the necessary "suspension" of your "operations" produces a "Rental Value" loss payable under this policy, we will pay for the actual loss of "Rental Value" you incur during the period that:

(a) Begins on the date property is actually repaired, rebuilt or replaced and tenantability is restored; and

(b) Ends on the earlier of:

(i) The date you could restore tenant occupancy, with reasonable speed, to the level which would generate the "Rental Value" that would have existed if no direct physical loss or damage had occurred; or

(ii) 30 consecutive days after the date determined in **(2)(a)** above.

However, Extended Business Income does not apply to loss of "Rental Value" incurred as a result of unfavorable business conditions caused by the impact of the Covered Cause of Loss in the area where the described premises are located.

Loss of "Rental Value" must be caused by direct physical loss or damage at the described premises caused by or resulting from any Covered Cause of Loss.

d. Interruption Of Computer Operations

(1) Under this Additional Coverage, electronic data has the meaning described under Additional Limitation – Interruption Of Computer Operations.

(2) Subject to all provisions of this Additional Coverage, you may extend the insurance that applies to Business Income and Extra Expense to apply to a "suspension" of "operations" caused by an interruption in computer operations due to destruction or corruption of electronic data due to a Covered Cause of Loss.

(3) With respect to the coverage provided under this Additional Coverage, the Covered Causes of Loss are subject to the following:

(a) If the Causes Of Loss – Special Form applies, coverage under this Additional Coverage – Interruption Of Computer Operations is limited to the "specified causes of loss" as defined in that form, and Collapse as set forth in that form.

(b) If the Causes Of Loss – Broad Form applies, coverage under this Additional Coverage – Interruption Of Computer Operations includes Collapse as set forth in that form.

(c) If the Causes Of Loss Form is endorsed to add a Covered Cause of Loss, the additional Covered Cause of Loss does not apply to the coverage provided under this Additional Coverage – Interruption Of Computer Operations.

(d) The Covered Causes of Loss include a virus, harmful code or similar instruction introduced into or enacted on a computer system (including electronic data) or a network to which it is connected, designed to damage or destroy any part of the system or disrupt its normal operation. But there is no coverage for an interruption related to manipulation of a computer system (including electronic data) by any employee, including a temporary or leased employee, or by an entity retained by you or for you to inspect, design, install, maintain, repair or replace that system.

(4) The most we will pay under this Additional Coverage – Interruption of Computer Operations is $2,500 for all loss sustained and expense incurred in any one policy year, regardless of the number of interruptions or the number of premises, locations or computer systems involved. If loss payment relating to the first interruption does not exhaust this amount, then the balance is available for loss or expense sustained or incurred as a result of subsequent interruptions in that policy year. A balance remaining at the end of a policy year does not increase the amount of insurance in the next policy year. With respect to any interruption which begins in one policy year and continues or results in additional loss or expense in a subsequent policy year(s), all loss and expense is deemed to be sustained or incurred in the policy year in which the interruption began.

(5) This Additional Coverage – Interruption in Computer Operations does not apply to loss sustained or expense incurred after the end of the "period of restoration", even if the amount of insurance stated in **(4)** above has not been exhausted.

6. Coverage Extension

If a Coinsurance percentage of 50% or more is shown in the Declarations, you may extend the insurance provided by this Coverage Part as follows:

NEWLY ACQUIRED LOCATIONS

a. You may extend your Business Income and Extra Expense Coverages to apply to property at any location you acquire other than fairs or exhibitions.

b. The most we will pay under this Extension, for the sum of Business Income loss and Extra Expense incurred, is $100,000 at each location.

       CP 00 30 06 07   ☐

Commercial Property

c. Insurance under this Extension for each newly acquired location will end when any of the following first occurs:

(1) This policy expires;

(2) 30 days expire after you acquire or begin to construct the property; or

(3) You report values to us.

We will charge you additional premium for values reported from the date you acquire the property.

The Additional Condition, Coinsurance, does not apply to this Extension.

B. Limits Of Insurance

The most we will pay for loss in any one occurrence is the applicable Limit of Insurance shown in the Declarations.

Payments under the following coverages will not increase the applicable Limit of Insurance:

1. Alterations And New Buildings;

2. Civil Authority;

3. Extra Expense; or

4. Extended Business Income.

The amounts of insurance stated in the Interruption Of Computer Operations Additional Coverage and the Newly Acquired Locations Coverage Extension apply in accordance with the terms of those coverages and are separate from the Limit(s) of Insurance shown in the Declarations for any other coverage.

C. Loss Conditions

The following conditions apply in addition to the Common Policy Conditions and the Commercial Property Conditions.

1. Appraisal

If we and you disagree on the amount of Net Income and operating expense or the amount of loss, either may make written demand for an appraisal of the loss. In this event, each party will select a competent and impartial appraiser.

The two appraisers will select an umpire. If they cannot agree, either may request that selection be made by a judge of a court having jurisdiction. The appraisers will state separately the amount of Net Income and operating expense or amount of loss. If they fail to agree, they will submit their differences to the umpire. A decision agreed to by any two will be binding. Each party will:

a. Pay its chosen appraiser; and

b. Bear the other expenses of the appraisal and umpire equally.

If there is an appraisal, we will still retain our right to deny the claim.

2. Duties In The Event Of Loss

a. You must see that the following are done in the event of loss:

(1) Notify the police if a law may have been broken.

(2) Give us prompt notice of the direct physical loss or damage. Include a description of the property involved.

(3) As soon as possible, give us a description of how, when, and where the direct physical loss or damage occurred.

(4) Take all reasonable steps to protect the Covered Property from further damage, and keep a record of your expenses necessary to protect the Covered Property, for consideration in the settlement of the claim. This will not increase the Limit of Insurance. However, we will not pay for any subsequent loss or damage resulting from a cause of loss that is not a Covered Cause of Loss. Also, if feasible, set the damaged property aside and in the best possible order for examination.

(5) As often as may be reasonably required, permit us to inspect the property proving the loss or damage and examine your books and records.

Also permit us to take samples of damaged and undamaged property for inspection, testing and analysis, and permit us to make copies from your books and records.

(6) Send us a signed, sworn proof of loss containing the information we request to investigate the claim. You must do this within 60 days after our request. We will supply you with the necessary forms.

(7) Cooperate with us in the investigation or settlement of the claim.

(8) If you intend to continue your business, you must resume all or part of your "operations" as quickly as possible.

b. We may examine any insured under oath, while not in the presence of any other insured and at such times as may be reasonably required, about any matter relating to this insurance or the claim, including an insured's books and records. In the event of an examination, an insured's answers must be signed.

3. Loss Determination

a. The amount of Business Income loss will be determined based on:

(1) The Net Income of the business before the direct physical loss or damage occurred;

(2) The likely Net Income of the business if no physical loss or damage had occurred, but not including any Net Income that would likely have been earned as a result of an increase in the volume of business due to favorable business conditions caused by the impact of the Covered Cause of Loss on customers or on other businesses;

(3) The operating expenses, including payroll expenses, necessary to resume "operations" with the same quality of service that existed just before the direct physical loss or damage; and

(4) Other relevant sources of information, including:

(a) Your financial records and accounting procedures;

(b) Bills, invoices and other vouchers; and

(c) Deeds, liens or contracts.

b. The amount of Extra Expense will be determined based on:

(1) All expenses that exceed the normal operating expenses that would have been incurred by "operations" during the "period of restoration" if no direct physical loss or damage had occurred. We will deduct from the total of such expenses:

(a) The salvage value that remains of any property bought for temporary use during the "period of restoration", once "operations" are resumed; and

(b) Any Extra Expense that is paid for by other insurance, except for insurance that is written subject to the same plan, terms, conditions and provisions as this insurance; and

(2) Necessary expenses that reduce the Business Income loss that otherwise would have been incurred.

c. Resumption Of Operations

We will reduce the amount of your:

(1) Business Income loss, other than Extra Expense, to the extent you can resume your "operations", in whole or in part, by using damaged or undamaged property (including merchandise or stock) at the described premises or elsewhere.

(2) Extra Expense loss to the extent you can return "operations" to normal and discontinue such Extra Expense.

d. If you do not resume "operations", or do not resume "operations" as quickly as possible, we will pay based on the length of time it would have taken to resume "operations" as quickly as possible.

4. Loss Payment

We will pay for covered loss within 30 days after we receive the sworn proof of loss, if you have complied with all of the terms of this Coverage Part and:

a. We have reached agreement with you on the amount of loss; or

b. An appraisal award has been made.

D. Additional Condition

COINSURANCE

If a Coinsurance percentage is shown in the Declarations, the following condition applies in addition to the Common Policy Conditions and the Commercial Property Conditions.

We will not pay the full amount of any Business Income loss if the Limit of Insurance for Business Income is less than:

1. The Coinsurance percentage shown for Business Income in the Declarations; times

2. The sum of:

a. The Net Income (Net Profit or Loss before income taxes), and

b. Operating expenses, including payroll expenses,

that would have been earned or incurred (had no loss occurred) by your "operations" at the described premises for the 12 months following the inception, or last previous anniversary date, of this policy (whichever is later).

Commercial Property

Instead, we will determine the most we will pay using the following steps:

Step **(1)**: Multiply the Net Income and operating expense for the 12 months following the inception, or last previous anniversary date, of this policy by the Coinsurance percentage;

Step **(2)**: Divide the Limit of Insurance for the described premises by the figure determined in Step **(1)**; and

Step **(3)**: Multiply the total amount of loss by the figure determined in Step **(2)**.

We will pay the amount determined in Step **(3)** or the limit of insurance, whichever is less. For the remainder, you will either have to rely on other insurance or absorb the loss yourself.

In determining operating expenses for the purpose of applying the Coinsurance condition, the following expenses, if applicable, shall be deducted from the total of all operating expenses:

(1) Prepaid freight – outgoing;

(2) Returns and allowances;

(3) Discounts;

(4) Bad debts;

(5) Collection expenses;

(6) Cost of raw stock and factory supplies consumed (including transportation charges);

(7) Cost of merchandise sold (including transportation charges);

(8) Cost of other supplies consumed (including transportation charges);

(9) Cost of services purchased from outsiders (not employees) to resell, that do not continue under contract;

(10) Power, heat and refrigeration expenses that do not continue under contract (if Form **CP 15 11** is attached);

(11) All ordinary payroll expenses or the amount of payroll expense excluded (if Form **CP 15 10** is attached); and

(12) Special deductions for mining properties (royalties unless specifically included in coverage; actual depletion commonly known as unit or cost depletion – not percentage depletion; welfare and retirement fund charges based on tonnage; hired trucks).

EXAMPLE #1 (UNDERINSURANCE)

When: The Net Income and operating expenses for the 12 months following the inception, or last previous anniversary date, of this policy at the described premises would have been: $ 400,000

The Coinsurance percentage is: 50%

The Limit of Insurance is: $ 150,000

The amount of loss is: $ 80,000

Step **(1)**: $400,000 x 50% = $200,000

(the minimum amount of insurance to meet your Coinsurance requirements)

Step **(2)**: $150,000 ÷ $200,000 = .75

Step **(3)**: $80,000 x .75 = $60,000

We will pay no more than $60,000. The remaining $20,000 is not covered.

EXAMPLE #2 (ADEQUATE INSURANCE)

When: The Net Income and operating expenses for the 12 months following the inception, or last previous anniversary date, of this policy at the described premises would have been: $ 400,000

The Coinsurance percentage is: 50%

The Limit of Insurance is: $ 200,000

The amount of loss is: $ 80,000

The minimum amount of insurance to meet your Coinsurance requirement is $200,000 ($400,000 x 50%). Therefore, the Limit of Insurance in this example is adequate and no penalty applies. We will pay no more than $80,000 (amount of loss).

This condition does not apply to Extra Expense Coverage.

E. Optional Coverages

If shown as applicable in the Declarations, the following Optional Coverages apply separately to each item.

1. Maximum Period Of Indemnity

a. The Additional Condition, Coinsurance, does not apply to this Coverage Form at the described premises to which this Optional Coverage applies.

b. The most we will pay for the total of Business Income loss and Extra Expense is the lesser of:

    (1) The amount of loss sustained and expenses incurred during the 120 days immediately following the beginning of the "period of restoration"; or

    (2) The Limit of Insurance shown in the Declarations.

2. Monthly Limit Of Indemnity

  a. The Additional Condition, Coinsurance, does not apply to this Coverage Form at the described premises to which this Optional Coverage applies.

  b. The most we will pay for loss of Business Income in each period of 30 consecutive days after the beginning of the "period of restoration" is:

    (1) The Limit of Insurance, multiplied by

    (2) The fraction shown in the Declarations for this Optional Coverage.

EXAMPLE

When:	The Limit of Insurance is:	$ 120,000
	The fraction shown in the Declarations for this Optional Coverage is:	1/4
	The most we will pay for loss in each period of 30 consecutive days is:	$ 30,000
	($120,000 x 1/4 = $30,000)	
	If, in this example, the actual amount of loss is:	
	Days 1–30:	$ 40,000
	Days 31–60:	$ 20,000
	Days 61–90:	$ 30,000
		$ 90,000
	We will pay:	
	Days 1–30:	$ 30,000
	Days 31–60:	$ 20,000
	Days 61–90:	$ 30,000
		$ 80,000

The remaining $10,000 is not covered.

3. Business Income Agreed Value

  a. To activate this Optional Coverage:

    (1) A Business Income Report/Work Sheet must be submitted to us and must show financial data for your "operations":

      (a) During the 12 months prior to the date of the Work Sheet; and

      (b) Estimated for the 12 months immediately following the inception of this Optional Coverage.

    (2) The Declarations must indicate that the Business Income Agreed Value Optional Coverage applies, and an Agreed Value must be shown in the Declarations. The Agreed Value should be at least equal to:

      (a) The Coinsurance percentage shown in the Declarations; multiplied by

      (b) The amount of Net Income and operating expenses for the following 12 months you report on the Work Sheet.

  b. The Additional Condition, Coinsurance, is suspended until:

    (1) 12 months after the effective date of this Optional Coverage; or

    (2) The expiration date of this policy;

    whichever occurs first.

  c. We will reinstate the Additional Condition, Coinsurance, automatically if you do not submit a new Work Sheet and Agreed Value:

    (1) Within 12 months of the effective date of this Optional Coverage; or

    (2) When you request a change in your Business Income Limit of Insurance.

  d. If the Business Income Limit of Insurance is less than the Agreed Value, we will not pay more of any loss than the amount of loss multiplied by:

    (1) The Business Income Limit of Insurance; divided by

    (2) The Agreed Value.

Commercial Property

EXAMPLE

When: The Limit of Insurance is: $ 100,000
        The Agreed Value is: $ 200,000
        The amount of loss is: $ 80,000

Step **(1)**: $100,000 ÷ $200,000 = .50

Step **(2)**: .50 x $80,000 = $40,000

We will pay $40,000. The remaining $40,000 is not covered.

4. Extended Period Of Indemnity

Under Paragraph **A.5.c., Extended Business Income,** the number 30 in Subparagraphs **(1)(b)** and **(2)(b)** is replaced by the number shown in the Declarations for this Optional Coverage.

F. Definitions

1. "Finished stock" means stock you have manufactured.

"Finished stock" also includes whiskey and alcoholic products being aged, unless there is a Coinsurance percentage shown for Business Income in the Declarations.

"Finished stock" does not include stock you have manufactured that is held for sale on the premises of any retail outlet insured under this Coverage Part.

2. "Operations" means:

a. Your business activities occurring at the described premises; and

b. The tenantability of the described premises, if coverage for Business Income Including "Rental Value" or "Rental Value" applies.

3. "Period of restoration" means the period of time that:

a. Begins:

(1) 72 hours after the time of direct physical loss or damage for Business Income Coverage; or

(2) Immediately after the time of direct physical loss or damage for Extra Expense Coverage;

caused by or resulting from any Covered Cause of Loss at the described premises; and

b. Ends on the earlier of:

(1) The date when the property at the described premises should be repaired, rebuilt or replaced with reasonable speed and similar quality; or

(2) The date when business is resumed at a new permanent location.

"Period of restoration" does not include any increased period required due to the enforcement of any ordinance or law that:

(1) Regulates the construction, use or repair, or requires the tearing down, of any property; or

(2) Requires any insured or others to test for, monitor, clean up, remove, contain, treat, detoxify or neutralize, or in any way respond to, or assess the effects of "pollutants".

The expiration date of this policy will not cut short the "period of restoration".

4. "Pollutants" means any solid, liquid, gaseous or thermal irritant or contaminant, including smoke, vapor, soot, fumes, acids, alkalis, chemicals and waste. Waste includes materials to be recycled, reconditioned or reclaimed.

5. "Rental Value" means Business Income that consists of:

a. Net Income (Net Profit or Loss before income taxes) that would have been earned or incurred as rental income from tenant occupancy of the premises described in the Declarations as furnished and equipped by you, including fair rental value of any portion of the described premises which is occupied by you; and

b. Continuing normal operating expenses incurred in connection with that premises, including:

(1) Payroll; and

(2) The amount of charges which are the legal obligation of the tenant(s) but would otherwise be your obligations.

6. "Suspension" means:

a. The slowdown or cessation of your business activities; or

b. That a part or all of the described premises is rendered untenantable, if coverage for Business Income Including "Rental Value" or "Rental Value" applies.

Commercial Inland Marine Insurance

Inland marine insurance grew out of ocean marine cargo insurance to meet new coverage needs that emerged in the early twentieth century. Today the category covers a wide range of loss exposures whose common link is an element of transportation or communication. Examples of inland marine exposures are property in domestic transit, property in the custody of a bailee, mobile equipment, buildings in the course of construction, computer equipment, and cable TV systems.

In many states (depending on state insurance regulations), some types of commercial inland marine insurance are nonfiled, meaning that insurers are not required to file their forms or rates with regulatory authorities. Being exempt from filing requirements allows insurers to tailor inland marine forms and rates to fit particular loss exposures that are not adequately insured under standard commercial property forms.

The American Association of Insurance Services (AAIS) and Insurance Services Office, Inc. (ISO) both publish policy forms and endorsements for the filed and the nonfiled classes of inland marine. The AAIS forms reprinted in the *Handbook* are only a small sampling of the many commercial inland marine forms in existence.

AAIS
IM 7250 04 04
Page 1 of 12

TRANSPORTATION COVERAGE

AGREEMENT

In return for "your" payment of the required premium, "we" provide the coverage described herein subject to all the "terms" of the Transportation Coverage. This coverage is also subject to the "schedule of coverages" and additional policy conditions relating to assignment or transfer of rights or duties, cancellation, changes or modifications, inspections, and examination of books and records.

Endorsements and schedules may also apply. They are identified on the "schedule of coverages".

Refer to Definitions for words and phrases that have special meaning. These words and phrases are shown in quotation marks or bold type.

DEFINITIONS

1. The words "you" and "your" mean the persons or organizations named as the insured on the declarations.

2. The words "we", "us", and "our" mean the company providing this coverage.

3. "Aircraft" means any one aircraft, airplane, helicopter, dirigible, or any machine capable of flight.

4. "Carrier for hire" means any one vehicle, truck, trailer, semitrailer, or combination of these pulled by one power unit operated by a carrier for hire.

5. "Limit" means the amount of coverage that applies.

6. "Owned vehicle" means any one vehicle, truck, trailer, semitrailer, or combination of these pulled by one power unit owned by "you" or leased by "you" and that is operated by "you".

7. "Perishable stock" means property preserved and maintained under controlled conditions and susceptible to loss or damage if the controlled conditions change.

8. "Pollutant" means:

    a. any solid, liquid, gaseous, thermal, or radioactive irritant or contaminant, including acids, alkalis, chemicals, fumes, smoke, soot, vapor, and waste. Waste includes materials to be recycled, reclaimed, or reconditioned, as well as disposed of; and

    b. electrical or magnetic emissions, whether visible or invisible, and sound emissions.

9. "Railroad car" means any one railroad car, boxcar, tank car, flat car, or similar rolling stock including any railroad car transporting property in or on one or more trucks, trailers, semitrailers, or other containers.

10. "Schedule of coverages" means:

    a. all pages labeled schedule of coverages or schedules which pertain to this coverage; and

    b. declarations or supplemental declarations which pertain to this coverage.

11. "Specified perils" means the perils of:

    a. fire;

    b   lightning; windstorm; hail;

    c. collision, overturn, or derailment of a transporting conveyance;

AAIS
IM 7250 04 04
Page 2 of 12

d.   collapse of a bridge or culvert; and

e.   theft.

12. "Spoilage" means any detrimental change in physical state of "perishable stock". Detrimental change includes, but is not limited to, thawing of frozen goods, warming of refrigerated goods, solidification of liquid material.

13. "Terminal" means a building where covered property is transferred between vehicles or between vehicles and other transporting conveyances.

The transfer of covered property is limited to:

a.   loading and unloading; and

b.   any temporary storage associated with the transfer of property.

14. "Terms" means all provisions, limitations, exclusions, conditions, and definitions that apply.

15. "Train" means one or more railroad cars, boxcars, tank cars, flat cars, or similar rolling stock connected together and pulled by one or more locomotives.

16. "Transit" means the shipment of covered property that:

a.   begins at the point of shipment to a specific destination;

b.   includes the ordinary reasonable and necessary stops, interruptions, delays, or transfers incidental to the route and method of shipment, including rest periods taken by the driver(s); and

c.   ends upon acceptance of the goods by or on behalf of the consignee at the specified destination.

PROPERTY COVERED

"We" cover the following property unless the property is excluded or subject to limitations.

1.   **Property In A Terminal --**

a.   **Coverage** -- "We" cover direct physical loss caused by a covered peril to property described on the "schedule of coverages" while at a "terminal" location.

b.   **Coverage Limitations --**

1)   "We" only cover described property while:

a)   at a "terminal" location that is described on the "schedule of coverages" or within 100 feet of the described "terminal"; and

b)   the property is in due course of "transit".

2)   If property described on the "schedule of coverages" includes property of others, "we" only cover property of others to the extent of "your" legal liability for direct physical loss caused by a covered peril.

2.   **Property In Transit --**

a.   **Coverage** -- "We" cover direct physical loss caused by a covered peril to property described on the "schedule of coverages" while in due course of "transit" including loading and unloading.

b.   **Coverage Limitations --**

1)   "We" only cover described property while in due course of "transit" when a "limit" for one or more of the following modes of transportation is indicated on the "schedule of coverages":

a)   Aircraft;
b)   Owned Vehicle;

AAIS
IM 7250 04 04
Page 3 of 12

c) Carrier For Hire; or
d) Railroad.

2) If property described on the "schedule of coverages" includes property of others, "we" only cover property of others to the extent of "your" legal liability for direct physical loss caused by a covered peril.

3) "We" only cover loading and unloading if the described property is loaded from or unloaded onto a sidewalk, street, loading dock, or similar area that is adjacent to the indicated mode of transportation.

PROPERTY NOT COVERED

1. **Art, Antiques And Fur** -- "We" do not cover objects of art, antiques, or fur garments.

2. **Carrier For Hire** -- "We" do not cover property of others that "you" are responsible for as:

   a. a carrier for hire; or

   b. an arranger of transportation; this includes carloader, consolidator, broker, freight forwarder, or shipping association.

3. **Contraband** -- "We" do not cover contraband or property in the course of illegal transportation or trade.

4. **Exports And Imports** -- "We" do not cover exported or imported property:

   a. that is covered under any ocean marine cargo policy that anyone has obtained to cover exports or imports; or

   b. while on an ocean or air conveyance.

5. **Jewelry, Stones And Metals** -- "We" do not cover jewelry, precious or semi-precious stones, gold, silver, platinum, or other precious metals or alloys.

6. **Lease Agreement** -- "We" do not cover property for which "you" are contractually liable under a lease agreement with any transportation carrier.

7. **Live Animals** -- "We" do not cover animals including cattle or poultry unless death is caused or made necessary by a "specified peril".

8. **Mail** -- "We" do not cover mail shipments in the custody of the U.S. Postal Service.

9. **Money And Securities** -- "We" do not cover accounts, bills, currency, food stamps, or other evidences of debt, lottery tickets not held for sale, money, notes, or securities.

10. **Samples** -- "We" do not cover samples while in the custody of a sales representative.

11. **Storage** -- "We" do not cover property held in storage.

COVERAGE EXTENSIONS

Provisions That Apply To Coverage Extensions -- The following Coverage Extensions indicate an applicable "limit". This "limit" may also be shown on the "schedule of coverages".

If a different "limit" is indicated on the "schedule of coverages", that "limit" will apply instead of the "limit" shown below.

AAIS
IM 7250 04 04
Page 4 of 12

However, if no "limit" is indicated for a Coverage Extension, coverage is provided up to the full "limit" for the applicable covered property unless a different "limit" is indicated on the "schedule of coverages".

Unless otherwise indicated, the coverages provided below are part of and not in addition to the applicable "limit" for coverage described under Property Covered.

The "limit" provided under a Coverage Extension cannot be combined or added to the "limit" for any other Coverage Extension or Supplemental Coverage including a Coverage Extension or Supplemental Coverage that is added to this policy by endorsement.

If coinsurance provisions are part of this policy, the following coverage extensions are not subject to and not considered in applying coinsurance conditions.

1.   **Debris Removal** --

a.   **Coverage** -- "We" pay the cost to remove the debris of covered property that is caused by a covered peril.

b.   **We Do Not Cover** -- This coverage does not include costs to:

1)   extract "pollutants" from land or water; or
2)   remove, restore, or replace polluted land or water.

c.   **Limit** -- "We" do not pay any more under this coverage than 25% of the amount "we" pay for the direct physical loss. "We" will not pay more for loss to property and debris removal combined than the "limit" for the damaged property.

d.   **Additional Limit** -- "We" pay up to an additional $5,000 for debris removal expense when the debris removal expense exceeds 25% of the amount "we" pay for direct physical loss or when the loss to property and debris removal combined exceeds the "limit" for the damaged property.

e.   **You Must Report Your Expenses** -- "We" do not pay any expenses unless they are reported to "us" in writing within 180 days from the date of direct physical loss to covered property.

2.   **Emergency Removal** --

a.   **Coverage** -- "We" pay for any direct physical loss to covered property while it is being moved or being stored to prevent a loss caused by a covered peril.

b.   **Time Limitation** -- This coverage applies for up to 365 days after the property is first moved. Also, this coverage does not extend past the date on which this policy expires.

SUPPLEMENTAL COVERAGES

Provisions That Apply To Supplemental Coverages -- The following Supplemental Coverages indicate an applicable "limit". This "limit" may also be shown on the "schedule of coverages".

If a different "limit" is indicated on the "schedule of coverages", that "limit" will apply instead of the "limit" shown below.

However, if no "limit" is indicated for a Supplemental Coverage, coverage is provided up to the full "limit" for the applicable covered property unless a different "limit" is indicated on the "schedule of coverages".

Unless otherwise indicated, a "limit" for a Supplemental Coverage provided below is separate from, and not part of, the applicable "limit" for coverage described under Property Covered.

The "limit" available for coverage described under a Supplemental Coverage:

a.   is the only "limit" available for the described coverage; and

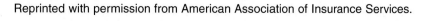

Comm. Inland Marine

AAIS
IM 7250 04 04
Page 5 of 12

b. is not the sum of the "limit" indicated for a Supplemental Coverage and the "limit" for coverage described under Property Covered.

The "limit" provided under a Supplemental Coverage cannot be combined or added to the "limit" for any other Supplemental Coverage or Coverage Extension including a Supplemental Coverage or Coverage Extension that is added to this policy by endorsement.

If coinsurance provisions are part of this policy, the following supplemental coverages are not subject to and not considered in applying coinsurance conditions.

1. **Pollutant Cleanup And Removal** --

    a. **Coverage** -- "We" pay "your" expense to extract "pollutants" from land or water if the discharge, dispersal, seepage, migration, release, or escape of the "pollutants" is caused by a covered peril that occurs during the policy period.

    b. **Time Limitation** -- The expenses to extract "pollutants" are paid only if they are reported to "us" in writing within 180 days from the date the covered peril occurs.

    c. **We Do Not Cover** -- "We" do not pay the cost of testing, evaluating, observing, or recording the existence, level, or effects of "pollutants".

        However, "we" pay the cost of testing which is necessary for the extraction of "pollutants" from land or water.

    d. **Limit** -- The most "we" pay for each location is $10,000 for the sum of all such expenses arising out of a covered peril occurring during each separate 12-month period of this policy.

2. **Property You Have Sold** --

    a. **Coverage** -- "We" pay for direct physical loss caused by a covered peril to covered property that "you" have sold and are shipping at the owner's risk.

    b. **Coverage Limitation** -- "We" only cover property that "you" have sold when the shipment has been rejected by the owner because:

        1) the property is damaged; and
        2) the owner of the property has refused to pay "you".

3. **Rejected Shipments** --

    a. **Coverage** -- "We" pay for direct physical loss caused by a covered peril to outgoing shipments of covered property that have been rejected by the consignee, including shipments that are not deliverable.

    b. **Coverage Limitation** -- "We" only cover rejected shipments while the property is:

        1) in due course of "transit" back to "you"; or
        2) awaiting return shipment to "you".

    c. **Time Limitation** -- This supplemental coverage will end ten days after delivery has been attempted or made to the consignee unless the covered property is in due course of "transit" back to "you".

PERILS COVERED

"We" cover risks of direct physical loss unless the loss is limited or caused by a peril that is excluded.

AAIS
IM 7250 04 04
Page 6 of 12

PERILS EXCLUDED

1. "We" do not pay for loss or damage caused directly or indirectly by one or more of the following excluded causes or events. Such loss or damage is excluded regardless of other causes or events that contribute to or aggravate the loss, whether such causes or events act to produce the loss before, at the same time as, or after the excluded causes or events.

    a. **Civil Authority** -- "We" do not pay for loss caused by order of any civil authority, including seizure, confiscation, destruction, or quarantine of property.

        "We" do cover loss resulting from acts of destruction by the civil authority to prevent the spread of fire, unless the fire is caused by a peril excluded under this coverage.

    b. **Nuclear Hazard** -- "We" do not pay for loss caused by or resulting from a nuclear reaction, nuclear radiation, or radioactive contamination (whether controlled or uncontrolled; whether caused by natural, accidental, or artificial means). Loss caused by nuclear hazard is not considered loss caused by fire, explosion, or smoke. Direct loss by fire resulting from the nuclear hazard is covered.

    c. **War And Military Action** -- "We" do not pay for loss caused by:

        1) war, including undeclared war or civil war; or
        2) a warlike action by a military force, including action taken to prevent or defend against an actual or expected attack, by any government, sovereign, or other authority using military personnel or other agents; or
        3) insurrection, rebellion, revolution, or unlawful seizure of power including action taken by governmental authority to prevent or defend against any of these.

    With regard to any action that comes within the "terms" of this exclusion and involves nuclear reaction, nuclear radiation, or radioactive contamination, this War and Military Action Exclusion will apply in place of the Nuclear Hazard Exclusion.

2. "We" do not pay for loss or damage that is caused by or results from one or more of the following:

    a. **Contamination Or Deterioration** -- "We" do not pay for loss caused by contamination or deterioration including corrosion; decay; fungus; mildew; mold; rot; rust; or any quality, fault, or weakness in the covered property that causes it to damage or destroy itself.

        But if contamination or deterioration results in a "specified peril", "we" do cover the loss or damage caused by that "specified peril".

    b. **Criminal, Fraudulent, Dishonest, Or Illegal Acts** -- "We" do not pay for loss caused by or resulting from criminal, fraudulent, dishonest, or illegal acts committed alone or in collusion with another by:

        1) "you";
        2) others who have an interest in the property;
        3) others to whom "you" entrust the property;
        4) "your" partners, officers, directors, trustees, joint venturers, or "your" members or managers if "you" are a limited liability company; or
        5) the employees or agents of 1), 2), 3), or 4) above, whether or not they are at work.

        This exclusion does not apply to acts of destruction by "your" employees, but "we" do not pay for theft by employees.

        This exclusion does not apply to covered property in the custody of a carrier for hire.

Comm. Inland Marine

c. **Loss Of Use** -- "We" do not pay for loss caused by or resulting from loss of use, delay, or loss of market.

d. **Missing Property** -- "We" do not pay for missing property where the only proof of loss is unexplained or mysterious disappearance of covered property, or shortage of property discovered on taking inventory, or any other instance where there is no physical evidence to show what happened to the covered property.

This exclusion does not apply to covered property in the custody of a carrier for hire.

e. **Pollutants** -- "We" do not pay for loss caused by or resulting from release, discharge, seepage, migration, dispersal, or escape of "pollutants":

1) unless the release, discharge, seepage, migration, dispersal, or escape is caused by a "specified peril"; or
2) except as specifically provided under the Supplemental Coverages - Pollutant Cleanup and Removal.

"We" do cover any resulting loss caused by a "specified peril".

f. **Spoilage** -- "We" do not pay for loss to "perishable stock" caused by "spoilage".

g. **Temperature/Humidity** -- "We" do not pay for loss caused by dryness, dampness, humidity, or changes in or extremes of temperature.

But if dryness, dampness, humidity, or changes in or extremes of temperature results in a "specified peril", "we" do cover the loss or damage caused by that "specified peril".

h. **Voluntary Parting** -- "We" do not pay for loss caused by or resulting from voluntary parting with title to or possession of any property because of any fraudulent scheme, trick, or false pretense.

"We" do cover loss to covered property caused by false bills of lading or shipping receipts that "you" accept in good faith.

i. **Wear And Tear** -- "We" do not pay for loss caused by wear and tear, marring, or scratching.

But if wear and tear, marring, or scratching results in a "specified peril", "we" do cover the loss or damage caused by that "specified peril".

WHAT MUST BE DONE IN CASE OF LOSS

1. **Notice** -- In case of a loss, "you" must:

   a. give "us" or "our" agent prompt notice including a description of the property involved ("we" may request written notice); and

   b. give notice to the police when the act that causes the loss is a crime.

2. **You Must Protect Property** -- "You" must take all reasonable steps to protect covered property at and after an insured loss to avoid further loss.

   a. **Payment Of Reasonable Costs** -- "We" do pay the reasonable costs incurred by "you" for necessary repairs or emergency measures performed solely to protect covered property from further damage by a peril insured against if a peril insured against has already caused a loss to covered property. "You" must keep an accurate record of such costs. "Our" payment of reasonable costs does not increase the "limit".

AAIS
IM 7250 04 04
Page 8 of 12

b. **We Do Not Pay** -- "We" do not pay for such repairs or emergency measures performed on property which has not been damaged by a peril insured against.

3. **Proof Of Loss** -- "You" must send "us", within 60 days after "our" request, a signed, sworn proof of loss. This must include the following information:

a. the time, place, and circumstances of the loss;

b. other policies of insurance that may cover the loss;

c. "your" interest and the interests of all others in the property involved, including all mortgages and liens;

d. changes in title of the covered property during the policy period; and

e. estimates, specifications, inventories, and other reasonable information that "we" may require to settle the loss.

4. **Examination** -- "You" must submit to examination under oath in matters connected with the loss as often as "we" reasonably request and give "us" sworn statements of the answers. If more than one person is examined, "we" have the right to examine and receive statements separately and not in the presence of others.

5. **Records** -- "You" must produce records, including tax returns and bank microfilms of all canceled checks relating to value, loss, and expense and permit copies and extracts to be made of them as often as "we" reasonably request.

6. **Damaged Property** -- "You" must exhibit the damaged and undamaged property as often as "we" reasonably request and allow "us" to inspect or take samples of the property.

7. **Volunteer Payments** -- "You" must not, except at "your" own expense, voluntarily make any payments, assume any obligations, pay or offer any rewards, or incur any other expenses except as respects protecting property from further damage.

8. **Abandonment** -- "You" may not abandon the property to "us" without "our" written consent.

9. **Cooperation** -- "You" must cooperate with "us" in performing all acts required by this policy.

VALUATION

1. **Value Of Covered Property** -- The value of covered property is based on the following:

a. **Invoice** -- The value of covered property is based on the invoice amount plus accrued costs, pre-paid charges, and charges since shipment.

b. **Actual Cash Value** -- In the absence of an invoice the value of covered property will be based on the actual cash value at the time of loss (with a deduction for depreciation).

2. **Pair Or Set** -- The value of a lost or damaged article which is part of a pair or set is based on a reasonable proportion of the value of the entire pair or set. The loss is not considered a total loss of the pair or set.

3. **Loss To Parts** -- The value of a lost or damaged part of an item that consists of several parts when it is complete is based on the value of only the lost or damaged part or the cost to repair or replace it.

Comm. Inland Marine

AAIS
IM 7250 04 04
Page 9 of 12

HOW MUCH WE PAY

1. **Insurable Interest** -- "We" do not cover more than "your" insurable interest in any property.

2. **Deductible** -- "We" pay only that part of "your" loss over the deductible amount indicated on the "schedule of coverages" in any one occurrence.

3. **Loss Settlement Terms** -- Subject to paragraphs 1., 2., 4., and 5. under How Much We Pay:

    a. **We Pay The Lesser Of** -- "We" pay the lesser of:

        1) the amount determined under Valuation;
        2) the cost to repair, replace, or rebuild the property with material of like kind and quality to the extent practicable; or
        3) the "limit" that applies to the mode of transportation or "terminal" location indicated on the "schedule of coverages".

    b. **Catastrophe Limit** -- In no event will "we" pay more than the catastrophe "limit" indicated on the "schedule of coverages" regardless if a loss involves:

        1) one or more modes of transportation;
        2) one or more "terminal" locations; or
        3) any combination of modes of transportation or "terminal" locations.

    c. **When A Railroad Is Transporting A Trailer** -- When a railroad is transporting a truck, trailer, or semitrailer, the "limit" for "railroad car" applies. In no event will "we" combine the "limit" for "railroad car" with the "limit" for:

        1) "owned vehicle"; or
        2) "carrier for hire".

    d. **When A Trailer Is At A Terminal** -- When a truck, trailer, or semitrailer is situated within a "terminal" building or within 100 feet of a "terminal" building, the "limit" for the "terminal" location applies. In no event will "we" combine the "limit" for a "terminal" location with the "limit" for:

        1) "owned vehicle"; or
        2) "carrier for hire".

4. **Insurance Under More Than One Coverage** -- If more than one coverage of this policy insures the same loss, "we" pay no more than the actual claim, loss, or damage sustained.

5. **Insurance Under More Than One Policy** --

    a. **Proportional Share** -- "You" may have another policy subject to the same "terms" as this policy. If "you" do, "we" will pay "our" share of the covered loss. "Our" share is the proportion that the applicable "limit" under this policy bears to the "limit" of all policies covering on the same basis.

    b. **Excess Amount** -- If there is another policy covering the same loss, other than that described above, "we" pay only for the amount of covered loss in excess of the amount due from that other policy, whether "you" can collect on it or not. But "we" do not pay more than the applicable "limit".

AAIS
IM 7250 04 04
Page 10 of 12

LOSS PAYMENT

1. **Loss Payment Options --**

   a. **Our Options --** In the event of loss covered by this coverage form, "we" have the following options:

      1) pay the value of the lost or damaged property;
      2) pay the cost of repairing or replacing the lost or damaged property;
      3) rebuild, repair, or replace the property with other property of equivalent kind and quality, to the extent practicable, within a reasonable time; or
      4) take all or any part of the property at the agreed or appraised value.

   b. **Notice Of Our Intent To Rebuild, Repair, Or Replace --** "We" must give "you" notice of "our" intent to rebuild, repair, or replace within 30 days after receipt of a duly executed proof of loss.

2. **Your Losses --**

   a. **Adjustment And Payment Of Loss --** "We" adjust all losses with "you". Payment will be made to "you" unless another loss payee is named in the policy.

   b. **Conditions For Payment Of Loss --** An insured loss will be payable 30 days after:

      1) a satisfactory proof of loss is received; and
      2) the amount of the loss has been established either by written agreement with "you" or the filing of an appraisal award with "us".

3. **Property Of Others --**

   a. **Adjustment And Payment Of Loss To Property Of Others --** Losses to property of others may be adjusted with and paid to:

      1) "you" on behalf of the owner; or
      2) the owner.

   b. **We Do Not Have To Pay You If We Pay The Owner --** If "we" pay the owner, "we" do not have to pay "you". "We" may also choose to defend any suits brought by the owners at "our" expense.

OTHER CONDITIONS

1. **Appraisal --** If "you" and "we" do not agree on the amount of the loss or the value of covered property, either party may demand that these amounts be determined by appraisal.

   If either makes a written demand for appraisal, each will select a competent, independent appraiser and notify the other of the appraiser's identity within 20 days of receipt of the written demand. The two appraisers will then select a competent, impartial umpire. If the two appraisers are unable to agree upon an umpire within 15 days, "you" or "we" can ask a judge of a court of record in the state where the property is located to select an umpire.

   The appraisers will then determine and state separately the amount of each loss.

   The appraisers will also determine the value of covered property items at the time of the loss, if requested.

Comm. Inland Marine

AAIS
IM 7250 04 04
Page 11 of 12

If the appraisers submit a written report of any agreement to "us", the amount agreed upon will be the amount of the loss. If the appraisers fail to agree within a reasonable time, they will submit only their differences to the umpire. Written agreement so itemized and signed by any two of these three, sets the amount of the loss.

Each appraiser will be paid by the party selecting that appraiser. Other expenses of the appraisal and the compensation of the umpire will be paid equally by "you" and "us".

2. **Benefit To Others** -- Insurance under this coverage shall not directly or indirectly benefit anyone having custody of "your" property.

3. **Conformity With Statute** -- When a condition of this coverage is in conflict with an applicable law, that condition is amended to conform to that law.

4. **Estates** -- This provision applies only if the insured is an individual.

   a. **Your Death** -- On "your" death, "we" cover the following as an insured:

      1) the person who has custody of "your" property until a legal representative is qualified and appointed; or
      2) "your" legal representative.

      This person or organization is an insured only with respect to property covered by this coverage.

   b. **Policy Period Is Not Extended** -- This coverage does not extend past the policy period indicated on the declarations.

5. **Misrepresentation, Concealment, Or Fraud** -- This coverage is void as to "you" and any other insured if, before or after a loss:

   a. "you" or any other insured have willfully concealed or misrepresented:

      1) a material fact or circumstance that relates to this insurance or the subject thereof; or

      2) "your" interest herein; or

   b. there has been fraud or false swearing by "you" or any other insured with regard to a matter that relates to this insurance or the subject thereof.

6. **Policy Period** -- "We" pay for a covered loss that occurs during the policy period.

7. **Recoveries** -- If "we" pay "you" for the loss and lost or damaged property is recovered, or payment is made by those responsible for the loss, the following provisions apply:

   a. "you" must notify "us" promptly if "you" recover property or receive payment;

   b. "we" must notify "you" promptly if "we" recover property or receive payment;

   c. any recovery expenses incurred by either are reimbursed first;

   d. "you" may keep the recovered property but "you" must refund to "us" the amount of the claim paid, or any lesser amount to which "we" agree; and

   e. if the claim paid is less than the agreed loss due to a deductible or other limiting "terms" of this policy, any recovery will be pro rated between "you" and "us" based on "our" respective interest in the loss.

8. **Restoration Of Limits** -- A loss "we" pay under this coverage does not reduce the applicable "limits".

9. **Subrogation** -- If "we" pay for a loss, "we" may require "you" to assign to "us" "your" right of recovery against others. "You" must do all that is necessary to secure "our" rights. "We" do not pay for a loss if "you" impair this right to recover.

   "You" may waive "your" right to recover from others in writing before a loss occurs.

Reprinted with permission from American Association of Insurance Services.

AAIS
IM 7250 04 04
Page 12 of 12

10. **Suit Against Us** -- No one may bring a legal action against "us" under this coverage unless:

    a.   all of the "terms" of this coverage have been complied with; and

    b.   the suit has been brought within two years after "you" first have knowledge of the loss.

    If any applicable law makes this limitation invalid, then suit must begin within the shortest period permitted by law.

11. **Territorial Limits** -- "We" cover property while:

    a.   at a location within; or

    b.   in "transit" between or within

    the United States of America, its territories and possessions, Canada, and Puerto Rico.

12. **Carriers For Hire** -- "You" may accept bills of lading or shipping receipts issued by carriers for hire that limit their liability to less than the actual cash value of the covered property.

IM 7250 04 04

Comm. Inland Marine

AAIS
IM 7005 04 04
Page 1 of 2

SCHEDULE OF COVERAGES
CONTRACTORS' EQUIPMENT

(The entries required to complete this schedule
will be shown below or on the "schedule of coverages".)

PROPERTY COVERED

(check one)

[X] Scheduled Equipment (Refer to Equipment Schedule)

[   ] Schedule On File

	Limit
Catastrophe Limit -- The most "we" pay for loss in any one occurrence is:	$ 3,000,000

COVERAGE EXTENSIONS

Additional Debris Removal Expenses	$ 5,000

SUPPLEMENTAL COVERAGES

Employee Tools	$ 5,000
Equipment Leased or Rented From Others	$ 25,000

Newly Purchased Equipment (check one)

[ ] Percentage of Catastrophe Limit	30%
[ ] Dollar Limit	$

Pollutant Cleanup and Removal	$ 25,000

Rental Reimbursement

-- Reimbursement Limit	$ 5,000
-- Waiting Period	72 hours

Spare Parts and Fuel	$ 5,000

AAIS
IM 7005 04 04
Page 2 of 2

COINSURANCE

(check one)

[X] 80%   [ ] 90%   [ ] 100%   [ ] Other _____%

REPORTING CONDITIONS

(check if applicable)

[ ] **Equipment Leased or Rented From Others**

    -- Reporting Rate $

    -- Deposit Premium $

    -- Minimum Premium $

VALUATION

(check if applicable)

[ ] Actual Cash Value   [X] Replacement Cost

[ ] Indicated on Equipment Schedule

DEDUCTIBLE

(check one)

[X] Flat Deductible Amount $ 1,000

[ ] Percentage Deductible   _____%

    Maximum Deductible Amount $

    Minimum Deductible Amount $

OPTIONAL COVERAGES AND ENDORSEMENTS

IM 7025, Fraud and Deceit
IM 7023, Equipment Loaned to Others

IM 7005 04 04

Copyright, American Association of Insurance Services, Inc., 2004

Comm. Inland Marine

AAIS
IM 7030 04 04

EQUIPMENT SCHEDULE
CONTRACTORS' EQUIPMENT

(The entries required to complete this schedule
will be shown below or on the "schedule of coverages".)

EQUIPMENT SCHEDULE

Item No.	Description of Equipment	Limit
1.	Clark backhoe – ser. 89337Ke45	$25,000
2.	Dyno Grader – mod. 4125654N	$22,000
3.	Dana tractor – ser. M0098825L2	$35,000
4.	Clark front end loader – ser. Pag784002	$26,000

IM 7030 04 04

AAIS
IM 7000 04 04
Page 1 of 13

CONTRACTORS' EQUIPMENT COVERAGE

AGREEMENT

In return for "your" payment of the required premium, "we" provide the coverage described herein subject to all the "terms" of the Contractors' Equipment Coverage. This coverage is also subject to the "schedule of coverages" and additional policy conditions relating to assignment or transfer of rights or duties, cancellation, changes or modifications, inspections, and examination of books and records.

Endorsements and schedules may also apply. They are identified on the "schedule of coverages".

Refer to Definitions for words and phrases that have special meaning. These words and phrases are shown in quotation marks or bold type.

DEFINITIONS

1. The words "you" and "your" mean the persons or organizations named as the insured on the declarations.

2. The words "we", "us", and "our" mean the company providing this coverage.

3. "Contractors' equipment" means machinery, equipment, and tools of a mobile nature that "you" use in "your" contracting, installation, erection, repair, or moving operations or projects.

    "Contractors' equipment" also means:

    a. self-propelled vehicles designed and used primarily to carry mounted equipment; or

    b. vehicles designed for highway use that are unlicensed and not operated on public roads.

4. "Equipment schedule" means a schedule of "contractors' equipment" that is attached to this policy and that describes each piece of covered equipment.

5. "Jobsite" means any location, project, or work site where "you" are in the process of construction, installation, erection, repair, or moving.

6. "Limit" means the amount of coverage that applies.

7. "Pollutant" means:

    a. any solid, liquid, gaseous, thermal, or radioactive irritant or contaminant, including acids, alkalis, chemicals, fumes, smoke, soot, vapor, and waste. Waste includes materials to be recycled, reclaimed, or reconditioned, as well as disposed of; and

    b. electrical or magnetic emissions, whether visible or invisible, and sound emissions.

8. "Schedule of coverages" means:

    a. all pages labeled schedule of coverages or schedules which pertain to this coverage; and

    b. declarations or supplemental declarations which pertain to this coverage.

9. "Sinkhole collapse" means the sudden settlement or collapse of earth supporting the covered property into subterranean voids created by the action of water on a limestone or similar rock formation. It does not include the value of the land or the cost of filling sinkholes.

Comm. Inland Marine

10. "Specified perils" means aircraft; civil commotion; explosion; falling objects; fire; hail; leakage from fire extinguishing equipment; lightning; riot; "sinkhole collapse"; smoke; sonic boom; vandalism; vehicles; "volcanic action"; water damage; weight of ice, snow, or sleet; and windstorm.

Falling objects does not include loss to:

a. personal property in the open; or

b. the interior of buildings or structures or to personal property inside buildings or structures unless the exterior of the roofs or walls are first damaged by a falling object.

Water damage means the sudden or accidental discharge or leakage of water or steam as a direct result of breaking or cracking of a part of the system or appliance containing the water or steam.

11. "Terms" means all provisions, limitations, exclusions, conditions, and definitions that apply.

12. "Volcanic action" means airborne volcanic blast or airborne shock waves; ash, dust, or particulate matter; or lava flow.

Volcanic action does not include the cost to remove ash, dust, or particulate matter that does not cause direct physical loss to the covered property.

PROPERTY COVERED

"We" cover the following property unless the property is excluded or subject to limitations.

1. **Scheduled Equipment --**

a. **Coverage** -- "We" cover direct physical loss caused by a covered peril to:

1) "your" "contractors' equipment"; and

2) "contractors' equipment" of others in "your" care, custody, or control.

b. **Coverage Limitation** -- "We" only cover "your" "contractors' equipment" and "contractors' equipment" of others:

1) that are described on the "equipment schedule"; and

2) when Scheduled Equipment is indicated on the "schedule of coverages".

2. **Schedule On File --**

a. **Coverage** -- "We" cover direct physical loss caused by a covered peril to:

1) "your" "contractors' equipment"; and

2) "contractors' equipment" of others in "your" care, custody, or control.

b. **Coverage Limitation** -- "We" only cover "your" "contractors' equipment" and "contractors' equipment" of others:

1) that are listed in a schedule which "you" must submit to "us" and "we" keep on file, the schedule must contain a description of each item to be covered and a "limit" for each item; and

2) when Schedule on File is indicated on the "schedule of coverages".

PROPERTY NOT COVERED

1. **Aircraft Or Watercraft** -- "We" do not cover aircraft or watercraft.

2. **Contraband** -- "We" do not cover contraband or property in the course of illegal transportation or trade.

3. **Leased Or Rented Property** -- "We" do not cover property that "you" lease or rent to others.

AAIS
IM 7000 04 04
Page 3 of 13

4. **Loaned Property** -- "We" do not cover property that "you" loan to others.

5. **Underground Mining Operations** -- "We" do not cover property while stored or operated underground in connection with any mining operations.

6. **Vehicles** -- "We" do not cover automobiles, motor trucks, tractors, trailers, and similar conveyances designed for highway use and used for over the road transportation of people or cargo. However, this does not include:

    a. self-propelled vehicles designed and used primarily to carry mounted equipment; or

    b. vehicles designed for highway use that are unlicensed and not operated on public roads.

7. **Waterborne Property** -- "We" do not cover property while waterborne except while in transit in the custody of a carrier for hire.

COVERAGE EXTENSIONS

Provisions That Apply To Coverage Extensions -- The following Coverage Extensions indicate an applicable "limit". This "limit" may also be shown on the "schedule of coverages".

If a different "limit" is indicated on the "schedule of coverages", that "limit" will apply instead of the "limit" shown below.

However, if no "limit" is indicated for a Coverage Extension, coverage is provided up to the full "limit" for the applicable covered property unless a different "limit" is indicated on the "schedule of coverages".

Unless otherwise indicated, the coverages provided below are part of and not in addition to the applicable "limit" for coverage described under Property Covered.

The "limit" provided under a Coverage Extension cannot be combined or added to the "limit" for any other Coverage Extension or Supplemental Coverage including a Coverage Extension or Supplemental Coverage that is added to this policy by endorsement.

If coinsurance provisions are part of this policy, the following coverage extensions are not subject to and not considered in applying coinsurance conditions.

Debris Removal --

1. **Coverage** -- "We" pay the cost to remove the debris of covered property that is caused by a covered peril.

2. **We Do Not Cover** -- This coverage does not include costs to:

    a. extract "pollutants" from land or water; or

    b. remove, restore, or replace polluted land or water.

3. **Limit** -- "We" do not pay any more under this coverage than 25% of the amount "we" pay for the direct physical loss. "We" will not pay more for loss to property and debris removal combined than the "limit" for the damaged property.

4. **Additional Limit** -- "We" pay up to an additional $5,000 for debris removal expense when the debris removal expense exceeds 25% of the amount "we" pay for direct physical loss or when the loss to property and debris removal combined exceeds the "limit" for the damaged property.

5. **You Must Report Your Expenses** -- "We" do not pay any expenses unless they are reported to "us" in writing within 180 days from the date of direct physical loss to covered property.

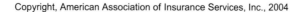

Comm. Inland Marine

AAIS
IM 7000 04 04
Page 4 of 13

SUPPLEMENTAL COVERAGES

Provisions That Apply To Supplemental Coverages -- The following Supplemental Coverages indicate an applicable "limit". This "limit" may also be shown on the "schedule of coverages".

If a different "limit" is indicated on the "schedule of coverages", that "limit" will apply instead of the "limit" shown below.

However, if no "limit" is indicated for a Supplemental Coverage, coverage is provided up to the full "limit" for the applicable covered property unless a different "limit" is indicated on the "schedule of coverages".

Unless otherwise indicated, a "limit" for a Supplemental Coverage provided below is separate from, and not part of, the applicable "limit" for coverage described under Property Covered.

The "limit" available for coverage described under a Supplemental Coverage:

a. is the only "limit" available for the described coverage; and

b. is not the sum of the "limit" indicated for a Supplemental Coverage and the "limit" for coverage described under Property Covered.

The "limit" provided under a Supplemental Coverage cannot be combined or added to the "limit" for any other Supplemental Coverage or Coverage Extension including a Supplemental Coverage or Coverage Extension that is added to this policy by endorsement.

If coinsurance provisions are part of this policy, the following supplemental coverages are not subject to and not considered in applying coinsurance conditions.

1. **Employee Tools** --

  a. **Coverage** -- "We" cover direct physical loss caused by a covered peril to tools owned by "your" employees.

  b. **Coverage Limitation** -- "We" only cover tools owned by "your" employees while at a:

    1) premises that "you" own or operate; or
    2) "jobsite".

  c. **Limit** -- The most "we" pay in any one occurrence for loss to employee tools is $5,000.

2. **Equipment Leased Or Rented From Others** --

  a. **Coverage** -- "We" cover direct physical loss caused by a covered peril to "contractors' equipment" that "you" have leased or rented from others.

  b. **Limit** -- The most "we" pay in any one occurrence for equipment leased or rented from others is $25,000.

3. **Newly Purchased Property** --

  a. **Coverage** -- "We" cover direct physical loss caused by a covered peril to additional "contractors' equipment" that "you" purchase during the policy period.

  b. **Limit** -- The most that "we" pay for any loss under this supplemental coverage is the least of the:

    1) actual cash value of the covered property; or
    2) "limit" for newly purchased property indicated on the "schedule of coverages". If no "limit" is indicated, then 30% of the Catastrophe Limit indicated on the "schedule of coverages" applies to this coverage.

c. **Time Limitation** -- "We" extend coverage to the additional "contractors' equipment" that "you" purchase for up to 60 days.

This supplemental coverage will end when any of the following first occur:

1) this policy expires;
2) 60 days after "you" obtain the additional "contractors' equipment"; or
3) "you" report the additional "contractors' equipment" to "us".

d. **Additional Premium** -- "You" must pay any additional premium due from the date "you" purchase the additional "contractors' equipment".

4. **Pollutant Cleanup And Removal** --

a. **Coverage** -- "We" pay "your" expense to extract "pollutants" from land or water if the discharge, dispersal, seepage, migration, release, or escape of the "pollutants" is caused by a covered peril that occurs during the policy period.

b. **Time Limitation** -- The expenses to extract "pollutants" are paid only if they are reported to "us" in writing within 180 days from the date the covered peril occurs.

c. **We Do Not Cover** -- "We" do not pay the cost of testing, evaluating, observing, or recording the existence, level, or effects of "pollutants".

However, "we" pay the cost of testing which is necessary for the extraction of "pollutants" from land or water.

d. **Limit** -- The most "we" pay for each location is $25,000 for the sum of all such expenses arising out of a covered peril occurring during each separate 12-month period of this policy.

5. **Rental Reimbursement** --

a. **Coverage** -- In the event of a direct physical loss by a covered peril to "your" "contractors' equipment", "we" reimburse "you" for "your" expense to rent similar equipment while "your" equipment is inoperable.

The deductible amount indicated on the "schedule of coverages" does not apply to a loss covered under this supplemental coverage.

b. **Waiting Period** -- "We" will not reimburse "you" for the rental of equipment until after the first 72-hours (unless otherwise indicated on the "schedule of coverages") following the direct physical loss to "your" "contractors' equipment" caused by a covered peril.

c. **Incurred Rental Expenses** -- After the waiting period has passed, "we" will only reimburse "you" for the rental expenses that "you" actually incur.

d. **Coverage After Expiration Date** -- "We" will continue to reimburse "you" for the rental of equipment after the expiration date of this coverage, provided the loss occurred before the expiration date.

e. **Coverage Limitations** -- "We" will not reimburse "you":

1) if "you" can continue or resume "your" operations with similar equipment that is available to "you" at no additional expense to "you"; or
2) for the rental expense of any equipment unless "you" make every reasonable effort to repair, replace, or rebuild the inoperable equipment after the loss by a covered peril occurs.

f. **Limit** -- The most "we" reimburse "you" in any one occurrence for rental expenses is $5,000.

Comm. Inland Marine

AAIS
IM 7000 04 04
Page 6 of 13

6. **Spare Parts And Fuel --**

   a. **Coverage** -- "We" cover direct physical loss caused by a covered peril to:

      1) spare parts and accessories for "contractors' equipment"; and
      2) fluids for vehicles and "contractors' equipment"; fluids include gasoline, oil, and hydraulic fluid.

   b. **Limit** -- The most "we" pay in any one occurrence for loss to spare parts and accessories is $5,000.

PERILS COVERED

"We" cover risks of direct physical loss unless the loss is limited or caused by a peril that is excluded.

PERILS EXCLUDED

1. "We" do not pay for loss or damage caused directly or indirectly by one or more of the following excluded causes or events. Such loss or damage is excluded regardless of other causes or events that contribute to or aggravate the loss, whether such causes or events act to produce the loss before, at the same time as, or after the excluded causes or events.

   a. **Civil Authority** -- "We" do not pay for loss caused by order of any civil authority, including seizure, confiscation, destruction, or quarantine of property.

   "We" do cover loss resulting from acts of destruction by the civil authority to prevent the spread of fire, unless the fire is caused by a peril excluded under this coverage.

   b. **Nuclear Hazard** -- "We" do not pay for loss caused by or resulting from a nuclear reaction, nuclear radiation, or radioactive contamination (whether controlled or uncontrolled; whether caused by natural, accidental, or artificial means). Loss caused by nuclear hazard is not considered loss caused by fire, explosion, or smoke. Direct loss by fire resulting from the nuclear hazard is covered.

   c. **War And Military Action** -- "We" do not pay for loss caused by:

      1) war, including undeclared war or civil war; or
      2) a warlike action by a military force, including action taken to prevent or defend against an actual or expected attack, by any government, sovereign, or other authority using military personnel or other agents; or
      3) insurrection, rebellion, revolution, or unlawful seizure of power including action taken by governmental authority to prevent or defend against any of these.

   With regard to any action that comes within the "terms" of this exclusion and involves nuclear reaction, nuclear radiation, or radioactive contamination, this War and Military Action Exclusion will apply in place of the Nuclear Hazard Exclusion.

2. "We" do not pay for loss or damage that is caused by or results from one or more of the following:

   a. **Contamination or Deterioration** -- "We" do not pay for loss caused by contamination or deterioration including corrosion, decay, fungus, mildew, mold, rot, rust, or any quality, fault, or weakness in the covered property that causes it to damage or destroy itself.

   But if contamination or deterioration results in a covered peril, "we" do cover the loss or damage caused by that covered peril.

AAIS
IM 7000 04 04
Page 7 of 13

b. **Criminal, Fraudulent, Dishonest Or Illegal Acts** -- "We" do not pay for loss caused by or resulting from criminal, fraudulent, dishonest, or illegal acts committed alone or in collusion with another by:

1) "you";
2) others who have an interest in the property;
3) others to whom "you" entrust the property;
4) "your" partners, officers, directors, trustees, joint venturers, or "your" members or managers if "you" are a limited liability company; or
5) the employees or agents of 1), 2), 3), or 4) above, whether or not they are at work.

This exclusion does not apply to acts of destruction by "your" employees, but "we" do not pay for theft by employees.

This exclusion does not apply to covered property in the custody of a carrier for hire.

c. **Loss Of Use** -- "We" do not pay for loss caused by or resulting from loss of use, delay, or loss of market.

d. **Mechanical Breakdown** -- "We" do not pay for loss caused by any mechanical, structural, or electrical breakdown or malfunction including a breakdown or malfunction resulting from a structural, mechanical, or reconditioning process.

But if a mechanical, structural, or electrical breakdown or malfunction results in a covered peril, "we" do cover the loss or damage caused by that covered peril.

e. **Missing Property** -- "We" do not pay for missing property where the only proof of loss is unexplained or mysterious disappearance of covered property, or shortage of property discovered on taking inventory, or any other instance where there is no physical evidence to show what happened to the covered property.

This exclusion does not apply to covered property in the custody of a carrier for hire.

f. **Pollutants** -- "We" do not pay for loss caused by or resulting from release, discharge, seepage, migration, dispersal, or escape of "pollutants":

1) unless the release, discharge, seepage, migration, dispersal, or escape is caused by a "specified peril"; or
2) except as specifically provided under the Supplemental Coverages - Pollutant Cleanup and Removal.

"We" do cover any resulting loss caused by a "specified peril".

g. **Temperature/Humidity** -- "We" do not pay for loss caused by dryness, dampness, humidity, or changes in or extremes of temperature.

But if dryness, dampness, humidity, or changes in or extremes of temperature results in a covered peril, "we" do cover the loss or damage caused by that covered peril.

h. **Voluntary Parting** -- "We" do not pay for loss caused by or resulting from voluntary parting with title to or possession of any property because of any fraudulent scheme, trick, or false pretense.

AAIS
IM 7000 04 04
Page 8 of 13

i.   **Wear And Tear** -- "We" do not pay for loss caused by wear and tear, marring, or scratching.

But if wear and tear, marring, or scratching results in a covered peril, "we" do cover the loss or damage caused by that covered peril.

WHAT MUST BE DONE IN CASE OF LOSS

1.   **Notice** -- In case of a loss, "you" must:

a.   give "us" or "our" agent prompt notice including a description of the property involved ("we" may request written notice); and

b.   give notice to the police when the act that causes the loss is a crime.

2.   **You Must Protect Property** -- "You" must take all reasonable steps to protect covered property at and after an insured loss to avoid further loss.

a.   **Payment of Reasonable Costs** -- "We" do pay the reasonable costs incurred by "you" for necessary repairs or emergency measures performed solely to protect covered property from further damage by a peril insured against if a peril insured against has already caused a loss to covered property. "You" must keep an accurate record of such costs. "Our" payment of reasonable costs does not increase the "limit".

b.   **We Do Not Pay** -- "We" do not pay for such repairs or emergency measures performed on property which has not been damaged by a peril insured against.

3.   **Proof Of Loss** -- "You" must send "us", within 60 days after "our" request, a signed, sworn proof of loss. This must include the following information:

a.   the time, place, and circumstances of the loss;

b.   other policies of insurance that may cover the loss;

c.   "your" interest and the interests of all others in the property involved, including all mortgages and liens;

d.   changes in title of the covered property during the policy period; and

e.   estimates, specifications, inventories, and other reasonable information that "we" may require to settle the loss.

4.   **Examination** -- "You" must submit to examination under oath in matters connected with the loss as often as "we" reasonably request and give "us" sworn statements of the answers. If more than one person is examined, "we" have the right to examine and receive statements separately and not in the presence of others.

5.   **Records** -- "You" must produce records, including tax returns and bank microfilms of all canceled checks relating to value, loss, and expense and permit copies and extracts to be made of them as often as "we" reasonably request.

6.   **Damaged Property** -- "You" must exhibit the damaged and undamaged property as often as "we" reasonably request and allow "us" to inspect or take samples of the property.

7.   **Volunteer Payments** -- "You" must not, except at "your" own expense, voluntarily make any payments, assume any obligations, pay or offer any rewards, or incur any other expenses except as respects protecting property from further damage.

8.   **Abandonment** -- "You" may not abandon the property to "us" without "our" written consent.

9.   **Cooperation** -- "You" must cooperate with "us" in performing all acts required by this policy.

AAIS
IM 7000 04 04
Page 9 of 13

VALUATION

1. **Actual Cash Value** -- The value of covered property will be based on the actual cash value at the time of the loss (with a deduction for depreciation) unless replacement cost is indicated on the "schedule of coverages".

2. **Replacement Cost** -- The value of covered property will be based on the replacement cost without any deduction for depreciation unless Actual Cash Value is indicated on the "schedule of coverages".

   a. **Replacement Cost Limitation** -- The replacement cost is limited to the cost of repair or replacement with similar materials and used for the same purpose. The payment will not exceed the amount "you" spend to repair or replace the damaged or destroyed property.

   b. **Replacement Cost Does Not Apply Until Repair Or Replacement** -- Replacement cost valuation does not apply until the damaged or destroyed property is repaired or replaced.

   c. **Time Limitation** -- "You" may make a claim for actual cash value before repair or replacement takes place, and later for the replacement cost if "you" notify "us" of "your" intent within 180 days after the loss.

3. **Pair Or Set** -- The value of a lost or damaged article which is part of a pair or set is based on a reasonable proportion of the value of the entire pair or set. The loss is not considered a total loss of the pair or set.

4. **Loss To Parts** -- The value of a lost or damaged part of an item that consists of several parts when it is complete is based on the value of only the lost or damaged part or the cost to repair or replace it.

HOW MUCH WE PAY

1. **Insurable Interest** -- "We" do not cover more than "your" insurable interest in any property.

2. **Flat Deductible** -- "We" pay only that part of "your" loss over the deductible amount indicated on the "schedule of coverages" in any one occurrence unless Percentage Deductible is indicated on the "schedule of coverages".

3. **Percentage Deductible** -- When a percentage deductible is indicated on the "schedule of coverages", "we" pay only that part of "your" loss over the deductible amount as determined below.

   a. **Determining The Deductible Amount** -- The deductible amount is determined by applying the percentage indicated on the "schedule of coverages" to the value of the covered property that is involved in the loss. The value is determined by the provisions described under the Valuation section of this policy.

   b. **Two Or More Items** -- If a loss involves two or more pieces of equipment, the percentage indicated on the "schedule of coverages" will apply only to the covered property with the highest value.

   c. **Minimum and Maximum Deductible** -- The percentage deductible will not exceed the Maximum Deductible amount and will not be less than the Minimum Deductible amount indicated on the "schedule of coverages".

4. **Loss Settlement Terms** -- Subject to paragraphs 1., 2., 3., 5., 6., and 7. under How Much We Pay, "we" pay the lesser of:

   a. the amount determined under Valuation;

Comm. Inland Marine

AAIS
IM 7000 04 04
Page 10 of 13

b. the cost to repair, replace, or rebuild the property with material of like kind and quality to the extent practicable; or

c. the "limit" that applies to the covered property. However, the most "we" pay for loss in any one occurrence is the Catastrophe Limit indicated on the "schedule of coverages".

5. **Coinsurance** --

a. **When Coinsurance Applies** -- "We" only pay a part of the loss if the "limit" is less than the percentage of the value of the covered property that is indicated on the "schedule of coverages".

b. **How We Determine Our Part Of The Loss** -- "Our" part of the loss is determined using the following steps:

1) multiply the percent indicated on the "schedule of coverages" by the value of the covered property at the time of loss;
2) divide the "limit" for covered property by the result determined in b.1) above;
3) multiply the total amount of loss, after the application of any deductible, by the result determined in b.2) above.

The most "we" pay is the amount determined in b.3) above or the "limit", whichever is less. "We" do not pay any remaining part of the loss.

c. **If There Is More Than One Limit** -- If there is more than one "limit" indicated on the "schedule of coverages" for this coverage part, this procedure applies separately to each "limit".

d. **If There Is Only One Limit** -- If there is only one "limit" indicated on the "schedule of coverages" for this coverage, this procedure applies to the total of all covered property to which the "limit" applies.

e. **When Coinsurance Does Not Apply** -- Conditions for coinsurance do not apply unless a coinsurance percentage is indicated on the "schedule of coverages".

6. **Insurance Under More Than One Coverage** -- If more than one coverage of this policy insures the same loss, "we" pay no more than the actual claim, loss, or damage sustained.

7. **Insurance Under More Than One Policy** --

a. **Proportional Share** -- "You" may have another policy subject to the same "terms" as this policy. If "you" do, "we" will pay "our" share of the covered loss. "Our" share is the proportion that the applicable "limit" under this policy bears to the "limit" of all policies covering on the same basis.

b. **Excess Amount** -- If there is another policy covering the same loss, other than that described above, "we" pay only for the amount of covered loss in excess of the amount due from that other policy, whether "you" can collect on it or not. But "we" do not pay more than the applicable "limit".

LOSS PAYMENT

1. **Loss Payment Options** --

a. **Our Options** -- In the event of loss covered by this coverage form, "we" have the following options:

1) pay the value of the lost or damaged property;
2) pay the cost of repairing or replacing the lost or damaged property;

AAIS
IM 7000 04 04
Page 11 of 13

3) rebuild, repair, or replace the property with other property of equivalent kind and quality, to the extent practicable, within a reasonable time; or

4) take all or any part of the property at the agreed or appraised value.

b. **Notice Of Our Intent To Rebuild, Repair, Or Replace** -- "We" must give "you" notice of "our" intent to rebuild, repair, or replace within 30 days after receipt of a duly executed proof of loss.

2. **Your Losses** --

a. **Adjustment And Payment Of Loss** -- "We" adjust all losses with "you". Payment will be made to "you" unless another loss payee is named in the policy.

b. **Conditions For Payment Of Loss** -- An insured loss will be payable 30 days after:

1) a satisfactory proof of loss is received, and

2) the amount of the loss has been established either by written agreement with "you" or the filing of an appraisal award with "us".

3. **Property Of Others** --

a. **Adjustment And Payment of Loss To Property of Others** -- Losses to property of others may be adjusted with and paid to:

1) "you" on behalf of the owner; or

2) the owner.

b. **We Do Not Have To Pay You If We Pay The Owner** -- If "we" pay the owner, "we" do not have to pay "you". "We" may also choose to defend any suits brought by the owners at "our" expense.

REPORTING CONDITIONS

Equipment Leased Or Rented From Others -- If indicated on the "schedule of coverages", the following reporting conditions apply.

1. **Reports** --

a. **You Will Report To Us** -- Within 30 days after the end of the policy period, "you" will report to "us" the total amount of "your" expenditures for "contractors' equipment" that "you" lease or rent from others.

b. **Cancellation** -- If this policy is canceled, "you" will report the total amount of expenditures up to and including the date of cancellation.

2. **Premium Computation And Adjustment** --

a. The premium will be adjusted at the end of the policy period. The total computed premium will be determined by multiplying "your" total equipment expenditures by the reporting rate indicated on the "schedule of coverages" for Equipment Leased or Rented From Others.

b. "We" will compare the total computed premium to the deposit premium. If it is more than the deposit premium, "you" will pay "us" the difference. If it is less than the deposit premium, "we" will pay "you" the difference subject to the minimum premium indicated on the "schedule of coverages".

3. **Provisions That Affect How Much We Pay** -- The following provisions apply to reports that are submitted and may affect How Much We Pay:

a. **Failure To Submit Reports** -- If "you" have failed to submit the required reports or no report has been submitted, the most "we" will pay is 90% of the "limit".

Comm. Inland Marine

AAIS
IM 7000 04 04
Page 12 of 13

b. **Reported Values Are Less Than The Full Value** -- If "your" last report before a loss shows less than the actual value of "your" expenditures for "contractors' equipment" that "you" lease or rent from others, "we" will only pay a part of the loss. "We" will not pay a greater portion of the loss, prior to the application of the deductible, than the total expenditures "you" reported divided by "your" actual expenditures for "contractors' equipment" that "you" lease or rent from others during the reporting period.

c. **We Will Not Pay More Than The Limit** -- "We" will not pay more than the applicable "limit" regardless of any reported value used in computing the premium.

OTHER CONDITIONS

1. **Appraisal** -- If "you" and "we" do not agree on the amount of the loss or the value of covered property, either party may demand that these amounts be determined by appraisal.

   If either makes a written demand for appraisal, each will select a competent, independent appraiser and notify the other of the appraiser's identity within 20 days of receipt of the written demand. The two appraisers will then select a competent, impartial umpire. If the two appraisers are unable to agree upon an umpire within 15 days, "you" or "we" can ask a judge of a court of record in the state where the property is located to select an umpire.

   The appraisers will then determine and state separately the amount of each loss.

The appraisers will also determine the value of covered property items at the time of the loss, if requested.

If the appraisers submit a written report of any agreement to "us", the amount agreed upon will be the amount of the loss. If the appraisers fail to agree within a reasonable time, they will submit only their differences to the umpire. Written agreement so itemized and signed by any two of these three, sets the amount of the loss.

Each appraiser will be paid by the party selecting that appraiser. Other expenses of the appraisal and the compensation of the umpire will be paid equally by "you" and "us".

2. **Benefit to Others** -- Insurance under this coverage will not directly or indirectly benefit anyone having custody of "your" property.

3. **Conformity With Statute** -- When a condition of this coverage is in conflict with an applicable law, that condition is amended to conform to that law.

4. **Estates** -- This provision applies only if the insured is an individual.

   a. **Your Death** -- On "your" death, "we" cover the following as an insured:

      1) the person who has custody of "your" property until a legal representative is qualified and appointed; or
      2) "your" legal representative.

      This person or organization is an insured only with respect to property covered by this coverage.

   b. **Policy Period Is Not Extended** -- This coverage does not extend past the policy period indicated on the declarations.

AAIS
IM 7000 04 04
Page 13 of 13

5. **Misrepresentation, Concealment, Or Fraud** -- This coverage is void as to "you" and any other insured if, before or after a loss:

   a. "you" or any other insured have willfully concealed or misrepresented:

      1) a material fact or circumstance that relates to this insurance or the subject thereof; or
      2) "your" interest herein.

   b. there has been fraud or false swearing by "you" or any other insured with regard to a matter that relates to this insurance or the subject thereof.

6. **Policy Period** -- "We" pay for a covered loss that occurs during the policy period.

7. **Recoveries** -- If "we" pay "you" for the loss and lost or damaged property is recovered, or payment is made by those responsible for the loss, the following provisions apply:

   a. "you" must notify "us" promptly if "you" recover property or receive payment;

   b. "we" must notify "you" promptly if "we" recover property or receive payment;

   c. any recovery expenses incurred by either are reimbursed first;

   d. "you" may keep the recovered property but "you" must refund to "us" the amount of the claim paid or any lesser amount to which "we" agree; and

   e. if the claim paid is less than the agreed loss due to a deductible or other limiting "terms" of this policy, any recovery will be pro rated between "you" and "us" based on "our" respective interest in the loss.

8. **Restoration Of Limits** -- A loss "we" pay under this coverage does not reduce the applicable "limit" unless it is a total loss to a scheduled item. In the event of a total loss to a scheduled item, "we" refund the unearned premium on that item.

9. **Subrogation** -- If "we" pay for a loss, "we" may require "you" to assign to "us" "your" right of recovery against others. "You" must do all that is necessary to secure "our" rights. "We" do not pay for a loss if "you" impair this right to recover.

   "You" may waive "your" right to recover from others in writing before a loss occurs.

10. **Suit Against Us** -- No one may bring a legal action against "us" under this coverage unless:

    a. all of the "terms" of this coverage have been complied with; and

    b. the suit has been brought within two years after "you" first have knowledge of the loss.

       If any applicable law makes this limitation invalid, then suit must begin within the shortest period permitted by law.

11. **Territorial Limits** -- "We" cover property while it is in the United States of America, its territories and possessions, Canada, and Puerto Rico.

IM 7000 04 04

Comm. Inland Marine

AAIS
IM 7014 04 04
Page 1 of 1

This endorsement changes the
Contractors' Equipment Coverage
-- PLEASE READ THIS CAREFULLY --

RENTAL REIMBURSEMENT ENDORSEMENT

(The entries required to complete this endorsement
will be shown below or on the "schedule of coverages".)

SCHEDULE

	Limit

The most "we" pay in any one occurrence for
rental reimbursement expense is: $_____

Waiting Period _____

SUPPLEMENTAL COVERAGES

Rental Reimbursement --

1. **Coverage** -- In the event of a direct physical loss by a covered peril to "your" "contractors' equipment", "we" reimburse "you" for "your" expense to rent similar equipment while "your" equipment is inoperable. The deductible amount indicated on the "schedule of coverages" does not apply to a loss covered under this supplemental coverage.

2. **Waiting Period** -- "We" will not reimburse "you" for the rental of equipment until after the first 72 hours (unless otherwise indicated on the schedule) following the direct physical loss to "your" "contractors' equipment" caused by a covered peril.

3. **Incurred Rental Expenses** -- After the waiting period has passed, "we" will only reimburse "you" for the rental expenses that "you" actually incur.

4. **Coverage After Expiration Date** -- "We" will continue to reimburse "you" for the rental of equipment after the expiration date of this coverage, provided the loss occurred before the expiration date.

5. **Coverage Limitations** -- "We" will not reimburse "you":

   a. if "you" can continue or resume "your" operations with similar equipment that is available to "you" at no additional expense to "you"; or

   b. for the rental expense of any equipment unless "you" make every reasonable effort to repair, replace, or rebuild the inoperable equipment after the loss by a covered peril occurs.

IM 7014 04 04

Ocean Marine Insurance

Ocean marine insurance is principally insurance on vessels and their cargoes. The three main types of ocean marine insurance are hull insurance, protection and indemnity (P&I) insurance, and cargo insurance. In addition, insurers write ocean marine policies to cover various maritime enterprises such as ship builders and repairers, terminal operators, offshore oil and gas exploration and production facilities, boat dealers, and marinas.

Hull insurance is mainly property insurance covering loss of or damage to vessels and their equipment. Hull insurance often includes collision liability insurance as well, covering the insured's liability for damage to other vessels and their cargoes resulting from collision with the insured vessel. One of the most commonly used hull insurance forms in the United States market is the American Institute Hull Clauses form, which is reprinted herein. ("American Institute" refers to the American Institute of Marine Underwriters, an association that develops marine policy forms in addition to providing marine insurance educational programs.)

Protection and indemnity (P&I) insurance covers a wide range of liability exposures and miscellaneous expenses (such as fines and penalties) that a shipowner might incur. The most notable liability exposures covered by P&I are injuries to crew members and other persons on board the insured vessel, injuries to persons on board other vessels struck by the insured vessel, damage to property struck by the insured vessel, and the insured shipowner's liability for damage to cargo being carried by the insured vessel. The American Institute of Marine Underwriters' Protection and Indemnity Clauses are reprinted in the *Handbook* as an example of a P&I form.

Cargo insurance covers a shipper's or consignee's interest in property being transported by vessels. Ocean marine cargo insurance also covers the insured goods during land transit that connects with the ocean conveyance. An ocean cargo policy can also be extended to cover inland-only shipments and international air shipments. The type of cargo policy written for frequent shippers, referred to as an open cargo policy, covers all shipments made by the insured. For infrequent shippers, a trip transit policy can be obtained to cover a specified shipment only.

1   **American Institute Hull Clauses (September 29, 2009)**
2
3   To be attached to and form a part of Policy No. ....
4   of the ....
5
6   The terms and conditions of the following clauses are to be regarded as substituted for those of the policy form to which they are
7   attached, the latter being hereby waived, except provisions required by law to be inserted in the Policy. All captions are inserted only for
8   purposes of reference and shall not be used to interpret the clauses to which they apply.

9   **ASSURED**
10   This Policy insures ....
11   ....
12   .... hereinafter referred to as the Assured.
13   If claim is made under this Policy by anyone other than the Owner of the Vessel, such person shall not be entitled to recover to a
14   greater extent than would the Owner, had claim been made by the Owner as an Assured named in this Policy.

15   Underwriters waive any right of subrogation against affiliated, subsidiary or interrelated companies of the Assured, provided that such
16   waiver shall not apply in the event of a collision between the Vessel and any vessel owned, demise chartered or otherwise controlled by any
17   of the aforesaid companies, or with respect to any loss, damage or expense against which such companies are insured.

18   **LOSS PAYEE**
19   Loss, if any, payable to ....
20   .... or order.
21   Provided, however, Underwriters shall pay claims to others as set forth in the Collision Liability clause and may make direct payment
22   to persons providing security for the release of the Vessel in Salvage cases.

23   **VESSEL**
24   The Subject Matter of this insurance is the Vessel called the ....
25   or by whatsoever name or names the said Vessel is or shall be called, which for purposes of this insurance shall consist of and be limited to
26   her hull, launches, lifeboats, rafts, furniture, bunkers, stores, supplies, tackle, fittings, equipment, apparatus, machinery, boilers,
27   refrigerating machinery, insulation, motor generators and other electrical machinery. Each vessel deemed to be separately insured. In the
28   event that more than one vessel is insured by the policy to which these clauses are attached, all such clauses shall apply as though a
29   separate policy has been issued with respect to each vessel.
30   In the event any equipment or apparatus not owned by the Assured is installed for use on board the Vessel and the Assured has
31   assumed responsibility therefor, it shall also be considered part of the Subject Matter and the aggregate value thereof shall be included in
32   the Agreed Value.
33   Notwithstanding the foregoing, cargo containers, barges and lighters shall not be considered a part of the Subject Matter of this
34   insurance.

35   This insurance also covers loss or damage to parts temporarily removed from the vessel, where such loss or damage is caused by an
36   insured peril occurring during the policy period.

37   **DURATION OF RISK**
38   From the .... day of ....20............, time
39   to the .... day of ....20.........., time.
40   Should the Vessel at the expiration of this Policy be in distress, she shall, provided previous notice be given to the Underwriters, be
41   held covered at a pro rata monthly premium until moored safely afloat in a port of refuge.
42   In the event of payment by the Underwriters for Total Loss of the Vessel this Policy shall thereupon automatically terminate.

43   **AGREED VALUE**
44   The Vessel, for so much as concerns the Assured, by agreement between the Assured and the Underwriters in this Policy, is and shall
45   be valued at ....Dollars.

46   **AMOUNT INSURED HEREUNDER**
47   ....Dollars.

48   **DEDUCTIBLE**
49   Notwithstanding anything in this Policy to the contrary, there shall be deducted from the aggregate of all claims (including claims
50   under the Sue and Labor clause and claims under the Collision Liability clause) arising out of each separate accident, the sum of
51    $.........................,unless the accident results in a Total Loss of the Vessel in which case this clause shall not apply. A recovery from other
52   interests, however, shall not operate to exclude claims under this Policy provided the aggregate of such claims arising out of one separate
53   accident if unreduced by such recovery exceeds that sum. For the purpose of this clause each accident shall be treated separately, but it is
54   agreed that (a) a sequence of damages arising from the same accident shall be treated as due to that accident and (b) all heavy weather
55   damage, or damage caused by contact with floating ice, which occurs during a single sea passage between two successive ports shall be
56   treated as though due to one accident.

57 **PREMIUM**
58   The Underwriters to be paid in consideration of this insurance ....
59 .... Dollars being at the annual rate of .... per cent, which premium shall be due on attachment. If
60 the Vessel is insured under this Policy for a period of less than one year at pro rata of the annual rate, full annual premium shall be
61 considered earned and immediately due and payable in the event of Total Loss of the Vessel **from a peril insured hereunder**.

62 **RETURNS OF PREMIUM**
63 Premium returnable as follows:
64   Pro rata daily net in the event of termination under the Change of Ownership clause;
65   Pro rata monthly net for each uncommenced month if it be mutually agreed to cancel this Policy;
66   For each period of 30 consecutive days the Vessel may be laid up in port for account of the Assured,
67 .... cents per cent. net not under repair, or
68 .... cents per cent. net under repair;
69 provided always that:
70   (a)   a Total Loss of the Vessel has not occurred during the currency of this Policy;
71   (b)   in no case shall a return for lay-up be allowed when the Vessel is lying in exposed or unprotected waters or in any location not
72   approved by the Underwriters;
73   (c)   in the event of any amendment of the annual rate, the above rates of return shall be adjusted accordingly;
74   (d)   in no case shall a return be allowed when the Vessel is used as a storage ship or for lighting purposes; and
75   (e)   in no case shall a return be allowed if the vessel is under repair due to a loss insured hereunder.
76   If the Vessel is laid up for a period of 30 consecutive days, a part only of which attaches under this Policy, the Underwriters shall pay
77 such proportion of the return due in respect of a full period of 30 days as the number of days attaching hereto bears to 30. Should the lay-up
78 period exceed 30 consecutive days, the Assured shall have the option to elect the period of 30 consecutive days for which a return is
79 recoverable.

80 **NON-PAYMENT OF PREMIUM**
81   In the event of non-payment of premium 30 days after attachment, or of any additional premium when due, this Policy may be
82 cancelled by the Underwriters upon 10 days written or **electronic** notice sent to the Assured at his last known address or in care of the
83 broker who negotiated this Policy. Such proportion of the premium, however, as shall have been earned up to the time of cancellation shall
84 be payable. In the event of Total Loss of the Vessel occurring prior to any cancellation or termination of this Policy, full annual premium
85 shall be considered earned.

86 **ADVENTURE**
87   Beginning the adventure upon the Vessel, as above, and so shall continue and endure during the period aforesaid, as employment may
88 offer, in port or at sea, in docks and graving docks, and on ways, gridirons and pontoons, at all times, in all places, and on all occasions,
89 services and trades; with leave to sail or navigate with or without pilots, to go on trial trips and to assist and tow vessels or craft in distress,
90 but the Vessel may not be towed, except as is customary or when in need of assistance, nor shall the Vessel render assistance or undertake
91 towage or salvage services under contract previously arranged by the Assured, the Owners, the Managers or the Charterers of the Vessel,
92 nor shall the Vessel, in the course of trading operations, engage in loading or discharging cargo at sea, from or into another vessel other
93 than a barge, lighter or similar craft used principally in harbors or inland waters. The phrase "engage in loading or discharging cargo at
94 sea" shall include while approaching, leaving or alongside, or while another vessel is approaching, leaving or alongside the Vessel.
95   The Vessel is held covered in case of any breach of conditions as to cargo, trade, locality, towage or salvage activities, or date of sailing,
96 or loading or discharging cargo at sea, provided (a) notice is given to the Underwriters immediately following receipt of knowledge thereof
97 by the Assured, and (b) any amended terms of cover and any additional premium required by the Underwriters are agreed to by the
98 Assured.

99 **PERILS**
100   Touching the Adventures and Perils which the Underwriters are contented to bear and take upon themselves, they are of the Seas,
101 Men-of-War, Fire, Lightning, Earthquake, Enemies, Pirates, Rovers, Assailing Thieves, Jettisons, Letters of Mart and Counter-Mart,
102 Surprisals, Takings at Sea, Arrests, Restraints and Detainments of all Kings, Princes and Peoples, of what nation, condition or quality
103 soever, Barratry of the Master and Mariners and of all other like Perils, Losses and Misfortunes that have or shall come to the Hurt,
104 Detriment or Damage of the Vessel, or any part thereof, excepting, however, such of the foregoing perils as may be excluded by provisions
105 elsewhere in the Policy or by endorsement thereon.

106 **ADDITIONAL PERILS (INCHAMAREE)**
107   Subject to the conditions of this Policy, this insurance also covers loss of or damage to the Vessel directly caused by the following:
108   Accidents in loading, discharging or handling cargo, or in bunkering;
109   Accidents in going on or off, or while on drydocks, graving docks, ways, gridirons or pontoons;
110   Explosions on shipboard or elsewhere;
111   Breakdown of motor generators or other electrical machinery and electrical connections thereto, bursting of boilers, breakage of
112   shafts, or any latent defect in the machinery or hull, (excluding the cost and expense of replacing or repairing the defective part);
113   Breakdown of or accidents to nuclear installations or reactors not on board the insured Vessel;
114   Contact with aircraft, rockets or similar missiles, or with any land conveyance;
115   Negligence of Charterers and/or Repairers, provided such Charterers and/or Repairers are not an Assured hereunder;
116   Negligence of Masters, Officers, Crew or Pilots;
117 provided such loss or damage has not resulted from want of due diligence by the Assured, the Owners or Managers of the Vessel, or any of
118 them. Masters, Officers, Crew or Pilots are not to be considered Owners within the meaning of this clause should they hold shares in the
119 Vessel.

120   **DELIBERATE DAMAGE (ENVIRONMENTAL HAZARD)**
121   Subject to the conditions of this Policy, this insurance also covers loss of or damage to the Vessel directly caused by governmental
122   authorities acting for the public welfare to prevent or mitigate an environmental hazard, or threat thereof, resulting directly from damage to
123   the Vessel for which the Underwriters are liable under this Policy, provided such act of governmental authorities has not resulted from want
124   of due diligence by the Assured, the Owners, or Managers of the Vessel or any of them to prevent or mitigate such hazard or threat.
125   Masters, Officers, Crew or Pilots are not to be considered Owners within the meaning of this clause should they hold shares in the Vessel.

126   **CLAIMS (GENERAL PROVISIONS)**
127   In the event of any accident or occurrence which could give rise to a claim under this Policy, prompt notice thereof shall be given **to**
128   the Underwriters and as soon as possible after the Assured has, or the Owners or Managers have, become aware or have knowledge of such
129   loss, damage, liability or expense, and
130   (a)   notwithstanding the foregoing requirement of prompt notice of all claims to the Underwriters, and without altering or amending
131   such prompt notice requirement, any claims under this Policy shall be barred if notice of the claim is not given to the Underwriters for
132   any reason within twelve months after the Assured has, or the Owners or Managers of the Vessel have, become aware or have
133   knowledge of the occurrence of the loss, damage, liability or expense giving rise to the claim, unless the Assured reasonably believes
134   that such loss, damage liability or expense will not give rise to a claim, the Underwriters agree to waive this time bar in writing, or
135   notice was properly given to the Underwriters on any subsequent policy year and it is later determined that the loss, damage, liability
136   or expense should be apportioned over multiple policy years, including earlier years;
137   (b)   where practicable, the Underwriters shall be advised prior to survey, so that they may appoint their own surveyor, if they so
138   desire;
139   (c)   the Underwriters shall be entitled to decide where the Vessel shall proceed for docking and/or repair (allowance to be made to
140   the Assured for the actual additional expense of the voyage arising from compliance with the Underwriters' requirement);
141   (d)   the Underwriters shall have the right of veto in connection with any repair firm proposed;
142   (e)   the Underwriters may take tenders, or may require in writing that tenders be taken for the repair of the Vessel, in which event,
143   upon acceptance of a tender with the approval of the Underwriters, an allowance shall be made at the rate of 30 per cent. per annum
144   on the amount insured, for each day or pro rata for part of a day, for time lost between the issuance of invitations to tender and the
145   acceptance of a tender, to the extent that such time is lost solely as the result of tenders having been taken and provided the tender is
146   accepted without delay after receipt of the Underwriters' approval.
147   Due credit shall be given against the allowances in (c) and (e) above for any amount recovered:
148   1.   in respect of fuel, stores, and wages and maintenance of the Master, Officers or Crew allowed in General or Particular Average;
149   and
150   2.   from third parties in respect of damages for detention and/or loss of profit and/or running expenses;
151   for the period covered by the allowances or any part thereof.
152   No claim shall be allowed in Particular Average for wages and maintenance of the Master, Officers or Crew, except when incurred
153   solely for the necessary removal of the Vessel from one port to another for average repairs or for trial trips to test average repairs, in which
154   cases wages and maintenance will be allowed only while the Vessel is under way. This exclusion shall not apply to overtime or similar
155   extraordinary payments to the Master, Officers or Crew incurred in shifting the Vessel for tank cleaning or repairs or while specifically
156   engaged in these activities, either in port or at sea.
157   Upon the request of the Underwriters, the Assured must provide or make available information or documentation from the
158   classification society reasonably requested by Underwriters concerning the condition of the Vessel before and during the policy period.
159   Additionally, the Assured shall authorize the Underwriters to obtain such information directly from the classification society and from the
160   relevant authorities in the country where the Vessel is registered or has been through port state control. Prompt notice shall be given to the
161   assured whenever such requests for information are made.
162   General and Particular Average shall be payable without deduction, new for old.
163   The expense of sighting the bottom after stranding shall be paid, if reasonably incurred especially for that purpose, even if no damage
164   be found.
165   No claim shall in any case be allowed in respect of scraping or painting the Vessel's bottom.
166   In the event of loss or damage to equipment or apparatus not owned by the Assured but installed for use on board the Vessel and for
167   which the Assured has assumed responsibility, claim shall not exceed (1) the amount the Underwriters would pay if the Assured were
168   owner of such equipment or apparatus, or (2) the contractual responsibility assumed by the Assured to the owners or lessors thereof,
169   whichever shall be less.
170   No claim for unrepaired damages shall be allowed, except to the extent that the aggregate damage caused by perils insured against
171   during the period of the Policy and left unrepaired at the expiration of the Policy shall be demonstrated by the Assured to have diminished
172   the actual market value of the Vessel on that date if undamaged by such perils.
173   Claims become time-barred after ten years from the end of the calendar year during which the loss or damage giving rise to any claim
174   under this policy took place, unless the Underwriters agree to an extension in writing, which agreement shall not be unreasonably refused.
175   However, this time bar shall not become effective until ninety days after notice of the time bar has been given to the Assured by the
176   Underwriters, which notice may be given within six months of the expiry of the limitation period, or thereafter. If notice is given within six
177   months of the expiry of the limitation period, the limitation expiry date shall be ten years after the date on which the loss or damage took
178   place, or ninety days after the Assured's receipt of the notice, whichever is later. As respects claims for third-party liability, such claims
179   shall not become time-barred before the time when the liability claim against the assured becomes time-barred. The ten-year limitation
180   shall not apply to claims where notice was properly given to the underwriters on any subsequent policy year and it is later determined that
181   the loss, damage, liability or expense should be apportioned over multiple policy years, including earlier years.

182   **GENERAL AVERAGE AND SALVAGE**
183   General Average and Salvage shall be payable as provided in the contract of affreightment, or failing such provision or there be no
184   contract of affreightment, payable at the Assured's election either in accordance with York-Antwerp Rules 1974 or 1994, or as agreed, or
185   with the Laws and Usages of the Port of New York. Provided always that when an adjustment according to the laws and usages of the port
186   of destination is properly demanded by the owners of the cargo, General Average shall be paid accordingly.

187 In the event of salvage, towage or other assistance being rendered to the Vessel by any vessel belonging in part or in whole to the
188 same Owners or Charterers, the value of such services (without regard to the common ownership or control of the vessels) shall be
189 ascertained by arbitration in the manner provided for under the Collision Liability clause in this Policy, and the amount so awarded so far
190 as applicable to the interest hereby insured shall constitute a charge under this Policy.
191 When the contributory value of the Vessel is greater than the Agreed Value herein, the liability of the Underwriters for General
192 Average contribution (except in respect to amounts made good to the Vessel), or Salvage, shall not exceed that proportion of the total
193 contribution due from the Vessel which the amount insured hereunder bears to the contributory value, and if, because of damage for which
194 the Underwriters are liable as Particular Average, the value of the Vessel has been reduced for the purpose of contribution, the amount of
195 such Particular Average damage recoverable under this Policy shall first be deducted from the amount insured hereunder, and the
196 Underwriters shall then be liable only for the proportion which such net amount bears to the contributory value.

TOTAL LOSS

198 In ascertaining whether the Vessel is a constructive Total Loss the Agreed Value shall be taken as the repaired value and nothing in
199 respect of the damaged or break-up value of the Vessel or wreck shall be taken into account.
200 There shall be no recovery for a constructive Total Loss hereunder unless the expense of recovering and repairing the Vessel would
201 exceed the Agreed Value. In making this determination, only expenses incurred or to be incurred by reason of a single accident or a
202 sequence of damages arising from the same accident shall be taken into account, but expenses incurred prior to tender of abandonment shall
203 not be considered if such are to be claimed separately under the Sue and Labor clause.
204 In the event of Total Loss (actual or constructive), no claim is to be made by the Underwriters for freight, whether notice of
205 abandonment has been given or not.
206 In no case shall the Underwriters be liable for unrepaired damage in addition to a subsequent Total Loss sustained during the period
207 covered by this Policy.

SUE AND LABOR

209 And in case of any Loss or Misfortune, it shall be lawful and necessary for the Assured, their Factors, Servants and Assigns, to sue,
210 labor and travel for, in and about the defense, safeguard and recovery of the Vessel, or any part thereof, without prejudice to this insurance,
211 to the charges whereof the Underwriters will contribute their proportion as provided below. And it is expressly declared and agreed that no
212 acts of the Underwriters or Assured in recovering, saving or preserving the Vessel shall be considered as a waiver or acceptance of
213 abandonment.
214 In the event of expenditure under the Sue and Labor clause, the Underwriters shall pay the proportion of such expenses that the
215 amount insured hereunder bears to the Agreed Value, or that the amount insured hereunder (less loss and/or damage payable under this
216 Policy) bears to the actual value of the salved property, whichever proportion shall be less; provided always that their liability for such
217 expenses shall not exceed their proportionate part of the Agreed Value.
218 If claim for Total Loss is admitted under this Policy and sue and labor expenses have been reasonably incurred in excess of any
219 proceeds realized or value recovered, the amount payable under this Policy will be the proportion of such excess that the amount insured
220 hereunder (without deduction for loss or damage) bears to the Agreed Value or to the sound value of the Vessel at the time of the accident,
221 whichever value was greater; provided always that Underwriters' liability for such expenses shall not exceed their proportionate part of the
222 Agreed Value. The foregoing shall also apply to expenses reasonably incurred in salving or attempting to salve the Vessel and other
223 property to the extent that such expenses shall be regarded as having been incurred in respect of the Vessel.

COLLISION LIABILITY

225 And it is further agreed that:
226 (a) if the Vessel shall come into collision with any other ship or vessel, and the Assured or the Surety in consequence of the Vessel
227 being at fault shall become liable to pay and shall pay by way of damages to any other person or persons any sum or sums in
228 respect of such collision, the Underwriters will pay the Assured or the Surety, whichever shall have paid, such proportion of such
229 sum or sums so paid as their respective subscriptions hereto bear to the Agreed Value, provided always that their liability in
230 respect to any one such collision shall not exceed their proportionate part of the Agreed Value;
231 (b) in cases where, with the consent in writing of a majority (in amount) of Hull Underwriters, the liability of the Vessel has been
232 contested, or proceedings have been taken to limit liability, the Underwriters will also pay a like proportion of the costs which
233 the Assured shall thereby incur or be compelled to pay.

234 When both vessels are to blame, then, unless the liability of the owners or charterers of one or both such vessels becomes limited by
235 law, claims under the Collision Liability clause shall be settled on the principle of Cross-Liabilities as if the owners or charterers of each
236 vessel had been compelled to pay to the owners or charterers of the other of such vessels such one-half or other proportion of the latter's
237 damages as may have been properly allowed in ascertaining the balance or sum payable by or to the Assured in consequence of such
238 collision.
239 The principles involved in this clause shall apply to the case where both vessels are the property, in part or in whole, of the same
240 owners or charterers, all questions of responsibility and amount of liability as between the two vessels being left to the decision of a single
241 Arbitrator, if the parties can agree upon a single Arbitrator, or failing such agreement, to the decision of Arbitrators, one to be appointed by
242 the Assured and one to be appointed by the majority (in amount) of Hull Underwriters interested; the two Arbitrators chosen to choose a
243 third Arbitrator before entering upon the reference, and the decision of such single Arbitrator, or of any two of such three Arbitrators,
244 appointed as above, to be final and binding.
245 Provided always that this clause shall in no case extend to any sum which the Assured or the Surety may become liable to pay or shall
246 pay in consequence of, or with respect to:
247 (a) removal or disposal of obstructions, wrecks or their cargoes under statutory powers or otherwise pursuant to law;
248 (b) injury to real or personal property of every description;
249 (c) the discharge, spillage, emission or leakage of oil, petroleum products, chemicals or other substances of any kind or description
250 whatsoever;
251 (d) cargo or other property on or the engagements of the Vessel;

Ocean Marine

252   (e) loss of life, personal injury or illness.
253   Provided further that exclusions (b) and (c) above shall not apply to injury to other vessels or property thereon except to the extent that
254   such injury arises out of any action taken to avoid, minimize or remove any discharge, spillage, emission or leakage described in (c) above.

PILOTAGE AND TOWAGE
256   This insurance shall not be prejudiced by reason of any contract limiting in whole or in part the liability of pilots, tugs, towboats, or
257   their owners when the Assured or the agent of the Assured accepts such contract in accordance with established local practice.
258   Where in accordance with such practice, pilotage or towage services are provided under contracts requiring the Assured or the agent
259   of the Assured:
260   (a) to assume liability for damage resulting from collision of the Vessel insured with any other ship or vessel, including the towing
261   vessel, or
262   (b) to indemnify those providing the pilotage or towage services against loss or liability for any such damages,
263   it is agreed that amounts paid by the Assured or Surety pursuant to such assumed obligations shall be deemed payments "by way of
264   damages to any other person or persons" and to have been paid "in consequence of the Vessel being at fault" within the meaning of the
265   Collision Liability clause in this Policy to the extent that such payments would have been covered if the Vessel had been legally
266   responsible in the absence of any agreement. Provided always that in no event shall the aggregate amount of liability of the Underwriters
267   under the Collision Liability clause, including this clause, be greater than the amount of any statutory limitation of liability to which owners
268   are entitled or would be entitled if liability under any contractual obligation referred to in this clause were included among the liabilities
269   subject to such statutory limitations.

CHANGE OF OWNERSHIP
271   In the event of any change, voluntary or otherwise, in the ownership or flag of the Vessel, or if the Vessel be placed under new
272   management, or be chartered on a bareboat basis or requisitioned on that basis, or if the Classification Society of the Vessel or her class
273   therein be changed, cancelled, or withdrawn, then, unless the Underwriters agree thereto in writing, this Policy shall automatically
274   terminate at the time of such change of ownership, flag, management, charter, requisition or classification; provided, however, that:
275   (a) if the Vessel has cargo on board and has already sailed from her loading port, or is at sea in ballast, such automatic termination
276   shall, if required, be deferred until arrival at final port of discharge if with cargo, or at port of destination if in ballast;
277   (b) in the event of an involuntary temporary transfer by requisition or otherwise, without the prior execution of a written agreement
278   by the Assured, such automatic termination shall occur fifteen days after such transfer.
279   This insurance shall not inure to the benefit of any transferee or charterer of the Vessel and, if a loss payable hereunder should occur
280   between the time of change or transfer and any deferred automatic termination, the Underwriters shall be subrogated to all of the rights of
281   the Assured against the transferee or charterer in respect of all or part of such loss as is recoverable from the transferee or charterer, and in
282   the proportion which the amount insured hereunder bears to the Agreed Value.
283   The term "new management" as used above refers only to the transfer of the management of the Vessel from one firm of corporation
284   to another, and it shall not apply to any internal changes within the offices of the Assured.

ADDITIONAL INSURANCES
286   It is a condition of this Policy that no additional insurance against the risk of Total Loss of the Vessel shall be effected to operate
287   during the currency of this Policy by or for account of the Assured, Owners, Managers, Operators or Mortgagees except on the interests
288   and up to the amounts enumerated in the following Sections (a) to (g), inclusive, and no such insurance shall be subject to P.P.I., F.I.A. or
289   other like term on any interests whatever excepting those enumerated in Section (a); provided always and notwithstanding the limitation on
290   recovery in the Assured clause a breach of this condition shall not afford the Underwriters any defense to a claim by a Mortgagee who has
291   accepted this Policy without knowledge of such breach:
292   (a) DISBURSEMENTS, MANAGERS' COMMISSIONS, PROFITS OR EXCESS OR INCREASED VALUE OF HULL AND
293   MACHINERY, AND/OR SIMILAR INTERESTS HOWEVER DESCRIBED, AND FREIGHT (INCLUDING CHARTERED
294   FREIGHT OR ANTICIPATED FREIGHT) INSURED FOR TIME. An amount not exceeding in the aggregate 25% of the
295   Agreed Value.
296   (b) FREIGHT OR HIRE, UNDER CONTRACTS FOR VOYAGE. An amount not exceeding the gross freight or hire for the current
297   cargo passage and next succeeding cargo passage (such insurance to include, if required, a preliminary and an intermediate
298   ballast passage) plus the charges of insurance. In the case of a voyage charter where payment is made on a time basis, the
299   amount shall be calculated on the estimated duration of the voyage, subject to the limitation of two cargo passages as laid down
300   herein. Any amount permitted under this Section shall be reduced, as the freight or hire is earned, by the gross amount so earned.
301   Any freight or hire to be earned under the form of Charters described in (d) below shall not be permitted under this Section (b) if
302   any part thereof is insured as permitted under said Section (d).
303   (c) ANTICIPATED FREIGHT IF THE VESSEL SAILS IN BALLAST AND NOT UNDER CHARTER. An amount not exceeding
304   the anticipated gross freight on next cargo passage, such amount to be reasonably estimated on the basis of the current rate of
305   freight at time of insurance, plus the charges of insurance. Provided, however, that no insurance shall be permitted by this
306   Section if any insurance is effected as permitted under Section (b).
307   (d) TIME CHARTER HIRE OR CHARTER HIRE FOR SERIES OF VOYAGES. An amount not exceeding 50% of the gross hire
308   which is to be earned under the charter in a period not exceeding 18 months. Any amount permitted under this Section shall be
309   reduced as the hire is earned under the charter by 50% of the gross amount so earned but, where the charter is for a period
310   exceeding 18 months, the amount insured need not be reduced while it does not exceed 50% of the gross hire still to be earned
311   under the charter. An insurance permitted by this Section may begin on the signing of the charter.
312   (e) PREMIUMS. An amount not exceeding the actual premiums of all interest insured for a period not exceeding 12 months
313   (excluding premiums insured as permitted under the foregoing Sections but including, if required, the premium or estimated calls
314   on any Protection and Indemnity or War Risks and Strikes insurance) reducing pro rata monthly.
315   (f) RETURNS OF PREMIUM. An amount not exceeding the actual returns which are recoverable subject to "and arrival" or
316   equivalent provision under any policy of insurance.

317   (g)   INSURANCE IRRESPECTIVE OF AMOUNT AGAINST: Risks excluded by War, Strikes and Related Exclusions clause; risks
318   enumerated in the American Institute War Risks and Strikes Clauses; and General Average and Salvage Disbursements.

319 **WAR STRIKES AND RELATED EXCLUSIONS**
320 The following conditions shall be paramount and shall supersede and nullify any contrary provisions of the Policy.
321 This Policy does not cover any loss, damage or expense caused by, resulting from, or incurred as a consequence of:
322   (a)   Capture, seizure, arrest, restraint, detainment, confiscation or expropriation or any attempt thereat; or
323   (b)   Any taking of the Vessel, by requisition or otherwise, whether in time of peace or war and whether lawful or otherwise; or
324   (c)   Any mine, bomb or torpedo not carried as cargo on board the Vessel; or
325   (d)   Any weapon of war employing atomic or nuclear fission and/or fusion or other like reaction or radioactive force or matter; or
326   (e)   Civil war, revolution, rebellion, insurrection, or civil strife arising therefrom, or piracy; or
327   (f)   Strikes, lockouts, political or labor disturbances, civil commotions, riots, martial law, military or usurped power; or
328   (g)   Any act perpetrated by terrorists or any act carried out by any person or persons acting primarily from a political, religious or
329   ideological motive; or
330   (h)   Any threat of terrorist activity, actual or perceived, including closure of ports or blockage of waterways resulting therefrom; or
331   (i)   Malicious acts or vandalism, unless committed by the Master or Mariners and not excluded elsewhere under this War Strikes and
332   Related Exclusions clause; or
333   (j)   Hostilities or warlike operations (whether there be a declaration of war or not) but this subparagraph (j) not to exclude collision
334   or contact with aircraft, rockets or similar missiles, or with any fixed or floating object, or stranding, heavy weather, fire or
335   explosion unless caused directly by a hostile act by or against a belligerent power, which act is independent of the nature of the
336   voyage or service which the Vessel concerned or, in the case of a collision, any other vessel involved therein, is performing. As
337   used herein, "power" includes any authority maintaining naval, military or air forces in association with a power.
338 If war risks or other risks excluded by this clause are hereafter insured by endorsement on this Policy, such endorsement shall
339 supersede the above conditions only to the extent that the terms of such endorsement are inconsistent therewith and only while such
340 endorsement remains in force.

AIMU
Protection and Indemnity (P and I) Clauses
June 2, 1983

To be attached to and form part of Policy No.................. of.......................(hereinafter "the Underwriters").   1

....   2

THE FOLLOWING CLAUSES ARE SUBSTITUTED FOR THOSE OF THE POLICY FORM TO WHICH   3
THEY ARE ATTACHED, THE LATTER BEING VOID, EXCEPT FOR THOSE PROVISIONS REQUIRED   4
BY LAW. CAPTIONS, BELOW, ARE FOR EASE OF REFERENCE ONLY AND ARE NOT TO BE USED TO   5
INTERPRET THE CLAUSES.   6

ASSURED

This Policy insures   7

....   8
(hereinafter, "the Assured"). The Underwriters waive all rights of subrogation against affiliated or subsidiary compa-   9
nies of the Assured but only to the extent that the liabilities of such companies are uninsured.   10

VESSEL

The Underwriters will indemnify the Assured in respect of the matters set forth at lines 46 through 76, below, subject   11
to all other terms hereof, in respect of the............................ of ....gross registered tons (hereinafter, the   12
"Vessel"). If more than one Vessel is named, all clauses shall apply as though a separate Policy had been issued for   13
each Vessel.   14

DURATION OF RISK

This Policy attaches on........................, 19....., at............ o'clock........................time and expires on   15
........................, 19....., at..........o'clock.........................time. Should the Vessel be at sea at the expiration of   16
this Policy, or in distress, or at a port of refuge or call, she shall be held covered until she reaches her port of destina-   17
tion, provided prior notice be given to the Underwriters and provided the Assured agrees to any amended terms of   18
cover and additional premium if required by the Underwriters.   19

LIMIT OF LIABILITY

Liability hereunder in respect of all consequences of any one casualty or occurrence, including defense costs, shall not   20
exceed the sum of $ less any applicable deductible, regardless of how many separate injuries or   21
claims arise out of such casualty or occurrence.   22

DEDUCTIBLES

There shall be deducted from the total amount payable by the Underwriters with respect to all claims, including costs   23
of defense and expenses, arising from any one casualty or occurrence: 24
    a) $........................with respect to those claims for loss of life, bodily injury or illness, and   25
    b) $........................with respect to all other claims;   26
PROVIDED, HOWEVER, that the maximum deductible for any one casualty or occurrence shall not exceed the   27
greater of the foregoing amounts.   28

PREMIUM

The Underwriters are to be paid premium of $ for this insurance, payable as follows: 29

....   30

....   31

RETURN PREMIUM

If the Vessel is sold, demise chartered or requisitioned this Policy shall terminate on the date and at the hour when   32
such disposition of the Vessel is effective and the Underwriters will return premium on a pro rata daily net basis for the   33
unexpired term. If the Policy is cancelled by the Assured, the Underwriters will return premium on the usual short rate   34
daily net basis for the unexpired term. If the Policy is cancelled by the Underwriters they will return premium on a pro   35
rata daily net basis for the unexpired term.   36

CANCELLATION

The Policy may be cancelled by the Underwriters or by the Assured upon fifteen days written or telegraphic notice.   37
The Underwriters may send notice to the Assured's last address known to them, or to the broker of record at the time   38
when notice is given. At noon local time at the place of the sending of the notice on the fifteenth day after such notice   39
shall have been mailed, telegraphed or telexed, the Policy shall cease to be in effect. The Policy may also be cancelled   40
at any time by mutual agreement of the Assured and the Underwriters.   41

TRADING WARRANTY

Warranted that the Vessel shall be confined to   42

.... 43

.... 44

.... 45

INDEMNITY

Subject to all exclusions and other terms of this Policy the Underwriters agree to indemnify the Assured for any sums 46
which the Assured, as owner of the Vessel, shall have become liable to pay, and shall have paid, in respect of any 47
casualty or occurrence during the currency of the Policy but only in consequence of any of the matters set forth here- 48
under PROVIDED, however, that if the interest of the Assured is or includes interests other than owner of the Vessel, 49
the Underwriters' liability shall not be greater than if the Assured was the owner entitled to all defenses and limita- 50
tions of liability to which a shipowner is entitled: 51

(1) Loss of life and bodily injury or illness; but excluding amounts paid under any compensation act. 52

(2) Hospital, medical or other expenses necessarily and reasonably incurred with respect to loss of life, bodily injury 53
to, or illness of, any person. 54

(3) Crew member burial expense not to exceed $1,000 per person. 55

(4) Repatriation expenses of crew member, excepting such as arise from the termination of any agreement in 56
accordance with its terms, or the sale of the Vessel or other voluntary act of the Assured. Wages may be included 57
in such expenses when a statute requires payment of wages while awaiting and during repatriation. 58

(5) Damage to any fixed or movable object or property, howsoever caused, excluding however, damage to another 59
vessel or any property aboard it caused by collision with the Vessel. 60

(6) Cost or expense of, or incidental to, any attempted or actual removal or disposal of obstructions, wrecks or their 61
cargoes under statutory power or otherwise pursuant to law, PROVIDED, however, that there shall be deducted from 62
such claim for cost or expenses, the value of any salvage from the wreck inuring to the benefit of the Assured or any 63
subrogee thereof. 64

(7) Fines and penalties, including expenses reasonably incurred in avoiding or mitigating same, for the violation of 65
any of the laws of the United States, or any State thereof, or of any foreign country; PROVIDED, however, that the 66
Underwriters shall not be liable to indemnify the Assured against any such fines or penalties resulting directly or 67
indirectly from the failure, neglect, or default of the Assured or his managing officers or managing agents to exercise 68
the highest degree of diligence to prevent a violation of any such laws. 69

(8) Extraordinary expense arising from an outbreak of contagious disease, PROVIDED that the Vessel was not 70
ordered by anyone acting on behalf of the Assured to proceed to a port where such disease was known or supposed 71
to exist. 72

(9) Costs incurred with the written consent of the Underwriters, or reasonably incurred prior to receipt of advices 73
from Underwriters, for investigation and defense of claims, valid or not, within the scope of the Policy. 74

(10) Port charges incurred solely for the purpose of putting in to land an injured or sick seaman or passenger, and the 75
net loss to the Assured in respect of bunkers, insurance, stores and provisions as the result of the deviation. 76

EXCLUSIONS

Notwithstanding anything to the contrary elsewhere herein the Underwriters will not indemnify the Assured in 77
respect of any of the following matters: 78

(A) Any liability assumed under contract or otherwise. 79

(B) Liability imposed on the Assured as punitive or exemplary damages, however described. 80

(C) Any liability for any loss of, damage to, or expense in respect of, cargo or other property (including baggage and 81
    personal effects of passengers, mail and parcel post) carried, to be carried or which had been carried on board 82
    the Vessel, EXCEPT, HOWEVER, such liability imposed under the doctrine of cross liabilities for cargo on 83
    board the Vessel for which there is no coverage under any other policy held by the Assured. 84

(D) Any liability or claim for, or any loss of, damage to, or expense in respect of property owned, leased, chartered 85
    or hired by the Assured. 86

(E) Engagement in unlawful trade or performance of an unlawful act with knowledge of the Assured. 87

(F) Cancellation or breach of any contract. 88

(G) Bad debts. 89

(H) Fraud, dishonesty or insolvency of the Assured, its agents or others. 90

(I) Salvage charges, special charges, general average, freight, detention, demurrage or loss of use, of the Vessel. 91

Ocean Marine

(J) Any liability for, or any loss, damage, or expense arising from or accruing by reason of the towage of any other   92
vessel or craft other than emergency towage of a vessel in distress at sea to a port or place of safety, EXCEPT,   93
HOWEVER, this exclusion shall not apply to claims for loss of life, or bodily injury to, or illness or any person.   94
Emergency towage is deemed to be towage undertaken as a salvage service while the Vessel is on a voyage wholly   95
unrelated to performance of such service.   96

(K) Any liability for, or any loss, damage or expense while engaged in, or resulting from, any commercial diving   97
operation or service from the Vessel, EXCEPT, HOWEVER, any liability incurred when the Vessel's crew is   98
engaged in inspection or repair of the Vessel which could not be deferred until commercial divers were available.   99

(L) Any liability for, or any loss, damage, injury or expense resulting from nuclear radiation, fission or fusion,   100
whether such loss, damage, injury or expense has been caused directly or indirectly or has arisen from any matter   101
for which the Assured has responsibility or otherwise, and whether the nuclear event be controlled or un-   102
controlled.   103

(M) Any liability for, or any loss, damage, injury or expense caused by, resulting from or incurred by reason of any   104
one or more of the following: 105

1) Capture, seizure, arrest, taking, restraint, detainment, confiscation, preemption, requisition or national-   106
ization, or the consequences thereof or any attempt thereat, whether in time of peace or war and whether   107
lawful or otherwise;   108

2) Any weapon of war employing atomic or nuclear fission and/or fusion or other reaction or radioactive   109
force or matter, or by any mine, bomb or torpedo;   110

3) Hostilities or warlike operations (whether there by a declaration of war or not), but the phrase, "hostilities   111
or warlike operations (whether there be a declaration of war or not)", shall not exclude collision or contact   112
with aircraft, rockets or similar missiles or with any fixed or floating object, stranding, heavy weather, fire   113
or explosion unless caused directly (independently of the nature of the voyage or service which the watercraft   114
concerned or in the case of a collision, any other vessel involved herein, is performing) by a hostile act by   115
or against a belligerent power; for the purpose of the foregoing, power includes any authority maintaining   116
naval, military or air forces in association with a power. In addition to the foregoing exclusions, this in-   117
surance shall not cover any loss, damage or expense to which a warlike act or the use of military or naval   118
weapons is a contributing cause, whether or not the Assured's liability therefor is based on negligence or   119
otherwise, and whether in time of peace or war. The embarkation, carriage and disembarkation of troops,   120
combatants, or material of war, or the placement of the watercraft in jeopardy as an act or measure of war   121
taken in the actual process of a military engagement, with or without the consent of the Assured, shall be   122
considered a warlike act for the purposes of this Policy.   123

4) The consequences of civil war, revolution, rebellion, insurrection, military or usurped power, the imposition   124
of martial law, or civil strife arising therefrom, or piracy; or from any loss, damage or expense caused by   125
or resulting directly or indirectly from the act or acts of one or more persons, whether or not agents of a   126
sovereign power, carried out for political, ideological or terrorist purposes, and whether any loss, damage   127
or expense resulting therefrom is accidental or intentional.   128

5) Malicious acts or vandalism, strikes, lockouts, political or labor disturbances, civil commotions, riots, or   129
the acts of any person or persons taking part in such occurrence or disorder.   130

(N) Any liability for, or any loss, damage, cost, expense, fine or penalty of any kind or nature whatsoever, whether   131
statutory or otherwise, incurred by or imposed on the Assured, directly or indirectly, in consequence of, or with   132
respect to, the actual or potential discharge, emission, spillage or leakage upon or into the seas, waters, land or   133
air, of substances of any kind or nature whatsoever.   134

GENERAL CONDITIONS
NOTICE OF LOSS

It is a condition of this Policy that the Assured give prompt notice to the Underwriters of any casualty or occurrence   135
which may result in a claim under this Policy.   136

FORWARDING OF PROCESS

It is a condition of this Policy that the Assured forward to the Underwriters, promptly upon receipt, copies of all   137
communications, legal process and pleadings relating to any casualty or occurrence which may result in a claim under   138
this Policy.   139

SETTLEMENT OF CLAIMS

1) It is a condition of the Policy that the Assured shall not make any admission of nor agree to assume any liability   140
either before or after any casualty or occurrence which may result in a claim under this Policy.   141

2) It is a condition of this Policy that the Assured shall take such steps to minimize and avoid liability, before and after   142
any casualty or occurrence, as would be taken by a prudent uninsured person.   143

3) The Underwriters shall have the option of naming the attorneys who shall represent the Assured in the prose-   144
cution or defense of any litigation or negotiations between the Assured and third parties concerning any claim   145
covered by this Policy, and in any event, the Underwriters shall direct the progress of such litigation or nego-   146
tiations.   147

4) If the Assured shall fail, or refuse, to settle any claim as authorized by the Underwriters, the liability of the Under- 148
writers shall be limited to the amount for which settlement could have been made plus legal fees and disbursements 149
incurred to the date the Assured fails or refuses to settle any such claim, less the amount of any deductible provided 150
for in this Policy. If thereafter any amount is recovered against the Assured in excess of the amount of any settle- 151
ment authorized by the Underwriters (less the deductible), such excess amount, plus any additional legal fees and 152
disbursements, shall be solely for account of the Assured. 153

CLAIM COOPERATION

The Assured shall aid in securing information, evidence, obtaining witnesses, and shall cooperate with the Under- 154
writers in the defense of any claim or suit or in the appeal from any judgment, in respect of any casualty or occurence 155
as hereinbefore provided. 156

SUBROGATION

The Underwriters shall be subrogated to all the rights which the Assured may have against any other person or entity, 157
in respect of any payment made under this Policy, to the extent of such payment, and the Assured shall, upon the 158
request of the Underwriters, execute and shall deliver such instruments and papers as the Underwriters shall require 159
and do whatever else is necessary to secure such rights. In the event of any agreement or act, past or future, by the 160
Assured, whereby any right of recovery of the Assured against any person or entity is released or lost to which the 161
Underwriters on payment of loss would be entitled to subrogation, but for such agreement or act, the Underwriters 162
shall be relieved of liability under this Policy to the extent that their rights of subrogation have been impaired 163
thereby; in such event the right of the Underwriters to retain or collect any premium paid or due hereunder shall 164
not be affected. The Underwriters shall not be liable for the costs and expenses of prosecuting any claim or suit 165
unless the same shall have been incurred with the written consent of the Underwriters, or the Underwriters shall 166
be satisfied that such approval could not have been obtained under the circumstances without unreasonable delay 167
and that such costs and expenses were reasonably and properly incurred, such costs and expenses being subject to 168
the deductible. The Underwriters shall be entitled to take credit for any profit accruing to the Assured by reason 169
of any negligence or wrongful act of the Assured's servants or agents, up to the measure of their loss, or to recover 170
for their own account from third parties any damage that may be provable by reason of such negligence or 171
wrongful act. 172

OTHER INSURANCE

Provided that where the Assured is, irrespective of this insurance, covered or protected against any loss or claim 173
which would otherwise have been paid by the Underwriters under this Policy, there shall be no contribution or par- 174
ticipation by the Underwriters on the basis of excess, contributing, deficiency, concurrent, or double insurance 175
or otherwise. 176

ASSIGNMENTS

Neither this Policy nor any claim or demand against the Underwriters under this Policy shall be assigned or trans- 177
ferred, and no person, excepting a legally appointed Receiver of the property of the Assured, shall acquire any right 178
against the Underwriters by virtue of this insurance without the express consent of the Underwriters endorsed hereon. 179
This Policy shall cease to be in effect 10 days after appointment of a Receiver, Trustee or any other transferee of the 180
Assured's assets. 181

TIME FOR SUIT CLAUSE

No action shall lie against the Underwriters for the recovery of any loss sustained by the Assured unless such action 182
be brought against the Underwriters within one year after the final judgment or decree is entered in the litigation 183
against the Assured, OR in case the claim against the Underwriters accrues without the entry of such final judgment 184
or decree, unless such action be brought within one year from the date of the payment by the Assured of such claim, 185
PROVIDED, however, that where such limitation of time is prohibited by the law of the State wherein this Policy 186
is issued, then, and only in that event, no action under this Policy shall be sustainable unless commenced within the 187
shortest limitation permitted under the law of such State. 188

AIMU
Protection and Indemnity (P and I) Clauses
Cargo Liability Endorsement
June 2, 1983

ENDORSEMENT to be attached to and made part of Policy No............................ of...................................... 1

.... 2

In consideration of the payment of an additional premium of $................. , and subject to the limit of liability, the 3
deductible amount for claims other than for loss of life, bodily injury or illness, the exclusions, the conditions and the 4
other terms of this Policy, this Policy is hereby extended to indemnify the Assured for any sum which the Assured, as 5
owner of the Vessel shall have become liable to pay and shall have paid, in respect of any claim for loss, damage or 6
expense in respect of cargo, including baggage and personal effects of passengers, on board the Vessel, carried, to be 7
carried, or which had been carried on board the Vessel SUBJECT ALSO to the Special Limits of Liability herein- 8
after provided. 9

The Underwriters expressly agree to indemnify the Assured for any sums which the Assured is unable to recover 10
as cargo's proportion of general average, salvage charges and special charges from any other source PROVIDED that 11
cargo's proportion shall be determined as if the contract of carriage or charter party contained the New Jason Clause. 12

EXCLUSIONS

Notwithstanding anything to the contrary contained in this Endorsement, the Underwriters shall not be required 13
to indemnify the Assured for any liability for, or any loss, damage or expense arising out of or in connection with: 14

a) The custody, care, carriage or delivery of specie, bullion, precious stones, precious metals, jewelry, furs, bank 15
   notes, bonds or other negotiable documents or similar valuable property, unless specially agreed to by the 16
   Underwriters and accepted for transportation under a form of contract approved in writing by the 17
   Underwriters. 18

b) The custody, care, carriage or delivery of mail and parcel post. 19

c) The custody, care, carriage or delivery of any cargo requiring refrigeration, unless the space, apparatus and 20
   means used for such care, custody, carriage and delivery thereof have been surveyed under working conditions 21
   by a classification surveyor or other competent disinterested surveyor before the commencement of each round 22
   voyage and found in all respects fit, and unless the said cargo be accepted for transportation under a form of 23
   contract approved in writing by the Underwriters. 24

d) The stowage of under deck cargo on deck or stowage of cargo in spaces not suitable for its carriage, unless the 25
   Assured shall show that he has taken every reasonable precaution to prevent such stowage. 26

e) Any deviation not authorized by the contract of affreightment, and known to the Assured in time to insure 27
   specifically the liability therefor, unless notice thereof is given to the Underwriters who agree in writing that 28
   such other insurance is unnecessary. 29

f) The refund of, or inability to collect, freight on cargo short delivered, whether or not prepaid or whether or not 30
   included in the claim and paid by the Assured. 31

g) The issuance of Bills of Lading or similar documents of title which, to the knowledge of the Assured, 32
   improperly describe the goods, their condition or quantity, their packing or their containers. 33

h) The delivery of cargo without surrender of Bills of Lading or similar documents of title. 34

i) Any unlawful act of the Assured or conversion of cargo or other property by the Assured. 35

SPECIAL LIMITS OF LIABILITY

It is specially further agreed and understood that under this Endorsement and subject always to the limit of 36
liability of the Policy to which this Endorsement is attached, 37

A) with respect to cargo, not property of the Assured, carried by the Vessel, the liability of the Underwriters   38
shall be limited: 39

    (i) to the minimum liabilities and obligations imposed upon the Assured by the U.S. Carriage of   40
Goods by Sea Act, April 16, 1936, regardless of whether the carriage is subject to the said Act,   41
and,   42

    (ii) as may be reduced by any other lawful protective clauses commonly in use in the particular trade in   43
which the Vessel is engaged,   44

regardless of whether the Assured or the Vessel assumes any greater liabilities or obligations;   45

B) with respect to cargo, property of the Assured, carried by the Vessel, the liability of the Underwriters shall   46
be limited: 47

    (i)   as hereinbefore provided under the preceding clauses A(i) and A(ii),   48

    (ii) subject however to reduction by the amount which would be recoverable for the loss under the usual   49
form of All Risks Cargo Policy if fully insured,   50

    (iii) regardless of whether such Policy had been obtained;   51

C) with respect to baggage and personal effects carried by the Vessel, the liability of the Underwriters shall in   52
no event exceed the lesser of that which would be imposed upon the Assured in the absence of contract   53
or that provided in the contract between the owner of the property and the Assured or Vessel.   54

All other terms and conditions remain unchanged.

....

Dated...

Commercial Crime Insurance

Commercial crime insurance covers causes of loss that are not covered in commercial property forms. These causes of loss include, but are not limited to, theft committed by employees, burglary, robbery, theft, forgery, computer fraud, and extortion.

Crime insurance also covers two important types of property that commercial property forms exclude: money and securities. Crime insurance on money and securities covers destruction or disappearance in addition to theft.

Various advisory organizations, including the American Association of Insurance Services (AAIS), Insurance Services Office, Inc. (ISO), and The Surety & Fidelity Association of America (SFAA) have developed commercial crime forms for the use of their member companies. The form reprinted in the *Handbook* is the ISO Commercial Crime Coverage Form, which includes optional insuring agreements for several commonly purchased crime coverages. Additional crime coverages can be added by endorsement. A slightly different ISO form is available for insuring governmental entities.

CRIME AND FIDELITY
CR 00 21 05 06

COMMERCIAL CRIME COVERAGE FORM
(LOSS SUSTAINED FORM)

Various provisions in this policy restrict coverage. Read the entire policy carefully to determine rights, duties and what is or is not covered.

Throughout this policy the words "you" and "your" refer to the Named Insured shown in the Declarations. The words "we", "us" and "our" refer to the Company providing this insurance.

Other words and phrases that appear in quotation marks have special meaning. Refer to Section **F.** Definitions.

A. Insuring Agreements

Coverage is provided under the following Insuring Agreements for which a Limit of Insurance is shown in the Declarations and applies to loss that you sustain resulting directly from an "occurrence" taking place during the Policy Period shown in the Declarations, except as provided in Condition **E.1.k.** or **E.1.l.**, which is "discovered" by you during the Policy Period shown in the Declarations or during the period of time provided in the Extended Period To Discover Loss Condition **E.1.g.:**

1. Employee Theft

We will pay for loss of or damage to "money", "securities" and "other property" resulting directly from "theft" committed by an "employee", whether identified or not, acting alone or in collusion with other persons.

For the purposes of this Insuring Agreement, "theft" shall also include forgery.

2. Forgery Or Alteration

a. We will pay for loss resulting directly from "forgery" or alteration of checks, drafts, promissory notes, or similar written promises, orders or directions to pay a sum certain in "money" that are:

(1) Made or drawn by or drawn upon you; or

(2) Made or drawn by one acting as your agent;

or that are purported to have been so made or drawn.

For the purposes of this Insuring Agreement, a substitute check as defined in the Check Clearing for the 21st Century Act shall be treated the same as the original it replaced.

b. If you are sued for refusing to pay any instrument covered in Paragraph **2.a.,** on the basis that it has been forged or altered, and you have our written consent to defend against the suit, we will pay for any reasonable legal expenses that you incur and pay in that defense. The amount that we will pay is in addition to the Limit of Insurance applicable to this Insuring Agreement.

3. Inside The Premises – Theft Of Money And Securities

a. We will pay for loss of "money" and "securities" inside the "premises" or "banking premises":

(1) Resulting directly from "theft" committed by a person present inside such "premises" or "banking premises"; or

(2) Resulting directly from disappearance or destruction.

b. We will pay for loss from damage to the "premises" or its exterior resulting directly from an actual or attempted "theft" of "money" and "securities", if you are the owner of the "premises" or are liable for damage to it.

c. We will pay for loss of or damage to a locked safe, vault, cash register, cash box or cash drawer located inside the "premises" resulting directly from an actual or attempted "theft" of or unlawful entry into those containers.

4. Inside The Premises – Robbery Or Safe Burglary Of Other Property

a. We will pay for loss of or damage to "other property":

(1) Inside the "premises" resulting directly from an actual or attempted "robbery" of a "custodian"; or

(2) Inside the "premises" in a safe or vault resulting directly from an actual or attempted "safe burglary".

b. We will pay for loss from damage to the "premises" or its exterior resulting directly from an actual or attempted "robbery" or "safe burglary" of "other property", if you are the owner of the "premises" or are liable for damage to it.

c. We will pay for loss of or damage to a locked safe or vault located inside the "premises" resulting directly from an actual or attempted "robbery" or "safe burglary".

5. Outside The Premises

a. We will pay for loss of "money" and "securities" outside the "premises" in the care and custody of a "messenger" or an armored motor vehicle company resulting directly from "theft", disappearance or destruction.

b. We will pay for loss of or damage to "other property" outside the "premises" in the care and custody of a "messenger" or an armored motor vehicle company resulting directly from an actual or attempted "robbery".

6. Computer Fraud

We will pay for loss of or damage to "money", "securities" and "other property" resulting directly from the use of any computer to fraudulently cause a transfer of that property from inside the "premises" or "banking premises":

a. To a person (other than a "messenger") outside those "premises"; or

b. To a place outside those "premises".

7. Funds Transfer Fraud

We will pay for loss of "funds" resulting directly from a "fraudulent instruction" directing a financial institution to transfer, pay or deliver "funds" from your "transfer account".

8. Money Orders And Counterfeit Money

We will pay for loss resulting directly from your having accepted in good faith, in exchange for merchandise, "money" or services:

a. Money orders issued by any post office, express company or bank that are not paid upon presentation; or

b. "Counterfeit money" that is acquired during the regular course of business.

B. Limit Of Insurance

The most we will pay for all loss resulting directly from an "occurrence" is the applicable Limit of Insurance shown in the Declarations.

If any loss is covered under more than one Insuring Agreement or Coverage, the most we will pay for such loss shall not exceed the largest Limit of Insurance available under any one of those Insuring Agreements or Coverages.

C. Deductible

We will not pay for loss resulting directly from an "occurrence" unless the amount of loss exceeds the Deductible Amount shown in the Declarations. We will then pay the amount of loss in excess of the Deductible Amount, up to the Limit of Insurance.

D. Exclusions

1. This insurance does not cover:

a. Acts Committed By You, Your Partners Or Your Members

Loss resulting from "theft" or any other dishonest act committed by:

(1) You; or

(2) Any of your partners or "members";

whether acting alone or in collusion with other persons.

b. Acts Of Employees Learned Of By You Prior To The Policy Period

Loss caused by an "employee" if the "employee" had also committed "theft" or any other dishonest act prior to the effective date of this insurance and you or any of your partners, "members", "managers", officers, directors or trustees, not in collusion with the "employee", learned of that "theft" or dishonest act prior to the Policy Period shown in the Declarations.

c. Acts Of Employees, Managers, Directors, Trustees Or Representatives

Loss resulting from "theft" or any other dishonest act committed by any of your "employees", "managers", directors, trustees or authorized representatives:

(1) Whether acting alone or in collusion with other persons; or

(2) While performing services for you or otherwise;

except when covered under Insuring Agreement **A.1.**

d. Confidential Information

Loss resulting from:

(1) The unauthorized disclosure of your confidential information including, but not limited to, patents, trade secrets, processing methods or customer lists; or

(2) The unauthorized use or disclosure of confidential information of another person or entity which is held by you including, but not limited to, financial information, personal information, credit card information or similar non-public information.

e. Governmental Action

Loss resulting from seizure or destruction of property by order of governmental authority.

f. Indirect Loss

Loss that is an indirect result of an "occurrence" covered by this insurance including, but not limited to, loss resulting from:

(1) Your inability to realize income that you would have realized had there been no loss of or damage to "money", "securities" or "other property".

(2) Payment of damages of any type for which you are legally liable. But, we will pay compensatory damages arising directly from a loss covered under this insurance.

(3) Payment of costs, fees or other expenses you incur in establishing either the existence or the amount of loss under this insurance.

g. Legal Fees, Costs And Expenses

Fees, costs and expenses incurred by you which are related to any legal action, except when covered under Insuring Agreement **A.2.**

h. Nuclear Hazard

Loss or damage resulting from nuclear reaction or radiation, or radioactive contamination, however caused.

i. Pollution

Loss or damage caused by or resulting from pollution. Pollution means the discharge, dispersal, seepage, migration, release or escape of any solid, liquid, gaseous or thermal irritant or contaminant, including smoke, vapor, soot, fumes, acids, alkalis, chemicals and waste. Waste includes materials to be recycled, reconditioned or reclaimed.

j. War And Military Action

Loss or damage resulting from:

(1) War, including undeclared or civil war;

(2) Warlike action by a military force, including action in hindering or defending against an actual or expected attack, by any government, sovereign or other authority using military personnel or other agents; or

(3) Insurrection, rebellion, revolution, usurped power, or action taken by governmental authority in hindering or defending against any of these.

2. Insuring Agreement **A.1.** does not cover:

a. Inventory Shortages

Loss, or that part of any loss, the proof of which as to its existence or amount is dependent upon:

(1) An inventory computation; or

(2) A profit and loss computation.

However, where you establish wholly apart from such computations that you have sustained a loss, then you may offer your inventory records and actual physical count of inventory in support of the amount of loss claimed.

b. Trading

Loss resulting from trading, whether in your name or in a genuine or fictitious account.

c. Warehouse Receipts

Loss resulting from the fraudulent or dishonest signing, issuing, canceling or failing to cancel, a warehouse receipt or any papers connected with it.

3. Insuring Agreements **A.3.**, **A.4.** and **A.5.** do not cover:

a. Accounting Or Arithmetical Errors Or Omissions

Loss resulting from accounting or arithmetical errors or omissions.

b. Exchanges Or Purchases

Loss resulting from the giving or surrendering of property in any exchange or purchase.

c. Fire

Loss or damage resulting from fire, however caused, except:

(1) Loss of or damage to "money" and "securities"; and

(2) Loss from damage to a safe or vault.

d. Money Operated Devices

Loss of property contained in any money operated device unless the amount of "money" deposited in it is recorded by a continuous recording instrument in the device.

e. Motor Vehicles Or Equipment And Accessories

Loss of or damage to motor vehicles, trailers or semi-trailers or equipment and accessories attached to them.

f. Transfer Or Surrender Of Property

(1) Loss of or damage to property after it has been transferred or surrendered to a person or place outside the "premises" or "banking premises":

(a) On the basis of unauthorized instructions;

(b) As a result of a threat to do bodily harm to any person;

(c) As a result of a threat to do damage to any property;

(d) As a result of a threat to introduce a denial of service attack into your computer system;

(e) As a result of a threat to introduce a virus or other malicious instruction into your computer system which is designed to damage, destroy or corrupt data or computer programs stored within your computer system;

(f) As a result of a threat to contaminate, pollute or render substandard your products or goods; or

(g) As a result of a threat to disseminate, divulge or utilize:

(i) Your confidential information; or

(ii) Weaknesses in the source code within your computer system.

(2) But, this Exclusion does not apply under Insuring Agreement **A.5.** to loss of "money", "securities" or "other property" while outside the "premises" in the care and custody of a "messenger" if you:

(a) Had no knowledge of any threat at the time the conveyance began; or

(b) Had knowledge of a threat at the time the conveyance began, but the loss was not related to the threat.

g. Vandalism

Loss from damage to the "premises" or its exterior, or to any safe, vault, cash register, cash box, cash drawer or "other property" by vandalism or malicious mischief.

h. Voluntary Parting Of Title To Or Possession Of Property

Loss resulting from your, or anyone acting on your express or implied authority, being induced by any dishonest act to voluntarily part with title to or possession of any property.

4. Insuring Agreement **A.6.** does not cover:

a. Credit Card Transactions

Loss resulting from the use or purported use of credit, debit, charge, access, convenience, identification, stored-value or other cards or the information contained on such cards.

b. Funds Transfer Fraud

Loss resulting from a "fraudulent instruction" directing a financial institution to transfer, pay or deliver "funds" from your "transfer account".

c. Inventory Shortages

Loss, or that part of any loss, the proof of which as to its existence or amount is dependent upon:

(1) An inventory computation; or

(2) A profit and loss computation.

5. Insuring Agreement **A.7.** does not cover:

COMPUTER FRAUD

Loss resulting from the use of any computer to fraudulently cause a transfer of "money", "securities" or "other property".

E. Conditions

The following Conditions apply in addition to the Common Policy Conditions:

1. Conditions Applicable To All Insuring Agreements

a. Additional Premises Or Employees

If, while this insurance is in force, you establish any additional "premises" or hire additional "employees", other than through consolidation or merger with, or purchase or acquisition of assets or liabilities of, another entity, such "premises" and "employees" shall automatically be covered under this insurance. Notice to us of an increase in the number of "premises" or "employees" need not be given and no additional premium need be paid for the remainder of the Policy Period shown in the Declarations.

b. Concealment, Misrepresentation Or Fraud

This insurance is void in any case of fraud by you as it relates to this insurance at any time. It is also void if you or any other Insured, at any time, intentionally conceal or misrepresent a material fact concerning:

(1) This insurance;

(2) The property covered under this insurance;

(3) Your interest in the property covered under this insurance; or

(4) A claim under this insurance.

c. Consolidation – Merger Or Acquisition

If you consolidate or merge with, or purchase or acquire the assets or liabilities of, another entity:

(1) You must give us written notice as soon as possible and obtain our written consent to extend the coverage provided by this insurance to such consolidated or merged entity or such purchased or acquired assets or liabilities. We may condition our consent by requiring payment of an additional premium; but

(2) For the first 90 days after the effective date of such consolidation, merger or purchase or acquisition of assets or liabilities, the coverage provided by this insurance shall apply to such consolidated or merged entity or such purchased or acquired assets or liabilities, provided that all "occurrences" causing or contributing to a loss involving such consolidation, merger or purchase or acquisition of assets or liabilities, must take place after the effective date of such consolidation, merger or purchase or acquisition of assets or liabilities.

d. Cooperation

You must cooperate with us in all matters pertaining to this insurance as stated in its terms and conditions.

e. Duties In The Event Of Loss

After you "discover" a loss or a situation that may result in loss of or damage to "money", "securities" or "other property" you must:

(1) Notify us as soon as possible. If you have reason to believe that any loss (except for loss covered under Insuring Agreement **A.1.** or **A.2.**) involves a violation of law, you must also notify the local law enforcement authorities.

(2) Submit to examination under oath at our request and give us a signed statement of your answers.

(3) Produce for our examination all pertinent records.

(4) Give us a detailed, sworn proof of loss within 120 days.

(5) Cooperate with us in the investigation and settlement of any claim.

f. Employee Benefit Plans

(1) The "employee benefit plans" shown in the Declarations (hereinafter referred to as Plan) are included as Insureds under Insuring Agreement **A.1.**

(2) If any Plan is insured jointly with any other entity under this insurance, you or the Plan Administrator must select a Limit of Insurance for Insuring Agreement **A.1.** that is sufficient to provide a Limit of Insurance for each Plan that is at least equal to that required if each Plan were separately insured.

(3) With respect to loss sustained or "discovered" by any such Plan, Insuring Agreement **A.1.** is replaced by the following:

We will pay for loss of or damage to "funds" and "other property" resulting directly from fraudulent or dishonest acts committed by an "employee", whether identified or not, acting alone or in collusion with other persons.

(4) If the first Named Insured is an entity other than a Plan, any payment we make for loss sustained by any Plan will be made to the Plan sustaining the loss.

(5) If two or more Plans are insured under this insurance, any payment we make for loss:

  (a) Sustained by two or more Plans; or

  (b) Of commingled "funds" or "other property" of two or more Plans;

  resulting directly from an "occurrence" will be made to each Plan sustaining loss in the proportion that the Limit of Insurance required for each Plan bears to the total Limit of Insurance of all Plans sustaining loss.

(6) The Deductible Amount applicable to Insuring Agreement **A.1.** does not apply to loss sustained by any Plan.

g. Extended Period To Discover Loss

We will pay for loss that you sustained prior to the effective date of cancellation of this insurance, which is "discovered" by you:

(1) No later than 1 year from the date of that cancellation. However, this extended period to "discover" loss terminates immediately upon the effective date of any other insurance obtained by you, whether from us or another insurer, replacing in whole or in part the coverage afforded under this insurance, whether or not such other insurance provides coverage for loss sustained prior to its effective date.

(2) No later than 1 year from the date of that cancellation with regard to any "employee benefit plans".

h. Joint Insured

(1) If more than one Insured is named in the Declarations, the first Named Insured will act for itself and for every other Insured for all purposes of this insurance. If the first Named Insured ceases to be covered, then the next Named Insured will become the first Named Insured.

(2) If any Insured, or partner, "member" or officer of that Insured has knowledge of any information relevant to this insurance, that knowledge is considered knowledge of every Insured.

(3) An "employee" of any Insured is considered to be an "employee" of every Insured.

(4) If this insurance or any of its coverages is cancelled as to any Insured, loss sustained by that Insured is covered only if it is "discovered" by you:

  (a) No later than 1 year from the date of that cancellation. However, this extended period to "discover" loss terminates immediately upon the effective date of any other insurance obtained by that Insured, whether from us or another insurer, replacing in whole or in part the coverage afforded under this insurance, whether or not such other insurance provides coverage for loss sustained prior to its effective date.

  (b) No later than 1 year from the date of that cancellation with regard to any "employee benefit plans".

(5) We will not pay more for loss sustained by more than one Insured than the amount we would pay if all such loss had been sustained by one Insured.

(6) Payment by us to the first Named Insured for loss sustained by any Insured, other than an "employee benefit plan", shall fully release us on account of such loss.

i. Legal Action Against Us

You may not bring any legal action against us involving loss:

(1) Unless you have complied with all the terms of this insurance;

(2) Until 90 days after you have filed proof of loss with us; and

(3) Unless brought within 2 years from the date you "discovered" the loss.

If any limitation in this Condition is prohibited by law, such limitation is amended so as to equal the minimum period of limitation provided by such law.

j. Liberalization

If we adopt any revision that would broaden the coverage under this insurance without additional premium within 45 days prior to or during the Policy Period shown in the Declarations, the broadened coverage will immediately apply to this insurance.

k. Loss Sustained During Prior Insurance Issued By Us Or Any Affiliate

(1) Loss Sustained Partly During This Insurance And Partly During Prior Insurance

If you "discover" loss during the Policy Period shown in the Declarations, resulting directly from an "occurrence" taking place:

(a) Partly during the Policy Period shown in the Declarations; and

(b) Partly during the Policy Period(s) of any prior cancelled insurance that we or any affiliate issued to you or any predecessor in interest;

and this insurance became effective at the time of cancellation of the prior insurance, we will first settle the amount of loss that you sustained during this Policy Period. We will then settle the remaining amount of loss that you sustained during the Policy Period(s) of the prior insurance.

(2) Loss Sustained Entirely During Prior Insurance

If you "discover" loss during the Policy Period shown in the Declarations, resulting directly from an "occurrence" taking place entirely during the Policy Period(s) of any prior cancelled insurance that we or any affiliate issued to you or any predecessor in interest, we will pay for the loss, provided:

(a) This insurance became effective at the time of cancellation of the prior insurance; and

(b) The loss would have been covered under this insurance had it been in effect at the time of the "occurrence".

We will first settle the amount of loss that you sustained during the most recent prior insurance. We will then settle any remaining amount of loss that you sustained during the Policy Period(s) of any other prior insurance.

(3) In settling loss subject to this Condition:

(a) The most we will pay for the entire loss is the highest single Limit of Insurance applicable during the period of loss, whether such limit was written under this insurance or was written under the prior insurance issued by us.

(b) We will apply the applicable Deductible Amount shown in the Declarations to the amount of loss sustained under this insurance. If no loss was sustained under this insurance, we will apply the Deductible Amount shown in the Declarations to the amount of loss sustained under the most recent prior insurance.

If the Deductible Amount is larger than the amount of loss sustained under this insurance, or the most recent prior insurance, we will apply the remaining Deductible Amount to the remaining amount of loss sustained during the prior insurance.

We will not apply any other Deductible Amount that may have been applicable to the loss.

(4) The following examples demonstrate how we will settle losses subject to this Condition **E.1.k.**:

EXAMPLE NO. 1:

The insured sustained a covered loss of $10,000 resulting directly from an "occurrence" taking place during the terms of Policy **A** and Policy **B**.

POLICY A

The current policy. Written at a Limit of Insurance of $50,000 and a Deductible Amount of $5,000.

POLICY B

Issued prior to Policy **A**. Written at a Limit of Insurance of $50,000 and a Deductible Amount of $5,000.

The amount of loss sustained under Policy **A** is $2,500 and under Policy **B** is $7,500.

The highest single Limit of Insurance applicable to this entire loss is $50,000 written under Policy **A**. The Policy **A** Deductible Amount of $5,000 applies. The loss is settled as follows:

1. The amount of loss sustained under Policy **A** ($2,500) is settled first. The amount we will pay is nil ($0.00) because the amount of loss is less than the Deductible Amount (i.e., $2,500 loss - $5,000 deductible = $0.00).

2. The remaining amount of loss sustained under Policy **B** ($7,500) is settled next. The amount recoverable is $5,000 after the remaining Deductible Amount from Policy **A** of $2,500 is applied to the loss (i.e., $7,500 loss - $2,500 deductible = $5,000).

The most we will pay for this loss is $5,000.

EXAMPLE NO. 2:

The insured sustained a covered loss of $250,000 resulting directly from an "occurrence" taking place during the terms of Policy **A** and Policy **B**.

POLICY A

The current policy. Written at a Limit of Insurance of $125,000 and a Deductible Amount of $10,000.

POLICY B

Issued prior to Policy **A**. Written at a Limit of Insurance of $150,000 and a Deductible Amount of $25,000.

The amount of loss sustained under Policy **A** is $175,000 and under Policy **B** is $75,000.

The highest single Limit of Insurance applicable to this entire loss is $150,000 written under Policy **B**. The Policy **A** Deductible Amount of $10,000 applies. The loss is settled as follows:

1. The amount of loss sustained under Policy **A** ($175,000) is settled first. The amount we will pay is the Policy **A** Limit of $125,000 because $175,000 loss - $10,000 deductible = $165,000 which is greater than the $125,000 policy limit.

2. The remaining amount of loss sustained under Policy **B** ($75,000) is settled next. The amount we will pay is $25,000 (i.e., $150,000 Policy **B** limit - $125,000 paid under Policy **A** = $25,000).

The most we will pay for this loss is $150,000.

EXAMPLE NO. 3:

The insured sustained a covered loss of $2,000,000 resulting directly from an "occurrence" taking place during the terms of Policies **A**, **B**, **C** and **D**.

POLICY A

The current policy. Written at a Limit of Insurance of $1,000,000 and a Deductible Amount of $100,000.

POLICY B

Issued prior to Policy **A**. Written at a Limit of Insurance of $750,000 and a Deductible Amount of $75,000.

POLICY C

Issued prior to Policy **B**. Written at a Limit of Insurance of $500,000 and a Deductible Amount of $50,000.

POLICY D

Issued prior to Policy **C**. Written at a Limit of Insurance of $500,000 and a Deductible Amount of $50,000.

The amount of loss sustained under Policy **A** is $350,000, under Policy **B** is $250,000, under Policy **C** is $600,000 and under Policy **D** is $800,000.

The highest single Limit of Insurance applicable to this entire loss is $1,000,000 written under Policy **A**. The Policy **A** Deductible Amount of $100,000 applies. The loss is settled as follows:

1. The amount of loss sustained under Policy **A** ($350,000) is settled first. The amount we will pay is $250,000 (i.e., $350,000 loss - $100,000 deductible = $250,000).

2. The amount of loss sustained under Policy **B** ($250,000) is settled next. The amount we will pay is $250,000 (no deductible is applied).

3. The amount of loss sustained under Policy **C** ($600,000) is settled next. The amount we will pay is $500,000, the policy limit (no deductible is applied).

4. We will not make any further payment under Policy **D** as the maximum amount payable under the highest single Limit of Insurance applying to the loss of $1,000,000 under Policy **A** has been satisfied.

The most we will pay for this loss is $1,000,000.

l. Loss Sustained During Prior Insurance Not Issued By Us Or Any Affiliate

(1) If you "discover" loss during the Policy Period shown in the Declarations, resulting directly from an "occurrence" taking place during the Policy Period of any prior cancelled insurance that was issued to you or a predecessor in interest by another company, and the period of time to discover loss under that insurance had expired, we will pay for the loss under this insurance, provided:

(a) This insurance became effective at the time of cancellation of the prior insurance; and

(b) The loss would have been covered under this insurance had it been in effect at the time of the "occurrence".

(2) In settling loss subject to this Condition:

(a) The most we will pay for the entire loss is the lesser of the Limits of Insurance applicable during the period of loss, whether such limit was written under this insurance or was written under the prior cancelled insurance.

(b) We will apply the applicable Deductible Amount shown in the Declarations to the amount of loss sustained under the prior cancelled insurance.

(3) The insurance provided under this Condition is subject to the following:

(a) If loss covered under this Condition is also partially covered under Condition **E.1.k.**, the amount recoverable under this Condition is part of, not in addition to, the amount recoverable under Condition **E.1.k.**

(b) For loss covered under this Condition that is not subject to Paragraph **(3)(a),** the amount recoverable under this Condition is part of, not in addition to, the Limit of Insurance applicable to the loss covered under this insurance and is limited to the lesser of the amount recoverable under:

(i) This insurance as of its effective date; or

(ii) The prior cancelled insurance had it remained in effect.

m. Other Insurance

If other valid and collectible insurance is available to you for loss covered under this insurance, our obligations are limited as follows:

(1) Primary Insurance

When this insurance is written as primary insurance, and:

(a) You have other insurance subject to the same terms and conditions as this insurance, we will pay our share of the covered loss. Our share is the proportion that the applicable Limit of Insurance shown in the Declarations bears to the total limit of all insurance covering the same loss.

(b) You have other insurance covering the same loss other than that described in Paragraph **(1)(a),** we will only pay for the amount of loss that exceeds:

(i) The Limit of Insurance and Deductible Amount of that other insurance, whether you can collect on it or not; or

(ii) The Deductible Amount shown in the Declarations;

whichever is greater. Our payment for loss is subject to the terms and conditions of this insurance.

(2) Excess Insurance

(a) When this insurance is written excess over other insurance, we will only pay for the amount of loss that exceeds the Limit of Insurance and Deductible Amount of that other insurance, whether you can collect on it or not. Our payment for loss is subject to the terms and conditions of this insurance.

(b) However, if loss covered under this insurance is subject to a Deductible, we will reduce the Deductible Amount shown in the Declarations by the sum total of all such other insurance plus any Deductible Amount applicable to that other insurance.

n. Ownership Of Property; Interests Covered

The property covered under this insurance is limited to property:

(1) That you own or lease; or

(2) That you hold for others whether or not you are legally liable for the loss of such property.

However, this insurance is for your benefit only. It provides no rights or benefits to any other person or organization. Any claim for loss that is covered under this insurance must be presented by you.

o. Records

You must keep records of all property covered under this insurance so we can verify the amount of any loss.

p. Recoveries

(1) Any recoveries, whether effected before or after any payment under this insurance, whether made by us or you, shall be applied net of the expense of such recovery:

(a) First, to you in satisfaction of your covered loss in excess of the amount paid under this insurance;

(b) Second, to us in satisfaction of amounts paid in settlement of your claim;

(c) Third, to you in satisfaction of any Deductible Amount; and

(d) Fourth, to you in satisfaction of any loss not covered under this insurance.

(2) Recoveries do not include any recovery:

(a) From insurance, suretyship, reinsurance, security or indemnity taken for our benefit; or

(b) Of original "securities" after duplicates of them have been issued.

q. Territory

This insurance covers loss that you sustain resulting directly from an "occurrence" taking place within the United States of America (including its territories and possessions), Puerto Rico and Canada.

r. Transfer Of Your Rights Of Recovery Against Others To Us

You must transfer to us all your rights of recovery against any person or organization for any loss you sustained and for which we have paid or settled. You must also do everything necessary to secure those rights and do nothing after loss to impair them.

s. Valuation – Settlement

(1) The value of any loss for purposes of coverage under this policy shall be determined as follows:

(a) Loss of "money" but only up to and including its face value. We will, at your option, pay for loss of "money" issued by any country other than the United States of America:

(i) At face value in the "money" issued by that country; or

(ii) In the United States of America dollar equivalent determined by the rate of exchange published in *The Wall Street Journal* on the day the loss was "discovered".

(b) Loss of "securities" but only up to and including their value at the close of business on the day the loss was "discovered". We may, at our option:

(i) Pay the market value of such "securities" or replace them in kind, in which event you must assign to us all your rights, title and interest in and to those "securities"; or

(ii) Pay the cost of any Lost Securities Bond required in connection with issuing duplicates of the "securities". However, we will be liable only for the payment of so much of the cost of the bond as would be charged for a bond having a penalty not exceeding the lesser of the:

i. Market value of the "securities" at the close of business on the day the loss was "discovered"; or

ii. The Limit of Insurance applicable to the "securities".

(c) Loss of or damage to "other property" or loss from damage to the "premises" or its exterior for the replacement cost of the property without deduction for depreciation. However, we will not pay more than the least of the following:

(i) The cost to replace the lost or damaged property with property of comparable material and quality and used for the same purpose;

(ii) The amount you actually spend that is necessary to repair or replace the lost or damaged property; or

(iii) The Limit of Insurance applicable to the lost or damaged property.

With regard to Paragraphs **s.(1)(c)(i)** through **s.(1)(c)(iii),** we will not pay on a replacement cost basis for any loss or damage:

i. Until the lost or damaged property is actually repaired or replaced; and

ii. Unless the repairs or replacement are made as soon as reasonably possible after the loss or damage.

If the lost or damaged property is not repaired or replaced, we will pay on an actual cash value basis.

(2) We will, at your option, settle loss or damage to property other than "money":

(a) In the "money" of the country in which the loss or damage occurred; or

(b) In the United States of America dollar equivalent of the "money" of the country in which the loss or damage occurred determined by the rate of exchange published in *The Wall Street Journal* on the day the loss was "discovered".

(3) Any property that we pay for or replace becomes our property.

2. Conditions Applicable To Insuring Agreement A.1.

a. Termination As To Any Employee

This Insuring Agreement terminates as to any "employee":

(1) As soon as:

(a) You; or

(b) Any of your partners, "members", "managers", officers, directors, or trustees not in collusion with the "employee";

learn of "theft" or any other dishonest act committed by the "employee" whether before or after becoming employed by you.

(2) On the date specified in a notice mailed to the first Named Insured. That date will be at least 30 days after the date of mailing.

We will mail or deliver our notice to the first Named Insured's last mailing address known to us. If notice is mailed, proof of mailing will be sufficient proof of notice.

b. Territory

We will pay for loss caused by any "employee" while temporarily outside the territory specified in the Territory Condition **E.1.q.** for a period of not more than 90 consecutive days.

3. Conditions Applicable To Insuring Agreement A.2.

a. Deductible Amount

The Deductible Amount does not apply to legal expenses paid under Insuring Agreement **A.2.**

b. Electronic And Mechanical Signatures

We will treat signatures that are produced or reproduced electronically, mechanically or by other means the same as handwritten signatures.

c. Proof Of Loss

You must include with your proof of loss any instrument involved in that loss, or, if that is not possible, an affidavit setting forth the amount and cause of loss.

d. **Territory**

We will cover loss that you sustain resulting directly from an "occurrence" taking place anywhere in the world. Territory Condition **E.1.q.** does not apply to Insuring Agreement **A.2.**

4. **Conditions Applicable To Insuring Agreements A.4. And A.5.**

a. **Armored Motor Vehicle Companies**

Under Insuring Agreement **A.5.**, we will only pay for the amount of loss you cannot recover:

(1) Under your contract with the armored motor vehicle company; and

(2) From any insurance or indemnity carried by, or for the benefit of customers of, the armored motor vehicle company.

b. **Special Limit Of Insurance For Specified Property**

We will only pay up to $5,000 for any one "occurrence" of loss of or damage to:

(1) Precious metals, precious or semi-precious stones, pearls, furs, or completed or partially completed articles made of or containing such materials that constitute the principal value of such articles; or

(2) Manuscripts, drawings, or records of any kind, or the cost of reconstructing them or reproducing any information contained in them.

5. **Conditions Applicable To Insuring Agreement A.6.**

a. **Special Limit Of Insurance For Specified Property**

We will only pay up to $5,000 for any one "occurrence" of loss of or damage to manuscripts, drawings, or records of any kind, or the cost of reconstructing them or reproducing any information contained in them.

b. **Territory**

We will cover loss that you sustain resulting directly from an "occurrence" taking place anywhere in the world. Territory Condition **E.1.q.** does not apply to Insuring Agreement **A.6.**

F. **Definitions**

1. "Banking premises" means the interior of that portion of any building occupied by a banking institution or similar safe depository.

2. "Counterfeit money" means an imitation of "money" that is intended to deceive and to be taken as genuine.

3. "Custodian" means you, or any of your partners or "members", or any "employee" while having care and custody of property inside the "premises", excluding any person while acting as a "watchperson" or janitor.

4. "Discover" or "discovered" means the time when you first become aware of facts which would cause a reasonable person to assume that a loss of a type covered by this insurance has been or will be incurred, regardless of when the act or acts causing or contributing to such loss occurred, even though the exact amount or details of loss may not then be known.

"Discover" or "discovered" also means the time when you first receive notice of an actual or potential claim in which it is alleged that you are liable to a third party under circumstances which, if true, would constitute a loss under this insurance

5. "Employee":

a. "Employee" means:

(1) Any natural person:

(a) While in your service and for the first 30 days immediately after termination of service, unless such termination is due to "theft" or any dishonest act committed by the "employee";

(b) Who you compensate directly by salary, wages or commissions; and

(c) Who you have the right to direct and control while performing services for you;

(2) Any natural person who is furnished temporarily to you:

(a) To substitute for a permanent "employee" as defined in Paragraph **a.(1)**, who is on leave; or

(b) To meet seasonal or short-term work load conditions;

while that person is subject to your direction and control and performing services for you, excluding, however, any such person while having care and custody of property outside the "premises";

(3) Any natural person who is leased to you under a written agreement between you and a labor leasing firm, to perform duties related to the conduct of your business, but does not mean a temporary employee as defined in Paragraph **a.(2)**;

(4) Any natural person who is:

(a) A trustee, officer, employee, administrator or manager, except an administrator or manager who is an independent contractor, of any "employee benefit plan"; and

(b) A director or trustee of yours while that person is engaged in handling "funds" or "other property" of any "employee benefit plan";

(5) Any natural person who is a former "employee", partner, "member", "manager", director or trustee retained as a consultant while performing services for you;

(6) Any natural person who is a guest student or intern pursuing studies or duties, excluding, however, any such person while having care and custody of property outside the "premises";

(7) Any "employee" of an entity merged or consolidated with you prior to the effective date of this policy; or

(8) Any of your "managers", directors or trustees while:

(a) Performing acts within the scope of the usual duties of an "employee"; or

(b) Acting as a member of any committee duly elected or appointed by resolution of your board of directors or board of trustees to perform specific, as distinguished from general, directorial acts on your behalf.

b. "Employee" does not mean:

Any agent, broker, factor, commission merchant, consignee, independent contractor or representative of the same general character not specified in Paragraph **5.a.**

6. "Employee benefit plan" means any welfare or pension benefit plan shown in the Declarations that you sponsor and which is subject to the Employee Retirement Income Security Act of 1974 (ERISA) and any amendments thereto.

7. "Forgery" means the signing of the name of another person or organization with intent to deceive; it does not mean a signature which consists in whole or in part of one's own name signed with or without authority, in any capacity, for any purpose.

8. "Fraudulent instruction" means:

a. An electronic, telegraphic, cable, teletype, telefacsimile or telephone instruction which purports to have been transmitted by you, but which was in fact fraudulently transmitted by someone else without your knowledge or consent;

b. A written instruction (other than those described in Insuring Agreement **A.2.**) issued by you, which was forged or altered by someone other than you without your knowledge or consent, or which purports to have been issued by you, but was in fact fraudulently issued without your knowledge or consent; or

c. An electronic, telegraphic, cable, teletype, telefacsimile, telephone or written instruction initially received by you which purports to have been transmitted by an "employee" but which was in fact fraudulently transmitted by someone else without your or the "employee's" knowledge or consent.

9. "Funds" means "money" and "securities".

10. "Manager" means a person serving in a directorial capacity for a limited liability company.

11. "Member" means an owner of a limited liability company represented by its membership interest, who also may serve as a "manager".

12. "Messenger" means you, or a relative of yours, or any of your partners or "members", or any "employee" while having care and custody of property outside the "premises".

13. "Money" means:

a. Currency, coins and bank notes in current use and having a face value; and

b. Travelers checks, register checks and money orders held for sale to the public.

14. "Occurrence" means:

a. Under Insuring Agreement **A.1.:**

(1) An individual act;

(2) The combined total of all separate acts whether or not related; or

Commercial Crime

(3) A series of acts whether or not related;

committed by an "employee" acting alone or in collusion with other persons, during the Policy Period shown in the Declarations, except as provided under Condition **E.1.k.** or **E.1.l.**

b. Under Insuring Agreement **A.2.:**

(1) An individual act;

(2) The combined total of all separate acts whether or not related; or

(3) A series of acts whether or not related;

committed by a person acting alone or in collusion with other persons, involving one or more instruments, during the Policy Period shown in the Declarations, except as provided under Condition **E.1.k.** or **E.1.l.**

c. Under All Other Insuring Agreements:

(1) An individual act or event;

(2) The combined total of all separate acts or events whether or not related; or

(3) A series of acts or events whether or not related;

committed by a person acting alone or in collusion with other persons, or not committed by any person, during the Policy Period shown in the Declarations, except as provided under Condition **E.1.k.** or **E.1.l.**

15. "Other property" means any tangible property other than "money" and "securities" that has intrinsic value. "Other property" does not include computer programs, electronic data or any property specifically excluded under this insurance.

16. "Premises" means the interior of that portion of any building you occupy in conducting your business.

17. "Robbery" means the unlawful taking of property from the care and custody of a person by one who has:

a. Caused or threatened to cause that person bodily harm; or

b. Committed an obviously unlawful act witnessed by that person.

18. "Safe burglary" means the unlawful taking of:

a. Property from within a locked safe or vault by a person unlawfully entering the safe or vault as evidenced by marks of forcible entry upon its exterior; or

b. A safe or vault from inside the "premises".

19. "Securities" means negotiable and nonnegotiable instruments or contracts representing either "money" or property and includes:

a. Tokens, tickets, revenue and other stamps (whether represented by actual stamps or unused value in a meter) in current use; and

b. Evidences of debt issued in connection with credit or charge cards, which cards are not issued by you;

but does not include "money".

20. "Theft" means the unlawful taking of property to the deprivation of the Insured.

21. "Transfer account" means an account maintained by you at a financial institution from which you can initiate the transfer, payment or delivery of "funds":

a. By means of electronic, telegraphic, cable, teletype, telefacsimile or telephone instructions communicated directly through an electronic funds transfer system; or

b. By means of written instructions (other than those described in Insuring Agreement **A.2.**) establishing the conditions under which such transfers are to be initiated by such financial institution through an electronic funds transfer system.

22. "Watchperson" means any person you retain specifically to have care and custody of property inside the "premises" and who has no other duties.

Equipment Breakdown Insurance

Equipment breakdown insurance (traditionally known as boiler and machinery insurance) covers loss resulting from the accidental breakdown of almost any type of equipment that operates under pressure or that controls, transmits, transforms, or uses mechanical or electrical power. Examples of such equipment are steam boilers and other pressure vessels; electrical generating and transmitting equipment; pumps, compressors, turbines, and engines; air conditioning and refrigeration systems; production machinery used in manufacturing operations; and electrically powered office equipment such as computers, telephone systems, and copiers.

Although the types of equipment just listed are covered property under commercial property forms such as the Building and Personal Property Coverage Form (BPP), the BPP covers such equipment only against the perils covered by the causes of loss forms used with the BPP. The causes of loss forms exclude electrical breakdown, mechanical breakdown, and steam boiler explosion, all of which can damage the equipment and sometimes the other property around it.

Equipment breakdown coverage can fill this gap, covering physical damage to both the covered equipment and other property of the insured that results from the accidental breakdown of covered equipment. Equipment breakdown insurance can also cover loss of business income, extra expenses, and other losses resulting from such physical damage.

The Equipment Breakdown Coverage Form reprinted in this section can be used either in a monoline equipment breakdown policy or to add equipment breakdown coverage to a commercial package policy. An alternative approach used by some insurers is to build equipment breakdown coverage into their commercial property coverage forms by eliminating particular exclusions from those forms and adding provisions for equipment breakdown coverage.

EQUIPMENT BREAKDOWN PROTECTION COVERAGE FORM

Various provisions in this policy restrict coverage. Read the entire policy carefully to determine rights, duties and what is and is not covered.

Throughout this policy, the words "you" and "your" refer to the Named Insured shown in the Declarations. The words "we", "us" and "our" refer to the Company providing this insurance.

Other words and phrases that appear in quotation marks have special meaning. Refer to Section **F** – Definitions.

A. Coverage

1. Covered Cause Of Loss

Covered Cause of Loss is a "Breakdown" to "Covered Equipment".

2. Coverages Provided

Each of the following coverages is provided if either a limit or the word INCLUDED is shown for that coverage in the Declarations. If neither a limit nor the word INCLUDED is shown, then that coverage is not provided.

These coverages apply only to that portion of the loss or damage that is a direct result of a Covered Cause of Loss.

a. Property Damage

We will pay for direct damage to "Covered Property" located at the premises described in the Declarations.

b. Expediting Expenses

With respect to direct damage to "Covered Property", we will pay for the extra cost you necessarily incur to:

(1) Make temporary repairs; and

(2) Expedite the permanent repairs or replacement of the damaged property.

c. Business Income And Extra Expense Or Extra Expense Only

(1) We will pay:

(a) Your actual loss of "Business Income" during the "Period of Restoration"; and

(b) The "Extra Expense" you necessarily incur to operate your business during the "Period of Restoration".

However, if coverage for "Extra Expense" only is indicated in the Declarations, then coverage for "Business Income" is not provided.

We will consider the experience of your business before the "Breakdown" and the probable experience you would have had without the "Breakdown" in determining the amount of our payment.

(2) If you have coverage for "Business Income" and "Extra Expense" or "Extra Expense" only and:

(a) If a number of days is shown in the Declarations for Extended Period Of Restoration Coverage, it will replace the five consecutive days in the definition of "Period of Restoration".

(b) If you have coverage for Ordinance or Law, then the "Period of Restoration" is extended to include the additional period of time required for demolition, removal, repair, remodeling or reconstruction.

(c) If "Media" are damaged or "Data" are lost or corrupted, we will pay your actual loss of "Business Income" and/or "Extra Expense" during the time necessary to:

(i) Research, replace or restore the damaged "Media" or lost or corrupted "Data"; and

(ii) Reprogram instructions used in any covered "Computer Equipment".

There shall be no coverage for any "Media" or "Data" that we determine are not or cannot be replaced or restored.

Unless a higher limit is shown in the Declarations, we will pay the lesser of your actual loss of "Business Income" and/or "Extra Expense" up to 30 days after the "Period of Restoration", or $25,000.

          □

d. Spoilage Damage

(1) We will pay for the spoilage damage to raw materials, property in process or finished products, provided all of the following conditions are met:

(a) The raw materials, property in process or finished products must be in storage or in the course of being manufactured;

(b) You must own or be legally liable under written contract for the raw materials, property in process or finished products; and

(c) The spoilage damage must be due to the lack or excess of power, light, heat, steam or refrigeration.

(2) We will also pay any necessary expenses you incur to reduce the amount of loss under this coverage. We will pay such expenses to the extent that they do not exceed the amount of loss that otherwise would have been payable under this coverage form.

e. Utility Interruption

If you have coverage for "Business Income" and "Extra Expense", "Extra Expense" only or Spoilage Damage, that coverage is extended to include loss resulting from the interruption of utility services, provided all of the following conditions are met:

(1) The interruption is the direct result of a "Breakdown" to "Covered Equipment" owned, operated or controlled by the local private or public utility or distributor that directly generates, transmits, distributes or provides utility services which you receive;

(2) The "Covered Equipment" is used to supply electric power, communication services, air conditioning, heating, gas, sewer, water or steam to your premises; and

(3) The interruption of utility service to your premises lasts at least the consecutive period of time shown in the Declarations. Once this waiting period is met, coverage will commence at the initial time of the interruption and will be subject to all applicable deductibles.

f. Newly Acquired Premises

We will automatically provide coverage at newly acquired premises you have purchased or leased. This coverage begins at the time you acquire the property and continues for a period not exceeding the number of days indicated in the Declarations for Newly Acquired Premises, under the following conditions:

(1) You must inform us, in writing, of the newly acquired premises as soon as practicable;

(2) You agree to pay an additional premium as determined by us;

(3) The coverage for these premises will be subject to the same terms, conditions, exclusions and limitations as other insured premises; and

(4) If the coverages and deductibles vary for existing premises, then the coverages for the newly acquired premises will be the broadest coverage and highest limits and deductible applicable to the existing premises.

g. Ordinance Or Law Coverage

The following applies despite the Ordinance Or Law Exclusion and provided these increases in loss are necessitated by the enforcement of any laws or ordinances that are in force at the time of the "Breakdown", which regulate the demolition, construction, repair or use of the building or structure. With respect to the building or structure that was damaged as a result of a "Breakdown":

(1) We will pay for:

(a) The loss in value of the undamaged portion of the building or structure as a consequence of enforcement of an ordinance or law that requires the demolition of undamaged parts of the same building or structure;

(b) Your actual cost to demolish and clear the site of the undamaged parts of the same building or structure as a consequence of enforcement of an ordinance or law that requires the demolition of such undamaged property; and

© Insurance Services Office, Inc., 2010   EB 00 20 09 11

(c) The increased cost actually and necessarily expended to:

(i) Repair or reconstruct the damaged or destroyed portions of the building or structure; and

(ii) Reconstruct or remodel the undamaged portion of that building or structure with buildings or structures of like materials, height, floor area and style for like occupancy, whether or not demolition is required on:

i. The same premises or on another premises if you so elect. However, if you rebuild at another premises, the most we will pay is the increased cost of construction that we would have paid to rebuild at the same premises; or

ii. Another premises if the relocation is required by the ordinance or law. The most we will pay is the increased cost of construction at the new premises.

(2) We will not pay for any:

(a) Demolition or site clearing until the undamaged portions of the buildings or structures are actually demolished;

(b) Increase in loss until the damaged or destroyed buildings or structures are actually rebuilt or replaced and approved by the regulating government agency;

(c) Loss due to any ordinance or law that:

(i) You were required to comply with before the loss, even if the building was undamaged; and

(ii) You failed to comply with;

(d) Increase in loss, excess of the amount required to meet the minimum requirement of any ordinance or law enforcement at the time of the "Breakdown";

(e) Increase in loss resulting from a substance declared to be hazardous to health or environment by any government agency;

(f) Loss or expense sustained due to the enforcement of any ordinance or law which requires the demolition, repair, replacement, reconstruction, remodeling or remediation of property due to the presence, growth, proliferation, spread or any activity of "Fungus", wet or dry rot; or

(g) Costs associated with the enforcement of any ordinance or law which requires any insured or others to test for, monitor, clean up, remove, contain, treat, detoxify or neutralize, or in any way respond to or assess the effects of "Fungus", wet or dry rot.

(3) If:

(a) The building or structure is damaged by a "Breakdown" that is covered under this policy;

(b) There is other physical damage that is not covered under this policy; and

(c) The building damage in its entirety results in enforcement of ordinance or law;

then we will not pay the full amount of the loss under this coverage. Instead, we will pay only that proportion of such loss, meaning the proportion that the covered "Breakdown" loss bears to the total physical damage.

But if the building or structure sustains direct physical damage that is not covered under this policy and such damage is the subject of the ordinance or law, then there is no Ordinance Or Law Coverage under this Coverage Part even if the building has also sustained damage by a covered "Breakdown".

h. Errors And Omissions

We will pay for any loss or damage, which is not otherwise payable under this Coverage Part, solely because of the items listed below:

(1) Any error or unintentional omission in the description or location of property as insured under this Coverage Part or in any subsequent amendments;

(2) Any failure through error to include any premises owned or occupied by you at the inception date of this Coverage Part; or

(3) Any error or unintentional omission by you that results in cancellation of any premises insured under this policy.

No coverage is provided as a result of any error or unintentional omission by you in the reporting of values or the coverage you requested.

It is a condition of this coverage that such errors or unintentional omissions shall be reported and corrected when discovered. The policy premium will be adjusted accordingly to reflect the date the premises should have been added had no error or omission occurred.

i. Brands And Labels

(1) If branded or labeled merchandise that is "Covered Property" is damaged by a "Breakdown", we may take all or any part of the property at an agreed or appraised value. If so, you may:

(a) Stamp the word SALVAGE on the merchandise or its containers if the stamp will not physically damage the merchandise; or

(b) Remove the brands or labels if doing so will not physically damage the merchandise. You must relabel the merchandise or its containers to comply with any law.

(2) We will pay reasonable costs you incur to perform the activity described in Paragraphs **(1)(a)** and **(1)(b),** but the total we pay for these costs and the value of the damaged property will not exceed the applicable Limit of Insurance on such property.

j. Contingent Business Income And Extra Expense Or Extra Expense Only Coverage

(1) Subject to the same terms and conditions, the "Business Income" and "Extra Expense" or "Extra Expense" only coverage provided by this Coverage Part is extended to cover your loss, if any, resulting from a "Breakdown" to "Covered Equipment" at a premises shown in the Declarations, that is not owned or operated by you which:

(a) Wholly or partially prevents the delivery of services or materials shown in the Declarations to you or from you to others for your account; or

(b) Results in the loss of sales at your premises shown in the Declarations.

(2) You shall use your influence to induce the contributing or recipient premises to make use of any other machinery, equipment, supplies or premises available in order to resume operations and delivery of services or materials to you, or the acceptance of products or services from you. You shall cooperate with the contributing or recipient premises to this effect in every way, but not financially unless authorized by us.

B. Exclusions

We will not pay for loss or damage caused directly or indirectly by any of the following. Such loss or damage is excluded, regardless of any other cause or event that contributes concurrently or in any sequence to the loss.

The exclusions apply whether or not the loss event results in widespread damage or affects a substantial area.

1. Ordinance Or Law

Increase in loss from the enforcement of any ordinance, law, rule, regulation or ruling which restricts or regulates the repair, replacement, alteration, use, operation, construction, installation, cleanup or disposal of "Covered Property".

However, the words use and operation shall be eliminated as respects a covered "Breakdown" to electrical supply and emergency generating equipment located on the premises of a hospital.

2. Earth Movement

Earth movement, including but not limited to earthquake, landslide, land subsidence, mine subsidence or volcanic action.

3. Water

a. Flood, surface water, waves (including tidal wave and tsunami), tides, tidal water, overflow of any body of water, or spray from any of these, all whether or not driven by wind (including storm surge);

b. Mudslide or mudflow;

c. Water that backs up or overflows or is otherwise discharged from a sewer, drain, sump, sump pump or related equipment;

d. Water damage caused by the discharge or leakage of a sprinkler system or domestic water piping;

e. Water under the ground surface pressing on, or flowing or seeping through:

(1) Foundations, walls, floors or paved surfaces;

(2) Basements, whether paved or not;

(3) Doors, windows or other openings; or

f. Waterborne material carried or otherwise moved by any of the water referred to in Paragraph **a.**, **c.** or **e.**, or material carried or otherwise moved by mudslide or mudflow.

This exclusion applies, regardless of whether any of the above, in Paragraphs **a.** through **f.**, is caused by an act of nature or is otherwise caused. An example of a situation to which this exclusion applies is the situation where a dam, levee, seawall or other boundary or containment system fails in whole or in part, for any reason, to contain the water.

4. Nuclear Hazard

Nuclear reaction or radiation, or radioactive contamination, however caused.

5. War Or Military Action

a. War, including undeclared or civil war;

b. Warlike action by a military force, including action in hindering or defending against an actual or expected attack, by any government, sovereign or other authority using military personnel or other agents; or

c. Insurrection, rebellion, revolution, usurped power or action taken by governmental authority in hindering or defending against any of these.

6. An explosion. However, we will pay for loss or damage caused by an explosion of "Covered Equipment" of a kind specified in **a.** through **g.** below, if not otherwise excluded in this Section **B.**:

a. Steam boiler;

b. Electric steam generator;

c. Steam piping;

d. Steam turbine;

e. Steam engine;

f. Gas turbine; or

g. Moving or rotating machinery when such explosion is caused by centrifugal force or mechanical breakdown.

7. Fire or combustion explosion including those that:

a. Result in a "Breakdown";

b. Occur at the same time as a "Breakdown"; or

c. Ensue from a "Breakdown".

8. "Fungus", Wet Rot And Dry Rot

Presence, growth, proliferation, spread or activity of "Fungus", wet or dry rot. However, if a "Breakdown" occurs, we will pay the resulting loss or damage.

This exclusion does not apply to the extent that coverage for "Fungus", wet rot or dry rot is provided elsewhere in this coverage form and then only for that portion of any loss or damage resulting from the presence, growth, proliferation, spread or activity of "Fungus", wet or dry rot as a result of a "Breakdown".

9. Any virus, bacterium or other microorganism that induces or is capable of inducing physical distress, illness or disease. However:

a. If a "Breakdown" occurs, we will pay the resulting loss or damage;

b. This exclusion does not apply to loss or damage caused by or resulting from "Fungus", wet rot or dry rot. Such loss or damage is addressed in Exclusion **B.8.**;

c. Regardless of the application of this exclusion to any particular loss, the provisions of this Exclusion **9.** do not serve to create coverage for any loss that would otherwise be excluded under this coverage form.

10. Explosion within the furnace of a chemical recovery type boiler or within the passage from the furnace to the atmosphere.

11. Damage to "Covered Equipment" undergoing a pressure or electrical test.

12. Water or other means used to extinguish a fire, even when the attempt is unsuccessful.

13. Depletion, deterioration, corrosion, erosion or wear and tear. However, if a "Breakdown" occurs, we will pay the resulting loss or damage.

14. A "Breakdown" that is caused by any of the following causes of loss if coverage for that cause of loss is provided by another policy of insurance you have, whether collectible or not:

a. Aircraft or vehicles;

b. Freezing caused by cold weather;

c. Lightning;

d. Sinkhole collapse;

e. Smoke;

f. Riot, civil commotion or vandalism; or

g. Weight of snow, ice or sleet.

15. A "Breakdown" that is caused by windstorm or hail.

16. A delay in, or an interruption of, any business, manufacturing or processing activity except as provided by the "Business Income" and "Extra Expense", "Extra Expense" only and Utility Interruption coverages.

17. With respect to "Business Income" and "Extra Expense", "Extra Expense" only and Utility Interruption coverages, the following additional exclusions shall apply:

a. The business that would not or could not have been carried on if the "Breakdown" had not occurred;

b. Your failure to use due diligence and dispatch and all reasonable means to operate your business as nearly normal as practicable at the premises shown in the Declarations; or

c. The suspension, lapse or cancellation of a contract following a "Breakdown" extending beyond the time business could have resumed if the contract had not lapsed, been suspended or canceled.

18. Any indirect loss following a "Breakdown" to "Covered Equipment" that results from the lack or excess of power, light, heat, steam or refrigeration except as provided by the "Business Income" and "Extra Expense", "Extra Expense" only, Spoilage Damage and Utility Interruption coverages.

19. With respect to Utility Interruption Coverage, any loss resulting from the following additional causes of loss whether or not coverage for that cause of loss is provided by another policy you have:

a. Acts of sabotage;

b. Collapse;

c. Deliberate act(s) of load shedding by the supplying utility;

d. Freezing caused by cold weather;

e. Impact of aircraft, missile or vehicle;

f. Impact of objects falling from an aircraft or missile;

g. Lightning;

h. Riot, civil commotion or vandalism;

i. Sinkhole collapse;

j. Smoke; or

k. Weight of snow, ice or sleet.

20. Any indirect result of a "Breakdown" to "Covered Equipment" except as provided by the "Business Income" and "Extra Expense", "Extra Expense" only, Spoilage Damage and Utility Interruption coverages.

21. Neglect by you to use all reasonable means to save and preserve "Covered Property" from further damage at and after the time of the loss.

C. Limits Of Insurance

1. The most we will pay for any and all coverages for loss or damage from any "One Breakdown" is the applicable Limit Of Insurance shown in the Declarations.

2. Any payment made will not be increased if more than one insured is shown in the Declarations.

3. For each coverage in Paragraph **A.2.**, if:

a. INCLUDED is shown in the Declarations, the limit for such coverage is part of, not in addition to, the Limit per Breakdown.

b. A limit is shown in the Declarations, we will not pay more than the Limit Of Insurance for each such coverage.

4. For any "Covered Equipment" that is:

a. Used solely to supply utility services to your premises;

b. Owned by a public or private utility;

c. Not in your care, custody or control and for which you are legally liable; and

d. Covered under this coverage form;

the Limit of Insurance for Property Damage stated in the Declarations is replaced by the sum of one dollar.

If you are a public or private utility, **4.b.** is replaced by the following:

b. Owned by a public or private utility other than you.

5. Unless a higher limit or INCLUDED is shown in the Declarations, the most we will pay for direct damage as a direct result of a "Breakdown" to "Covered Equipment" is $25,000 for each of the following. The limits are part of, not in addition to, the Limit of Insurance for Property Damage or Limit per Breakdown.

a. Ammonia Contamination

The spoilage to "Covered Property" contaminated by ammonia, including any salvage expense.

b. Consequential Loss

The reduction in the value of undamaged "Stock" parts of a product which becomes unmarketable. The reduction in value must be caused by a physical loss or damage to another part of the product.

c. Data And Media

Your cost to research, replace or restore damaged "Data" or "Media" including the cost to reprogram instructions used in any "Computer Equipment".

d. Hazardous Substance

Any additional expenses incurred by you for the cleanup, repair or replacement or disposal of "Covered Property" that is damaged, contaminated or polluted by a "Hazardous Substance".

As used here, additional expenses mean the additional cost incurred over and above the amount that we would have paid had no "Hazardous Substance" been involved with the loss.

Ammonia is not considered to be a "Hazardous Substance" as respects this limitation.

This coverage applies despite the operation of the Ordinance Or Law Exclusion.

e. Water Damage

The damage to "Covered Property" by water including any salvage expenses.

If "Fungus", wet or dry rot results from damage by water as limited in this paragraph, loss or damage attributable to "Fungus", wet or dry rot will be:

(1) Limited as described in Paragraphs **C.6.a.(1)** through **C.6.a.(5);** and

(2) Part of the Water Damage limit, not in addition to it.

6. Limited Coverage For "Fungus", Wet Rot And Dry Rot

a. Property Damage

We will pay for loss or damage by "Fungus", wet or dry rot only when the "Fungus", wet or dry rot is the direct result of a "Breakdown" to "Covered Equipment" that occurs during the policy period. As used in this Limited Coverage, the term loss or damage means:

(1) Direct physical loss or damage to "Covered Property" caused by "Fungus", wet or dry rot including the cost of removal of the "Fungus", wet or dry rot;

(a) The cost to tear out and replace any "Covered Property" as needed to gain access to the "Fungus", wet or dry rot; and

(b) The cost of testing performed after removal, repair, replacement or restoration of the damaged property is completed, provided there is a reason to believe that "Fungus", wet or dry rot is present.

(2) The coverage described under Paragraph **6.a.(1)** of this Limited Coverage is limited to $15,000. Regardless of the number of claims, this limit is the most we will pay for the total of all loss or damage arising out of all occurrences of "Breakdown" to "Covered Equipment" which take place within the 12-month period starting with the beginning of the present annual policy period. With respect to a particular occurrence of loss which results in "Fungus", wet or dry rot, we will not pay more than a total of $15,000 even if the "Fungus", wet or dry rot continues to be present or active or recurs in a later policy period.

(3) The coverage provided under this Limited Coverage does not increase the applicable Limit of Insurance on any "Covered Property". If a particular occurrence results in loss or damage by "Fungus", wet or dry rot, and other loss or damage, we will not pay more, for the total of all loss or damage, than the applicable Limit of Insurance on the affected "Covered Property".

If there is covered loss or damage to "Covered Property" not caused by "Fungus", wet or dry rot, loss payment will not be limited by the terms of this Limited Coverage, except to the extent that "Fungus", wet or dry rot causes an increase in the loss. Any such increase in the loss will be subject to the terms of this Limited Coverage.

(4) If a Revised Limit is shown in the Declarations, the amount of $15,000 in Paragraph **6.a.(2)** is replaced by the amount indicated in the Declarations.

(5) If the Declarations indicates that the Separate Premises Option applies, then the amount of coverage ($15,000, unless a higher amount is shown in the Declarations) is made applicable to separate premises as described in the Declarations. For each premises so described, the amount of coverage is an annual aggregate limit, subject to the terms set forth in Paragraph **6.a.(2).**

b. Business Income And Extra Expense Or Extra Expense Only

(1) If you have coverage for "Business Income" and "Extra Expense" or "Extra Expense" only, then Paragraph **b.(1)(a)** or **b.(1)(b)** applies, provided that the incurred loss or expense satisfies the terms and conditions applicable to the "Business Income" and "Extra Expense" or "Extra Expense" only coverage.

(a) If:

(i) The "Breakdown"; or

(ii) Any damage from water resulting from the "Breakdown";

which resulted in "Fungus", wet or dry rot, does not in itself generate a loss of "Business Income" or an "Extra Expense", but the loss of "Business Income" or "Extra Expense" is solely due to loss or damage to property caused by "Fungus", wet or dry rot, then our payment under "Business Income" and "Extra Expense" or "Extra Expense" only is limited to the amount of loss and/or expense sustained in a period of not more than 30 days. The days need not be consecutive.

(b) If a covered loss of "Business Income" or an "Extra Expense" was caused by loss or damage other than "Fungus", wet or dry rot, but remediation of "Fungus", wet or dry rot prolongs the "Period of Restoration", we will pay for loss and/or expense sustained during the delay (regardless of when such a delay occurs during the "Period of Restoration"), but such coverage is limited to 30 days. The days need not be consecutive.

(2) If a Revised Number of Days is shown in the Declarations, the number of days (30) in Paragraph **b.(1)(a)** or **b.(1)(b)** is replaced by the number of days indicated in the Declarations.

c. If you have coverage for Ordinance Or Law, then with respect to Property Damage, "Business Income" and "Extra Expense" or "Extra Expense" only, we will not pay under the Ordinance Or Law Coverage for:

(1) Loss or expense sustained due to the enforcement of any ordinance or law which requires the demolition, repair, replacement, reconstruction, remodeling or remediation of property due to the presence, growth, proliferation, spread or any activity of "Fungus", wet or dry rot; or

(2) The costs associated with the enforcement of any ordinance or law which requires any insured or others to test for, monitor, clean up, remove, contain, treat, detoxify or neutralize, or in any way respond to or assess the effects of "Fungus", wet or dry rot.

7. Increased Cost Of Loss And Related Expenses For "Green" Upgrades

a. Property Damage

Coverage is extended to include the additional loss or damage and related expenses incurred by you that are attributable to "Green" upgrades as a direct result of a "Breakdown" to "Covered Equipment" that occurs during the policy period. As provided in this "Green" upgrades coverage, we will pay for:

(1) Additional expense to repair or replace the damaged "Covered Property" except raw materials, property in process, finished goods and "Stock";

(2) Related additional expenses to:

(a) Reuse or salvage the damaged "Covered Property";

(b) Remove, transport and dispose of the recyclable damaged "Covered Property" and its construction waste to appropriate sites; and

(c) Replace the damaged portions of roof section(s) of buildings or structures with a vegetated roof in accordance with the recommended procedures of a "Green standards-setter";

(3) Additional reasonable and customary expense to hire the services of an accredited architect or engineer with respect to any necessary design and engineering recommendations in the course of repair or replacement of damaged portions of the building; and

(4) Additional reasonable expense to pay:

(a) Fees imposed by the "Green standards-setter" in order to determine if certification or recertification is appropriate according to the organization's standard;

(b) Fees to test "Covered Equipment" following its repair or installation as replacements, when such testing is undertaken in the course of submitting to the certification or recertification process; and

(c) After repair or reconstruction is completed, to flush out the renovated space and/or conduct air quality testing of the renovated space in accordance with the recommended procedures of a "Green standards-setter" and for the purpose of mitigating indoor air quality deficiencies resulting from the repair or reconstruction of the "Covered Property".

As used here, additional expenses are limited to the additional cost incurred over and above the amount that we would have paid had no "Green" upgrades been involved with the loss.

In addition, we will not pay for any:

(i) Further modification if the "Covered Property" fails to obtain certification, recertification or a specific level of certification; or

(ii) Additional cost to repair or replace damaged property solely for the purpose of achieving points toward certification or recertification of the property by a "Green standards-setter".

Unless a different limit or INCLUDED is shown in the Declarations, the most we pay under this "Green" upgrades coverage is an amount equal to 25% of the total Property Damage loss otherwise recoverable, subject to a maximum limit of $100,000.

b. Business Income And Extra Expense Or Extra Expense Only

If you have coverage for "Business Income" and "Extra Expense" or "Extra Expense" only and the terms and conditions applicable to the "Business Income" and "Extra Expense" or "Extra Expense" only coverage are satisfied, then:

(1) If the remediation of the damaged "Covered Property" using "Green" upgrades prolongs the "Period of Restoration", we will pay for loss and/or expense sustained during the delay (regardless of when such a delay occurs during the "Period of Restoration"), but such coverage is limited to 30 days. The days need not be consecutive.

(2) If a Revised Number of Days is shown in the Declarations, the number of days (30) in Paragraph **b.(1)** is replaced by the number of days indicated in the Declarations.

(3) As used here, the prolonged "Period of Restoration" is limited to the additional days incurred over and above the amount needed had no "Green" upgrades been involved with the loss.

c. The coverage provided under this "Green" upgrades coverage:

(1) Does not increase any of the applicable Limits of Insurance;

(2) Applies despite the operation of the Ordinance Or Law Exclusion; and

(3) Does not reduce the coverage otherwise applicable for repair or replacement of "Covered Property" that qualified as "Green" prior to loss or damage, with comparable materials and products.

D. Deductibles

1. Application Of Deductibles

We will not pay for loss or damage resulting from any "One Breakdown" until the amount of covered loss or damage exceeds the deductible shown in the Declarations for each applicable coverage. We will then pay the amount of covered loss or damage in excess of the deductible, up to the applicable Limit of Insurance.

Deductibles apply separately for each applicable coverage except if:

a. A deductible is shown as COMBINED for any of the coverages in the Declarations, then we will first subtract the combined deductible amount from the aggregate amount of any loss to which the combined deductible applies; or

b. More than one "Covered Equipment" is involved in "One Breakdown", then only one deductible, the highest, shall apply for each of the applicable coverages.

2. Determination Of Deductibles

a. Dollar Deductible

If a dollar deductible is shown in the Declarations, we will first subtract the deductible amount from any loss we would otherwise pay.

b. Time Deductible

If a time deductible is shown in the Declarations, we will not be liable for any loss under that coverage that occurs during that specified time period immediately following a "Breakdown". If a time deductible is shown in days, each day shall mean 24 consecutive hours.

c. Multiple Of Daily Value Deductible

If a multiple of daily value is shown in the Declarations, this deductible will be calculated as follows:

(1) For the entire premises where the loss occurred, determine the total amount of "Business Income" that would have been earned during the "Period of Restoration" had no "Breakdown" taken place.

(2) Divide the result in Paragraph **(1)** by the number of days the business would have been open during the "Period of Restoration". The result is the daily value.

(3) Multiply the daily value in Paragraph **(2)** by the number of days shown in the Declarations. We will first subtract this deductible amount from any loss we would otherwise pay. We will then pay the amount of loss or damage in excess of the deductible, up to the applicable Limit of Insurance.

d. Percentage Of Loss Deductible

If a deductible is expressed as a percentage of loss in the Declarations, we will not be liable for the indicated percentage of gross amount of loss or damage (prior to the applicable deductible or coinsurance) insured under the applicable coverage.

e. Minimum Or Maximum Deductibles

(1) If:

(a) A minimum dollar amount deductible is shown in the Declarations; and

(b) The dollar amount of the Multiple of Daily Value or the Percentage of Loss Deductible is less than the Minimum Deductible;

then the Minimum Deductible amount shown in the Declarations will be the applicable deductible.

(2) If:

(a) A maximum dollar amount deductible is shown in the Declarations; and

(b) The dollar amount of the Multiple of Daily Value or the Percentage of Loss Deductible is greater than the Maximum Deductible;

then the Maximum Deductible amount shown in the Declarations will be the applicable deductible.

E. Equipment Breakdown Protection Conditions

The following conditions apply in addition to the Common Policy Conditions:

1. Loss Conditions

a. Abandonment

There can be no abandonment of any property to us.

b. Appraisal

If we and you disagree on the value of the property or the amount of loss, either may make written demand for an appraisal of the loss. In this event, each party will select a competent and impartial appraiser. The two appraisers will select an umpire. If they cannot agree, either may request that the selection be made by a judge of a court having jurisdiction. The appraisers will state separately the value of the property and amount of loss. If they fail to agree, they will submit their differences to the umpire. A decision agreed to by any two will be binding.

Each party will:

(1) Pay its chosen appraiser; and

(2) Bear the other expenses of the appraisal and umpire equally.

If there is an appraisal, we will still retain our right to deny the claim.

c. Defense

We may elect to defend you against suits arising from claims of owners of property. We will do this at our expense.

d. Duties In The Event Of Loss Or Damage

(1) You must see that the following are done in the event of loss or damage to "Covered Property":

(a) Give us a prompt notice of the loss or damage. Include a description of the property involved.

(b) As soon as possible, give us a description of how, when and where the loss or damage occurred.

(c) Allow us a reasonable time and opportunity to examine the property and premises before repairs are undertaken or physical evidence of the "Breakdown" is removed. But you must take whatever measures are necessary to protect the property and premises from further damage.

(d) As often as may be reasonably required, permit us to inspect the property proving the loss or damage and examine your books and records.

Also, permit us to take samples of damaged and undamaged property for inspection, testing and analysis, and permit us to make copies from your books and records.

(e) Send us a signed, sworn proof of loss containing the information we request to investigate the claim. You must do this within 60 days after our request. We will supply you with the necessary forms.

(f) Cooperate with us in the investigation or settlement of the claim.

(2) We may examine any insured under oath, while not in the presence of any other insured and at such times as may be reasonably required, about any matter relating to this insurance or the claim, including an insured's books and records. In the event of an examination, an insured's answers must be signed.

e. Insurance Under Two Or More Coverages

If two or more of this policy's coverages apply to the same loss or damage, we will not pay more than the actual amount of the loss or damage.

f. Legal Action Against Us

No one may bring a legal action against us under this Coverage Part unless:

(1) There has been full compliance with all the terms of this Coverage Part; and

(2) The action is brought within two years after the date of the "Breakdown"; or

(3) We agree in writing that you have an obligation to pay for damage to "Covered Property" of others or until the amount of that obligation has been determined by final judgment or arbitration award. No one has the right under this policy to bring us into any action to determine your liability.

g. Loss Payable Clause

(1) We will pay you and the loss payee shown in the Declarations for loss due to a "Breakdown" to "Covered Equipment", as interests may appear. The insurance covers the interest of the loss payee unless the loss results from conversion, secretion or embezzlement on your part.

(2) We may cancel the policy as allowed by the Cancellation Condition. Cancellation ends this agreement as to the loss payee's interest. If we cancel, we will mail you and the loss payee the same advance notice.

(3) If we make any payment to the loss payee, we will obtain their rights against any other party.

h. Other Insurance

(1) You may have other insurance subject to the same plan, terms, conditions and provisions as the insurance under this Coverage Part. If you do, we will pay our share of the covered loss or damage. Our share is the proportion that the applicable Limit of Insurance under this Coverage Part bears to the Limits of Insurance of all insurance covering on the same basis.

(2) If there is other insurance covering the same loss or damage, other than that described in Paragraph (1), we will pay only for the amount of covered loss or damage in excess of the amount due from that other insurance, whether you can collect on it or not. But we will not pay more than the applicable Limit of Insurance.

i. Privilege To Adjust With Owner

In the event of loss or damage involving property of others in your care, custody or control, we have the right to settle the loss or damage with the owner of the property. A receipt for payment from the owner of that property will satisfy any claim of yours against us.

j. Reducing Your Loss

As soon as possible after a "Breakdown", you must:

(1) Resume business, partially or completely;

(2) Make up for lost business within a reasonable period of time. This reasonable period does not necessarily end when operations are resumed; and

(3) Make use of every reasonable means to reduce or avert loss, including:

(a) Working extra time or overtime at the premises or at another premises you own or acquire to carry on the same operations;

(b) Utilizing the property and/or services of other concerns;

(c) Using merchandise or other property, such as surplus machinery, duplicate parts, equipment, supplies and surplus or reserve stock you own, control or can obtain; or

(d) Salvaging the damaged "Covered Property".

k. Transfer Of Rights Of Recovery Against Others To Us

If any person or organization to or for whom we make payment under this Coverage Part has rights to recover damages from another, those rights are transferred to us to the extent of our payment.

That person or organization must do everything necessary to secure our rights and must do nothing after loss to impair them. But you may waive your rights against another party in writing:

(1) Prior to a loss to your "Covered Property" or covered income.

(2) After a loss to your "Covered Property" or covered income only if, at time of loss, that party is one of the following:

(a) Someone insured by this insurance;

(b) A business firm:

(i) Owned or controlled by you; or

(ii) That owns or controls you; or

(c) Your tenant.

This will not restrict your insurance.

l. Valuation

(1) We will determine the value of "Covered Property" in the event of loss or damage as follows:

(a) The cost to repair, rebuild or replace the damaged property with property of the same kind, capacity, size or quality on the same site or another site, whichever is the less costly; or

(b) The cost actually and necessarily expended in repairing, rebuilding or replacing on the same site or another site, whichever is the less costly;

except we will not pay for such damaged property that is obsolete and useless to you.

(2) If you elect or we require that the repair or replacement of the damaged "Covered Equipment" be done in a manner that enhances safety while maintaining the existing function, then we will pay, subject to the limit of insurance, up to an additional 25% of the property damage amount for the "Covered Equipment" otherwise recoverable.

(3) If:

(a) Any damaged "Covered Property" is protected by an extended warranty, or maintenance or service contract; and

(b) That warranty or contract becomes void or unusable due to a "Breakdown";

we will reimburse you for the unused costs of nonrefundable, nontransferable warranties or contracts.

(4) Unless we agree otherwise in writing, if you do not repair or replace the damaged property within 24 months following the date of the "Breakdown", then we will pay only the smaller of the:

(a) Cost it would have taken to repair or replace; or

(b) Actual cash value at the time of the "Breakdown".

(5) If all of the following conditions are met, property held by you for sale will be valued at the selling price as if no loss or damage had occurred, less any discounts you offered and expenses you otherwise would have had:

(a) The property was manufactured by you;

(b) The selling price of the property is more than the replacement cost of the property; and

(c) You are unable to replace the property before its anticipated sale.

(6) We will pay for loss to damaged "Data" or "Media" as follows:

(a) Replacement cost for "Data" or "Media" that are mass produced and commercially available; and

(b) The cost you actually spend to reproduce the records on blank material for all other "Data" or "Media", including the cost of gathering or assembling information for such reproduction.

However, we will not pay for "Data" or "Media" that we determine are not or cannot be replaced with "Data" or "Media" of like kind and quality or property of similar functional use.

(7) We will determine the value of "Covered Property" under Spoilage Damage Coverage as follows:

(a) For raw materials, the replacement cost;

(b) For property in process, the replacement cost of the raw materials, the labor expended and the proper proportion of overhead charges; and

(c) For finished products, the selling price, as if no loss or damage had occurred, less any discounts you offered and expenses you otherwise would have had.

(8) Any salvage value of property obtained for temporary repairs or use following a "Breakdown" which remains after repairs are completed will be taken into consideration in the adjustment of any loss.

m. The following additional conditions apply to the "Business Income" and "Extra Expense" coverage:

(1) Annual Reports

You must complete an Annual Report of Values form approved by us once each year. Your reports must reach us within three months of the annual report date shown in the Declarations and each anniversary of that date.

(2) Adjustment Of Premium

Upon receipt of the annual reports of values you furnish us, we will determine the amount of premium we earned for the past year. If the amount determined is more than the premium we have already charged for this coverage, you must pay the difference. If the amount determined is less than the premium we originally charged, we will refund the difference. However, the amount we return will not exceed 75% of the premium we originally charged.

(3) Coinsurance

This Coinsurance Condition applies only if we did not receive your Annual Report of Values form within three months of the due date as outlined in Paragraph **(1).**

(a) We will not pay the full amount of any loss if:

  (i) The "Business Income Actual Annual Value" at the time of loss is greater than the "Business Income Estimated Annual Value" shown in your latest report; or

  (ii) Your report was received by us more than three months after the due date, or your report is overdue.

(b) Instead, we will determine the most we will pay using the following steps:

  (i) Divide the "Business Income Estimated Annual Value" by the "Business Income Actual Annual Value" at the time of the "Breakdown";

  (ii) Multiply the total amount of the covered loss of "Business Income" by the figure determined in Step **(i)**; and

  (iii) Subtract any applicable deductible from the amount determined in Step **(ii).**

  We will pay the amount determined in Step **(iii)** or the "Business Income" and "Extra Expense" limit of insurance, whichever is less. For the remainder, you will either have to rely on other insurance or absorb the loss yourself.

  If coverage is provided for more than one premises, then this Coinsurance Condition applies separately to each premises.

2. General Conditions

a. Additional Insured

If a person or organization is designated in this Coverage Part as an additional insured, we will consider them to be an insured under this Coverage Part to the extent of their interest.

b. Bankruptcy

The bankruptcy or insolvency of you or your estate will not relieve us of our obligation under this Coverage Part.

c. Concealment, Misrepresentation Or Fraud

This Coverage Part is void in any case of fraud, intentional concealment or misrepresentation of a material fact by you or any other insured, at any time, concerning:

(1) This Coverage Part;

(2) The "Covered Property";

(3) Your interest in the "Covered Property"; or

(4) A claim under this Coverage Part.

d. Liberalization

If we adopt any standard form revision for general use that would broaden coverage in this Coverage Part without additional premium, the broadened coverage will immediately apply to this Coverage Part if the revision is effective within 45 days prior to or during the policy period.

e. Mortgageholder

(1) The term mortgageholder includes trustee.

(2) We will pay for direct damage to "Covered Property" due to a "Breakdown" to "Covered Equipment" to each mortgageholder shown in the Declarations in their order of precedence, as interests may appear.

(3) The mortgageholder has the right to receive loss payment even if the mortgageholder has started foreclosure or similar action on the "Covered Property".

(4) If we deny your claim because of your acts or because you have failed to comply with the terms of this Coverage Part, the mortgageholder will still have the right to receive loss payment if the mortgageholder:

  (a) Pays any premium due under this Coverage Part at our request if you have failed to do so;

  (b) Submits a signed, sworn proof of loss within 60 days after receiving notice from us of your failure to do so; and

  (c) Has notified us of any change in ownership or material change in risk known to the mortgageholder.

  All of the terms of this Coverage Part will then apply directly to the mortgageholder.

(5) If we pay the mortgageholder for any loss and deny payment to you because of your acts or because you have failed to comply with the terms of this Coverage Part:

  (a) The mortgageholder's rights under the mortgage will be transferred to us to the extent of the amount we pay; and

  (b) The mortgageholder's right to recover the full amount of the mortgageholder's claim will not be impaired.

  At our option, we may pay to the mortgageholder the whole principal on the mortgage plus any accrued interest. In this event, your mortgage and note will be transferred to us and you will pay your remaining mortgage debt to us.

(6) If we cancel this policy, we will give written notice to the mortgageholder at least:

  (a) 10 days before the effective date of cancellation if we cancel for nonpayment of premium; or

  (b) 30 days before the effective date of cancellation if we cancel for any other reason.

(7) If we do not renew this policy, we will give written notice to the mortgageholder at least 10 days before the expiration date of this policy.

(8) If we suspend coverage, it will also be suspended as respects the mortgageholder. We will give written notice of the suspension to the mortgageholder.

f. No Benefit To Bailee

No person or organization, other than you, having custody of "Covered Property" will benefit from this insurance.

g. Policy Period, Coverage Territory

Under this Coverage Part:

(1) We cover loss or damage commencing:

  (a) During the policy period shown in the Declarations; and

  (b) Within the coverage territory.

(2) The coverage territory is:

  (a) The United States of America (including its territories and possessions);

  (b) Puerto Rico; and

  (c) Canada.

h. Premium And Adjustments

You shall report to us 100% of the total insurable values at each premises every year as of the anniversary date. The values shall be reported separately for each of the coverages provided. Premium for each anniversary will be promulgated for the ensuing period on the basis of rates in effect at the anniversary date and for all values at risk.

You agree to keep the applicable records for each policy year available for inspection by our representatives at all times during business hours, during the respective policy year, and for a period of 12 months after the end of the respective policy year or after cancellation of this Coverage Part.

i. Suspension

Whenever "Covered Equipment" is found to be in, or exposed to, a dangerous condition, any of our representatives may immediately suspend the insurance against loss from a "Breakdown" to that "Covered Equipment". This can be done by delivering or mailing a written notice of suspension to:

(1) Your last known address; or

(2) The address where the "Covered Equipment" is located.

Once suspended in this way, your insurance can be reinstated only by an endorsement for that "Covered Equipment".

If we suspend your insurance, you will get a pro rata refund of premium for that "Covered Equipment". But the suspension will be effective even if we have not yet made or offered a refund.

3. Joint Or Disputed Loss Agreement

a. This condition is intended to facilitate payment of insurance proceeds when:

  (1) Both a commercial property policy and this equipment breakdown protection policy are in effect;

  (2) Damage occurs to Covered Property that is insured by the commercial property policy and this equipment breakdown protection policy; and

  (3) There is disagreement between the insurers as to whether there is coverage or as to the amount of the loss to be paid, if any, by each insurer under its own policies.

b. This condition does not apply if:

  (1) Both the commercial property insurer(s) and we do not admit to any liability; and

  (2) Neither the commercial property insurer(s) nor we contend that coverage applies under the other insurer's policy.

c. The provisions of this condition apply only if all of the following requirements are met:

  (1) The commercial property policy carried by the Named Insured, insuring the Covered Property, contains a similar provision at the time of the loss or damage, with substantially the same requirements, procedures and conditions as contained in this condition;

  (2) The damage to the Covered Property was caused by a loss for which:

    (a) Both the commercial property insurer(s) and we admit to some liability for payment under the respective policies; or

    (b) Either:

      (i) The commercial property insurer(s) does not admit to any liability for payment, while we contend that:

        i. All liability exists under the commercial property policy; or

        ii. Some liability exists under both the commercial property policy and this equipment breakdown protection policy;

      (ii) We do not admit to any liability for payment, while the commercial property insurer(s) contends that:

        i. All liability exists under this equipment breakdown protection coverage policy; or

        ii. Some liability exists under both the commercial property policy and this equipment breakdown protection policy; or

      (iii) Both the commercial property insurer(s) and we:

        i. Do not admit to any liability for payment; and

        ii. Contend that some or all liability exists under the other insurer's policy; and

    (c) The total amount of the loss is agreed to by you, the commercial property insurer(s) and us.

d. If the requirements listed in Paragraph **c.** above are satisfied, we and the commercial property insurer(s) will make payments to the extent, and in the manner, described as follows:

  (1) We will pay, after your written request, the entire amount of loss that we have agreed as being covered, if any, by this equipment breakdown protection policy and one-half (1/2) the amount of the loss that is in disagreement.

  (2) The commercial property insurer(s) will pay, after your written request, the entire amount of loss that they have agreed as being covered, if any, by the commercial property policy and one-half (1/2) the amount of loss that is in disagreement.

  (3) Payments by the insurers of the amounts that are in disagreement, as described in Paragraphs **(1)** and **(2)**, do not alter, waive or surrender any rights of any insurer against any other with regard to the portion of the loss for which each insurer is liable.

  (4) The amount in disagreement to be paid by us under this condition shall not exceed the amount payable under the equivalent Loss Agreement(s) of the commercial property policy.

  (5) The amount to be paid under this condition shall not exceed the amount we would have paid had no commercial property policy been in effect at the time of loss. In no event will we pay more than the applicable Limit Of Insurance shown in the Declarations.

  (6) Acceptance by you of sums paid under this condition does not alter, waive or surrender any other rights against us.

e. Arbitration

  (1) If the circumstances described in Paragraph **c.(2)(a)** exist and the commercial property insurer(s) and we agree to submit our differences to arbitration, the commercial property insurer(s) and we will determine the amount each will pay and will pay the insured within 90 days. Arbitration will then take place within 90 days after payment of the loss under the terms of this condition.

(2) If any of the circumstances described in Paragraph **c.(2)(b)** exist, then the commercial property insurer(s) and we agree to submit our differences to arbitration within 90 days after payment of the loss under the terms of this condition.

(3) You agree to cooperate with any arbitration procedures. There will be three arbitrators: one will be appointed by us, and another will be appointed by the commercial property insurer(s). The two arbitrators will select a third arbitrator. If they cannot agree, either may request that selection be made by a judge of a court having jurisdiction. A decision agreed to by two of the three arbitrators will be binding on both parties. Judgment on any award can be entered in any court that has jurisdiction.

f. Final Settlement Between Insurers

The insurer(s) found responsible for the greater percentage of the ultimate loss must return the excess contribution to the other insurer(s). In addition, the insurer(s) found responsible for the greater portion of the loss must pay Liquidated Damages to the other insurer(s) on the amount of the excess contribution of the other insurer(s). Liquidated Damages are defined as interest from the date the insured invokes this Agreement to the date the insurer(s) that contributed the excess amount is reimbursed. The interest is calculated at 1.5 times the highest prime rate from the Money Rates column of the Wall Street Journal during the period of the Liquidated Damages. Arbitration expenses are not a part of the excess contribution for which Liquidated Damages are calculated. Arbitration expenses will be apportioned between insurers on the same basis that the ultimate loss is apportioned.

F. Definitions

1. "Breakdown":

a. Means the following direct physical loss that causes damage to "Covered Equipment" and necessitates its repair or replacement:

(1) Failure of pressure or vacuum equipment;

(2) Mechanical failure including rupture or bursting caused by centrifugal force; or

(3) Electrical failure including arcing;

unless such loss or damage is otherwise excluded within this coverage form.

b. Does not mean or include:

(1) Malfunction including but not limited to adjustment, alignment, calibration, cleaning or modification;

(2) Defects, erasures, errors, limitations or viruses in computer equipment and programs including the inability to recognize and process any date or time or provide instructions to "Covered Equipment";

(3) Leakage at any valve, fitting, shaft seal, gland packing, joint or connection;

(4) Damage to any vacuum tube, gas tube, or brush;

(5) Damage to any structure or foundation supporting the "Covered Equipment" or any of its parts;

(6) The functioning of any safety or protective device; or

(7) The cracking of any part on an internal combustion gas turbine exposed to the products of combustion.

2. "Business Income" means the:

a. Net Income (Net Profit or Loss before income taxes) that would have been earned or incurred; and

b. Continuing normal operating expenses incurred, including payroll.

3. "Business Income Actual Annual Value" means the sum of the Net Income and continuing normal operating expenses incurred, including payroll that would have been earned had the "Breakdown" not occurred.

4. "Business Income Estimated Annual Value" means the sum of the Net Income and continuing normal operating expenses incurred, including payroll as estimated by you in the most recent Annual Report of Values form on file with us.

5. "Computer Equipment" means:

a. Your programmable electronic equipment that is used to store, retrieve and process data; and

b. Associated peripheral equipment that provides communication including input and output functions such as printing or auxiliary functions such as data transmission.

It does not include "Data" or "Media".

6. "Covered Equipment":

a. Means and includes any:

(1) Equipment built to operate under internal pressure or vacuum other than weight of contents;

(2) Electrical or mechanical equipment that is used in the generation, transmission or utilization of energy;

(3) Communication equipment and "Computer Equipment"; and

(4) Equipment in Paragraphs (1), (2) and (3) that is owned by a public or private utility and used solely to supply utility services to your premises.

However, if Coverage **A.2.e.** Utility Interruption is provided, then Paragraph **6.a.(4)** does not apply.

Except for Paragraph **6.a.(4)**, Utility Interruption and Contingent "Business Income" and "Extra Expense" or "Extra Expense" only coverages, the "Covered Equipment" must be located at a premises described in the Declarations and be owned, leased or operated under your control.

b. Does not mean or include any:

(1) "Media";

(2) Part of pressure or vacuum equipment that is not under internal pressure of its contents or internal vacuum;

(3) Insulating or refractory material, but not excluding the glass lining of any "Covered Equipment";

(4) Nonmetallic pressure or vacuum equipment, unless it is constructed and used in accordance with the American Society of Mechanical Engineers (A.S.M.E.) code or another appropriate and approved code;

(5) Catalyst;

(6) Vessels, piping and other equipment that is buried belowground and requires the excavation of materials to inspect, remove, repair or replace;

(7) Structure, foundation, cabinet or compartment supporting or containing the "Covered Equipment" or part of the "Covered Equipment" including penstock, draft tube or well casing;

(8) Vehicle, aircraft, self-propelled equipment or floating vessel including any "Covered Equipment" that is mounted upon or used solely with any one or more vehicle(s), aircraft, self-propelled equipment or floating vessel;

(9) Dragline, excavation or construction equipment including any "Covered Equipment" that is mounted upon or used solely with any one or more dragline(s), excavation or construction equipment;

(10) Felt, wire, screen, die, extrusion plate, swing hammer, grinding disc, cutting blade, nonelectrical cable, chain, belt, rope, clutch plate, brake pad, nonmetal part or any part or tool subject to periodic replacement;

(11) Machine or apparatus used solely for research, diagnosis, medication, surgical, therapeutic, dental or pathological purposes including any "Covered Equipment" that is mounted upon or used solely with any one or more machine(s) or apparatus unless Diagnostic Equipment is shown as INCLUDED in the Declarations; or

(12) Equipment or any part of such equipment manufactured by you for sale.

7. "Covered Property" means any property that:

a. You own; or

b. Is in your care, custody or control and for which you are legally liable.

8. "Data" means:

a. Programmed and recorded material stored on "Media"; and

b. Programming records used for electronic data processing, or electronically controlled equipment.

9. "Extra Expense" means the additional cost you incur to operate your business during the "Period of Restoration" over and above the cost that you normally would have incurred to operate the business during the same period had no "Breakdown" occurred.

10. "Fungus" means any type or form of fungus, including mold or mildew and any mycotoxins, spores, scents or by-products produced or released by fungi.

Equipment Breakdown

       EB 00 20 09 11   □

11. "Green" means enhanced energy efficiency or use of environmentally-preferable, sustainable materials, products or methods in design, construction, manufacture or operation, as recognized by a "Green standards-setter".

12. "Green standards-setter" means an organization or governmental agency which produces and maintains guidelines related to "Green" products and practices. "Green standards-setters" include but are not limited to:

   a. The Leadership in Energy and Environmental Design (LEED®) program of the U.S. Green Building Council;

   b. ENERGY STAR, a joint program of the U.S. Environmental Protection Agency and the U.S. Department of Energy; and

   c. Green Globes™, a program of the Green Building Initiative.

13. "Hazardous Substance" means any substance other than ammonia that has been declared to be hazardous to health by a government agency.

14. "Media" means electronic data processing or storage media such as films, tapes, discs, drums or cells.

15. "One Breakdown" means if an initial "Breakdown" causes other "Breakdowns", all will be considered "One Breakdown". All "Breakdowns" at any one premises that manifest themselves at the same time and are the direct result of the same cause will be considered "One Breakdown".

16. "Period of Restoration" means the period of time that:

   a. Begins at the time of the "Breakdown" or 24 hours before we receive notice of "Breakdown", whichever is later; and

   b. Ends five consecutive days after the date when the damaged property at the premises described in the Declarations is repaired or replaced with reasonable speed and similar quality.

17. "Stock" means merchandise held in storage or for sale, raw materials, property in process or finished products including supplies used in their packing or shipping.

Businessowners Insurance

Many organizations are insured under businessowners policies instead of the more cumbersome type of commercial package policy that includes multiple coverage parts such as commercial property, equipment breakdown, crime, inland marine, and commercial general liability.

Typically, businessowners policies provide, in one form, most of the property and liability coverages needed by small to medium-sized businesses. A businessowners policy ordinarily includes building and personal property coverage, business income and extra expense coverage, selected crime and inland marine coverages, and equipment breakdown coverage. Liability coverage, like that of the Commercial General Liability Coverage Form, is also included in the policy. Hired and nonowned auto liability coverage and various professional liability endorsements can be added as needed.

The Businessowners Coverage Form of Insurance Services Office, Inc. (ISO) is reprinted in the *Handbook* as an example. Many insurers develop their own businessowners forms that differ to varying degrees from the ISO form. Please note that forms corresponding to the 2006 Businessowners Program and the 2010 Businessowners Program are included for reference purposes

2000 EDITION

BUSINESSOWNERS
BP 00 03 01 06

BUSINESSOWNERS COVERAGE FORM

Various provisions in this policy restrict coverage. Read the entire policy carefully to determine rights, duties and what is and is not covered.

Throughout this Coverage Form the words "you" and "your" refer to the Named Insured shown in the Declarations. The words "we", "us" and "our" refer to the Company providing this insurance.

In Section **II** – Liability, the word "insured" means any person or organization qualifying as such under Paragraph **C.** Who Is An Insured.

Other words and phrases that appear in quotation marks have special meaning. Refer to Paragraph **H.** Property Definitions in Section **I** – Property and Paragraph **F.** Liability And Medical Expenses Definitions in Section **II** – Liability.

SECTION I – PROPERTY

A. Coverage

We will pay for direct physical loss of or damage to Covered Property at the premises described in the Declarations caused by or resulting from any Covered Cause of Loss.

1. Covered Property

Covered Property includes Buildings as described under Paragraph **a.** below, Business Personal Property as described under Paragraph **b.** below, or both, depending on whether a Limit of Insurance is shown in the Declarations for that type of property. Regardless of whether coverage is shown in the Declarations for Buildings, Business Personal Property, or both, there is no coverage for property described under Paragraph **2.** Property Not Covered.

a. Buildings, meaning the buildings and structures at the premises described in the Declarations, including:

(1) Completed additions;

(2) Fixtures, including outdoor fixtures;

(3) Permanently installed:

(a) Machinery; and

(b) Equipment;

(4) Your personal property in apartments, rooms or common areas furnished by you as landlord;

(5) Personal property owned by you that is used to maintain or service the buildings or structures or the premises, including:

(a) Fire extinguishing equipment;

(b) Outdoor furniture;

(c) Floor coverings; and

(d) Appliances used for refrigerating, ventilating, cooking, dishwashing or laundering;

(6) If not covered by other insurance:

(a) Additions under construction, alterations and repairs to the buildings or structures;

(b) Materials, equipment, supplies and temporary structures, on or within 100 feet of the described premises, used for making additions, alterations or repairs to the buildings or structures.

b. Business Personal Property located in or on the buildings at the described premises or in the open (or in a vehicle) within 100 feet of the described premises, including:

(1) Property you own that is used in your business;

(2) Property of others that is in your care, custody or control, except as otherwise provided in Loss Payment Property Loss Condition Paragraph **E.5.d.(3)(b);**

(3) Tenant's improvements and betterments. Improvements and betterments are fixtures, alterations, installations or additions:

(a) Made a part of the building or structure you occupy but do not own; and

(b) You acquired or made at your expense but cannot legally remove;

(4) Leased personal property which you have a contractual responsibility to insure, unless otherwise provided for under Paragraph **1.b.(2);** and

(5) Exterior building glass, if you are a tenant and no Limit of Insurance is shown in the Declarations for Building property. The glass must be owned by you or in your care, custody or control.

2. Property Not Covered

Covered Property does not include:

a. Aircraft, automobiles, motortrucks and other vehicles subject to motor vehicle registration;

b. "Money" or "securities" except as provided in the:

(1) Money and Securities Optional Coverage; or

(2) Employee Dishonesty Optional Coverage;

c. Contraband, or property in the course of illegal transportation or trade;

d. Land (including land on which the property is located), water, growing crops or lawns;

e. Outdoor fences, radio or television antennas (including satellite dishes) and their lead-in wiring, masts or towers, signs (other than signs attached to buildings), trees, shrubs or plants, all except as provided in the:

(1) Outdoor Property Coverage Extension; or

(2) Outdoor Signs Optional Coverage;

f. Watercraft (including motors, equipment and accessories) while afloat;

g. Accounts, bills, food stamps, other evidences of debt, accounts receivable or "valuable papers and records"; except as otherwise provided in this policy;

h. "Computer(s)" which are permanently installed or designed to be permanently installed in any aircraft, watercraft, motortruck or other vehicle subject to motor vehicle registration. This paragraph does not apply to "computer(s)" while held as "stock";

i. "Electronic Data", except as provided under Additional Coverages – Electronic Data. This Paragraph **i.** does not apply to your "stock" of prepackaged software.

3. Covered Causes Of Loss

Risks of direct physical loss unless the loss is:

a. Excluded in Paragraph **B.** Exclusions in Section **I**; or

b. Limited in Paragraph **4.** Limitations in Section **I.**

4. Limitations

a. We will not pay for loss of or damage to:

(1) Steam boilers, steam pipes, steam engines or steam turbines caused by or resulting from any condition or event inside such equipment. But we will pay for loss of or damage to such equipment caused by or resulting from an explosion of gases or fuel within the furnace of any fired vessel or within the flues or passages through which the gases of combustion pass.

(2) Hot water boilers or other water heating equipment caused by or resulting from any condition or event inside such boilers or equipment, other than an explosion.

(3) Property that is missing, where the only evidence of the loss or damage is a shortage disclosed on taking inventory, or other instances where there is no physical evidence to show what happened to the property. This limitation does not apply to the Optional Coverage for Money and Securities.

(4) Property that has been transferred to a person or to a place outside the described premises on the basis of unauthorized instructions.

(5) The interior of any building or structure caused by or resulting from rain, snow, sleet, ice, sand or dust, whether driven by wind or not, unless:

(a) The building or structure first sustains damage by a Covered Cause of Loss to its roof or walls through which the rain, snow, sleet, ice, sand or dust enters; or

(b) The loss or damage is caused by or results from thawing of snow, sleet or ice on the building or structure.

b. We will not pay for loss of or damage to fragile articles such as glassware, statuary, marble, chinaware and porcelain, if broken, unless caused by the "specified causes of loss" or building glass breakage. This restriction does not apply to:

(1) Glass that is part of the exterior or interior of a building or structure;

(2) Containers of property held for sale; or

(3) Photographic or scientific instrument lenses.

c. For loss or damage by theft, the following types of property are covered only up to the limits shown:

(1) $2,500 for furs, fur garments and garments trimmed with fur.

(2) $2,500 for jewelry, watches, watch movements, jewels, pearls, precious and semi-precious stones, bullion, gold, silver, platinum and other precious alloys or metals. This limit does not apply to jewelry and watches worth $100 or less per item.

(3) $2,500 for patterns, dies, molds and forms.

5. Additional Coverages

a. Debris Removal

(1) Subject to Paragraphs **(3)** and **(4)**, we will pay your expense to remove debris of Covered Property caused by or resulting from a Covered Cause of Loss that occurs during the policy period. The expenses will be paid only if they are reported to us in writing within 180 days of the date of direct physical loss or damage.

(2) Debris Removal does not apply to costs to:

(a) Extract "pollutants" from land or water; or

(b) Remove, restore or replace polluted land or water.

(3) Subject to the exceptions in Paragraph **(4)**, the following provisions apply:

(a) The most that we will pay for the total of direct physical loss or damage plus debris removal expense is the Limit of Insurance applicable to the Covered Property that has sustained loss or damage.

(b) Subject to Paragraph **(a)** above, the amount we will pay for debris removal expense is limited to 25% of the sum of the deductible plus the amount that we pay for direct physical loss or damage to the Covered Property that has sustained loss or damage.

(4) We will pay up to an additional $10,000 for debris removal expense, for each location, in any one occurrence of physical loss or damage to Covered Property, if one or both of the following circumstances apply:

(a) The total of the actual debris removal expense plus the amount we pay for direct physical loss or damage exceeds the Limit of Insurance on the Covered Property that has sustained loss or damage.

(b) The actual debris removal expense exceeds 25% of the sum of the deductible plus the amount that we pay for direct physical loss or damage to the Covered Property that has sustained loss or damage.

Therefore, if Paragraphs **(4)(a)** and/or **(4)(b)** apply, our total payment for direct physical loss or damage and debris removal expense may reach but will never exceed the Limit of Insurance on the Covered Property that has sustained loss or damage, plus $10,000.

(5) Examples

Example #1

Limit of Insurance	$ 90,000
Amount of Deductible	$ 500
Amount of Loss	$ 50,000
Amount of Loss Payable	$ 49,500
($50,000 – $500)	
Debris Removal Expense	$ 10,000
Debris Removal Expense Payable	$ 10,000
($10,000 is 20% of $50,000)	

The debris removal expense is less than 25% of the sum of the loss payable plus the deductible. The sum of the loss payable and the debris removal expense ($49,500 + $10,000 = $59,500) is less than the Limit of Insurance. Therefore the full amount of debris removal expense is payable in accordance with the terms of Paragraph **(3)**.

Example #2

Limit of Insurance	$ 90,000
Amount of Deductible	$ 500
Amount of Loss	$ 80,000
Amount of Loss Payable	$ 79,500
	($80,000 – $500)
Debris Removal Expense	$ 30,000
Debris Removal Expense Payable	
Basic Amount	$ 10,500
Additional Amount	$ 10,000

The basic amount payable for debris removal expense under the terms of Paragraph **(3)** is calculated as follows: $80,000 ($79,500 + $500) x .25 = $20,000; capped at $10,500). The cap applies because the sum of the loss payable ($79,500) and the basic amount payable for debris removal expense ($10,500) cannot exceed the Limit of Insurance ($90,000).

The additional amount payable for debris removal expense is provided in accordance with the terms of Paragraph **(4)**, because the debris removal expense ($30,000) exceeds 25% of the loss payable plus the deductible ($30,000 is 37.5% of $80,000), and because the sum of the loss payable and debris removal expense ($79,500 + $30,000 = $109,500) would exceed the Limit of Insurance ($90,000). The additional amount of covered debris removal expense is $10,000, the maximum payable under Paragraph **(4)**. Thus the total payable for debris removal expense in this example is $20,500; $9,500 of the debris removal expense is not covered.

b. Preservation Of Property

If it is necessary to move Covered Property from the described premises to preserve it from loss or damage by a Covered Cause of Loss, we will pay for any direct physical loss of or damage to that property:

(1) While it is being moved or while temporarily stored at another location; and

(2) Only if the loss or damage occurs within 30 days after the property is first moved.

c. Fire Department Service Charge

When the fire department is called to save or protect Covered Property from a Covered Cause of Loss, we will pay up to $2,500, unless a different limit is shown in the Declarations, for your liability for fire department service charges:

(1) Assumed by contract or agreement prior to loss; or

(2) Required by local ordinance.

d. Collapse

(1) With respect to buildings:

(a) Collapse means an abrupt falling down or caving in of a building or any part of a building with the result that the building or part of the building cannot be occupied for its intended purpose;

(b) A building or any part of a building that is in danger of falling down or caving in is not considered to be in a state of collapse;

(c) A part of a building that is standing is not considered to be in a state of collapse even if it has separated from another part of the building; and

(d) A building that is standing or any part of a building that is standing is not considered to be in a state of collapse even if it shows evidence of cracking, bulging, sagging, bending, leaning, settling, shrinkage or expansion.

(2) We will pay for direct physical loss or damage to Covered Property, caused by collapse of a building or any part of a building that is insured under this policy or that contains Covered Property insured under this policy, if the collapse is caused by one or more of the following:

(a) The "specified causes of loss" or breakage of building glass, all only as insured against in this policy;

(b) Decay that is hidden from view, unless the presence of such decay is known to an insured prior to collapse;

(c) Insect or vermin damage that is hidden from view, unless the presence of such damage is known to an insured prior to collapse;

© ISO Properties, Inc., 2004

(d) Weight of people or personal property;

(e) Weight of rain that collects on a roof; or

(f) Use of defective material or methods in construction, remodeling or renovation if the collapse occurs during the course of the construction, remodeling or renovation. However, if the collapse occurs after construction, remodeling or renovation is complete and is caused in part by a cause of loss listed in Paragraphs **(a)** through **(e),** we will pay for the loss or damage even if use of defective material or methods in construction, remodeling or renovation, contributes to the collapse.

The criteria set forth in Paragraphs **(1)(a)** through **(1)(d)** do not limit the coverage otherwise provided under this Additional Coverage for the causes of loss listed in Paragraphs **(2)(a), (2)(d)** and **(2)(e).**

(3) With respect to the following property:

(a) Awnings;

(b) Gutters and downspouts;

(c) Yard fixtures;

(d) Outdoor swimming pools;

(e) Piers, wharves and docks;

(f) Beach or diving platforms or appurtenances;

(g) Retaining walls; and

(h) Walks, roadways and other paved surfaces;

if the collapse is caused by a cause of loss listed in Paragraphs **(2)(b)** through **(2)(f),** we will pay for loss or damage to that property only if such loss or damage is a direct result of the collapse of a building insured under this policy and the property is Covered Property under this policy.

(4) If personal property abruptly falls down or caves in and such collapse is not the result of collapse of a building, we will pay for loss or damage to Covered Property caused by such collapse of personal property only if:

(a) The collapse was caused by a cause of loss listed in Paragraphs **(2)(a)** through **(2)(f)** of this Additional Coverage;

(b) The personal property which collapses is inside a building; and

(c) The property which collapses is not of a kind listed in Paragraph **(3)** above, regardless of whether that kind of property is considered to be personal property or real property.

The coverage stated in this Paragraph **(4)** does not apply to personal property if marring and/or scratching is the only damage to that personal property caused by the collapse.

Collapse of personal property does not mean cracking, bulging, sagging, bending, leaning, settling, shrinkage or expansion.

(5) This Additional Coverage, Collapse, will not increase the Limits of Insurance provided in this policy.

e. Water Damage, Other Liquids, Powder Or Molten Material Damage

If loss or damage caused by or resulting from covered water or other liquid, powder or molten material occurs, we will also pay the cost to tear out and replace any part of the building or structure to repair damage to the system or appliance from which the water or other substance escapes.

We will not pay the cost to repair any defect that caused the loss or damage; but we will pay the cost to repair or replace damaged parts of fire extinguishing equipment if the damage:

(1) Results in discharge of any substance from an automatic fire protection system; or

(2) Is directly caused by freezing.

f. Business Income

(1) Business Income

(a) We will pay for the actual loss of Business Income you sustain due to the necessary suspension of your "operations" during the "period of restoration". The suspension must be caused by direct physical loss of or damage to property at the described premises. The loss or damage must be caused by or result from a Covered Cause of Loss. With respect to loss of or damage to personal property in the open or personal property in a vehicle, the described premises include the area within 100 feet of the site at which the described premises are located.

With respect to the requirements set forth in the preceding paragraph, if you occupy only part of the site at which the described premises are located, your premises means:

(i) The portion of the building which you rent, lease or occupy; and

(ii) Any area within the building or on the site at which the described premises are located, if that area services, or is used to gain access to, the described premises.

(b) We will only pay for loss of Business Income that you sustain during the "period of restoration" and that occurs within 12 consecutive months after the date of direct physical loss or damage. We will only pay for ordinary payroll expenses for 60 days following the date of direct physical loss or damage, unless a greater number of days is shown in the Declarations.

(c) Business Income means the:

(i) Net Income (Net Profit or Loss before income taxes) that would have been earned or incurred if no physical loss or damage had occurred, but not including any Net Income that would likely have been earned as a result of an increase in the volume of business due to favorable business conditions caused by the impact of the Covered Cause of Loss on customers or on other businesses; and

(ii) Continuing normal operating expenses incurred, including payroll.

(d) Ordinary payroll expenses:

(i) Mean payroll expenses for all your employees except:

i. Officers;

ii. Executives;

iii. Department Managers;

iv. Employees under contract; and

v. Additional Exemptions shown in the Declarations as:

- Job Classifications; or

- Employees.

(ii) Include:

i. Payroll;

ii. Employee benefits, if directly related to payroll;

iii. FICA payments you pay;

iv. Union dues you pay; and

v. Workers' compensation premiums.

(2) Extended Business Income

(a) If the necessary suspension of your "operations" produces a Business Income loss payable under this policy, we will pay for the actual loss of Business Income you incur during the period that:

(i) Begins on the date property except finished stock is actually repaired, rebuilt or replaced and "operations" are resumed; and

(ii) Ends on the earlier of:

i. The date you could restore your "operations", with reasonable speed, to the level which would generate the Business Income amount that would have existed if no direct physical loss or damage had occurred; or

ii. 30 consecutive days after the date determined in Paragraph **(a)(i)** above, unless a greater number of consecutive days is shown in the Declarations.

© ISO Properties, Inc., 2004   **BP 00 03 01 06**   ☐

However, Extended Business Income does not apply to loss of Business Income incurred as a result of unfavorable business conditions caused by the impact of the Covered Cause of Loss in the area where the described premises are located.

(b) Loss of Business Income must be caused by direct physical loss or damage at the described premises caused by or resulting from any Covered Cause of Loss.

(3) With respect to the coverage provided in this Additional Coverage, suspension means:

(a) The partial slowdown or complete cessation of your business activities; or

(b) That a part or all of the described premises is rendered untenantable, if coverage for Business Income applies.

(4) This Additional Coverage is not subject to the Limits of Insurance of Section I – Property.

g. Extra Expense

(1) We will pay necessary Extra Expense you incur during the "period of restoration" that you would not have incurred if there had been no direct physical loss or damage to property at the described premises. The loss or damage must be caused by or result from a Covered Cause of Loss. With respect to loss of or damage to personal property in the open or personal property in a vehicle, the described premises include the area within 100 feet of the site at which the described premises are located.

With respect to the requirements set forth in the preceding paragraph, if you occupy only part of the site at which the described premises are located, your premises means:

(a) The portion of the building which you rent, lease or occupy; and

(b) Any area within the building or on the site at which the described premises are located, if that area services, or is used to gain access to, the described premises.

(2) Extra Expense means expense incurred:

(a) To avoid or minimize the suspension of business and to continue "operations":

(i) At the described premises; or

(ii) At replacement premises or at temporary locations, including relocation expenses, and costs to equip and operate the replacement or temporary locations.

(b) To minimize the suspension of business if you cannot continue "operations".

(c) To:

(i) Repair or replace any property; or

(ii) Research, replace or restore the lost information on damaged "valuable papers and records"

to the extent it reduces the amount of loss that otherwise would have been payable under this Additional Coverage or Additional Coverage **f.** Business Income.

(3) With respect to the coverage provided in this Additional Coverage, suspension means:

(a) The partial slowdown or complete cessation of your business activities; or

(b) That a part or all of the described premises is rendered untenantable, if coverage for Business Income applies.

(4) We will only pay for Extra Expense that occurs within 12 consecutive months after the date of direct physical loss or damage. This Additional Coverage is not subject to the Limits of Insurance of Section I – Property.

h. Pollutant Clean Up And Removal

We will pay your expense to extract "pollutants" from land or water at the described premises if the discharge, dispersal, seepage, migration, release or escape of the "pollutants" is caused by or results from a Covered Cause of Loss that occurs during the policy period. The expenses will be paid only if they are reported to us in writing within 180 days of the date on which the Covered Cause of Loss occurs.

This Additional Coverage does not apply to costs to test for, monitor or assess the existence, concentration or effects of "pollutants". But we will pay for testing which is performed in the course of extracting the "pollutants" from the land or water.

The most we will pay for each location under this Additional Coverage is $10,000 for the sum of all such expenses arising out of Covered Causes of Loss occurring during each separate 12 month period of this policy.

i. Civil Authority

We will pay for the actual loss of Business Income you sustain and necessary Extra Expense caused by action of civil authority that prohibits access to the described premises due to direct physical loss of or damage to property, other than at the described premises, caused by or resulting from any Covered Cause of Loss.

The coverage for Business Income will begin 72 hours after the time of that action and will apply for a period of up to three consecutive weeks after coverage begins.

The coverage for necessary Extra Expense will begin immediately after the time of that action and ends:

(1) 3 consecutive weeks after the time of that action; or

(2) When your Business Income coverage ends;

whichever is later.

The definitions of Business Income and Extra Expense contained in the Business Income and Extra Expense Additional Coverages also apply to this Civil Authority Additional Coverage. The Civil Authority Additional Coverage is not subject to the Limits of Insurance of Section I – Property.

j. Money Orders And "Counterfeit Money"

We will pay for loss resulting directly from your having accepted in good faith, in exchange for merchandise, "money" or services:

(1) Money orders issued by any post office, express company or bank that are not paid upon presentation; or

(2) "Counterfeit money" that is acquired during the regular course of business.

The most we will pay for any loss under this Additional Coverage is $1,000.

k. Forgery Or Alteration

(1) We will pay for loss resulting directly from forgery or alteration of, any check, draft, promissory note, bill of exchange or similar written promise of payment in "money", that you or your agent has issued, or that was issued by someone who impersonates you or your agent.

(2) If you are sued for refusing to pay the check, draft, promissory note, bill of exchange or similar written promise of payment in "money", on the basis that it has been forged or altered, and you have our written consent to defend against the suit, we will pay for any reasonable legal expenses that you incur in that defense.

(3) For the purpose of this coverage, check includes a substitute check as defined in the Check Clearing for the 21st Century Act, and will be treated the same as the original it replaced.

(4) The most we will pay for any loss, including legal expenses, under this Additional Coverage is $2,500, unless a higher Limit of Insurance is shown in the Declarations.

l. Increased Cost Of Construction

(1) This Additional Coverage applies only to buildings insured on a replacement cost basis.

(2) In the event of damage by a Covered Cause of Loss to a building that is Covered Property, we will pay the increased costs incurred to comply with enforcement of an ordinance or law in the course of repair, rebuilding or replacement of damaged parts of that property, subject to the limitations stated in Paragraphs **(3)** through **(9)** of this Additional Coverage.

(3) The ordinance or law referred to in Paragraph **(2)** of this Additional Coverage is an ordinance or law that regulates the construction or repair of buildings or establishes zoning or land use requirements at the described premises, and is in force at the time of loss.

(4) Under this Additional Coverage, we will not pay any costs due to an ordinance or law that:

(a) You were required to comply with before the loss, even when the building was undamaged; and

(b) You failed to comply with.

(5) Under this Additional Coverage, we will not pay for:

(a) The enforcement of any ordinance or law which requires demolition, repair, replacement, reconstruction, remodeling or remediation of property due to contamination by "pollutants" or due to the presence, growth, proliferation, spread or any activity of "fungi", wet or dry rot or bacteria; or

(b) Any costs associated with the enforcement of an ordinance or law which requires any insured or others to test for, monitor, clean up, remove, contain, treat, detoxify or neutralize, or in any way respond to or assess the effects of "pollutants", "fungi", wet or dry rot or bacteria.

(6) The most we will pay under this Additional Coverage, for each described building insured under Section I – Property, is $10,000. If a damaged building(s) is covered under a blanket Limit of Insurance which applies to more than one building or item of property, then the most we will pay under this Additional Coverage, for each damaged building, is $10,000.

The amount payable under this Additional Coverage is additional insurance.

(7) With respect to this Additional Coverage:

(a) We will not pay for the Increased Cost of Construction:

(i) Until the property is actually repaired or replaced, at the same or another premises; and

(ii) Unless the repairs or replacement are made as soon as reasonably possible after the loss or damage, not to exceed two years. We may extend this period in writing during the two years.

(b) If the building is repaired or replaced at the same premises, or if you elect to rebuild at another premises, the most we will pay for the Increased Cost of Construction is the increased cost of construction at the same premises.

(c) If the ordinance or law requires relocation to another premises, the most we will pay for the Increased Cost of Construction is the increased cost of construction at the new premises.

(8) This Additional Coverage is not subject to the terms of the Ordinance Or Law Exclusion, to the extent that such Exclusion would conflict with the provisions of this Additional Coverage.

(9) The costs addressed in the Loss Payment Property Loss Condition in Section I – Property do not include the increased cost attributable to enforcement of an ordinance or law. The amount payable under this Additional Coverage, as stated in Paragraph **(6)** of this Additional Coverage, is not subject to such limitation.

m. Business Income From Dependent Properties

(1) We will pay for the actual loss of Business Income you sustain due to physical loss or damage at the premises of a dependent property caused by or resulting from any Covered Cause of Loss.

However, this Additional Coverage does not apply when the only loss to dependent property is loss or damage to "electronic data", including destruction or corruption of "electronic data". If the dependent property sustains loss or damage to "electronic data" and other property, coverage under this Additional Coverage will not continue once the other property is repaired, rebuilt or replaced.

The most we will pay under this Additional Coverage is $5,000 unless a higher Limit of Insurance is indicated in the Declarations.

(2) We will reduce the amount of your Business Income loss, other than Extra Expense, to the extent you can resume "operations", in whole or in part, by using any other available:

(a) Source of materials; or

(b) Outlet for your products.

(3) If you do not resume "operations", or do not resume "operations" as quickly as possible, we will pay based on the length of time it would have taken to resume "operations" as quickly as possible.

(4) Dependent property means property owned by others whom you depend on to:

(a) Deliver materials or services to you, or to others for your account. But services does not mean water, communication or power supply services;

(b) Accept your products or services;

(c) Manufacture your products for delivery to your customers under contract for sale; or

(d) Attract customers to your business.

The dependent property must be located in the coverage territory of this policy.

(5) The coverage period for Business Income under this Additional Coverage:

(a) Begins 72 hours after the time of direct physical loss or damage caused by or resulting from any Covered Cause of Loss at the premises of the dependent property; and

(b) Ends on the date when the property at the premises of the dependent property should be repaired, rebuilt or replaced with reasonable speed and similar quality.

(6) The Business Income coverage period, as stated in Paragraph **(5)**, does not include any increased period required due to the enforcement of any ordinance or law that:

(a) Regulates the construction, use or repair, or requires the tearing down of any property; or

(b) Requires any insured or others to test for, monitor, clean up, remove, contain, treat, detoxify or neutralize, or in any way respond to, or assess the effects of "pollutants".

The expiration date of this policy will not reduce the Business Income coverage period.

(7) The definition of Business Income contained in the Business Income Additional Coverage also applies to this Business Income From Dependent Properties Additional Coverage.

n. Glass Expenses

(1) We will pay for expenses incurred to put up temporary plates or board up openings if repair or replacement of damaged glass is delayed.

(2) We will pay for expenses incurred to remove or replace obstructions when repairing or replacing glass that is part of a building. This does not include removing or replacing window displays.

o. Fire Extinguisher Systems Recharge Expense

(1) We will pay:

(a) The cost of recharging or replacing, whichever is less, your fire extinguishers and fire extinguishing systems (including hydrostatic testing if needed) if they are discharged on or within 100 feet of the described premises; and

(b) For loss or damage to Covered Property if such loss or damage is the result of an accidental discharge of chemicals from a fire extinguisher or a fire extinguishing system.

(2) No coverage will apply if the fire extinguishing system is discharged during installation or testing.

(3) The most we will pay under this Additional Coverage is $5,000 in any one occurrence.

p. Electronic Data

(1) Subject to the provisions of this Additional Coverage, we will pay for the cost to replace or restore "electronic data" which has been destroyed or corrupted by a Covered Cause of Loss. To the extent that "electronic data" is not replaced or restored, the loss will be valued at the cost of replacement of the media on which the "electronic data" was stored, with blank media of substantially identical type.

(2) The Covered Causes of Loss applicable to Business Personal Property include a virus, harmful code or similar instruction introduced into or enacted on a computer system (including "electronic data") or a network to which it is connected, designed to damage or destroy any part of the system or disrupt its normal operation. But there is no coverage for loss or damage caused by or resulting from manipulation of a computer system (including "electronic data") by any employee, including a temporary or leased employee, or by an entity retained by you, or for you, to inspect, design, install, modify, maintain, repair or replace that system.

(3) The most we will pay under this Additional Coverage – Electronic Data for all loss or damage sustained in any one policy year, regardless of the number of occurrences of loss or damage or the number of premises, locations or computer systems involved, is $10,000, unless a higher Limit of Insurance is shown in the Declarations. If loss payment on the first occurrence does not exhaust this amount, then the balance is available for subsequent loss or damage sustained in, but not after, that policy year. With respect to an occurrence which begins in one policy year and continues or results in additional loss or damage in a subsequent policy year(s), all loss or damage is deemed to be sustained in the policy year in which the occurrence began.

q. Interruption Of Computer Operations

(1) Subject to all provisions of this Additional Coverage, you may extend the insurance that applies to Business Income and Extra Expense to apply to a suspension of "operations" caused by an interruption in computer operations due to destruction or corruption of "electronic data" due to a Covered Cause of Loss.

(2) With respect to the coverage provided under this Additional Coverage, the Covered Causes of Loss are subject to the following:

(a) Coverage under this Additional Coverage – Interruption Of Computer Operations is limited to the "specified causes of loss" and Collapse.

(b) If the Businessowners Coverage Form is endorsed to add a Covered Cause of Loss, the additional Covered Cause of Loss does not apply to the coverage provided under this Additional Coverage.

(c) The Covered Causes of Loss include a virus, harmful code or similar instruction introduced into or enacted on a computer system (including "electronic data") or a network to which it is connected, designed to damage or destroy any part of the system or disrupt its normal operation. But there is no coverage for an interruption related to manipulation of a computer system (including "electronic data") by any employee, including a temporary or leased employee, or by an entity retained by you, or for you, to inspect, design, install, modify, maintain, repair or replace that system.

(3) The most we will pay under this Additional Coverage – Interruption Of Computer Operations for all loss sustained and expense incurred in any one policy year, regardless of the number of interruptions or the number of premises, locations or computer systems involved, is $10,000 unless a higher Limit of Insurance is shown in the Declarations. If loss payment relating to the first interruption does not exhaust this amount, then the balance is available for loss or expense sustained or incurred as a result of subsequent interruptions in that policy year. A balance remaining at the end of a policy year does not increase the amount of insurance in the next policy year. With respect to any interruption which begins in one policy year and continues or results in additional loss or expense in a subsequent policy year(s), all loss and expense is deemed to be sustained or incurred in the policy year in which the interruption began.

(4) This Additional Coverage – Interruption Of Computer Operations does not apply to loss sustained or expense incurred after the end of the "period of restoration", even if the amount of insurance stated in **(3)** above has not been exhausted.

(5) Coverage for Business Income does not apply when a suspension of "operations" is caused by destruction or corruption of "electronic data", or any loss or damage to "electronic data", except as provided under Paragraphs **(1)** through **(4)** of this Additional Coverage.

(6) Coverage for Extra Expense does not apply when action is taken to avoid or minimize a suspension of "operations" caused by destruction or corruption of "electronic data", or any loss or damage to "electronic data", except as provided under Paragraphs **(1)** through **(4)** of this Additional Coverage.

r. Limited Coverage For "Fungi", Wet Rot, Dry Rot And Bacteria

(1) The coverage described in Paragraphs **r.(2)** and **r.(6)** only applies when the "fungi", wet or dry rot or bacteria are the result of a "specified cause of loss" other than fire or lightning that occurs during the policy period and only if all reasonable means were used to save and preserve the property from further damage at the time of and after that occurrence.

(2) We will pay for loss or damage by "fungi", wet or dry rot or bacteria. As used in this Limited Coverage, the term loss or damage means:

(a) Direct physical loss or damage to Covered Property caused by "fungi", wet or dry rot or bacteria, including the cost of removal of the "fungi", wet or dry rot or bacteria;

(b) The cost to tear out and replace any part of the building or other property as needed to gain access to the "fungi", wet or dry rot or bacteria; and

(c) The cost of testing performed after removal, repair, replacement or restoration of the damaged property is completed, provided there is a reason to believe that "fungi", wet or dry rot or bacteria are present.

(3) The coverage described under this Limited Coverage is limited to $15,000. Regardless of the number of claims, this limit is the most we will pay for the total of all loss or damage arising out of all occurrences of "specified causes of loss" (other than fire or lightning) which take place in a 12-month period (starting with the beginning of the present annual policy period). With respect to a particular occurrence of loss which results in "fungi", wet or dry rot or bacteria, we will not pay more than the total of $15,000 even if the "fungi", wet or dry rot or bacteria continues to be present or active, or recurs, in a later policy period.

(4) The coverage provided under this Limited Coverage does not increase the applicable Limit of Insurance on any Covered Property. If a particular occurrence results in loss or damage by "fungi", wet or dry rot or bacteria, and other loss or damage, we will not pay more, for the total of all loss or damage, than the applicable Limit of Insurance on the affected Covered Property.

If there is covered loss or damage to Covered Property, not caused by "fungi", wet or dry rot or bacteria, loss payment will not be limited by the terms of this Limited Coverage, except to the extent that "fungi", wet or dry rot or bacteria causes an increase in the loss. Any such increase in the loss will be subject to the terms of this Limited Coverage.

(5) The terms of this Limited Coverage do not increase or reduce the coverage provided under the Water Damage, Other Liquids, Powder Or Molten Material Damage or Collapse Additional Coverages.

(6) The following applies only if Business Income and/or Extra Expense Coverage applies to the described premises and only if the suspension of "operations" satisfies all the terms and conditions of the applicable Business Income and/or Extra Expense Additional Coverage.

(a) If the loss which resulted in "fungi", wet or dry rot or bacteria does not in itself necessitate a suspension of "operations", but such suspension is necessary due to loss or damage to property caused by "fungi", wet or dry rot or bacteria, then our payment under the Business Income and/or Extra Expense is limited to the amount of loss and/or expense sustained in a period of not more than 30 days. The days need not be consecutive.

(b) If a covered suspension of "operations" was caused by loss or damage other than "fungi", wet or dry rot or bacteria, but remediation of "fungi", wet or dry rot or bacteria prolongs the "period of restoration", we will pay for loss and/or expense sustained during the delay (regardless of when such a delay occurs during the "period of restoration"), but such coverage is limited to 30 days. The days need not be consecutive.

© ISO Properties, Inc., 2004

6. Coverage Extensions

In addition to the Limits of Insurance of Section I – Property, you may extend the insurance provided by this policy as provided below.

Except as otherwise provided, the following Extensions apply to property located in or on the building described in the Declarations or in the open (or in a vehicle) within 100 feet of the described premises, unless a higher Limit of Insurance is shown in the Declarations.

a. Newly Acquired Or Constructed Property

(1) Buildings

If this policy covers Buildings, you may extend that insurance to apply to:

(a) Your new buildings while being built on the described premises; and

(b) Buildings you acquire at premises other than the one described, intended for:

(i) Similar use as the building described in the Declarations; or

(ii) Use as a warehouse.

The most we will pay for loss or damage under this Extension is $250,000 at each building.

(2) Business Personal Property

If this policy covers Business Personal Property, you may extend that insurance to apply to:

(a) Business Personal Property, including such property that you newly acquire, at any location you acquire;

(b) Business Personal Property, including such property that you newly acquire, located at your newly constructed or acquired buildings at the location described in the Declarations; or

(c) Business Personal Property that you newly acquire, located at the described premises.

This Extension does not apply to personal property that you temporarily acquire in the course of installing or performing work on such property or your wholesale activities.

The most we will pay for loss or damage under this Extension is $100,000 at each building.

(3) Period Of Coverage

With respect to insurance on or at each newly acquired or constructed property, coverage will end when any of the following first occurs:

(a) This policy expires;

(b) 30 days expire after you acquire the property or begin construction of that part of the building that would qualify as covered property; or

(c) You report values to us.

We will charge you additional premium for values reported from the date you acquire the property or begin construction of that part of the building that would qualify as covered property.

b. Personal Property Off Premises

You may extend the insurance provided by this policy to apply to your Covered Property, other than "money" and "securities", "valuable papers and records" or accounts receivable, while it is in the course of transit or at a premises you do not own, lease or operate. The most we will pay for loss or damage under this Extension is $10,000.

c. Outdoor Property

You may extend the insurance provided by this policy to apply to your outdoor fences, radio and television antennas (including satellite dishes), signs (other than signs attached to buildings), trees, shrubs and plants, including debris removal expense. Loss or damage must be caused by or result from any of the following causes of loss:

(1) Fire;

(2) Lightning;

(3) Explosion;

(4) Riot or Civil Commotion; or

(5) Aircraft.

The most we will pay for loss or damage under this Extension is $2,500, but not more than $500 for any one tree, shrub or plant.

d. Personal Effects

You may extend the insurance that applies to Business Personal Property to apply to personal effects owned by you, your officers, your partners or "members", your "managers" or your employees. This extension does not apply to:

(1) Tools or equipment used in your business; or

(2) Loss or damage by theft.

The most we will pay for loss or damage under this Extension is $2,500 at each described premises.

e. Valuable Papers And Records

(1) You may extend the insurance that applies to Business Personal Property to apply to direct physical loss or damage to "valuable papers and records" that you own, or that are in your care, custody or control caused by or resulting from a Covered Cause of Loss. This Coverage Extension includes the cost to research, replace or restore the lost information on "valuable papers and records" for which duplicates do not exist.

(2) This Coverage Extension does not apply to:

(a) Property held as samples or for delivery after sale; and

(b) Property in storage away from the premises shown in the Declarations.

(3) The most we will pay under this Coverage Extension for loss or damage to "valuable papers and records" in any one occurrence at the described premises is $10,000, unless a higher Limit of Insurance for "valuable papers and records" is shown in the Declarations.

For "valuable papers and records" not at the described premises, the most we will pay is $5,000.

(4) Loss or damage to "valuable papers and records" will be valued at the cost of restoration or replacement of the lost or damaged information. To the extent that the contents of the "valuable papers and records" are not restored, the "valuable papers and records" will be valued at the cost of replacement with blank materials of substantially identical type.

(5) Paragraph **B.** Exclusions in Section I – Property does not apply to this Coverage Extension except for:

(a) Paragraph **B.1.c.,** Governmental Action;

(b) Paragraph **B.1.d.,** Nuclear Hazard;

(c) Paragraph **B.1.f.,** War And Military Action;

(d) Paragraph **B.2.f.,** Dishonesty;

(e) Paragraph **B.2.g.,** False Pretense;

(f) Paragraph **B.2.m.(2),** Errors Or Omissions; and

(g) Paragraph **B.3.**

f. Accounts Receivable

(1) You may extend the insurance that applies to Business Personal Property to apply to accounts receivable. We will pay:

(a) All amounts due from your customers that you are unable to collect;

(b) Interest charges on any loan required to offset amounts you are unable to collect pending our payment of these amounts;

(c) Collection expenses in excess of your normal collection expenses that are made necessary by loss or damage; and

(d) Other reasonable expenses that you incur to re-establish your records of accounts receivable;

that result from direct physical loss or damage by any Covered Cause of Loss to your records of accounts receivable.

(2) The most we will pay under this Coverage Extension for loss or damage in any one occurrence at the described premises is $10,000, unless a higher Limit of Insurance for accounts receivable is shown in the Declarations.

For accounts receivable not at the described premises, the most we will pay is $5,000.

(3) Paragraph **B.** Exclusions in Section I – Property does not apply to this Coverage Extension except for:

(a) Paragraph **B.1.c.,** Governmental Action;

       BP 00 03 01 06   □

(b) Paragraph **B.1.d.,** Nuclear Hazard;

(c) Paragraph **B.1.f.,** War And Military Action;

(d) Paragraph **B.2.f.,** Dishonesty;

(e) Paragraph **B.2.g.,** False Pretense;

(f) Paragraph **B.3.;** and

(g) Paragraph **B.5.,** Accounts Receivable Exclusion.

B. Exclusions

1. We will not pay for loss or damage caused directly or indirectly by any of the following. Such loss or damage is excluded regardless of any other cause or event that contributes concurrently or in any sequence to the loss. These exclusions apply whether or not the loss event results in widespread damage or affects a substantial area.

   a. **Ordinance Or Law**

   (1) The enforcement of any ordinance or law:

   (a) Regulating the construction, use or repair of any property; or

   (b) Requiring the tearing down of any property, including the cost of removing its debris.

   (2) This exclusion, Ordinance Or Law, applies whether the loss results from:

   (a) An ordinance or law that is enforced even if the property has not been damaged; or

   (b) The increased costs incurred to comply with an ordinance or law in the course of construction, repair, renovation, remodeling or demolition of property or removal of its debris, following a physical loss to that property.

   b. **Earth Movement**

   (1) Earthquake, including any earth sinking, rising or shifting related to such event;

   (2) Landslide, including any earth sinking, rising or shifting related to such event;

   (3) Mine subsidence, meaning subsidence of a man-made mine, whether or not mining activity has ceased;

   (4) Earth sinking (other than sinkhole collapse), rising or shifting including soil conditions which cause settling, cracking or other disarrangement of foundations or other parts of realty. Soil conditions include contraction, expansion, freezing, thawing, erosion, improperly compacted soil and the action of water under the ground surface.

   But if Earth Movement, as described in Paragraphs **(1)** through **(4)** above, results in fire or explosion, we will pay for the loss or damage caused by that fire or explosion.

   (5) Volcanic eruption, explosion or effusion. But if volcanic eruption, explosion or effusion results in fire, building glass breakage or volcanic action, we will pay for the loss or damage caused by that fire, building glass breakage or volcanic action.

   Volcanic action means direct loss or damage resulting from the eruption of a volcano when the loss or damage is caused by:

   (a) Airborne volcanic blast or airborne shock waves;

   (b) Ash, dust or particulate matter; or

   (c) Lava flow.

   All volcanic eruptions that occur within any 168-hour period will constitute a single occurrence.

   Volcanic action does not include the cost to remove ash, dust or particulate matter that does not cause direct physical loss of or damage to Covered Property.

   c. **Governmental Action**

   Seizure or destruction of property by order of governmental authority.

   But we will pay for loss or damage caused by or resulting from acts of destruction ordered by governmental authority and taken at the time of a fire to prevent its spread, if the fire would be covered under this policy.

   d. **Nuclear Hazard**

   Nuclear reaction or radiation, or radioactive contamination, however caused.

   But if nuclear reaction or radiation, or radioactive contamination, results in fire, we will pay for the loss or damage caused by that fire.

e. Power Failure

The failure of power or other utility service supplied to the described premises, however caused, if the failure occurs away from the described premises. Failure includes lack of sufficient capacity and reduction in supply.

But if the failure of power or other utility service results in a Covered Cause of Loss, we will pay for the loss or damage caused by that Covered Cause of Loss.

This exclusion does not apply to loss or damage to "computer(s)" and "electronic data".

f. War And Military Action

(1) War, including undeclared or civil war;

(2) Warlike action by a military force, including action in hindering or defending against an actual or expected attack, by any government, sovereign or other authority using military personnel or other agents; or

(3) Insurrection, rebellion, revolution, usurped power, or action taken by governmental authority in hindering or defending against any of these.

g. Water

(1) Flood, surface water, waves, tides, tidal waves, overflow of any body of water, or their spray, all whether driven by wind or not;

(2) Mudslide or mudflow;

(3) Water that backs up or overflows from a sewer, drain or sump; or

(4) Water under the ground surface pressing on, or flowing or seeping through:

   (a) Foundations, walls, floors or paved surfaces;

   (b) Basements, whether paved or not; or

   (c) Doors, windows or other openings.

But if Water, as described in Paragraphs (1) through (4), results in fire, explosion or sprinkler leakage, we will pay for the loss or damage caused by that fire, explosion or sprinkler leakage.

h. Certain Computer-Related Losses

(1) The failure, malfunction or inadequacy of:

   (a) Any of the following, whether belonging to any insured or to others:

     (i) "Computer" hardware, including microprocessors or other electronic data processing equipment as may be described elsewhere in this policy;

     (ii) "Computer" application software or other "electronic media and records" as may be described elsewhere in this policy;

     (iii) "Computer" operating systems and related software;

     (iv) "Computer" networks;

     (v) Microprocessors ("computer" chips) not part of any "computer" system; or

     (vi) Any other computerized or electronic equipment or components; or

   (b) Any other products, and any services, data or functions that directly or indirectly use or rely upon, in any manner, any of the items listed in Paragraph (a) above;

due to the inability to correctly recognize, distinguish, interpret or accept one or more dates or times. An example is the inability of computer software to recognize the year 2000.

(2) Any advice, consultation, design, evaluation, inspection, installation, maintenance, repair, replacement or supervision provided or done by you or for you to determine, rectify or test for, any potential or actual problems described in Paragraph (1) above.

However, if excluded loss or damage, as described in Paragraph (1) above results in a "specified cause of loss" under Section I – Property, we will pay only for the loss or damage caused by such "specified cause of loss".

We will not pay for repair, replacement or modification of any items in Paragraph (1)(a) or (1)(b) to correct any deficiencies or change any features.

i. **"Fungi", Wet Rot, Dry Rot And Bacteria**

Presence, growth, proliferation, spread or any activity of "fungi", wet or dry rot or bacteria.

But if "fungi", wet or dry rot or bacteria result in a "specified cause of loss", we will pay for the loss or damage caused by that "specified cause of loss".

This exclusion does not apply:

(1) When "fungi", wet or dry rot or bacteria result from fire or lightning; or

(2) To the extent that coverage is provided in the Additional Coverage – Limited Coverage For "Fungi", Wet Rot, Dry Rot And Bacteria (contained in the Limited Fungi or Bacteria Coverage) if any, with respect to loss or damage by a cause of loss other than fire or lightning.

2. We will not pay for loss or damage caused by or resulting from any of the following:

a. **Electrical Apparatus**

Artificially generated electrical current, including electric arcing, that disturbs electrical devices, appliances or wires.

But if artificially generated electrical current results in fire, we will pay for the loss or damage caused by fire.

We will pay for loss or damage to "computer(s)" due to artificially generated electrical current if such loss or damage is caused by or results from:

(1) An occurrence that took place within 100 feet of the described premises; or

(2) Interruption of electric power supply, power surge, blackout or brownout if the cause of such occurrence took place within 100 feet of the described premises.

b. **Consequential Losses**

Delay, loss of use or loss of market.

c. **Smoke, Vapor, Gas**

Smoke, vapor or gas from agricultural smudging or industrial operations.

d. **Steam Apparatus**

Explosion of steam boilers, steam pipes, steam engines or steam turbines owned or leased by you, or operated under your control. But if explosion of steam boilers, steam pipes, steam engines or steam turbines results in fire or combustion explosion, we will pay for the loss or damage caused by that fire or combustion explosion. We will also pay for loss or damage caused by or resulting from the explosion of gases or fuel within the furnace of any fired vessel or within the flues or passages through which the gases of combustion pass.

e. **Frozen Plumbing**

Water, other liquids, powder or molten material that leaks or flows from plumbing, heating, air conditioning or other equipment (except fire protective systems) caused by or resulting from freezing, unless:

(1) You do your best to maintain heat in the building or structure; or

(2) You drain the equipment and shut off the supply if the heat is not maintained.

f. **Dishonesty**

Dishonest or criminal acts by you, anyone else with an interest in the property, or any of your or their partners, "members", officers, "managers", employees, directors, trustees, authorized representatives or anyone to whom you entrust the property for any purpose:

(1) Acting alone or in collusion with others; or

(2) Whether or not occurring during the hours of employment.

This exclusion does not apply to acts of destruction by your employees; but theft by employees is not covered.

With respect to accounts receivable and "valuable papers and records", this exclusion does not apply to carriers for hire.

This exclusion does not apply to coverage that is provided under the Employee Dishonesty Optional Coverage.

g. False Pretense

Voluntary parting with any property by you or anyone else to whom you have entrusted the property if induced to do so by any fraudulent scheme, trick, device or false pretense.

h. Exposed Property

Rain, snow, ice or sleet to personal property in the open.

i. Collapse

Collapse, except as provided in the Additional Coverage for Collapse. But if collapse results in a Covered Cause of Loss, we will pay for the loss or damage caused by that Covered Cause of Loss.

j. Pollution

We will not pay for loss or damage caused by or resulting from the discharge, dispersal, seepage, migration, release or escape of "pollutants" unless the discharge, dispersal, seepage, migration, release or escape is itself caused by any of the "specified causes of loss". But if the discharge, dispersal, seepage, migration, release or escape of "pollutants" results in a "specified cause of loss", we will pay for the loss or damage caused by that "specified cause of loss".

k. Neglect

Neglect of an insured to use all reasonable means to save and preserve property from further damage at and after the time of loss.

l. Other Types Of Loss

(1) Wear and tear;

(2) Rust or other corrosion, decay, deterioration, hidden or latent defect or any quality in property that causes it to damage or destroy itself;

(3) Smog;

(4) Settling, cracking, shrinking or expansion;

(5) Nesting or infestation, or discharge or release of waste products or secretions, by insects, birds, rodents or other animals;

(6) Mechanical breakdown, including rupture or bursting caused by centrifugal force.

This exclusion does not apply with respect to the breakdown of "computer(s)";

(7) The following causes of loss to personal property:

(a) Dampness or dryness of atmosphere;

(b) Changes in or extremes of temperature; or

(c) Marring or scratching.

But if an excluded cause of loss that is listed in Paragraphs **(1)** through **(7)** above results in a "specified cause of loss" or building glass breakage, we will pay for the loss or damage caused by that "specified cause of loss" or building glass breakage.

m. Errors Or Omissions

Errors or omissions in:

(1) Programming, processing or storing data, as described under "electronic data" or in any "computer" operations; or

(2) Processing or copying "valuable papers and records".

However, we will pay for direct physical loss or damage caused by resulting fire or explosion if these causes of loss would be covered by this coverage form.

n. Installation, Testing, Repair

Errors or deficiency in design, installation, testing, maintenance, modification or repair of your "computer" system including "electronic data".

However, we will pay for direct physical loss or damage caused by resulting fire or explosion if these causes of loss would be covered by this coverage form.

o. Electrical Disturbance

Electrical or magnetic injury, disturbance or erasure of "electronic data", except as provided for under the Additional Coverages of Section I – Property.

However, we will pay for direct loss or damage caused by lightning.

p. Continuous Or Repeated Seepage Or Leakage Of Water

Continuous or repeated seepage or leakage of water, or the presence or condensation of humidity, moisture or vapor, that occurs over a period of 14 days or more.

3. We will not pay for loss or damage caused by or resulting from any of the following Paragraphs **a.** through **c.** But if an excluded cause of loss that is listed in Paragraphs **a.** through **c.** results in a Covered Cause of Loss, we will pay for the loss or damage caused by that Covered Cause of Loss.

   a. **Weather Conditions**

   Weather conditions. But this exclusion only applies if weather conditions contribute in any way with a cause or event excluded in Paragraph **B.1.** above to produce the loss or damage.

   b. **Acts Or Decisions**

   Acts or decisions, including the failure to act or decide, of any person, group, organization or governmental body.

   c. **Negligent Work**

   Faulty, inadequate or defective:

   (1) Planning, zoning, development, surveying, siting;

   (2) Design, specifications, workmanship, repair, construction, renovation, remodeling, grading, compaction;

   (3) Materials used in repair, construction, renovation or remodeling; or

   (4) Maintenance;

   of part or all of any property on or off the described premises.

4. **Business Income And Extra Expense Exclusions**

   a. We will not pay for:

   (1) Any Extra Expense, or increase of Business Income loss, caused by or resulting from:

   (a) Delay in rebuilding, repairing or replacing the property or resuming "operations", due to interference at the location of the rebuilding, repair or replacement by strikers or other persons; or

   (b) Suspension, lapse or cancellation of any license, lease or contract. But if the suspension, lapse or cancellation is directly caused by the suspension of "operations", we will cover such loss that affects your Business Income during the "period of restoration".

   (2) Any other consequential loss.

   b. With respect to this exclusion, suspension means:

   (1) The partial slowdown or complete cessation of your business activities; and

   (2) That a part or all of the described premises is rendered untenantable, if coverage for Business Income applies.

5. **Accounts Receivable Exclusion**

   The following additional exclusion applies to the Accounts Receivable Coverage Extension:

   We will not pay for:

   a. Loss or damage caused by or resulting from alteration, falsification, concealment or destruction of records of accounts receivable done to conceal the wrongful giving, taking or withholding of "money", "securities" or other property.

   This exclusion applies only to the extent of the wrongful giving, taking or withholding.

   b. Loss or damage caused by or resulting from bookkeeping, accounting or billing errors or omissions.

   c. Any loss or damage that requires any audit of records or any inventory computation to prove its factual existence.

C. Limits Of Insurance

1. The most we will pay for loss or damage in any one occurrence is the applicable Limit of Insurance of Section I – Property shown in the Declarations.

2. The most we will pay for loss of or damage to outdoor signs attached to buildings is $1,000 per sign in any one occurrence.

3. The limits applicable to the Coverage Extensions and the Fire Department Service Charge and Pollutant Clean Up and Removal Additional Coverages are in addition to the Limits of Insurance of Section I – Property.

4. **Building Limit – Automatic Increase**

   a. The Limit of Insurance for Buildings will automatically increase by the annual percentage shown in the Declarations.

   b. The amount of increase will be:

   (1) The Building limit that applied on the most recent of the policy inception date, the policy anniversary date, or any other policy change amending the Building limit, times

   (2) The percentage of annual increase shown in the Declarations, expressed as a decimal (example: 8% is .08), times

(3) The number of days since the beginning of the current policy year, or the effective date of the most recent policy change amending the Building limit, divided by 365.

Example:

If: The applicable Building limit is $100,000. The annual percentage increase is 8%. The number of days since the beginning of the policy year (or last policy change) is 146.

The amount of increase is

$100,000 x .08 x 146 ÷ 365 = $3,200.

5. Business Personal Property Limit – Seasonal Increase

a. The Limit of Insurance for Business Personal Property will automatically increase by 25% to provide for seasonal variations.

b. This increase will apply only if the Limit of Insurance shown for Business Personal Property in the Declarations is at least 100% of your average monthly values during the lesser of:

(1) The 12 months immediately preceding the date the loss or damage occurs; or

(2) The period of time you have been in business as of the date the loss or damage occurs.

D. Deductibles

1. We will not pay for loss or damage in any one occurrence until the amount of loss or damage exceeds the Deductible shown in the Declarations. We will then pay the amount of loss or damage in excess of the Deductible up to the applicable Limit of Insurance of Section I – Property.

2. Regardless of the amount of the Deductible, the most we will deduct from any loss or damage for Glass and under all of the following Optional Coverages in any one occurrence is the Optional Coverage/Glass Deductible shown in the Declarations:

a. Money and Securities;

b. Employee Dishonesty; and

c. Outdoor Signs.

But this Optional Coverage/Glass Deductible will not increase the Deductible shown in the Declarations. This Deductible will be used to satisfy the requirements of the Deductible in the Declarations.

3. No deductible applies to the following Additional Coverages:

a. Fire Department Service Charge;

b. Business Income;

c. Extra Expense;

d. Civil Authority; and

e. Fire Extinguisher Systems Recharge Expense.

E. Property Loss Conditions

1. Abandonment

There can be no abandonment of any property to us.

2. Appraisal

If we and you disagree on the amount of loss, either may make written demand for an appraisal of the loss. In this event, each party will select a competent and impartial appraiser. The two appraisers will select an umpire. If they cannot agree, either may request that selection be made by a judge of a court having jurisdiction. The appraisers will state separately the amount of loss. If they fail to agree, they will submit their differences to the umpire. A decision agreed to by any two will be binding. Each party will:

a. Pay its chosen appraiser; and

b. Bear the other expenses of the appraisal and umpire equally.

If there is an appraisal, we will still retain our right to deny the claim.

3. Duties In The Event Of Loss Or Damage

a. You must see that the following are done in the event of loss or damage to Covered Property:

(1) Notify the police if a law may have been broken.

(2) Give us prompt notice of the loss or damage. Include a description of the property involved.

(3) As soon as possible, give us a description of how, when and where the loss or damage occurred.

(4) Take all reasonable steps to protect the Covered Property from further damage, and keep a record of your expenses necessary to protect the Covered Property, for consideration in the settlement of the claim. This will not increase the Limits of Insurance of Section I – Property. However, we will not pay for any subsequent loss or damage resulting from a cause of loss that is not a Covered Cause of Loss. Also, if feasible, set the damaged property aside and in the best possible order for examination.

(5) At our request, give us complete inventories of the damaged and undamaged property. Include quantities, costs, values and amount of loss claimed.

(6) As often as may be reasonably required, permit us to inspect the property proving the loss or damage and examine your books and records.

Also permit us to take samples of damaged and undamaged property for inspection, testing and analysis, and permit us to make copies from your books and records.

(7) Send us a signed, sworn proof of loss containing the information we request to investigate the claim. You must do this within 60 days after our request. We will supply you with the necessary forms.

(8) Cooperate with us in the investigation or settlement of the claim.

(9) Resume all or part of your "operations" as quickly as possible.

b. We may examine any insured under oath, while not in the presence of any other insured and at such times as may be reasonably required, about any matter relating to this insurance or the claim, including an insured's books and records. In the event of an examination, an insured's answers must be signed.

4. Legal Action Against Us

No one may bring a legal action against us under this insurance unless:

a. There has been full compliance with all of the terms of this insurance; and

b. The action is brought within 2 years after the date on which the direct physical loss or damage occurred.

5. Loss Payment

In the event of loss or damage covered by this policy:

a. At our option, we will either:

(1) Pay the value of lost or damaged property;

(2) Pay the cost of repairing or replacing the lost or damaged property;

(3) Take all or any part of the property at an agreed or appraised value; or

(4) Repair, rebuild or replace the property with other property of like kind and quality, subject to Paragraph **d.(1)(e)** below.

b. We will give notice of our intentions within 30 days after we receive the sworn proof of loss.

c. We will not pay you more than your financial interest in the Covered Property.

d. Except as provided in Paragraphs **(2)** through **(7)** below, we will determine the value of Covered Property as follows:

(1) At replacement cost without deduction for depreciation, subject to the following:

(a) If, at the time of loss, the Limit of Insurance on the lost or damaged property is 80% or more of the full replacement cost of the property immediately before the loss, we will pay the cost to repair or replace, after application of the deductible and without deduction for depreciation, but not more than the least of the following amounts:

(i) The Limit of Insurance under Section I – Property that applies to the lost or damaged property;

(ii) The cost to replace, on the same premises, the lost or damaged property with other property:

i. Of comparable material and quality; and

ii. Used for the same purpose; or

(iii) The amount that you actually spend that is necessary to repair or replace the lost or damaged property.

If a building is rebuilt at a new premises, the cost is limited to the cost which would have been incurred had the building been built at the original premises.

(b) If, at the time of loss, the Limit of Insurance applicable to the lost or damaged property is less than 80% of the full replacement cost of the property immediately before the loss, we will pay the greater of the following amounts, but not more than the Limit of Insurance that applies to the property:

   (i) The actual cash value of the lost or damaged property; or

   (ii) A proportion of the cost to repair or replace the lost or damaged property, after application of the deductible and without deduction for depreciation. This proportion will equal the ratio of the applicable Limit of Insurance to 80% of the cost of repair or replacement.

(c) You may make a claim for loss or damage covered by this insurance on an actual cash value basis instead of on a replacement cost basis. In the event you elect to have loss or damage settled on an actual cash value basis, you may still make a claim on a replacement cost basis if you notify us of your intent to do so within 180 days after the loss or damage.

(d) We will not pay on a replacement cost basis for any loss or damage:

   (i) Until the lost or damaged property is actually repaired or replaced; and

   (ii) Unless the repairs or replacement are made as soon as reasonably possible after the loss or damage.

   However, if the cost to repair or replace the damaged building property is $2,500 or less, we will settle the loss according to the provisions of Paragraphs **d.(1)(a)** and **d.(1)(b)** above whether or not the actual repair or replacement is complete.

(e) The cost to repair, rebuild or replace does not include the increased cost attributable to enforcement of any ordinance or law regulating the construction, use or repair of any property.

(2) If the "Actual Cash Value – Buildings" option applies, as shown in the Declarations, Paragraph **(1)** above does not apply to Buildings. Instead, we will determine the value of Buildings at actual cash value.

(3) The following property at actual cash value:

   (a) Used or second-hand merchandise held in storage or for sale;

   (b) Property of others. However, if an item(s) of personal property of others is subject to a written contract which governs your liability for loss or damage to that item(s), then valuation of that item(s) will be based on the amount for which you are liable under such contract, but not to exceed the lesser of the replacement cost of the property or the applicable Limit of Insurance;

   (c) Household contents, except personal property in apartments or rooms furnished by you as landlord;

   (d) Manuscripts; and

   (e) Works of art, antiques or rare articles, including etchings, pictures, statuary, marble, bronzes, porcelain and bric-a-brac.

(4) Glass at the cost of replacement with safety glazing material if required by law.

(5) Tenants' Improvements and Betterments at:

   (a) Replacement cost if you make repairs promptly.

   (b) A proportion of your original cost if you do not make repairs promptly. We will determine the proportionate value as follows:

     (i) Multiply the original cost by the number of days from the loss or damage to the expiration of the lease; and

     (ii) Divide the amount determined in **(i)** above by the number of days from the installation of improvements to the expiration of the lease.

   If your lease contains a renewal option, the expiration of the renewal option period will replace the expiration of the lease in this procedure.

(c) Nothing if others pay for repairs or replacement.

(6) Applicable only to the Optional Coverages:

(a) "Money" at its face value; and

(b) "Securities" at their value at the close of business on the day the loss is discovered.

(7) Applicable only to Accounts Receivable:

(a) If you cannot accurately establish the amount of accounts receivable outstanding as of the time of loss or damage:

(i) We will determine the total of the average monthly amounts of accounts receivable for the 12 months immediately preceding the month in which the loss or damage occurs; and

(ii) We will adjust that total for any normal fluctuations in the amount of accounts receivable for the month in which the loss or damage occurred or for any demonstrated variance from the average for that month.

(b) The following will be deducted from the total amount of accounts receivable, however that amount is established:

(i) The amount of the accounts for which there is no loss or damage;

(ii) The amount of the accounts that you are able to re-establish or collect;

(iii) An amount to allow for probable bad debts that you are normally unable to collect; and

(iv) All unearned interest and service charges.

e. Our payment for loss of or damage to personal property of others will only be for the account of the owners of the property. We may adjust losses with the owners of lost or damaged property if other than you. If we pay the owners, such payments will satisfy your claims against us for the owners' property. We will not pay the owners more than their financial interest in the Covered Property.

f. We may elect to defend you against suits arising from claims of owners of property. We will do this at our expense.

g. We will pay for covered loss or damage within 30 days after we receive the sworn proof of loss, provided you have complied with all of the terms of this policy, and

(1) We have reached agreement with you on the amount of loss; or

(2) An appraisal award has been made.

6. **Recovered Property**

If either you or we recover any property after loss settlement, that party must give the other prompt notice. At your option, you may retain the property. But then you must return to us the amount we paid to you for the property. We will pay recovery expenses and the expenses to repair the recovered property, subject to the Limits of Insurance of Section I – Property.

7. **Resumption Of Operations**

We will reduce the amount of your:

a. Business Income loss, other than Extra Expense, to the extent you can resume your "operations", in whole or in part, by using damaged or undamaged property (including merchandise or stock) at the described premises or elsewhere.

b. Extra Expense loss to the extent you can return "operations" to normal and discontinue such Extra Expense.

8. **Vacancy**

a. **Description Of Terms**

(1) As used in this Vacancy Condition, the term building and the term vacant have the meanings set forth in Paragraphs (a) and (b) below:

(a) When this policy is issued to a tenant, and with respect to that tenant's interest in Covered Property, building means the unit or suite rented or leased to the tenant. Such building is vacant when it does not contain enough business personal property to conduct customary operations.

(b) When this policy is issued to the owner or general lessee of a building, building means the entire building. Such building is vacant unless at least 31% of its total square footage is:

(i) Rented to a lessee or sub-lessee and used by the lessee or sub-lessee to conduct its customary operations; and/or

(ii) Used by the building owner to conduct customary operations.

(2) Buildings under construction or renovation are not considered vacant.

b. Vacancy Provisions

If the building where loss or damage occurs has been vacant for more than 60 consecutive days before that loss or damage occurs:

(1) We will not pay for any loss or damage caused by any of the following even if they are Covered Causes of Loss:

(a) Vandalism;

(b) Sprinkler leakage, unless you have protected the system against freezing;

(c) Building glass breakage;

(d) Water damage;

(e) Theft; or

(f) Attempted theft.

(2) With respect to Covered Causes of Loss other than those listed in Paragraphs **(1)(a)** through **(1)(f)** above, we will reduce the amount we would otherwise pay for the loss or damage by 15%.

F. Property General Conditions

1. Control Of Property

Any act or neglect of any person other than you beyond your direction or control will not affect this insurance.

The breach of any condition of this Coverage Form at any one or more locations will not affect coverage at any location where, at the time of loss or damage, the breach of condition does not exist.

2. Mortgageholders

a. The term "mortgageholder" includes trustee.

b. We will pay for covered loss of or damage to buildings or structures to each mortgageholder shown in the Declarations in their order of precedence, as interests may appear.

c. The mortgageholder has the right to receive loss payment even if the mortgageholder has started foreclosure or similar action on the building or structure.

d. If we deny your claim because of your acts or because you have failed to comply with the terms of this policy, the mortgageholder will still have the right to receive loss payment if the mortgageholder:

(1) Pays any premium due under this policy at our request if you have failed to do so;

(2) Submits a signed, sworn proof of loss within 60 days after receiving notice from us of your failure to do so; and

(3) Has notified us of any change in ownership, occupancy or substantial change in risk known to the mortgageholder.

All of the terms of this policy will then apply directly to the mortgageholder.

e. If we pay the mortgageholder for any loss or damage and deny payment to you because of your acts or because you have failed to comply with the terms of this policy:

(1) The mortgageholder's rights under the mortgage will be transferred to us to the extent of the amount we pay; and

(2) The mortgageholder's right to recover the full amount of the mortgageholder's claim will not be impaired.

At our option, we may pay to the mortgageholder the whole principal on the mortgage plus any accrued interest. In this event, your mortgage and note will be transferred to us and you will pay your remaining mortgage debt to us.

f. If we cancel this policy, we will give written notice to the mortgageholder at least:

(1) 10 days before the effective date of cancellation if we cancel for your non-payment of premium; or

(2) 30 days before the effective date of cancellation if we cancel for any other reason.

g. If we elect not to renew this policy, we will give written notice to the mortgageholder at least 10 days before the expiration date of this policy.

3. No Benefit To Bailee

No person or organization, other than you, having custody of Covered Property will benefit from this insurance.

4. Policy Period, Coverage Territory

Under Section **I** – Property:

a. We cover loss or damage commencing:

(1) During the policy period shown in the Declarations; and

(2) Within the coverage territory or, with respect to property in transit, while it is between points in the coverage territory.

b. The coverage territory is:

(1) The United States of America (including its territories and possessions);

© ISO Properties, Inc., 2004 **BP 00 03 01 06** □

(2) Puerto Rico; and

(3) Canada.

G. Optional Coverages

If shown as applicable in the Declarations, the following Optional Coverages also apply. These coverages are subject to the terms and conditions applicable to property coverage in this policy, except as provided below.

1. Outdoor Signs

a. We will pay for direct physical loss of or damage to all outdoor signs at the described premises:

(1) Owned by you; or

(2) Owned by others but in your care, custody or control.

b. Paragraph **A.3.**, Covered Causes Of Loss, and Paragraph **B.**, Exclusions in Section **I** – Property, do not apply to this Optional Coverage, except for:

(1) Paragraph **B.1.c.**, Governmental Action;

(2) Paragraph **B.1.d.**, Nuclear Hazard; and

(3) Paragraph **B.1.f.**, War And Military Action.

c. We will not pay for loss or damage caused by or resulting from:

(1) Wear and tear;

(2) Hidden or latent defect;

(3) Rust;

(4) Corrosion; or

(5) Mechanical breakdown.

d. The most we will pay for loss or damage in any one occurrence is the Limit of Insurance for Outdoor Signs shown in the Declarations.

e. The provisions of this Optional Coverage supersede all other references to outdoor signs in this policy.

2. Money And Securities

a. We will pay for loss of "money" and "securities" used in your business while at a bank or savings institution, within your living quarters or the living quarters of your partners or any employee having use and custody of the property, at the described premises, or in transit between any of these places, resulting directly from:

(1) Theft, meaning any act of stealing;

(2) Disappearance; or

(3) Destruction.

b. In addition to the Limitations and Exclusions applicable to Section **I** – Property, we will not pay for loss:

(1) Resulting from accounting or arithmetical errors or omissions;

(2) Due to the giving or surrendering of property in any exchange or purchase; or

(3) Of property contained in any "money"-operated device unless the amount of "money" deposited in it is recorded by a continuous recording instrument in the device.

c. The most we will pay for loss in any one occurrence is:

(1) The limit shown in the Declarations for Inside the Premises for "money" and "securities" while:

(a) In or on the described premises; or

(b) Within a bank or savings institution; and

(2) The limit shown in the Declarations for Outside the Premises for "money" and "securities" while anywhere else.

d. All loss:

(1) Caused by one or more persons; or

(2) Involving a single act or series of related acts;

is considered one occurrence.

e. You must keep records of all "money" and "securities" so we can verify the amount of any loss or damage.

3. Employee Dishonesty

a. We will pay for direct loss of or damage to Business Personal Property and "money" and "securities" resulting from dishonest acts committed by any of your employees acting alone or in collusion with other persons (except you or your partner) with the manifest intent to:

(1) Cause you to sustain loss or damage; and also

(2) Obtain financial benefit (other than salaries, commissions, fees, bonuses, promotions, awards, profit sharing, pensions or other employee benefits earned in the normal course of employment) for:

(a) Any employee; or

(b) Any other person or organization.

b. We will not pay for loss or damage:

(1) Resulting from any dishonest or criminal act that you or any of your partners or "members" commit whether acting alone or in collusion with other persons.

(2) Resulting from any dishonest act committed by any of your employees (except as provided in Paragraph **a.**), "managers" or directors:

(a) Whether acting alone or in collusion with other persons; or

(b) While performing services for you or otherwise.

(3) The only proof of which as to its existence or amount is:

(a) An inventory computation; or

(b) A profit and loss computation.

c. The most we will pay for loss or damage in any one occurrence is the Limit of Insurance for Employee Dishonesty shown in the Declarations.

d. All loss or damage:

(1) Caused by one or more persons; or

(2) Involving a single act or series of acts;

is considered one occurrence.

e. If any loss is covered:

(1) Partly by this insurance; and

(2) Partly by any prior cancelled or terminated insurance that we or any affiliate had issued to you or any predecessor in interest;

the most we will pay is the larger of the amount recoverable under this insurance or the prior insurance.

We will pay only for loss or damage you sustain through acts committed or events occurring during the Policy Period. Regardless of the number of years this policy remains in force or the number of premiums paid, no Limit of Insurance cumulates from year to year or period to period.

f. This Optional Coverage is cancelled as to any employee immediately upon discovery by:

(1) You; or

(2) Any of your partners, "members", "managers", officers or directors not in collusion with the employee;

of any dishonest act committed by that employee before or after being hired by you.

g. We will pay only for covered loss or damage sustained during the policy period and discovered no later than one year from the end of the policy period.

h. If you (or any predecessor in interest) sustained loss or damage during the policy period of any prior insurance that you could have recovered under that insurance except that the time within which to discover loss or damage had expired, we will pay for it under this Optional Coverage, provided:

(1) This Optional Coverage became effective at the time of cancellation or termination of the prior insurance; and

(2) The loss or damage would have been covered by this Optional Coverage had it been in effect when the acts or events causing the loss or damage were committed or occurred.

i. The insurance under Paragraph **h.** above is part of, not in addition to, the Limit of Insurance applying to this Optional Coverage and is limited to the lesser of the amount recoverable under:

(1) This Optional Coverage as of its effective date; or

(2) The prior insurance had it remained in effect.

j. With respect to the Employee Dishonesty Optional Coverage in Paragraph **G.3.**, employee means:

(1) Any natural person:

(a) While in your service or for 30 days after termination of service;

(b) Who you compensate directly by salary, wages or commissions; and

(c) Who you have the right to direct and control while performing services for you:

(2) Any natural person who is furnished temporarily to you:

(a) To substitute for a permanent employee as defined in Paragraph **(1)** above, who is on leave; or

(b) To meet seasonal or short-term work load conditions:

(3) Any natural person who is leased to you under a written agreement between you and a labor leasing firm, to perform duties related to the conduct of your business, but does not mean a temporary employee as defined in Paragraph **(2)** above;

(4) Any natural person who is a former employee, director, partner, member, manager, representative or trustee retained as a consultant while performing services for you; or

(5) Any natural person who is a guest student or intern pursuing studies or duties, excluding, however, any such person while having care and custody of property outside any building you occupy in conducting your business.

But employee does not mean:

(1) Any agent, broker, factor, commission merchant, consignee, independent contractor or representative of the same general character; or

(2) Any "manager", director or trustee except while performing acts coming within the usual duties of an employee.

4. Mechanical Breakdown

a. We will pay for direct damage to Covered Property caused by an Accident to an Object. The Object must be:

(1) Owned by you or in your care, custody or control; and

(2) At the described premises.

b. Accident means a sudden and accidental breakdown of the Object or a part of the Object. At the time the breakdown occurs, it must manifest itself by physical damage to the Object that necessitates repair or replacement.

c. None of the following is an Accident:

(1) Depletion, deterioration, corrosion or erosion;

(2) Wear and tear;

(3) Leakage at any valve, fitting, shaft seal, gland packing, joint or connection;

(4) Breakdown of any vacuum tube, gas tube or brush;

(5) Breakdown of any "computer", including "computer(s)" used to operate production type machinery or equipment;

(6) Breakdown of any structure or foundation supporting the Object or any of its parts;

(7) The functioning of any safety or protective device; or

(8) The explosion of gases or fuel within the furnace of any Object or within the flues or passages through which the gases of combustion pass.

d. Object means any of the following equipment:

(1) Boiler and Pressure Vessels:

(a) Steam heating boilers and condensate return tanks used with them;

(b) Hot water heating boilers and expansion tanks used with them;

(c) Hot water supply boilers;

(d) Other fired or unfired vessels used for maintenance or service of the described premises but not used for processing or manufacturing;

(e) Steam boiler piping, valves, fittings, traps and separators, but only if they:

(i) Are on your premises or between parts of your premises;

(ii) Contain steam or condensate of steam; and

(iii) Are not part of any other vessel or apparatus;

(f) Feed water piping between any steam boiler and a feed pump or injector.

(2) Air Conditioning Units – Any air conditioning unit that has a capacity of 60,000 Btu or more, including:

(a) Inductors, convectors and coils that make use of a refrigerant and form part of a cooling, humidity control or space heating system;

(b) Interconnecting piping, valves and fittings containing only a refrigerant, water, brine or other solution;

(c) Vessels heated directly or indirectly that:

(i) Form part of an absorption type system; and

(ii) Function as a generator, regenerator or concentrator;

(d) Compressors, pumps, fans and blowers used solely with the system together with their driving electric motors; and

(e) Control equipment used solely with the system.

e. Object does not mean:

(1) As Boiler and Pressure Vessels:

(a) Equipment that is not under internal vacuum or internal pressure other than weight of contents;

(b) Boiler settings;

(c) Insulating or refractory material; or

(d) Electrical, reciprocating or rotating apparatus within or forming a part of the boiler or vessel.

(2) As Air Conditioning Units, any:

(a) Vessel, cooling tower, reservoir or other source of cooling water for a condenser or compressor, or any water piping leading to or from that source; or

(b) Wiring or piping leading to or from the unit.

f. We will not pay for an Accident to any Object while being tested.

g. Suspension

Whenever an Object is found to be in, or exposed to, a dangerous condition, any of our representatives may immediately suspend the insurance against loss from an Accident to that Object. This can be done by delivering or mailing a written notice of suspension to:

(1) Your last known address; or

(2) The address where the Object is located.

If we suspend your insurance, you will get a pro rata refund of premium. But the suspension will be effective even if we have not yet made or offered a refund.

H. Property Definitions

1. "Computer" means:

a. Programmable electronic equipment that is used to store, retrieve and process data; and

b. Associated peripheral equipment that provides communication, including input and output functions such as printing and auxiliary functions such as data transmission.

"Computer" does not include those used to operate production type machinery or equipment.

2. "Counterfeit money" means an imitation of "money" that is intended to deceive and to be taken as genuine.

3. "Electronic data" means information, facts or computer programs stored as or on, created or used on, or transmitted to or from computer software (including systems and applications software), on hard or floppy disks, CD-ROMs, tapes, drives, cells, data processing devices or any other repositories of computer software which are used with electronically controlled equipment. The term computer programs, referred to in the foregoing description of electronic data, means a set of related electronic instructions which direct the operations and functions of a "computer" or device connected to it, which enable the "computer" or device to receive, process, store, retrieve or send data.

4. "Fungi" means any type or form of fungus, including mold or mildew, and any mycotoxins, spores, scents or by-products produced or released by fungi.

5. "Manager" means a person serving in a directorial capacity for a limited liability company.

6. "Member" means an owner of a limited liability company represented by its membership interest, who also may serve as a "manager".

7. "Money" means:

a. Currency, coins and bank notes in current use and having a face value; and

b. Travelers checks, register checks and money orders held for sale to the public.

8. "Operations" means your business activities occurring at the described premises.

9. "Period of restoration":

a. Means the period of time that:

(1) Begins:

(a) 72 hours after the time of direct physical loss or damage for Business Income Coverage; or

(b) Immediately after the time of direct physical loss or damage for Extra Expense Coverage;

caused by or resulting from any Covered Cause of Loss at the described premises; and

(2) Ends on the earlier of:

(a) The date when the property at the described premises should be repaired, rebuilt or replaced with reasonable speed and similar quality; or

(b) The date when business is resumed at a new permanent location.

b. Does not include any increased period required due to the enforcement of any ordinance or law that:

(1) Regulates the construction, use or repair, or requires the tearing down of any property; or

(2) Requires any insured or others to test for, monitor, clean up, remove, contain, treat, detoxify or neutralize, or in any way respond to or assess the effects of "pollutants".

The expiration date of this policy will not cut short the "period of restoration".

10. "Pollutants" means any solid, liquid, gaseous or thermal irritant or contaminant, including smoke, vapor, soot, fumes, acids, alkalis, chemicals and waste. Waste includes materials to be recycled, reconditioned or reclaimed.

11. "Securities" means negotiable and non-negotiable instruments or contracts representing either "money" or other property and includes:

a. Tokens, tickets, revenue and other stamps (whether represented by actual stamps or unused value in a meter) in current use; and

b. Evidences of debt issued in connection with credit or charge cards, which cards are not issued by you;

but does not include "money".

12. "Specified causes of loss" means the following:

Fire; lightning; explosion; windstorm or hail; smoke; aircraft or vehicles; riot or civil commotion; vandalism; leakage from fire extinguishing equipment; sinkhole collapse; volcanic action; falling objects; weight of snow, ice or sleet; water damage.

a. Sinkhole collapse means the sudden sinking or collapse of land into underground empty spaces created by the action of water on limestone or dolomite. This cause of loss does not include:

(1) The cost of filling sinkholes; or

(2) Sinking or collapse of land into man-made underground cavities.

b. Falling objects does not include loss of or damage to:

(1) Personal property in the open; or

(2) The interior of a building or structure, or property inside a building or structure, unless the roof or an outside wall of the building or structure is first damaged by a falling object.

c. Water damage means accidental discharge or leakage of water or steam as the direct result of the breaking apart or cracking of any part of a system or appliance (other than a sump system including its related equipment and parts) containing water or steam.

13. "Stock" means merchandise held in storage or for sale, raw materials and in-process or finished goods, including supplies used in their packing or shipping.

14. "Valuable papers and records" means inscribed, printed or written:

a. Documents;

b. Manuscripts; and

c. Records;

including abstracts, books, deeds, drawings, films, maps or mortgages.

But "valuable papers and records" does not mean "money" or "securities".

SECTION II – LIABILITY

A. Coverages

1. Business Liability

a. We will pay those sums that the insured becomes legally obligated to pay as damages because of "bodily injury", "property damage" or "personal and advertising injury" to which this insurance applies. We will have the right and duty to defend the insured against any "suit" seeking those damages. However, we will have no duty to defend the insured against any "suit" seeking damages for "bodily injury", "property damage" or "personal and advertising injury", to which this insurance does not apply. We may at our discretion, investigate any "occurrence" and settle any claim or "suit" that may result. But:

(1) The amount we will pay for damages is limited as described in Paragraph **D.** – Liability And Medical Expenses Limits Of Insurance in Section **II** – Liability; and

(2) Our right and duty to defend end when we have used up the applicable Limit of Insurance in the payment of judgments or settlements or medical expenses.

No other obligation or liability to pay sums or perform acts or services is covered unless explicitly provided for under Paragraph **f.** Coverage Extension – Supplementary Payments.

b. This insurance applies:

(1) To "bodily injury" and "property damage" only if:

(a) The "bodily injury" or "property damage" is caused by an "occurrence" that takes place in the "coverage territory";

(b) The "bodily injury" or "property damage" occurs during the policy period; and

(c) Prior to the policy period, no insured listed under Paragraph **C.1.** Who Is An Insured and no "employee" authorized by you to give or receive notice of an "occurrence" or claim, knew that the "bodily injury" or "property damage" had occurred, in whole or in part. If such a listed insured or authorized "employee" knew, prior to the policy period, that the "bodily injury" or "property damage" occurred, then any continuation, change or resumption of such "bodily injury" or "property damage" during or after the policy period will be deemed to have been known before the policy period.

(2) To "personal and advertising injury" caused by an offense arising out of your business, but only if the offense was committed in the "coverage territory" during the policy period.

c. "Bodily injury" or "property damage" which occurs during the policy period and was not, prior to the policy period, known to have occurred by any insured listed under Paragraph **C.1.** Who Is An Insured or any "employee" authorized by you to give or receive notice of an "occurrence" or claim, includes any continuation, change or resumption of "bodily injury" or "property damage" after the end of the policy period.

d. "Bodily injury" or "property damage" will be deemed to have been known to have occurred at the earliest time when any insured listed under Paragraph **C.1.** Who Is An Insured or any "employee" authorized by you to give or receive notice of an "occurrence" or claim:

(1) Reports all, or any part, of the "bodily injury" or "property damage" to us or any other insurer;

(2) Receives a written or verbal demand or claim for damages because of the "bodily injury" or "property damage"; or

(3) Becomes aware by any other means that "bodily injury" or "property damage" has occurred or has begun to occur.

e. Damages because of "bodily injury" include damages claimed by any person or organization for care, loss of services or death resulting at any time from the "bodily injury".

f. Coverage Extension – Supplementary Payments

(1) We will pay, with respect to any claim we investigate or settle, or any "suit" against an insured we defend:

(a) All expenses we incur.

(b) Up to $250 for cost of bail bonds required because of accidents or traffic law violations arising out of the use of any vehicle to which Business Liability Coverage for "bodily injury" applies. We do not have to furnish these bonds.

(c) The cost of bonds to release attachments, but only for bond amounts within our Limit of Insurance. We do not have to furnish these bonds.

(d) All reasonable expenses incurred by the insured at our request to assist us in the investigation or defense of the claim or "suit", including actual loss of earnings up to $250 a day because of time off from work.

(e) All costs taxed against the insured in the "suit".

(f) Prejudgment interest awarded against the insured on that part of the judgment we pay. If we make an offer to pay the Limit of Insurance, we will not pay any prejudgment interest based on that period of time after the offer.

(g) All interest on the full amount of any judgment that accrues after entry of the judgment and before we have paid, offered to pay, or deposited in court the part of the judgment that is within our Limit of Insurance.

These payments will not reduce the limit of liability.

(2) If we defend an insured against a "suit" and an indemnitee of the insured is also named as a party to the "suit", we will defend that indemnitee if all of the following conditions are met:

(a) The "suit" against the indemnitee seeks damages for which the insured has assumed the liability of the indemnitee in a contract or agreement that is an "insured contract";

(b) This insurance applies to such liability assumed by the insured;

(c) The obligation to defend, or the cost of the defense of, that indemnitee, has also been assumed by the insured in the same "insured contract";

(d) The allegations in the "suit" and the information we know about the "occurrence" are such that no conflict appears to exist between the interests of the insured and the interests of the indemnitee;

(e) The indemnitee and the insured ask us to conduct and control the defense of that indemnitee against such "suit" and agree that we can assign the same counsel to defend the insured and the indemnitee; and

(f) The indemnitee:

(i) Agrees in writing to:

i. Cooperate with us in the investigation, settlement or defense of the "suit";

ii. Immediately send us copies of any demands, notices, summonses or legal papers received in connection with the "suit";

iii. Notify any other insurer whose coverage is available to the indemnitee; and

iv. Cooperate with us with respect to coordinating other applicable insurance available to the indemnitee; and

(ii) Provides us with written authorization to:

i. Obtain records and other information related to the "suit"; and

ii. Conduct and control the defense of the indemnitee in such "suit".

(3) So long as the conditions in Paragraph **(2)** are met, attorneys' fees incurred by us in the defense of that indemnitee, necessary litigation expenses incurred by us and necessary litigation expenses incurred by the indemnitee at our request will be paid as Supplementary Payments. Notwithstanding the provisions of Paragraph **B.1.b.(2)** Exclusions in Section **II** – Liability, such payments will not be deemed to be damages for "bodily injury" and "property damage" and will not reduce the Limits of Insurance.

Our obligation to defend an insured's indemnitee and to pay for attorneys' fees and necessary litigation expenses as Supplementary Payments ends when:

(a) We have used up the applicable Limit of Insurance in the payment of judgments or settlements; or

(b) The conditions set forth above, or the terms of the agreement described in Paragraph **(2)(f)** above are no longer met.

2. Medical Expenses

a. We will pay medical expenses as described below for "bodily injury" caused by an accident:

(1) On premises you own or rent;

(2) On ways next to premises you own or rent; or

(3) Because of your operations;

provided that:

(a) The accident takes place in the "coverage territory" and during the policy period;

(b) The expenses are incurred and reported to us within one year of the date of the accident; and

(c) The injured person submits to examination, at our expense, by physicians of our choice as often as we reasonably require.

b. We will make these payments regardless of fault. These payments will not exceed the Limits of Insurance of Section **II** – Liability. We will pay reasonable expenses for:

(1) First aid administered at the time of an accident;

(2) Necessary medical, surgical, x-ray and dental services, including prosthetic devices; and

(3) Necessary ambulance, hospital, professional nursing and funeral services.

B. Exclusions

1. Applicable To Business Liability Coverage

This insurance does not apply to:

a. Expected Or Intended Injury

"Bodily injury" or "property damage" expected or intended from the standpoint of the insured. This exclusion does not apply to "bodily injury" resulting from the use of reasonable force to protect persons or property.

b. Contractual Liability

"Bodily injury" or "property damage" for which the insured is obligated to pay damages by reason of the assumption of liability in a contract or agreement. This exclusion does not apply to liability for damages:

(1) That the insured would have in the absence of the contract or agreement; or

(2) Assumed in a contract or agreement that is an "insured contract", provided the "bodily injury" or "property damage" occurs subsequent to the execution of the contract or agreement. Solely for the purposes of liability assumed in an "insured contract", reasonable attorney fees and necessary litigation expenses incurred by or for a party other than an insured are deemed to be damages because of "bodily injury" or "property damage", provided:

(a) Liability to such party for, or for the cost of, that party's defense has also been assumed in the same "insured contract"; and

(b) Such attorney fees and litigation expenses are for defense of that party against a civil or alternative dispute resolution proceeding in which damages to which this insurance applies are alleged.

c. Liquor Liability

"Bodily injury" or "property damage" for which any insured may be held liable by reason of:

(1) Causing or contributing to the intoxication of any person;

(2) The furnishing of alcoholic beverages to a person under the legal drinking age or under the influence of alcohol; or

(3) Any statute, ordinance or regulation relating to the sale, gift, distribution or use of alcoholic beverages.

This exclusion applies only if you are in the business of manufacturing, distributing, selling, serving or furnishing alcoholic beverages.

d. Workers' Compensation And Similar Laws

Any obligation of the insured under a workers' compensation, disability benefits or unemployment compensation law or any similar law.

e. Employer's Liability

"Bodily injury" to:

(1) An "employee" of the insured arising out of and in the course of:

(a) Employment by the insured; or

(b) Performing duties related to the conduct of the insured's business; or

(2) The spouse, child, parent, brother or sister of that "employee" as a consequence of Paragraph **(1)** above.

This exclusion applies:

(1) Whether the insured may be liable as an employer or in any other capacity; and

(2) To any obligation to share damages with or repay someone else who must pay damages because of the injury.

This exclusion does not apply to liability assumed by the insured under an "insured contract".

f. Pollution

(1) "Bodily injury" or "property damage" arising out of the actual, alleged or threatened discharge, dispersal, seepage, migration, release or escape of "pollutants":

(a) At or from any premises, site or location which is or was at any time owned or occupied by, or rented or loaned to, any insured. However, this subparagraph does not apply to:

(i) "Bodily injury" if sustained within a building and caused by smoke, fumes, vapor or soot produced by or originating from equipment that is used to heat, cool or dehumidify the building, or equipment that is used to heat water for personal use, by the building's occupants or their guests;

(ii) "Bodily injury" or "property damage" for which you may be held liable, if you are a contractor and the owner or lessee of such premises, site or location has been added to your policy as an additional insured with respect to your ongoing operations performed for that additional insured at that premises, site or location and such premises, site or location is not and never was owned or occupied by, or rented or loaned to, any insured, other than that additional insured; or

(iii) "Bodily injury" or "property damage" arising out of heat, smoke or fumes from a "hostile fire";

(b) At or from any premises, site or location which is or was at any time used by or for any insured or others for the handling, storage, disposal, processing or treatment of waste;

(c) Which are or were at any time transported, handled, stored, treated, disposed of, or processed as waste by or for:

(i) Any insured; or

(ii) Any person or organization for whom you may be legally responsible; or

(d) At or from any premises, site or location on which any insured or any contractors or subcontractors working directly or indirectly on any insured's behalf are performing operations if the "pollutants" are brought on or to the premises, site or location in connection with such operations by such insured, contractor or subcontractor. However, this subparagraph does not apply to:

(i) "Bodily injury" or "property damage" arising out of the escape of fuels, lubricants or other operating fluids which are needed to perform the normal electrical, hydraulic or mechanical functions necessary for the operation of "mobile equipment" or its parts, if such fuels, lubricants or other operating fluids escape from a vehicle part designed to hold, store or receive them. This exception does not apply if the "bodily injury" or "property damage" arises out of the intentional discharge, dispersal or release of the fuels, lubricants or other operating fluids, or if such fuels, lubricants or other operating fluids are brought on or to the premises, site or location with the intent that they be discharged, dispersed or released as part of the operations being performed by such insured, contractor or subcontractor;

(ii) "Bodily injury" or "property damage" sustained within a building and caused by the release of gases, fumes or vapors from materials brought into that building in connection with operations being performed by you or on your behalf by a contractor or subcontractor; or

(iii) "Bodily injury" or "property damage" arising out of heat, smoke or fumes from a "hostile fire".

(e) At or from any premises, site or location on which any insured or any contractors or subcontractors working directly or indirectly on any insured's behalf are performing operations if the operations are to test for, monitor, clean up, remove, contain, treat, detoxify or neutralize, or in any way respond to, or assess the effects of, "pollutants".

(2) Any loss, cost or expense arising out of any:

  (a) Request, demand, order or statutory or regulatory requirement that any insured or others test for, monitor, clean up, remove, contain, treat, detoxify or neutralize, or in any way respond to, or assess the effects of, "pollutants"; or

  (b) Claim or "suit" by or on behalf of a governmental authority for damages because of testing for, monitoring, cleaning up, removing, containing, treating, detoxifying or neutralizing, or in any way responding to, or assessing the effects of, "pollutants".

However, this paragraph does not apply to liability for damages because of "property damage" that the insured would have in the absence of such request, demand, order or statutory or regulatory requirement or such claim or "suit" by or on behalf of a governmental authority.

g. Aircraft, Auto Or Watercraft

"Bodily injury" or "property damage" arising out of the ownership, maintenance, use or entrustment to others of any aircraft, "auto" or watercraft owned or operated by or rented or loaned to any insured. Use includes operation and "loading or unloading".

This exclusion applies even if the claims allege negligence or other wrongdoing in the supervision, hiring, employment, training or monitoring of others by an insured, if the "occurrence" which caused the "bodily injury" or "property damage" involved the ownership, maintenance, use or entrustment to others of any aircraft, "auto" or watercraft that is owned or operated by or rented or loaned to any insured.

This exclusion does not apply to:

(1) A watercraft while ashore on premises you own or rent;

(2) A watercraft you do not own that is:

  (a) Less than 51 feet long; and

  (b) Not being used to carry persons or property for a charge;

(3) Parking an "auto" on, or on the ways next to, premises you own or rent, provided the "auto" is not owned by or rented or loaned to you or the insured;

(4) Liability assumed under any "insured contract" for the ownership, maintenance or use of aircraft or watercraft; or

(5) "Bodily injury" or "property damage" arising out of:

  (a) The operation of machinery or equipment that is attached to, or part of, a land vehicle that would qualify under the definition of "mobile equipment" if it were not subject to a compulsory or financial responsibility law or other motor vehicle insurance or motor vehicle registration law where it is licensed or principally garaged; or

  (b) The operation of any of the following machinery or equipment:

    (i) Cherry pickers and similar devices mounted on automobile or truck chassis and used to raise or lower workers; and

    (ii) Air compressors, pumps and generators, including spraying, welding, building cleaning, geophysical exploration, lighting and well servicing equipment.

h. Mobile Equipment

"Bodily injury" or "property damage" arising out of:

(1) The transportation of "mobile equipment" by an "auto" owned or operated by or rented or loaned to any insured; or

(2) The use of "mobile equipment" in, or while in practice for, or while being prepared for, any prearranged racing, speed, demolition or stunting activity.

i. War

"Bodily injury", "property damage" or "personal and advertising injury", however caused, arising, directly or indirectly, out of:

(1) War, including undeclared civil war;

(2) Warlike action by a military force, including action in hindering or defending against an actual or expected attack, by any government, sovereign or other authority using military personnel or other agents; or

(3) Insurrection, rebellion, revolution, usurped power, or action taken by government authority in hindering or defending against any of these.

j. Professional Services

"Bodily injury", "property damage" or "personal and advertising injury" caused by the rendering or failure to render any professional service. This includes but is not limited to:

(1) Legal, accounting or advertising services;

(2) Preparing, approving, or failing to prepare or approve maps, drawings, opinions, reports, surveys, change orders, designs or specifications;

(3) Supervisory, inspection or engineering services;

(4) Medical, surgical, dental, x-ray or nursing services treatment, advice or instruction;

(5) Any health or therapeutic service treatment, advice or instruction;

(6) Any service, treatment, advice or instruction for the purpose of appearance or skin enhancement, hair removal or replacement or personal grooming;

(7) Optometry or optical or hearing aid services including the prescribing, preparation, fitting, demonstration or distribution of ophthalmic lenses and similar products or hearing aid devices;

(8) Body piercing services; and

(9) Services in the practice of pharmacy.

k. Damage To Property

"Property damage" to:

(1) Property you own, rent or occupy, including any costs or expenses incurred by you, or any other person, organization or entity, for repair, replacement, enhancement, restoration or maintenance of such property for any reason, including prevention of injury to a person or damage to another's property;

(2) Premises you sell, give away or abandon, if the "property damage" arises out of any part of those premises;

(3) Property loaned to you;

(4) Personal property in the care, custody or control of the insured;

(5) That particular part of real property on which you or any contractor or subcontractor working directly or indirectly on your behalf is performing operations, if the "property damage" arises out of those operations; or

(6) That particular part of any property that must be restored, repaired or replaced because "your work" was incorrectly performed on it.

Paragraphs **(1)**, **(3)** and **(4)** of this exclusion do not apply to "property damage" (other than damage by fire) to premises, including the contents of such premises, rented to you for a period of 7 or fewer consecutive days. A separate Limit of Insurance applies to Damage To Premises Rented To You as described in Paragraph **D.** Liability And Medical Expenses Limit Of Insurance in Section **II** – Liability.

Paragraph **(2)** of this exclusion does not apply if the premises are "your work" and were never occupied, rented or held for rental by you.

Paragraphs **(3)**, **(4)**, **(5)** and **(6)** of this exclusion do not apply to liability assumed under a sidetrack agreement.

Paragraph **(6)** of this exclusion does not apply to "property damage" included in the "products-completed operations hazard".

l. Damage To Your Product

"Property damage" to "your product" arising out of it or any part of it.

m. Damage To Your Work

"Property damage" to "your work" arising out of it or any part of it and included in the "products-completed operations hazard".

This exclusion does not apply if the damaged work or the work out of which the damage arises was performed on your behalf by a subcontractor.

n. Damage To Impaired Property Or Property Not Physically Injured

"Property damage" to "impaired property" or property that has not been physically injured, arising out of:

(1) A defect, deficiency, inadequacy or dangerous condition in "your product" or "your work"; or

(2) A delay or failure by you or anyone acting on your behalf to perform a contract or agreement in accordance with its terms.

This exclusion does not apply to the loss of use of other property arising out of sudden and accidental physical injury to "your product" or "your work" after it has been put to its intended use.

o. Recall Of Products, Work Or Impaired Property

Damages claimed for any loss, cost or expense incurred by you or others for the loss of use, withdrawal, recall, inspection, repair, replacement, adjustment, removal or disposal of:

(1) "Your product";

(2) "Your work"; or

(3) "Impaired property";

if such product, work or property is withdrawn or recalled from the market or from use by any person or organization because of a known or suspected defect, deficiency, inadequacy or dangerous condition in it.

p. Personal And Advertising Injury

"Personal and advertising injury":

(1) Caused by or at the direction of the insured with the knowledge that the act would violate the rights of another and would inflict "personal and advertising injury";

(2) Arising out of oral or written publication of material, if done by or at the direction of the insured with knowledge of its falsity;

(3) Arising out of oral or written publication of material whose first publication took place before the beginning of the policy period;

(4) For which the insured has assumed liability in a contract or agreement. This exclusion does not apply to liability for damages that the insured would have in the absence of the contract or agreement;

(5) Arising out of a breach of contract, except an implied contract to use another's advertising idea in your "advertisement";

(6) Arising out of the failure of goods, products or services to conform with any statement of quality or performance made in your "advertisement";

(7) Arising out of the wrong description of the price of goods, products or services stated in your "advertisement";

(8) Committed by an insured whose business is:

   (a) Advertising, broadcasting, publishing or telecasting;

(b) Designing or determining content of web-sites for others; or

(c) An Internet search, access, content or service provider.

However, this exclusion does not apply to Paragraphs **14.a., b.** and **c.** of "personal and advertising injury" under Paragraph **F.** Liability And Medical Expenses Definitions.

For the purposes of this exclusion, the placing of frames, borders or links, or advertising, for you or others anywhere on the Internet, by itself, is not considered the business of advertising, broadcasting, publishing or telecasting.

(9) Arising out of the actual, alleged or threatened discharge, dispersal, seepage, migration, release or escape of "pollutants" at any time;

(10) With respect to any loss, cost or expense arising out of any:

   (a) Request, demand or order that any insured or others test for, monitor, clean-up, remove, contain, treat, detoxify or neutralize or in any way respond to, or assess the effects of, "pollutants"; or

   (b) Claim or "suit" by or on behalf of a governmental authority for damages because of testing for, monitoring, cleaning up, removing, containing, treating, detoxifying or neutralizing or in any way responding to, or assessing the effects of, "pollutants".

(11) Arising out of an electronic chatroom or bulletin board the insured hosts, owns or over which the insured exercises control;

(12) Arising out of the infringement of copyright, patent, trademark, trade secret or other intellectual property rights.

However, this exclusion does not apply to infringement, in your "advertisement", of copyright, trade dress or slogan.

(13) Arising out of the unauthorized use of another's name or product in your e-mail address, domain name or metatags, or any other similar tactics to mislead another's potential customers.

q. Electronic Data

Damages arising out of the loss of, loss of use of, damage to, corruption of, inability to access, or inability to manipulate electronic data.

As used in this exclusion, electronic data means information, facts or programs stored as or on, created or used on, or transmitted to or from computer software, including systems and applications software, hard or floppy disks, CD-ROMs, tapes, drives, cells, data processing devices or any other media which are used with electronically controlled equipment.

r. Criminal Acts

"Personal and advertising injury" arising out of a criminal act committed by or at the direction of the insured.

s. Distribution Of Material In Violation Of Statutes

"Bodily injury", "property damage", or "personal and advertising injury" arising directly or indirectly out of any action or omission that violates or is alleged to violate:

(1) The Telephone Consumer Protection Act (TCPA), including any amendment of or addition to such law; or

(2) The CAN-SPAM Act of 2003, including any amendment of or addition to such law; or

(3) Any statute, ordinance or regulation, other than the TCPA or CAN-SPAM Act of 2003, that prohibits or limits the sending, transmitting, communicating or distribution of material or information.

Exclusions **c., d., e., f., g., h., i., k., l., m., n.** and **o.** in Section **II** – Liability do not apply to damage by fire to premises while rented to you, or temporarily occupied by you with permission of the owner. A separate Damage To Premises Rented To You Limit of Insurance applies to this coverage as described in Paragraph **D.** Liability And Medical Expenses Limits of Insurance in Section **II** – Liability.

2. Applicable To Medical Expenses Coverage

We will not pay expenses for "bodily injury":

a. To any insured, except "volunteer workers".

b. To a person hired to do work for or on behalf of any insured or a tenant of any insured.

c. To a person injured on that part of premises you own or rent that the person normally occupies.

d. To a person, whether or not an "employee" of any insured, if benefits for the "bodily injury" are payable or must be provided under a workers' compensation or disability benefits law or a similar law.

e. To a person injured while practicing, instructing or participating in any physical exercises or games, sports or athletic contests.

f. Included within the "products-completed operations hazard".

g. Excluded under Business Liability Coverage.

3. Applicable To Both Business Liability Coverage And Medical Expenses Coverage – Nuclear Energy Liability Exclusion

This insurance does not apply:

a. Under Business Liability Coverage, to "bodily injury" or "property damage":

(1) With respect to which an insured under the policy is also an insured under a nuclear energy liability policy issued by the Nuclear Energy Liability Insurance Association, Mutual Atomic Energy Liability Underwriters or Nuclear Insurance Association of Canada, or would be an insured under any such policy but for its termination upon exhaustion of its limit of liability; or

(2) Resulting from the "hazardous properties" of "nuclear material" and with respect to which:

(a) Any person or organization is required to maintain financial protection pursuant to the Atomic Energy Act of 1954, or any law amendatory thereof; or

(b) The insured is, or had this policy not been issued would be, entitled to indemnity from the United States of America, or any agency thereof, under any agreement entered into by the United States of America, or any agency thereof, with any person or organization.

b. Under Medical Expenses Coverage, to expenses incurred with respect to "bodily injury" resulting from the "hazardous properties" of "nuclear material" and arising out of the operation of a "nuclear facility" by any person or organization.

c. Under Business Liability Coverage, to "bodily injury" or "property damage" resulting from the "hazardous properties" of the "nuclear material"; if:

(1) The "nuclear material":

(a) Is at any "nuclear facility" owned by, or operated by or on behalf of, an insured; or

(b) Has been discharged or dispersed therefrom;

(2) The "nuclear material" is contained in "spent fuel" or "waste" at any time possessed, handled, used, processed, stored, transported or disposed of by or on behalf of an insured; or

(3) The "bodily injury" or "property damage" arises out of the furnishing by an insured of services, materials, parts or equipment in connection with the planning, construction, maintenance, operation or use of any "nuclear facility"; but if such facility is located within the United States of America, its territories or possessions or Canada, this Exclusion **(3)** applies only to "property damage" to such "nuclear facility" and any property thereat.

d. As used in this exclusion:

(1) "By-product material" has the meaning given it in the Atomic Energy Act of 1954 or in any law amendatory thereof;

(2) "Hazardous properties" include radioactive, toxic or explosive properties;

(3) "Nuclear facility" means:

(a) Any "nuclear reactor";

(b) Any equipment or device designed or used for:

(i) Separating the isotopes of uranium or plutonium;

(ii) Processing or utilizing "spent fuel"; or

(iii) Handling, processing or packaging "waste";

(c) Any equipment or device used for the processing, fabricating or alloying of "special nuclear material" if at any time the total amount of such material in the custody of the insured at the premises where such equipment or device is located consists of or contains more than 25 grams of plutonium or uranium 233 or any combination thereof, or more than 250 grams of uranium 235;

(d) Any structure, basin, excavation, premises or place prepared or used for the storage or disposal of "waste";

and includes the site on which any of the foregoing is located, all operations conducted on such site and all premises used for such operations;

(4) "Nuclear material" means "source material", "special nuclear material" or "by-product material";

(5) "Nuclear reactor" means any apparatus designed or used to sustain nuclear fission in a self-supporting chain reaction or to contain a critical mass of fissionable material;

(6) "Property damage" includes all forms of radioactive contamination of property;

(7) "Source material" has the meaning given it in the Atomic Energy Act of 1954 or in any law amendatory thereof;

(8) "Special nuclear material" has the meaning given it in the Atomic Energy Act of 1954 or in any law amendatory thereof;

(9) "Spent fuel" means any fuel element or fuel component, solid or liquid, which has been used or exposed to radiation in a "nuclear reactor";

(10) "Waste" means any waste material:

(a) Containing "by-product material" other than the tailings or wastes produced by the extraction or concentration of uranium or thorium from any ore processed primarily for its "source material" content; and

(b) Resulting from the operation by any person or organization of any "nuclear facility" included under Paragraphs **(a)** and **(b)** of the definition of "nuclear facility".

C. Who Is An Insured

1. If you are designated in the Declarations as:

a. An individual, you and your spouse are insureds, but only with respect to the conduct of a business of which you are the sole owner.

b. A partnership or joint venture, you are an insured. Your members, your partners and their spouses are also insureds, but only with respect to the conduct of your business.

c. A limited liability company, you are an insured. Your members are also insureds, but only with respect to the conduct of your business. Your managers are insureds, but only with respect to their duties as your managers.

d. An organization other than a partnership, joint venture or limited liability company, you are an insured. Your "executive officers" and directors are insureds, but only with respect to their duties as your officers or directors. Your stockholders are also insureds, but only with respect to their liability as stockholders.

2. Each of the following is also an insured:

a. Your "volunteer workers" only while performing duties related to the conduct of your business, or your "employees", other than either your "executive officers" (if you are an organization other than a partnership, joint venture or limited liability company) or your managers (if you are a limited liability company), but only for acts within the scope of their employment by you or while performing duties related to the conduct of your business. However, none of these "employees" or "volunteer workers" are insureds for:

(1) "Bodily injury" or "personal and advertising injury":

(a) To you, to your partners or members (if you are a partnership or joint venture), to your members (if you are a limited liability company), or to a co-"employee" while in the course of his or her employment or performing duties related to the conduct of your business, or to your other "volunteer workers" while performing duties related to the conduct of your business;

(b) To the spouse, child, parent, brother or sister of that co-"employee" as a consequence of Paragraph **(a)** above;

(c) For which there is any obligation to share damages with or repay someone else who must pay damages because of the injury described in Paragraph **(a)** or **(b)**; or

(d) Arising out of his or her providing or failing to provide professional health care services.

(2) "Property damage" to property:

(a) Owned, occupied or used by,

(b) Rented to, in the care, custody or control of, or over which physical control is being exercised for any purpose by

you, any of your "employees", "volunteer workers", any partner or member (if you are a partnership or joint venture), or any member (if you are a limited liability company).

b. Any person (other than your "employee" or "volunteer worker"), or any organization while acting as your real estate manager.

c. Any person or organization having proper temporary custody of your property if you die, but only:

(1) With respect to liability arising out of the maintenance or use of that property; and

(2) Until your legal representative has been appointed.

d. Your legal representative if you die, but only with respect to duties as such. That representative will have all your rights and duties under this policy.

No person or organization is an insured with respect to the conduct of any current or past partnership, joint venture or limited liability company that is not shown as a Named Insured in the Declarations.

D. Liability And Medical Expenses Limits Of Insurance

1. The Limits of Insurance of Section **II** – Liability shown in the Declarations and the rules below fix the most we will pay regardless of the number of:

a. Insureds;

b. Claims made or "suits" brought; or

c. Persons or organizations making claims or bringing "suits".

2. The most we will pay for the sum of all damages because of all:

a. "Bodily injury", "property damage" and medical expenses arising out of any one "occurrence"; and

b. "Personal and advertising injury" sustained by any one person or organization;

is the Liability and Medical Expenses limit shown in the Declarations. But the most we will pay for all medical expenses because of "bodily injury" sustained by any one person is the Medical Expenses limit shown in the Declarations.

3. The most we will pay under Business Liability Coverage for damages because of "property damage" to a premises while rented to you or in the case of fire while rented to you or temporarily occupied by you with permission of the owner is the applicable Damage To Premises Rented To You limit shown for that premises in the Declarations. For a premises temporarily occupied by you, the applicable limit will be the highest Damage To Premises Rented To You limit shown in the Declarations.

4. **Aggregate Limits**

The most we will pay for:

a. All "bodily injury" and "property damage" that is included in the "products-completed operations hazard" is twice the Liability and Medical Expenses limit.

b. All:

(1) "Bodily injury" and "property damage" except damages because of "bodily injury" or "property damage" included in the "products-completed operations hazard";

(2) Plus medical expenses;

(3) Plus all "personal and advertising injury" caused by offenses committed;

is twice the Liability and Medical Expenses limit.

Subject to Paragraph **a.** or **b.** above, whichever applies, the Damage To Premises Rented To You Limit is the most we will pay for damages because of "property damage" to any one premises, while rented to you, or in the case of fire, while rented to you or temporarily occupied by you with permission of the owner.

The Limits of Insurance of Section II – Liability apply separately to each consecutive annual period and to any remaining period of less than 12 months, starting with the beginning of the policy period shown in the Declarations, unless the policy period is extended after issuance for an additional period of less than 12 months. In that case, the additional period will be deemed part of the last preceding period for purposes of determining the Limits of Insurance.

E. Liability And Medical Expenses General Conditions

1. **Bankruptcy**

Bankruptcy or insolvency of the insured or of the insured's estate will not relieve us of our obligations under this policy.

2. **Duties In The Event Of Occurrence, Offense, Claim Or Suit**

a. You must see to it that we are notified as soon as practicable of an "occurrence" or an offense which may result in a claim. To the extent possible, notice should include:

(1) How, when and where the "occurrence" or offense took place;

(2) The names and addresses of any injured persons and witnesses; and

(3) The nature and location of any injury or damage arising out of the "occurrence" or offense.

b. If a claim is made or "suit" is brought against any insured, you must:

(1) Immediately record the specifics of the claim or "suit" and the date received; and

(2) Notify us as soon as practicable.

You must see to it that we receive written notice of the claim or "suit" as soon as practicable.

c. You and any other involved insured must:

(1) Immediately send us copies of any demands, notices, summonses or legal papers received in connection with the claim or "suit";

(2) Authorize us to obtain records and other information;

(3) Cooperate with us in the investigation, or settlement of the claim or defense against the "suit"; and

(4) Assist us, upon our request, in the enforcement of any right against any person or organization that may be liable to the insured because of injury or damage to which this insurance may also apply.

d. No insured will, except at that insured's own cost, voluntarily make a payment, assume any obligation, or incur any expense, other than for first aid, without our consent.

3. **Legal Action Against Us**

No person or organization has a right under this policy:

a. To join us as a party or otherwise bring us into a "suit" asking for damages from an insured; or

b. To sue us on this policy unless all of its terms have been fully complied with.

A person or organization may sue us to recover on an agreed settlement or on a final judgment against an insured; but we will not be liable for damages that are not payable under the terms of this policy or that are in excess of the applicable Limit of Insurance. An agreed settlement means a settlement and release of liability signed by us, the insured and the claimant or the claimant's legal representative.

4. Separation Of Insureds

Except with respect to the Limits of Insurance of Section **II** – Liability, and any rights or duties specifically assigned in this policy to the first Named Insured, this insurance applies:

a. As if each Named Insured were the only Named Insured; and

b. Separately to each insured against whom claim is made or "suit" is brought.

F. Liability And Medical Expenses Definitions

1. "Advertisement" means a notice that is broadcast or published to the general public or specific market segments about your goods, products or services for the purpose of attracting customers or supporters. For the purposes of this definition:

a. Notices that are published include material placed on the Internet or on similar electronic means of communication; and

b. Regarding web-sites, only that part of a web-site that is about your goods, products or services for the purposes of attracting customers or supporters is considered an advertisement.

2. "Auto" means:

a. A land motor vehicle, trailer or semitrailer designed for travel on public roads, including any attached machinery or equipment; or

b. Any other land vehicle that is subject to a compulsory or financial responsibility law or other motor vehicle insurance or motor vehicle registration law where it is licensed or principally garaged.

However, "auto" does not include "mobile equipment".

3. "Bodily injury" means bodily injury, sickness or disease sustained by a person, including death resulting from any of these at any time.

4. "Coverage territory" means:

a. The United States of America (including its territories and possessions), Puerto Rico and Canada;

b. International waters or airspace, but only if the injury or damage occurs in the course of travel or transportation between any places included in Paragraph **a.** above; or

c. All other parts of the world if the injury or damage arises out of:

(1) Goods or products made or sold by you in the territory described in Paragraph **a.** above;

(2) The activities of a person whose home is in the territory described in Paragraph **a.** above, but is away for a short time on your business; or

(3) "Personal and advertising injury" offenses that take place through the Internet or similar electronic means of communication;

provided the insured's responsibility to pay damages is determined in a "suit" on the merits in the territory described in Paragraph **a.** above or in a settlement we agree to.

5. "Employee" includes a "leased worker". "Employee" does not include a "temporary worker".

6. "Executive officer" means a person holding any of the officer positions created by your charter, constitution, by-laws or any other similar governing document.

7. "Hostile fire" means one which becomes uncontrollable or breaks out from where it was intended to be.

8. "Impaired property" means tangible property, other than "your product" or "your work", that cannot be used or is less useful because:

a. It incorporates "your product" or "your work" that is known or thought to be defective, deficient, inadequate or dangerous; or

b. You have failed to fulfill the terms of a contract or agreement;

if such property can be restored to use by:

(1) The repair, replacement, adjustment or removal of "your product" or "your work"; or

(2) Your fulfilling the terms of the contract or agreement.

9. "Insured contract" means:

a. A contract for a lease of premises. However, that portion of the contract for a lease of premises that indemnifies any person or organization for damage by fire to premises while rented to you or temporarily occupied by you with permission of the owner is not an "insured contract";

b. A sidetrack agreement;

c. Any easement or license agreement, except in connection with construction or demolition operations on or within 50 feet of a railroad;

d. An obligation, as required by ordinance, to indemnify a municipality, except in connection with work for a municipality;

e. An elevator maintenance agreement;

f. That part of any other contract or agreement pertaining to your business (including an indemnification of a municipality in connection with work performed for a municipality) under which you assume the tort liability of another party to pay for "bodily injury" or "property damage" to a third person or organization. Tort liability means a liability that would be imposed by law in the absence of any contract or agreement.

Paragraph **f.** does not include that part of any contract or agreement:

(1) That indemnifies a railroad for "bodily injury" or "property damage" arising out of construction or demolition operations, within 50 feet of any railroad property and affecting any railroad bridge or trestle, tracks, road beds, tunnel, underpass or crossing;

(2) That indemnifies an architect, engineer or surveyor for injury or damage arising out of:

(a) Preparing, approving or failing to prepare or approve maps, drawings, opinions, reports, surveys, change orders, designs or specifications; or

(b) Giving directions or instructions, or failing to give them, if that is the primary cause of the injury or damage; or

(3) Under which the insured, if an architect, engineer or surveyor, assumes liability for an injury or damage arising out of the insured's rendering or failure to render professional services, including those listed in Paragraph **(2)** above and supervisory, inspection or engineering services.

10. "Leased worker" means a person leased to you by a labor leasing firm under an agreement between you and the labor leasing firm, to perform duties related to the conduct of your business. "Leased worker" does not include a "temporary worker".

11. "Loading or unloading" means the handling of property:

a. After it is moved from the place where it is accepted for movement into or onto an aircraft, watercraft or "auto";

b. While it is in or on an aircraft, watercraft or "auto"; or

c. While it is being moved from an aircraft, watercraft or "auto" to the place where it is finally delivered;

but "loading or unloading" does not include the movement of property by means of a mechanical device, other than a hand truck, that is not attached to the aircraft, watercraft or "auto".

12. "Mobile equipment" means any of the following types of land vehicles, including any attached machinery or equipment:

a. Bulldozers, farm machinery, forklifts and other vehicles designed for use principally off public roads;

b. Vehicles maintained for use solely on or next to premises you own or rent;

c. Vehicles that travel on crawler treads;

d. Vehicles, whether self-propelled or not, on which are permanently mounted:

(1) Power cranes, shovels, loaders, diggers or drills; or

(2) Road construction or resurfacing equipment such as graders, scrapers or rollers;

e. Vehicles not described in Paragraph **a., b., c.** or **d.** above that are not self-propelled and are maintained primarily to provide mobility to permanently attached equipment of the following types:

(1) Air compressors, pumps and generators, including spraying, welding, building cleaning, geophysical exploration, lighting and well servicing equipment; or

(2) Cherry pickers and similar devices used to raise or lower workers;

f. Vehicles not described in Paragraph **a., b., c.** or **d.** above maintained primarily for purposes other than the transportation of persons or cargo.

However, self-propelled vehicles with the following types of permanently attached equipment are not "mobile equipment" but will be considered "autos":

(1) Equipment designed primarily for:

(a) Snow removal;

(b) Road maintenance, but not construction or resurfacing; or

(c) Street cleaning;

(2) Cherry pickers and similar devices mounted on automobile or truck chassis and used to raise or lower workers; and

(3) Air compressors, pumps and generators, including spraying, welding, building cleaning, geophysical exploration, lighting and well servicing equipment.

However, "mobile equipment" does not include land vehicles that are subject to a compulsory or financial responsibility law or other motor vehicle insurance or motor vehicle registration law where they are licensed or principally garaged. Land vehicles subject to a compulsory or financial responsibility law or other motor vehicle insurance law are considered "autos".

13. "Occurrence" means an accident, including continuous or repeated exposure to substantially the same general harmful conditions.

14. "Personal and advertising injury" means injury, including consequential "bodily injury", arising out of one or more of the following offenses:

a. False arrest, detention or imprisonment;

b. Malicious prosecution;

c. The wrongful eviction from, wrongful entry into, or invasion of the right of private occupancy of a room, dwelling or premises that a person occupies, committed by or on behalf of its owner, landlord or lessor;

d. Oral or written publication, in any manner, of material that slanders or libels a person or organization or disparages a person's or organization's goods, products or services;

e. Oral or written publication, in any manner, of material that violates a person's right of privacy;

f. The use of another's advertising idea in your "advertisement"; or

g. Infringing upon another's copyright, trade dress or slogan in your "advertisement".

15. "Pollutants" mean any solid, liquid, gaseous or thermal irritant or contaminant, including smoke, vapor, soot, fumes, acids, alkalis, chemicals and waste. Waste includes materials to be recycled, reconditioned or reclaimed.

16. "Products-completed operations hazard":

a. Includes all "bodily injury" and "property damage" occurring away from premises you own or rent and arising out of "your product" or "your work" except:

(1) Products that are still in your physical possession; or

(2) Work that has not yet been completed or abandoned. However, "your work" will be deemed completed at the earliest of the following times:

(a) When all of the work called for in your contract has been completed.

(b) When all of the work to be done at the job site has been completed if your contract calls for work at more than one job site.

(c) When that part of the work done at the job site has been put to its intended use by any other person or organization other than another contractor or subcontractor working on the same project.

Work that may need service, maintenance, correction, repair or replacement, but which is otherwise complete, will be treated as completed.

The "bodily injury" or "property damage" must occur away from premises you own or rent, unless your business includes the selling, handling or distribution of "your product" for consumption on premises you own or rent.

b. Does not include "bodily injury" or "property damage" arising out of:

(1) The transportation of property, unless the injury or damage arises out of a condition in or on a vehicle not owned or operated by you, and that condition was created by the "loading or unloading" of that vehicle by any insured; or

(2) The existence of tools, uninstalled equipment or abandoned or unused materials.

17. "Property damage" means:

a. Physical injury to tangible property, including all resulting loss of use of that property. All such loss of use shall be deemed to occur at the time of the physical injury that caused it; or

b. Loss of use of tangible property that is not physically injured. All such loss of use shall be deemed to occur at the time of the "occurrence" that caused it.

For the purposes of this insurance, electronic data is not tangible property.

As used in this definition, electronic data means information, facts or programs stored as, created or used on, or transmitted to or from computer software, including systems and applications software, hard or floppy disks, CD-ROMs, tapes, drives, cells, data processing devices or any other media which are used with electronically controlled equipment.

18. "Suit" means a civil proceeding in which damages because of "bodily injury", "property damage", or "personal and advertising injury" to which this insurance applies are alleged. "Suit" includes:

a. An arbitration proceeding in which such damages are claimed and to which the insured must submit or does submit with our consent; or

b. Any other alternative dispute resolution proceeding in which such damages are claimed and to which the insured submits with our consent.

19. "Temporary worker" means a person who is furnished to you to substitute for a permanent "employee" on leave or to meet seasonal or short-term workload conditions.

20. "Volunteer worker" means a person who is not your "employee", and who donates his or her work and acts at the direction of and within the scope of duties determined by you, and is not paid a fee, salary or other compensation by you or anyone else for their work performed for you.

21. "Your product":

a. Means:

(1) Any goods or products, other than real property, manufactured, sold, handled, distributed or disposed of by:

(a) You;

(b) Others trading under your name; or

(c) A person or organization whose business or assets you have acquired; and

(2) Containers (other than vehicles), materials, parts or equipment furnished in connection with such goods or products.

b. Includes:

(1) Warranties or representations made at any time with respect to the fitness, quality, durability, performance or use of "your product"; and

(2) The providing of or failure to provide warnings or instructions.

c. Does not include vending machines or other property rented to or located for the use of others but not sold.

22. "Your work":

a. Means:

(1) Work or operations performed by you or on your behalf; and

(2) Materials, parts or equipment furnished in connection with such work or operations.

b. Includes:

(1) Warranties or representations made at any time with respect to the fitness, quality, durability, performance or use of "your work"; and

(2) The providing of or failure to provide warnings or instructions.

SECTION III – COMMON POLICY CONDITIONS (APPLICABLE TO SECTION I – PROPERTY AND SECTION II – LIABILITY)

A. Cancellation

1. The first Named Insured shown in the Declarations may cancel this policy by mailing or delivering to us advance written notice of cancellation.

2. We may cancel this policy by mailing or delivering to the first Named Insured written notice of cancellation at least:

a. 5 days before the effective date of cancellation if any one of the following conditions exists at any building that is Covered Property in this policy;

(1) The building has been vacant or unoccupied 60 or more consecutive days. This does not apply to:

(a) Seasonal unoccupancy; or

(b) Buildings in the course of construction, renovation or addition.

Buildings with 65% or more of the rental units or floor area vacant or unoccupied are considered unoccupied under this provision.

(2) After damage by a Covered Cause of Loss, permanent repairs to the building:

(a) Have not started, and

(b) Have not been contracted for,

within 30 days of initial payment of loss.

(3) The building has:

(a) An outstanding order to vacate;

(b) An outstanding demolition order; or

(c) Been declared unsafe by governmental authority.

(4) Fixed and salvageable items have been or are being removed from the building and are not being replaced. This does not apply to such removal that is necessary or incidental to any renovation or remodeling.

(5) Failure to:

(a) Furnish necessary heat, water, sewer service or electricity for 30 consecutive days or more, except during a period of seasonal unoccupancy; or

(b) Pay property taxes that are owing and have been outstanding for more than one year following the date due, except that this provision will not apply where you are in a bona fide dispute with the taxing authority regarding payment of such taxes.

b. 10 days before the effective date of cancellation if we cancel for nonpayment of premium.

c. 30 days before the effective date of cancellation if we cancel for any other reason.

3. We will mail or deliver our notice to the first Named Insured's last mailing address known to us.

4. Notice of cancellation will state the effective date of cancellation. The policy period will end on that date.

5. If this policy is cancelled, we will send the first Named Insured any premium refund due. If we cancel, the refund will be pro rata. If the first Named Insured cancels, the refund may be less than pro rata. The cancellation will be effective even if we have not made or offered a refund.

6. If notice is mailed, proof of mailing will be sufficient proof of notice.

B. Changes

This policy contains all the agreements between you and us concerning the insurance afforded. The first Named Insured shown in the Declarations is authorized to make changes in the terms of this policy with our consent. This policy's terms can be amended or waived only by endorsement issued by us and made a part of this policy.

C. Concealment, Misrepresentation Or Fraud

This policy is void in any case of fraud by you as it relates to this policy at any time. It is also void if you or any other insured, at any time, intentionally conceal or misrepresent a material fact concerning:

1. This policy;

2. The Covered Property;

3. Your interest in the Covered Property; or

4. A claim under this policy.

D. Examination Of Your Books And Records

We may examine and audit your books and records as they relate to this policy at any time during the policy period and up to three years afterward.

E. Inspections And Surveys

1. We have the right to:

a. Make inspections and surveys at any time;

b. Give you reports on the conditions we find; and

c. Recommend changes.

2. We are not obligated to make any inspections, surveys, reports or recommendations and any such actions we do undertake relate only to insurability and the premiums to be charged. We do not make safety inspections. We do not undertake to perform the duty of any person or organization to provide for the health or safety of workers or the public. And we do not warrant that conditions:

a. Are safe and healthful; or

b. Comply with laws, regulations, codes or standards.

3. Paragraphs **1.** and **2.** of this condition apply not only to us, but also to any rating, advisory, rate service or similar organization which makes insurance inspections, surveys, reports or recommendations.

4. Paragraph **2.** of this condition does not apply to any inspections, surveys, reports or recommendations we may make relative to certification, under state or municipal statutes, ordinances or regulations, of boilers, pressure vessels or elevators.

F. Insurance Under Two Or More Coverages

If two or more of this policy's coverages apply to the same loss or damage, we will not pay more than the actual amount of the loss or damage.

G. Liberalization

If we adopt any revision that would broaden the coverage under this policy without additional premium within 45 days prior to or during the policy period, the broadened coverage will immediately apply to this policy.

H. Other Insurance

1. If there is other insurance covering the same loss or damage, we will pay only for the amount of covered loss or damage in excess of the amount due from that other insurance, whether you can collect on it or not. But we will not pay more than the applicable Limit of Insurance of Section I – Property.

2. Business Liability Coverage is excess over:

   a. Any other insurance that insures for direct physical loss or damage; or

   b. Any other primary insurance available to you covering liability for damages arising out of the premises or operations for which you have been added as an additional insured by attachment of an endorsement.

3. When this insurance is excess, we will have no duty under Business Liability Coverage to defend any claim or "suit" that any other insurer has a duty to defend. If no other insurer defends, we will undertake to do so; but we will be entitled to the insured's rights against all those other insurers.

I. Premiums

1. The first Named Insured shown in the Declarations:

   a. Is responsible for the payment of all premiums; and

   b. Will be the payee for any return premiums we pay.

2. The premium shown in the Declarations was computed based on rates in effect at the time the policy was issued. On each renewal, continuation or anniversary of the effective date of this policy, we will compute the premium in accordance with our rates and rules then in effect.

3. With our consent, you may continue this policy in force by paying a continuation premium for each successive one-year period. The premium must be:

   a. Paid to us prior to the anniversary date; and

   b. Determined in accordance with Paragraph 2. above.

   Our forms then in effect will apply. If you do not pay the continuation premium, this policy will expire on the first anniversary date that we have not received the premium.

4. Undeclared exposures or change in your business operation, acquisition or use of locations may occur during the policy period that are not shown in the Declarations. If so, we may require an additional premium. That premium will be determined in accordance with our rates and rules then in effect.

J. Premium Audit

1. This policy is subject to audit if a premium designated as an advance premium is shown in the Declarations. We will compute the final premium due when we determine your actual exposures.

2. Premium shown in this policy as advance premium is a deposit premium only. At the close of each audit period we will compute the earned premium for that period and send notice to the first Named Insured. The due date for audit premiums is the date shown as the due date on the bill. If the sum of the advance and audit premiums paid for the policy period is greater than the earned premium, we will return the excess to the first Named Insured.

3. The first Named Insured must keep records of the information we need for premium computation, and send us copies at such times as we may request.

K. Transfer Of Rights Of Recovery Against Others To Us

1. Applicable to Businessowners Property Coverage:

   If any person or organization to or for whom we make payment under this policy has rights to recover damages from another, those rights are transferred to us to the extent of our payment. That person or organization must do everything necessary to secure our rights and must do nothing after loss to impair them. But you may waive your rights against another party in writing:

   a. Prior to a loss to your Covered Property.

   b. After a loss to your Covered Property only if, at time of loss, that party is one of the following:

      (1) Someone insured by this insurance;

      (2) A business firm:

         (a) Owned or controlled by you; or

         (b) That owns or controls you; or

      (3) Your tenant.

   You may also accept the usual bills of lading or shipping receipts limiting the liability of carriers.

   This will not restrict your insurance.

 □

2. Applicable to Businessowners Liability Coverage:

If the insured has rights to recover all or part of any payment we have made under this policy, those rights are transferred to us. The insured must do nothing after loss to impair them. At our request, the insured will bring "suit" or transfer those rights to us and help us enforce them. This condition does not apply to Medical Expenses Coverage.

L. Transfer Of Your Rights And Duties Under This Policy

Your rights and duties under this policy may not be transferred without our written consent except in the case of death of an individual Named Insured.

If you die, your rights and duties will be transferred to your legal representative but only while acting within the scope of duties as your legal representative. Until your legal representative is appointed, anyone having proper temporary custody of your property will have your rights and duties but only with respect to that property.

2010 EDITION

BUSINESSOWNERS
BP 00 03 01 10

BUSINESSOWNERS COVERAGE FORM

Various provisions in this policy restrict coverage. Read the entire policy carefully to determine rights, duties and what is and is not covered.

Throughout this Coverage Form the words "you" and "your" refer to the Named Insured shown in the Declarations. The words "we", "us" and "our" refer to the Company providing this insurance.

In Section **II** – Liability, the word "insured" means any person or organization qualifying as such under Paragraph **C.** Who Is An Insured.

Other words and phrases that appear in quotation marks have special meaning. Refer to Paragraph **H.** Property Definitions in Section **I** – Property and Paragraph **F.** Liability And Medical Expenses Definitions in Section **II** – Liability.

SECTION I – PROPERTY

A. Coverage

We will pay for direct physical loss of or damage to Covered Property at the premises described in the Declarations caused by or resulting from any Covered Cause of Loss.

1. Covered Property

Covered Property includes Buildings as described under Paragraph **a.** below, Business Personal Property as described under Paragraph **b.** below, or both, depending on whether a Limit of Insurance is shown in the Declarations for that type of property. Regardless of whether coverage is shown in the Declarations for Buildings, Business Personal Property, or both, there is no coverage for property described under Paragraph **2.** Property Not Covered.

a. Buildings, meaning the buildings and structures at the premises described in the Declarations, including:

(1) Completed additions;

(2) Fixtures, including outdoor fixtures;

(3) Permanently installed:

(a) Machinery; and

(b) Equipment;

(4) Your personal property in apartments, rooms or common areas furnished by you as landlord;

(5) Personal property owned by you that is used to maintain or service the buildings or structures or the premises, including:

(a) Fire extinguishing equipment;

(b) Outdoor furniture;

(c) Floor coverings; and

(d) Appliances used for refrigerating, ventilating, cooking, dishwashing or laundering;

(6) If not covered by other insurance:

(a) Additions under construction, alterations and repairs to the buildings or structures;

(b) Materials, equipment, supplies and temporary structures, on or within 100 feet of the described premises, used for making additions, alterations or repairs to the buildings or structures.

b. Business Personal Property located in or on the buildings at the described premises or in the open (or in a vehicle) within 100 feet of the described premises, including:

(1) Property you own that is used in your business;

(2) Property of others that is in your care, custody or control, except as otherwise provided in Loss Payment Property Loss Condition Paragraph **E.5.d.(3)(b);**

(3) Tenant's improvements and betterments. Improvements and betterments are fixtures, alterations, installations or additions:

(a) Made a part of the building or structure you occupy but do not own; and

(b) You acquired or made at your expense but cannot legally remove;

(4) Leased personal property which you have a contractual responsibility to insure, unless otherwise provided for under Paragraph **1.b.(2);** and

(5) Exterior building glass, if you are a tenant and no Limit of Insurance is shown in the Declarations for Building property. The glass must be owned by you or in your care, custody or control.

2. **Property Not Covered**

Covered Property does not include:

a. Aircraft, automobiles, motortrucks and other vehicles subject to motor vehicle registration;

b. "Money" or "securities" except as provided in the:

(1) Money And Securities Optional Coverage; or

(2) Employee Dishonesty Optional Coverage;

c. Contraband, or property in the course of illegal transportation or trade;

d. Land (including land on which the property is located), water, growing crops or lawns;

e. Outdoor fences, radio or television antennas (including satellite dishes) and their lead-in wiring, masts or towers, signs (other than signs attached to buildings), trees, shrubs or plants, all except as provided in the:

(1) Outdoor Property Coverage Extension; or

(2) Outdoor Signs Optional Coverage;

f. Watercraft (including motors, equipment and accessories) while afloat;

g. Accounts, bills, food stamps, other evidences of debt, accounts receivable or "valuable papers and records"; except as otherwise provided in this policy;

h. "Computer(s)" which are permanently installed or designed to be permanently installed in any aircraft, watercraft, motortruck or other vehicle subject to motor vehicle registration. This paragraph does not apply to "computer(s)" while held as "stock";

i. "Electronic data", except as provided under Additional Coverages – Electronic Data. This Paragraph i. does not apply to your "stock" of prepackaged software.

j. Animals, unless owned by others and boarded by you, or if owned by you, only as "stock" while inside of buildings.

3. **Covered Causes Of Loss**

Risks of direct physical loss unless the loss is:

a. Excluded in Paragraph B. Exclusions in Section I; or

b. Limited in Paragraph 4. Limitations in Section I.

4. **Limitations**

a. We will not pay for loss of or damage to:

(1) Steam boilers, steam pipes, steam engines or steam turbines caused by or resulting from any condition or event inside such equipment. But we will pay for loss of or damage to such equipment caused by or resulting from an explosion of gases or fuel within the furnace of any fired vessel or within the flues or passages through which the gases of combustion pass.

(2) Hot water boilers or other water heating equipment caused by or resulting from any condition or event inside such boilers or equipment, other than an explosion.

(3) Property that is missing, where the only evidence of the loss or damage is a shortage disclosed on taking inventory, or other instances where there is no physical evidence to show what happened to the property. This limitation does not apply to the Optional Coverage for Money and Securities.

(4) Property that has been transferred to a person or to a place outside the described premises on the basis of unauthorized instructions.

(5) The interior of any building or structure caused by or resulting from rain, snow, sleet, ice, sand or dust, whether driven by wind or not, unless:

(a) The building or structure first sustains damage by a Covered Cause of Loss to its roof or walls through which the rain, snow, sleet, ice, sand or dust enters; or

(b) The loss or damage is caused by or results from thawing of snow, sleet or ice on the building or structure.

b. We will not pay for loss of or damage to the following types of property unless caused by the "specified causes of loss" or building glass breakage:

(1) Animals, and then only if they are killed or their destruction is made necessary.

(2) Fragile articles such as glassware, statuary, marble, chinaware and porcelain, if broken. This restriction does not apply to:

(a) Glass that is part of the exterior or interior of a building or structure;

(b) Containers of property held for sale; or

(c) Photographic or scientific instrument lenses.

c. For loss or damage by theft, the following types of property are covered only up to the limits shown:

(1) $2,500 for furs, fur garments and garments trimmed with fur.

(2) $2,500 for jewelry, watches, watch movements, jewels, pearls, precious and semiprecious stones, bullion, gold, silver, platinum and other precious alloys or metals. This limit does not apply to jewelry and watches worth $100 or less per item.

(3) $2,500 for patterns, dies, molds and forms.

5. Additional Coverages

a. Debris Removal

(1) Subject to Paragraphs **(3)** and **(4)**, we will pay your expense to remove debris of Covered Property caused by or resulting from a Covered Cause of Loss that occurs during the policy period. The expenses will be paid only if they are reported to us in writing within 180 days of the date of direct physical loss or damage.

(2) Debris Removal does not apply to costs to:

(a) Extract "pollutants" from land or water; or

(b) Remove, restore or replace polluted land or water.

(3) Subject to the exceptions in Paragraph **(4)**, the following provisions apply:

(a) The most that we will pay for the total of direct physical loss or damage plus debris removal expense is the Limit of Insurance applicable to the Covered Property that has sustained loss or damage.

(b) Subject to Paragraph **(a)** above, the amount we will pay for debris removal expense is limited to 25% of the sum of the deductible plus the amount that we pay for direct physical loss or damage to the Covered Property that has sustained loss or damage.

(4) We will pay up to an additional $10,000 for debris removal expense, for each location, in any one occurrence of physical loss or damage to Covered Property, if one or both of the following circumstances apply:

(a) The total of the actual debris removal expense plus the amount we pay for direct physical loss or damage exceeds the Limit of Insurance on the Covered Property that has sustained loss or damage.

(b) The actual debris removal expense exceeds 25% of the sum of the deductible plus the amount that we pay for direct physical loss or damage to the Covered Property that has sustained loss or damage.

Therefore, if Paragraphs **(4)(a)** and/or **(4)(b)** apply, our total payment for direct physical loss or damage and debris removal expense may reach but will never exceed the Limit of Insurance on the Covered Property that has sustained loss or damage, plus $10,000.

(5) Examples

Example #1

Limit of Insurance	$ 90,000
Amount of Deductible	$ 500
Amount of Loss	$ 50,000
Amount of Loss Payable	$ 49,500
	($50,000 – $500)
Debris Removal Expense	$ 10,000
Debris Removal Expense Payable	$ 10,000
($10,000 is 20% of $50,000)	

The debris removal expense is less than 25% of the sum of the loss payable plus the deductible. The sum of the loss payable and the debris removal expense ($49,500 + $10,000 = $59,500) is less than the Limit of Insurance. Therefore the full amount of debris removal expense is payable in accordance with the terms of Paragraph **(3)**.

Example #2

Limit of Insurance	$ 90,000
Amount of Deductible	$ 500
Amount of Loss	$ 80,000
Amount of Loss Payable	$ 79,500
	($80,000 – $500)
Debris Removal Expense	$ 30,000
Debris Removal Expense Payable	
Basic Amount	$ 10,500
Additional Amount	$ 10,000

The basic amount payable for debris removal expense under the terms of Paragraph **(3)** is calculated as follows: $80,000 ($79,500 + $500) x .25 = $20,000; capped at $10,500). The cap applies because the sum of the loss payable ($79,500) and the basic amount payable for debris removal expense ($10,500) cannot exceed the Limit of Insurance ($90,000).

The additional amount payable for debris removal expense is provided in accordance with the terms of Paragraph **(4)**, because the debris removal expense ($30,000) exceeds 25% of the loss payable plus the deductible ($30,000 is 37.5% of $80,000), and because the sum of the loss payable and debris removal expense ($79,500 + $30,000 = $109,500) would exceed the Limit of Insurance ($90,000). The additional amount of covered debris removal expense is $10,000, the maximum payable under Paragraph **(4).** Thus the total payable for debris removal expense in this example is $20,500; $9,500 of the debris removal expense is not covered.

b. Preservation Of Property

If it is necessary to move Covered Property from the described premises to preserve it from loss or damage by a Covered Cause of Loss, we will pay for any direct physical loss of or damage to that property:

(1) While it is being moved or while temporarily stored at another location; and

(2) Only if the loss or damage occurs within 30 days after the property is first moved.

c. Fire Department Service Charge

When the fire department is called to save or protect Covered Property from a Covered Cause of Loss, we will pay up to $2,500, unless a different limit is shown in the Declarations, for your liability for fire department service charges:

(1) Assumed by contract or agreement prior to loss; or

(2) Required by local ordinance.

d. Collapse

The coverage provided under this Additional Coverage – Collapse applies only to an abrupt collapse as described and limited in Paragraphs **d.(1)** through **d.(7).**

(1) For the purpose of this Additional Coverage – Collapse, abrupt collapse means an abrupt falling down or caving in of a building or any part of a building with the result that the building or part of the building cannot be occupied for its intended purpose.

(2) We will pay for direct physical loss or damage to Covered Property, caused by abrupt collapse of a building or any part of a building that is insured under this policy or that contains Covered Property insured under this policy, if such collapse is caused by one or more of the following:

(a) Building decay that is hidden from view, unless the presence of such decay is known to an insured prior to collapse;

(b) Insect or vermin damage that is hidden from view, unless the presence of such damage is known to an insured prior to collapse;

(c) Use of defective material or methods in construction, remodeling or renovation if the abrupt collapse occurs during the course of the construction, remodeling or renovation.

(d) Use of defective material or methods in construction, remodeling or renovation if the abrupt collapse occurs after the construction, remodeling or renovation is complete, but only if the collapse is caused in part by:

(i) A cause of loss listed in Paragraph **(2)(a)** or **(2)(b);**

(ii) One or more of the "specified causes of loss";

(iii) Breakage of building glass;

(iv) Weight of people or personal property; or

(v) Weight of rain that collects on a roof.

(3) This Additional Coverage – Collapse does **not** apply to:

(a) A building or any part of a building that is in danger of falling down or caving in;

(b) A part of a building that is standing, even if it has separated from another part of the building; or

(c) A building that is standing or any part of a building that is standing, even if it shows evidence of cracking, bulging, sagging, bending, leaning, settling, shrinkage or expansion.

(4) With respect to the following property:

(a) Awnings;

(b) Gutters and downspouts;

(c) Yard fixtures;

(d) Outdoor swimming pools;

(e) Piers, wharves and docks;

(f) Beach or diving platforms or appurtenances;

(g) Retaining walls; and

(h) Walks, roadways and other paved surfaces;

if an abrupt collapse is caused by a cause of loss listed in Paragraphs **(2)(a)** through **(2)(d),** we will pay for loss or damage to that property only if such loss or damage is a direct result of the abrupt collapse of a building insured under this policy and the property is Covered Property under this policy.

(5) If personal property abruptly falls down or caves in and such collapse is **not** the result of abrupt collapse of a building, we will pay for loss or damage to Covered Property caused by such collapse of personal property only if:

(a) The collapse of personal property was caused by a cause of loss listed in Paragraphs **(2)(a)** through **(2)(d)** of this Additional Coverage;

(b) The personal property which collapses is inside a building; and

(c) The property which collapses is not of a kind listed in Paragraph **(4),** regardless of whether that kind of property is considered to be personal property or real property.

The coverage stated in this Paragraph **(5)** does not apply to personal property if marring and/or scratching is the only damage to that personal property caused by the collapse.

(6) This Additional Coverage – Collapse does not apply to personal property that has not abruptly fallen down or caved in, even if the personal property shows evidence of cracking, bulging, sagging, bending, leaning, settling, shrinkage or expansion.

(7) This Additional Coverage – Collapse will not increase the Limits of Insurance provided in this policy.

(8) The term Covered Cause of Loss includes the Additional Coverage – Collapse as described and limited in Paragraphs **d.(1)** through **d.(7).**

e. Water Damage, Other Liquids, Powder Or Molten Material Damage

If loss or damage caused by or resulting from covered water or other liquid, powder or molten material occurs, we will also pay the cost to tear out and replace any part of the building or structure to repair damage to the system or appliance from which the water or other substance escapes.

We will not pay the cost to repair any defect that caused the loss or damage; but we will pay the cost to repair or replace damaged parts of fire extinguishing equipment if the damage:

(1) Results in discharge of any substance from an automatic fire protection system; or

(2) Is directly caused by freezing.

f. Business Income

(1) Business Income

(a) We will pay for the actual loss of Business Income you sustain due to the necessary suspension of your "operations" during the "period of restoration". The suspension must be caused by direct physical loss of or damage to property at the described premises. The loss or damage must be caused by or result from a Covered Cause of Loss. With respect to loss of or damage to personal property in the open or personal property in a vehicle, the described premises include the area within 100 feet of the site at which the described premises are located.

With respect to the requirements set forth in the preceding paragraph, if you occupy only part of the site at which the described premises are located, your premises means:

(i) The portion of the building which you rent, lease or occupy; and

(ii) Any area within the building or on the site at which the described premises are located, if that area services, or is used to gain access to, the described premises.

(b) We will only pay for loss of Business Income that you sustain during the "period of restoration" and that occurs within 12 consecutive months after the date of direct physical loss or damage. We will only pay for ordinary payroll expenses for 60 days following the date of direct physical loss or damage, unless a greater number of days is shown in the Declarations.

(c) Business Income means the:

(i) Net Income (Net Profit or Loss before income taxes) that would have been earned or incurred if no physical loss or damage had occurred, but not including any Net Income that would likely have been earned as a result of an increase in the volume of business due to favorable business conditions caused by the impact of the Covered Cause of Loss on customers or on other businesses; and

(ii) Continuing normal operating expenses incurred, including payroll.

(d) Ordinary payroll expenses:

(i) Means payroll expenses for all your employees except:

  i. Officers;

  ii. Executives;

  iii. Department Managers;

  iv. Employees under contract; and

  v. Additional Exemptions shown in the Declarations as:

    ● Job Classifications; or

    ● Employees.

(ii) Include:

  i. Payroll;

  ii. Employee benefits, if directly related to payroll;

  iii. FICA payments you pay;

  iv. Union dues you pay; and

  v. Workers' compensation premiums.

(2) Extended Business Income

(a) If the necessary suspension of your "operations" produces a Business Income loss payable under this policy, we will pay for the actual loss of Business Income you incur during the period that:

(i) Begins on the date property except finished stock is actually repaired, rebuilt or replaced and "operations" are resumed; and

(ii) Ends on the earlier of:

  i. The date you could restore your "operations", with reasonable speed, to the level which would generate the Business Income amount that would have existed if no direct physical loss or damage had occurred; or

  ii. 30 consecutive days after the date determined in Paragraph **(a)(i)** above, unless a greater number of consecutive days is shown in the Declarations.

However, Extended Business Income does not apply to loss of Business Income incurred as a result of unfavorable business conditions caused by the impact of the Covered Cause of Loss in the area where the described premises are located.

(b) Loss of Business Income must be caused by direct physical loss or damage at the described premises caused by or resulting from any Covered Cause of Loss.

(3) With respect to the coverage provided in this Additional Coverage, suspension means:

(a) The partial slowdown or complete cessation of your business activities; or

(b) That a part or all of the described premises is rendered untenantable, if coverage for Business Income applies.

(4) This Additional Coverage is not subject to the Limits of Insurance of Section I – Property.

g. Extra Expense

(1) We will pay necessary Extra Expense you incur during the "period of restoration" that you would not have incurred if there had been no direct physical loss or damage to property at the described premises. The loss or damage must be caused by or result from a Covered Cause of Loss. With respect to loss of or damage to personal property in the open or personal property in a vehicle, the described premises include the area within 100 feet of the site at which the described premises are located.

With respect to the requirements set forth in the preceding paragraph, if you occupy only part of the site at which the described premises are located, your premises means:

(a) The portion of the building which you rent, lease or occupy; and

(b) Any area within the building or on the site at which the described premises are located, if that area services, or is used to gain access to, the described premises.

(2) Extra Expense means expense incurred:

(a) To avoid or minimize the suspension of business and to continue "operations":

(i) At the described premises; or

(ii) At replacement premises or at temporary locations, including relocation expenses, and costs to equip and operate the replacement or temporary locations.

(b) To minimize the suspension of business if you cannot continue "operations".

(c) To:

(i) Repair or replace any property; or

(ii) Research, replace or restore the lost information on damaged "valuable papers and records";

to the extent it reduces the amount of loss that otherwise would have been payable under this Additional Coverage or Additional Coverage **f.** Business Income.

(3) With respect to the coverage provided in this Additional Coverage, suspension means:

(a) The partial slowdown or complete cessation of your business activities; or

(b) That a part or all of the described premises is rendered untenantable, if coverage for Business Income applies.

(4) We will only pay for Extra Expense that occurs within 12 consecutive months after the date of direct physical loss or damage. This Additional Coverage is not subject to the Limits of Insurance of Section I – Property.

h. Pollutant Clean-up And Removal

We will pay your expense to extract "pollutants" from land or water at the described premises if the discharge, dispersal, seepage, migration, release or escape of the "pollutants" is caused by or results from a Covered Cause of Loss that occurs during the policy period. The expenses will be paid only if they are reported to us in writing within 180 days of the date on which the Covered Cause of Loss occurs.

This Additional Coverage does not apply to costs to test for, monitor or assess the existence, concentration or effects of "pollutants". But we will pay for testing which is performed in the course of extracting the "pollutants" from the land or water.

The most we will pay for each location under this Additional Coverage is $10,000 for the sum of all such expenses arising out of Covered Causes of Loss occurring during each separate 12-month period of this policy.

i. Civil Authority

When a Covered Cause of Loss causes damage to property other than property at the described premises, we will pay for the actual loss of Business Income you sustain and necessary Extra Expense caused by action of civil authority that prohibits access to the described premises, provided that both of the following apply:

(1) Access to the area immediately surrounding the damaged property is prohibited by civil authority as a result of the damage, and the described premises are within that area but are not more than one mile from the damaged property; and

(2) The action of civil authority is taken in response to dangerous physical conditions resulting from the damage or continuation of the Covered Cause of Loss that caused the damage, or the action is taken to enable a civil authority to have unimpeded access to the damaged property.

Civil Authority coverage for Business Income will begin 72 hours after the time of the first action of civil authority that prohibits access to the described premises and will apply for a period of up to four consecutive weeks from the date on which such coverage began.

Civil Authority coverage for necessary Extra Expense will begin immediately after the time of the first action of civil authority that prohibits access to the described premises and will end:

(1) Four consecutive weeks after the date of that action; or

(2) When your Civil Authority coverage for Business Income ends;

whichever is later.

The definitions of Business Income and Extra Expense contained in the Business Income and Extra Expense Additional Coverages also apply to this Civil Authority Additional Coverage. The Civil Authority Additional Coverage is not subject to the Limits of Insurance of Section **I** – Property.

j. Money Orders And "Counterfeit Money"

We will pay for loss resulting directly from your having accepted in good faith, in exchange for merchandise, "money" or services:

(1) Money orders issued by any post office, express company or bank that are not paid upon presentation; or

(2) "Counterfeit money" that is acquired during the regular course of business.

The most we will pay for any loss under this Additional Coverage is $1,000.

k. Forgery Or Alteration

(1) We will pay for loss resulting directly from forgery or alteration of, any check, draft, promissory note, bill of exchange or similar written promise of payment in "money", that you or your agent has issued, or that was issued by someone who impersonates you or your agent.

(2) If you are sued for refusing to pay the check, draft, promissory note, bill of exchange or similar written promise of payment in "money", on the basis that it has been forged or altered, and you have our written consent to defend against the suit, we will pay for any reasonable legal expenses that you incur in that defense.

(3) For the purpose of this coverage, check includes a substitute check as defined in the Check Clearing for the 21st Century Act, and will be treated the same as the original it replaced.

(4) The most we will pay for any loss, including legal expenses, under this Additional Coverage is $2,500, unless a higher Limit of Insurance is shown in the Declarations.

l. Increased Cost Of Construction

(1) This Additional Coverage applies only to buildings insured on a replacement cost basis.

(2) In the event of damage by a Covered Cause of Loss to a building that is Covered Property, we will pay the increased costs incurred to comply with enforcement of an ordinance or law in the course of repair, rebuilding or replacement of damaged parts of that property, subject to the limitations stated in Paragraphs **(3)** through **(9)** of this Additional Coverage.

(3) The ordinance or law referred to in Paragraph **(2)** of this Additional Coverage is an ordinance or law that regulates the construction or repair of buildings or establishes zoning or land use requirements at the described premises, and is in force at the time of loss.

(4) Under this Additional Coverage, we will not pay any costs due to an ordinance or law that:

(a) You were required to comply with before the loss, even when the building was undamaged; and

(b) You failed to comply with.

(5) Under this Additional Coverage, we will not pay for:

(a) The enforcement of any ordinance or law which requires demolition, repair, replacement, reconstruction, remodeling or remediation of property due to contamination by "pollutants" or due to the presence, growth, proliferation, spread or any activity of "fungi", wet rot or dry rot; or

(b) Any costs associated with the enforcement of an ordinance or law which requires any insured or others to test for, monitor, clean up, remove, contain, treat, detoxify or neutralize, or in any way respond to or assess the effects of "pollutants", "fungi", wet rot or dry rot.

(6) The most we will pay under this Additional Coverage, for each described building insured under Section I – Property, is $10,000. If a damaged building(s) is covered under a blanket Limit of Insurance which applies to more than one building or item of property, then the most we will pay under this Additional Coverage, for each damaged building, is $10,000.

The amount payable under this Additional Coverage is additional insurance.

(7) With respect to this Additional Coverage:

(a) We will not pay for the Increased Cost of Construction:

(i) Until the property is actually repaired or replaced, at the same or another premises; and

(ii) Unless the repairs or replacement are made as soon as reasonably possible after the loss or damage, not to exceed two years. We may extend this period in writing during the two years.

(b) If the building is repaired or replaced at the same premises, or if you elect to rebuild at another premises, the most we will pay for the Increased Cost of Construction is the increased cost of construction at the same premises.

(c) If the ordinance or law requires relocation to another premises, the most we will pay for the Increased Cost of Construction is the increased cost of construction at the new premises.

(8) This Additional Coverage is not subject to the terms of the Ordinance Or Law Exclusion, to the extent that such Exclusion would conflict with the provisions of this Additional Coverage.

(9) The costs addressed in the Loss Payment Property Loss Condition in Section I – Property do not include the increased cost attributable to enforcement of an ordinance or law. The amount payable under this Additional Coverage, as stated in Paragraph **(6)** of this Additional Coverage, is not subject to such limitation.

m. Business Income From Dependent Properties

(1) We will pay for the actual loss of Business Income you sustain due to physical loss or damage at the premises of a dependent property caused by or resulting from any Covered Cause of Loss.

However, this Additional Coverage does not apply when the only loss to dependent property is loss or damage to "electronic data", including destruction or corruption of "electronic data". If the dependent property sustains loss or damage to "electronic data" and other property, coverage under this Additional Coverage will not continue once the other property is repaired, rebuilt or replaced.

The most we will pay under this Additional Coverage is $5,000 unless a higher Limit of Insurance is indicated in the Declarations.

(2) We will reduce the amount of your Business Income loss, other than Extra Expense, to the extent you can resume "operations", in whole or in part, by using any other available:

(a) Source of materials; or

(b) Outlet for your products.

(3) If you do not resume "operations", or do not resume "operations" as quickly as possible, we will pay based on the length of time it would have taken to resume "operations" as quickly as possible.

(4) Dependent property means property owned by others whom you depend on to:

   (a) Deliver materials or services to you, or to others for your account. But services does not mean water, communication or power supply services;

   (b) Accept your products or services;

   (c) Manufacture your products for delivery to your customers under contract for sale; or

   (d) Attract customers to your business.

   The dependent property must be located in the coverage territory of this policy.

(5) The coverage period for Business Income under this Additional Coverage:

   (a) Begins 72 hours after the time of direct physical loss or damage caused by or resulting from any Covered Cause of Loss at the premises of the dependent property; and

   (b) Ends on the date when the property at the premises of the dependent property should be repaired, rebuilt or replaced with reasonable speed and similar quality.

(6) The Business Income coverage period, as stated in Paragraph **(5),** does not include any increased period required due to the enforcement of any ordinance or law that:

   (a) Regulates the construction, use or repair, or requires the tearing down of any property; or

   (b) Requires any insured or others to test for, monitor, clean up, remove, contain, treat, detoxify or neutralize, or in any way respond to, or assess the effects of "pollutants".

   The expiration date of this policy will not reduce the Business Income coverage period.

(7) The definition of Business Income contained in the Business Income Additional Coverage also applies to this Business Income From Dependent Properties Additional Coverage.

n. Glass Expenses

(1) We will pay for expenses incurred to put up temporary plates or board up openings if repair or replacement of damaged glass is delayed.

(2) We will pay for expenses incurred to remove or replace obstructions when repairing or replacing glass that is part of a building. This does not include removing or replacing window displays.

o. Fire Extinguisher Systems Recharge Expense

(1) We will pay:

   (a) The cost of recharging or replacing, whichever is less, your fire extinguishers and fire extinguishing systems (including hydrostatic testing if needed) if they are discharged on or within 100 feet of the described premises; and

   (b) For loss or damage to Covered Property if such loss or damage is the result of an accidental discharge of chemicals from a fire extinguisher or a fire extinguishing system.

(2) No coverage will apply if the fire extinguishing system is discharged during installation or testing.

(3) The most we will pay under this Additional Coverage is $5,000 in any one occurrence.

p. Electronic Data

(1) Subject to the provisions of this Additional Coverage, we will pay for the cost to replace or restore "electronic data" which has been destroyed or corrupted by a Covered Cause of Loss. To the extent that "electronic data" is not replaced or restored, the loss will be valued at the cost of replacement of the media on which the "electronic data" was stored, with blank media of substantially identical type.

(2) The Covered Causes of Loss applicable to Business Personal Property include a computer virus, harmful code or similar instruction introduced into or enacted on a computer system (including "electronic data") or a network to which it is connected, designed to damage or destroy any part of the system or disrupt its normal operation. But there is no coverage for loss or damage caused by or resulting from manipulation of a computer system (including "electronic data") by any employee, including a temporary or leased employee, or by an entity retained by you, or for you, to inspect, design, install, modify, maintain, repair or replace that system.

(3) The most we will pay under this Additional Coverage – Electronic Data for all loss or damage sustained in any one policy year, regardless of the number of occurrences of loss or damage or the number of premises, locations or computer systems involved, is $10,000, unless a higher Limit of Insurance is shown in the Declarations. If loss payment on the first occurrence does not exhaust this amount, then the balance is available for subsequent loss or damage sustained in, but not after, that policy year. With respect to an occurrence which begins in one policy year and continues or results in additional loss or damage in a subsequent policy year(s), all loss or damage is deemed to be sustained in the policy year in which the occurrence began.

q. Interruption Of Computer Operations

(1) Subject to all provisions of this Additional Coverage, you may extend the insurance that applies to Business Income and Extra Expense to apply to a suspension of "operations" caused by an interruption in computer operations due to destruction or corruption of "electronic data" due to a Covered Cause of Loss.

(2) With respect to the coverage provided under this Additional Coverage, the Covered Causes of Loss are subject to the following:

(a) Coverage under this Additional Coverage – Interruption Of Computer Operations is limited to the "specified causes of loss" and Collapse.

(b) If the Businessowners Coverage Form is endorsed to add a Covered Cause of Loss, the additional Covered Cause of Loss does not apply to the coverage provided under this Additional Coverage.

(c) The Covered Causes of Loss include a computer virus, harmful code or similar instruction introduced into or enacted on a computer system (including "electronic data") or a network to which it is connected, designed to damage or destroy any part of the system or disrupt its normal operation. But there is no coverage for an interruption related to manipulation of a computer system (including "electronic data") by any employee, including a temporary or leased employee, or by an entity retained by you, or for you, to inspect, design, install, modify, maintain, repair or replace that system.

(3) The most we will pay under this Additional Coverage – Interruption Of Computer Operations for all loss sustained and expense incurred in any one policy year, regardless of the number of interruptions or the number of premises, locations or computer systems involved, is $10,000 unless a higher Limit of Insurance is shown in the Declarations. If loss payment relating to the first interruption does not exhaust this amount, then the balance is available for loss or expense sustained or incurred as a result of subsequent interruptions in that policy year. A balance remaining at the end of a policy year does not increase the amount of insurance in the next policy year. With respect to any interruption which begins in one policy year and continues or results in additional loss or expense in a subsequent policy year(s), all loss and expense is deemed to be sustained or incurred in the policy year in which the interruption began.

(4) This Additional Coverage – Interruption Of Computer Operations does not apply to loss sustained or expense incurred after the end of the "period of restoration", even if the amount of insurance stated in **(3)** above has not been exhausted.

(5) Coverage for Business Income does not apply when a suspension of "operations" is caused by destruction or corruption of "electronic data", or any loss or damage to "electronic data", except as provided under Paragraphs **(1)** through **(4)** of this Additional Coverage.

Businessowners

(6) Coverage for Extra Expense does not apply when action is taken to avoid or minimize a suspension of "operations" caused by destruction or corruption of "electronic data", or any loss or damage to "electronic data", except as provided under Paragraphs **(1)** through **(4)** of this Additional Coverage.

r. Limited Coverage For "Fungi", Wet Rot Or Dry Rot

(1) The coverage described in Paragraphs **r.(2)** and **r.(6)** only applies when the "fungi", wet rot or dry rot are the result of a "specified cause of loss" other than fire or lightning that occurs during the policy period and only if all reasonable means were used to save and preserve the property from further damage at the time of and after that occurrence.

(2) We will pay for loss or damage by "fungi", wet rot or dry rot. As used in this Limited Coverage, the term loss or damage means:

(a) Direct physical loss or damage to Covered Property caused by "fungi", wet rot or dry rot, including the cost of removal of the "fungi", wet rot or dry rot;

(b) The cost to tear out and replace any part of the building or other property as needed to gain access to the "fungi", wet rot or dry rot; and

(c) The cost of testing performed after removal, repair, replacement or restoration of the damaged property is completed, provided there is a reason to believe that "fungi", wet rot or dry rot are present.

(3) The coverage described under this Limited Coverage is limited to $15,000. Regardless of the number of claims, this limit is the most we will pay for the total of all loss or damage arising out of all occurrences of "specified causes of loss" (other than fire or lightning) which take place in a 12-month period (starting with the beginning of the present annual policy period). With respect to a particular occurrence of loss which results in "fungi", wet rot or dry rot, we will not pay more than the total of $15,000 even if the "fungi", wet rot or dry rot continues to be present or active, or recurs, in a later policy period.

(4) The coverage provided under this Limited Coverage does not increase the applicable Limit of Insurance on any Covered Property. If a particular occurrence results in loss or damage by "fungi", wet rot or dry rot, and other loss or damage, we will not pay more, for the total of all loss or damage, than the applicable Limit of Insurance on the affected Covered Property.

If there is covered loss or damage to Covered Property, not caused by "fungi", wet rot or dry rot, loss payment will not be limited by the terms of this Limited Coverage, except to the extent that "fungi", wet rot or dry rot causes an increase in the loss. Any such increase in the loss will be subject to the terms of this Limited Coverage.

(5) The terms of this Limited Coverage do not increase or reduce the coverage provided under the Water Damage, Other Liquids, Powder Or Molten Material Damage or Collapse Additional Coverages.

(6) The following applies only if Business Income and/or Extra Expense Coverage applies to the described premises and only if the suspension of "operations" satisfies all the terms and conditions of the applicable Business Income and/or Extra Expense Additional Coverage.

(a) If the loss which resulted in "fungi", wet rot or dry rot does not in itself necessitate a suspension of "operations", but such suspension is necessary due to loss or damage to property caused by "fungi", wet rot or dry rot, then our payment under the Business Income and/or Extra Expense is limited to the amount of loss and/or expense sustained in a period of not more than 30 days. The days need not be consecutive.

(b) If a covered suspension of "operations" was caused by loss or damage other than "fungi", wet rot or dry rot, but remediation of "fungi", wet rot or dry rot prolongs the "period of restoration", we will pay for loss and/or expense sustained during the delay (regardless of when such a delay occurs during the "period of restoration"), but such coverage is limited to 30 days. The days need not be consecutive.

6. Coverage Extensions

In addition to the Limits of Insurance of Section I – Property, you may extend the insurance provided by this policy as provided below.

Except as otherwise provided, the following Extensions apply to property located in or on the building described in the Declarations or in the open (or in a vehicle) within 100 feet of the described premises.

a. Newly Acquired Or Constructed Property

(1) Buildings

If this policy covers Buildings, you may extend that insurance to apply to:

(a) Your new buildings while being built on the described premises; and

(b) Buildings you acquire at premises other than the one described, intended for:

(i) Similar use as the building described in the Declarations; or

(ii) Use as a warehouse.

The most we will pay for loss or damage under this Extension is $250,000 at each building.

(2) Business Personal Property

If this policy covers Business Personal Property, you may extend that insurance to apply to:

(a) Business Personal Property, including such property that you newly acquire, at any location you acquire;

(b) Business Personal Property, including such property that you newly acquire, located at your newly constructed or acquired buildings at the location described in the Declarations; or

(c) Business Personal Property that you newly acquire, located at the described premises.

This Extension does not apply to personal property that you temporarily acquire in the course of installing or performing work on such property or your wholesale activities.

The most we will pay for loss or damage under this Extension is $100,000 at each building.

(3) Period Of Coverage

With respect to insurance on or at each newly acquired or constructed property, coverage will end when any of the following first occurs:

(a) This policy expires;

(b) 30 days expire after you acquire the property or begin construction of that part of the building that would qualify as covered property; or

(c) You report values to us.

We will charge you additional premium for values reported from the date you acquire the property or begin construction of that part of the building that would qualify as covered property.

b. Personal Property Off-premises

You may extend the insurance provided by this policy to apply to your Covered Property, other than "money" and "securities", "valuable papers and records" or accounts receivable, while it is in the course of transit or at a premises you do not own, lease or operate. The most we will pay for loss or damage under this Extension is $10,000.

c. Outdoor Property

You may extend the insurance provided by this policy to apply to your outdoor fences, radio and television antennas (including satellite dishes), signs (other than signs attached to buildings), trees, shrubs and plants, including debris removal expense. Loss or damage must be caused by or result from any of the following causes of loss:

(1) Fire;

(2) Lightning;

(3) Explosion;

(4) Riot or Civil Commotion; or

(5) Aircraft.

The most we will pay for loss or damage under this Extension is $2,500, unless a higher Limit of Insurance for Outdoor Property is shown in the Declarations, but not more than $1,000 for any one tree, shrub or plant.

d. Personal Effects

You may extend the insurance that applies to Business Personal Property to apply to personal effects owned by you, your officers, your partners or "members", your "managers" or your employees. This extension does not apply to:

(1) Tools or equipment used in your business; or

(2) Loss or damage by theft.

The most we will pay for loss or damage under this Extension is $2,500 at each described premises.

e. Valuable Papers And Records

(1) You may extend the insurance that applies to Business Personal Property to apply to direct physical loss or damage to "valuable papers and records" that you own, or that are in your care, custody or control caused by or resulting from a Covered Cause of Loss. This Coverage Extension includes the cost to research, replace or restore the lost information on "valuable papers and records" for which duplicates do not exist.

(2) This Coverage Extension does not apply to:

(a) Property held as samples or for delivery after sale; and

(b) Property in storage away from the premises shown in the Declarations.

(3) The most we will pay under this Coverage Extension for loss or damage to "valuable papers and records" in any one occurrence at the described premises is $10,000, unless a higher Limit of Insurance for "valuable papers and records" is shown in the Declarations.

For "valuable papers and records" not at the described premises, the most we will pay is $5,000.

(4) Loss or damage to "valuable papers and records" will be valued at the cost of restoration or replacement of the lost or damaged information. To the extent that the contents of the "valuable papers and records" are not restored, the "valuable papers and records" will be valued at the cost of replacement with blank materials of substantially identical type.

(5) Paragraph **B.** Exclusions in Section I – Property does not apply to this Coverage Extension except for:

(a) Paragraph **B.1.c.,** Governmental Action;

(b) Paragraph **B.1.d.,** Nuclear Hazard;

(c) Paragraph **B.1.f.,** War And Military Action;

(d) Paragraph **B.2.f.,** Dishonesty;

(e) Paragraph **B.2.g.,** False Pretense;

(f) Paragraph **B.2.m.(2),** Errors Or Omissions; and

(g) Paragraph **B.3.**

f. Accounts Receivable

(1) You may extend the insurance that applies to Business Personal Property to apply to accounts receivable. We will pay:

(a) All amounts due from your customers that you are unable to collect;

(b) Interest charges on any loan required to offset amounts you are unable to collect pending our payment of these amounts;

(c) Collection expenses in excess of your normal collection expenses that are made necessary by loss or damage; and

(d) Other reasonable expenses that you incur to reestablish your records of accounts receivable;

that result from direct physical loss or damage by any Covered Cause of Loss to your records of accounts receivable.

(2) The most we will pay under this Coverage Extension for loss or damage in any one occurrence at the described premises is $10,000, unless a higher Limit of Insurance for accounts receivable is shown in the Declarations.

For accounts receivable not at the described premises, the most we will pay is $5,000.

(3) Paragraph **B.** Exclusions in Section I – Property does not apply to this Coverage Extension except for:

(a) Paragraph **B.1.c.,** Governmental Action;

(b) Paragraph **B.1.d.,** Nuclear Hazard;

(c) Paragraph **B.1.f.,** War And Military Action;

(d) Paragraph **B.2.f.,** Dishonesty;

(e) Paragraph **B.2.g.,** False Pretense;

(f) Paragraph **B.3.;** and

(g) Paragraph **B.6.,** Accounts Receivable Exclusion.

B. Exclusions

1. We will not pay for loss or damage caused directly or indirectly by any of the following. Such loss or damage is excluded regardless of any other cause or event that contributes concurrently or in any sequence to the loss. These exclusions apply whether or not the loss event results in widespread damage or affects a substantial area.

   a. Ordinance Or Law

   (1) The enforcement of any ordinance or law:

   (a) Regulating the construction, use or repair of any property; or

   (b) Requiring the tearing down of any property, including the cost of removing its debris.

   (2) This exclusion, Ordinance Or Law, applies whether the loss results from:

   (a) An ordinance or law that is enforced even if the property has not been damaged; or

   (b) The increased costs incurred to comply with an ordinance or law in the course of construction, repair, renovation, remodeling or demolition of property or removal of its debris, following a physical loss to that property.

   b. Earth Movement

   (1) Earthquake, including any earth sinking, rising or shifting related to such event;

   (2) Landslide, including any earth sinking, rising or shifting related to such event;

   (3) Mine subsidence, meaning subsidence of a man-made mine, whether or not mining activity has ceased;

   (4) Earth sinking (other than sinkhole collapse), rising or shifting including soil conditions which cause settling, cracking or other disarrangement of foundations or other parts of realty. Soil conditions include contraction, expansion, freezing, thawing, erosion, improperly compacted soil and the action of water under the ground surface.

   But if Earth Movement, as described in Paragraphs (1) through (4) above, results in fire or explosion, we will pay for the loss or damage caused by that fire or explosion.

   (5) Volcanic eruption, explosion or effusion. But if volcanic eruption, explosion or effusion results in fire, building glass breakage or volcanic action, we will pay for the loss or damage caused by that fire, building glass breakage or volcanic action.

   Volcanic action means direct loss or damage resulting from the eruption of a volcano when the loss or damage is caused by:

   (a) Airborne volcanic blast or airborne shock waves;

   (b) Ash, dust or particulate matter; or

   (c) Lava flow.

   All volcanic eruptions that occur within any 168-hour period will constitute a single occurrence.

   Volcanic action does not include the cost to remove ash, dust or particulate matter that does not cause direct physical loss of or damage to Covered Property.

   c. Governmental Action

   Seizure or destruction of property by order of governmental authority.

   But we will pay for loss or damage caused by or resulting from acts of destruction ordered by governmental authority and taken at the time of a fire to prevent its spread, if the fire would be covered under this policy.

   d. Nuclear Hazard

   Nuclear reaction or radiation, or radioactive contamination, however caused.

   But if nuclear reaction or radiation, or radioactive contamination, results in fire, we will pay for the loss or damage caused by that fire.

   e. Utility Services

   The failure of power, communication, water or other utility service supplied to the described premises, however caused, if the failure:

   (1) Originates away from the described premises; or

   (2) Originates at the described premises, but only if such failure involves equipment used to supply the utility service to the described premises from a source away from the described premises.

   Failure of any utility service includes lack of sufficient capacity and reduction in supply.

Loss or damage caused by a surge of power is also excluded, if the surge would not have occurred but for an event causing a failure of power.

But if the failure or surge of power, or the failure of communication, water or other utility service, results in a Covered Cause of Loss, we will pay for the loss or damage caused by that Covered Cause of Loss.

Communication services include but are not limited to service relating to Internet access or access to any electronic, cellular or satellite network.

This exclusion does not apply to loss or damage to "computer(s)" and "electronic data".

f. **War And Military Action**

(1) War, including undeclared or civil war;

(2) Warlike action by a military force, including action in hindering or defending against an actual or expected attack, by any government, sovereign or other authority using military personnel or other agents; or

(3) Insurrection, rebellion, revolution, usurped power, or action taken by governmental authority in hindering or defending against any of these.

g. **Water**

(1) Flood, surface water, waves (including tidal wave and tsunami), tides, tidal water, overflow of any body of water, or spray from any of these, all whether or not driven by wind (including storm surge);

(2) Mudslide or mudflow;

(3) Water that backs up or overflows or is otherwise discharged from a sewer, drain, sump, sump pump or related equipment;

(4) Water under the ground surface pressing on, or flowing or seeping through:

(a) Foundations, walls, floors or paved surfaces;

(b) Basements, whether paved or not; or

(c) Doors, windows or other openings; or

(5) Waterborne material carried or otherwise moved by any of the water referred to in Paragraph (1), (3) or (4), or material carried or otherwise moved by mudslide or mudflow.

This exclusion applies regardless of whether any of the above, in Paragraphs (1) through (5), is caused by an act of nature or is otherwise caused. An example of a situation to which this exclusion applies is the situation where a dam, levee, seawall or other boundary or containment system fails in whole or in part, for any reason, to contain the water.

But if any of the above, in Paragraphs (1) through (5), results in fire, explosion or sprinkler leakage, we will pay for the loss or damage caused by that fire, explosion or sprinkler leakage.

h. **Certain Computer-related Losses**

(1) The failure, malfunction or inadequacy of:

(a) Any of the following, whether belonging to any insured or to others:

(i) "Computer" hardware, including microprocessors or other electronic data processing equipment as may be described elsewhere in this policy;

(ii) "Computer" application software or other "electronic data" as may be described elsewhere in this policy;

(iii) "Computer" operating systems and related software;

(iv) "Computer" networks;

(v) Microprocessors ("computer" chips) not part of any "computer" system; or

(vi) Any other computerized or electronic equipment or components; or

(b) Any other products, and any services, data or functions that directly or indirectly use or rely upon, in any manner, any of the items listed in Paragraph (a) above;

due to the inability to correctly recognize, distinguish, interpret or accept one or more dates or times. An example is the inability of computer software to recognize the year 2000.

(2) Any advice, consultation, design, evaluation, inspection, installation, maintenance, repair, replacement or supervision provided or done by you or for you to determine, rectify or test for, any potential or actual problems described in Paragraph (1) above.

However, if excluded loss or damage, as described in Paragraph **(1)** above results in a "specified cause of loss" under Section **I** – Property, we will pay only for the loss or damage caused by such "specified cause of loss".

We will not pay for repair, replacement or modification of any items in Paragraph **(1)(a)** or **(1)(b)** to correct any deficiencies or change any features.

i. "Fungi", Wet Rot Or Dry Rot

Presence, growth, proliferation, spread or any activity of "fungi", wet rot or dry rot.

But if "fungi", wet rot or dry rot result in a "specified cause of loss", we will pay for the loss or damage caused by that "specified cause of loss".

This exclusion does not apply:

(1) When "fungi", wet rot or dry rot result from fire or lightning; or

(2) To the extent that coverage is provided in the Limited Coverage For "Fungi", Wet Rot Or Dry Rot Additional Coverage, with respect to loss or damage by a cause of loss other than fire or lightning.

j. Virus Or Bacteria

(1) Any virus, bacterium or other microorganism that induces or is capable of inducing physical distress, illness or disease.

(2) However, the exclusion in Paragraph **(1)** does not apply to loss or damage caused by or resulting from "fungi", wet rot or dry rot. Such loss or damage is addressed in Exclusion **i.;**

(3) With respect to any loss or damage subject to the exclusion in Paragraph **(1),** such exclusion supersedes any exclusion relating to "pollutants".

2. We will not pay for loss or damage caused by or resulting from any of the following:

a. Electrical Apparatus

Artificially generated electrical, magnetic or electromagnetic energy that damages, disturbs, disrupts or otherwise interferes with any:

(1) Electrical or electronic wire, device, appliance, system or network; or

(2) Device, appliance, system or network utilizing cellular or satellite technology.

For the purpose of this exclusion, electrical, magnetic or electromagnetic energy includes but is not limited to:

(1) Electrical current, including arcing;

(2) Electrical charge produced or conducted by a magnetic or electromagnetic field;

(3) Pulse of electromagnetic energy; or

(4) Electromagnetic waves or microwaves.

But if fire results, we will pay for the loss or damage caused by fire.

We will pay for loss or damage to "computer(s)" due to artificially generated electrical, magnetic or electromagnetic energy if such loss or damage is caused by or results from:

(1) An occurrence that took place within 100 feet of the described premises; or

(2) Interruption of electric power supply, power surge, blackout or brownout if the cause of such occurrence took place within 100 feet of the described premises.

b. Consequential Losses

Delay, loss of use or loss of market.

c. Smoke, Vapor, Gas

Smoke, vapor or gas from agricultural smudging or industrial operations.

d. Steam Apparatus

Explosion of steam boilers, steam pipes, steam engines or steam turbines owned or leased by you, or operated under your control. But if explosion of steam boilers, steam pipes, steam engines or steam turbines results in fire or combustion explosion, we will pay for the loss or damage caused by that fire or combustion explosion. We will also pay for loss or damage caused by or resulting from the explosion of gases or fuel within the furnace of any fired vessel or within the flues or passages through which the gases of combustion pass.

e. Frozen Plumbing

Water, other liquids, powder or molten material that leaks or flows from plumbing, heating, air conditioning or other equipment (except fire protective systems) caused by or resulting from freezing, unless:

(1) You do your best to maintain heat in the building or structure; or

(2) You drain the equipment and shut off the supply if the heat is not maintained.

f. Dishonesty

Dishonest or criminal acts by you, anyone else with an interest in the property, or any of your or their partners, "members", officers, "managers", employees, directors, trustees, authorized representatives or anyone to whom you entrust the property for any purpose:

(1) Acting alone or in collusion with others; or

(2) Whether or not occurring during the hours of employment.

This exclusion does not apply to acts of destruction by your employees; but theft by employees is not covered.

With respect to accounts receivable and "valuable papers and records", this exclusion does not apply to carriers for hire.

This exclusion does not apply to coverage that is provided under the Employee Dishonesty Optional Coverage.

g. False Pretense

Voluntary parting with any property by you or anyone else to whom you have entrusted the property if induced to do so by any fraudulent scheme, trick, device or false pretense.

h. Exposed Property

Rain, snow, ice or sleet to personal property in the open.

i. Collapse

(1) Collapse, including any of the following conditions of property or any part of the property:

(a) An abrupt falling down or caving in;

(b) Loss of structural integrity, including separation of parts of the property or property in danger of falling down or caving in; or

(c) Any cracking, bulging, sagging, bending, leaning, settling, shrinkage or expansion as such condition relates to Paragraph **i.(1)(a)** or **i.(1)(b)**.

But if collapse results in a Covered Cause of Loss at the described premises, we will pay for the loss or damage caused by that Covered Cause of Loss.

(2) This Exclusion **i.**, does not apply:

(a) To the extent that coverage is provided under the Additional Coverage – Collapse; or

(b) To collapse caused by one or more of the following:

(i) The "specified causes of loss";

(ii) Breakage of building glass;

(iii) Weight of rain that collects on a roof; or

(iv) Weight of people or personal property.

j. Pollution

We will not pay for loss or damage caused by or resulting from the discharge, dispersal, seepage, migration, release or escape of "pollutants" unless the discharge, dispersal, seepage, migration, release or escape is itself caused by any of the "specified causes of loss". But if the discharge, dispersal, seepage, migration, release or escape of "pollutants" results in a "specified cause of loss", we will pay for the loss or damage caused by that "specified cause of loss".

k. Neglect

Neglect of an insured to use all reasonable means to save and preserve property from further damage at and after the time of loss.

l. Other Types Of Loss

(1) Wear and tear;

(2) Rust or other corrosion, decay, deterioration, hidden or latent defect or any quality in property that causes it to damage or destroy itself;

(3) Smog;

(4) Settling, cracking, shrinking or expansion;

(5) Nesting or infestation, or discharge or release of waste products or secretions, by insects, birds, rodents or other animals;

(6) Mechanical breakdown, including rupture or bursting caused by centrifugal force.

This exclusion does not apply with respect to the breakdown of "computer(s)";

(7) The following causes of loss to personal property:

(a) Dampness or dryness of atmosphere;

(b) Changes in or extremes of temperature; or

(c) Marring or scratching.

But if an excluded cause of loss that is listed in Paragraphs **(1)** through **(7)** above results in a "specified cause of loss" or building glass breakage, we will pay for the loss or damage caused by that "specified cause of loss" or building glass breakage.

m. Errors Or Omissions

Errors or omissions in:

(1) Programming, processing or storing data, as described under "electronic data" or in any "computer" operations; or

(2) Processing or copying "valuable papers and records".

However, we will pay for direct physical loss or damage caused by resulting fire or explosion if these causes of loss would be covered by this coverage form.

n. Installation, Testing, Repair

Errors or deficiency in design, installation, testing, maintenance, modification or repair of your "computer" system including "electronic data".

However, we will pay for direct physical loss or damage caused by resulting fire or explosion if these causes of loss would be covered by this coverage form.

o. Electrical Disturbance

Electrical or magnetic injury, disturbance or erasure of "electronic data", except as provided for under the Additional Coverages of Section **I** – Property.

However, we will pay for direct loss or damage caused by lightning.

p. Continuous Or Repeated Seepage Or Leakage Of Water

Continuous or repeated seepage or leakage of water, or the presence or condensation of humidity, moisture or vapor, that occurs over a period of 14 days or more.

3. We will not pay for loss or damage caused by or resulting from any of the following Paragraphs **a.** through **c.** But if an excluded cause of loss that is listed in Paragraphs **a.** through **c.** results in a Covered Cause of Loss, we will pay for the loss or damage caused by that Covered Cause of Loss.

a. Weather Conditions

Weather conditions. But this exclusion only applies if weather conditions contribute in any way with a cause or event excluded in Paragraph **B.1.** above to produce the loss or damage.

b. Acts Or Decisions

Acts or decisions, including the failure to act or decide, of any person, group, organization or governmental body.

c. Negligent Work

Faulty, inadequate or defective:

(1) Planning, zoning, development, surveying, siting;

(2) Design, specifications, workmanship, repair, construction, renovation, remodeling, grading, compaction;

(3) Materials used in repair, construction, renovation or remodeling; or

(4) Maintenance;

of part or all of any property on or off the described premises.

4. Additional Exclusion

The following applies only to the property specified in this Additional Exclusion.

Loss Or Damage To Products

We will not pay for loss or damage to any merchandise, goods or other product caused by or resulting from error or omission by any person or entity (including those having possession under an arrangement where work or a portion of the work is outsourced) in any stage of the development, production or use of the product, including planning, testing, processing, packaging, installation, maintenance or repair. This exclusion applies to any effect that compromises the form, substance or quality of the product. But if such error or omission results in a Covered Cause of Loss, we will pay for the loss or damage caused by that Covered Cause of Loss.

5. Business Income And Extra Expense Exclusions

a. We will not pay for:

(1) Any Extra Expense, or increase of Business Income loss, caused by or resulting from:

(a) Delay in rebuilding, repairing or replacing the property or resuming "operations", due to interference at the location of the rebuilding, repair or replacement by strikers or other persons; or

(b) Suspension, lapse or cancellation of any license, lease or contract. But if the suspension, lapse or cancellation is directly caused by the suspension of "operations", we will cover such loss that affects your Business Income during the "period of restoration" and any extension of the "period of restoration" in accordance with the terms of the Extended Business Income Additional Coverage.

(2) Any other consequential loss.

b. With respect to this exclusion, suspension means:

(1) The partial slowdown or complete cessation of your business activities; and

(2) That a part or all of the described premises is rendered untenantable, if coverage for Business Income applies.

6. Accounts Receivable Exclusion

The following additional exclusion applies to the Accounts Receivable Coverage Extension:

We will not pay for:

a. Loss or damage caused by or resulting from alteration, falsification, concealment or destruction of records of accounts receivable done to conceal the wrongful giving, taking or withholding of "money", "securities" or other property.

This exclusion applies only to the extent of the wrongful giving, taking or withholding.

b. Loss or damage caused by or resulting from bookkeeping, accounting or billing errors or omissions.

c. Any loss or damage that requires any audit of records or any inventory computation to prove its factual existence.

C. Limits Of Insurance

1. The most we will pay for loss or damage in any one occurrence is the applicable Limits of Insurance of Section I – Property shown in the Declarations.

2. The most we will pay for loss of or damage to outdoor signs attached to buildings is $1,000 per sign in any one occurrence.

3. The amounts of insurance applicable to the Coverage Extensions and the following Additional Coverages apply in accordance with the terms of such coverages and are in addition to the Limits of Insurance of Section I – Property:

a. Fire Department Service Charge;

b. Pollutant Clean-up And Removal;

c. Increased Cost Of Construction;

d. Business Income From Dependent Properties;

e. Electronic Data; and

f. Interruption Of Computer Operations.

4. Building Limit – Automatic Increase

a. In accordance with Paragraph **C.4.b.**, the Limit of Insurance for Buildings will automatically increase by 8%, unless a different percentage of annual increase is shown in the Declarations.

b. The amount of increase is calculated as follows:

(1) Multiply the Building limit that applied on the most recent of the policy inception date, the policy anniversary date, or any other policy change amending the Building limit by:

(a) The percentage of annual increase shown in the Declarations, expressed as a decimal (example: 7% is .07); or

(b) .08, if no percentage of annual increase is shown in the Declarations; and

(2) Multiply the number calculated in accordance with **b.(1)** by the number of days since the beginning of the current policy year, or the effective date of the most recent policy change amending the Building limit, divided by 365.

Example:

If:

The applicable Building limit is $100,000. The annual percentage increase is 8%. The number of days since the beginning of the policy year (or last policy change) is 146.

The amount of increase is

$100,000 x .08 x 146 ÷ 365 = $3,200.

5. Business Personal Property Limit – Seasonal Increase

a. Subject to Paragraph **5.b.**, the Limit of Insurance for Business Personal Property is automatically increased by:

(1) The Business Personal Property – Seasonal Increase percentage shown in the Declarations; or

(2) 25% if no Business Personal Property – Seasonal Increase percentage is shown in the Declarations;

to provide for seasonal variances.

b. The increase described in Paragraph **5.a** will apply only if the Limit of Insurance shown for Business Personal Property in the Declarations is at least 100% of your average monthly values during the lesser of:

   (1) The 12 months immediately preceding the date the loss or damage occurs; or

   (2) The period of time you have been in business as of the date the loss or damage occurs.

D. Deductibles

1. We will not pay for loss or damage in any one occurrence until the amount of loss or damage exceeds the Deductible shown in the Declarations. We will then pay the amount of loss or damage in excess of the Deductible up to the applicable Limit of Insurance of Section I – Property.

2. Regardless of the amount of the Deductible, the most we will deduct from any loss or damage under all of the following Optional Coverages in any one occurrence is the Optional Coverage Deductible shown in the Declarations:

   a. Money and Securities;

   b. Employee Dishonesty;

   c. Outdoor Signs; and

   d. Forgery or Alteration.

But this Optional Coverage Deductible will not increase the Deductible shown in the Declarations. This Deductible will be used to satisfy the requirements of the Deductible in the Declarations.

3. No deductible applies to the following Additional Coverages:

   a. Fire Department Service Charge;

   b. Business Income;

   c. Extra Expense;

   d. Civil Authority; and

   e. Fire Extinguisher Systems Recharge Expense.

E. Property Loss Conditions

1. Abandonment

There can be no abandonment of any property to us.

2. Appraisal

If we and you disagree on the amount of loss, either may make written demand for an appraisal of the loss. In this event, each party will select a competent and impartial appraiser. The two appraisers will select an umpire. If they cannot agree, either may request that selection be made by a judge of a court having jurisdiction. The appraisers will state separately the amount of loss. If they fail to agree, they will submit their differences to the umpire. A decision agreed to by any two will be binding. Each party will:

   a. Pay its chosen appraiser; and

   b. Bear the other expenses of the appraisal and umpire equally.

If there is an appraisal, we will still retain our right to deny the claim.

3. Duties In The Event Of Loss Or Damage

   a. You must see that the following are done in the event of loss or damage to Covered Property:

     (1) Notify the police if a law may have been broken.

     (2) Give us prompt notice of the loss or damage. Include a description of the property involved.

     (3) As soon as possible, give us a description of how, when and where the loss or damage occurred.

     (4) Take all reasonable steps to protect the Covered Property from further damage, and keep a record of your expenses necessary to protect the Covered Property, for consideration in the settlement of the claim. This will not increase the Limits of Insurance of Section I – Property. However, we will not pay for any subsequent loss or damage resulting from a cause of loss that is not a Covered Cause of Loss. Also, if feasible, set the damaged property aside and in the best possible order for examination.

     (5) At our request, give us complete inventories of the damaged and undamaged property. Include quantities, costs, values and amount of loss claimed.

     (6) As often as may be reasonably required, permit us to inspect the property proving the loss or damage and examine your books and records.

Also permit us to take samples of damaged and undamaged property for inspection, testing and analysis, and permit us to make copies from your books and records.

(7) Send us a signed, sworn proof of loss containing the information we request to investigate the claim. You must do this within 60 days after our request. We will supply you with the necessary forms.

(8) Cooperate with us in the investigation or settlement of the claim.

(9) Resume all or part of your "operations" as quickly as possible.

b. We may examine any insured under oath, while not in the presence of any other insured and at such times as may be reasonably required, about any matter relating to this insurance or the claim, including an insured's books and records. In the event of an examination, an insured's answers must be signed.

4. Legal Action Against Us

No one may bring a legal action against us under this insurance unless:

a. There has been full compliance with all of the terms of this insurance; and

b. The action is brought within two years after the date on which the direct physical loss or damage occurred.

5. Loss Payment

In the event of loss or damage covered by this policy:

a. At our option, we will either:

(1) Pay the value of lost or damaged property;

(2) Pay the cost of repairing or replacing the lost or damaged property;

(3) Take all or any part of the property at an agreed or appraised value; or

(4) Repair, rebuild or replace the property with other property of like kind and quality, subject to Paragraph **d.(1)(e)** below.

b. We will give notice of our intentions within 30 days after we receive the sworn proof of loss.

c. We will not pay you more than your financial interest in the Covered Property.

d. Except as provided in Paragraphs **(2)** through **(7)** below, we will determine the value of Covered Property as follows:

(1) At replacement cost without deduction for depreciation, subject to the following:

(a) If, at the time of loss, the Limit of Insurance on the lost or damaged property is 80% or more of the full replacement cost of the property immediately before the loss, we will pay the cost to repair or replace, after application of the deductible and without deduction for depreciation, but not more than the least of the following amounts:

(i) The Limit of Insurance under Section I – Property that applies to the lost or damaged property;

(ii) The cost to replace, on the same premises, the lost or damaged property with other property:

  i. Of comparable material and quality; and

  ii. Used for the same purpose; or

(iii) The amount that you actually spend that is necessary to repair or replace the lost or damaged property.

If a building is rebuilt at a new premises, the cost is limited to the cost which would have been incurred had the building been built at the original premises.

(b) If, at the time of loss, the Limit of Insurance applicable to the lost or damaged property is less than 80% of the full replacement cost of the property immediately before the loss, we will pay the greater of the following amounts, but not more than the Limit of Insurance that applies to the property:

(i) The actual cash value of the lost or damaged property; or

(ii) A proportion of the cost to repair or replace the lost or damaged property, after application of the deductible and without deduction for depreciation. This proportion will equal the ratio of the applicable Limit of Insurance to 80% of the cost of repair or replacement.

(c) You may make a claim for loss or damage covered by this insurance on an actual cash value basis instead of on a replacement cost basis. In the event you elect to have loss or damage settled on an actual cash value basis, you may still make a claim on a replacement cost basis if you notify us of your intent to do so within 180 days after the loss or damage.

(d) We will not pay on a replacement cost basis for any loss or damage:

(i) Until the lost or damaged property is actually repaired or replaced; and

(ii) Unless the repairs or replacement are made as soon as reasonably possible after the loss or damage.

However, if the cost to repair or replace the damaged building property is $2,500 or less, we will settle the loss according to the provisions of Paragraphs **d.(1)(a)** and **d.(1)(b)** above whether or not the actual repair or replacement is complete.

(e) The cost to repair, rebuild or replace does not include the increased cost attributable to enforcement of any ordinance or law regulating the construction, use or repair of any property.

(2) If the Actual Cash Value – Buildings option applies, as shown in the Declarations, Paragraph **(1)** above does not apply to Buildings. Instead, we will determine the value of Buildings at actual cash value.

(3) The following property at actual cash value:

(a) Used or secondhand merchandise held in storage or for sale;

(b) Property of others. However, if an item(s) of personal property of others is subject to a written contract which governs your liability for loss or damage to that item(s), then valuation of that item(s) will be based on the amount for which you are liable under such contract, but not to exceed the lesser of the replacement cost of the property or the applicable Limit of Insurance;

(c) Household contents, except personal property in apartments or rooms furnished by you as landlord;

(d) Manuscripts; and

(e) Works of art, antiques or rare articles, including etchings, pictures, statuary, marble, bronzes, porcelain and bric-a-brac.

(4) Glass at the cost of replacement with safety glazing material if required by law.

(5) Tenants' Improvements and Betterments at:

(a) Replacement cost if you make repairs promptly.

(b) A proportion of your original cost if you do not make repairs promptly. We will determine the proportionate value as follows:

(i) Multiply the original cost by the number of days from the loss or damage to the expiration of the lease; and

(ii) Divide the amount determined in **(i)** above by the number of days from the installation of improvements to the expiration of the lease.

If your lease contains a renewal option, the expiration of the renewal option period will replace the expiration of the lease in this procedure.

(c) Nothing if others pay for repairs or replacement.

(6) Applicable only to the Optional Coverages:

(a) "Money" at its face value; and

(b) "Securities" at their value at the close of business on the day the loss is discovered.

(7) Applicable only to Accounts Receivable:

(a) If you cannot accurately establish the amount of accounts receivable outstanding as of the time of loss or damage:

(i) We will determine the total of the average monthly amounts of accounts receivable for the 12 months immediately preceding the month in which the loss or damage occurs; and

(ii) We will adjust that total for any normal fluctuations in the amount of accounts receivable for the month in which the loss or damage occurred or for any demonstrated variance from the average for that month.

(b) The following will be deducted from the total amount of accounts receivable, however that amount is established:

(i) The amount of the accounts for which there is no loss or damage;

(ii) The amount of the accounts that you are able to reestablish or collect;

(iii) An amount to allow for probable bad debts that you are normally unable to collect; and

(iv) All unearned interest and service charges.

e. Our payment for loss of or damage to personal property of others will only be for the account of the owners of the property. We may adjust losses with the owners of lost or damaged property if other than you. If we pay the owners, such payments will satisfy your claims against us for the owners' property. We will not pay the owners more than their financial interest in the Covered Property.

f. We may elect to defend you against suits arising from claims of owners of property. We will do this at our expense.

g. We will pay for covered loss or damage within 30 days after we receive the sworn proof of loss, provided you have complied with all of the terms of this policy; and

(1) We have reached agreement with you on the amount of loss; or

(2) An appraisal award has been made.

h. A party wall is a wall that separates and is common to adjoining buildings that are owned by different parties. In settling covered losses involving a party wall, we will pay a proportion of the loss to the party wall based on your interest in the wall in proportion to the interest of the owner of the adjoining building. However, if you elect to repair or replace your building and the owner of the adjoining building elects not to repair or replace that building, we will pay you the full value of the loss to the party wall, subject to all applicable policy provisions including Limits of Insurance and all other provisions of this Loss Payment Condition. Our payment under the provisions of this paragraph does not alter any right of subrogation we may have against any entity, including the owner or insurer of the adjoining building, and does not alter the terms of the Transfer Of Rights Of Recovery Against Others To Us Condition in this policy.

6. Recovered Property

If either you or we recover any property after loss settlement, that party must give the other prompt notice. At your option, you may retain the property. But then you must return to us the amount we paid to you for the property. We will pay recovery expenses and the expenses to repair the recovered property, subject to the Limits of Insurance of Section I – Property.

7. Resumption Of Operations

We will reduce the amount of your:

a. Business Income loss, other than Extra Expense, to the extent you can resume your "operations", in whole or in part, by using damaged or undamaged property (including merchandise or stock) at the described premises or elsewhere.

b. Extra Expense loss to the extent you can return "operations" to normal and discontinue such Extra Expense.

8. Vacancy

a. Description Of Terms

(1) As used in this Vacancy Condition, the term building and the term vacant have the meanings set forth in Paragraphs **(a)** and **(b)** below:

(a) When this policy is issued to a tenant, and with respect to that tenant's interest in Covered Property, building means the unit or suite rented or leased to the tenant. Such building is vacant when it does not contain enough business personal property to conduct customary operations.

(b) When this policy is issued to the owner or general lessee of a building, building means the entire building. Such building is vacant unless at least 31% of its total square footage is:

(i) Rented to a lessee or sublessee and used by the lessee or sublessee to conduct its customary operations; and/or

(ii) Used by the building owner to conduct customary operations.

(2) Buildings under construction or renovation are not considered vacant.

b. Vacancy Provisions

If the building where loss or damage occurs has been vacant for more than 60 consecutive days before that loss or damage occurs:

(1) We will not pay for any loss or damage caused by any of the following even if they are Covered Causes of Loss:

(a) Vandalism;

(b) Sprinkler leakage, unless you have protected the system against freezing;

(c) Building glass breakage;

(d) Water damage;

(e) Theft; or

(f) Attempted theft.

(2) With respect to Covered Causes of Loss other than those listed in Paragraphs **(1)(a)** through **(1)(f)** above, we will reduce the amount we would otherwise pay for the loss or damage by 15%.

F. Property General Conditions

1. Control Of Property

Any act or neglect of any person other than you beyond your direction or control will not affect this insurance.

The breach of any condition of this Coverage Form at any one or more locations will not affect coverage at any location where, at the time of loss or damage, the breach of condition does not exist.

2. Mortgageholders

a. The term "mortgageholder" includes trustee.

b. We will pay for covered loss of or damage to buildings or structures to each mortgageholder shown in the Declarations in their order of precedence, as interests may appear.

c. The mortgageholder has the right to receive loss payment even if the mortgageholder has started foreclosure or similar action on the building or structure.

d. If we deny your claim because of your acts or because you have failed to comply with the terms of this policy, the mortgageholder will still have the right to receive loss payment if the mortgageholder:

(1) Pays any premium due under this policy at our request if you have failed to do so;

(2) Submits a signed, sworn proof of loss within 60 days after receiving notice from us of your failure to do so; and

(3) Has notified us of any change in ownership, occupancy or substantial change in risk known to the mortgageholder.

All of the terms of this policy will then apply directly to the mortgageholder.

e. If we pay the mortgageholder for any loss or damage and deny payment to you because of your acts or because you have failed to comply with the terms of this policy:

(1) The mortgageholder's rights under the mortgage will be transferred to us to the extent of the amount we pay; and

(2) The mortgageholder's right to recover the full amount of the mortgageholder's claim will not be impaired.

At our option, we may pay to the mortgageholder the whole principal on the mortgage plus any accrued interest. In this event, your mortgage and note will be transferred to us and you will pay your remaining mortgage debt to us.

f. If we cancel this policy, we will give written notice to the mortgageholder at least:

(1) 10 days before the effective date of cancellation if we cancel for your nonpayment of premium; or

(2) 30 days before the effective date of cancellation if we cancel for any other reason.

g. If we elect not to renew this policy, we will give written notice to the mortgageholder at least 10 days before the expiration date of this policy.

3. No Benefit To Bailee

No person or organization, other than you, having custody of Covered Property will benefit from this insurance.

4. Policy Period, Coverage Territory

Under Section I – Property:

a. We cover loss or damage commencing:

(1) During the policy period shown in the Declarations; and

(2) Within the coverage territory or, with respect to property in transit, while it is between points in the coverage territory.

b. The coverage territory is:

(1) The United States of America (including its territories and possessions);

(2) Puerto Rico; and

(3) Canada.

G. Optional Coverages

If shown as applicable in the Declarations, the following Optional Coverages also apply. These coverages are subject to the terms and conditions applicable to property coverage in this policy, except as provided below.

1. Outdoor Signs

a. We will pay for direct physical loss of or damage to all outdoor signs at the described premises:

(1) Owned by you; or

(2) Owned by others but in your care, custody or control.

b. Paragraph **A.3.,** Covered Causes Of Loss, and Paragraph **B.,** Exclusions in Section I – Property, do not apply to this Optional Coverage, except for:

(1) Paragraph **B.1.c.,** Governmental Action;

(2) Paragraph **B.1.d.,** Nuclear Hazard; and

(3) Paragraph **B.1.f.,** War And Military Action.

c. We will not pay for loss or damage caused by or resulting from:

(1) Wear and tear;

(2) Hidden or latent defect;

(3) Rust;

(4) Corrosion; or

(5) Mechanical breakdown.

d. The most we will pay for loss or damage in any one occurrence is the Limit of Insurance for Outdoor Signs shown in the Declarations.

e. The provisions of this Optional Coverage supersede all other references to outdoor signs in this policy.

2. Money And Securities

a. We will pay for loss of "money" and "securities" used in your business while at a bank or savings institution, within your living quarters or the living quarters of your partners or any employee having use and custody of the property, at the described premises, or in transit between any of these places, resulting directly from:

(1) Theft, meaning any act of stealing;

(2) Disappearance; or

(3) Destruction.

b. In addition to the Limitations and Exclusions applicable to Section I – Property, we will not pay for loss:

(1) Resulting from accounting or arithmetical errors or omissions;

(2) Due to the giving or surrendering of property in any exchange or purchase; or

(3) Of property contained in any "money"-operated device unless the amount of "money" deposited in it is recorded by a continuous recording instrument in the device.

c. The most we will pay for loss in any one occurrence is:

(1) The limit shown in the Declarations for Inside the Premises for "money" and "securities" while:

(a) In or on the described premises; or

(b) Within a bank or savings institution; and

(2) The limit shown in the Declarations for Outside the Premises for "money" and "securities" while anywhere else.

d. All loss:

(1) Caused by one or more persons; or

(2) Involving a single act or series of related acts;

is considered one occurrence.

e. You must keep records of all "money" and "securities" so we can verify the amount of any loss or damage.

3. Employee Dishonesty

a. We will pay for direct loss of or damage to Business Personal Property and "money" and "securities" resulting from dishonest acts committed by any of your employees acting alone or in collusion with other persons (except you or your partner) with the manifest intent to:

(1) Cause you to sustain loss or damage; and also

(2) Obtain financial benefit (other than salaries, commissions, fees, bonuses, promotions, awards, profit sharing, pensions or other employee benefits earned in the normal course of employment) for:

(a) Any employee; or

(b) Any other person or organization.

b. We will not pay for loss or damage:

(1) Resulting from any dishonest or criminal act that you or any of your partners or "members" commit whether acting alone or in collusion with other persons.

(2) Resulting from any dishonest act committed by any of your employees (except as provided in Paragraph **a.**), "managers" or directors:

(a) Whether acting alone or in collusion with other persons; or

(b) While performing services for you or otherwise.

(3) The only proof of which as to its existence or amount is:

(a) An inventory computation; or

(b) A profit and loss computation.

c. The most we will pay for loss or damage in any one occurrence is the Limit of Insurance for Employee Dishonesty shown in the Declarations.

d. All loss or damage:

(1) Caused by one or more persons; or

(2) Involving a single act or series of acts;

is considered one occurrence.

e. If any loss is covered:

(1) Partly by this insurance; and

(2) Partly by any prior cancelled or terminated insurance that we or any affiliate had issued to you or any predecessor in interest;

the most we will pay is the larger of the amount recoverable under this insurance or the prior insurance.

We will pay only for loss or damage you sustain through acts committed or events occurring during the policy period. Regardless of the number of years this policy remains in force or the number of premiums paid, no Limit of Insurance cumulates from year to year or period to period.

f. This Optional Coverage is cancelled as to any employee immediately upon discovery by:

(1) You; or

(2) Any of your partners, "members", "managers", officers or directors not in collusion with the employee;

of any dishonest act committed by that employee before or after being hired by you.

g. We will pay only for covered loss or damage sustained during the policy period and discovered no later than one year from the end of the policy period.

h. If you (or any predecessor in interest) sustained loss or damage during the policy period of any prior insurance that you could have recovered under that insurance except that the time within which to discover loss or damage had expired, we will pay for it under this Optional Coverage, provided:

(1) This Optional Coverage became effective at the time of cancellation or termination of the prior insurance; and

(2) The loss or damage would have been covered by this Optional Coverage had it been in effect when the acts or events causing the loss or damage were committed or occurred.

i. The insurance under Paragraph **h.** above is part of, not in addition to, the Limit of Insurance applying to this Optional Coverage and is limited to the lesser of the amount recoverable under:

(1) This Optional Coverage as of its effective date; or

(2) The prior insurance had it remained in effect.

j. With respect to the Employee Dishonesty Optional Coverage in Paragraph **G.3.**, employee means:

(1) Any natural person:

(a) While in your service or for 30 days after termination of service;

(b) Who you compensate directly by salary, wages or commissions; and

(c) Who you have the right to direct and control while performing services for you;

(2) Any natural person who is furnished temporarily to you:

(a) To substitute for a permanent employee as defined in Paragraph **(1)** above, who is on leave; or

(b) To meet seasonal or short-term workload conditions;

(3) Any natural person who is leased to you under a written agreement between you and a labor leasing firm, to perform duties related to the conduct of your business, but does not mean a temporary employee as defined in Paragraph **(2)** above;

(4) Any natural person who is a former employee, director, partner, member, manager, representative or trustee retained as a consultant while performing services for you; or

(5) Any natural person who is a guest student or intern pursuing studies or duties, excluding, however, any such person while having care and custody of property outside any building you occupy in conducting your business.

But employee does not mean:

(1) Any agent, broker, factor, commission merchant, consignee, independent contractor or representative of the same general character; or

(2) Any "manager", director or trustee except while performing acts coming within the usual duties of an employee.

4. Equipment Breakdown Protection Coverage

a. We will pay for direct loss of or damage to Covered Property caused by or resulting from a mechanical breakdown or electrical failure to pressure, mechanical or electrical machinery and equipment.

Mechanical breakdown or electrical failure to pressure, mechanical or electrical machinery and equipment does not mean any:

(1) Malfunction including but not limited to adjustment, alignment, calibration, cleaning or modification;

(2) Leakage at any valve, fitting, shaft seal, gland packing, joint or connection;

(3) Damage to any vacuum tube, gas tube, or brush; or

(4) The functioning of any safety or protective device.

b. Paragraphs **A.4.a.(1)** and **A.4.a.(2), Limitations,** do not apply to this Optional Coverage.

c. With respect to the coverage provided by this Optional Coverage, the following exclusions in Paragraph **B. Exclusions** do not apply:

(1) Paragraph **B.2.a. Electrical Apparatus;**

(2) Paragraph **B.2.d. Steam Apparatus;** and

(3) Paragraph **B.2.l.(6) Mechanical Breakdown.**

d. With respect to the coverage provided by this Optional Coverage, Paragraph **G.1.c.(5)** of the **Outdoor Sign Optional Coverage** does not apply.

e. If a dollar deductible is shown in the Declarations for this Optional Coverage, we will first subtract the applicable deductible amount from any loss we would otherwise pay. We will then pay the amount of loss in excess of the applicable deductible up to the applicable limit for this coverage.

If no optional deductible is chosen for this Optional Coverage, the Property Deductible shown in the Declarations applies.

          □

f. With respect to **Additional Coverages 5.f. Business Income** and **5.g. Extra Expense**, if the 72-hour time period in the definition of "period of restoration" (hereinafter referred to as time deductible) is amended for this Optional Coverage as shown in the Declarations, we will not pay for any Business Income loss that occurs during the consecutive number of hours shown as the time deductible in the Declarations immediately following a mechanical breakdown or electrical failure. If a time deductible is shown in days, each day shall mean 24 consecutive hours.

As respects the coverage provided by this Optional Coverage, any time deductible shown in the Declarations for Equipment Breakdown Protection Coverage supersedes any time deductible otherwise applicable to the Business Income coverage provided by this policy.

g. With respect to the coverage provided by this Optional Coverage, Paragraph **H. Property Definitions** is amended as follows:

1. "Computer" means:

a. Programmable electronic equipment that is used to store, retrieve and process data; and

b. Associated peripheral equipment that provides communication, including input and output functions such as printing and auxiliary functions such as data transmission.

"Computer" includes those used to operate production type machinery or equipment.

h. Whenever any covered pressure, mechanical or electrical machinery and equipment is found to be in, or exposed to, a dangerous condition, any of our representatives may suspend coverage provided by this Optional Coverage for loss from a mechanical breakdown or electrical failure to that pressure, mechanical or electrical machinery and equipment.

However, coverage provided by this Optional Coverage may be reinstated for loss from a mechanical breakdown or electrical failure to that pressure, mechanical or electrical machinery and equipment if the reasons for the suspension are found by any of our representatives to no longer exist.

We may suspend or reinstate this Optional coverage by mailing or delivering a written notification regarding the suspension or reinstatement to:

(1) Your last known address; or

(2) The address where the pressure, mechanical or electrical machinery and equipment is located.

This notification will indicate the effective date of the suspension or reinstatement.

If the coverage provided by this Optional Coverage is not reinstated, you will get a pro rata refund of premium. But the suspension will be effective even if we have not yet made or offered a refund.

H. Property Definitions

1. "Computer" means:

a. Programmable electronic equipment that is used to store, retrieve and process data; and

b. Associated peripheral equipment that provides communication, including input and output functions such as printing and auxiliary functions such as data transmission.

"Computer" does not include those used to operate production type machinery or equipment.

2. "Counterfeit money" means an imitation of "money" that is intended to deceive and to be taken as genuine.

3. "Electronic data" means information, facts or computer programs stored as or on, created or used on, or transmitted to or from computer software (including systems and applications software), on hard or floppy disks, CD-ROMs, tapes, drives, cells, data processing devices or any other repositories of computer software which are used with electronically controlled equipment. The term computer programs, referred to in the foregoing description of electronic data, means a set of related electronic instructions which direct the operations and functions of a "computer" or device connected to it, which enable the "computer" or device to receive, process, store, retrieve or send data.

4. "Fungi" means any type or form of fungus, including mold or mildew, and any mycotoxins, spores, scents or by-products produced or released by fungi.

5. "Manager" means a person serving in a directorial capacity for a limited liability company.

6. "Member" means an owner of a limited liability company represented by its membership interest, who also may serve as a "manager".

7. "Money" means:

    a. Currency, coins and bank notes in current use and having a face value; and

    b. Travelers checks, register checks and money orders held for sale to the public.

8. "Operations" means your business activities occurring at the described premises.

9. "Period of restoration":

    a. Means the period of time that:

        (1) Begins:

            (a) 72 hours after the time of direct physical loss or damage for Business Income Coverage; or

            (b) Immediately after the time of direct physical loss or damage for Extra Expense Coverage;

        caused by or resulting from any Covered Cause of Loss at the described premises; and

        (2) Ends on the earlier of:

            (a) The date when the property at the described premises should be repaired, rebuilt or replaced with reasonable speed and similar quality; or

            (b) The date when business is resumed at a new permanent location.

    b. Does not include any increased period required due to the enforcement of any ordinance or law that:

        (1) Regulates the construction, use or repair, or requires the tearing down of any property; or

        (2) Requires any insured or others to test for, monitor, clean up, remove, contain, treat, detoxify or neutralize, or in any way respond to or assess the effects of "pollutants".

    The expiration date of this policy will not cut short the "period of restoration".

10. "Pollutants" means any solid, liquid, gaseous or thermal irritant or contaminant, including smoke, vapor, soot, fumes, acids, alkalis, chemicals and waste. Waste includes materials to be recycled, reconditioned or reclaimed.

11. "Securities" means negotiable and non-negotiable instruments or contracts representing either "money" or other property and includes:

    a. Tokens, tickets, revenue and other stamps (whether represented by actual stamps or unused value in a meter) in current use; and

    b. Evidences of debt issued in connection with credit or charge cards, which cards are not issued by you;

but does not include "money".

12. "Specified causes of loss" means the following:

Fire; lightning; explosion; windstorm or hail; smoke; aircraft or vehicles; riot or civil commotion; vandalism; leakage from fire extinguishing equipment; sinkhole collapse; volcanic action; falling objects; weight of snow, ice or sleet; water damage.

    a. Sinkhole collapse means the sudden sinking or collapse of land into underground empty spaces created by the action of water on limestone or dolomite. This cause of loss does not include:

        (1) The cost of filling sinkholes; or

        (2) Sinking or collapse of land into man-made underground cavities.

    b. Falling objects does not include loss of or damage to:

        (1) Personal property in the open; or

        (2) The interior of a building or structure, or property inside a building or structure, unless the roof or an outside wall of the building or structure is first damaged by a falling object.

    c. Water damage means accidental discharge or leakage of water or steam as the direct result of the breaking apart or cracking of any part of a system or appliance (other than a sump system including its related equipment and parts) containing water or steam.

13. "Stock" means merchandise held in storage or for sale, raw materials and in-process or finished goods, including supplies used in their packing or shipping.

14. "Valuable papers and records" means inscribed, printed or written:

    a. Documents;

    b. Manuscripts; and

    c. Records;

including abstracts, books, deeds, drawings, films, maps or mortgages.

But "valuable papers and records" does not mean "money" or "securities".

© Insurance Services Office, Inc., 2009   **BP 00 03 01 10**   ▫

SECTION II – LIABILITY

A. Coverages

1. Business Liability

a. We will pay those sums that the insured becomes legally obligated to pay as damages because of "bodily injury", "property damage" or "personal and advertising injury" to which this insurance applies. We will have the right and duty to defend the insured against any "suit" seeking those damages. However, we will have no duty to defend the insured against any "suit" seeking damages for "bodily injury", "property damage" or "personal and advertising injury" to which this insurance does not apply. We may, at our discretion, investigate any "occurrence" or any offense and settle any claim or "suit" that may result. But:

   (1) The amount we will pay for damages is limited as described in Paragraph **D. – Liability And Medical Expenses Limits Of Insurance** in Section **II** – Liability; and

   (2) Our right and duty to defend end when we have used up the applicable Limit of Insurance in the payment of judgments or settlements or medical expenses.

   No other obligation or liability to pay sums or perform acts or services is covered unless explicitly provided for under Paragraph **f. Coverage Extension – Supplementary Payments.**

b. This insurance applies:

   (1) To "bodily injury" and "property damage" only if:

      (a) The "bodily injury" or "property damage" is caused by an "occurrence" that takes place in the "coverage territory";

      (b) The "bodily injury" or "property damage" occurs during the policy period; and

      (c) Prior to the policy period, no insured listed under Paragraph **C.1.** Who Is An Insured and no "employee" authorized by you to give or receive notice of an "occurrence" or claim, knew that the "bodily injury" or "property damage" had occurred, in whole or in part. If such a listed insured or authorized "employee" knew, prior to the policy period, that the "bodily injury" or "property damage" occurred, then any continuation, change or resumption of such "bodily injury" or "property damage" during or after the policy period will be deemed to have been known before the policy period.

   (2) To "personal and advertising injury" caused by an offense arising out of your business, but only if the offense was committed in the "coverage territory" during the policy period.

c. "Bodily injury" or "property damage" which occurs during the policy period and was not, prior to the policy period, known to have occurred by any insured listed under Paragraph **C.1.** Who Is An Insured or any "employee" authorized by you to give or receive notice of an "occurrence" or claim, includes any continuation, change or resumption of "bodily injury" or "property damage" after the end of the policy period.

d. "Bodily injury" or "property damage" will be deemed to have been known to have occurred at the earliest time when any insured listed under Paragraph **C.1.** Who Is An Insured or any "employee" authorized by you to give or receive notice of an "occurrence" or claim:

   (1) Reports all, or any part, of the "bodily injury" or "property damage" to us or any other insurer;

   (2) Receives a written or verbal demand or claim for damages because of the "bodily injury" or "property damage"; or

   (3) Becomes aware by any other means that "bodily injury" or "property damage" has occurred or has begun to occur.

e. Damages because of "bodily injury" include damages claimed by any person or organization for care, loss of services or death resulting at any time from the "bodily injury".

f. **Coverage Extension – Supplementary Payments**

(1) We will pay, with respect to any claim we investigate or settle, or any "suit" against an insured we defend:

(a) All expenses we incur.

(b) Up to $250 for cost of bail bonds required because of accidents or traffic law violations arising out of the use of any vehicle to which Business Liability Coverage for "bodily injury" applies. We do not have to furnish these bonds.

(c) The cost of bonds to release attachments, but only for bond amounts within our Limit of Insurance. We do not have to furnish these bonds.

(d) All reasonable expenses incurred by the insured at our request to assist us in the investigation or defense of the claim or "suit", including actual loss of earnings up to $250 a day because of time off from work.

(e) All court costs taxed against the insured in the "suit". However, these payments do not include attorneys' fees or attorneys' expenses taxed against the insured.

(f) Prejudgment interest awarded against the insured on that part of the judgment we pay. If we make an offer to pay the Limit of Insurance, we will not pay any prejudgment interest based on that period of time after the offer.

(g) All interest on the full amount of any judgment that accrues after entry of the judgment and before we have paid, offered to pay, or deposited in court the part of the judgment that is within our Limit of Insurance.

These payments will not reduce the limit of liability.

(2) If we defend an insured against a "suit" and an indemnitee of the insured is also named as a party to the "suit", we will defend that indemnitee if all of the following conditions are met:

(a) The "suit" against the indemnitee seeks damages for which the insured has assumed the liability of the indemnitee in a contract or agreement that is an "insured contract";

(b) This insurance applies to such liability assumed by the insured;

(c) The obligation to defend, or the cost of the defense of, that indemnitee, has also been assumed by the insured in the same "insured contract";

(d) The allegations in the "suit" and the information we know about the "occurrence" are such that no conflict appears to exist between the interests of the insured and the interests of the indemnitee;

(e) The indemnitee and the insured ask us to conduct and control the defense of that indemnitee against such "suit" and agree that we can assign the same counsel to defend the insured and the indemnitee; and

(f) The indemnitee:

(i) Agrees in writing to:

i. Cooperate with us in the investigation, settlement or defense of the "suit";

ii. Immediately send us copies of any demands, notices, summonses or legal papers received in connection with the "suit";

iii. Notify any other insurer whose coverage is available to the indemnitee; and

iv. Cooperate with us with respect to coordinating other applicable insurance available to the indemnitee; and

(ii) Provides us with written authorization to:

i. Obtain records and other information related to the "suit"; and

ii. Conduct and control the defense of the indemnitee in such "suit".

(3) So long as the conditions in Paragraph **(2)** are met, attorneys' fees incurred by us in the defense of that indemnitee, necessary litigation expenses incurred by us and necessary litigation expenses incurred by the indemnitee at our request will be paid as Supplementary Payments. Notwithstanding the provisions of Paragraph **B.1.b.(2)** Exclusions in Section **II** – Liability, such payments will not be deemed to be damages for "bodily injury" and "property damage" and will not reduce the Limits of Insurance.

Our obligation to defend an insured's indemnitee and to pay for attorneys' fees and necessary litigation expenses as Supplementary Payments ends when:

(a) We have used up the applicable Limit of Insurance in the payment of judgments or settlements; or

(b) The conditions set forth above, or the terms of the agreement described in Paragraph **(2)(f)** above are no longer met.

2. Medical Expenses

a. We will pay medical expenses as described below for "bodily injury" caused by an accident:

(1) On premises you own or rent;

(2) On ways next to premises you own or rent; or

(3) Because of your operations;

provided that:

(a) The accident takes place in the "coverage territory" and during the policy period;

(b) The expenses are incurred and reported to us within one year of the date of the accident; and

(c) The injured person submits to examination, at our expense, by physicians of our choice as often as we reasonably require.

b. We will make these payments regardless of fault. These payments will not exceed the Limits of Insurance of Section **II** – Liability. We will pay reasonable expenses for:

(1) First aid administered at the time of an accident;

(2) Necessary medical, surgical, x-ray and dental services, including prosthetic devices; and

(3) Necessary ambulance, hospital, professional nursing and funeral services.

B. Exclusions

1. Applicable To Business Liability Coverage

This insurance does not apply to:

a. Expected Or Intended Injury

"Bodily injury" or "property damage" expected or intended from the standpoint of the insured. This exclusion does not apply to "bodily injury" resulting from the use of reasonable force to protect persons or property.

b. Contractual Liability

"Bodily injury" or "property damage" for which the insured is obligated to pay damages by reason of the assumption of liability in a contract or agreement. This exclusion does not apply to liability for damages:

(1) That the insured would have in the absence of the contract or agreement; or

(2) Assumed in a contract or agreement that is an "insured contract", provided the "bodily injury" or "property damage" occurs subsequent to the execution of the contract or agreement. Solely for the purposes of liability assumed in an "insured contract", reasonable attorney fees and necessary litigation expenses incurred by or for a party other than an insured are deemed to be damages because of "bodily injury" or "property damage", provided:

(a) Liability to such party for, or for the cost of, that party's defense has also been assumed in the same "insured contract"; and

(b) Such attorney fees and litigation expenses are for defense of that party against a civil or alternative dispute resolution proceeding in which damages to which this insurance applies are alleged.

c. Liquor Liability

"Bodily injury" or "property damage" for which any insured may be held liable by reason of:

(1) Causing or contributing to the intoxication of any person;

(2) The furnishing of alcoholic beverages to a person under the legal drinking age or under the influence of alcohol; or

(3) Any statute, ordinance or regulation relating to the sale, gift, distribution or use of alcoholic beverages.

This exclusion applies only if you are in the business of manufacturing, distributing, selling, serving or furnishing alcoholic beverages.

d. Workers' Compensation And Similar Laws

Any obligation of the insured under a workers' compensation, disability benefits or unemployment compensation law or any similar law.

e. Employer's Liability

"Bodily injury" to:

(1) An "employee" of the insured arising out of and in the course of:

(a) Employment by the insured; or

(b) Performing duties related to the conduct of the insured's business; or

(2) The spouse, child, parent, brother or sister of that "employee" as a consequence of Paragraph **(1)** above.

This exclusion applies:

(1) Whether the insured may be liable as an employer or in any other capacity; and

(2) To any obligation to share damages with or repay someone else who must pay damages because of the injury.

This exclusion does not apply to liability assumed by the insured under an "insured contract".

f. Pollution

(1) "Bodily injury" or "property damage" arising out of the actual, alleged or threatened discharge, dispersal, seepage, migration, release or escape of "pollutants":

(a) At or from any premises, site or location which is or was at any time owned or occupied by, or rented or loaned to, any insured. However, this subparagraph does not apply to:

(i) "Bodily injury" if sustained within a building and caused by smoke, fumes, vapor or soot produced by or originating from equipment that is used to heat, cool or dehumidify the building, or equipment that is used to heat water for personal use, by the building's occupants or their guests;

(ii) "Bodily injury" or "property damage" for which you may be held liable, if you are a contractor and the owner or lessee of such premises, site or location has been added to your policy as an additional insured with respect to your ongoing operations performed for that additional insured at that premises, site or location and such premises, site or location is not and never was owned or occupied by, or rented or loaned to, any insured, other than that additional insured; or

(iii) "Bodily injury" or "property damage" arising out of heat, smoke or fumes from a "hostile fire";

(b) At or from any premises, site or location which is or was at any time used by or for any insured or others for the handling, storage, disposal, processing or treatment of waste;

(c) Which are or were at any time transported, handled, stored, treated, disposed of, or processed as waste by or for:

    (i) Any insured; or

    (ii) Any person or organization for whom you may be legally responsible; or

(d) At or from any premises, site or location on which any insured or any contractors or subcontractors working directly or indirectly on any insured's behalf are performing operations if the "pollutants" are brought on or to the premises, site or location in connection with such operations by such insured, contractor or subcontractor. However, this subparagraph does not apply to:

    (i) "Bodily injury" or "property damage" arising out of the escape of fuels, lubricants or other operating fluids which are needed to perform the normal electrical, hydraulic or mechanical functions necessary for the operation of "mobile equipment" or its parts, if such fuels, lubricants or other operating fluids escape from a vehicle part designed to hold, store or receive them. This exception does not apply if the "bodily injury" or "property damage" arises out of the intentional discharge, dispersal or release of the fuels, lubricants or other operating fluids, or if such fuels, lubricants or other operating fluids are brought on or to the premises, site or location with the intent that they be discharged, dispersed or released as part of the operations being performed by such insured, contractor or subcontractor;

    (ii) "Bodily injury" or "property damage" sustained within a building and caused by the release of gases, fumes or vapors from materials brought into that building in connection with operations being performed by you or on your behalf by a contractor or subcontractor; or

    (iii) "Bodily injury" or "property damage" arising out of heat, smoke or fumes from a "hostile fire".

(e) At or from any premises, site or location on which any insured or any contractors or subcontractors working directly or indirectly on any insured's behalf are performing operations if the operations are to test for, monitor, clean up, remove, contain, treat, detoxify or neutralize, or in any way respond to, or assess the effects of, "pollutants".

(2) Any loss, cost or expense arising out of any:

(a) Request, demand, order or statutory or regulatory requirement that any insured or others test for, monitor, clean up, remove, contain, treat, detoxify or neutralize, or in any way respond to, or assess the effects of, "pollutants"; or

(b) Claim or "suit" by or on behalf of a governmental authority for damages because of testing for, monitoring, cleaning up, removing, containing, treating, detoxifying or neutralizing, or in any way responding to, or assessing the effects of, "pollutants".

However, this paragraph does not apply to liability for damages because of "property damage" that the insured would have in the absence of such request, demand, order or statutory or regulatory requirement or such claim or "suit" by or on behalf of a governmental authority.

g. Aircraft, Auto Or Watercraft

"Bodily injury" or "property damage" arising out of the ownership, maintenance, use or entrustment to others of any aircraft, "auto" or watercraft owned or operated by or rented or loaned to any insured. Use includes operation and "loading or unloading".

This exclusion applies even if the claims allege negligence or other wrongdoing in the supervision, hiring, employment, training or monitoring of others by an insured, if the "occurrence" which caused the "bodily injury" or "property damage" involved the ownership, maintenance, use or entrustment to others of any aircraft, "auto" or watercraft that is owned or operated by or rented or loaned to any insured.

This exclusion does not apply to:

(1) A watercraft while ashore on premises you own or rent;

(2) A watercraft you do not own that is:

(a) Less than 51 feet long; and

(b) Not being used to carry persons or property for a charge;

(3) Parking an "auto" on, or on the ways next to, premises you own or rent, provided the "auto" is not owned by or rented or loaned to you or the insured;

(4) Liability assumed under any "insured contract" for the ownership, maintenance or use of aircraft or watercraft; or

(5) "Bodily injury" or "property damage" arising out of:

(a) The operation of machinery or equipment that is attached to, or part of, a land vehicle that would qualify under the definition of "mobile equipment" if it were not subject to a compulsory or financial responsibility law or other motor vehicle insurance or motor vehicle registration law where it is licensed or principally garaged; or

(b) The operation of any of the following machinery or equipment:

(i) Cherry pickers and similar devices mounted on automobile or truck chassis and used to raise or lower workers; and

(ii) Air compressors, pumps and generators, including spraying, welding, building cleaning, geophysical exploration, lighting and well servicing equipment.

h. Mobile Equipment

"Bodily injury" or "property damage" arising out of:

(1) The transportation of "mobile equipment" by an "auto" owned or operated by or rented or loaned to any insured; or

(2) The use of "mobile equipment" in, or while in practice for, or while being prepared for, any prearranged racing, speed, demolition or stunting activity.

i. War

"Bodily injury", "property damage" or "personal and advertising injury", however caused, arising, directly or indirectly, out of:

(1) War, including undeclared civil war;

(2) Warlike action by a military force, including action in hindering or defending against an actual or expected attack, by any government, sovereign or other authority using military personnel or other agents; or

(3) Insurrection, rebellion, revolution, usurped power, or action taken by government authority in hindering or defending against any of these.

j. Professional Services

"Bodily injury", "property damage" or "personal and advertising injury" caused by the rendering or failure to render any professional service. This includes but is not limited to:

(1) Legal, accounting or advertising services;

(2) Preparing, approving, or failing to prepare or approve maps, drawings, opinions, reports, surveys, change orders, designs or specifications;

(3) Supervisory, inspection or engineering services;

(4) Medical, surgical, dental, x-ray or nursing services treatment, advice or instruction;

(5) Any health or therapeutic service treatment, advice or instruction;

(6) Any service, treatment, advice or instruction for the purpose of appearance or skin enhancement, hair removal or replacement or personal grooming;

(7) Optometry or optical or hearing aid services including the prescribing, preparation, fitting, demonstration or distribution of ophthalmic lenses and similar products or hearing aid devices;

(8) Body piercing services; and

(9) Services in the practice of pharmacy.

This exclusion applies even if the claims allege negligence or other wrongdoing in the supervision, hiring, employment, training or monitoring of others by an insured, if the "occurrence" which caused the "bodily injury" or "property damage", or the offense which caused the "personal and advertising injury", involved the rendering or failure to render of any professional service.

k. Damage To Property

"Property damage" to:

(1) Property you own, rent or occupy, including any costs or expenses incurred by you, or any other person, organization or entity, for repair, replacement, enhancement, restoration or maintenance of such property for any reason, including prevention of injury to a person or damage to another's property;

(2) Premises you sell, give away or abandon, if the "property damage" arises out of any part of those premises;

(3) Property loaned to you;

(4) Personal property in the care, custody or control of the insured;

(5) That particular part of real property on which you or any contractor or subcontractor working directly or indirectly on your behalf is performing operations, if the "property damage" arises out of those operations; or

(6) That particular part of any property that must be restored, repaired or replaced because "your work" was incorrectly performed on it.

Paragraphs **(1)**, **(3)** and **(4)** of this exclusion do not apply to "property damage" (other than damage by fire) to premises, including the contents of such premises, rented to you for a period of seven or fewer consecutive days. A separate Limit of Insurance applies to Damage To Premises Rented To You as described in Paragraph **D.** Liability And Medical Expenses Limit Of Insurance in Section **II** – Liability.

Paragraph **(2)** of this exclusion does not apply if the premises are "your work" and were never occupied, rented or held for rental by you.

Paragraphs **(3)**, **(4)**, **(5)** and **(6)** of this exclusion do not apply to liability assumed under a sidetrack agreement.

Paragraph **(6)** of this exclusion does not apply to "property damage" included in the "products-completed operations hazard".

l. Damage To Your Product

"Property damage" to "your product" arising out of it or any part of it.

m. Damage To Your Work

"Property damage" to "your work" arising out of it or any part of it and included in the "products-completed operations hazard".

This exclusion does not apply if the damaged work or the work out of which the damage arises was performed on your behalf by a subcontractor.

n. Damage To Impaired Property Or Property Not Physically Injured

"Property damage" to "impaired property" or property that has not been physically injured, arising out of:

(1) A defect, deficiency, inadequacy or dangerous condition in "your product" or "your work"; or

(2) A delay or failure by you or anyone acting on your behalf to perform a contract or agreement in accordance with its terms.

This exclusion does not apply to the loss of use of other property arising out of sudden and accidental physical injury to "your product" or "your work" after it has been put to its intended use.

o. Recall Of Products, Work Or Impaired Property

Damages claimed for any loss, cost or expense incurred by you or others for the loss of use, withdrawal, recall, inspection, repair, replacement, adjustment, removal or disposal of:

(1) "Your product";

(2) "Your work"; or

(3) "Impaired property";

if such product, work or property is withdrawn or recalled from the market or from use by any person or organization because of a known or suspected defect, deficiency, inadequacy or dangerous condition in it.

p. Personal And Advertising Injury

"Personal and advertising injury":

(1) Caused by or at the direction of the insured with the knowledge that the act would violate the rights of another and would inflict "personal and advertising injury";

(2) Arising out of oral or written publication of material, if done by or at the direction of the insured with knowledge of its falsity;

(3) Arising out of oral or written publication of material whose first publication took place before the beginning of the policy period;

(4) For which the insured has assumed liability in a contract or agreement. This exclusion does not apply to liability for damages that the insured would have in the absence of the contract or agreement;

(5) Arising out of a breach of contract, except an implied contract to use another's advertising idea in your "advertisement";

(6) Arising out of the failure of goods, products or services to conform with any statement of quality or performance made in your "advertisement";

(7) Arising out of the wrong description of the price of goods, products or services stated in your "advertisement";

(8) Committed by an insured whose business is:

(a) Advertising, broadcasting, publishing or telecasting;

(b) Designing or determining content of websites for others; or

(c) An Internet search, access, content or service provider.

However, this exclusion does not apply to Paragraphs **14.a.**, **b.** and **c.** of "personal and advertising injury" under Paragraph **F.** Liability And Medical Expenses Definitions.

For the purposes of this exclusion, the placing of frames, borders or links, or advertising, for you or others anywhere on the Internet, by itself, is not considered the business of advertising, broadcasting, publishing or telecasting.

(9) Arising out of the actual, alleged or threatened discharge, dispersal, seepage, migration, release or escape of "pollutants" at any time;

(10) With respect to any loss, cost or expense arising out of any:

(a) Request, demand or order that any insured or others test for, monitor, clean-up, remove, contain, treat, detoxify or neutralize or in any way respond to, or assess the effects of, "pollutants"; or

(b) Claim or "suit" by or on behalf of a governmental authority for damages because of testing for, monitoring, cleaning up, removing, containing, treating, detoxifying or neutralizing or in any way responding to, or assessing the effects of, "pollutants".

(11) Arising out of an electronic chatroom or bulletin board the insured hosts, owns or over which the insured exercises control;

(12) Arising out of the infringement of copyright, patent, trademark, trade secret or other intellectual property rights. Under this exclusion, such other intellectual property rights do not include the use of another's advertising idea in your "advertisement".

However, this exclusion does not apply to infringement, in your "advertisement", of copyright, trade dress or slogan.

(13) Arising out of the unauthorized use of another's name or product in your e-mail address, domain name or metatags, or any other similar tactics to mislead another's potential customers.

q. Electronic Data

Damages arising out of the loss of, loss of use of, damage to, corruption of, inability to access, or inability to manipulate electronic data.

As used in this exclusion, electronic data means information, facts or computer programs stored as or on, created or used on, or transmitted to or from computer software (including systems and applications software), on hard or floppy disks, CD-ROMs, tapes, drives, cells, data processing devices or any other repositories of computer software which are used with electronically controlled equipment. The term computer programs, referred to in the foregoing description of electronic data, means a set of related electronic instructions which direct the operations and functions of a computer or device connected to it, which enable the computer or device to receive, process, store, retrieve or send data.

r. Criminal Acts

"Personal and advertising injury" arising out of a criminal act committed by or at the direction of the insured.

s. Recording And Distribution Of Material Or Information In Violation Of Law

"Bodily injury", "property damage", or "personal and advertising injury" arising directly or indirectly out of any action or omission that violates or is alleged to violate:

(1) The Telephone Consumer Protection Act (TCPA), including any amendment of or addition to such law;

(2) The CAN-SPAM Act of 2003, including any amendment of or addition to such law;

(3) The Fair Credit Reporting Act (FCRA), and any amendment of or addition to such law, including the Fair and Accurate Credit Transaction Act (FACTA); or

(4) Any federal, state or local statute, ordinance or regulation, other than the TCPA, CAN-SPAM Act of 2003 or FCRA and their amendments and additions, that addresses, prohibits, or limits the printing, dissemination, disposal, collecting, recording, sending, transmitting, communicating or distribution of material or information.

Exclusions **c.**, **d.**, **e.**, **f.**, **g.**, **h.**, **i.**, **k.**, **l.**, **m.**, **n.** and **o.** in Section **II** – Liability do not apply to damage by fire to premises while rented to you, or temporarily occupied by you with permission of the owner. A separate Damage To Premises Rented To You Limit of Insurance applies to this coverage as described in Paragraph **D.** Liability And Medical Expenses Limits of Insurance in Section **II** – Liability.

2. Applicable To Medical Expenses Coverage

We will not pay expenses for "bodily injury":

a. To any insured, except "volunteer workers".

b. To a person hired to do work for or on behalf of any insured or a tenant of any insured.

c. To a person injured on that part of premises you own or rent that the person normally occupies.

d. To a person, whether or not an "employee" of any insured, if benefits for the "bodily injury" are payable or must be provided under a workers' compensation or disability benefits law or a similar law.

e. To a person injured while practicing, instructing or participating in any physical exercises or games, sports or athletic contests.

f. Included within the "products-completed operations hazard".

g. Excluded under Business Liability Coverage.

3. Applicable To Both Business Liability Coverage And Medical Expenses Coverage – Nuclear Energy Liability Exclusion

This insurance does not apply:

a. Under Business Liability Coverage, to "bodily injury" or "property damage":

(1) With respect to which an insured under the policy is also an insured under a nuclear energy liability policy issued by the Nuclear Energy Liability Insurance Association, Mutual Atomic Energy Liability Underwriters or Nuclear Insurance Association of Canada, or would be an insured under any such policy but for its termination upon exhaustion of its limit of liability; or

(2) Resulting from the "hazardous properties" of "nuclear material" and with respect to which:

(a) Any person or organization is required to maintain financial protection pursuant to the Atomic Energy Act of 1954, or any law amendatory thereof; or

(b) The insured is, or had this policy not been issued would be, entitled to indemnity from the United States of America, or any agency thereof, under any agreement entered into by the United States of America, or any agency thereof, with any person or organization.

b. Under Medical Expenses Coverage, to expenses incurred with respect to "bodily injury" resulting from the "hazardous properties" of "nuclear material" and arising out of the operation of a "nuclear facility" by any person or organization.

c. Under Business Liability Coverage, to "bodily injury" or "property damage" resulting from the "hazardous properties" of the "nuclear material"; if:

(1) The "nuclear material":

(a) Is at any "nuclear facility" owned by, or operated by or on behalf of, an insured; or

(b) Has been discharged or dispersed therefrom;

(2) The "nuclear material" is contained in "spent fuel" or "waste" at any time possessed, handled, used, processed, stored, transported or disposed of by or on behalf of an insured; or

(3) The "bodily injury" or "property damage" arises out of the furnishing by an insured of services, materials, parts or equipment in connection with the planning, construction, maintenance, operation or use of any "nuclear facility"; but if such facility is located within the United States of America, its territories or possessions or Canada, this Exclusion **(3)** applies only to "property damage" to such "nuclear facility" and any property thereat.

d. As used in this exclusion:

(1) "By-product material" has the meaning given it in the Atomic Energy Act of 1954 or in any law amendatory thereof;

(2) "Hazardous properties" include radioactive, toxic or explosive properties;

(3) "Nuclear facility" means:

(a) Any "nuclear reactor";

(b) Any equipment or device designed or used for:

(i) Separating the isotopes of uranium or plutonium;

(ii) Processing or utilizing "spent fuel"; or

(iii) Handling, processing or packaging "waste";

(c) Any equipment or device used for the processing, fabricating or alloying of "special nuclear material" if at any time the total amount of such material in the custody of the insured at the premises where such equipment or device is located consists of or contains more than 25 grams of plutonium or uranium 233 or any combination thereof, or more than 250 grams of uranium 235;

(d) Any structure, basin, excavation, premises or place prepared or used for the storage or disposal of "waste";

and includes the site on which any of the foregoing is located, all operations conducted on such site and all premises used for such operations;

(4) "Nuclear material" means "source material", "special nuclear material" or "by-product material";

(5) "Nuclear reactor" means any apparatus designed or used to sustain nuclear fission in a self-supporting chain reaction or to contain a critical mass of fissionable material;

(6) "Property damage" includes all forms of radioactive contamination of property;

(7) "Source material" has the meaning given it in the Atomic Energy Act of 1954 or in any law amendatory thereof;

(8) "Special nuclear material" has the meaning given it in the Atomic Energy Act of 1954 or in any law amendatory thereof;

(9) "Spent fuel" means any fuel element or fuel component, solid or liquid, which has been used or exposed to radiation in a "nuclear reactor";

(10) "Waste" means any waste material:

(a) Containing "by-product material" other than the tailings or wastes produced by the extraction or concentration of uranium or thorium from any ore processed primarily for its "source material" content; and

(b) Resulting from the operation by any person or organization of any "nuclear facility" included under Paragraphs **(a)** and **(b)** of the definition of "nuclear facility".

C. Who Is An Insured

1. If you are designated in the Declarations as:

a. An individual, you and your spouse are insureds, but only with respect to the conduct of a business of which you are the sole owner.

b. A partnership or joint venture, you are an insured. Your members, your partners and their spouses are also insureds, but only with respect to the conduct of your business.

c. A limited liability company, you are an insured. Your members are also insureds, but only with respect to the conduct of your business. Your managers are insureds, but only with respect to their duties as your managers.

d. An organization other than a partnership, joint venture or limited liability company, you are an insured. Your "executive officers" and directors are insureds, but only with respect to their duties as your officers or directors. Your stockholders are also insureds, but only with respect to their liability as stockholders.

e. A trust, you are an insured. Your trustees are also insureds, but only with respect to their duties as trustees.

2. Each of the following is also an insured:

a. Your "volunteer workers" only while performing duties related to the conduct of your business, or your "employees", other than either your "executive officers" (if you are an organization other than a partnership, joint venture or limited liability company) or your managers (if you are a limited liability company), but only for acts within the scope of their employment by you or while performing duties related to the conduct of your business. However, none of these "employees" or "volunteer workers" are insureds for:

(1) "Bodily injury" or "personal and advertising injury":

(a) To you, to your partners or members (if you are a partnership or joint venture), to your members (if you are a limited liability company), or to a co-"employee" while in the course of his or her employment or performing duties related to the conduct of your business, or to your other "volunteer workers" while performing duties related to the conduct of your business;

(b) To the spouse, child, parent, brother or sister of that co-"employee" as a consequence of Paragraph **(a)** above;

(c) For which there is any obligation to share damages with or repay someone else who must pay damages because of the injury described in Paragraph **(a)** or **(b)**; or

(d) Arising out of his or her providing or failing to provide professional health care services.

(2) "Property damage" to property:

(a) Owned, occupied or used by,

(b) Rented to, in the care, custody or control of, or over which physical control is being exercised for any purpose by

you, any of your "employees", "volunteer workers", any partner or member (if you are a partnership or joint venture), or any member (if you are a limited liability company).

b. Any person (other than your "employee" or "volunteer worker"), or any organization while acting as your real estate manager.

c. Any person or organization having proper temporary custody of your property if you die, but only:

(1) With respect to liability arising out of the maintenance or use of that property; and

(2) Until your legal representative has been appointed.

d. Your legal representative if you die, but only with respect to duties as such. That representative will have all your rights and duties under this policy.

No person or organization is an insured with respect to the conduct of any current or past partnership, joint venture or limited liability company that is not shown as a Named Insured in the Declarations.

D. Liability And Medical Expenses Limits Of Insurance

1. The Limits of Insurance of Section **II** – Liability shown in the Declarations and the rules below fix the most we will pay regardless of the number of:

a. Insureds;

b. Claims made or "suits" brought; or

c. Persons or organizations making claims or bringing "suits".

2. The most we will pay for the sum of all damages because of all:

a. "Bodily injury", "property damage" and medical expenses arising out of any one "occurrence"; and

b. "Personal and advertising injury" sustained by any one person or organization;

is the Liability and Medical Expenses limit shown in the Declarations. But the most we will pay for all medical expenses because of "bodily injury" sustained by any one person is the Medical Expenses limit shown in the Declarations.

3. The most we will pay under Business Liability Coverage for damages because of "property damage" to a premises while rented to you or in the case of fire while rented to you or temporarily occupied by you with permission of the owner is the applicable Damage To Premises Rented To You limit shown for that premises in the Declarations. For a premises temporarily occupied by you, the applicable limit will be the highest Damage To Premises Rented To You limit shown in the Declarations.

4. **Aggregate Limits**

The most we will pay for:

a. All "bodily injury" and "property damage" that is included in the "products-completed operations hazard" is twice the Liability and Medical Expenses limit.

b. All:

(1) "Bodily injury" and "property damage" except damages because of "bodily injury" or "property damage" included in the "products-completed operations hazard";

(2) Plus medical expenses;

(3) Plus all "personal and advertising injury" caused by offenses committed;

is twice the Liability and Medical Expenses limit.

Subject to Paragraph **a.** or **b.** above, whichever applies, the Damage To Premises Rented To You Limit is the most we will pay for damages because of "property damage" to any one premises, while rented to you, or in the case of fire, while rented to you or temporarily occupied by you with permission of the owner.

The Limits of Insurance of Section **II** – Liability apply separately to each consecutive annual period and to any remaining period of less than 12 months, starting with the beginning of the policy period shown in the Declarations, unless the policy period is extended after issuance for an additional period of less than 12 months. In that case, the additional period will be deemed part of the last preceding period for purposes of determining the Limits of Insurance.

E. **Liability And Medical Expenses General Conditions**

1. **Bankruptcy**

Bankruptcy or insolvency of the insured or of the insured's estate will not relieve us of our obligations under this policy.

2. **Duties In The Event Of Occurrence, Offense, Claim Or Suit**

a. You must see to it that we are notified as soon as practicable of an "occurrence" or an offense which may result in a claim. To the extent possible, notice should include:

(1) How, when and where the "occurrence" or offense took place;

(2) The names and addresses of any injured persons and witnesses; and

(3) The nature and location of any injury or damage arising out of the "occurrence" or offense.

b. If a claim is made or "suit" is brought against any insured, you must:

(1) Immediately record the specifics of the claim or "suit" and the date received; and

(2) Notify us as soon as practicable.

You must see to it that we receive written notice of the claim or "suit" as soon as practicable.

c. You and any other involved insured must:

(1) Immediately send us copies of any demands, notices, summonses or legal papers received in connection with the claim or "suit";

(2) Authorize us to obtain records and other information;

(3) Cooperate with us in the investigation or settlement of the claim or defense against the "suit"; and

(4) Assist us, upon our request, in the enforcement of any right against any person or organization that may be liable to the insured because of injury or damage to which this insurance may also apply.

d. No insured will, except at that insured's own cost, voluntarily make a payment, assume any obligation, or incur any expense, other than for first aid, without our consent.

3. **Legal Action Against Us**

No person or organization has a right under this policy:

a. To join us as a party or otherwise bring us into a "suit" asking for damages from an insured; or

b. To sue us on this policy unless all of its terms have been fully complied with.

 □

A person or organization may sue us to recover on an agreed settlement or on a final judgment against an insured; but we will not be liable for damages that are not payable under the terms of this policy or that are in excess of the applicable Limit of Insurance. An agreed settlement means a settlement and release of liability signed by us, the insured and the claimant or the claimant's legal representative.

4. **Separation Of Insureds**

Except with respect to the Limits of Insurance of Section **II** – Liability, and any rights or duties specifically assigned in this policy to the first Named Insured, this insurance applies:

a. As if each Named Insured were the only Named Insured; and

b. Separately to each insured against whom claim is made or "suit" is brought.

F. **Liability And Medical Expenses Definitions**

1. "Advertisement" means a notice that is broadcast or published to the general public or specific market segments about your goods, products or services for the purpose of attracting customers or supporters. For the purposes of this definition:

a. Notices that are published include material placed on the Internet or on similar electronic means of communication; and

b. Regarding websites, only that part of a website that is about your goods, products or services for the purposes of attracting customers or supporters is considered an advertisement.

2. "Auto" means:

a. A land motor vehicle, trailer or semitrailer designed for travel on public roads, including any attached machinery or equipment; or

b. Any other land vehicle that is subject to a compulsory or financial responsibility law or other motor vehicle insurance or motor vehicle registration law where it is licensed or principally garaged.

However, "auto" does not include "mobile equipment".

3. "Bodily injury" means bodily injury, sickness or disease sustained by a person, including death resulting from any of these at any time.

4. "Coverage territory" means:

a. The United States of America (including its territories and possessions), Puerto Rico and Canada;

b. International waters or airspace, but only if the injury or damage occurs in the course of travel or transportation between any places included in Paragraph **a.** above; or

c. All other parts of the world if the injury or damage arises out of:

(1) Goods or products made or sold by you in the territory described in Paragraph **a.** above;

(2) The activities of a person whose home is in the territory described in Paragraph **a.** above, but is away for a short time on your business; or

(3) "Personal and advertising injury" offenses that take place through the Internet or similar electronic means of communication;

provided the insured's responsibility to pay damages is determined in a "suit" on the merits in the territory described in Paragraph **a.** above or in a settlement we agree to.

5. "Employee" includes a "leased worker". "Employee" does not include a "temporary worker".

6. "Executive officer" means a person holding any of the officer positions created by your charter, constitution, bylaws or any other similar governing document.

7. "Hostile fire" means one which becomes uncontrollable or breaks out from where it was intended to be.

8. "Impaired property" means tangible property, other than "your product" or "your work", that cannot be used or is less useful because:

a. It incorporates "your product" or "your work" that is known or thought to be defective, deficient, inadequate or dangerous; or

b. You have failed to fulfill the terms of a contract or agreement;

if such property can be restored to use by:

(1) The repair, replacement, adjustment or removal of "your product" or "your work"; or

(2) Your fulfilling the terms of the contract or agreement.

9. "Insured contract" means:

a. A contract for a lease of premises. However, that portion of the contract for a lease of premises that indemnifies any person or organization for damage by fire to premises while rented to you or temporarily occupied by you with permission of the owner is not an "insured contract";

b. A sidetrack agreement;

c. Any easement or license agreement, except in connection with construction or demolition operations on or within 50 feet of a railroad;

d. An obligation, as required by ordinance, to indemnify a municipality, except in connection with work for a municipality;

e. An elevator maintenance agreement;

f. That part of any other contract or agreement pertaining to your business (including an indemnification of a municipality in connection with work performed for a municipality) under which you assume the tort liability of another party to pay for "bodily injury" or "property damage" to a third person or organization. Tort liability means a liability that would be imposed by law in the absence of any contract or agreement.

Paragraph **f.** does not include that part of any contract or agreement:

(1) That indemnifies a railroad for "bodily injury" or "property damage" arising out of construction or demolition operations, within 50 feet of any railroad property and affecting any railroad bridge or trestle, tracks, roadbeds, tunnel, underpass or crossing;

(2) That indemnifies an architect, engineer or surveyor for injury or damage arising out of:

(a) Preparing, approving or failing to prepare or approve maps, drawings, opinions, reports, surveys, change orders, designs or specifications; or

(b) Giving directions or instructions, or failing to give them, if that is the primary cause of the injury or damage; or

(3) Under which the insured, if an architect, engineer or surveyor, assumes liability for an injury or damage arising out of the insured's rendering or failure to render professional services, including those listed in Paragraph **(2)** above and supervisory, inspection or engineering services.

10. "Leased worker" means a person leased to you by a labor leasing firm under an agreement between you and the labor leasing firm, to perform duties related to the conduct of your business. "Leased worker" does not include a "temporary worker".

11. "Loading or unloading" means the handling of property:

a. After it is moved from the place where it is accepted for movement into or onto an aircraft, watercraft or "auto";

b. While it is in or on an aircraft, watercraft or "auto"; or

c. While it is being moved from an aircraft, watercraft or "auto" to the place where it is finally delivered;

but "loading or unloading" does not include the movement of property by means of a mechanical device, other than a hand truck, that is not attached to the aircraft, watercraft or "auto".

12. "Mobile equipment" means any of the following types of land vehicles, including any attached machinery or equipment:

a. Bulldozers, farm machinery, forklifts and other vehicles designed for use principally off public roads;

b. Vehicles maintained for use solely on or next to premises you own or rent;

c. Vehicles that travel on crawler treads;

d. Vehicles, whether self-propelled or not, on which are permanently mounted:

(1) Power cranes, shovels, loaders, diggers or drills; or

(2) Road construction or resurfacing equipment such as graders, scrapers or rollers;

e. Vehicles not described in Paragraph **a.**, **b.**, **c.** or **d.** above that are not self-propelled and are maintained primarily to provide mobility to permanently attached equipment of the following types:

(1) Air compressors, pumps and generators, including spraying, welding, building cleaning, geophysical exploration, lighting and well servicing equipment; or

(2) Cherry pickers and similar devices used to raise or lower workers;

f. Vehicles not described in Paragraph **a.**, **b.**, **c.** or **d.** above maintained primarily for purposes other than the transportation of persons or cargo.

However, self-propelled vehicles with the following types of permanently attached equipment are not "mobile equipment" but will be considered "autos":

(1) Equipment designed primarily for:

(a) Snow removal;

(b) Road maintenance, but not construction or resurfacing; or

(c) Street cleaning;

(2) Cherry pickers and similar devices mounted on automobile or truck chassis and used to raise or lower workers; and

(3) Air compressors, pumps and generators, including spraying, welding, building cleaning, geophysical exploration, lighting and well servicing equipment.

However, "mobile equipment" does not include land vehicles that are subject to a compulsory or financial responsibility law or other motor vehicle insurance or motor vehicle registration law where they are licensed or principally garaged. Land vehicles subject to a compulsory or financial responsibility law or other motor vehicle insurance law or motor vehicle registration law are considered "autos".

13. "Occurrence" means an accident, including continuous or repeated exposure to substantially the same general harmful conditions.

14. "Personal and advertising injury" means injury, including consequential "bodily injury", arising out of one or more of the following offenses:

a. False arrest, detention or imprisonment;

b. Malicious prosecution;

c. The wrongful eviction from, wrongful entry into, or invasion of the right of private occupancy of a room, dwelling or premises that a person occupies, committed by or on behalf of its owner, landlord or lessor;

d. Oral or written publication, in any manner, of material that slanders or libels a person or organization or disparages a person's or organization's goods, products or services;

e. Oral or written publication, in any manner, of material that violates a person's right of privacy;

f. The use of another's advertising idea in your "advertisement"; or

g. Infringing upon another's copyright, trade dress or slogan in your "advertisement".

15. "Pollutants" mean any solid, liquid, gaseous or thermal irritant or contaminant, including smoke, vapor, soot, fumes, acids, alkalis, chemicals and waste. Waste includes materials to be recycled, reconditioned or reclaimed.

16. "Products-completed operations hazard":

a. Includes all "bodily injury" and "property damage" occurring away from premises you own or rent and arising out of "your product" or "your work" except:

(1) Products that are still in your physical possession; or

(2) Work that has not yet been completed or abandoned. However, "your work" will be deemed completed at the earliest of the following times:

(a) When all of the work called for in your contract has been completed.

(b) When all of the work to be done at the job site has been completed if your contract calls for work at more than one job site.

(c) When that part of the work done at the job site has been put to its intended use by any other person or organization other than another contractor or subcontractor working on the same project.

Work that may need service, maintenance, correction, repair or replacement, but which is otherwise complete, will be treated as completed.

The "bodily injury" or "property damage" must occur away from premises you own or rent, unless your business includes the selling, handling or distribution of "your product" for consumption on premises you own or rent.

b. Does not include "bodily injury" or "property damage" arising out of:

(1) The transportation of property, unless the injury or damage arises out of a condition in or on a vehicle not owned or operated by you, and that condition was created by the "loading or unloading" of that vehicle by any insured; or

(2) The existence of tools, uninstalled equipment or abandoned or unused materials.

17. "Property damage" means:

a. Physical injury to tangible property, including all resulting loss of use of that property. All such loss of use shall be deemed to occur at the time of the physical injury that caused it; or

b. Loss of use of tangible property that is not physically injured. All such loss of use shall be deemed to occur at the time of the "occurrence" that caused it.

For the purposes of this insurance, electronic data is not tangible property.

As used in this definition, electronic data means information, facts or programs stored as, created or used on, or transmitted to or from computer software, including systems and applications software, hard or floppy disks, CD-ROMs, tapes, drives, cells, data processing devices or any other media which are used with electronically controlled equipment.

18. "Suit" means a civil proceeding in which damages because of "bodily injury", "property damage", or "personal and advertising injury" to which this insurance applies are alleged. "Suit" includes:

   a. An arbitration proceeding in which such damages are claimed and to which the insured must submit or does submit with our consent; or

   b. Any other alternative dispute resolution proceeding in which such damages are claimed and to which the insured submits with our consent.

19. "Temporary worker" means a person who is furnished to you to substitute for a permanent "employee" on leave or to meet seasonal or short-term workload conditions.

20. "Volunteer worker" means a person who is not your "employee", and who donates his or her work and acts at the direction of and within the scope of duties determined by you, and is not paid a fee, salary or other compensation by you or anyone else for their work performed for you.

21. "Your product":

   a. Means:

      (1) Any goods or products, other than real property, manufactured, sold, handled, distributed or disposed of by:

         (a) You;

         (b) Others trading under your name; or

         (c) A person or organization whose business or assets you have acquired; and

      (2) Containers (other than vehicles), materials, parts or equipment furnished in connection with such goods or products.

   b. Includes:

      (1) Warranties or representations made at any time with respect to the fitness, quality, durability, performance or use of "your product"; and

   (2) The providing of or failure to provide warnings or instructions.

   c. Does not include vending machines or other property rented to or located for the use of others but not sold.

22. "Your work":

   a. Means:

      (1) Work or operations performed by you or on your behalf; and

      (2) Materials, parts or equipment furnished in connection with such work or operations.

   b. Includes:

      (1) Warranties or representations made at any time with respect to the fitness, quality, durability, performance or use of "your work"; and

      (2) The providing of or failure to provide warnings or instructions.

SECTION III – COMMON POLICY CONDITIONS (APPLICABLE TO SECTION I – PROPERTY AND SECTION II – LIABILITY)

A. Cancellation

   1. The first Named Insured shown in the Declarations may cancel this policy by mailing or delivering to us advance written notice of cancellation.

   2. We may cancel this policy by mailing or delivering to the first Named Insured written notice of cancellation at least:

      a. Five days before the effective date of cancellation if any one of the following conditions exists at any building that is Covered Property in this policy;

         (1) The building has been vacant or unoccupied 60 or more consecutive days. This does not apply to:

            (a) Seasonal unoccupancy; or

            (b) Buildings in the course of construction, renovation or addition.

            Buildings with 65% or more of the rental units or floor area vacant or unoccupied are considered unoccupied under this provision.

         (2) After damage by a Covered Cause of Loss, permanent repairs to the building:

            (a) Have not started, and

            (b) Have not been contracted for,

            within 30 days of initial payment of loss.

         (3) The building has:

            (a) An outstanding order to vacate;

© Insurance Services Office, Inc., 2009   □

(b) An outstanding demolition order; or

(c) Been declared unsafe by governmental authority.

(4) Fixed and salvageable items have been or are being removed from the building and are not being replaced. This does not apply to such removal that is necessary or incidental to any renovation or remodeling.

(5) Failure to:

(a) Furnish necessary heat, water, sewer service or electricity for 30 consecutive days or more, except during a period of seasonal unoccupancy; or

(b) Pay property taxes that are owing and have been outstanding for more than one year following the date due, except that this provision will not apply where you are in a bona fide dispute with the taxing authority regarding payment of such taxes.

b. 10 days before the effective date of cancellation if we cancel for nonpayment of premium.

c. 30 days before the effective date of cancellation if we cancel for any other reason.

3. We will mail or deliver our notice to the first Named Insured's last mailing address known to us.

4. Notice of cancellation will state the effective date of cancellation. The policy period will end on that date.

5. If this policy is cancelled, we will send the first Named Insured any premium refund due. If we cancel, the refund will be pro rata. If the first Named Insured cancels, the refund may be less than pro rata. The cancellation will be effective even if we have not made or offered a refund.

6. If notice is mailed, proof of mailing will be sufficient proof of notice.

B. Changes

This policy contains all the agreements between you and us concerning the insurance afforded. The first Named Insured shown in the Declarations is authorized to make changes in the terms of this policy with our consent. This policy's terms can be amended or waived only by endorsement issued by us and made a part of this policy.

C. Concealment, Misrepresentation Or Fraud

This policy is void in any case of fraud by you as it relates to this policy at any time. It is also void if you or any other insured, at any time, intentionally conceal or misrepresent a material fact concerning:

1. This policy;

2. The Covered Property;

3. Your interest in the Covered Property; or

4. A claim under this policy.

D. Examination Of Your Books And Records

We may examine and audit your books and records as they relate to this policy at any time during the policy period and up to three years afterward.

E. Inspections And Surveys

1. We have the right to:

a. Make inspections and surveys at any time;

b. Give you reports on the conditions we find; and

c. Recommend changes.

2. We are not obligated to make any inspections, surveys, reports or recommendations and any such actions we do undertake relate only to insurability and the premiums to be charged. We do not make safety inspections. We do not undertake to perform the duty of any person or organization to provide for the health or safety of workers or the public. And we do not warrant that conditions:

a. Are safe and healthful; or

b. Comply with laws, regulations, codes or standards.

3. Paragraphs **1.** and **2.** of this condition apply not only to us, but also to any rating, advisory, rate service or similar organization which makes insurance inspections, surveys, reports or recommendations.

4. Paragraph **2.** of this condition does not apply to any inspections, surveys, reports or recommendations we may make relative to certification, under state or municipal statutes, ordinances or regulations, of boilers, pressure vessels or elevators.

F. Insurance Under Two Or More Coverages

If two or more of this policy's coverages apply to the same loss or damage, we will not pay more than the actual amount of the loss or damage.

G. Liberalization

If we adopt any revision that would broaden the coverage under this policy without additional premium within 45 days prior to or during the policy period, the broadened coverage will immediately apply to this policy.

H. Other Insurance

1. If there is other insurance covering the same loss or damage, we will pay only for the amount of covered loss or damage in excess of the amount due from that other insurance, whether you can collect on it or not. But we will not pay more than the applicable Limit of Insurance of Section I – Property.

2. Business Liability Coverage is excess over:

   a. Any other insurance that insures for direct physical loss or damage; or

   b. Any other primary insurance available to you covering liability for damages arising out of the premises or operations for which you have been added as an additional insured by attachment of an endorsement.

3. When this insurance is excess, we will have no duty under Business Liability Coverage to defend any claim or "suit" that any other insurer has a duty to defend. If no other insurer defends, we will undertake to do so, but we will be entitled to the insured's rights against all those other insurers.

I. Premiums

1. The first Named Insured shown in the Declarations:

   a. Is responsible for the payment of all premiums; and

   b. Will be the payee for any return premiums we pay.

2. The premium shown in the Declarations was computed based on rates in effect at the time the policy was issued. On each renewal, continuation or anniversary of the effective date of this policy, we will compute the premium in accordance with our rates and rules then in effect.

3. With our consent, you may continue this policy in force by paying a continuation premium for each successive one-year period. The premium must be:

   a. Paid to us prior to the anniversary date; and

   b. Determined in accordance with Paragraph 2. above.

Our forms then in effect will apply. If you do not pay the continuation premium, this policy will expire on the first anniversary date that we have not received the premium.

4. Undeclared exposures or change in your business operation, acquisition or use of locations may occur during the policy period that are not shown in the Declarations. If so, we may require an additional premium. That premium will be determined in accordance with our rates and rules then in effect.

J. Premium Audit

1. This policy is subject to audit if a premium designated as an advance premium is shown in the Declarations. We will compute the final premium due when we determine your actual exposures.

2. Premium shown in this policy as advance premium is a deposit premium only. At the close of each audit period we will compute the earned premium for that period and send notice to the first Named Insured. The due date for audit premiums is the date shown as the due date on the bill. If the sum of the advance and audit premiums paid for the policy period is greater than the earned premium, we will return the excess to the first Named Insured.

3. The first Named Insured must keep records of the information we need for premium computation, and send us copies at such times as we may request.

K. Transfer Of Rights Of Recovery Against Others To Us

1. Applicable to Businessowners Property Coverage:

   If any person or organization to or for whom we make payment under this policy has rights to recover damages from another, those rights are transferred to us to the extent of our payment. That person or organization must do everything necessary to secure our rights and must do nothing after loss to impair them. But you may waive your rights against another party in writing:

   a. Prior to a loss to your Covered Property.

   b. After a loss to your Covered Property only if, at time of loss, that party is one of the following:

      (1) Someone insured by this insurance;

      (2) A business firm:

         (a) Owned or controlled by you; or

         (b) That owns or controls you; or

      (3) Your tenant.

You may also accept the usual bills of lading or shipping receipts limiting the liability of carriers.

This will not restrict your insurance.

2. Applicable to Businessowners Liability Coverage:

If the insured has rights to recover all or part of any payment we have made under this policy, those rights are transferred to us. The insured must do nothing after loss to impair them. At our request, the insured will bring "suit" or transfer those rights to us and help us enforce them. This condition does not apply to Medical Expenses Coverage.

L. Transfer Of Your Rights And Duties Under This Policy

Your rights and duties under this policy may not be transferred without our written consent except in the case of death of an individual Named Insured.

If you die, your rights and duties will be transferred to your legal representative but only while acting within the scope of duties as your legal representative. Until your legal representative is appointed, anyone having proper temporary custody of your property will have your rights and duties but only with respect to that property.

Farm Insurance

Some insurers offer specialized package policies for covering the property and liability loss exposures of farms. (The word "farms," as used here, includes ranches.) These specialized policies are called either farm insurance policies or farmowners policies. A typical farm policy covering a farm family might include coverages for the following:

- The insured's dwelling
- Appurtenant private structures (such as a detached garage)
- Household personal property (excluding personal property used in farming)
- Loss of use of the above categories of property
- Scheduled farm personal property
- Unscheduled farm personal property
- Barns and other farm structures

The first four coverages are essentially the same as Coverages A through D of a homeowners policy, and the last three coverages insure property used in farming, with an option for covering farm personal property with a separate limit for each type or class of property or with one limit for all covered property. If the policy covers a farm that is owned by an agribusiness corporation, the personal coverages can be omitted.

In addition to property coverage, a farm policy ordinarily includes liability coverage for both the family's personal liability loss exposures and the liability loss exposures arising out of farming operations.

This section of the *Handbook* reprints two forms from the farm insurance program of Insurance Services Office, Inc. (ISO). The Farm Personal Property Coverage Form contains provisions for insuring farm personal property (excluding household personal property). The Causes of Loss Form—Farm Property describes the covered perils. The other ISO forms that might be included in a farm policy are as follows:

- The Farm Dwellings, Appurtenant Structures and Household Personal Property Coverage Form provides the equivalent of Coverages A through D of a homeowners policy.
- The Barns, Outbuildings and Other Farm Structures Coverage Form can be used to insure all types of farm buildings and structures other than the dwelling and private garages.
- The Other Farm Provisions Form contains general provisions that apply to the various coverage forms that might be attached.
- The Farm Liability Coverage Form covers both personal and farming liability exposures.

Farm

FARM
FP 00 13 09 03

FARM PROPERTY – FARM PERSONAL PROPERTY COVERAGE FORM

Various provisions in this policy restrict coverage. Read the entire policy carefully to determine rights, duties and what is and is not covered.

Throughout this Coverage Form, the words "you" and "your" refer to the Named Insured shown in the Declarations. If the Named Insured shown in the Declarations and spouse are members of the same household, the words "you" and "your" also refer to the spouse. The words "we", "us" and "our" refer to the Company providing this insurance.

Other words and phrases that appear in quotation marks have special meaning. Refer to the Definitions Section of the Farm Property – Other Farm Provisions Form – Additional Coverages, Conditions, Definitions.

SECTION I – COVERAGES

COVERAGE E – SCHEDULED FARM PERSONAL PROPERTY

A. Coverage

We will pay for direct physical loss of or damage to Covered Property at the "insured location" described in the Declarations, or elsewhere as expressly provided below, caused by or resulting from any Covered Cause of Loss.

1. Covered Property

All of the following are Covered Property under Coverage **E** of this Coverage Form, provided a Limit of Insurance is shown in the Declarations for the specific type of property:

a. Grain, threshed seeds and beans, ground feed, silage, and manufactured and blended "livestock" feed in buildings or structures or in sacks, wagons or trucks.

b. Grain in stacks, shocks, swaths or piles in the open, but for this property fire and lightning, vandalism, vehicles and theft are the only Covered Causes of Loss.

c. Hay, straw and fodder:

(1) In buildings or structures; and

(2) In stacks, windrows or bales, but for this property fire or lightning, windstorm or hail, vandalism, vehicles and theft are the only Covered Causes of Loss.

A stack means hay, straw or fodder in one area separated by a clear space of 100 feet or more from any other hay, straw or fodder in the open.

d. Farm products, materials and supplies shown in the Declarations. These include farm materials and related packing materials and containers usual to the operations of a farm, but not hay, grain or any growing crops.

e. "Poultry" (excluding turkeys unless specified):

(1) In the open; or

(2) In any building designated for "poultry" in the Declarations.

But for this property, the Basic or Broad Covered Causes of Loss are the only Covered Causes of Loss.

f. Trays, boxes and box shook, each item or set in the proportion that its value bears to the total value of all trays, boxes and box shook covered under this Coverage Form.

g. Computers and related software used principally as aids in farm management.

But an item of software is Covered Property only up to the amount required to replace it as a prepackaged program, or in unexposed or blank form, whichever is greater.

h. Miscellaneous equipment, usual or incidental to the operation of a farm (including machinery, vehicles, tools, and supplies of all kinds), covered under a single Limit of Insurance shown for Miscellaneous Equipment in the Declarations.

But such miscellaneous farm equipment does not include:

(1) Threshing machines, tractors, combines, corn pickers, hay balers, harvesters, peanut diggers, potato diggers and pickers, cotton pickers, crop driers or sawmill equipment;

(2) Automobiles, trucks, motorcycles, motorized bicycles or tricycles, mopeds, dirt bikes, snowmobiles, four-wheel all-terrain vehicles; mobile homes, house trailers; vehicles primarily designed and licensed for road use (other than farm wagons and farm trailers); watercraft or aircraft; or the equipment, tires or parts of any of these;

(3) Liquefied petroleum or manufactured gas or fuel, or their containers;

(4) Bulk milk tanks, bulk feed tanks or bins attached to buildings or structures; barn cleaners, pasteurizers or boilers; any permanent fixtures within or attached to a building;

(5) Brooders;

(6) Fences, windchargers, windmills or their towers;

(7) Outdoor radio or television equipment or wiring; private power and light poles;

(8) Irrigation equipment;

(9) Portable buildings and portable structures;

(10) Household personal property or property usual to a "dwelling"; or

(11) Property more specifically covered under another Coverage or Coverage Form of this or any other policy.

i. Farm machinery, vehicles and equipment that you borrow or rent, whether or not under a written contract, except while on the premises of its owner. The borrowed or rented property must be:

(1) Usual or incidental to farming operations;

(2) In your care, custody or control; and

(3) Property in which you have no interest as owner or lienholder.

But Covered Property does not include borrowed or rented property of the following types:

(1) Automobiles, trucks, motorcycles, motorized bicycles or tricycles, mopeds, dirt bikes, snowmobiles, four-wheel all-terrain vehicles; mobile homes, house trailers; vehicles primarily designed and licensed for road use (other than farm wagons and farm trailers); watercraft or aircraft; or the equipment, tires or parts of any of these; or

(2) Dealers' demonstration machinery, vehicles or equipment.

j. Farm machinery, vehicles and equipment which are individually described and specifically covered in the Declarations, while on or away from the "insured location", except while in the custody of a common or contract carrier.

k. "Livestock" on or away from the "insured location", but for this property the Basic or Broad Covered Causes of Loss are the only Covered Causes of Loss.

But we do not cover "livestock" while:

(1) In the custody of a common or contract carrier;

(2) At public stockyards, sales barns or sales yards; or

(3) At packing plants or slaughterhouses.

l. Bees, but for this property the Basic or Broad Covered Causes of Loss are the only Covered Causes of Loss.

m. Worms, but for this property the Basic or Broad Covered Causes of Loss are the only Covered Causes of Loss.

n. Fish, but for this property the Basic or Broad Covered Causes of Loss are the only Covered Causes of Loss.

o. Other animals, but for this property the Basic or Broad Covered Causes of Loss are the only Covered Causes of Loss.

p. Portable buildings and portable structures that you own.

2. Property Not Covered

Under Coverage **E,** Covered Property does not include:

a. Growing crops, trees, plants, shrubs or lawns;

b. Household personal property or property usual to a "dwelling";

c. Magnetic recording or storage media for electronic data processing, such as cell, disc, drum, film and tape, over or above their replacement value:

(1) As prepackaged software programs; or

(2) In unexposed or blank form;

whichever is greater;

d. Any permanent fixtures within or attached to a building; or

e. Outdoor radio or television equipment or wiring; private power and light poles.

3. Special Limits Of Insurance Under Coverage E

Under Coverage **E,** certain individual items of "farm personal property" are subject to Special Limits of Insurance. These Special Limits are part of, not in addition to, the applicable Limits of Insurance shown in the Declarations.

© ISO Properties, Inc., 2002   **FP 00 13 09 03**   □

a. If no specific stack limit is shown in the Declarations for hay, straw or fodder in the open, the Limit will be $10,000 on any one stack.

b. For covered "poultry", the Limit of Insurance per bird under any provision of this Coverage Form applicable to "poultry" will be its cash market value as of the time of loss.

c. The Limit of Insurance on any one item of miscellaneous equipment is $3,000.

d. The most we will pay for loss of or damage to any one head of "livestock" (other than animals individually described and specifically covered under this coverage) is the least of the following amounts:

   (1) 120% of the amount obtained by dividing the total insurance on the class and type of animal involved by the number of head of that class and type owned by you as of the time of loss;

   (2) The actual cash value of the animal destroyed or damaged; or

   (3) $2,000.

   Each horse, mule or head of cattle under one year of age as of time of loss will be counted as 1/2 head.

B. Coverage E Conditions

Coverage **E** is subject to the following Loss Conditions as well as to the Farm Property Conditions (see Farm Property – Other Farm Provisions Form – Additional Coverages, Conditions, Definitions) and the Common Policy Conditions.

LOSS CONDITIONS

1. Portable Buildings And Portable Structures That You Own

The most we will pay for loss of or damage to this property in any one occurrence is the proportion that the applicable Limit of Insurance shown in the Declarations bears to the value of all portable buildings and portable structures you own as of the time of loss.

2. Pro Rata Distribution – Applicable Only to Grain, Hay, Straw and Fodder, to Farm Machinery, Vehicles and Equipment, and to Poultry in Unheated Buildings.

This Condition applies only if Scheduled "farm personal property" is covered at more than one "insured location". The Limit of Insurance for any category of covered "farm personal property" mentioned in the heading of this Condition will apply at any one "insured location" in the proportion that the value of Covered Property in that category at that location bears to the value of all Covered Property in that category at all "insured locations".

EXAMPLE #1 (ADEQUATE INSURANCE)

The property in the given category is located at locations 1, 2, 3 and 4. Total value is:	$130,000
The overall Limit of Insurance for this category is:	$150,000
No loss at location 1, 2 or 3; loss at location 4 is:	$12,000
Value of property in this category at location 4 is:	$45,000
The deductible is:	$250
Loss minus deductible ($12,000 – $250) is:	$11,750

Steps In Computing Loss Payment	
A. Value of property in this category at location 4:	$45,000
B. Value of such property at all four locations:	$130,000
C. Ratio of A to B ($45,000 ÷ $130,000):	9/26 or 34.6%
D. Proportion of Limit of Insurance available for covering the loss (C x $150,000):	$51,900
Therefore, the proportion of the Limit of Insurance available for payment of the $12,000 loss (after subtraction of deductible) is adequate and the full loss less the deductible is payable.	
We will pay no more than:	$11,750
i.e., the $12,000 amount of loss minus the deductible of $250.	

EXAMPLE #2 (UNDERINSURANCE)

The property in the given category is located in silos at locations 1 and 2. Total value is:	$18,000
Value at location 1 is:	$10,000
Value at location 2 is:	$8,000
The overall Limit of Insurance for this category is:	$15,000
The deductible is:	$500
No loss at location 1; loss at location 2 is:	$7,500
Loss minus deductible ($7,500 − $500) is:	$7,000

Steps In Computing Loss Payment	
A. Value of property in this category at location 2:	$8,000
B. Value of such property at both locations:	$18,000
C. Ratio of A to B ($8,000 ÷ $18,000):	4/9 or 44.4%
D. Proportion of Limit of Insurance available for covering the loss (C x $15,000):	$6,660
E. Determination of payment amount: compare D ($6,660) with loss-minus-deductible ($7,000).	
We will pay no more than:	$6,660
The remaining $840 is not covered.	

3. **Livestock, Poultry, Bees, Fish, Worms and Other Animals**

   With respect to "livestock", "poultry", bees, fish, worms, and other animals, the term loss means death or destruction caused by, resulting from or made necessary by a Covered Cause of Loss.

4. **Valuation**

   In the event of loss of or damage to covered "farm personal property", we will settle at actual cash value as of time of loss, but we will not pay more than the amount necessary for repair or replacement.

5. **Coverage Territory**

   We cover loss or damage commencing within the coverage territory. The coverage territory is:

   a. The United States of America;

   b. Puerto Rico; and

   c. Canada.

COVERAGE F – UNSCHEDULED FARM PERSONAL PROPERTY

A. **Coverage**

   We will pay for direct physical loss of or damage to Covered Property at the "insured location" described in the Declarations, or elsewhere as expressly provided below, caused by or resulting from any Covered Cause of Loss.

   1. **Covered Property**

      All of the following are Covered Property under Coverage **F** of this Coverage Form, provided a Limit of Insurance is shown in the Declarations:

      a. All items of "farm personal property" on the "insured location", except for items specified under Paragraph **2.** Property Not Covered.

         But for "livestock", the Basic or Broad Covered Causes of Loss are the only Covered Causes of Loss; and

      b. The following items of "farm personal property" away from the "insured location":

         (1) Grain, ground feed, fertilizer, fodder, hay, herbicides, manufactured and blended "livestock" feed, pesticides, silage, straw, threshed beans and threshed seeds, except while:

            (a) Being stored or processed in commercial drying plants, manufacturing plants, public elevators, seed houses or warehouses; or

            (b) In the custody of a common or contract carrier.

         (2) "Livestock", except while:

            (a) In the custody of a common or contract carrier;

            (b) At public stockyards, sales barns or yards; or

            (c) At packing plants or slaughterhouses.

            But for "livestock", the Basic or Broad Covered Causes of Loss are the only Covered Causes of Loss.

         (3) Farm machinery, equipment, implements, tools and supplies, except:

            (a) Items specified under Paragraph **2.** Property Not Covered; or

            (b) While in the custody of a common or contract carrier.

           FP 00 13 09 03

2. **Property Not Covered**

Covered Property does not include:

a. Household or personal property usual to a "dwelling";

b. Magnetic recording or storage media for electronic data processing, such as cell, disc, drum, file and tape, over or above their replacement value:

(1) As prepackaged software programs; or

(2) In unexposed or blank form;

whichever is greater;

c. Animals other than "livestock";

d. "Poultry", bees, fish or worms;

e. Racehorses, show horses or show ponies;

f. Any of the following while being stored or processed in manufacturing plants, public elevators, warehouses, seed houses or commercial drying plants: grain, threshed seeds, threshed beans, hay, straw, fodder, silage, ground feed, herbicides, fertilizer, manufactured or blended "livestock" feed;

g. Trees, plants, shrubs or lawns;

h. Tobacco, cotton, vegetables, root crops, potatoes, bulbs, fruit or nursery stock;

i. Crops in the open, except to the extent provided for in the applicable Coverage Extension in Section **II** of this Coverage Form;

j. Contents of chicken fryer or broiler houses, laying houses, "poultry" brooder or duck or turkey houses;

k. Automobiles, trucks, motorcycles, motorized bicycles or tricycles, mopeds, dirt bikes, snowmobiles, four-wheel all-terrain vehicles; mobile homes, house trailers; vehicles primarily designed and licensed for road use (other than farm wagons and farm trailers); watercraft or aircraft; or the equipment, tires or parts of any of these;

l. Fences; windmills or windchargers or their towers;

m. Bulk milk tanks, bulk feed tanks or bins attached to buildings or structures; barn cleaners, pasteurizers or boilers; any permanent fixtures within or attached to a building;

n. Outdoor radio or television equipment;

o. Portable buildings or portable structures;

p. Irrigation equipment;

q. Property separately described and specifically covered in whole or in part under another Coverage or Coverage Form of this or any other policy;

r. Cotton pickers and harvester-thresher combines; or

s. Any property shown in the Declarations under the heading Other Property Not Covered Under Coverage **F.**

3. **Special Limits Of Insurance Under Coverage F**

Under Coverage **F,** individual "livestock" are subject to Special Limits of Insurance. These Special Limits are part of, not in addition to, the applicable Limit of Insurance shown in the Declarations.

The most we will pay for loss of or damage to any one head of "livestock" is:

a. $1,000 on any horse, mule or head of cattle under one year of age as of time of loss; and

b. $2,000 on any head of "livestock" not included under Paragraph **a.** above.

If it becomes necessary to impose the penalty provided for in the first paragraph of the Coverage **F** Loss Condition – Coinsurance (see Paragraph **B.2.** below), no amount used as the actual cash value of an animal will exceed the applicable Limit of Insurance specified above.

B. **Coverage F Conditions**

Coverage **F** is subject to the following Loss Conditions as well as to the Farm Property Conditions (see the Farm Property – Other Farm Provisions Form – Additional Coverages, Conditions, Definitions) and the Common Policy Conditions.

LOSS CONDITIONS

1. **Livestock**

With respect to "livestock", the term loss means death or destruction caused by, resulting from or made necessary by a covered cause of loss.

2. **Coinsurance**

You must maintain insurance on unscheduled "farm personal property" to the extent of at least 80% of its actual cash value as of the time of loss. If you fail to do this, the percentage we pay of any loss will be the result produced by dividing the Limit of Insurance actually carried by the required Limit of Insurance.

The following provision applies in the event of loss of or damage to machinery or equipment within 30 days after the purchase of additional or replacement machinery or equipment.

If the Limit of Insurance actually carried becomes inadequate due to the purchase of additional or replacement machinery or equipment, then, up to $100,000 of the value of the newly purchased additional machinery or equipment and $75,000 of the value of the newly purchased replacement machinery or equipment will be omitted in determining the required Limit of Insurance.

3. Valuation

In the event of loss of or damage to covered "farm personal property", we will settle at actual cash value as of time of loss, but we will not pay more than the amount necessary for repair or replacement.

4. Coverage Territory

We cover loss or damage commencing within the coverage territory. The coverage territory is:

a. The United States of America;

b. Puerto Rico; and

c. Canada.

SECTION II – COVERAGE EXTENSIONS

A. Property In The Custody Of A Common Or Contract Carrier

This Coverage Extension applies to Coverages **E** and **F**.

Coverage is extended to apply to "farm personal property", insured under Coverage **E** or Coverage **F**, while in the custody of a common or contract carrier, for up to a total of $1,000 under each of these Coverages. However, if a higher limit is specified in the Declarations for Coverage **E** or Coverage **F** – Property in the Custody of a Common or Contract Carrier, the higher limit will apply to the Coverage(s) specified, instead of $1,000.

B. Covered Property Away From The "Insured Location"

This Coverage Extension applies to Coverage **E**.

1. Coverage is extended to apply to Covered Property while away from the "insured location", for up to a certain percentage of the Limit of Insurance shown in the Declarations for the specific type of property, as follows:

a. 25%, for Miscellaneous Equipment Usual or Incidental to the Operation of a Farm; or

b. 10%, for other types of property.

2. This Coverage Extension is part of, not in addition to, the applicable Limit of Insurance or Special Limit of Insurance.

3. This Coverage Extension does not apply to:

a. "Livestock" or individually insured farm machinery, vehicles or equipment which are described in Paragraph **1.j.** or **1.k.** of Covered Property;

b. Property while in the custody of a common or contract carrier;

c. Property stored or being processed in manufacturing plants, public elevators, warehouses, seed houses or commercial drying plants; or

d. Property in public sales barns or public sales yards.

4. Under this Coverage Extension, the greatest proportion we will pay of any one loss is the proportion we would have paid if every policy covering the property involved in the loss had provided the same coverage as this Coverage Extension.

C. Replacement Machinery, Vehicles And Equipment Newly Purchased

This Coverage Extension applies to Coverage **E**.

A Special Limit of Insurance equal to $75,000 plus the corresponding limit specified in the Declarations for individually scheduled items of Farm Machinery, Vehicles and Equipment applies to any item of property purchased as a replacement of such machinery, vehicle or equipment.

The additional $75,000 coverage will end:

1. 30 days after the date of purchase of the replacement item; or

2. When this policy expires;

whichever comes first.

In no event will we pay more than the actual cash value as of the time of loss.

A newly purchased vehicle or item of machinery or equipment is covered under this Coverage Extension only to the extent that it is not covered under another Coverage or Coverage Form of this or any other policy of the "insured".

D. Additional Machinery, Vehicles And Equipment Newly Purchased

This Coverage Extension applies to Coverage **E**.

1. Coverage on such items of farm equipment, machinery and vehicles such as tractors, combines, harvesters, corn pickers and hay balers, will extend to apply to newly purchased additional farm equipment, machinery and vehicles.

Farm

2. The most we will pay under this Coverage Extension is $100,000 for loss of or damage to all such Newly Purchased Additional Farm Equipment, Machinery and Vehicles. This $100,000 Limit is part of, not in addition to, the applicable Limit of Insurance.

3. When values for Newly Purchased Additional Farm Equipment, Machinery and Vehicles are reported under this Coverage Extension, additional premium for these values will be due and payable from the date of purchase.

4. None of the following is covered under this Coverage Extension:

   a. Automobiles, trucks, motorcycles, motorized bicycles or tricycles, mopeds, dirt bikes, snowmobiles; four-wheel all-terrain vehicles; mobile homes or house trailers; vehicles primarily designed and licensed for road use (other than farm wagons and farm trailers); watercraft; aircraft; or their equipment, tires or parts;

   b. Liquefied petroleum or manufactured gas or fuel, or their containers;

   c. Brooders, fences, windchargers, windmills or their towers; or

   d. Any farm equipment, machinery, or vehicles purchased as replacements of equipment, machinery, vehicles or equipment specifically described in the Declarations.

5. This Coverage Extension will end:

   a. 30 days after the date of acquisition of the additional item; or

   b. When this policy expires;

   whichever comes first.

6. Newly Purchased Additional Farm Equipment, Machinery and Vehicles are covered under this Coverage Extension only to the extent that they are not covered under another Coverage or Coverage Form of this or any other policy of the "insured".

E. Additional Acquired Livestock

This Coverage Extension applies to Coverage **E**.

1. If Coverage **E** covers "livestock":

   a. Specifically declared and described in the Coverage **E** Declarations; or

   b. With separate Limits of Insurance per class shown in the Coverage **E** Declarations;

   we will cover additional "livestock" you acquire during the policy period, for up to 30 days from acquisition.

2. The most we will pay under this Coverage Extension is the lesser of:

   a. The actual cash value of the additional "livestock"; or

   b. 25% of the total of the Limits of Insurance shown in the Coverage **E** Declarations for:

      (1) Specifically declared and described "livestock"; and

      (2) "Livestock" with separate limits per class.

3. You must report the additional "livestock" within 30 days from the date of acquisition and pay any additional premium due. If you do not report such property, coverage will end 30 days after the date of acquisition.

F. Thirty-Day Additional Limit On Borrowed Or Rented Farm Machinery, Vehicles, Equipment

This Coverage Extension applies to Coverage **E**.

1. The Limit of Insurance, if any, shown in the Declarations for Farm Machinery, Vehicles, Equipment Borrowed Or Rented With Or Without A Written Contract will be increased by $10,000, which will apply in any one occurrence to loss of or damage only to such items, as described and limited in Paragraph **A.1.i.** in Section **I**, that you borrow or rent after the beginning of the policy period. However, if a higher additional Limit of Insurance is specified in the Declarations, the higher Limit will apply.

2. Insurance under this Coverage Extension will end:

   a. Thirty days after the Covered Property is borrowed or rented; or

   b. When this policy expires;

   whichever comes first.

3. If any property covered under this Coverage Extension remains in your possession for a period of more than thirty days, you must report value for it, and additional premium will be due and payable from the thirty-first day after you took possession.

G. Farm Products In The Open – Coverage Against Certain Causes Of Loss

This Coverage Extension applies to Coverage **F**.

You may apply up to 10% of the Limit of Insurance shown in the Declarations for "farm personal property" to cover the following in the open:

1. Grain in piles, shocks, stacks or swaths;

2. Hay, straw and fodder in stacks, windrows or bales; but the most we will pay for loss or damage is $10,000 for any one stack of hay, straw or fodder.

A stack means hay, straw or fodder in one area separated by a clear space of 100 feet or more from any other hay, straw or fodder in the open.

Fire or lightning, windstorm or hail, vandalism, vehicles and theft are the only Covered Causes of Loss for the property named in Paragraphs **1.** and **2.** above.

3. Unharvested barley, corn, oats, rye, wheat and other grains, flax, soy beans and sunflowers (but not on seed or forage crops, straw or stubble).

Fire or lightning is the only Covered Cause of Loss for this property.

This Extension is part of, not in addition to, the applicable Limit of Insurance.

SECTION III – ADDITIONAL COVERAGES

A. Cost Of Restoring Farm Operations Records

For any one loss we will pay up to $2,000 to cover your cost to research, replace or restore the lost information on farm operations records damaged by a Covered Cause of Loss.

But if a higher Limit of Insurance is specified in the Declarations, the higher limit will apply.

No deductible applies to this Additional Coverage.

B. Extra Expense

If a Limit of Insurance is shown in the Declarations for Extra Expense Coverage, we will pay, up to that Limit of Insurance, the actual and necessary expenses you incur to resume normal farming operations interrupted as the result of direct physical loss of or damage to Covered Property by a Covered Cause of Loss.

Coverage for such extra expense is not limited by the expiration of this policy. But, we will not pay extra expense you incur after the period required for repair, rebuilding or replacement of Covered Property.

Extra Expense Coverage does not include loss caused by or resulting from the enforcement of any ordinance or law which requires any "insured" or others to test for, monitor, clean up, remove, contain, treat, detoxify, neutralize, or in any way respond to, or assess the effects of, "pollutants".

No deductible applies to this Additional Coverage.

C. Other Additional Coverages

For other Additional Coverages, see the Farm Property – Other Farm Provisions Form – Additional Coverages, Conditions, Definitions.

SECTION IV – OTHER PROVISIONS

A. Covered Causes Of Loss, Exclusions And Limitations

See the Causes of Loss Form – Farm Property, for Basic, Broad or Special coverage as shown in the Declarations.

B. Limits Of Insurance

See the Farm Property – Other Farm Provisions Form – Additional Coverages, Conditions, Definitions.

C. Deductible

See the Farm Property – Other Farm Provisions Form – Additional Coverages, Conditions, Definitions.

FARM
FP 10 60 02 09

CAUSES OF LOSS FORM – FARM PROPERTY

Words and phrases that appear in quotation marks have special meaning. Refer to the Definitions Section of the Farm Property – Other Farm Provisions Form – Additional Coverages, Conditions, Definitions.

A. Covered Causes Of Loss

Covered Causes Of Loss means the causes as described and limited under either Paragraph **B.** or **C.** or **D.** below in accordance with a corresponding entry of either Basic or Broad or Special, respectively, on the Declarations opposite each Coverage or property to which this insurance applies. Covered Causes of Loss are also limited by the Exclusions in Section **E.**

However, certain property is covered only for particular causes of loss, as listed under the following items: the Coverage Extension to Coverage **A;** Paragraphs **1.b., 1.c.(2), 1.e., 1.k., 1.l., 1.m., 1.n.** and **1.o.** of Coverage **E** Covered Property; Paragraphs **1.a.** and **1.b.(2)** of Coverage **F** Covered Property; **G.** of the Coverage Extensions to Coverage **F;** and Paragraph **B.** of the Coverage Extensions to Coverage **G.**

B. Covered Causes Of Loss – Basic

Subject to the provisions in Section **A.,** when Basic is shown in the Declarations, Covered Causes of Loss means the following:

1. Fire Or Lightning

We will not pay for loss of or damage to buildings, or contents usual to a tobacco barn, if that loss or damage:

a. Results from the use of open fire for curing or drying tobacco in the barn; and

b. Occurs during, or within the five-day period following, open-fire curing or drying.

2. Windstorm Or Hail, but not including:

a. Frost or cold weather;

b. Ice (other than hail), snow or sleet, whether driven by wind or not; or

c. Loss of or damage to:

(1) The interior of any building or structure, or the property inside a building or structure, caused by rain, snow, sleet, sand or dust, whether driven by wind or not, unless the building or structure first sustains wind or hail damage to its roof or walls through which the rain, snow, sleet, sand or dust enters; or

(2) Watercraft or their trailers, furnishings, equipment or outboard motors unless within a fully enclosed building.

(3) Under Coverage **E** or Coverage **F:**

(a) "Livestock" or "poultry" when caused by running into streams, ponds or ditches, or against fences or other objects; or from smothering; or resulting directly or indirectly from fright;

(b) "Livestock" or "poultry" when caused by freezing or smothering in blizzards or snowstorms; or

(c) Dairy or farm products in the open other than hay, straw or fodder.

3. Explosion, including the explosion of gases or fuel within the furnace of any fired vessel or within the flues or passages of such a vessel from which the gases of combustion pass.

But under Coverages **E, F** and **G** this Cause of Loss does not include loss or damage caused by or resulting from:

a. Explosion of alcohol stills, steam boilers, steam pipes, steam engines or steam turbines owned or leased by you, or operated under your control;

b. Electric arcing;

c. Rupture or bursting of water pipes;

d. Rupture, bursting or operation of pressure relief devices; or

e. Rupture or bursting due to expansion or swelling of the contents of any building or structure caused by or resulting from water.

4. Riot Or Civil Commotion, including:

a. Acts of striking employees while occupying the "insured location"; and

b. Looting occurring at the time and place of a riot or civil commotion.

5. Aircraft, meaning only loss or damage caused by or resulting from:

a. Contact of an aircraft, spacecraft or self-propelled missile with Covered Property or with a building or structure containing Covered Property; or

b. Objects falling from aircraft.

    ☐

6. **Vehicles,** meaning only loss or damage caused by contact of a vehicle, or of an object thrown up by a vehicle, with Covered Property or with a building or structure containing Covered Property.

This Cause of Loss does not include loss or damage to:

a. "Livestock"; or

b. A fence, driveway or walk.

However, we will provide coverage under this Cause of Loss if the fence, driveway or walk is appurtenant to a covered "dwelling" and the vehicle that caused the loss or damage was not owned or operated by a resident of the "dwelling".

7. **Smoke,** causing sudden and accidental loss or damage, including the emission or puffback of smoke, soot, fumes or vapors from a boiler, furnace or related equipment.

This Cause of Loss does not include loss or damage by smoke from agricultural smudging or industrial operations.

8. **Vandalism**

This Cause of Loss does not include loss of or damage to:

a. A building or structure, or its contents, if the building or structure has been "vacant" for more than 30 consecutive days immediately before the loss;

b. Any device or instrument, for the transmitting, recording, receiving or reproduction of sound or pictures, that is operated by power from the electrical system of a motor vehicle or mobile agricultural vehicle, unless it is:

(1) Covered Property; and

(2) Permanently installed in the motor vehicle or mobile agricultural vehicle; or

c. While in or upon a motor vehicle or mobile agricultural vehicle, any tape, wire, record, disc or other medium for use with any device or instrument that transmits, records, receives or reproduces sound or pictures and that is operated by power from the electrical system of the motor vehicle or mobile agricultural vehicle.

9. **Theft,** including attempted theft and loss of property from a known location when it is likely that the property has been stolen.

This Cause of Loss does not include loss caused by or resulting from theft:

a. Due to unauthorized instructions to transfer property to any person or to any place;

b. Under Coverage **A, B** or **G:**

In or from a building or structure under construction, or of materials and supplies for use in such construction, until the building or structure is completed and occupied;

c. Under Coverage **A, B** or **C:**

(1) From that part of your principal residence, including its grounds and appurtenant structures, which you rent to someone who is not an "insured";

(2) With respect to household personal property away from the "insured location", of:

(a) Property at any residence owned by, rented to, or occupied by, an "insured", except while an "insured" is temporarily residing there.

But property of a student who is an "insured" is covered at a residence away from home provided the student has been there at any time during the 45 days immediately preceding the loss;

(b) Any watercraft, its furnishings, equipment or outboard motors; or

(c) Trailers or campers;

d. Under Coverage **E** or **F:**

(1) Discovered on taking inventory;

(2) Due to wrongful conversion or embezzlement;

(3) Due to disappearance of any "farm personal property" unless there is evidence that the property was stolen; or

(4) Due to acceptance of counterfeit money, fraudulent post office or express money orders, or checks or promissory notes not paid upon presentation;

e. Of any device or instrument for the transmitting, recording, receiving or reproduction of sound or pictures, that is operated by power from the electrical system of a motor vehicle or mobile agricultural vehicle, unless it is:

(1) Covered Property; and

(2) Permanently installed in the motor vehicle or mobile agricultural vehicle; or

© Insurance Services Office, Inc., 2008 **FP 10 60 02 09** □

f. While in or upon a motor vehicle or mobile agricultural vehicle, of any tape, wire, record, disc or other medium for use with any device or instrument that transmits, records, receives or reproduces sound or pictures and that is operated by power from the electrical system of the motor vehicle or mobile agricultural vehicle.

10. **Sinkhole Collapse,** meaning loss or damage caused by the sudden sinking or collapse of land into underground empty spaces created by the action of water on limestone or dolomite. This Cause of Loss does not include:

   a. The cost of filling sinkholes; or

   b. Sinking or collapse of land into man-made underground cavities.

11. **Volcanic Action,** meaning direct loss or damage resulting from the eruption of a volcano when the loss or damage is caused by:

   a. Airborne volcanic blast or airborne shock waves;

   b. Ash, dust or particulate matter; or

   c. Lava flow.

   All volcanic eruptions that occur within any 168-hour period will constitute a single occurrence.

   This Cause of Loss does not include the cost to remove ash, dust or particulate matter that does not cause direct physical loss or damage to the Covered Property.

12. **Collision – Coverages E And F Only**

   a. **Causing Damage To Covered Farm Machinery**

      We will pay for loss of or damage to covered farm machinery caused by collision or overturn of that machinery. Collision means accidental contact of the farm machinery with another vehicle or object.

      Under this Cause of Loss we will not pay for loss or damage:

      (1) To tires or tubes unless the damage is coincidental with other damage to the farm machinery or implement; or

      (2) Caused by foreign objects taken into any farm machine or mechanical harvester.

   b. **Causing Death Of Covered Livestock**

      We will pay for loss of covered "livestock" caused by:

      (1) Collision or overturn of a vehicle on which the "livestock" are being transported. Collision means accidental contact of that vehicle with another vehicle or object; or

      (2) "Livestock" running into or being struck by a vehicle while the "livestock" are crossing, moving along or standing in a public road.

      But we will not pay for loss if a vehicle owned or operated by an "insured":

      (1) Collides with the vehicle on which the "livestock" are being transported; or

      (2) Strikes "livestock" crossing, moving along or standing in a public road.

   c. **Causing Damage To Other Farm Personal Property**

      We will pay for loss of or damage to covered "farm personal property" (other than that described in Paragraph **a.** or **b.** above) in or upon a motor vehicle, caused by collision or overturn of that vehicle. Collision means accidental contact of the motor vehicle with another vehicle or object.

13. **Earthquake Loss To "Livestock"**

14. **Flood Loss To "Livestock"**

   We will pay for loss or damage to "livestock" caused by or resulting from flood, surface water, waves (including tidal wave and tsunami), tides, tidal water, overflow of any body of water, or spray from any of these, all whether or not driven by wind (including storm surge).

C. **Covered Causes Of Loss – Broad**

   Subject to the provisions in Section **A.,** when Broad is shown in the Declarations, Covered Causes of Loss means the Covered Causes of Loss under Section **B.** Covered Causes Of Loss – Basic, plus the following:

15. **Electrocution Of Covered Livestock**

16. **Attacks On Covered Livestock By Dogs Or Wild Animals**

   This Cause of Loss does not include loss or damage:

   a. To sheep; or

   b. Caused by dogs or wild animals owned by you, your employees or other persons residing on the "insured location".

17. **Accidental Shooting Of Covered Livestock**

This Cause of Loss does not include loss or damage caused by you, any other "insured", your employees, or other persons residing on the "insured location".

18. **Drowning Of Covered Livestock From External Causes**

This Cause of Loss does not include loss resulting from the drowning of swine under 30 days old.

19. **Loading/Unloading Accidents,** meaning sudden, unforeseen and unintended events causing or necessitating death of covered "livestock" and occurring while they are being unloaded from or loaded onto vehicles used or to be used to transport them.

This Cause of Loss does not include loss caused by or resulting from disease.

20. **Breakage Of Glass Or Safety Glazing Material** that is part of a building or structure, storm door or storm window.

Under this Cause of Loss, we will not pay for loss if the building or structure which contained the glass, including door or window glass, has been "vacant" for more than 30 consecutive days immediately before the loss.

21. **Falling Objects**

But we will not pay for loss or damage to:

a. Personal property in the open;

b. The interior of a building or structure, or property inside a building or structure, unless the roof or an outside wall of the building or structure is first damaged by a falling object; or

c. The falling object itself.

22. **Weight Of Ice, Snow Or Sleet** causing damage to a building or to any property inside a building.

But under this Cause of Loss we will not pay for loss by pressure or weight of water in any form, whether driven by wind or not, to any:

a. Foundation or retaining wall;

b. Pavement or patio;

c. Awning;

d. Fence;

e. Outdoor equipment;

f. Swimming pool; or

g. Bulkhead, dock, pier or wharf.

23. **Sudden And Accidental Tearing Apart,** cracking, burning or bulging of a steam or hot water heating system, an air conditioning or automatic fire protective system, or an appliance for heating water.

Under this Cause of Loss we will not pay for loss or damage caused by or resulting from freezing.

24. **Accidental Discharge Or Leakage Of Water Or Steam** from within a plumbing, heating, air conditioning or other system or appliance that is located on the "insured location" and contains water or steam.

Under this Cause of Loss we will pay for loss of or damage to covered personal property provided that Broad is shown in the Declarations for the coverage applicable to that personal property. If any part of a building or structure to which Coverage **A, B** or **G** applies must be torn out and replaced so that repairs can be made to the damaged system or appliance, we will also pay the necessary costs involved, provided that Broad is shown in the Declarations for the coverage applying to that building or structure.

We will not pay:

a. For loss or damage caused by discharge or leakage from a sump or related equipment and parts, including overflow due to sump pump failure or excessive volume of water;

b. The cost to repair any defect that caused the loss or damage;

c. For loss or damage caused by discharge or leakage in a building or structure "vacant" for more than 30 consecutive days immediately before the loss;

d. For loss or damage caused by or resulting from freezing; or

e. For loss or damage caused by or resulting from discharge or leakage from roof drains, gutters, downspouts or similar fixtures or equipment.

25. Freezing of a plumbing, heating, air conditioning or automatic fire protective system or of a household appliance but only if you have used reasonable care to:

a. Maintain heat in the building or structure; or

b. Shut off the water supply and drain all systems or appliances of water.

However, if the building or structure is protected by an automatic fire protective system, you must use reasonable care to continue the water supply and maintain heat in the building or structure for coverage to apply.

A plumbing system does not include a roof drain, gutter, downspout or similar fixtures or equipment.

26. **Sudden And Accidental Damage** from artificially generated electrical current – Applicable Only to Coverages **A, B, C** and **D.**

This Cause of Loss does not include loss of or damage to:

a. Tubes, transistors or integrated circuitry that are a part of appliances, fixtures, computers, home entertainment units or other types of electronic apparatus. Integrated circuitry includes, but is not limited to, chips, transformers, resistors, diodes, wafers and rectifiers; or

b. Laser or infrared devices used to operate or assist in the operation of any appliances, fixtures, computers, home entertainment units or other types of electronic apparatus.

D. Covered Causes Of Loss – Special

Subject to the provisions in Section **A.,** when Special is shown in the Declarations, Covered Causes of Loss means Risks Of Direct Physical Loss unless the loss is excluded in the following paragraphs or in Section **E.** Exclusions.

1. We will not pay for loss or damage caused by or resulting from:

a. Fire, if that loss or damage is sustained by buildings or contents usual to tobacco barns as the result of using open fire for curing or drying tobacco in the barn, and occurs:

(1) While tobacco is being fired; or

(2) Within the five-day period following tobacco firing in the barn;

b. Collapse, except as provided in the Additional Coverage entitled Collapse. But if collapse results in a Covered Cause of Loss at the "insured location", we will pay for the loss or damage caused by that Covered Cause of Loss;

c. Windstorm or hail to:

(1) Dairy or farm products in the open;

(2) Watercraft or their trailers, furnishings, equipment or outboard motors, unless within a fully enclosed building;

d. Rain, snow, ice or sleet to personal property in the open;

e. Rain, snow, sleet, sand or dust, whether driven by wind or not, to the interior of any building or structure or the property inside a building or structure, unless the building or structure first sustains wind or hail damage to its roof or walls through which the rain, snow, sleet, sand or dust enters;

f. Freezing, thawing, or pressure or weight of water or ice whether or not driven by wind, to any:

(1) Footing, foundation, bulkhead, wall, or any other structure or device that supports all or part of any property covered under Coverages **A, B** or **G;**

(2) Retaining wall or bulkhead that does not support all or part of a building or structure;

(3) Pavement or patio;

(4) Fence;

(5) Swimming pool; or

(6) Dock, pier or wharf;

g. Discharge or overflow of water or steam from within a plumbing, heating, air conditioning or automatic fire protective system or from within a household appliance:

(1) That occurs on the "insured location", but is caused by discharge that takes place off the "insured location";

(2) Caused by or resulting from freezing. This provision does not apply if you have used reasonable care to:

(a) Maintain heat in the building or structure; or

(b) Shut off the water supply and drain all systems or appliances of water.

However, if the building or structure is protected by an automatic fire protective system, you must use reasonable care to continue the water supply and maintain heat in the building or structure for coverage to apply.

(3) Due to any cause other than freezing and occurring in a building or structure "vacant" for more than 30 consecutive days immediately before the loss;

h. Any of the following occurrences, if they take place in buildings or structures covered under Coverage **G** or if the property destroyed or damaged is "farm personal property":

   (1) Explosion of alcohol stills, steam boilers, steam pipes or steam engines, if you own, lease or operate them;

   (2) Conditions or events (other than explosions) inside hot water boilers or other heating equipment, to the extent that they cause loss or damage to these boilers or equipment;

   (3) Rupture, bursting or operating of pressure relief devices; or

   (4) Rupture or bursting due to expansion of the contents of any building or structure, if the expansion is caused by or results from water.

   But this exclusion does not apply to loss or damage caused by explosion of gases or fuel within the furnace of any fired vessel or within the flues or passages through which the gases of combustion pass;

i. Under Coverage **A, B** or **C,** theft from that part of your principal residence, including its grounds and appurtenant structures, which you rent to someone who is not an "insured";

j. Under Coverage **B** or **G,** theft in or from a building or structure under construction, or of materials and supplies for use in such construction until the building or structure is completed and occupied;

k. Under Coverage **A, B** or **C,** theft of the following property away from the "insured location":

   (1) Property at any residence owned by, rented to, or occupied by, an "insured", except while an "insured" is temporarily residing there.

   But we will pay for loss by theft of the property of a student who is an "insured" from a residence away from home, provided the student was there at any time during the 45 days immediately preceding the loss.

   (2) Any watercraft, its furnishings, equipment or outboard motors; or

   (3) Trailers or campers;

l. Inventory shortage;

m. Disappearance of any "farm personal property" or portable building or structure unless there is evidence that the property was stolen;

n. Voluntary parting with any property by you or anyone else to whom you have entrusted the property if induced to do so by any fraudulent scheme, trick, device or false pretense;

o. Unauthorized instructions to transfer property to any person or to any place;

p. Theft of or vandalism to:

   (1) Any device or instrument, for the transmitting, recording, receiving or reproduction of sound or pictures, that is operated by power from the electrical system of a motor vehicle or mobile agricultural vehicle, unless it is:

      (a) Covered Property; and

      (b) Permanently installed in the motor vehicle or mobile agricultural vehicle.

   (2) While in or upon a motor vehicle or mobile agricultural vehicle, any tape, wire, record, disc or other medium for use with any device or instrument that transmits, records, receives or reproduces sound or pictures and that is operated by power from the electrical system of the motor vehicle or mobile agricultural vehicle;

q. Vandalism or breakage of glass or safety glazing material, if the building or structure was "vacant" for more than 30 consecutive days immediately before the loss;

r. Dishonest or criminal acts committed by you, any of your partners, employees (including leased employees), directors, trustees, authorized representatives or anyone to whom you entrust the property for any purpose, regardless of whether:

   (1) That person acts alone or in collusion with others; or

   (2) The act is committed during the hours of employment.

   This exclusion does not apply to loss by acts of destruction committed by your striking employees (including leased employees), but it does apply to employee (including leased employee) theft;

s. Transport of "farm personal property", except to the extent of the coverage afforded under Covered Causes of Loss – Basic and Broad;

t. Any cause included in the following list if that loss or damage is sustained by farm machinery:

(1) Collision, upset or overturn of farm machinery or equipment, to the extent of any loss of or damage to the tires or inner tubes of such machinery or equipment. But we will pay for the loss of or damage to the tires or inner tubes if the same accident causes other covered loss to the same machinery or equipment.

(2) Foreign objects being taken into any farm machine or mechanical harvester;

u. Artificially generated electric current, including electric arcing, that disturbs any electrical devices, appliances or wires; or under Coverages **A**, **B**, **C** and **D**, any tubes, transistors or integrated circuitry that are a part of appliances, fixtures, computers, home entertainment units or other types of electronic apparatus, or laser or infrared devices used to operate or assist in the operation of any appliances, fixtures, computers, home entertainment units or other types of electronic apparatus. Integrated circuitry includes, but is not limited to, chips, transformers, resistors, diodes, wafers and rectifiers.

But:

(1) Under Coverages **A**, **B**, **C** and **D**, we will pay for loss of or damage to electric devices, appliances or wires, provided the damage is sudden and accidental.

(2) If artificially generated electric current results in fire, we will pay for the loss or damage caused by that fire;

v. Smoke, vapor or gas from agricultural smudging or industrial operations, to any building, structure or personal property;

w. The following causes of loss to any building, structure or personal property:

(1) Wear and tear;

(2) Rust, corrosion, fungus, decay, deterioration, hidden or latent defect or any quality in property that causes it to damage or destroy itself;

(3) Smog;

(4) Settling, cracking, shrinking or expansion;

(5) Nesting or infestation, or discharge or release of waste products or secretions, by birds, vermin, rodents, insects or domestic animals.

(6) Mechanical breakdown, including rupture or bursting caused by centrifugal force;

(7) Dampness or dryness of atmosphere;

(8) Changes in temperature or extremes of heat or cold, including freezing. But this exclusion does not apply to freezing of a plumbing, heating, air conditioning or automatic fire protective system or freezing of a household appliance, if you have used reasonable care to:

(a) Maintain heat in the building or structure; or

(b) Shut off the water supply and drain all systems or appliances of water.

However, if the building or structure is protected by an automatic fire protective system, you must use reasonable care to continue the water supply and maintain heat in the building or structure for coverage to apply;

(9) Marring or scratching.

But if an excluded cause of loss that is listed in Paragraphs **w.(1)** through **w.(9)** results in a "specified cause of loss" or building glass breakage, we will pay for the loss or damage caused by that "specified cause of loss" or building glass breakage.

2. We will not pay for loss or damage caused by or resulting from any of the following, Paragraphs **2.a.** through **2.c.** But if an excluded cause of loss that is listed in Paragraphs **2.a.** through **2.c.** results in a Covered Cause of Loss, we will pay for the loss or damage caused by that Covered Cause of Loss.

a. Weather conditions. But this exclusion applies only if weather conditions contribute in any way with a cause or event excluded in Section **E.** Exclusions to produce the loss or damage.

b. Acts or decisions, including the failure to act or decide, of any person, group, organization or governmental body.

c. Faulty, inadequate or defective:

(1) Planning, zoning, development, surveying, siting;

(2) Design, specifications, workmanship, repair, construction, renovation, remodeling, grading, compaction;

(3) Materials used in repair, construction, renovation or remodeling; or

(4) Maintenance;

of part or all of any property on or off the "insured location".

3. We will not pay for loss or damage caused by or resulting from the discharge, dispersal, seepage, migration, release or escape of "pollutants" unless the discharge, dispersal, seepage, migration, release or escape is itself caused by any of the "specified causes of loss". But if the discharge, dispersal, seepage, migration, release or escape of "pollutants" results in a "specified cause of loss", we will pay for the loss or damage caused by that "specified cause of loss".

Under Paragraphs **1.**, **2.** and **3.**, any ensuing loss to property described in Coverages **A** and **B** not precluded by any other provision in this policy is covered.

E. Exclusions

The following Exclusions apply when any or all of the Covered Causes of Loss, Basic, Broad or Special, are specified in the Declarations.

We will not pay for loss or damage caused directly or indirectly by any of the following. Such loss or damage is excluded regardless of any other cause or event that contributes concurrently or in any sequence to the loss.

1. Ordinance Or Law

The enforcement of any ordinance or law:

a. Regulating the construction, use or repair of any property; or

b. Requiring the tearing down of any property, including the cost of removing its debris.

This exclusion, Ordinance or Law, applies whether the loss results from:

a. An ordinance or law that is enforced even if the property has not been damaged; or

b. The increased costs incurred to comply with an ordinance or law in the course of construction, repair, renovation, remodeling or demolition of property, or removal of its debris, following a physical loss to that property.

2. Earth Movement

a. Earthquake, including any earth sinking, rising or shifting related to such event;

b. Landslide, including any earth sinking, rising or shifting related to such event;

c. Mine subsidence, meaning subsidence of a man-made mine, whether or not mining activity has ceased;

d. Earth sinking (other than sinkhole collapse), rising or shifting including soil conditions that cause settling, cracking or other disarrangement of foundations or other parts of realty. Soil conditions include contraction, expansion, freezing, thawing, erosion, improperly compacted soil and the action of water under the ground surface.

This exclusion applies whether the Earth Movement, as described in Paragraphs **a.** through **d.** above, is caused by human or animal forces or any act of nature.

But:

(1) If Earth Movement, as described in Paragraphs **a.** through **d.** above, results in fire or explosion, we will pay for the loss or damage caused by that fire or explosion; or

(2) If:

(a) Loss or damage to farm machinery, vehicles and equipment covered for the Special Causes of Loss; or

(b) Loss to "livestock";

is caused by earthquake, as described in **a.** above, this Earth Movement exclusion does not apply to such loss or damage.

e. Volcanic eruption, explosion or effusion. But if volcanic eruption, explosion or effusion results in fire or volcanic action, we will pay for the loss or damage caused by that fire or volcanic action.

Volcanic action means direct loss or damage resulting from the eruption of a volcano when the loss or damage is caused by:

(1) Airborne volcanic blast or airborne shock waves;

(2) Ash, dust or particulate matter; or

(3) Lava flow.

All volcanic eruptions that occur within any 168-hour period will constitute a single occurrence.

Volcanic action does not include the cost to remove ash, dust or particulate matter that does not cause direct physical loss or damage to Covered Property.

3. Governmental Action

Seizure or destruction of property by order of governmental authority.

Farm

© Insurance Services Office, Inc., 2008   FP 10 60 02 09   □

But we will pay for loss or damage caused by or resulting from acts of destruction ordered by governmental authority and taken at the time of a fire to prevent its spread, if the fire would be covered under this Coverage Form.

4. Intentional Loss

We will not pay for loss or damage arising out of any act an "insured" commits or conspires to commit with the intent to cause a loss.

In the event of such loss, no "insured" is entitled to coverage, even "insureds" who did not commit or conspire to commit the act causing the loss.

5. Nuclear Hazard

Nuclear reaction or radiation, or radioactive contamination, however caused.

But if nuclear reaction or radiation, or radioactive contamination, results in fire, we will pay for the loss or damage caused by that fire.

6. Utility Services

The failure of power or other utility service supplied to the "insured location", however caused, if the failure occurs away from the "insured location", except as provided under Coverage C. Failure includes lack of sufficient capacity and reduction in supply.

But if the failure of power or other utility service results in a Covered Cause of Loss, we will pay for the loss or damage caused by that Covered Cause of Loss.

7. Neglect

Neglect, meaning neglect of the "insured" to use all reasonable means to save and preserve property at and after the time of a loss.

8. War And Military Action

a. War, including undeclared or civil war;

b. Warlike action by a military force, including action in hindering or defending against an actual or expected attack, by any government, sovereign or other authority using military personnel or other agents; or

c. Insurrection, rebellion, revolution, usurped power, or action taken by governmental authority in hindering or defending against any of these.

9. Water

a. Flood, surface water, waves (including tidal wave and tsunami), tides, tidal water, overflow of any body of water, or spray from any of these, all whether or not driven by wind (including storm surge);

b. Mudslide or mudflow;

c. Water that backs up or overflows or is otherwise discharged from a sewer or drain;

d. Water that backs up or overflows or is otherwise discharged from a sump, sump pump or related equipment;

e. Water under the ground surface pressing on, or flowing or seeping through:

   (1) Foundations, walls, floors or paved surfaces;

   (2) Basements, whether paved or not; or

   (3) Doors, windows or other openings; or

f. Waterborne material carried or otherwise moved by any of the water referred to in Paragraph a., c., d. or e., or material carried or otherwise moved by mudslide or mudflow.

This exclusion applies regardless of whether any of the above, in Paragraphs a. through f., is caused by an act of nature or is otherwise caused. An example of a situation to which this exclusion applies is the situation where a dam, levee, seawall or other boundary or containment system fails in whole or in part, for any reason, to contain the water.

But:

   (1) If any of the above, in Paragraphs a. through f., results in fire, explosion or sprinkler leakage, we will pay for the loss or damage caused by that fire, explosion or sprinkler leakage; or

   (2) If loss or damage to:

      (a) Farm machinery, vehicles and equipment covered for the Special Causes of Loss; or

      (b) "Livestock";

   is caused by water as described in Paragraph a. above, this Water exclusion does not apply to such loss or damage.

Exclusions E.1. through E.9. apply whether or not the loss event results in widespread damage or affects a substantial area.

Commercial General Liability Insurance

Commercial general liability (CGL) insurance is the most basic, and often the most important, coverage for insuring commercial liability loss exposures. The loss exposures covered by CGL insurance are often characterized as premises, operations, products, and completed operations. With the exceptions of automobile liability exposures and workers compensation obligations, CGL insurance covers the majority of liability exposures facing many organizations.

The principal form used to provide CGL insurance is the Commercial General Liability Coverage Form of Insurance Services Office (ISO). The two versions of this form differ only with respect to their coverage triggers:

- The *occurrence* form covers bodily injury or property damage that occurs during the policy period, regardless of when claim is actually made against the insured.

- The *claims-made* form covers bodily injury or property damage that occurs after the retroactive date stated in the policy but only if claim for the injury or damage is first made at some time during the policy period (or during an extended reporting period, if applicable).

Because the claims-made version is seldom used, only the occurrence version of the CGL coverage form is included in the *Handbook*. Apart from the coverage trigger, both forms provide the same coverages, as follows.

Coverage A—Bodily Injury and Property Damage Liability: The insurer agrees to pay on behalf of the insured those sums that the insured becomes legally obligated to pay as damages because of bodily injury or property damage covered by the policy. The insurer also agrees to defend the insured against claims or suits alleging such damages. Several exclusions define the scope of coverage. Among the most important exclusions are those applying to intended injury, injury to employees of the insured, pollution, aircraft, automobiles, watercraft, and damage to the insured's own work or products.

Coverage B—Personal and Advertising Injury Liability: The insurer agrees to pay on behalf of the insured those sums that the insured becomes legally obligated to pay as damages because of personal and advertising injury to which the insurance applies. Personal and advertising injury includes such offenses as libel, slander, false arrest, wrongful eviction, and infringement of copyright.

Coverage C—Medical Payments: Medical payments insurance covers medical expenses, regardless of whether the insured is legally liable to pay them, for persons other than insureds who are injured on the insured's premises or because of the insured's operations.

POLICY NUMBER:

COMMERCIAL GENERAL LIABILITY
CG DS 01 10 01

COMMERCIAL GENERAL LIABILITY DECLARATIONS

Worthley Insurance Co.	A. M. Abel

NAMED INSURED: Barnley Corporation

MAILING ADDRESS: 2000 Industrial Highway

                                  Workingtown, PA 19000

POLICY PERIOD: FROM ____10/1/20X1____ TO ____10/1/20X2____ AT 12:01 A.M. TIME AT

YOUR MAILING ADDRESS SHOWN ABOVE

IN RETURN FOR THE PAYMENT OF THE PREMIUM, AND SUBJECT TO ALL THE TERMS OF THIS POLICY, WE AGREE WITH YOU TO PROVIDE THE INSURANCE AS STATED IN THIS POLICY.

LIMITS OF INSURANCE		
EACH OCCURRENCE LIMIT	$ 1,000,000	
DAMAGE TO PREMISES RENTED TO YOU LIMIT	$ 100,000	Any one premises
MEDICAL EXPENSE LIMIT	$ 5,000	Any one person
PERSONAL & ADVERTISING INJURY LIMIT	$ 1,000,000	Any one person or organization
GENERAL AGGREGATE LIMIT		$ 2,000,000
PRODUCTS/COMPLETED OPERATIONS AGGREGATE LIMIT		$ 2,000,000

RETROACTIVE DATE (CG 00 02 ONLY)

THIS INSURANCE DOES NOT APPLY TO "BODILY INJURY", "PROPERTY DAMAGE" OR "PERSONAL AND ADVERTISING INJURY" WHICH OCCURS BEFORE THE RETROACTIVE DATE, IF ANY, SHOWN BELOW.

RETROACTIVE DATE: _____

(ENTER DATE OR "NONE" IF NO RETROACTIVE DATE APPLIES)

DESCRIPTION OF BUSINESS

FORM OF BUSINESS:

☐ INDIVIDUAL   ☐ PARTNERSHIP   ☐ JOINT VENTURE   ☐ TRUST

☐ LIMITED LIABILITY COMPANY   ☒ ORGANIZATION, INCLUDING A CORPORATION (BUT NOT IN-
                                                      CLUDING A PARTNERSHIP, JOINT VENTURE OR LIMITED LIABILITY
                                                      COMPANY)

BUSINESS DESCRIPTION: _____Storm Door Manufacturing_____

CG DS 01 10 01   © ISO Properties, Inc., 2000   **Page 1 of 2**   ☐

ALL PREMISES YOU OWN, RENT OR OCCUPY	
LOCATION NUMBER	ADDRESS OF ALL PREMISES YOU OWN, RENT OR OCCUPY
1	2000 Industrial Highway Workingtown, PA 19000

CLASSIFICATION AND PREMIUM

LOCATION NUMBER	CLASSIFICATION	CODE NO.	PREMIUM BASE	RATE		ADVANCE PREMIUM	
				Prem/Ops	Prod/Comp Ops	Prem/Ops	Prod/Comp Ops
1	Glass or Glassware Mfg.	54077	$2,000,000	$1,018	$ 2.589	$ 2,036	$5,178

STATE TAX OR OTHER (if applicable) $ _____

TOTAL PREMIUM (SUBJECT TO AUDIT) $ _____

PREMIUM SHOWN IS PAYABLE:

AT INCEPTION $ ___XXX___

AT EACH ANNIVERSARY $ _____

(IF POLICY PERIOD IS MORE THAN ONE YEAR AND PREMIUM IS PAID IN ANNUAL INSTALLMENTS)

AUDIT PERIOD (IF APPLICABLE)	☒ ANNUALLY	☐ SEMI-ANNUALLY	☐ QUARTERLY	☐ MONTHLY

ENDORSEMENTS

ENDORSEMENTS ATTACHED TO THIS POLICY:

IL 00 21 04 98—Broad Form Nuclear Exclusion

Plus those listed on schedule

THESE DECLARATIONS, TOGETHER WITH THE COMMON POLICY CONDITIONS AND COVERAGE FORM(S) AND ANY ENDORSEMENT(S), COMPLETE THE ABOVE NUMBERED POLICY.

Countersigned:	10/1/20X1	By:	A.M. Abel
			(Authorized Representative)

NOTE

OFFICERS' FACSIMILE SIGNATURES MAY BE INSERTED HERE, ON THE POLICY COVER OR ELSEWHERE AT THE COMPANY'S OPTION.

COMMERCIAL GENERAL LIABILITY
CG 00 01 12 07

COMMERCIAL GENERAL LIABILITY COVERAGE FORM

Various provisions in this policy restrict coverage. Read the entire policy carefully to determine rights, duties and what is and is not covered.

Throughout this policy the words "you" and "your" refer to the Named Insured shown in the Declarations, and any other person or organization qualifying as a Named Insured under this policy. The words "we", "us" and "our" refer to the company providing this insurance.

The word "insured" means any person or organization qualifying as such under Section **II** – Who Is An Insured.

Other words and phrases that appear in quotation marks have special meaning. Refer to Section **V** – Definitions.

SECTION I – COVERAGES

COVERAGE A BODILY INJURY AND PROPERTY DAMAGE LIABILITY

1. Insuring Agreement

   a. We will pay those sums that the insured becomes legally obligated to pay as damages because of "bodily injury" or "property damage" to which this insurance applies. We will have the right and duty to defend the insured against any "suit" seeking those damages. However, we will have no duty to defend the insured against any "suit" seeking damages for "bodily injury" or "property damage" to which this insurance does not apply. We may, at our discretion, investigate any "occurrence" and settle any claim or "suit" that may result. But:

   (1) The amount we will pay for damages is limited as described in Section **III** – Limits Of Insurance; and

   (2) Our right and duty to defend ends when we have used up the applicable limit of insurance in the payment of judgments or settlements under Coverages **A** or **B** or medical expenses under Coverage **C**.

   No other obligation or liability to pay sums or perform acts or services is covered unless explicitly provided for under Supplementary Payments – Coverages **A** and **B**.

   b. This insurance applies to "bodily injury" and "property damage" only if:

   (1) The "bodily injury" or "property damage" is caused by an "occurrence" that takes place in the "coverage territory";

   (2) The "bodily injury" or "property damage" occurs during the policy period; and

   (3) Prior to the policy period, no insured listed under Paragraph **1.** of Section **II** – Who Is An Insured and no "employee" authorized by you to give or receive notice of an "occurrence" or claim, knew that the "bodily injury" or "property damage" had occurred, in whole or in part. If such a listed insured or authorized "employee" knew, prior to the policy period, that the "bodily injury" or "property damage" occurred, then any continuation, change or resumption of such "bodily injury" or "property damage" during or after the policy period will be deemed to have been known prior to the policy period.

   c. "Bodily injury" or "property damage" which occurs during the policy period and was not, prior to the policy period, known to have occurred by any insured listed under Paragraph **1.** of Section **II** – Who Is An Insured or any "employee" authorized by you to give or receive notice of an "occurrence" or claim, includes any continuation, change or resumption of that "bodily injury" or "property damage" after the end of the policy period.

   d. "Bodily injury" or "property damage" will be deemed to have been known to have occurred at the earliest time when any insured listed under Paragraph **1.** of Section **II** – Who Is An Insured or any "employee" authorized by you to give or receive notice of an "occurrence" or claim:

   (1) Reports all, or any part, of the "bodily injury" or "property damage" to us or any other insurer;

   (2) Receives a written or verbal demand or claim for damages because of the "bodily injury" or "property damage"; or

   (3) Becomes aware by any other means that "bodily injury" or "property damage" has occurred or has begun to occur.

e. Damages because of "bodily injury" include damages claimed by any person or organization for care, loss of services or death resulting at any time from the "bodily injury".

2. Exclusions

This insurance does not apply to:

a. Expected Or Intended Injury

"Bodily injury" or "property damage" expected or intended from the standpoint of the insured. This exclusion does not apply to "bodily injury" resulting from the use of reasonable force to protect persons or property.

b. Contractual Liability

"Bodily injury" or "property damage" for which the insured is obligated to pay damages by reason of the assumption of liability in a contract or agreement. This exclusion does not apply to liability for damages:

(1) That the insured would have in the absence of the contract or agreement; or

(2) Assumed in a contract or agreement that is an "insured contract", provided the "bodily injury" or "property damage" occurs subsequent to the execution of the contract or agreement. Solely for the purposes of liability assumed in an "insured contract", reasonable attorney fees and necessary litigation expenses incurred by or for a party other than an insured are deemed to be damages because of "bodily injury" or "property damage", provided:

(a) Liability to such party for, or for the cost of, that party's defense has also been assumed in the same "insured contract"; and

(b) Such attorney fees and litigation expenses are for defense of that party against a civil or alternative dispute resolution proceeding in which damages to which this insurance applies are alleged.

c. Liquor Liability

"Bodily injury" or "property damage" for which any insured may be held liable by reason of:

(1) Causing or contributing to the intoxication of any person;

(2) The furnishing of alcoholic beverages to a person under the legal drinking age or under the influence of alcohol; or

(3) Any statute, ordinance or regulation relating to the sale, gift, distribution or use of alcoholic beverages.

This exclusion applies only if you are in the business of manufacturing, distributing, selling, serving or furnishing alcoholic beverages.

d. Workers' Compensation And Similar Laws

Any obligation of the insured under a workers' compensation, disability benefits or unemployment compensation law or any similar law.

e. Employer's Liability

"Bodily injury" to:

(1) An "employee" of the insured arising out of and in the course of:

(a) Employment by the insured; or

(b) Performing duties related to the conduct of the insured's business; or

(2) The spouse, child, parent, brother or sister of that "employee" as a consequence of Paragraph **(1)** above.

This exclusion applies whether the insured may be liable as an employer or in any other capacity and to any obligation to share damages with or repay someone else who must pay damages because of the injury.

This exclusion does not apply to liability assumed by the insured under an "insured contract".

CGL

f. Pollution

(1) "Bodily injury" or "property damage" arising out of the actual, alleged or threatened discharge, dispersal, seepage, migration, release or escape of "pollutants":

(a) At or from any premises, site or location which is or was at any time owned or occupied by, or rented or loaned to, any insured. However, this subparagraph does not apply to:

(i) "Bodily injury" if sustained within a building and caused by smoke, fumes, vapor or soot produced by or originating from equipment that is used to heat, cool or dehumidify the building, or equipment that is used to heat water for personal use, by the building's occupants or their guests;

(ii) "Bodily injury" or "property damage" for which you may be held liable, if you are a contractor and the owner or lessee of such premises, site or location has been added to your policy as an additional insured with respect to your ongoing operations performed for that additional insured at that premises, site or location and such premises, site or location is not and never was owned or occupied by, or rented or loaned to, any insured, other than that additional insured; or

(iii) "Bodily injury" or "property damage" arising out of heat, smoke or fumes from a "hostile fire";

(b) At or from any premises, site or location which is or was at any time used by or for any insured or others for the handling, storage, disposal, processing or treatment of waste;

(c) Which are or were at any time transported, handled, stored, treated, disposed of, or processed as waste by or for:

(i) Any insured; or

(ii) Any person or organization for whom you may be legally responsible; or

(d) At or from any premises, site or location on which any insured or any contractors or subcontractors working directly or indirectly on any insured's behalf are performing operations if the "pollutants" are brought on or to the premises, site or location in connection with such operations by such insured, contractor or subcontractor. However, this subparagraph does not apply to:

(i) "Bodily injury" or "property damage" arising out of the escape of fuels, lubricants or other operating fluids which are needed to perform the normal electrical, hydraulic or mechanical functions necessary for the operation of "mobile equipment" or its parts, if such fuels, lubricants or other operating fluids escape from a vehicle part designed to hold, store or receive them. This exception does not apply if the "bodily injury" or "property damage" arises out of the intentional discharge, dispersal or release of the fuels, lubricants or other operating fluids, or if such fuels, lubricants or other operating fluids are brought on or to the premises, site or location with the intent that they be discharged, dispersed or released as part of the operations being performed by such insured, contractor or subcontractor;

(ii) "Bodily injury" or "property damage" sustained within a building and caused by the release of gases, fumes or vapors from materials brought into that building in connection with operations being performed by you or on your behalf by a contractor or subcontractor; or

(iii) "Bodily injury" or "property damage" arising out of heat, smoke or fumes from a "hostile fire".

(e) At or from any premises, site or location on which any insured or any contractors or subcontractors working directly or indirectly on any insured's behalf are performing operations if the operations are to test for, monitor, clean up, remove, contain, treat, detoxify or neutralize, or in any way respond to, or assess the effects of, "pollutants".

(2) Any loss, cost or expense arising out of any:

(a) Request, demand, order or statutory or regulatory requirement that any insured or others test for, monitor, clean up, remove, contain, treat, detoxify or neutralize, or in any way respond to, or assess the effects of, "pollutants"; or

(b) Claim or "suit" by or on behalf of a governmental authority for damages because of testing for, monitoring, cleaning up, removing, containing, treating, detoxifying or neutralizing, or in any way responding to, or assessing the effects of, "pollutants".

However, this paragraph does not apply to liability for damages because of "property damage" that the insured would have in the absence of such request, demand, order or statutory or regulatory requirement, or such claim or "suit" by or on behalf of a governmental authority.

g. Aircraft, Auto Or Watercraft

"Bodily injury" or "property damage" arising out of the ownership, maintenance, use or entrustment to others of any aircraft, "auto" or watercraft owned or operated by or rented or loaned to any insured. Use includes operation and "loading or unloading".

This exclusion applies even if the claims against any insured allege negligence or other wrongdoing in the supervision, hiring, employment, training or monitoring of others by that insured, if the "occurrence" which caused the "bodily injury" or "property damage" involved the ownership, maintenance, use or entrustment to others of any aircraft, "auto" or watercraft that is owned or operated by or rented or loaned to any insured.

This exclusion does not apply to:

(1) A watercraft while ashore on premises you own or rent;

(2) A watercraft you do not own that is:

(a) Less than 26 feet long; and

(b) Not being used to carry persons or property for a charge;

(3) Parking an "auto" on, or on the ways next to, premises you own or rent, provided the "auto" is not owned by or rented or loaned to you or the insured;

(4) Liability assumed under any "insured contract" for the ownership, maintenance or use of aircraft or watercraft; or

(5) "Bodily injury" or "property damage" arising out of:

(a) The operation of machinery or equipment that is attached to, or part of, a land vehicle that would qualify under the definition of "mobile equipment" if it were not subject to a compulsory or financial responsibility law or other motor vehicle insurance law in the state where it is licensed or principally garaged; or

(b) the operation of any of the machinery or equipment listed in Paragraph **f.(2)** or **f.(3)** of the definition of "mobile equipment".

h. Mobile Equipment

"Bodily injury" or "property damage" arising out of:

(1) The transportation of "mobile equipment" by an "auto" owned or operated by or rented or loaned to any insured; or

(2) The use of "mobile equipment" in, or while in practice for, or while being prepared for, any prearranged racing, speed, demolition, or stunting activity.

i. War

"Bodily injury" or "property damage", however caused, arising, directly or indirectly, out of:

(1) War, including undeclared or civil war;

(2) Warlike action by a military force, including action in hindering or defending against an actual or expected attack, by any government, sovereign or other authority using military personnel or other agents; or

(3) Insurrection, rebellion, revolution, usurped power, or action taken by governmental authority in hindering or defending against any of these.

j. Damage To Property

"Property damage" to:

(1) Property you own, rent, or occupy, including any costs or expenses incurred by you, or any other person, organization or entity, for repair, replacement, enhancement, restoration or maintenance of such property for any reason, including prevention of injury to a person or damage to another's property;

(2) Premises you sell, give away or abandon, if the "property damage" arises out of any part of those premises;

(3) Property loaned to you;

(4) Personal property in the care, custody or control of the insured;

(5) That particular part of real property on which you or any contractors or subcontractors working directly or indirectly on your behalf are performing operations, if the "property damage" arises out of those operations; or

(6) That particular part of any property that must be restored, repaired or replaced because "your work" was incorrectly performed on it.

Paragraphs **(1)**, **(3)** and **(4)** of this exclusion do not apply to "property damage" (other than damage by fire) to premises, including the contents of such premises, rented to you for a period of 7 or fewer consecutive days. A separate limit of insurance applies to Damage To Premises Rented To You as described in Section **III** – Limits Of Insurance.

Paragraph **(2)** of this exclusion does not apply if the premises are "your work" and were never occupied, rented or held for rental by you.

Paragraphs **(3)**, **(4)**, **(5)** and **(6)** of this exclusion do not apply to liability assumed under a sidetrack agreement.

Paragraph **(6)** of this exclusion does not apply to "property damage" included in the "products-completed operations hazard".

k. Damage To Your Product

"Property damage" to "your product" arising out of it or any part of it.

l. Damage To Your Work

"Property damage" to "your work" arising out of it or any part of it and included in the "products-completed operations hazard".

This exclusion does not apply if the damaged work or the work out of which the damage arises was performed on your behalf by a subcontractor.

m. Damage To Impaired Property Or Property Not Physically Injured

"Property damage" to "impaired property" or property that has not been physically injured, arising out of:

(1) A defect, deficiency, inadequacy or dangerous condition in "your product" or "your work"; or

(2) A delay or failure by you or anyone acting on your behalf to perform a contract or agreement in accordance with its terms.

This exclusion does not apply to the loss of use of other property arising out of sudden and accidental physical injury to "your product" or "your work" after it has been put to its intended use.

n. Recall Of Products, Work Or Impaired Property

Damages claimed for any loss, cost or expense incurred by you or others for the loss of use, withdrawal, recall, inspection, repair, replacement, adjustment, removal or disposal of:

(1) "Your product";

(2) "Your work"; or

(3) "Impaired property";

if such product, work, or property is withdrawn or recalled from the market or from use by any person or organization because of a known or suspected defect, deficiency, inadequacy or dangerous condition in it.

o. Personal And Advertising Injury

"Bodily injury" arising out of "personal and advertising injury".

p. Electronic Data

Damages arising out of the loss of, loss of use of, damage to, corruption of, inability to access, or inability to manipulate electronic data.

As used in this exclusion, electronic data means information, facts or programs stored as or on, created or used on, or transmitted to or from computer software, including systems and applications software, hard or floppy disks, CD-ROMS, tapes, drives, cells, data processing devices or any other media which are used with electronically controlled equipment.

q. Distribution Of Material In Violation Of Statutes

"Bodily injury" or "property damage" arising directly or indirectly out of any action or omission that violates or is alleged to violate:

(1) The Telephone Consumer Protection Act (TCPA), including any amendment of or addition to such law; or

(2) The CAN-SPAM Act of 2003, including any amendment of or addition to such law; or

(3) Any statute, ordinance or regulation, other than the TCPA or CAN-SPAM Act of 2003, that prohibits or limits the sending, transmitting, communicating or distribution of material or information.

Exclusions **c.** through **n.** do not apply to damage by fire to premises while rented to you or temporarily occupied by you with permission of the owner. A separate limit of insurance applies to this coverage as described in Section **III** – Limits Of Insurance.

COVERAGE B PERSONAL AND ADVERTISING INJURY LIABILITY

1. Insuring Agreement

a. We will pay those sums that the insured becomes legally obligated to pay as damages because of "personal and advertising injury" to which this insurance applies. We will have the right and duty to defend the insured against any "suit" seeking those damages. However, we will have no duty to defend the insured against any "suit" seeking damages for "personal and advertising injury" to which this insurance does not apply. We may, at our discretion, investigate any offense and settle any claim or "suit" that may result. But:

(1) The amount we will pay for damages is limited as described in Section **III** – Limits Of Insurance; and

(2) Our right and duty to defend end when we have used up the applicable limit of insurance in the payment of judgments or settlements under Coverages **A** or **B** or medical expenses under Coverage **C.**

No other obligation or liability to pay sums or perform acts or services is covered unless explicitly provided for under Supplementary Payments – Coverages **A** and **B.**

b. This insurance applies to "personal and advertising injury" caused by an offense arising out of your business but only if the offense was committed in the "coverage territory" during the policy period.

2. Exclusions

This insurance does not apply to:

a. Knowing Violation Of Rights Of Another

"Personal and advertising injury" caused by or at the direction of the insured with the knowledge that the act would violate the rights of another and would inflict "personal and advertising injury".

b. Material Published With Knowledge Of Falsity

"Personal and advertising injury" arising out of oral or written publication of material, if done by or at the direction of the insured with knowledge of its falsity.

c. Material Published Prior To Policy Period

"Personal and advertising injury" arising out of oral or written publication of material whose first publication took place before the beginning of the policy period.

d. Criminal Acts

"Personal and advertising injury" arising out of a criminal act committed by or at the direction of the insured.

e. Contractual Liability

"Personal and advertising injury" for which the insured has assumed liability in a contract or agreement. This exclusion does not apply to liability for damages that the insured would have in the absence of the contract or agreement.

f. Breach Of Contract

"Personal and advertising injury" arising out of a breach of contract, except an implied contract to use another's advertising idea in your "advertisement".

g. Quality Or Performance Of Goods – Failure To Conform To Statements

"Personal and advertising injury" arising out of the failure of goods, products or services to conform with any statement of quality or performance made in your "advertisement".

h. Wrong Description Of Prices

"Personal and advertising injury" arising out of the wrong description of the price of goods, products or services stated in your "advertisement".

i. Infringement Of Copyright, Patent, Trademark Or Trade Secret

"Personal and advertising injury" arising out of the infringement of copyright, patent, trademark, trade secret or other intellectual property rights. Under this exclusion, such other intellectual property rights do not include the use of another's advertising idea in your "advertisement".

However, this exclusion does not apply to infringement, in your "advertisement", of copyright, trade dress or slogan.

j. Insureds In Media And Internet Type Businesses

"Personal and advertising injury" committed by an insured whose business is:

(1) Advertising, broadcasting, publishing or telecasting;

(2) Designing or determining content of websites for others; or

(3) An Internet search, access, content or service provider.

However, this exclusion does not apply to Paragraphs **14.a.**, **b.** and **c.** of "personal and advertising injury" under the Definitions Section.

For the purposes of this exclusion, the placing of frames, borders or links, or advertising, for you or others anywhere on the Internet, is not by itself, considered the business of advertising, broadcasting, publishing or telecasting.

k. Electronic Chatrooms Or Bulletin Boards

"Personal and advertising injury" arising out of an electronic chatroom or bulletin board the insured hosts, owns, or over which the insured exercises control.

l. Unauthorized Use Of Another's Name Or Product

"Personal and advertising injury" arising out of the unauthorized use of another's name or product in your e-mail address, domain name or metatag, or any other similar tactics to mislead another's potential customers.

m. Pollution

"Personal and advertising injury" arising out of the actual, alleged or threatened discharge, dispersal, seepage, migration, release or escape of "pollutants" at any time.

n. Pollution-Related

Any loss, cost or expense arising out of any:

(1) Request, demand, order or statutory or regulatory requirement that any insured or others test for, monitor, clean up, remove, contain, treat, detoxify or neutralize, or in any way respond to, or assess the effects of, "pollutants"; or

(2) Claim or suit by or on behalf of a governmental authority for damages because of testing for, monitoring, cleaning up, removing, containing, treating, detoxifying or neutralizing, or in any way responding to, or assessing the effects of, "pollutants".

o. War

"Personal and advertising injury", however caused, arising, directly or indirectly, out of:

(1) War, including undeclared or civil war;

(2) Warlike action by a military force, including action in hindering or defending against an actual or expected attack, by any government, sovereign or other authority using military personnel or other agents; or

(3) Insurrection, rebellion, revolution, usurped power, or action taken by governmental authority in hindering or defending against any of these.

p. Distribution Of Material In Violation Of Statutes

"Personal and advertising injury" arising directly or indirectly out of any action or omission that violates or is alleged to violate:

(1) The Telephone Consumer Protection Act (TCPA), including any amendment of or addition to such law; or

(2) The CAN-SPAM Act of 2003, including any amendment of or addition to such law; or

(3) Any statute, ordinance or regulation, other than the TCPA or CAN-SPAM Act of 2003, that prohibits or limits the sending, transmitting, communicating or distribution of material or information.

COVERAGE C MEDICAL PAYMENTS

1. Insuring Agreement

a. We will pay medical expenses as described below for "bodily injury" caused by an accident:

(1) On premises you own or rent;

(2) On ways next to premises you own or rent; or

(3) Because of your operations;

provided that:

    (a) The accident takes place in the "coverage territory" and during the policy period;

    (b) The expenses are incurred and reported to us within one year of the date of the accident; and

    (c) The injured person submits to examination, at our expense, by physicians of our choice as often as we reasonably require.

b. We will make these payments regardless of fault. These payments will not exceed the applicable limit of insurance. We will pay reasonable expenses for:

(1) First aid administered at the time of an accident;

(2) Necessary medical, surgical, x-ray and dental services, including prosthetic devices; and

(3) Necessary ambulance, hospital, professional nursing and funeral services.

2. Exclusions

We will not pay expenses for "bodily injury":

a. Any Insured

To any insured, except "volunteer workers".

b. Hired Person

To a person hired to do work for or on behalf of any insured or a tenant of any insured.

c. Injury On Normally Occupied Premises

To a person injured on that part of premises you own or rent that the person normally occupies.

d. Workers Compensation And Similar Laws

To a person, whether or not an "employee" of any insured, if benefits for the "bodily injury" are payable or must be provided under a workers' compensation or disability benefits law or a similar law.

e. Athletics Activities

To a person injured while practicing, instructing or participating in any physical exercises or games, sports, or athletic contests.

f. Products-Completed Operations Hazard

Included within the "products-completed operations hazard".

g. Coverage A Exclusions

Excluded under Coverage **A**.

SUPPLEMENTARY PAYMENTS – COVERAGES A AND B

1. We will pay, with respect to any claim we investigate or settle, or any "suit" against an insured we defend:

a. All expenses we incur.

b. Up to $250 for cost of bail bonds required because of accidents or traffic law violations arising out of the use of any vehicle to which the Bodily Injury Liability Coverage applies. We do not have to furnish these bonds.

c. The cost of bonds to release attachments, but only for bond amounts within the applicable limit of insurance. We do not have to furnish these bonds.

d. All reasonable expenses incurred by the insured at our request to assist us in the investigation or defense of the claim or "suit", including actual loss of earnings up to $250 a day because of time off from work.

e. All court costs taxed against the insured in the "suit". However, these payments do not include attorneys' fees or attorneys' expenses taxed against the insured.

f. Prejudgment interest awarded against the insured on that part of the judgment we pay. If we make an offer to pay the applicable limit of insurance, we will not pay any prejudgment interest based on that period of time after the offer.

g. All interest on the full amount of any judgment that accrues after entry of the judgment and before we have paid, offered to pay, or deposited in court the part of the judgment that is within the applicable limit of insurance.

These payments will not reduce the limits of insurance.

2. If we defend an insured against a "suit" and an indemnitee of the insured is also named as a party to the "suit", we will defend that indemnitee if all of the following conditions are met:

a. The "suit" against the indemnitee seeks damages for which the insured has assumed the liability of the indemnitee in a contract or agreement that is an "insured contract";

b. This insurance applies to such liability assumed by the insured;

c. The obligation to defend, or the cost of the defense of, that indemnitee, has also been assumed by the insured in the same "insured contract";

d. The allegations in the "suit" and the information we know about the "occurrence" are such that no conflict appears to exist between the interests of the insured and the interests of the indemnitee;

e. The indemnitee and the insured ask us to conduct and control the defense of that indemnitee against such "suit" and agree that we can assign the same counsel to defend the insured and the indemnitee; and

f. The indemnitee:

(1) Agrees in writing to:

(a) Cooperate with us in the investigation, settlement or defense of the "suit";

(b) Immediately send us copies of any demands, notices, summonses or legal papers received in connection with the "suit";

(c) Notify any other insurer whose coverage is available to the indemnitee; and

(d) Cooperate with us with respect to coordinating other applicable insurance available to the indemnitee; and

(2) Provides us with written authorization to:

(a) Obtain records and other information related to the "suit"; and

(b) Conduct and control the defense of the indemnitee in such "suit".

So long as the above conditions are met, attorneys' fees incurred by us in the defense of that indemnitee, necessary litigation expenses incurred by us and necessary litigation expenses incurred by the indemnitee at our request will be paid as Supplementary Payments. Notwithstanding the provisions of Paragraph **2.b.(2)** of Section I – Coverage **A** – Bodily Injury And Property Damage Liability, such payments will not be deemed to be damages for "bodily injury" and "property damage" and will not reduce the limits of insurance.

Our obligation to defend an insured's indemnitee and to pay for attorneys' fees and necessary litigation expenses as Supplementary Payments ends when we have used up the applicable limit of insurance in the payment of judgments or settlements or the conditions set forth above, or the terms of the agreement described in Paragraph **f.** above, are no longer met.

SECTION II – WHO IS AN INSURED

1. If you are designated in the Declarations as:

   a. An individual, you and your spouse are insureds, but only with respect to the conduct of a business of which you are the sole owner.

   b. A partnership or joint venture, you are an insured. Your members, your partners, and their spouses are also insureds, but only with respect to the conduct of your business.

   c. A limited liability company, you are an insured. Your members are also insureds, but only with respect to the conduct of your business. Your managers are insureds, but only with respect to their duties as your managers.

   d. An organization other than a partnership, joint venture or limited liability company, you are an insured. Your "executive officers" and directors are insureds, but only with respect to their duties as your officers or directors. Your stockholders are also insureds, but only with respect to their liability as stockholders.

   e. A trust, you are an insured. Your trustees are also insureds, but only with respect to their duties as trustees.

2. Each of the following is also an insured:

   a. Your "volunteer workers" only while performing duties related to the conduct of your business, or your "employees", other than either your "executive officers" (if you are an organization other than a partnership, joint venture or limited liability company) or your managers (if you are a limited liability company), but only for acts within the scope of their employment by you or while performing duties related to the conduct of your business. However, none of these "employees" or "volunteer workers" are insureds for:

   (1) "Bodily injury" or "personal and advertising injury":

   (a) To you, to your partners or members (if you are a partnership or joint venture), to your members (if you are a limited liability company), to a co-"employee" while in the course of his or her employment or performing duties related to the conduct of your business, or to your other "volunteer workers" while performing duties related to the conduct of your business;

   (b) To the spouse, child, parent, brother or sister of that co-"employee" or "volunteer worker" as a consequence of Paragraph **(1)(a)** above;

   (c) For which there is any obligation to share damages with or repay someone else who must pay damages because of the injury described in Paragraphs **(1)(a)** or **(b)** above; or

   (d) Arising out of his or her providing or failing to provide professional health care services.

   (2) "Property damage" to property:

   (a) Owned, occupied or used by,

   (b) Rented to, in the care, custody or control of, or over which physical control is being exercised for any purpose by

   you, any of your "employees", "volunteer workers", any partner or member (if you are a partnership or joint venture), or any member (if you are a limited liability company).

b. Any person (other than your "employee" or "volunteer worker"), or any organization while acting as your real estate manager.

c. Any person or organization having proper temporary custody of your property if you die, but only:

   (1) With respect to liability arising out of the maintenance or use of that property; and

   (2) Until your legal representative has been appointed.

d. Your legal representative if you die, but only with respect to duties as such. That representative will have all your rights and duties under this Coverage Part.

3. Any organization you newly acquire or form, other than a partnership, joint venture or limited liability company, and over which you maintain ownership or majority interest, will qualify as a Named Insured if there is no other similar insurance available to that organization. However:

a. Coverage under this provision is afforded only until the 90th day after you acquire or form the organization or the end of the policy period, whichever is earlier;

b. Coverage **A** does not apply to "bodily injury" or "property damage" that occurred before you acquired or formed the organization; and

c. Coverage **B** does not apply to "personal and advertising injury" arising out of an offense committed before you acquired or formed the organization.

No person or organization is an insured with respect to the conduct of any current or past partnership, joint venture or limited liability company that is not shown as a Named Insured in the Declarations.

SECTION III – LIMITS OF INSURANCE

1. The Limits of Insurance shown in the Declarations and the rules below fix the most we will pay regardless of the number of:

a. Insureds;

b. Claims made or "suits" brought; or

c. Persons or organizations making claims or bringing "suits".

2. The General Aggregate Limit is the most we will pay for the sum of:

a. Medical expenses under Coverage **C**;

b. Damages under Coverage **A**, except damages because of "bodily injury" or "property damage" included in the "products-completed operations hazard"; and

c. Damages under Coverage **B**.

3. The Products-Completed Operations Aggregate Limit is the most we will pay under Coverage **A** for damages because of "bodily injury" and "property damage" included in the "products-completed operations hazard".

4. Subject to Paragraph **2.** above, the Personal and Advertising Injury Limit is the most we will pay under Coverage **B** for the sum of all damages because of all "personal and advertising injury" sustained by any one person or organization.

5. Subject to Paragraph **2.** or **3.** above, whichever applies, the Each Occurrence Limit is the most we will pay for the sum of:

a. Damages under Coverage **A**; and

b. Medical expenses under Coverage **C**

because of all "bodily injury" and "property damage" arising out of any one "occurrence".

6. Subject to Paragraph **5.** above, the Damage To Premises Rented To You Limit is the most we will pay under Coverage **A** for damages because of "property damage" to any one premises, while rented to you, or in the case of damage by fire, while rented to you or temporarily occupied by you with permission of the owner.

7. Subject to Paragraph **5.** above, the Medical Expense Limit is the most we will pay under Coverage **C** for all medical expenses because of "bodily injury" sustained by any one person.

The Limits of Insurance of this Coverage Part apply separately to each consecutive annual period and to any remaining period of less than 12 months, starting with the beginning of the policy period shown in the Declarations, unless the policy period is extended after issuance for an additional period of less than 12 months. In that case, the additional period will be deemed part of the last preceding period for purposes of determining the Limits of Insurance.

SECTION IV – COMMERCIAL GENERAL LIABILITY CONDITIONS

1. Bankruptcy

Bankruptcy or insolvency of the insured or of the insured's estate will not relieve us of our obligations under this Coverage Part.

2. Duties In The Event Of Occurrence, Offense, Claim Or Suit

a. You must see to it that we are notified as soon as practicable of an "occurrence" or an offense which may result in a claim. To the extent possible, notice should include:

   (1) How, when and where the "occurrence" or offense took place;

   (2) The names and addresses of any injured persons and witnesses; and

© ISO Properties, Inc., 2006   □

CGL

(3) The nature and location of any injury or damage arising out of the "occurrence" or offense.

b. If a claim is made or "suit" is brought against any insured, you must:

(1) Immediately record the specifics of the claim or "suit" and the date received; and

(2) Notify us as soon as practicable.

You must see to it that we receive written notice of the claim or "suit" as soon as practicable.

c. You and any other involved insured must:

(1) Immediately send us copies of any demands, notices, summonses or legal papers received in connection with the claim or "suit";

(2) Authorize us to obtain records and other information;

(3) Cooperate with us in the investigation or settlement of the claim or defense against the "suit"; and

(4) Assist us, upon our request, in the enforcement of any right against any person or organization which may be liable to the insured because of injury or damage to which this insurance may also apply.

d. No insured will, except at that insured's own cost, voluntarily make a payment, assume any obligation, or incur any expense, other than for first aid, without our consent.

3. Legal Action Against Us

No person or organization has a right under this Coverage Part:

a. To join us as a party or otherwise bring us into a "suit" asking for damages from an insured; or

b. To sue us on this Coverage Part unless all of its terms have been fully complied with.

A person or organization may sue us to recover on an agreed settlement or on a final judgment against an insured; but we will not be liable for damages that are not payable under the terms of this Coverage Part or that are in excess of the applicable limit of insurance. An agreed settlement means a settlement and release of liability signed by us, the insured and the claimant or the claimant's legal representative.

4. Other Insurance

If other valid and collectible insurance is available to the insured for a loss we cover under Coverages **A** or **B** of this Coverage Part, our obligations are limited as follows:

a. Primary Insurance

This insurance is primary except when Paragraph **b.** below applies. If this insurance is primary, our obligations are not affected unless any of the other insurance is also primary. Then, we will share with all that other insurance by the method described in Paragraph **c.** below.

b. Excess Insurance

(1) This insurance is excess over:

(a) Any of the other insurance, whether primary, excess, contingent or on any other basis:

(i) That is Fire, Extended Coverage, Builder's Risk, Installation Risk or similar coverage for "your work";

(ii) That is Fire insurance for premises rented to you or temporarily occupied by you with permission of the owner;

(iii) That is insurance purchased by you to cover your liability as a tenant for "property damage" to premises rented to you or temporarily occupied by you with permission of the owner; or

(iv) If the loss arises out of the maintenance or use of aircraft, "autos" or watercraft to the extent not subject to Exclusion **g.** of Section **I** – Coverage **A** – Bodily Injury And Property Damage Liability.

(b) Any other primary insurance available to you covering liability for damages arising out of the premises or operations, or the products and completed operations, for which you have been added as an additional insured by attachment of an endorsement.

(2) When this insurance is excess, we will have no duty under Coverages **A** or **B** to defend the insured against any "suit" if any other insurer has a duty to defend the insured against that "suit". If no other insurer defends, we will undertake to do so, but we will be entitled to the insured's rights against all those other insurers.

(3) When this insurance is excess over other insurance, we will pay only our share of the amount of the loss, if any, that exceeds the sum of:

(a) The total amount that all such other insurance would pay for the loss in the absence of this insurance; and

(b) The total of all deductible and self-insured amounts under all that other insurance.

(4) We will share the remaining loss, if any, with any other insurance that is not described in this Excess Insurance provision and was not bought specifically to apply in excess of the Limits of Insurance shown in the Declarations of this Coverage Part.

c. Method Of Sharing

If all of the other insurance permits contribution by equal shares, we will follow this method also. Under this approach each insurer contributes equal amounts until it has paid its applicable limit of insurance or none of the loss remains, whichever comes first.

If any of the other insurance does not permit contribution by equal shares, we will contribute by limits. Under this method, each insurer's share is based on the ratio of its applicable limit of insurance to the total applicable limits of insurance of all insurers.

5. Premium Audit

a. We will compute all premiums for this Coverage Part in accordance with our rules and rates.

b. Premium shown in this Coverage Part as advance premium is a deposit premium only. At the close of each audit period we will compute the earned premium for that period and send notice to the first Named Insured. The due date for audit and retrospective premiums is the date shown as the due date on the bill. If the sum of the advance and audit premiums paid for the policy period is greater than the earned premium, we will return the excess to the first Named Insured.

c. The first Named Insured must keep records of the information we need for premium computation, and send us copies at such times as we may request.

6. Representations

By accepting this policy, you agree:

a. The statements in the Declarations are accurate and complete;

b. Those statements are based upon representations you made to us; and

c. We have issued this policy in reliance upon your representations.

7. Separation Of Insureds

Except with respect to the Limits of Insurance, and any rights or duties specifically assigned in this Coverage Part to the first Named Insured, this insurance applies:

a. As if each Named Insured were the only Named Insured; and

b. Separately to each insured against whom claim is made or "suit" is brought.

8. Transfer Of Rights Of Recovery Against Others To Us

If the insured has rights to recover all or part of any payment we have made under this Coverage Part, those rights are transferred to us. The insured must do nothing after loss to impair them. At our request, the insured will bring "suit" or transfer those rights to us and help us enforce them.

9. When We Do Not Renew

If we decide not to renew this Coverage Part, we will mail or deliver to the first Named Insured shown in the Declarations written notice of the nonrenewal not less than 30 days before the expiration date.

If notice is mailed, proof of mailing will be sufficient proof of notice.

SECTION V – DEFINITIONS

1. "Advertisement" means a notice that is broadcast or published to the general public or specific market segments about your goods, products or services for the purpose of attracting customers or supporters. For the purposes of this definition:

a. Notices that are published include material placed on the Internet or on similar electronic means of communication; and

b. Regarding web-sites, only that part of a web-site that is about your goods, products or services for the purposes of attracting customers or supporters is considered an advertisement.

2. "Auto" means:

a. A land motor vehicle, trailer or semitrailer designed for travel on public roads, including any attached machinery or equipment; or

b. Any other land vehicle that is subject to a compulsory or financial responsibility law or other motor vehicle insurance law in the state where it is licensed or principally garaged.

However, "auto" does not include "mobile equipment".

 □

3. "Bodily injury" means bodily injury, sickness or disease sustained by a person, including death resulting from any of these at any time.

4. "Coverage territory" means:

   a. The United States of America (including its territories and possessions), Puerto Rico and Canada;

   b. International waters or airspace, but only if the injury or damage occurs in the course of travel or transportation between any places included in Paragraph **a.** above; or

   c. All other parts of the world if the injury or damage arises out of:

      (1) Goods or products made or sold by you in the territory described in Paragraph **a.** above;

      (2) The activities of a person whose home is in the territory described in Paragraph **a.** above, but is away for a short time on your business; or

      (3) "Personal and advertising injury" offenses that take place through the Internet or similar electronic means of communication

   provided the insured's responsibility to pay damages is determined in a "suit" on the merits, in the territory described in Paragraph **a.** above or in a settlement we agree to.

5. "Employee" includes a "leased worker". "Employee" does not include a "temporary worker".

6. "Executive officer" means a person holding any of the officer positions created by your charter, constitution, by-laws or any other similar governing document.

7. "Hostile fire" means one which becomes uncontrollable or breaks out from where it was intended to be.

8. "Impaired property" means tangible property, other than "your product" or "your work", that cannot be used or is less useful because:

   a. It incorporates "your product" or "your work" that is known or thought to be defective, deficient, inadequate or dangerous; or

   b. You have failed to fulfill the terms of a contract or agreement;

   if such property can be restored to use by the repair, replacement, adjustment or removal of "your product" or "your work" or your fulfilling the terms of the contract or agreement.

9. "Insured contract" means:

   a. A contract for a lease of premises. However, that portion of the contract for a lease of premises that indemnifies any person or organization for damage by fire to premises while rented to you or temporarily occupied by you with permission of the owner is not an "insured contract";

   b. A sidetrack agreement;

   c. Any easement or license agreement, except in connection with construction or demolition operations on or within 50 feet of a railroad;

   d. An obligation, as required by ordinance, to indemnify a municipality, except in connection with work for a municipality;

   e. An elevator maintenance agreement;

   f. That part of any other contract or agreement pertaining to your business (including an indemnification of a municipality in connection with work performed for a municipality) under which you assume the tort liability of another party to pay for "bodily injury" or "property damage" to a third person or organization. Tort liability means a liability that would be imposed by law in the absence of any contract or agreement.

   Paragraph **f.** does not include that part of any contract or agreement:

      (1) That indemnifies a railroad for "bodily injury" or "property damage" arising out of construction or demolition operations, within 50 feet of any railroad property and affecting any railroad bridge or trestle, tracks, road-beds, tunnel, underpass or crossing;

      (2) That indemnifies an architect, engineer or surveyor for injury or damage arising out of:

         (a) Preparing, approving, or failing to prepare or approve, maps, shop drawings, opinions, reports, surveys, field orders, change orders or drawings and specifications; or

         (b) Giving directions or instructions, or failing to give them, if that is the primary cause of the injury or damage; or

      (3) Under which the insured, if an architect, engineer or surveyor, assumes liability for an injury or damage arising out of the insured's rendering or failure to render professional services, including those listed in **(2)** above and supervisory, inspection, architectural or engineering activities.

10. "Leased worker" means a person leased to you by a labor leasing firm under an agreement between you and the labor leasing firm, to perform duties related to the conduct of your business. "Leased worker" does not include a "temporary worker".

11. "Loading or unloading" means the handling of property:

   a. After it is moved from the place where it is accepted for movement into or onto an aircraft, watercraft or "auto";

   b. While it is in or on an aircraft, watercraft or "auto"; or

   c. While it is being moved from an aircraft, watercraft or "auto" to the place where it is finally delivered;

   but "loading or unloading" does not include the movement of property by means of a mechanical device, other than a hand truck, that is not attached to the aircraft, watercraft or "auto".

12. "Mobile equipment" means any of the following types of land vehicles, including any attached machinery or equipment:

   a. Bulldozers, farm machinery, forklifts and other vehicles designed for use principally off public roads;

   b. Vehicles maintained for use solely on or next to premises you own or rent;

   c. Vehicles that travel on crawler treads;

   d. Vehicles, whether self-propelled or not, maintained primarily to provide mobility to permanently mounted:

      (1) Power cranes, shovels, loaders, diggers or drills; or

      (2) Road construction or resurfacing equipment such as graders, scrapers or rollers;

   e. Vehicles not described in Paragraph a., b., c. or d. above that are not self-propelled and are maintained primarily to provide mobility to permanently attached equipment of the following types:

      (1) Air compressors, pumps and generators, including spraying, welding, building cleaning, geophysical exploration, lighting and well servicing equipment; or

      (2) Cherry pickers and similar devices used to raise or lower workers;

   f. Vehicles not described in Paragraph a., b., c. or d. above maintained primarily for purposes other than the transportation of persons or cargo.

   However, self-propelled vehicles with the following types of permanently attached equipment are not "mobile equipment" but will be considered "autos":

   (1) Equipment designed primarily for:

      (a) Snow removal;

      (b) Road maintenance, but not construction or resurfacing; or

      (c) Street cleaning;

   (2) Cherry pickers and similar devices mounted on automobile or truck chassis and used to raise or lower workers; and

   (3) Air compressors, pumps and generators, including spraying, welding, building cleaning, geophysical exploration, lighting and well servicing equipment.

   However, "mobile equipment" does not include any land vehicles that are subject to a compulsory or financial responsibility law or other motor vehicle insurance law in the state where it is licensed or principally garaged. Land vehicles subject to a compulsory or financial responsibility law or other motor vehicle insurance law are considered "autos".

13. "Occurrence" means an accident, including continuous or repeated exposure to substantially the same general harmful conditions.

14. "Personal and advertising injury" means injury, including consequential "bodily injury", arising out of one or more of the following offenses:

   a. False arrest, detention or imprisonment;

   b. Malicious prosecution;

   c. The wrongful eviction from, wrongful entry into, or invasion of the right of private occupancy of a room, dwelling or premises that a person occupies, committed by or on behalf of its owner, landlord or lessor;

   d. Oral or written publication, in any manner, of material that slanders or libels a person or organization or disparages a person's or organization's goods, products or services;

   e. Oral or written publication, in any manner, of material that violates a person's right of privacy;

   f. The use of another's advertising idea in your "advertisement"; or

   g. Infringing upon another's copyright, trade dress or slogan in your "advertisement".

15. "Pollutants" mean any solid, liquid, gaseous or thermal irritant or contaminant, including smoke, vapor, soot, fumes, acids, alkalis, chemicals and waste. Waste includes materials to be recycled, reconditioned or reclaimed.

16. "Products-completed operations hazard":

   a. Includes all "bodily injury" and "property damage" occurring away from premises you own or rent and arising out of "your product" or "your work" except:

     (1) Products that are still in your physical possession; or

     (2) Work that has not yet been completed or abandoned. However, "your work" will be deemed completed at the earliest of the following times:

       (a) When all of the work called for in your contract has been completed.

       (b) When all of the work to be done at the job site has been completed if your contract calls for work at more than one job site.

       (c) When that part of the work done at a job site has been put to its intended use by any person or organization other than another contractor or subcontractor working on the same project.

     Work that may need service, maintenance, correction, repair or replacement, but which is otherwise complete, will be treated as completed.

   b. Does not include "bodily injury" or "property damage" arising out of:

     (1) The transportation of property, unless the injury or damage arises out of a condition in or on a vehicle not owned or operated by you, and that condition was created by the "loading or unloading" of that vehicle by any insured;

     (2) The existence of tools, uninstalled equipment or abandoned or unused materials; or

     (3) Products or operations for which the classification, listed in the Declarations or in a policy schedule, states that products-completed operations are subject to the General Aggregate Limit.

17. "Property damage" means:

   a. Physical injury to tangible property, including all resulting loss of use of that property. All such loss of use shall be deemed to occur at the time of the physical injury that caused it; or

   b. Loss of use of tangible property that is not physically injured. All such loss of use shall be deemed to occur at the time of the "occurrence" that caused it.

For the purposes of this insurance, electronic data is not tangible property.

As used in this definition, electronic data means information, facts or programs stored as or on, created or used on, or transmitted to or from computer software, including systems and applications software, hard or floppy disks, CD-ROMS, tapes, drives, cells, data processing devices or any other media which are used with electronically controlled equipment.

18. "Suit" means a civil proceeding in which damages because of "bodily injury", "property damage" or "personal and advertising injury" to which this insurance applies are alleged. "Suit" includes:

   a. An arbitration proceeding in which such damages are claimed and to which the insured must submit or does submit with our consent; or

   b. Any other alternative dispute resolution proceeding in which such damages are claimed and to which the insured submits with our consent.

19. "Temporary worker" means a person who is furnished to you to substitute for a permanent "employee" on leave or to meet seasonal or short-term workload conditions.

20. "Volunteer worker" means a person who is not your "employee", and who donates his or her work and acts at the direction of and within the scope of duties determined by you, and is not paid a fee, salary or other compensation by you or anyone else for their work performed for you.

21. "Your product":

   a. Means:

     (1) Any goods or products, other than real property, manufactured, sold, handled, distributed or disposed of by:

       (a) You;

       (b) Others trading under your name; or

       (c) A person or organization whose business or assets you have acquired; and

     (2) Containers (other than vehicles), materials, parts or equipment furnished in connection with such goods or products.

   b. Includes:

     (1) Warranties or representations made at any time with respect to the fitness, quality, durability, performance or use of "your product"; and

    (2) The providing of or failure to provide warnings or instructions.

  c. Does not include vending machines or other property rented to or located for the use of others but not sold.

22. "Your work":

  a. Means:

    (1) Work or operations performed by you or on your behalf; and

    (2) Materials, parts or equipment furnished in connection with such work or operations.

  b. Includes:

    (1) Warranties or representations made at any time with respect to the fitness, quality, durability, performance or use of "your work", and

    (2) The providing of or failure to provide warnings or instructions.

INTERLINE
IL 00 21 05 04

THIS ENDORSEMENT CHANGES THE POLICY. PLEASE READ IT CAREFULLY.

NUCLEAR ENERGY LIABILITY EXCLUSION ENDORSEMENT
(Broad Form)

This endorsement modifies insurance provided under the following:

COMMERCIAL AUTOMOBILE COVERAGE PART
COMMERCIAL GENERAL LIABILITY COVERAGE PART
FARM COVERAGE PART
LIQUOR LIABILITY COVERAGE PART
OWNERS AND CONTRACTORS PROTECTIVE LIABILITY COVERAGE PART
POLLUTION LIABILITY COVERAGE PART
PRODUCTS/COMPLETED OPERATIONS LIABILITY COVERAGE PART
PROFESSIONAL LIABILITY COVERAGE PART
RAILROAD PROTECTIVE LIABILITY COVERAGE PART

1. The insurance does not apply:

    A. Under any Liability Coverage, to "bodily injury" or "property damage":

    (1) With respect to which an "insured" under the policy is also an insured under a nuclear energy liability policy issued by Nuclear Energy Liability Insurance Association, Mutual Atomic Energy Liability Underwriters, Nuclear Insurance Association of Canada or any of their successors, or would be an insured under any such policy but for its termination upon exhaustion of its limit of liability; or

    (2) Resulting from the "hazardous properties" of "nuclear material" and with respect to which **(a)** any person or organization is required to maintain financial protection pursuant to the Atomic Energy Act of 1954, or any law amendatory thereof, or **(b)** the "insured" is, or had this policy not been issued would be, entitled to indemnity from the United States of America, or any agency thereof, under any agreement entered into by the United States of America, or any agency thereof, with any person or organization.

    B. Under any Medical Payments coverage, to expenses incurred with respect to "bodily injury" resulting from the "hazardous properties" of "nuclear material" and arising out of the operation of a "nuclear facility" by any person or organization.

    C. Under any Liability Coverage, to "bodily injury" or "property damage" resulting from "hazardous properties" of "nuclear material", if:

    (1) The "nuclear material" **(a)** is at any "nuclear facility" owned by, or operated by or on behalf of, an "insured" or **(b)** has been discharged or dispersed therefrom;

    (2) The "nuclear material" is contained in "spent fuel" or "waste" at any time possessed, handled, used, processed, stored, transported or disposed of, by or on behalf of an "insured"; or

    (3) The "bodily injury" or "property damage" arises out of the furnishing by an "insured" of services, materials, parts or equipment in connection with the planning, construction, maintenance, operation or use of any "nuclear facility", but if such facility is located within the United States of America, its territories or possessions or Canada, this exclusion **(3)** applies only to "property damage" to such "nuclear facility" and any property thereat.

2. As used in this endorsement:

"Hazardous properties" includes radioactive, toxic or explosive properties;

"Nuclear material" means "source material", "Special nuclear material" or "by-product material";

"Source material", "special nuclear material," and "by-product material" have the meanings given them in the Atomic Energy Act of 1954 or in any law amendatory thereof;

"Spent fuel" means any fuel element or fuel component, solid or liquid, which has been used or exposed to radiation in a "nuclear reactor";

"Waste" means any waste material **(a)** containing "by-product material" other than the tailings or wastes produced by the extraction or concentration of uranium or thorium from any ore processed primarily for its "source material" content, and **(b)** resulting from the operation by any person or organization of any "nuclear facility" included under the first two paragraphs of the definition of "nuclear facility".

"Nuclear facility" means:

(a) Any "nuclear reactor";

(b) Any equipment or device designed or used for **(1)** separating the isotopes of uranium or plutonium, **(2)** processing or utilizing "spent fuel", or **(3)** handling, processing or packaging "waste";

(c) Any equipment or device used for the processing, fabricating or alloying of "special nuclear material" if at any time the total amount of such material in the custody of the "insured" at the premises where such equipment or device is located consists of or contains more than 25 grams of plutonium or uranium 233 or any combination thereof, or more than 250 grams of uranium 235;

(d) Any structure, basin, excavation, premises or place prepared or used for the storage or disposal of "waste";

and includes the site on which any of the foregoing is located, all operations conducted on such site and all premises used for such operations;

"Nuclear reactor" means any apparatus designed or used to sustain nuclear fission in a self-supporting chain reaction or to contain a critical mass of fissionable material;

"Property damage" includes all forms of radioactive contamination of property.

CGL

COMMERCIAL GENERAL LIABILITY
CG 21 76 01 08

THIS ENDORSEMENT CHANGES THE POLICY. PLEASE READ IT CAREFULLY.

EXCLUSION OF PUNITIVE DAMAGES RELATED TO A CERTIFIED ACT OF TERRORISM

This endorsement modifies insurance provided under the following:

COMMERCIAL GENERAL LIABILITY COVERAGE PART
LIQUOR LIABILITY COVERAGE PART
OWNERS AND CONTRACTORS PROTECTIVE LIABILITY COVERAGE PART
POLLUTION LIABILITY COVERAGE PART
PRODUCTS/COMPLETED OPERATIONS LIABILITY COVERAGE PART
RAILROAD PROTECTIVE LIABILITY COVERAGE PART
UNDERGROUND STORAGE TANK POLICY

A. The following exclusion is added:

This insurance does not apply to:

TERRORISM PUNITIVE DAMAGES

Damages arising, directly or indirectly, out of a "certified act of terrorism" that are awarded as punitive damages.

B. The following definition is added:

"Certified act of terrorism" means an act that is certified by the Secretary of the Treasury, in concurrence with the Secretary of State and the Attorney General of the United States, to be an act of terrorism pursuant to the federal Terrorism Risk Insurance Act. The criteria contained in the Terrorism Risk Insurance Act for a "certified act of terrorism" include the following:

1. The act resulted in insured losses in excess of $5 million in the aggregate, attributable to all types of insurance subject to the Terrorism Risk Insurance Act; and

2. The act is a violent act or an act that is dangerous to human life, property or infrastructure and is committed by an individual or individuals as part of an effort to coerce the civilian population of the United States or to influence the policy or affect the conduct of the United States Government by coercion.

       □

POLICY NUMBER:

COMMERCIAL GENERAL LIABILITY
CG 21 80 01 08

THIS ENDORSEMENT CHANGES THE POLICY. PLEASE READ IT CAREFULLY.

CERTIFIED ACTS OF TERRORISM AGGREGATE LIMIT; CAP ON LOSSES FROM CERTIFIED ACTS OF TERRORISM

This endorsement modifies insurance provided under the following:

COMMERCIAL GENERAL LIABILITY COVERAGE PART

SCHEDULE

Certified Acts Of Terrorism Aggregate Limit: $
Information required to complete this Schedule, if not shown above, will be shown in the Declarations.

A. Coverage provided by this insurance for "bodily injury", "property damage" or "personal and advertising injury", arising out of a "certified act of terrorism", is subject to the Certified Acts Of Terrorism Aggregate Limit as described in Paragraph **B.** of this endorsement.

B. The following are added to **Section III – Limits Of Insurance:**

Subject to Paragraphs **2.** and **3.** of Section **III** – Limits Of Insurance, as applicable, the Certified Acts Of Terrorism Aggregate Limit shown in the Schedule of this endorsement is the most we will pay for all:

1. "Bodily injury" or "property damage" under Coverage **A;**

2. "Personal and advertising injury" under Coverage **B;** and

3. Medical payments under Coverage **C;**

arising out of all "certified acts of terrorism".

Paragraph **4.**, the Personal and Advertising Injury Limit, Paragraph **5.**, the Each Occurrence Limit, Paragraph **6.**, the Damage To Premises Rented To You Limit, and Paragraph **7.**, the Medical Expense Limit, of Section **III** – Limits Of Insurance continue to apply to damages arising out of a "certified act of terrorism". Those limits will only be available if, and to the extent that, limits are available under the Certified Acts Of Terrorism Aggregate Limit.

C. The following definition is added:

"Certified act of terrorism" means an act that is certified by the Secretary of the Treasury, in concurrence with the Secretary of State and the Attorney General of the United States, to be an act of terrorism pursuant to the federal Terrorism Risk Insurance Act. The criteria contained in the Terrorism Risk Insurance Act for a "certified act of terrorism" include the following:

1. The act resulted in insured losses in excess of $5 million in the aggregate, attributable to all types of insurance subject to the Terrorism Risk Insurance Act; and

2. The act is a violent act or an act that is dangerous to human life, property or infrastructure and is committed by an individual or individuals as part of an effort to coerce the civilian population of the United States or to influence the policy or affect the conduct of the United States Government by coercion.

D. If aggregate insured losses attributable to terrorist acts certified under the federal Terrorism Risk Insurance Act exceed $100 billion in a Program Year (January 1 through December 31) and we have met our insurer deductible under the Terrorism Risk Insurance Act, we shall not be liable for the payment of any portion of the amount of such losses that exceeds $100 billion, and in such case insured losses up to that amount are subject to pro rata allocation in accordance with procedures established by the Secretary of the Treasury.

CGL

Commercial Auto Insurance

The commercial auto forms of Insurance Services Office, Inc. (ISO) include the Business Auto Coverage Form, the Garage Coverage Form, the Truckers Coverage Form, and the Motor Carrier Coverage Form. All four forms include provisions for auto liability insurance and auto physical damage insurance. Other coverages—such as medical payments, uninsured motorists, and personal injury protection—can be added by endorsement.

The Business Auto Coverage Form is the most widely used of the four ISO commercial auto forms. It is designed to meet the needs of most types of businesses.

The Garage Coverage Form is designed to meet the needs of auto and trailer dealers. Because it can be difficult to separate the auto liability and general liability exposures of an auto dealer, the Garage Coverage Form provides liability coverage for both covered autos and garage locations/operations, including products and completed work. The form also provides garage-keepers coverage, which insures damage to customers' vehicles while in the insured's care, custody, or control. Finally, the Garage Coverage Form includes provisions for insuring the inventory of an auto dealer on either a reporting or a nonreporting basis.

The Truckers Coverage Form and the Motor Carrier Coverage Form are specifically designed for insuring the auto liability and physical damage exposures of individuals or firms in the business of transporting property of others. Both forms are similar. The Motor Carrier Coverage Form, which was introduced in 1993, is designed to accommodate changes in trucking regulation that occurred after the Truckers Coverage Form was developed in the late 1970s.

The *Handbook* reproduces the Business Auto Coverage Form and the Garage Coverage Form.

POLICY NUMBER:

BUSINESS AUTO DECLARATIONS

ITEM ONE

Company Name: Argot Insurance	**Producer Name:** The Smithson Agency
Named Insured: Barnley Corporation	**Mailing Address:** 2000 Industrial Highway Workingtown, PA 19000

Policy Period	
From: 10/1/20X1	
To: 10/1/20X2	At 12:01 AM Standard Time at your mailing address shown above
Previous Policy Number:	

Form Of Business:

[X] Corporation	[ ] Limited Liability Company	[ ] Individual
[ ] Partnership	[ ] Other:	

In return for the payment of the premium, and subject to all the terms of this policy, we agree with you to provide the insurance as stated in this policy.

Premium shown is payable at inception: $ XXX
Audit Period (If Applicable):   [X] Annually   [ ] Semiannually   [ ] Quarterly   [ ] Monthly

Endorsements Attached To This Policy
IL 00 17 – Common Policy Conditions (**IL 01 46** in Washington)
IL 00 21 – Nuclear Energy Liability Exclusion Endorsement

Countersignature Of Authorized Representative
Name: A. M. Abel
Title:
Signature:
Date: 10/1/20X1

Note

Officers' facsimile signatures may be inserted here, on the policy cover or elsewhere at the company's option.

ITEM TWO
Schedule Of Coverages And Covered Autos

This policy provides only those coverages where a charge is shown in the premium column below. Each of these coverages will apply only to those "autos" shown as covered "autos". **"Autos" are shown as covered "autos" for a particular coverage by the entry of one or more of the symbols from the Covered Autos Section of the Business Auto Coverage Form next to the name of the coverage.**

Coverages	Covered Autos	Limit	Premium
Liability	1	$ 1,000,000	$ XXX
Personal Injury Protection (Or Equivalent No-fault Coverage)	5	**Separately Stated In Each Personal Injury Protection Endorsement Minus** $ **Deductible**	$ XXX
Added Personal Injury Protection (Or Equivalent Added No-fault Coverage)		**Separately Stated In Each Added Personal Injury Protection Endorsement**	$
Property Protection Insurance (Michigan Only)		**Separately Stated In The Property Protection Insurance Endorsement Minus** $ **Deductible** **For Each Accident**	$
Auto Medical Payments		$	$
Medical Expense And Income Loss Benefits (Virginia Only)		**Separately Stated In The Medical Expense And Income Loss Benefits Endorsement**	$
Uninsured Motorists	6	$ 1,000,000	$ XXX
Underinsured Motorists (When Not Included In Uninsured Motorists Coverage)	6	$ 1,000,000	$ XXX

© Insurance Services Office, Inc., 2009   CA DS 03 03 10   □

Commercial Auto

ITEM TWO

Schedule Of Coverages And Covered Autos (Cont'd)

Coverages	Covered Autos	Limit	Premium
Physical Damage Comprehensive Coverage	*7, 8*	**Actual Cash Value Or Cost Of Repair, Whichever Is Less, Minus** **$ Deductible** **For Each Covered Auto, But No Deductible Applies To Loss Caused By Fire Or Lightning** **See Item Four for Hired or Borrowed Autos.**	$ XXX
Physical Damage Specified Causes Of Loss Coverage		**Actual Cash Value Or Cost Of Repair, Whichever Is Less, Minus** **$ Deductible** **For Each Covered Auto For Loss Caused By Mischief Or Vandalism** **See Item Four for Hired or Borrowed Autos.**	$
Physical Damage Collision Coverage	*7, 8*	**Actual Cash Value Or Cost Of Repair, Whichever Is Less, Minus** **$ Deductible** **For Each Covered Auto** **See Item Four for Hired or Borrowed Autos.**	$ XXX
Physical Damage Towing And Labor		**$ For Each Disablement Of A Private Passenger Auto**	$
			$ XXX
Premium For Endorsements			$
Estimated Total Premium*			$ XXX
*This policy may be subject to final audit.			

ITEM THREE

Schedule Of Covered Autos You Own

Covered Auto Number: 1	
Town And State Where The Covered Auto Will Be Principally Garaged: PA 041	

Covered Auto Description

Year: 20XX **Model:**	**Trade Name:** Lincoln Navigator
Body Type:	**Serial Number (S):** XXX
Vehicle Identification Number (VIN): XXX	

Purchased

Original Cost New: $ XXX

Actual Cost New Or Used: $ XXX   [X] New   [ ] Used

Classification

Radius Of Operation	Business Use s=service r=retail c=commercial	Size GVW, GCW Or Vehicle Seating Capacity	Age Group	Secondary Rating Classification	Code

Except For Towing, All Physical Damage Loss Is Payable To You And The Loss Payee Named Below According To Their Interests In The Auto At The Time Of The Loss:

ITEM THREE
Schedule Of Covered Autos You Own (Cont'd)

Coverages – Premiums, Limits And Deductibles		
(Absence of a deductible or limit entry in any column below means that the limit or deductible entry in the corresponding Item Two column applies instead.)		
Coverages	**Limit**	**Premium**
Liability	$	$ XXX
Personal Injury Protection	**Stated In Each Personal Injury Protection Endorsement Minus** $ **Deductible**	$ XXX
Added Personal Injury Protection	**Stated In Each Added Personal Injury Protection Endorsement**	$
Property Protection Insurance (Michigan Only)	**Stated In The Property Protection Insurance Endorsement Minus** $ **Deductible**	$
Auto Medical Payments	$	$
Medical Expense And Income Loss Benefits (Virginia Only)	**Stated In The Medical Expense And Income Loss Benefits Endorsement For Each Person**	$
Comprehensive	**Stated In Item Two Minus** $ **Deductible**	$ XXX
Specified Causes Of Loss	**Stated In Item Two Minus** $ **Deductible**	$
Collision	**Stated In Item Two Minus** $ **Deductible**	$ XXX
Towing And Labor	$ **Per Disablement**	$

ITEM THREE

Schedule Of Covered Autos You Own (Cont'd)

Covered Auto Number: 2
Town And State Where The Covered Auto Will Be Principally Garaged: PA 041

Covered Auto Description		
Year: 20XX	Model:	Trade Name: Acura Legend
Body Type:		Serial Number (S): XXX
Vehicle Identification Number (VIN): XXX		

Purchased		
Original Cost New: $ XXX		
Actual Cost New Or Used: $ XXX	[X] New	[ ] Used

Classification

Radius Of Operation	Business Use s=service r=retail c=commercial	Size GVW, GCW Or Vehicle Seating Capacity	Age Group	Secondary Rating Classification	Code

Except For Towing, All Physical Damage Loss Is Payable To You And The Loss Payee Named Below According To Their Interests In The Auto At The Time Of The Loss:

© Insurance Services Office, Inc., 2009   CA DS 03 03 10   ☐

Commercial Auto

ITEM THREE

Schedule Of Covered Autos You Own (Cont'd)

Coverages	Limit	Premium
Coverages – Premiums, Limits And Deductibles (Absence of a deductible or limit entry in any column below means that the limit or deductible entry in the corresponding Item Two column applies instead.)		
Liability	$	$ XXX
Personal Injury Protection	**Stated In Each Personal Injury Protection Endorsement Minus** $ **Deductible**	$ XXX
Added Personal Injury Protection	**Stated In Each Added Personal Injury Protection Endorsement**	$
Property Protection Insurance (Michigan Only)	**Stated In The Property Protection Insurance Endorsement Minus** $ **Deductible**	$
Auto Medical Payments	$	$
Medical Expense And Income Loss Benefits (Virginia Only)	**Stated In The Medical Expense And Income Loss Benefits Endorsement For Each Person**	$
Comprehensive	**Stated In Item Two Minus** $ **Deductible**	$ XXX
Specified Causes Of Loss	**Stated In Item Two Minus** $ **Deductible**	$
Collision	**Stated In Item Two Minus** $ **Deductible**	$ XXX
Towing And Labor	$ **Per Disablement**	$

ITEM THREE

Schedule Of Covered Autos You Own (Cont'd)

Covered Auto Number: 3

Town And State Where The Covered Auto Will Be Principally Garaged: PA 041

Covered Auto Description		
Year: 20XX	**Model:**	**Trade Name:** Saturn Ion
Body Type:		**Serial Number (S):** XXX
Vehicle Identification Number (VIN): XXX		

Purchased
Original Cost New: $ XXX
Actual Cost New Or Used: $ XXX   [X] New   [ ] Used

Classification					
Radius Of Operation	Business Use s=service r=retail c=commercial	Size GVW, GCW Or Vehicle Seating Capacity	Age Group	Secondary Rating Classification	Code

Except For Towing, All Physical Damage Loss Is Payable To You And The Loss Payee Named Below According To Their Interests In The Auto At The Time Of The Loss:

© Insurance Services Office, Inc., 2009   CA DS 03 03 10   ☐

Commercial Auto

ITEM THREE
Schedule Of Covered Autos You Own (Cont'd)

Coverages	Limit		Premium
Coverages – Premiums, Limits And Deductibles (Absence of a deductible or limit entry in any column below means that the limit or deductible entry in the corresponding Item Two column applies instead.)			
Liability	$		$
Personal Injury Protection	Stated In Each Personal Injury Protection Endorsement Minus	$ Deductible	$
Added Personal Injury Protection	Stated In Each Added Personal Injury Protection Endorsement		$
Property Protection Insurance (Michigan Only)	Stated In The Property Protection Insurance Endorsement Minus	$ Deductible	$
Auto Medical Payments	$		$
Medical Expense And Income Loss Benefits (Virginia Only)	Stated In The Medical Expense And Income Loss Benefits Endorsement For Each Person		$
Comprehensive	Stated In Item Two Minus	$ Deductible	$
Specified Causes Of Loss	Stated In Item Two Minus	$ Deductible	$
Collision	Stated In Item Two Minus	$ Deductible	$
Towing And Labor	$ Per Disablement		$

Total Premiums	
Liability	$
Personal Injury Protection	$
Added Personal Injury Protection	$
Property Protection Insurance (Michigan Only)	$
Auto Medical Payments	$
Medical Expense And Income Loss Benefits (Virginia Only)	$
Comprehensive	$
Specified Causes Of Loss	$
Collision	$
Towing And Labor	$

ITEM FOUR

Schedule Of Hired Or Borrowed Covered Auto Coverage And Premiums

Liability Coverage – Cost Of Hire Rating Basis For Autos Used In Your Motor Carrier Operations (Other Than Mobile Or Farm Equipment)		
Liability Coverage	**Estimated Annual Cost Of Hire For All States**	**Premium**
Primary Coverage	$	$ XXX
Excess Coverage	$	$
Total Premium		$ XXX

For "autos" used in your motor carrier operations, cost of hire means:

(a) The total dollar amount of costs you incurred for the hire of automobiles (includes "trailers" and semitrailers), and if not included therein,

(b) The total remunerations of all operators and drivers' helpers, of hired automobiles whether hired with a driver by lessor or an "employee" of the lessee, or any other third party, and

(c) The total dollar amount of any other costs (*i.e.*, repair, maintenance, fuel, etc.) directly associated with operating the hired automobiles whether such costs are absorbed by the "insured", paid to the lessor or owner, or paid to others.

Liability Coverage – Cost of Hire Rating Basis For Autos NOT Used In Your Motor Carrier Operations (Other Than Mobile Or Farm Equipment)			
Liability Coverage	**State**	**Estimated Annual Cost Of Hire For Each State**	**Premium**
Primary Coverage		$	$ XXX
Excess Coverage		$	$
Total Premium			$ XXX

For "autos" **NOT** used in your motor carrier operations, cost of hire means the total amount you incur for the hire of "autos" you don't own (not including "autos" you borrow or rent from your partners or "employees" or their family members). Cost of hire does not include charges for services performed by motor carriers of property or passengers.

CA DS 03 03 10   □

Commercial Auto

ITEM FOUR

Schedule Of Hired Or Borrowed Covered Auto Coverage And Premiums (Cont'd)

Physical Damage Coverages – Cost of Hire Rating Basis For All Autos (Other Than Mobile Or Farm Equipment)				
Coverage	State	Limit Of Insurance	Estimated Annual Cost Of Hire For Each State (Excluding Autos Hired With A Driver)	Premium
Comprehensive	PA	Actual Cash Value Or Cost Of Repair, Whichever Is Less, Minus $ _____ Deductible For Each Covered Auto, But No Deductible Applies To Loss Caused By Fire Or Lightning	$	$
Specified Causes Of Loss		Actual Cash Value Or Cost Of Repair, Whichever Is Less, Minus $ _____ Deductible For Each Covered Auto For Loss Caused By Mischief Or Vandalism	$	$
Collision		Actual Cash Value Or Cost Of Repair, Whichever Is Less, Minus $ _____ Deductible For Each Covered Auto	$	$
			Total Premium	$ XXX

For Physical Damage Coverages, cost of hire means the total amount you incur for the hire of "autos" you don't own (not including "autos" you borrow or rent from your partners or "employees" or their family members). Cost of hire does not include charges for any "auto" that is leased, hired, rented or borrowed with a driver.

ITEM FOUR

Schedule Of Hired Or Borrowed Covered Auto Coverage And Premiums (Cont'd)

Cost Of Hire Rating Basis For Mobile Or Farm Equipment – Other Than Physical Damage Coverages					
		Estimated Annual Cost Of Hire For Each State		Premium	
Coverage	State	Mobile Equipment	Farm Equipment	Mobile Equipment	Farm Equipment
Liability – Primary Coverage		$	$	$	$
Liability – Excess Coverage		$	$	$	$
Personal Injury Protection		$	$	$	$
Medical Expense Benefits (Virginia Only)		$	$	$	$
Income Loss Benefits (Virginia Only)		$	$	$	$
Auto Medical Payments		$	$	$	$
Total Premiums				$ XXX	$ XXX

Cost of hire means the total amount you incur for the hire of "autos" you don't own (not including "autos" you borrow or rent from your partners or "employees" or their family members). Cost of hire does not include charges for services performed by motor carriers of property or passengers.

Commercial Auto

ITEM FOUR

Schedule Of Hired Or Borrowed Covered Auto Coverage And Premiums (Cont'd)

Cost Of Hire Rating Basis For Mobile Or Farm Equipment – Physical Damage Coverages						
			Estimated Annual Cost Of Hire For Each State (Excluding Autos Hired With A Driver)		Premium	
Coverage	State	Limit Of Insurance	Mobile Equipment	Farm Equipment	Mobile Equipment	Farm Equipment
Comprehensive		Actual Cash Value Or Cost Of Repair, Whichever Is Less, Minus $_____ Ded. For Each Covered Auto, But No Deductible Applies To Loss Caused By Fire Or Lightning	$	$	$	$
Specified Causes Of Loss		Actual Cash Value Or Cost Of Repair, Whichever Is Less, Minus $_____ Ded. For Each Covered Auto For Loss Caused By Mischief Or Vandalism	$	$	$	$
Collision		Actual Cash Value Or Cost Of Repair, Whichever Is Less, Minus $_____ Ded. For Each Covered Auto	$	$	$	$
				Total Premiums	$	$

For Physical Damage Coverages, cost of hire means the total amount you incur for the hire of "autos" you don't own (not including "autos" you borrow or rent from your partners or "employees" or their family members). Cost of hire does not include charges for any auto that is leased, hired, rented or borrowed with a driver.

ITEM FOUR

Schedule Of Hired Or Borrowed Covered Auto Coverage And Premiums (Cont'd)

Coverage	Town and State Where The Job Site Is Located	Estimated Number Of Days Equipment Will Be Rented		Premium	
		Mobile Equipment	Farm Equipment	Mobile Equipment	Farm Equipment
Liability – Primary Coverage				$	$
Liability – Excess Coverage				$	$
Personal Injury Protection				$	$
Medical Expense Benefits (Virginia Only)				$	$
Income Loss Benefits (Virginia Only)				$	$
Auto Medical Payments				$	$
Total Premiums				$	$

© Insurance Services Office, Inc., 2009   CA DS 03 03 10   ☐

Commercial Auto

ITEM FIVE

Schedule For Non-ownership Liability

Named Insured's Business	Rating Basis	Number	Premium
Other Than Garage Service Operations And Other Than Social Service Agencies	**Number Of Employees**	32	$ XXX
	Number Of Partners (Active and Inactive)		$
Garage Service Operations	**Number Of Employees Whose Principal Duty Involves The Operation Of Autos**		$
	Number Of Partners (Active and Inactive)		$
Social Service Agencies	**Number Of Employees**		$
	Number Of Volunteers Who Regularly Use Autos To Transport Clients		$
	Number Of Partners (Active and Inactive)		$
		Total Premium	$ XXX

ITEM SIX

Schedule For Gross Receipts Or Mileage Basis

Address Of Business Headquarters Location:	
Type Of Risk (Check one): ☐ **Public Autos**	☐ **Leasing Or Rental Concerns**
Rating Basis (Check one): ☐ **Gross Receipts (Per $100)**	☐ **Mileage (Per Mile)**
Estimated Yearly (Gross Receipts Or Mileage):	
Premiums	
Liability	$
Personal Injury Protection	$
Added Personal Injury Protection	$
Property Protection Insurance (Michigan Only)	$
Auto Medical Payments	$
Medical Expense And Income Loss Benefits (Virginia Only)	$
Comprehensive	$
Specified Causes Of Loss	$
Collision	$
Towing And Labor	$

ITEM SIX

Schedule For Gross Receipts Or Mileage Basis (Cont'd)

Address Of Business Headquarters Location:	
Type Of Risk (Check one): ☐ **Public Autos** ☐ **Leasing Or Rental Concerns**	
Rating Basis (Check one): ☐ **Gross Receipts (Per $100)** ☐ **Mileage (Per Mile)**	
Estimated Yearly (Gross Receipts Or Mileage):	
Premiums	
Liability	$
Personal Injury Protection	$
Added Personal Injury Protection	$
Property Protection Insurance (Michigan Only)	$
Auto Medical Payments	$
Medical Expense And Income Loss Benefits (Virginia Only)	$
Comprehensive	$
Specified Causes Of Loss	$
Collision	$
Towing And Labor	$

Address Of Business Headquarters Location:	
Type Of Risk (Check one): ☐ **Public Autos** ☐ **Leasing Or Rental Concerns**	
Rating Basis (Check one): ☐ **Gross Receipts (Per $100)** ☐ **Mileage (Per Mile)**	
Estimated Yearly (Gross Receipts Or Mileage):	
Premiums	
Liability	$
Personal Injury Protection	$
Added Personal Injury Protection	$
Property Protection Insurance (Michigan Only)	$
Auto Medical Payments	$
Medical Expense And Income Loss Benefits (Virginia Only)	$
Comprehensive	$
Specified Causes Of Loss	$
Collision	$
Towing And Labor	$

       CA DS 03 03 10   ☐

Commercial Auto

When used as a premium basis:

FOR PUBLIC AUTOS

Gross receipts means the total amount earned by the named insured for transporting passengers, mail and merchandise.

Gross receipts does not include:

A. Amounts paid to air, sea or land carriers operating under their own permits.

B. Advertising revenue.

C. Taxes collected as a separate item and paid directly to the government.

D. C.O.D. collections for cost of mail or merchandise including collection fees.

Mileage means the total live and dead mileage of all revenue producing "autos" during the policy period.

FOR RENTAL OR LEASING CONCERNS

Gross receipts means the total amount earned by the named insured for the leasing or renting of "autos" to others without drivers.

Mileage means the total live and dead mileage of all "autos" you leased or rented to others without drivers.

COMMERCIAL AUTO
CA 00 01 03 10

BUSINESS AUTO COVERAGE FORM

Various provisions in this policy restrict coverage. Read the entire policy carefully to determine rights, duties and what is and is not covered.

Throughout this policy the words "you" and "your" refer to the Named Insured shown in the Declarations. The words "we", "us" and "our" refer to the company providing this insurance.

Other words and phrases that appear in quotation marks have special meaning. Refer to Section **V** – Definitions.

SECTION I – COVERED AUTOS

Item Two of the Declarations shows the "autos" that are covered "autos" for each of your coverages. The following numerical symbols describe the "autos" that may be covered "autos". The symbols entered next to a coverage on the Declarations designate the only "autos" that are covered "autos".

A. Description Of Covered Auto Designation Symbols

Symbol	Description Of Covered Auto Designation Symbols	
1	Any "Auto"	
2	Owned "Autos" Only	Only those "autos" you own (and for Liability Coverage any "trailers" you don't own while attached to power units you own). This includes those "autos" you acquire ownership of after the policy begins.
3	Owned Private Passenger "Autos" Only	Only the private passenger "autos" you own. This includes those private passenger "autos" you acquire ownership of after the policy begins.
4	Owned "Autos" Other Than Private Passenger "Autos" Only	Only those "autos" you own that are not of the private passenger type (and for Liability Coverage any "trailers" you don't own while attached to power units you own). This includes those "autos" not of the private passenger type you acquire ownership of after the policy begins.
5	Owned "Autos" Subject To No-fault	Only those "autos" you own that are required to have no-fault benefits in the state where they are licensed or principally garaged. This includes those "autos" you acquire ownership of after the policy begins provided they are required to have no-fault benefits in the state where they are licensed or principally garaged.
6	Owned "Autos" Subject To A Compulsory Uninsured Motorists Law	Only those "autos" you own that because of the law in the state where they are licensed or principally garaged are required to have and cannot reject Uninsured Motorists Coverage. This includes those "autos" you acquire ownership of after the policy begins provided they are subject to the same state uninsured motorists requirement.
7	Specifically Described "Autos"	Only those "autos" described in Item Three of the Declarations for which a premium charge is shown (and for Liability Coverage any "trailers" you don't own while attached to any power unit described in Item Three).
8	Hired "Autos" Only	Only those "autos" you lease, hire, rent or borrow. This does not include any "auto" you lease, hire, rent or borrow from any of your "employees", partners (if you are a partnership), members (if you are a limited liability company) or members of their households.
9	Non-owned "Autos" Only	Only those "autos" you do not own, lease, hire, rent or borrow that are used in connection with your business. This includes "autos" owned by your "employees", partners (if you are a partnership), members (if you are a limited liability company) or members of their households but only while used in your business or your personal affairs.

Commercial Auto

19	Mobile Equipment Subject To Compulsory Or Financial Responsibility Or Other Motor Vehicle Insurance Law Only	Only those "autos" that are land vehicles and that would qualify under the definition of "mobile equipment" under this policy if they were not subject to a compulsory or financial responsibility law or other motor vehicle insurance law where they are licensed or principally garaged.

B. Owned Autos You Acquire After The Policy Begins

1. If Symbols **1, 2, 3, 4, 5, 6** or **19** are entered next to a coverage in Item Two of the Declarations, then you have coverage for "autos" that you acquire of the type described for the remainder of the policy period.

2. But, if Symbol **7** is entered next to a coverage in Item Two of the Declarations, an "auto" you acquire will be a covered "auto" for that coverage only if:

   a. We already cover all "autos" that you own for that coverage or it replaces an "auto" you previously owned that had that coverage; and

   b. You tell us within 30 days after you acquire it that you want us to cover it for that coverage.

C. Certain Trailers, Mobile Equipment And Temporary Substitute Autos

If Liability Coverage is provided by this coverage form, the following types of vehicles are also covered "autos" for Liability Coverage:

1. "Trailers" with a load capacity of 2,000 pounds or less designed primarily for travel on public roads.

2. "Mobile equipment" while being carried or towed by a covered "auto".

3. Any "auto" you do not own while used with the permission of its owner as a temporary substitute for a covered "auto" you own that is out of service because of its:

   a. Breakdown;

   b. Repair;

   c. Servicing;

   d. "Loss"; or

   e. Destruction.

SECTION II – LIABILITY COVERAGE

A. Coverage

We will pay all sums an "insured" legally must pay as damages because of "bodily injury" or "property damage" to which this insurance applies, caused by an "accident" and resulting from the ownership, maintenance or use of a covered "auto".

We will also pay all sums an "insured" legally must pay as a "covered pollution cost or expense" to which this insurance applies, caused by an "accident" and resulting from the ownership, maintenance or use of covered "autos". However, we will only pay for the "covered pollution cost or expense" if there is either "bodily injury" or "property damage" to which this insurance applies that is caused by the same "accident".

We have the right and duty to defend any "insured" against a "suit" asking for such damages or a "covered pollution cost or expense". However, we have no duty to defend any "insured" against a "suit" seeking damages for "bodily injury" or "property damage" or a "covered pollution cost or expense" to which this insurance does not apply. We may investigate and settle any claim or "suit" as we consider appropriate. Our duty to defend or settle ends when the Liability Coverage Limit of Insurance has been exhausted by payment of judgments or settlements.

1. **Who Is An Insured**

   The following are "insureds":

   a. You for any covered "auto".

   b. Anyone else while using with your permission a covered "auto" you own, hire or borrow except:

      (1) The owner or anyone else from whom you hire or borrow a covered "auto".

   This exception does not apply if the covered "auto" is a "trailer" connected to a covered "auto" you own.

(2) Your "employee" if the covered "auto" is owned by that "employee" or a member of his or her household.

(3) Someone using a covered "auto" while he or she is working in a business of selling, servicing, repairing, parking or storing "autos" unless that business is yours.

(4) Anyone other than your "employees", partners (if you are a partnership), members (if you are a limited liability company) or a lessee or borrower or any of their "employees", while moving property to or from a covered "auto".

(5) A partner (if you are a partnership) or a member (if you are a limited liability company) for a covered "auto" owned by him or her or a member of his or her household.

c. Anyone liable for the conduct of an "insured" described above but only to the extent of that liability.

2. Coverage Extensions

a. Supplementary Payments

We will pay for the "insured":

(1) All expenses we incur.

(2) Up to $2,000 for cost of bail bonds (including bonds for related traffic law violations) required because of an "accident" we cover. We do not have to furnish these bonds.

(3) The cost of bonds to release attachments in any "suit" against the "insured" we defend, but only for bond amounts within our Limit of Insurance.

(4) All reasonable expenses incurred by the "insured" at our request, including actual loss of earnings up to $250 a day because of time off from work.

(5) All court costs taxed against the "insured" in any "suit" against the "insured" we defend. However, these payments do not include attorneys' fees or attorneys' expenses taxed against the "insured".

(6) All interest on the full amount of any judgment that accrues after entry of the judgment in any "suit" against the "insured" we defend, but our duty to pay interest ends when we have paid, offered to pay or deposited in court the part of the judgment that is within our Limit of Insurance.

These payments will not reduce the Limit of Insurance.

b. Out-of-state Coverage Extensions

While a covered "auto" is away from the state where it is licensed we will:

(1) Increase the Limit of Insurance for Liability Coverage to meet the limits specified by a compulsory or financial responsibility law of the jurisdiction where the covered "auto" is being used. This extension does not apply to the limit or limits specified by any law governing motor carriers of passengers or property.

(2) Provide the minimum amounts and types of other coverages, such as no-fault, required of out-of-state vehicles by the jurisdiction where the covered "auto" is being used.

We will not pay anyone more than once for the same elements of loss because of these extensions.

B. Exclusions

This insurance does not apply to any of the following:

1. Expected Or Intended Injury

"Bodily injury" or "property damage" expected or intended from the standpoint of the "insured".

2. Contractual

Liability assumed under any contract or agreement.

But this exclusion does not apply to liability for damages:

a. Assumed in a contract or agreement that is an "insured contract" provided the "bodily injury" or "property damage" occurs subsequent to the execution of the contract or agreement; or

b. That the "insured" would have in the absence of the contract or agreement.

3. Workers' Compensation

Any obligation for which the "insured" or the "insured's" insurer may be held liable under any workers' compensation, disability benefits or unemployment compensation law or any similar law.

4. Employee Indemnification And Employer's Liability

"Bodily injury" to:

a. An "employee" of the "insured" arising out of and in the course of:

(1) Employment by the "insured"; or

(2) Performing the duties related to the conduct of the "insured's" business; or

b. The spouse, child, parent, brother or sister of that "employee" as a consequence of Paragraph **a.** above.

This exclusion applies:

(1) Whether the "insured" may be liable as an employer or in any other capacity; and

(2) To any obligation to share damages with or repay someone else who must pay damages because of the injury.

But this exclusion does not apply to "bodily injury" to domestic "employees" not entitled to workers' compensation benefits or to liability assumed by the "insured" under an "insured contract". For the purposes of the coverage form, a domestic "employee" is a person engaged in household or domestic work performed principally in connection with a residence premises.

5. Fellow Employee

"Bodily injury" to:

a. Any fellow "employee" of the "insured" arising out of and in the course of the fellow "employee's" employment or while performing duties related to the conduct of your business; or

b. The spouse, child, parent, brother or sister of that fellow "employee" as a consequence of Paragraph **a.** above.

6. Care, Custody Or Control

"Property damage" to or "covered pollution cost or expense" involving property owned or transported by the "insured" or in the "insured's" care, custody or control. But this exclusion does not apply to liability assumed under a sidetrack agreement.

7. Handling Of Property

"Bodily injury" or "property damage" resulting from the handling of property:

a. Before it is moved from the place where it is accepted by the "insured" for movement into or onto the covered "auto"; or

b. After it is moved from the covered "auto" to the place where it is finally delivered by the "insured".

8. Movement Of Property By Mechanical Device

"Bodily injury" or "property damage" resulting from the movement of property by a mechanical device (other than a hand truck) unless the device is attached to the covered "auto".

9. Operations

"Bodily injury" or "property damage" arising out of the operation of:

a. Any equipment listed in Paragraphs **6.b.** and **6.c.** of the definition of "mobile equipment"; or

b. Machinery or equipment that is on, attached to or part of a land vehicle that would qualify under the definition of "mobile equipment" if it were not subject to a compulsory or financial responsibility law or other motor vehicle insurance law where it is licensed or principally garaged.

10. Completed Operations

"Bodily injury" or "property damage" arising out of your work after that work has been completed or abandoned.

In this exclusion, your work means:

a. Work or operations performed by you or on your behalf; and

b. Materials, parts or equipment furnished in connection with such work or operations.

Your work includes warranties or representations made at any time with respect to the fitness, quality, durability or performance of any of the items included in Paragraph **a.** or **b.** above.

Your work will be deemed completed at the earliest of the following times:

(1) When all of the work called for in your contract has been completed.

(2) When all of the work to be done at the site has been completed if your contract calls for work at more than one site.

(3) When that part of the work done at a job site has been put to its intended use by any person or organization other than another contractor or subcontractor working on the same project.

    CA 00 01 03 10   ☐

Work that may need service, maintenance, correction, repair or replacement, but which is otherwise complete, will be treated as completed.

11. **Pollution**

"Bodily injury" or "property damage" arising out of the actual, alleged or threatened discharge, dispersal, seepage, migration, release or escape of "pollutants":

a. That are, or that are contained in any property that is:

   (1) Being transported or towed by, handled or handled for movement into, onto or from the covered "auto";

   (2) Otherwise in the course of transit by or on behalf of the "insured"; or

   (3) Being stored, disposed of, treated or processed in or upon the covered "auto";

b. Before the "pollutants" or any property in which the "pollutants" are contained are moved from the place where they are accepted by the "insured" for movement into or onto the covered "auto"; or

c. After the "pollutants" or any property in which the "pollutants" are contained are moved from the covered "auto" to the place where they are finally delivered, disposed of or abandoned by the "insured".

Paragraph **a.** above does not apply to fuels, lubricants, fluids, exhaust gases or other similar "pollutants" that are needed for or result from the normal electrical, hydraulic or mechanical functioning of the covered "auto" or its parts, if:

   (1) The "pollutants" escape, seep, migrate or are discharged, dispersed or released directly from an "auto" part designed by its manufacturer to hold, store, receive or dispose of such "pollutants"; and

   (2) The "bodily injury", "property damage" or "covered pollution cost or expense" does not arise out of the operation of any equipment listed in Paragraphs **6.b.** and **6.c.** of the definition of "mobile equipment".

Paragraphs **b.** and **c.** above of this exclusion do not apply to "accidents" that occur away from premises owned by or rented to an "insured" with respect to "pollutants" not in or upon a covered "auto" if:

   (a) The "pollutants" or any property in which the "pollutants" are contained are upset, overturned or damaged as a result of the maintenance or use of a covered "auto"; and

   (b) The discharge, dispersal, seepage, migration, release or escape of the "pollutants" is caused directly by such upset, overturn or damage.

12. **War**

"Bodily injury" or "property damage" arising directly or indirectly out of:

a. War, including undeclared or civil war;

b. Warlike action by a military force, including action in hindering or defending against an actual or expected attack, by any government, sovereign or other authority using military personnel or other agents; or

c. Insurrection, rebellion, revolution, usurped power or action taken by governmental authority in hindering or defending against any of these.

13. **Racing**

Covered "autos" while used in any professional or organized racing or demolition contest or stunting activity, or while practicing for such contest or activity. This insurance also does not apply while that covered "auto" is being prepared for such a contest or activity.

C. **Limit Of Insurance**

Regardless of the number of covered "autos", "insureds", premiums paid, claims made or vehicles involved in the "accident", the most we will pay for the total of all damages and "covered pollution cost or expense" combined resulting from any one "accident" is the Limit of Insurance for Liability Coverage shown in the Declarations.

Commercial Auto

All "bodily injury", "property damage" and "covered pollution cost or expense" resulting from continuous or repeated exposure to substantially the same conditions will be considered as resulting from one "accident".

No one will be entitled to receive duplicate payments for the same elements of "loss" under this coverage form and any Medical Payments Coverage endorsement, Uninsured Motorists Coverage endorsement or Underinsured Motorists Coverage endorsement attached to this Coverage Part.

SECTION III – PHYSICAL DAMAGE COVERAGE

A. Coverage

1. We will pay for "loss" to a covered "auto" or its equipment under:

   a. **Comprehensive Coverage**

   From any cause except:

   (1) The covered "auto's" collision with another object; or

   (2) The covered "auto's" overturn.

   b. **Specified Causes Of Loss Coverage**

   Caused by:

   (1) Fire, lightning or explosion;

   (2) Theft;

   (3) Windstorm, hail or earthquake;

   (4) Flood;

   (5) Mischief or vandalism; or

   (6) The sinking, burning, collision or derailment of any conveyance transporting the covered "auto".

   c. **Collision Coverage**

   Caused by:

   (1) The covered "auto's" collision with another object; or

   (2) The covered "auto's" overturn.

2. **Towing**

   We will pay up to the limit shown in the Declarations for towing and labor costs incurred each time a covered "auto" of the private passenger type is disabled. However, the labor must be performed at the place of disablement.

3. **Glass Breakage – Hitting A Bird Or Animal – Falling Objects Or Missiles**

   If you carry Comprehensive Coverage for the damaged covered "auto", we will pay for the following under Comprehensive Coverage:

   a. Glass breakage;

   b. "Loss" caused by hitting a bird or animal; and

   c. "Loss" caused by falling objects or missiles.

   However, you have the option of having glass breakage caused by a covered "auto's" collision or overturn considered a "loss" under Collision Coverage.

4. **Coverage Extensions**

   a. **Transportation Expenses**

   We will pay up to $20 per day to a maximum of $600 for temporary transportation expense incurred by you because of the total theft of a covered "auto" of the private passenger type. We will pay only for those covered "autos" for which you carry either Comprehensive or Specified Causes Of Loss Coverage. We will pay for temporary transportation expenses incurred during the period beginning 48 hours after the theft and ending, regardless of the policy's expiration, when the covered "auto" is returned to use or we pay for its "loss".

   b. **Loss Of Use Expenses**

   For Hired Auto Physical Damage, we will pay expenses for which an "insured" becomes legally responsible to pay for loss of use of a vehicle rented or hired without a driver under a written rental contract or agreement. We will pay for loss of use expenses if caused by:

   (1) Other than collision only if the Declarations indicate that Comprehensive Coverage is provided for any covered "auto";

   (2) Specified Causes Of Loss only if the Declarations indicate that Specified Causes Of Loss Coverage is provided for any covered "auto"; or

   (3) Collision only if the Declarations indicate that Collision Coverage is provided for any covered "auto".

   However, the most we will pay for any expenses for loss of use is $20 per day, to a maximum of $600.

B. Exclusions

1. We will not pay for "loss" caused by or resulting from any of the following. Such "loss" is excluded regardless of any other cause or event that contributes concurrently or in any sequence to the "loss".

   a. **Nuclear Hazard**

   (1) The explosion of any weapon employing atomic fission or fusion; or

   (2) Nuclear reaction or radiation, or radioactive contamination, however caused.

b. War Or Military Action

   (1) War, including undeclared or civil war;

   (2) Warlike action by a military force, including action in hindering or defending against an actual or expected attack, by any government, sovereign or other authority using military personnel or other agents; or

   (3) Insurrection, rebellion, revolution, usurped power or action taken by governmental authority in hindering or defending against any of these.

2. We will not pay for "loss" to any covered "auto" while used in any professional or organized racing or demolition contest or stunting activity, or while practicing for such contest or activity. We will also not pay for "loss" to any covered "auto" while that covered "auto" is being prepared for such a contest or activity.

3. We will not pay for "loss" due and confined to:

   a. Wear and tear, freezing, mechanical or electrical breakdown.

   b. Blowouts, punctures or other road damage to tires.

This exclusion does not apply to such "loss" resulting from the total theft of a covered "auto".

4. We will not pay for "loss" to any of the following:

   a. Tapes, records, discs or other similar audio, visual or data electronic devices designed for use with audio, visual or data electronic equipment.

   b. Any device designed or used to detect speed-measuring equipment such as radar or laser detectors and any jamming apparatus intended to elude or disrupt speed-measurement equipment.

   c. Any electronic equipment, without regard to whether this equipment is permanently installed, that reproduces, receives or transmits audio, visual or data signals.

   d. Any accessories used with the electronic equipment described in Paragraph **c.** above.

5. Exclusions **4.c.** and **4.d.** do not apply to equipment designed to be operated solely by use of the power from the "auto's" electrical system that, at the time of "loss", is:

   a. Permanently installed in or upon the covered "auto";

   b. Removable from a housing unit which is permanently installed in or upon the covered "auto";

   c. An integral part of the same unit housing any electronic equipment described in Paragraphs **a.** and **b.** above; or

   d. Necessary for the normal operation of the covered "auto" or the monitoring of the covered "auto's" operating system.

6. We will not pay for "loss" to a covered "auto" due to "diminution in value".

C. Limit Of Insurance

1. The most we will pay for "loss" in any one "accident" is the lesser of:

   a. The actual cash value of the damaged or stolen property as of the time of the "loss"; or

   b. The cost of repairing or replacing the damaged or stolen property with other property of like kind and quality.

2. $1,000 is the most we will pay for "loss" in any one "accident" to all electronic equipment that reproduces, receives or transmits audio, visual or data signals which, at the time of "loss", is:

   a. Permanently installed in or upon the covered "auto" in a housing, opening or other location that is not normally used by the "auto" manufacturer for the installation of such equipment;

   b. Removable from a permanently installed housing unit as described in Paragraph **2.a.** above or is an integral part of that equipment; or

   c. An integral part of such equipment.

3. An adjustment for depreciation and physical condition will be made in determining actual cash value in the event of a total "loss".

4. If a repair or replacement results in better than like kind or quality, we will not pay for the amount of the betterment.

D. Deductible

For each covered "auto", our obligation to pay for, repair, return or replace damaged or stolen property will be reduced by the applicable deductible shown in the Declarations. Any Comprehensive Coverage deductible shown in the Declarations does not apply to "loss" caused by fire or lightning.

SECTION IV – BUSINESS AUTO CONDITIONS

The following conditions apply in addition to the Common Policy Conditions:

A. Loss Conditions

1. Appraisal For Physical Damage Loss

If you and we disagree on the amount of "loss", either may demand an appraisal of the "loss". In this event, each party will select a competent appraiser. The two appraisers will select a competent and impartial umpire. The appraisers will state separately the actual cash value and amount of "loss". If they fail to agree, they will submit their differences to the umpire. A decision agreed to by any two will be binding. Each party will:

a. Pay its chosen appraiser; and

b. Bear the other expenses of the appraisal and umpire equally.

If we submit to an appraisal, we will still retain our right to deny the claim.

2. Duties In The Event Of Accident, Claim, Suit Or Loss

We have no duty to provide coverage under this policy unless there has been full compliance with the following duties:

a. In the event of "accident", claim, "suit" or "loss", you must give us or our authorized representative prompt notice of the "accident" or "loss". Include:

(1) How, when and where the "accident" or "loss" occurred;

(2) The "insured's" name and address; and

(3) To the extent possible, the names and addresses of any injured persons and witnesses.

b. Additionally, you and any other involved "insured" must:

(1) Assume no obligation, make no payment or incur no expense without our consent, except at the "insured's" own cost.

(2) Immediately send us copies of any request, demand, order, notice, summons or legal paper received concerning the claim or "suit".

(3) Cooperate with us in the investigation or settlement of the claim or defense against the "suit".

(4) Authorize us to obtain medical records or other pertinent information.

(5) Submit to examination, at our expense, by physicians of our choice, as often as we reasonably require.

c. If there is "loss" to a covered "auto" or its equipment you must also do the following:

(1) Promptly notify the police if the covered "auto" or any of its equipment is stolen.

(2) Take all reasonable steps to protect the covered "auto" from further damage. Also keep a record of your expenses for consideration in the settlement of the claim.

(3) Permit us to inspect the covered "auto" and records proving the "loss" before its repair or disposition.

(4) Agree to examinations under oath at our request and give us a signed statement of your answers.

3. Legal Action Against Us

No one may bring a legal action against us under this coverage form until:

a. There has been full compliance with all the terms of this coverage form; and

b. Under Liability Coverage, we agree in writing that the "insured" has an obligation to pay or until the amount of that obligation has finally been determined by judgment after trial. No one has the right under this policy to bring us into an action to determine the "insured's" liability.

4. Loss Payment – Physical Damage Coverages

At our option we may:

a. Pay for, repair or replace damaged or stolen property;

b. Return the stolen property, at our expense. We will pay for any damage that results to the "auto" from the theft; or

c. Take all or any part of the damaged or stolen property at an agreed or appraised value.

If we pay for the "loss", our payment will include the applicable sales tax for the damaged or stolen property.

5. Transfer Of Rights Of Recovery Against Others To Us

If any person or organization to or for whom we make payment under this coverage form has rights to recover damages from another, those rights are transferred to us. That person or organization must do everything necessary to secure our rights and must do nothing after "accident" or "loss" to impair them.

B. General Conditions

1. Bankruptcy

Bankruptcy or insolvency of the "insured" or the "insured's" estate will not relieve us of any obligations under this coverage form.

2. Concealment, Misrepresentation Or Fraud

This coverage form is void in any case of fraud by you at any time as it relates to this coverage form. It is also void if you or any other "insured", at any time, intentionally conceal or misrepresent a material fact concerning:

a. This coverage form;

b. The covered "auto";

c. Your interest in the covered "auto"; or

d. A claim under this coverage form.

3. Liberalization

If we revise this coverage form to provide more coverage without additional premium charge, your policy will automatically provide the additional coverage as of the day the revision is effective in your state.

4. No Benefit To Bailee – Physical Damage Coverages

We will not recognize any assignment or grant any coverage for the benefit of any person or organization holding, storing or transporting property for a fee regardless of any other provision of this coverage form.

5. Other Insurance

a. For any covered "auto" you own, this coverage form provides primary insurance. For any covered "auto" you don't own, the insurance provided by this coverage form is excess over any other collectible insurance. However, while a covered "auto" which is a "trailer" is connected to another vehicle, the Liability Coverage this coverage form provides for the "trailer" is:

(1) Excess while it is connected to a motor vehicle you do not own.

(2) Primary while it is connected to a covered "auto" you own.

b. For Hired Auto Physical Damage Coverage, any covered "auto" you lease, hire, rent or borrow is deemed to be a covered "auto" you own. However, any "auto" that is leased, hired, rented or borrowed with a driver is not a covered "auto".

c. Regardless of the provisions of Paragraph **a.** above, this coverage form's Liability Coverage is primary for any liability assumed under an "insured contract".

d. When this coverage form and any other coverage form or policy covers on the same basis, either excess or primary, we will pay only our share. Our share is the proportion that the Limit of Insurance of our coverage form bears to the total of the limits of all the coverage forms and policies covering on the same basis.

6. Premium Audit

a. The estimated premium for this coverage form is based on the exposures you told us you would have when this policy began. We will compute the final premium due when we determine your actual exposures. The estimated total premium will be credited against the final premium due and the first Named Insured will be billed for the balance, if any. The due date for the final premium or retrospective premium is the date shown as the due date on the bill. If the estimated total premium exceeds the final premium due, the first Named Insured will get a refund.

b. If this policy is issued for more than one year, the premium for this coverage form will be computed annually based on our rates or premiums in effect at the beginning of each year of the policy.

7. Policy Period, Coverage Territory

Under this coverage form, we cover "accidents" and "losses" occurring:

a. During the policy period shown in the Declarations; and

b. Within the coverage territory.

The coverage territory is:

(1) The United States of America;

(2) The territories and possessions of the United States of America;

(3) Puerto Rico;

(4) Canada; and

(5) Anywhere in the world if:

(a) A covered "auto" of the private passenger type is leased, hired, rented or borrowed without a driver for a period of 30 days or less; and

(b) The "insured's" responsibility to pay damages is determined in a "suit" on the merits, in the United States of America, the territories and possessions of the United States of America, Puerto Rico or Canada or in a settlement we agree to.

We also cover "loss" to, or "accidents" involving, a covered "auto" while being transported between any of these places.

8. Two Or More Coverage Forms Or Policies Issued By Us

If this coverage form and any other coverage form or policy issued to you by us or any company affiliated with us applies to the same "accident", the aggregate maximum Limit of Insurance under all the coverage forms or policies shall not exceed the highest applicable Limit of Insurance under any one coverage form or policy. This condition does not apply to any coverage form or policy issued by us or an affiliated company specifically to apply as excess insurance over this coverage form.

SECTION V – DEFINITIONS

A. "Accident" includes continuous or repeated exposure to the same conditions resulting in "bodily injury" or "property damage".

B. "Auto" means:

1. A land motor vehicle, "trailer" or semitrailer designed for travel on public roads; or

2. Any other land vehicle that is subject to a compulsory or financial responsibility law or other motor vehicle insurance law where it is licensed or principally garaged.

However, "auto" does not include "mobile equipment".

C. "Bodily injury" means bodily injury, sickness or disease sustained by a person including death resulting from any of these.

D. "Covered pollution cost or expense" means any cost or expense arising out of:

1. Any request, demand, order or statutory or regulatory requirement that any "insured" or others test for, monitor, clean up, remove, contain, treat, detoxify or neutralize, or in any way respond to, or assess the effects of, "pollutants"; or

2. Any claim or "suit" by or on behalf of a governmental authority for damages because of testing for, monitoring, cleaning up, removing, containing, treating, detoxifying or neutralizing, or in any way responding to, or assessing the effects of, "pollutants".

"Covered pollution cost or expense" does not include any cost or expense arising out of the actual, alleged or threatened discharge, dispersal, seepage, migration, release or escape of "pollutants":

a. That are, or that are contained in any property that is:

(1) Being transported or towed by, handled or handled for movement into, onto or from the covered "auto";

(2) Otherwise in the course of transit by or on behalf of the "insured"; or

(3) Being stored, disposed of, treated or processed in or upon the covered "auto";

b. Before the "pollutants" or any property in which the "pollutants" are contained are moved from the place where they are accepted by the "insured" for movement into or onto the covered "auto"; or

c. After the "pollutants" or any property in which the "pollutants" are contained are moved from the covered "auto" to the place where they are finally delivered, disposed of or abandoned by the "insured".

Paragraph **a.** above does not apply to fuels, lubricants, fluids, exhaust gases or other similar "pollutants" that are needed for or result from the normal electrical, hydraulic or mechanical functioning of the covered "auto" or its parts, if:

(1) The "pollutants" escape, seep, migrate or are discharged, dispersed or released directly from an "auto" part designed by its manufacturer to hold, store, receive or dispose of such "pollutants"; and

(2) The "bodily injury", "property damage" or "covered pollution cost or expense" does not arise out of the operation of any equipment listed in Paragraph **6.b.** or **6.c.** of the definition of "mobile equipment".

© Insurance Services Office, Inc., 2009   CA 00 01 03 10   □

Paragraphs **b.** and **c.** above do not apply to "accidents" that occur away from premises owned by or rented to an "insured" with respect to "pollutants" not in or upon a covered "auto" if:

    (a) The "pollutants" or any property in which the "pollutants" are contained are upset, overturned or damaged as a result of the maintenance or use of a covered "auto"; and

    (b) The discharge, dispersal, seepage, migration, release or escape of the "pollutants" is caused directly by such upset, overturn or damage.

E. "Diminution in value" means the actual or perceived loss in market value or resale value which results from a direct and accidental "loss".

F. "Employee" includes a "leased worker". "Employee" does not include a "temporary worker".

G. "Insured" means any person or organization qualifying as an insured in the Who Is An Insured provision of the applicable coverage. Except with respect to the Limit of Insurance, the coverage afforded applies separately to each insured who is seeking coverage or against whom a claim or "suit" is brought.

H. "Insured contract" means:

    1. A lease of premises;

    2. A sidetrack agreement;

    3. Any easement or license agreement, except in connection with construction or demolition operations on or within 50 feet of a railroad;

    4. An obligation, as required by ordinance, to indemnify a municipality, except in connection with work for a municipality;

    5. That part of any other contract or agreement pertaining to your business (including an indemnification of a municipality in connection with work performed for a municipality) under which you assume the tort liability of another to pay for "bodily injury" or "property damage" to a third party or organization. Tort liability means a liability that would be imposed by law in the absence of any contract or agreement;

    6. That part of any contract or agreement entered into, as part of your business, pertaining to the rental or lease, by you or any of your "employees", of any "auto". However, such contract or agreement shall not be considered an "insured contract" to the extent that it obligates you or any of your "employees" to pay for "property damage" to any "auto" rented or leased by you or any of your "employees".

An "insured contract" does not include that part of any contract or agreement:

    a. That indemnifies a railroad for "bodily injury" or "property damage" arising out of construction or demolition operations, within 50 feet of any railroad property and affecting any railroad bridge or trestle, tracks, roadbeds, tunnel, underpass or crossing;

    b. That pertains to the loan, lease or rental of an "auto" to you or any of your "employees", if the "auto" is loaned, leased or rented with a driver; or

    c. That holds a person or organization engaged in the business of transporting property by "auto" for hire harmless for your use of a covered "auto" over a route or territory that person or organization is authorized to serve by public authority.

I. "Leased worker" means a person leased to you by a labor leasing firm under an agreement between you and the labor leasing firm to perform duties related to the conduct of your business. "Leased worker" does not include a "temporary worker".

J. "Loss" means direct and accidental loss or damage.

K. "Mobile equipment" means any of the following types of land vehicles, including any attached machinery or equipment:

    1. Bulldozers, farm machinery, forklifts and other vehicles designed for use principally off public roads;

    2. Vehicles maintained for use solely on or next to premises you own or rent;

    3. Vehicles that travel on crawler treads;

    4. Vehicles, whether self-propelled or not, maintained primarily to provide mobility to permanently mounted:

        a. Power cranes, shovels, loaders, diggers or drills; or

        b. Road construction or resurfacing equipment such as graders, scrapers or rollers;

    5. Vehicles not described in Paragraph **1.**, **2.**, **3.** or **4.** above that are not self-propelled and are maintained primarily to provide mobility to permanently attached equipment of the following types:

        a. Air compressors, pumps and generators, including spraying, welding, building cleaning, geophysical exploration, lighting and well-servicing equipment; or

        b. Cherry pickers and similar devices used to raise or lower workers; or

6. Vehicles not described in Paragraph **1.**, **2.**, **3.** or **4.** above maintained primarily for purposes other than the transportation of persons or cargo. However, self-propelled vehicles with the following types of permanently attached equipment are not "mobile equipment" but will be considered "autos":

   a. Equipment designed primarily for:

      (1) Snow removal;

      (2) Road maintenance, but not construction or resurfacing; or

      (3) Street cleaning;

   b. Cherry pickers and similar devices mounted on automobile or truck chassis and used to raise or lower workers; and

   c. Air compressors, pumps and generators, including spraying, welding, building cleaning, geophysical exploration, lighting or well-servicing equipment.

   However, "mobile equipment" does not include land vehicles that are subject to a compulsory or financial responsibility law or other motor vehicle insurance law where it is licensed or principally garaged. Land vehicles subject to a compulsory or financial responsibility law or other motor vehicle insurance law are considered "autos".

L. "Pollutants" means any solid, liquid, gaseous or thermal irritant or contaminant, including smoke, vapor, soot, fumes, acids, alkalis, chemicals and waste. Waste includes materials to be recycled, reconditioned or reclaimed.

M. "Property damage" means damage to or loss of use of tangible property.

N. "Suit" means a civil proceeding in which:

   1. Damages because of "bodily injury" or "property damage"; or

   2. A "covered pollution cost or expense";

   to which this insurance applies, are alleged.

   "Suit" includes:

      a. An arbitration proceeding in which such damages or "covered pollution costs or expenses" are claimed and to which the "insured" must submit or does submit with our consent; or

      b. Any other alternative dispute resolution proceeding in which such damages or "covered pollution costs or expenses" are claimed and to which the insured submits with our consent.

O. "Temporary worker" means a person who is furnished to you to substitute for a permanent "employee" on leave or to meet seasonal or short-term workload conditions.

P. "Trailer" includes semitrailer.

       CA 00 01 03 10   □

COMMERCIAL AUTO
CA 00 05 03 10

GARAGE COVERAGE FORM

Various provisions in this policy restrict coverage. Read the entire policy carefully to determine rights, duties and what is and is not covered.

Throughout this policy the words "you" and "your" refer to the Named Insured shown in the Declarations. The words "we", "us" and "our" refer to the company providing this insurance.

Other words and phrases that appear in quotation marks have special meaning. Refer to Section **VI** – Definitions.

SECTION I – COVERED AUTOS

Item Two of the Declarations shows the "autos" that are covered "autos" for each of your coverages. The following numerical symbols describe the "autos" that may be covered "autos". The symbols entered next to a coverage on the Declarations designate the only "autos" that are covered "autos".

A. Description Of Covered Auto Designation Symbols

Symbol	Description Of Covered Auto Designation Symbols	
21	Any "Auto"	
22	Owned "Autos" Only	Only those "autos" you own (and for Liability Coverage any "trailers" you don't own while attached to power units you own). This includes those "autos" you acquire ownership of after the policy begins.
23	Owned Private Passenger "Autos" Only	Only the private passenger "autos" you own. This includes those private passenger "autos" you acquire ownership of after the policy begins.
24	Owned "Autos" Other Than Private Passenger "Autos" Only	Only those "autos" you own that are not of the private passenger type (and for Liability Coverage any "trailers" you don't own while attached to power units you own). This includes those "autos" not of the private passenger type you acquire ownership of after the policy begins.
25	Owned "Autos" Subject To No-fault	Only those "autos" you own that are required to have no-fault benefits in the state where they are licensed or principally garaged. This includes those "autos" you acquire ownership of after the policy begins provided they are required to have no-fault benefits in the state where they are licensed or principally garaged.
26	Owned "Autos" Subject To A Compulsory Uninsured Motorists Law	Only those "autos" you own that because of the law in the state where they are licensed or principally garaged are required to have and cannot reject Uninsured Motorists Coverage. This includes those "autos" you acquire ownership of after the policy begins provided they are subject to the same state uninsured motorists requirement.
27	Specifically Described "Autos"	Only those "autos" described in Item Nine of the Declarations for which a premium charge is shown (and for Liability Coverage any "trailers" you don't own while attached to a power unit described in Item Nine).
28	Hired "Autos" Only	Only those "autos" you lease, hire, rent or borrow. This does not include any "auto" you lease, hire, rent or borrow from any of your "employees", partners (if you are a partnership), members (if you are a limited liability company) or members of their households.
29	Non-owned "Autos" Used In Your Garage Business	Any "auto" you do not own, lease, hire, rent or borrow used in connection with your garage business described in the Declarations. This includes "autos" owned by your "employees" or partners (if you are a partnership), members (if you are a limited liability company) or members of their households while used in your garage business.

Commercial Auto

Symbol		Description Of Covered Auto Designation Symbols
30	"Autos" Left With You For Service, Repair, Storage Or Safekeeping	Any customer's land motor vehicle or trailer or semitrailer while left with you for service, repair, storage or safekeeping. Customers include your "employees", and members of their households, who pay for the services performed.
31	Dealers "Autos" (Physical Damage Coverages)	Any "autos" and the interests in these "autos" described in Item Seven of the Declarations.

B. Owned Autos You Acquire After The Policy Begins

1. If Symbols **21, 22, 23, 24, 25** or **26** are entered next to a coverage in Item Two of the Declarations, then you have coverage for "autos" that you acquire of the type described for the remainder of the policy period.

2. But, if Symbol **27** is entered next to a coverage in Item Two of the Declarations, an "auto" you acquire will be a covered "auto" for that coverage only if:

   a. We already cover all "autos" that you own for that coverage or it replaces an "auto" you previously owned that had that coverage; and

   b. You tell us within 30 days after you acquire it that you want us to cover it for that coverage.

C. Certain Trailers And Temporary Substitute Autos

If Liability Coverage is provided by this coverage form, the following types of vehicles are also covered "autos" for Liability Coverage:

1. "Trailers" with a load capacity of 2,000 pounds or less designed primarily for travel on public roads.

2. Any "auto" you do not own while used with the permission of its owner as a temporary substitute for a covered "auto" you own that is out of service because of its:

   a. Breakdown;

   b. Repair;

   c. Servicing;

d. "Loss"; or

e. Destruction.

SECTION II – LIABILITY COVERAGE

A. Coverage

1. **"Garage Operations" – Other Than Covered "Autos"**

   a. We will pay all sums an "insured" legally must pay as damages because of "bodily injury" or "property damage" to which this insurance applies caused by an "accident" and resulting from "garage operations" other than the ownership, maintenance or use of covered "autos".

   We have the right and duty to defend any "insured" against a "suit" asking for these damages. However, we have no duty to defend any "insured" against a "suit" seeking damages for "bodily injury" or "property damage" to which this insurance does not apply. We may investigate and settle any claim or "suit" as we consider appropriate. Our duty to defend or settle ends when the applicable Liability Coverage Limit of Insurance – "Garage Operations" – Other Than Covered "Autos" has been exhausted by payment of judgments or settlements.

   b. This insurance applies to "bodily injury" and "property damage" only if:

      (1) The "accident" occurs in the coverage territory;

      (2) The "bodily injury" or "property damage" occurs during the policy period; and

(3) Prior to the policy period, no "insured" listed under Who Is An Insured and no "employee" authorized by you to give or receive notice of an "accident" or claim knew that the "bodily injury" or "property damage" had occurred, in whole or in part. If such a listed "insured" or authorized "employee" knew, prior to the policy period, that the "bodily injury" or "property damage" occurred, then any continuation, change or resumption of such "bodily injury" or "property damage" during or after the policy period will be deemed to have been known prior to the policy period.

c. "Bodily injury" or "property damage", which occurs during the policy period and was not, prior to the policy period, known to have occurred by any "insured" listed under Who Is An Insured or any "employee" authorized by you to give or receive notice of an "accident" or claim, includes any continuation, change or resumption of that "bodily injury" or "property damage" after the end of the policy period.

d. "Bodily injury" or "property damage" will be deemed to have been known to have occurred at the earliest time when any "insured" listed under Who Is An Insured or any "employee" authorized by you to give or receive notice of an "accident" or claim:

(1) Reports all, or any part, of the "bodily injury" or "property damage" to us or any other insurer;

(2) Receives a written or verbal demand or claim for damages because of the "bodily injury" or "property damage"; or

(3) Becomes aware by any other means that "bodily injury" or "property damage" has occurred or has begun to occur.

2. "Garage Operations" – Covered "Autos"

We will pay all sums an "insured" legally must pay as damages because of "bodily injury" or "property damage" to which this insurance applies, caused by an "accident" and resulting from "garage operations" involving the ownership, maintenance or use of covered "autos".

We will also pay all sums an "insured" legally must pay as a "covered pollution cost or expense" to which this insurance applies, caused by an "accident" and resulting from "garage operations" involving the ownership, maintenance or use of covered "autos". However, we will only pay for the "covered pollution cost or expense" if there is either "bodily injury" or "property damage" to which this insurance applies that is caused by the same "accident".

We have the right and duty to defend any "insured" against a "suit" asking for such damages or a "covered pollution cost or expense". However, we have no duty to defend any "insured" against a "suit" seeking damages for "bodily injury" or "property damage" or a "covered pollution cost or expense" to which this insurance does not apply. We may investigate and settle any claim or "suit" as we consider appropriate. Our duty to defend or settle ends when the Liability Coverage Limit of Insurance – "Garage Operations" – Covered "Autos" has been exhausted by payment of judgments or settlements.

3. Who Is An Insured

a. The following are "insureds" for covered "autos":

(1) You for any covered "auto".

(2) Anyone else while using with your permission a covered "auto" you own, hire or borrow except:

(a) The owner or anyone else from whom you hire or borrow a covered "auto". This exception does not apply if the covered "auto" is a "trailer" connected to a covered "auto" you own.

(b) Your "employee" if the covered "auto" is owned by that "employee" or a member of his or her household.

(c) Someone using a covered "auto" while he or she is working in a business of selling, servicing or repairing "autos" unless that business is your "garage operations".

Commercial Auto

(d) Your customers. However, if a customer of yours:

   (i) Has no other available insurance (whether primary, excess or contingent), they are an "insured" but only up to the compulsory or financial responsibility law limits where the covered "auto" is principally garaged.

   (ii) Has other available insurance (whether primary, excess or contingent) less than the compulsory or financial responsibility law limits where the covered "auto" is principally garaged, they are an "insured" only for the amount by which the compulsory or financial responsibility law limits exceed the limit of their other insurance.

(e) A partner (if you are a partnership) or a member (if you are a limited liability company) for a covered "auto" owned by him or her or a member of his or her household.

(3) Anyone liable for the conduct of an "insured" described above but only to the extent of that liability.

(4) Your "employee" while using a covered "auto" you do not own, hire or borrow in your business or your personal affairs.

b. The following are "insureds" for "garage operations" other than covered "autos":

(1) You.

(2) Your partners (if you are a partnership), members (if you are a limited liability company), "employees", directors or shareholders but only while acting within the scope of their duties.

4. Coverage Extensions

a. Supplementary Payments

We will pay for the "insured":

(1) All expenses we incur.

(2) Up to $2,000 for the cost of bail bonds (including bonds for related traffic law violations) required because of an "accident" we cover. We do not have to furnish these bonds.

(3) The cost of bonds to release attachments in any "suit" against the "insured" we defend, but only for bond amounts within our Limit of Insurance.

(4) All reasonable expenses incurred by the "insured" at our request, including actual loss of earnings up to $250 a day because of time off from work.

(5) All court costs taxed against the "insured" in any "suit" against the "insured" we defend. However, these payments do not include attorneys' fees or attorneys' expenses taxed against the "insured".

(6) All interest on the full amount of any judgment that accrues after entry of the judgment in any "suit" against the "insured" we defend; but our duty to pay interest ends when we have paid, offered to pay or deposited in court the part of the judgment that is within our Limit of Insurance.

These payments will not reduce the Limit of Insurance.

b. Out-of-state Coverage Extensions

While a covered "auto" is away from the state where it is licensed we will:

(1) Increase the Limit of Insurance for Liability Coverage to meet the limits specified by a compulsory or financial responsibility law of the jurisdiction where the covered "auto" is being used. This extension does not apply to the limit or limits specified by any law governing motor carriers of passengers or property.

(2) Provide the minimum amounts and types of other coverages, such as no-fault, required of out-of-state vehicles by the jurisdiction where the covered "auto" is being used.

We will not pay anyone more than once for the same elements of loss because of these extensions.

B. Exclusions

This insurance does not apply to any of the following:

1. Expected Or Intended Injury

"Bodily injury" or "property damage" expected or intended from the standpoint of the "insured". But for "garage operations" other than covered "autos" this exclusion does not apply to "bodily injury" resulting from the use of reasonable force to protect persons or property.

© Insurance Services Office, Inc., 2009   CA 00 05 03 10   □

2. Contractual

Liability assumed under any contract or agreement. But this exclusion does not apply to liability for damages:

a. Assumed in a contract or agreement that is an "insured contract" provided the "bodily injury" or "property damage" occurs subsequent to the execution of the contract or agreement; or

b. That the "insured" would have in the absence of the contract or agreement.

3. Workers' Compensation

Any obligation for which the "insured" or the "insured's" insurer may be held liable under any workers' compensation, disability benefits or unemployment compensation law or any similar law.

4. Employee Indemnification And Employer's Liability

"Bodily injury" to:

a. An "employee" of the "insured" arising out of and in the course of:

(1) Employment by the "insured"; or

(2) Performing the duties related to the conduct of the "insured's" business;

b. The spouse, child, parent, brother or sister of that "employee" as a consequence of Paragraph **a.** above;

c. A person arising out of any:

(1) Refusal to employ that person;

(2) Termination of that person's employment; or

(3) Employment-related practices, policies, acts or omissions, such as coercion, demotion, evaluation, reassignment, discipline, defamation, harassment, humiliation, discrimination or malicious prosecution directed at that person; or

d. The spouse, child, parent, brother or sister of that person as a consequence of "bodily injury" to that person at whom any of the employment-related practices described in Paragraph **c.(1)**, **(2)** or **(3)** above are directed.

This exclusion applies:

(1) Whether the injury-causing event described in Paragraph **c.(1)**, **(2)** or **(3)** above occurs before employment, during employment or after employment of that person;

(2) Whether the "insured" may be liable as an employer or in any other capacity; and

(3) To any obligation to share damages with or repay someone else who must pay damages because of the injury.

But this exclusion does not apply to "bodily injury" to domestic "employees" not entitled to workers' compensation benefits or to liability assumed by the "insured" under an "insured contract". For the purposes of the coverage form, a domestic "employee" is a person engaged in household or domestic work performed principally in connection with a residence premises.

5. Fellow Employee

"Bodily injury" to:

a. Any fellow "employee" of the "insured" arising out of and in the course of the fellow "employee's" employment or while performing duties related to the conduct of your business; or

b. The spouse, child, parent, brother or sister of that fellow "employee" as a consequence of Paragraph **a.** above.

6. Care, Custody Or Control

"Property damage" to or "covered pollution cost or expense" involving:

a. Property owned, rented or occupied by the "insured";

b. Property loaned to the "insured";

c. Property held for sale or being transported by the "insured"; or

d. Property in the "insured's" care, custody or control.

But this exclusion does not apply to liability assumed under a sidetrack agreement.

7. Leased Autos

Any covered "auto" while leased or rented to others. But this exclusion does not apply to a covered "auto" you rent to one of your customers while their "auto" is left with you for service or repair.

8. **Pollution Exclusion Applicable To "Garage Operations" – Other Than Covered "Autos"**

   a. "Bodily injury" or "property damage" arising out of the actual, alleged or threatened discharge, dispersal, seepage, migration, release or escape of "pollutants":

      (1) At or from any premises, site or location that is or was at any time owned or occupied by, or rented or loaned to, any "insured";

      (2) At or from any premises, site or location that is or was at any time used by or for any "insured" or others for the handling, storage, disposal, processing or treatment of waste;

      (3) At or from any premises, site or location on which any "insured" or any contractors or subcontractors working directly or indirectly on any "insured's" behalf are performing operations:

         (a) To test for, monitor, clean up, remove, contain, treat, detoxify or neutralize, or in any way respond to, or assess the effects of, the "pollutants"; or

         (b) If the "pollutants" are brought on or to the premises, site or location in connection with such operations by such "insured", contractor or subcontractor; or

      (4) That are or were at any time transported, handled, stored, treated, disposed of or processed as waste by or for any "insured" or any person or organization for whom you may be legally responsible.

      Paragraphs **a.(1)** and **a.(3)(b)** do not apply to "bodily injury" or "property damage" arising out of heat, smoke or fumes from a hostile fire. A hostile fire means one that becomes uncontrollable or breaks out from where it was intended to be.

      Paragraph **a.(1)** does not apply to "bodily injury" if sustained within a building and caused by smoke, fumes, vapor or soot produced by or originating from equipment that is used to heat, cool or dehumidify the building, or equipment that is used to heat water for personal use, by the building's occupants or their guests.

   Paragraph **a.(3)(b)** does not apply to "bodily injury" or "property damage" sustained within a building and caused by the release of gases, fumes or vapors from material brought into that building in connection with operations being performed by you or on your behalf by a contractor or subcontractor.

   b. Any loss, cost or expense arising out of any:

      (1) Request, demand, order or statutory or regulatory requirement that any "insured" or others test for, monitor, clean up, remove, contain, treat, detoxify or neutralize, or in any way respond to, or assess the effects of, "pollutants"; or

      (2) Claim or suit by or on behalf of a governmental authority for damages because of testing for, monitoring, cleaning up, removing, containing, treating, detoxifying or neutralizing, or in any way responding to, or assessing the effects of, "pollutants".

      However, this paragraph does not apply to liability for damages because of "property damage" that the "insured" would have in the absence of such request, demand, order or statutory or regulatory requirement, or such claim or "suit" by or on behalf of a governmental authority.

9. **Pollution Exclusion Applicable To "Garage Operations" – Covered "Autos"**

   "Bodily injury" or "property damage" arising out of the actual, alleged or threatened discharge, dispersal, seepage, migration, release or escape of "pollutants":

   a. That are, or that are contained in any property that is:

      (1) Being transported or towed by, handled or handled for movement into, onto or from, the covered "auto";

      (2) Otherwise in the course of transit by or on behalf of the "insured"; or

      (3) Being stored, disposed of, treated or processed in or upon the covered "auto";

   b. Before the "pollutants" or any property in which the "pollutants" are contained are moved from the place where they are accepted by the "insured" for movement into or onto the covered "auto"; or

c. After the "pollutants" or any property in which the "pollutants" are contained are moved from the covered "auto" to the place where they are finally delivered, disposed of or abandoned by the "insured".

Paragraph **a.** above does not apply to fuels, lubricants, fluids, exhaust gases or other similar "pollutants" that are needed for or result from the normal electrical, hydraulic or mechanical functioning of the covered "auto" or its parts, if the "pollutants" escape, seep, migrate or are discharged, dispersed or released directly from an "auto" part designed by its manufacturer to hold, store, receive or dispose of such "pollutants".

Paragraphs **b.** and **c.** above of this exclusion do not apply to "accidents" that occur away from premises owned by or rented to an "insured" with respect to "pollutants" not in or upon a covered "auto" if:

   (1) The "pollutants" or any property in which the "pollutants" are contained are upset, overturned or damaged as a result of the maintenance or use of a covered "auto"; and

   (2) The discharge, dispersal, seepage, migration, release or escape of the "pollutants" is caused directly by such upset, overturn or damage.

10. Racing

Covered "autos" while used in any professional or organized racing or demolition contest or stunting activity, or while practicing for such contest or activity. This insurance also does not apply while that covered "auto" is being prepared for such a contest or activity.

11. Watercraft Or Aircraft

Any watercraft or aircraft except watercraft while ashore on premises where you conduct "garage operations".

12. Defective Products

"Property damage" to any of your "products", if caused by a defect existing in your "products" or any part of your "products", at the time it was transferred to another.

13. Work You Performed

"Property damage" to "work you performed" if the "property damage" results from any part of the work itself or from the parts, materials or equipment used in connection with the work.

14. Loss Of Use

Loss of use of other property not physically damaged if caused by:

a. A delay or failure by you or anyone acting on your behalf to perform a contract or agreement in accordance with its terms.

b. A defect, deficiency, inadequacy or dangerous condition in your "products" or "work you performed". But this exclusion, **14.b.,** does not apply if the loss of use was caused by sudden and accidental damage to or destruction of your "products" or "work you performed" after they have been put to their intended use.

15. Products Recall

Damages claimed for any loss, cost or expense incurred by you or others for the loss of use, withdrawal, recall, inspection, repair, replacement, adjustment, removal or disposal of your "products" or "work you performed" or other property of which they form a part, if such product, work or property is withdrawn or recalled from the market or from use by any person or organization because of a known or suspected defect, deficiency, inadequacy or dangerous condition in it.

16. War

"Bodily injury" or "property damage" arising directly or indirectly out of:

a. War, including undeclared or civil war;

b. Warlike action by a military force, including action in hindering or defending against an actual or expected attack, by any government, sovereign or other authority using military personnel or other agents; or

c. Insurrection, rebellion, revolution, usurped power or action taken by governmental authority in hindering or defending against any of these.

17. Distribution Of Material In Violation Of Statutes Exclusion Applicable To "Garage Operations" – Other Than Covered "Autos"

"Bodily injury" or "property damage" arising directly or indirectly out of any action or omission that violates or is alleged to violate:

a. The Telephone Consumer Protection Act (TCPA), including any amendment of or addition to such law;

b. The CAN-SPAM Act of 2003, including any amendment of or addition to such law; or

c. Any statute, ordinance or regulation, other than the TCPA or CAN-SPAM Act of 2003, that prohibits or limits the sending, transmitting, communicating or distribution of material or information.

C. Limit Of Insurance

1. Aggregate Limit Of Insurance – "Garage Operations" – Other Than Covered "Autos"

For "garage operations" other than the ownership, maintenance or use of covered "autos", the following applies:

Regardless of the number of "insureds", claims made or "suits" brought or persons or organizations making claims or bringing "suits", the most we will pay for the sum of all damages involving "garage operations" other than "auto" is the Aggregate Limit of Insurance – "Garage Operations" – Other Than Covered "Autos" for Liability Coverage shown in the Declarations.

Damages payable under the Aggregate Limit of Insurance – "Garage Operations" – Other Than Covered "Autos" consist of damages resulting from "garage operations", other than the ownership, maintenance or use of the "autos" indicated in Section I of this coverage form as covered "autos", including the following coverages, if provided by endorsement:

a. "Personal injury" liability coverage;

b. "Personal and advertising injury" liability coverage;

c. Host liquor liability coverage;

d. Damage to rented premises liability coverage;

e. Incidental medical malpractice liability coverage;

f. Non-owned watercraft coverage; and

g. Broad form products coverage.

Damages payable under the Each "Accident" Limit of Insurance – "Garage Operations" – Other Than Covered "Autos" are not payable under the Each "Accident" Limit of Insurance – "Garage Operations" – Covered "Autos".

Subject to the above, the most we will pay for all damages resulting from all "bodily injury" and "property damage" resulting from any one "accident" is the Each "Accident" Limit of Insurance – "Garage Operations" – Other Than Covered "Autos" for Liability Coverage shown in the Declarations.

All "bodily injury" and "property damage" resulting from continuous or repeated exposure to substantially the same conditions will be considered as resulting from one "accident".

The Aggregate Limit of Insurance – "Garage Operations" Other Than Covered "Autos" applies separately to each consecutive annual period and to any remaining period of less than 12 months, starting with the beginning of the policy period shown in the Declarations, unless the policy period is extended after issuance for an additional period of less than 12 months. In that case, the additional period will be deemed part of the last preceding period for purposes of determining the Aggregate Limit of Insurance – "Garage Operations" – Other Than Covered "Autos".

2. Limit Of Insurance – "Garage Operations" – Covered "Autos"

For "accidents" resulting from "garage operations" involving the ownership, maintenance or use of covered "autos", the following applies:

Regardless of the number of covered "autos", "insureds", premiums paid, claims made or vehicles involved in the "accident", the most we will pay for the total of all damages and "covered pollution cost or expense" combined, resulting from any one "accident" involving a covered "auto" is the Each "Accident" Limit of Insurance – "Garage Operations" – Covered "Autos" for Liability Coverage shown in the Declarations.

Damages and "covered pollution cost or expense" payable under the Each "Accident" Limit of Insurance – "Garage Operations" – Covered "Autos" are not payable under the Each "Accident" Limit of Insurance – "Garage Operations" – Other Than Covered "Autos".

All "bodily injury", "property damage" and "covered pollution cost or expense" resulting from continuous or repeated exposure to substantially the same conditions will be considered as resulting from one "accident".

No one will be entitled to receive duplicate payments for the same elements of "loss" under this coverage form and any Medical Payments Coverage endorsement, Uninsured Motorists Coverage endorsement or Underinsured Motorists Coverage endorsement attached to this Coverage Part.

D. Deductible

We will deduct $100 from the damages in any "accident" resulting from "property damage" to an "auto" as a result of "work you performed" on that "auto".

© Insurance Services Office, Inc., 2009   CA 00 05 03 10   □

SECTION III – GARAGEKEEPERS COVERAGE

A. Coverage

1. We will pay all sums the "insured" legally must pay as damages for "loss" to a "customer's auto" or "customer's auto" equipment left in the "insured's" care while the "insured" is attending, servicing, repairing, parking or storing it in your "garage operations" under:

   a. Comprehensive Coverage

   From any cause except:

   (1) The "customer's auto's" collision with another object; or

   (2) The "customer's auto's" overturn.

   b. Specified Causes Of Loss Coverage

   Caused by:

   (1) Fire, lightning or explosion;

   (2) Theft; or

   (3) Mischief or vandalism.

   c. Collision Coverage

   Caused by:

   (1) The "customer's auto's" collision with another object; or

   (2) The "customer's auto's" overturn.

2. We have the right and duty to defend any "insured" against a "suit" asking for these damages. However, we have no duty to defend any "insured" against a "suit" seeking damages for any loss to which this insurance does not apply. We may investigate and settle any claim or "suit" as we consider appropriate. Our duty to defend or settle ends for a coverage when the Limit of Insurance for that coverage has been exhausted by payment of judgments or settlements.

3. **Who Is An Insured**

   The following are "insureds" for "loss" to "customer's autos" and "customer's auto" equipment:

   a. You.

   b. Your partners (if you are a partnership), members (if you are a limited liability company), "employees", directors or shareholders while acting within the scope of their duties as such.

4. **Coverage Extensions**

   The following apply as **Supplementary Payments.** We will pay for the "insured":

   a. All expenses we incur.

b. The cost of bonds to release attachments in any "suit" against the "insured" we defend, but only for bond amounts within our Limit of Insurance.

c. All reasonable expenses incurred by the "insured" at our request, including actual loss of earnings up to $250 a day because of time off from work.

d. All court costs taxed against the "insured" in any "suit" against the "insured" we defend. However, these payments do not include attorneys' fees or attorneys' expenses taxed against the "insured".

e. All interest on the full amount of any judgment that accrues after entry of the judgment in any "suit" against the "insured" we defend; but our duty to pay interest ends when we have paid, offered to pay or deposited in court the part of the judgment that is within our Limit of Insurance.

These payments will not reduce the Limit of Insurance.

B. Exclusions

1. This insurance does not apply to any of the following:

   a. Contractual Obligations

   Liability resulting from any contract or agreement by which the "insured" accepts responsibility for "loss". But this exclusion does not apply to liability for "loss" that the "insured" would have in the absence of the contract or agreement.

   b. Theft

   "Loss" due to theft or conversion caused in any way by you, your "employees" or by your shareholders.

   c. Defective Parts

   Defective parts or materials.

   d. Faulty Work

   Faulty "work you performed".

2. We will not pay for "loss" to any of the following:

   a. Tape decks or other sound-reproducing equipment unless permanently installed in a "customer's auto".

   b. Tapes, records or other sound-reproducing devices designed for use with sound-reproducing equipment.

Commercial Auto

c. Sound-receiving equipment designed for use as a citizens' band radio, two-way mobile radio or telephone or scanning monitor receiver, including its antennas and other accessories, unless permanently installed in the dash or console opening normally used by the "customer's auto" manufacturer for the installation of a radio.

d. Any device designed or used to detect speed-measuring equipment such as radar or laser detectors and any jamming apparatus intended to elude or disrupt speed-measuring equipment.

3. We will not pay for "loss" caused by or resulting from the following. Such "loss" is excluded regardless of any other cause or event that contributes concurrently or in any sequence to the "loss":

a. War, including undeclared or civil war;

b. Warlike action by a military force, including action in hindering or defending against an actual or expected attack, by any government, sovereign or other authority using military personnel or other agents; or

c. Insurrection, rebellion, revolution, usurped power, or action taken by governmental authority in hindering or defending against any of these.

C. **Limits Of Insurance And Deductibles**

1. Regardless of the number of "customer's autos", "insureds", premiums paid, claims made or "suits" brought, the most we will pay for each "loss" at each location is the Garagekeepers Coverage Limit of Insurance shown in the Declarations for that location. Prior to the application of this limit, the damages for "loss" that would otherwise be payable will be reduced by the applicable deductibles for "loss" caused by:

a. Collision; or

b. With respect to Garagekeepers Coverage Comprehensive or Specified Causes Of Loss Coverage:

(1) Theft or mischief or vandalism; or

(2) All perils.

2. The maximum deductible stated in the Declarations for Garagekeepers Coverage Comprehensive or Specified Causes Of Loss Coverage is the most that will be deducted for all "loss" in any one event caused by:

a. Theft or mischief or vandalism; or

b. All perils.

3. Sometimes to settle a claim or "suit", we may pay all or any part of the deductible. If this happens you must reimburse us for the deductible or that portion of the deductible that we paid.

SECTION IV – PHYSICAL DAMAGE COVERAGE

A. **Coverage**

1. We will pay for "loss" to a covered "auto" or its equipment under:

a. **Comprehensive Coverage**

From any cause except:

(1) The covered "auto's" collision with another object; or

(2) The covered "auto's" overturn.

b. **Specified Causes Of Loss Coverage**

Caused by:

(1) Fire, lightning or explosion;

(2) Theft;

(3) Windstorm, hail or earthquake;

(4) Flood;

(5) Mischief or vandalism; or

(6) The sinking, burning, collision or derailment of any conveyance transporting the covered "auto".

c. **Collision Coverage**

Caused by:

(1) The covered "auto's" collision with another object; or

(2) The covered "auto's" overturn.

2. **Glass Breakage – Hitting A Bird Or Animal – Falling Objects Or Missiles**

If you carry Comprehensive Coverage for the damaged covered "auto", we will pay for the following under Comprehensive Coverage:

a. Glass breakage;

b. "Loss" caused by hitting a bird or animal; and

c. "Loss" caused by falling objects or missiles.

However, you have the option of having glass breakage caused by a covered "auto's" collision or overturn considered a "loss" under Collision Coverage.

3. **Coverage Extension – Loss Of Use Expenses**

For Hired Auto Physical Damage, we will pay expenses for which an "insured" becomes legally responsible to pay for loss of use of a vehicle rented or hired without a driver, under a written rental contract or agreement. We will pay for loss of use expenses if caused by:

a. Other than collision only if the Declarations indicate that Comprehensive Coverage is provided for any covered "auto";

b. Specified Causes Of Loss only if the Declarations indicate that Specified Causes Of Loss Coverage is provided for any covered "auto"; or

c. Collision only if the Declarations indicate that Collision Coverage is provided for any covered "auto".

However, the most we will pay for any expenses for loss of use is $20 per day, to a maximum of $600.

B. **Exclusions**

1. We will not pay for "loss" caused by or resulting from any of the following. Such "loss" is excluded regardless of any other cause or event that contributes concurrently or in any sequence to the "loss".

   a. **Nuclear Hazard**

      (1) The explosion of any weapon employing atomic fission or fusion; or

      (2) Nuclear reaction or radiation, or radioactive contamination, however caused.

   b. **War Or Military Action**

      (1) War, including undeclared or civil war;

      (2) Warlike action by a military force, including action in hindering or defending against an actual or expected attack, by any government, sovereign or other authority using military personnel or other agents; or

      (3) Insurrection, rebellion, revolution, usurped power or action taken by governmental authority in hindering or defending against any of these.

2. We will not pay for "loss" to any of the following:

   a. Any covered "auto" leased or rented to others unless rented to one of your customers while their "auto" is left with you for service or repair.

   b. Any covered "auto" while used in any professional or organized racing or demolition contest or stunting activity, or while practicing for such contest or activity. We will also not pay for "loss" to any covered "auto" while that covered "auto" is being prepared for such contest or activity.

   c. Tapes, records, discs or other similar audio, visual or data electronic devices designed for use with audio, visual or data electronic equipment.

   d. Any device designed or used to detect speed measuring equipment such as radar or laser detectors and any jamming apparatus intended to elude or disrupt speed-measurement equipment.

   e. Any electronic equipment, without regard to whether this equipment is permanently installed, that reproduces, receives or transmits audio, visual or data signals.

   f. Any accessories used with the electronic equipment described in Paragraph **e.** above.

3. Exclusions **2.e.** and **2.f.** do not apply to equipment designed to be operated solely by use of the power from the "auto's" electrical system that, at the time of "loss", is:

   a. Permanently installed in or upon the covered "auto";

   b. Removable from a housing unit which is permanently installed in or upon the covered "auto";

   c. An integral part of the same unit housing any electronic equipment described in Paragraphs **a.** and **b.** above; or

   d. Necessary for the normal operation of the covered "auto" or the monitoring of the covered "auto's" operating system.

4. **False Pretense**

   We will not pay for "loss" to a covered "auto" caused by or resulting from:

   a. Someone causing you to voluntarily part with it by trick or scheme or under false pretenses; or

   b. Your acquiring an "auto" from a seller who did not have legal title.

5. We will not pay for:

   a. Your expected profit, including loss of market value or resale value.

b. "Loss" to any covered "auto" displayed or stored at any location not shown in Item Three of the Declarations if the "loss" occurs more than 45 days after your use of the location begins.

c. Under the Collision Coverage, "loss" to any covered "auto" while being driven or transported from the point of purchase or distribution to its destination if such points are more than 50 road miles apart.

d. Under the Specified Causes Of Loss Coverage, "loss" to any covered "auto" caused by or resulting from the collision or upset of any vehicle transporting it.

6. We will not pay for "loss" to a covered "auto" due to "diminution in value".

7. Other Exclusions

We will not pay for "loss" due and confined to:

a. Wear and tear, freezing, mechanical or electrical breakdown.

b. Blowouts, punctures or other road damage to tires.

This exclusion does not apply to such "loss" resulting from the total theft of a covered "auto".

C. Limits Of Insurance

1. The most we will pay for "loss" to any one covered "auto" is the lesser of:

a. The actual cash value of the damaged or stolen property as of the time of "loss"; or

b. The cost of repairing or replacing the damaged or stolen property with other property of like kind and quality.

2. $1,000 is the most we will pay for "loss" in any one "accident" to all electronic equipment that reproduces, receives or transmits audio, visual or data signals which, at the time of "loss", is:

a. Permanently installed in or upon the covered "auto" in a housing, opening or other location that is not normally used by the "auto" manufacturer for the installation of such equipment;

b. Removable from a permanently installed housing unit as described in Paragraph **2.a.** above; or

c. An integral part of such equipment.

3. An adjustment for depreciation and physical condition will be made in determining actual cash value in the event of a total "loss".

4. If a repair or replacement results in better than like kind or quality, we will not pay for the amount of the betterment.

5. The following provisions also apply:

a. Regardless of the number of covered "autos" involved in the "loss", the most we will pay for all "loss" at any one location is the amount shown in the Declarations for that location. Regardless of the number of covered "autos" involved in the "loss", the most we will pay for all "loss" in transit is the amount shown in the Declarations for "loss" in transit.

b. Quarterly Or Monthly Reporting Premium Basis

If, on the date of your last report, the actual value of the covered "autos" at the "loss" location exceeds what you last reported, when a "loss" occurs we will pay only a percentage of what we would otherwise be obligated to pay. We will determine this percentage by dividing your total reported value for the involved location by the total actual value at the "loss" location on the date of your last report.

If the first report due is delinquent on the date of "loss", the most we will pay will not exceed 75 percent of the Limit of Insurance shown in the Declarations for the applicable location.

c. Non-reporting Premium Basis

If, when "loss" occurs, the total value of your covered "autos" exceeds the Limit of Insurance shown in the Declarations, we will pay only a percentage of what we would otherwise be obligated to pay. We will determine this percentage by dividing the Limit of Insurance by the total actual value at the "loss" location at the time the "loss" occurred.

D. Deductible

For each covered "auto", our obligation to pay for, repair, return or replace damaged or stolen property will be reduced by the applicable deductible shown in the Declarations prior to the application of the Limit of Insurance shown in the Declarations, provided that:

1. The Comprehensive or Specified Causes Of Loss Coverage deductible applies only to "loss" caused by:

a. Theft or mischief or vandalism; or

b. All perils.

2. Regardless of the number of covered "autos" damaged or stolen, the per "loss" deductible for Comprehensive or Specified Causes Of Loss Coverage shown in the Declarations is the maximum deductible applicable for all "loss" in any one event caused by:

   a. Theft or mischief or vandalism; or

   b. All perils.

SECTION V – GARAGE CONDITIONS

The following conditions apply in addition to the Common Policy Conditions:

A. Loss Conditions

   1. Appraisal For Physical Damage Loss

   If you and we disagree on the amount of "loss", either may demand an appraisal of the "loss". In this event, each party will select a competent appraiser. The two appraisers will select a competent and impartial umpire.

   The appraisers will state separately the actual cash value and amount of "loss". If they fail to agree, they will submit their differences to the umpire. A decision agreed to by any two will be binding. Each party will:

   a. Pay its chosen appraiser; and

   b. Bear the other expenses of the appraisal and umpire equally.

   If we submit to an appraisal, we will still retain our right to deny the claim.

   2. Duties In The Event Of Accident, Claim, Suit Or Loss

   We have no duty to provide coverage under this policy unless there has been full compliance with the following duties:

   a. In the event of "accident", claim, "suit" or "loss", you must give us or our authorized representative prompt notice of the accident or "loss". Include:

   (1) How, when and where the "accident" or "loss" occurred;

   (2) The "insured's" name and address; and

   (3) To the extent possible, the names and addresses of any injured persons and witnesses.

   b. Additionally, you and any other involved "insured" must:

   (1) Assume no obligation, make no payment or incur no expense without our consent, except at the "insured's" own cost.

   (2) Immediately send us copies of any request, demand, order, notice, summons or legal paper received concerning the claim or "suit".

   (3) Cooperate with us in the investigation or settlement of the claim or defense against the "suit".

   (4) Authorize us to obtain medical records or other pertinent information.

   (5) Submit to examination at our expense, by physicians of our choice, as often as we reasonably require.

   c. If there is "loss" to a covered "auto" or its equipment you must also do the following:

   (1) Promptly notify the police if the covered "auto" or any of its equipment is stolen.

   (2) Take all reasonable steps to protect the covered "auto" from further damage. Also keep a record of your expenses for consideration in the settlement of the claim.

   (3) Permit us to inspect the covered "auto" and records proving the "loss" before its repair or disposition.

   (4) Agree to examinations under oath at our request and give us a signed statement of your answers.

   3. Legal Action Against Us

   No one may bring a legal action against us under this coverage form until:

   a. There has been full compliance with all the terms of this coverage form; and

   b. Under Liability Coverage, we agree in writing that the "insured" has an obligation to pay or until the amount of that obligation has finally been determined by judgment after trial. No one has the right under this policy to bring us into an action to determine the "insured's" liability.

   4. Loss Payment – Physical Damage Coverages

   At our option we may:

   a. Pay for, repair or replace damaged or stolen property;

   b. Return the stolen property, at our expense. We will pay for any damage that results to the "auto" from the theft; or

   c. Take all or any part of the damaged or stolen property at an agreed or appraised value.

If we pay for the "loss", our payment will include the applicable sales tax for the damaged or stolen property.

5. Transfer Of Rights Of Recovery Against Others To Us

If any person or organization to or for whom we make payment under this coverage form has rights to recover damages from another, those rights are transferred to us. That person or organization must do everything necessary to secure our rights and must do nothing after "accident" or "loss" to impair them.

B. General Conditions

1. Bankruptcy

Bankruptcy or insolvency of the "insured" or the "insured's" estate will not relieve us of any obligations under this coverage form.

2. Concealment, Misrepresentation Or Fraud

This coverage form is void in any case of fraud by you at any time as it relates to this coverage form. It is also void if you or any other "insured", at any time, intentionally conceals or misrepresents a material fact concerning:

a. This coverage form;

b. The covered "auto";

c. Your interest in the covered "auto"; or

d. A claim under this coverage form.

3. Liberalization

If we revise this coverage form to provide more coverage without additional premium charge, your policy will automatically provide the additional coverage as of the day the revision is effective in your state.

4. No Benefit To Bailee – Physical Damage Coverages

We will not recognize any assignment or grant any coverage for the benefit of any person or organization holding, storing or transporting property for a fee regardless of any other provision of this coverage form.

5. Other Insurance

a. For any covered "auto" you own, this coverage form provides primary insurance. For any covered "auto" you don't own, the insurance provided by this coverage form is excess over any other collectible insurance. However, while a covered "auto" which is a "trailer" is connected to another vehicle, the Liability Coverage this coverage form provides for the "trailer" is:

(1) Excess while it is connected to a motor vehicle you do not own.

(2) Primary while it is connected to a covered "auto" you own.

b. For Hired Auto Physical Damage Coverage, any covered "auto" you lease, hire, rent or borrow is deemed to be a covered "auto" you own. However, any "auto" that is leased, hired, rented or borrowed with a driver is not a covered "auto".

c. Regardless of the provisions of Paragraph **a.** above, this coverage form's Liability Coverage is primary for any liability assumed under an "insured contract".

d. When this coverage form and any other coverage form or policy covers on the same basis, either excess or primary, we will pay only our share. Our share is the proportion that the Limit of Insurance of our coverage form bears to the total of the limits of all the coverage forms and policies covering on the same basis.

6. Premium Audit

a. The estimated premium for this coverage form is based on the exposures you told us you would have when this policy began. We will compute the final premium due when we determine your actual exposures. The estimated total premium will be credited against the final premium due and the first Named Insured will be billed for the balance, if any. The due date for the final premium or retrospective premium is the date shown as the due date on the bill. If the estimated total premium exceeds the final premium due, the first Named Insured will get a refund.

b. If this policy is issued for more than one year, the premium for this coverage form will be computed annually based on our rates or premiums in effect at the beginning of each year of the policy.

7. Policy Period, Coverage Territory

Under this coverage form, we cover:

a. "Bodily injury", "property damage" and "losses" occurring; and

b. "Covered pollution cost or expense" arising out of "accidents" occurring;

during the policy period shown in the Declarations and within the coverage territory.

The coverage territory is:

(1) The United States of America;

(2) The territories and possessions of the United States of America;

(3) Puerto Rico;

(4) Canada; and

(5) Anywhere in the world if:

(a) A covered "auto" of the private passenger type is leased, hired, rented or borrowed without a driver for a period of 30 days or less; and

(b) The "insured's" responsibility to pay damages is determined in a "suit" on the merits, in the United States of America, the territories and possessions of the United States of America, Puerto Rico or Canada or in a settlement we agree to.

We also cover "bodily injury", "property damage", "covered pollution cost or expense" and "losses" while a covered "auto" is being transported between any of these places.

The coverage territory is extended to anywhere in the world if the "bodily injury" or "property damage" is caused by one of your "products" which is sold for use in the United States of America, its territories or possessions, Puerto Rico or Canada. The original "suit" for damages resulting from such "bodily injury" or "property damage" must be brought in one of these places.

8. Two Or More Coverage Forms Or Policies Issued By Us

If this coverage form and any other coverage form or policy issued to you by us or any company affiliated with us applies to the same "accident", the aggregate maximum Limit of Insurance under all the coverage forms or policies shall not exceed the highest applicable Limit of Insurance under any one coverage form or policy. This condition does not apply to any coverage form or policy issued by us or an affiliated company specifically to apply as excess insurance over this coverage form.

SECTION VI – DEFINITIONS

A. "Accident" includes continuous or repeated exposure to the same conditions resulting in "bodily injury" or "property damage".

B. "Auto" means a land motor vehicle, "trailer" or semitrailer.

C. "Bodily injury" means bodily injury, sickness or disease sustained by a person including death resulting from any of these.

D. "Covered pollution cost or expense" means any cost or expense arising out of:

1. Any request, demand, order or statutory or regulatory requirement that the "insured" or others test for, monitor, clean up, remove, contain, treat, detoxify or neutralize, or in any way respond to, or assess the effects of, "pollutants"; or

2. Any claim or "suit" by or on behalf of a governmental authority for damages because of testing for, monitoring, cleaning up, removing, containing, treating, detoxifying or neutralizing, or in any way responding to, or assessing the effects of, "pollutants".

"Covered pollution cost or expense" does not include any cost or expense arising out of the actual, alleged or threatened discharge, dispersal, seepage, migration, release or escape of "pollutants":

a. That are, or that are contained in any property that is:

(1) Being transported or towed by, handled, or handled for movement into, onto or from the covered "auto";

(2) Otherwise in the course of transit by or on behalf of the "insured"; or

(3) Being stored, disposed of, treated or processed in or upon the covered "auto";

b. Before the "pollutants" or any property in which the "pollutants" are contained are moved from the place where they are accepted by the "insured" for movement into or onto the covered "auto"; or

c. After the "pollutants" or any property in which the "pollutants" are contained are moved from the covered "auto" to the place where they are finally delivered, disposed of or abandoned by the "insured".

Paragraph **a.** above does not apply to fuels, lubricants, fluids, exhaust gases or other similar "pollutants" that are needed for or result from the normal electrical, hydraulic or mechanical functioning of the covered "auto" or its parts, if the "pollutants" escape, seep, migrate or are discharged, dispersed or released directly from an "auto" part designed by its manufacturer to hold, store, receive or dispose of such "pollutants".

Paragraphs **b.** and **c.** above do not apply to "accidents" that occur away from premises owned by or rented to an "insured" with respect to "pollutants" not in or upon a covered "auto" if:

   (1) The "pollutants" or any property in which the "pollutants" are contained are upset, overturned or damaged as a result of the maintenance or use of a covered "auto"; and

   (2) The discharge, dispersal, seepage, migration, release or escape of the "pollutants" is caused directly by such upset, overturn or damage.

E. "Customer's auto" means a land motor vehicle, "trailer" or semitrailer lawfully within your possession for service, repair, storage or safekeeping, with or without the vehicle owner's knowledge or consent. A "customer's auto" also includes any such vehicle left in your care by your "employees" and members of their households, who pay for services performed.

F. "Diminution in value" means the actual or perceived loss in market value or resale value which results from a direct and accidental "loss".

G. "Employee" includes a "leased worker". "Employee" does not include a "temporary worker".

H. "Garage operations" means the ownership, maintenance or use of locations for garage business and that portion of the roads or other accesses that adjoin these locations. "Garage operations" includes the ownership, maintenance or use of the "autos" indicated in Section I of this coverage form as covered "autos". "Garage operations" also include all operations necessary or incidental to a garage business.

I. "Insured" means any person or organization qualifying as an insured in the Who Is an Insured provision of the applicable coverage. Except with respect to the Limit of Insurance, the coverage afforded applies separately to each insured who is seeking coverage or against whom a claim or "suit" is brought.

J. "Insured contract" means:

  1. A lease of premises;

  2. A sidetrack agreement;

  3. Any easement or license agreement, except in connection with construction or demolition operations on or within 50 feet of a railroad;

  4. An obligation, as required by ordinance, to indemnify a municipality, except in connection with work for a municipality;

  5. That part of any other contract or agreement pertaining to your garage business (including an indemnification of a municipality in connection with work performed for a municipality) under which you assume the tort liability of another to pay for "bodily injury" or "property damage" to a third party or organization. Tort liability means a liability that would be imposed by law in the absence of any contract or agreement;

  6. An elevator maintenance agreement; or

  7. That part of any contract or agreement entered into, as part of your garage business, pertaining to the rental or lease, by you or any of your "employees", of any "auto". However, such contract or agreement shall not be considered an "insured contract" to the extent that it obligates you or any of your "employees" to pay "property damage" to any "auto" rented or leased by you or any of your "employees".

An "insured contract" does not include that part of any contract or agreement:

  a. That indemnifies an architect, engineer or surveyor for injury or damage arising out of:

    (1) Preparing, approving or failing to prepare or approve maps, drawings, opinions, reports, surveys, change orders, designs or specifications; or

    (2) Giving directions or instructions, or failing to give them, if that is the primary cause of the injury or damage.

  b. That indemnifies any person or organization for damage by fire to premises rented or loaned to you or temporarily occupied by you with permission of the owner.

  c. That pertains to the loan, lease or rental of an "auto", to you or any of your "employees" if the "auto" is loaned, leased or rented with a driver.

  d. That holds a person or organization engaged in the business of transporting property by "auto" for hire harmless for your use of a covered "auto" over a route or territory that person or organization is authorized to serve by public authority.

  e. That indemnifies a railroad for "bodily injury" or "property damage" arising out of construction or demolition operations, within 50 feet of any railroad property and affecting any railroad bridge or trestle, tracks, roadbeds, tunnel, underpass or crossing.

K. "Leased worker" means a person leased to you by a labor leasing firm under an agreement between you and the labor leasing firm to perform duties related to the conduct of your business. "Leased worker" does not include a "temporary worker".

L. "Loss" means direct and accidental loss or damage. But for Garagekeepers Coverage only, "loss" also includes any resulting loss of use.

M. "Pollutants" means any solid, liquid, gaseous or thermal irritant or contaminant, including smoke, vapor, soot, fumes, acids, alkalis, chemicals and waste. Waste includes materials to be recycled, reconditioned or reclaimed.

N. "Products" includes:

  1. The goods or products you made or sold in a garage business; and

  2. The providing of or failure to provide warnings or instructions.

O. "Property damage" means damage to or loss of use of tangible property.

P. "Suit" means a civil proceeding in which:

  1. Damages because of "bodily injury" or "property damage"; or

2. A "covered pollution cost or expense";

to which this insurance applies, are claimed.

"Suit" includes:

  a. An arbitration proceeding in which such damages or "covered pollution costs or expenses" are claimed and to which the "insured" must submit or does submit with our consent; or

  b. Any other alternative dispute resolution proceeding in which such damages or "covered pollution costs or expenses" are claimed and to which the insured submits with our consent.

Q. "Temporary worker" means a person who is furnished to you to substitute for a permanent "employee" on leave or to meet seasonal or short-term workload conditions.

R. "Trailer" includes semitrailer.

S. "Work you performed" includes:

  1. Work that someone performed on your behalf; and

  2. The providing of or failure to provide warnings or instructions.

Commercial Auto

Workers Compensation and Employers Liability Insurance

Each state of the United States has a workers compensation law requiring most employers in the state to provide medical, disability, and other benefits to employees or their family members because of occupational injury or disease to the employees. A workers compensation law also requires any employer with employees covered by the statute to obtain workers compensation insurance or to qualify as a self-insurer as defined in the law.

In most states, insurers writing workers compensation insurance use the Workers Compensation and Employers Liability Insurance Policy developed by the National Council on Compensation Insurance, an insurance advisory organization. The Workers Compensation section of the policy covers the insured's obligations to pay benefits required by the applicable workers compensation law(s). The Employers Liability section covers common-law suits made against the employer because of occupational injury or disease. Although workers compensation laws restrict the right of employees to sue their employers for occupational injury or disease, there are some situations in which a suit is allowed, and the Employers Liability section is designed to cover such claims.

The Workers Compensation and Employers Liability Insurance Policy, reprinted in the following section, can be extended by endorsement to cover obligations under other statutes, such as the U.S. Longshore and Harbor Workers' Compensation Act.

WORKERS COMPENSATION AND EMPLOYERS LIABILITY INSURANCE POLICY

INFORMATION PAGE

Insurer:

P O L I C Y   N O .

1. **The Insured:**   Barnley Corporation   ___ Individual   ___ Partnership
   Mailing address: 2000 Industrial Highway   X Corporation or   _____
                       Workingtown, PA 19000

   Other workplaces not shown above:

2. **The policy period is from**   10/1/20X1   **to**   10/1/20X2   **at the insured's mailing address.**

3.   **A.**   **Workers Compensation Insurance: Part One of the policy applies to the Workers Compensation Law of the states listed here:**   PA

     B.   **Employers Liability Insurance: Part Two of the policy applies to work in each state listed in Item 3.A. The limits of our liability under Part Two are:**

Bodily Injury by Accident	$ ___100,000___	**each accident**
Bodily Injury by Disease	$ ___500,000___	**policy limit**
Bodily Injury by Disease	$ ___100,000___	**each employee**

     C.   **Other States Insurance: Part Three of the policy applies to the states, if any, listed here:**

        All except those listed in Item 3A and ND, OH, WA, WV, WY and OR

     D.   **This policy includes these endorsements and schedules:**

        See Schedule

4.   **The premium for this policy will be determined by our Manuals of Rules, Classifications, Rates and Rating Plans. All information required below is subject to verification and change by audit.**

Classifications	Code No.	Premium Basis Total Estimated Annual Remuneration	Rate Per $100 of Remuneration	Estimated Annual Premium
Sheet Metal Shop	0454	300,000	11.53	34,590
Clerical Office	0953	275,000	.49	1,348
		Experience Modification of 1.382 Applied		13,728
		Estimated Premium Discount		(4,869)
		Total Estimated Annual Premium $		44,797

Minimum Premium $ 1,273   **Expense Constant $**   140

Countersigned by   _____ A. M. Abel _____
                              (authorized representative)

WC 00 00 01 A
© **1987 National Council on Compensation Insurance.**

WORKERS COMPENSATION AND EMPLOYERS LIABILITY INSURANCE POLICY   **WC 00 00 00 A**

1st Reprint   Effective April 1, 1992   **Standard**

WORKERS COMPENSATION AND EMPLOYERS LIABILITY INSURANCE POLICY

In return for the payment of the premium and subject to all terms of this policy, we agree with you as follows:

GENERAL SECTION

A. The Policy

This policy includes at its effective date the Information Page and all endorsements and schedules listed there. It is a contract of insurance between you (the employer named in Item 1 of the Information Page) and us (the insurer named on the Information Page). The only agreements relating to this insurance are stated in this policy. The terms of this policy may not be changed or waived except by endorsement issued by us to be part of this policy.

B. Who Is Insured

You are insured if you are an employer named in Item 1 of the Information Page. If that employer is a partnership, and if you are one of its partners, you are insured, but only in your capacity as an employer of the partnership's employees.

C. Workers Compensation Law

Workers Compensation Law means the workers or workmen's compensation law and occupational disease law of each state or territory named in Item 3.A. of the Information Page. It includes any amendments to that law which are in effect during the policy period. It does not include any federal workers or workmen's compensation law, any federal occupational disease law or the provisions of any law that provide nonoccupational disability benefits.

D. State

State means any state of the United States of America, and the District of Columbia.

E. Locations

This policy covers all of your workplaces listed in Items 1 or 4 of the Information Page; and it covers all other workplaces in Item 3.A. states unless you have other insurance or are self-insured for such workplaces.

PART ONE
WORKERS COMPENSATION INSURANCE

A. How This Insurance Applies

This workers compensation insurance applies to bodily injury by accident or bodily injury by disease. Bodily injury includes resulting death.

1. Bodily injury by accident must occur during the policy period.
2. Bodily injury by disease must be caused or aggravated by the conditions of your employment. The employee's last day of last exposure to the conditions causing or aggravating such bodily injury by disease must occur during the policy period.

B. We Will Pay

We will pay promptly when due the benefits required of you by the workers compensation law.

C. We Will Defend

We have the right and duty to defend at our expense any claim, proceeding or suit against you for benefits payable by this insurance. We have the right to investigate and settle these claims, proceedings or suits.

We have no duty to defend a claim, proceeding or suit that is not covered by this insurance.

D. We Will Also Pay

We will also pay these costs, in addition to other amounts payable under this insurance, as part of any claim, proceeding or suit we defend:

1. reasonable expenses incurred at our request, but not loss of earnings;
2. premiums for bonds to release attachments and for appeal bonds in bond amounts up to the amount payable under this insurance;
3. litigation costs taxed against you;
4. interest on a judgment as required by law until we offer the amount due under this insurance; and
5. expenses we incur.

E. Other Insurance

We will not pay more than our share of benefits and costs covered by this insurance and other

1 of 6

WC 00 00 00 A

WORKERS COMPENSATION AND EMPLOYERS LIABILITY INSURANCE POLICY

Standard   Effective April 1, 1992   **1st Reprint**

insurance or self-insurance. Subject to any limits of liability that may apply, all shares will be equal until the loss is paid. If any insurance or self-insurance is exhausted, the shares of all remaining insurance will be equal until the loss is paid.

F. Payments You Must Make

You are responsible for any payments in excess of the benefits regularly provided by the workers compensation law including those required because:

1. of your serious and willful misconduct;

2. you knowingly employ an employee in violation of law;

3. you fail to comply with a health or safety law or regulation; or

4. you discharge, coerce or otherwise discriminate against any employee in violation of the workers compensation law.

If we make any payments in excess of the benefits regularly provided by the workers compensation law on your behalf, you will reimburse us promptly.

G. Recovery From Others

We have your rights, and the rights of persons entitled to the benefits of this insurance, to recover our payments from anyone liable for the injury. You will do everything necessary to protect those rights for us and to help us enforce them.

H. Statutory Provisions

These statements apply where they are required by law.

1. As between an injured worker and us, we have notice of the injury when you have notice.

2. Your default or the bankruptcy or insolvency of you or your estate will not relieve us of our duties under this insurance after an injury occurs.

3. We are directly and primarily liable to any person entitled to the benefits payable by this insurance. Those persons may enforce our duties; so may an agency authorized by law. Enforcement may be against us or against you and us.

4. Jurisdiction over you is jurisdiction over us for purposes of the workers compensation law. We are bound by decisions against you under that law, subject to the provisions of this policy that are not in conflict with that law.

5. This insurance conforms to the parts of the workers compensation law that apply to:

a. benefits payable by this insurance;

b. special taxes, payments into security or other special funds, and assessments payable by us under that law.

6. Terms of this insurance that conflict with the workers compensation law are changed by this statement to conform to that law.

Nothing in these paragraphs relieves you of your duties under this policy.

PART TWO
EMPLOYERS LIABILITY INSURANCE

A. How This Insurance Applies

This employers liability insurance applies to bodily injury by accident or bodily injury by disease. Bodily injury includes resulting death.

1. The bodily injury must arise out of and in the course of the injured employee's employment by you.

2. The employment must be necessary or incidental to your work in a state or territory listed in Item 3.A. of the Information Page.

3. Bodily injury by accident must occur during the policy period.

4. Bodily injury by disease must be caused or aggravated by the conditions of your employment. The employee's last day of last exposure to the conditions causing or aggravating such bodily injury by disease must occur during the policy period.

5. If you are sued, the original suit and any related legal actions for damages for bodily injury by accident or by disease must be brought in the United States of America, its territories or possessions, or Canada.

B. We Will Pay

We will pay all sums you legally must pay as damages because of bodily injury to your employees, provided the bodily injury is covered by this Employers Liability Insurance.

The damages we will pay, where recovery is permitted by law, include damages:

1. for which you are liable to a third party by reason of a claim or suit against you by that third party to recover the damages claimed against such third party as a result of injury to your employee;

WORKERS COMPENSATION AND EMPLOYERS LIABILITY INSURANCE POLICY   WC 00 00 00 A

1st Reprint   Effective April 1, 1992   **Standard**

against such third party as a result of injury to your employee;

2. for care and loss of services; and

3. for consequential bodily injury to a spouse, child, parent, brother or sister of the injured employee;

provided that these damages are the direct consequence of bodily injury that arises out of and in the course of the injured employee's employment by you; and

4. because of bodily injury to your employee that arises out of and in the course of employment, claimed against you in a capacity other than as employer.

C. **Exclusions**

This insurance does not cover:

1. liability assumed under a contract. This exclusion does not apply to a warranty that your work will be done in a workmanlike manner;

2. punitive or exemplary damages because of bodily injury to an employee employed in violation of law;

3. bodily injury to an employee while employed in violation of law with your actual knowledge or the actual knowledge of any of your executive officers;

4. any obligation imposed by a workers compensation, occupational disease, unemployment compensation, or disability benefits law, or any similar law;

5. bodily injury intentionally caused or aggravated by you;

6. bodily injury occurring outside the United States of America, its territories or possessions, and Canada. This exclusion does not apply to bodily injury to a citizen or resident of the United States of America or Canada who is temporarily outside these countries;

7. damages arising out of coercion, criticism, demotion, evaluation, reassignment, discipline, defamation, harassment, humiliation, discrimination against or termination of any employee, or any personnel practices, policies, acts or omissions;

8. bodily injury to any person in work subject to the Longshore and Harbor Workers' Compensation Act (33 USC Sections 901–950), the Nonappropriated Fund Instrumentalities Act (5 USC Sections 8171–8173), the Outer Conti-

nental Shelf Lands Act (43 USC Sections 1331–1356), the Defense Base Act (42 USC Sections 1651–1654), the Federal Coal Mine Health and Safety Act of 1969 (30 USC Sections 901–942), any other federal workers or workmen's compensation law or other federal occupational disease law, or any amendments to these laws;

9. bodily injury to any person in work subject to the Federal Employers' Liability Act (45 USC Sections 51–60), any other federal laws obligating an employer to pay damages to an employee due to bodily injury arising out of or in the course of employment, or any amendments to those laws;

10. bodily injury to a master or member of the crew of any vessel;

11. fines or penalties imposed for violation of federal or state law; and

12. damages payable under the Migrant and Seasonal Agricultural Worker Protection Act (29 USC Sections 1801–1872) and under any other federal law awarding damages for violation of those laws or regulations issued thereunder, and any amendments to those laws.

D. **We Will Defend**

We have the right and duty to defend, at our expense, any claim, proceeding or suit against you for damages payable by this insurance. We have the right to investigate and settle these claims, proceedings and suits.

We have no duty to defend a claim, proceeding or suit that is not covered by this insurance. We have no duty to defend or continue defending after we have paid our applicable limit of liability under this insurance.

E. **We Will Also Pay**

We will also pay these costs, in addition to other amounts payable under this insurance, as part of any claim, proceeding, or suit we defend:

1. reasonable expenses incurred at our request, but not loss of earnings;

2. premiums for bonds to release attachments and for appeal bonds in bond amounts up to the limit of our liability under this insurance;

3. litigation costs taxed against you;

4. interest on a judgment as required by law until we offer the amount due under this insurance; and

5. expenses we incur.

3 of 6

WC 00 00 00 A

WORKERS COMPENSATION AND EMPLOYERS LIABILITY INSURANCE POLICY

Standard

Effective April 1, 1992

1st Reprint

F. Other Insurance

We will not pay more than our share of damages and costs covered by this insurance and other insurance or self-insurance. Subject to any limits of liability that apply, all shares will be equal until the loss is paid. If any insurance or self-insurance is exhausted, the shares of all remaining insurance and self-insurance will be equal until the loss is paid.

G. Limits of Liability

Our liability to pay for damages is limited. Our limits of liability are shown in Item 3.B. of the Information Page. They apply as explained below.

1. Bodily Injury by Accident. The limit shown for "bodily injury by accident—each accident" is the most we will pay for all damages covered by this insurance because of bodily injury to one or more employees in any one accident.

   A disease is not bodily injury by accident unless it results directly from bodily injury by accident.

2. Bodily Injury by Disease. The limit shown for "bodily injury by disease—policy limit" is the most we will pay for all damages covered by this insurance and arising out of bodily injury by disease, regardless of the number of employees who sustain bodily injury by disease. The limit shown for "bodily injury by disease—each employee" is the most we will pay for all damages because of bodily injury by disease to any one employee.

   Bodily injury by disease does not include disease that results directly from a bodily injury by accident.

3. We will not pay any claims for damages after we have paid the applicable limit of our liability under this insurance.

H. Recovery From Others

We have your rights to recover our payment from anyone liable for an injury covered by this insurance. You will do everything necessary to protect those rights for us and to help us enforce them.

I. Actions Against Us

There will be no right of action against us under this insurance unless:

1. You have complied with all the terms of this policy; and

2. The amount you owe has been determined with our consent or by actual trial and final judgment.

   This insurance does not give anyone the right to add us as a defendant in an action against you to determine your liability. The bankruptcy or insolvency of you or your estate will not relieve us of our obligations under this Part.

PART THREE
OTHER STATES INSURANCE

A. How This Insurance Applies

1. This other states insurance applies only if one or more states are shown in Item 3.C. of the Information Page.

2. If you begin work in any one of those states after the effective date of this policy and are not insured or are not self-insured for such work, all provisions of the policy will apply as though that state were listed in Item 3.A. of the Information Page.

3. We will reimburse you for the benefits required by the workers compensation law of that state if we are not permitted to pay the benefits directly to persons entitled to them.

4. If you have work on the effective date of this policy in any state not listed in Item 3.A. of the Information Page, coverage will not be afforded for that state unless we are notified within thirty days.

B. Notice

Tell us at once if you begin work in any state listed in Item 3.C. of the Information Page.

PART FOUR
YOUR DUTIES IF INJURY OCCURS

Tell us at once if injury occurs that may be covered by this policy. Your other duties are listed here.

1. Provide for immediate medical and other services required by the workers compensation law.

2. Give us or our agent the names and addresses of the injured persons and of witnesses, and other information we may need.

3. Promptly give us all notices, demands and legal

4 of 6

WORKERS COMPENSATION AND EMPLOYERS LIABILITY INSURANCE POLICY   **WC 00 00 00 A**

1st Reprint   Effective April 1, 1992   **Standard**

Workers Comp.

papers related to the injury, claim, proceeding or suit.

4. Cooperate with us and assist us, as we may request, in the investigation, settlement or defense of any claim, proceeding or suit.

5. Do nothing after an injury occurs that would interfere with our right to recover from others.

6. Do not voluntarily make payments, assume obligations or incur expenses, except at your own cost.

PART FIVE—PREMIUM

A. Our Manuals

All premium for this policy will be determined by our manuals of rules, rates, rating plans and classifications. We may change our manuals and apply the changes to this policy if authorized by law or a governmental agency regulating this insurance.

B. Classifications

Item 4 of the Information Page shows the rate and premium basis for certain business or work classifications. These classifications were assigned based on an estimate of the exposures you would have during the policy period. If your actual exposures are not properly described by those classifications, we will assign proper classifications, rates and premium basis by endorsement to this policy.

C. Remuneration

Premium for each work classification is determined by multiplying a rate times a premium basis. Remuneration is the most common premium basis. This premium basis includes payroll and all other remuneration paid or payable during the policy period for the services of:

1. all your officers and employees engaged in work covered by this policy; and

2. all other persons engaged in work that could make us liable under Part One (Workers Compensation Insurance) of this policy. If you do not have payroll records for these persons, the contract price for their services and materials may be used as the premium basis. This paragraph 2 will not apply if you give us proof that the employers of these persons lawfully secured their workers compensation obligations.

D. Premium Payments

You will pay all premium when due. You will pay the premium even if part or all of a workers compensation law is not valid.

E. Final Premium

The premium shown on the Information Page, schedules, and endorsements is an estimate. The final premium will be determined after this policy ends by using the actual, not the estimated, premium basis and the proper classifications and rates that lawfully apply to the business and work covered by this policy. If the final premium is more than the premium you paid to us, you must pay us the balance. If it is less, we will refund the balance to you. The final premium will not be less than the highest minimum premium for the classifications covered by this policy.

If this policy is canceled, final premium will be determined in the following way unless our manuals provide otherwise:

1. If we cancel, final premium will be calculated pro rata based on the time this policy was in force. Final premium will not be less than the pro rata share of the minimum premium.

2. If you cancel, final premium will be more than pro rata; it will be based on the time this policy was in force, and increased by our short-rate cancelation table and procedure. Final premium will not be less than the minimum premium.

F. Records

You will keep records of information needed to compute premium. You will provide us with copies of those records when we ask for them.

G. Audit

You will let us examine and audit all your records that relate to this policy. These records include ledgers, journals, registers, vouchers, contracts, tax reports, payroll and disbursement records, and programs for storing and retrieving data. We may conduct the audits during regular business hours during the policy period and within three years after the policy period ends. Information developed by audit will be used to determine final premium. Insurance rate service organizations have the same rights we have under this provision.

WC 00 00 00 A   **WORKERS COMPENSATION AND EMPLOYERS LIABILITY INSURANCE POLICY**

Standard   Effective April 1, 1992   **1st Reprint**

PART SIX—CONDITIONS

A. Inspection

We have the right, but are not obliged to inspect your workplaces at any time. Our inspections are not safety inspections. They relate only to the insurability of the workplaces and the premiums to be charged. We may give you reports on the conditions we find. We may also recommend changes. While they may help reduce losses, we do not undertake to perform the duty of any person to provide for the health or safety of your employees or the public. We do not warrant that your workplaces are safe or healthful or that they comply with laws, regulations, codes or standards. Insurance rate service organizations have the same rights we have under this provision.

B. Long Term Policy

If the policy period is longer than one year and sixteen days, all provisions of this policy will apply as though a new policy were issued on each annual anniversary that this policy is in force.

C. Transfer of Your Rights and Duties

Your rights or duties under this policy may not be transferred without our written consent.

If you die and we receive notice within thirty days after your death, we will cover your legal representative as insured.

D. Cancelation

1. You may cancel this policy. You must mail or deliver advance written notice to us stating when the cancelation is to take effect.

2. We may cancel this policy. We must mail or deliver to you not less than ten days advance written notice stating when the cancelation is to take effect. Mailing that notice to you at your mailing address shown in Item 1 of the Information Page will be sufficient to prove notice.

3. The policy period will end on the day and hour stated in the cancelation notice.

4. Any of these provisions that conflict with a law that controls the cancelation of the insurance in this policy is changed by this statement to comply with the law.

E. Sole Representative

The insured first named in Item 1 of the Information Page will act on behalf of all insureds to change this policy, receive return premium, and give or receive notice of cancelation.

6 of 6

Miscellaneous Commercial Insurance Policies

Although many policies could be included under this section title, those that are reprinted in this section of the *Handbook* represent some of the more important types of commercial insurance in addition to those that have been treated separately.

Directors and Officers Liability Insurance

The individuals who serve as the directors and officers of a corporation can be sued for breach of their corporate duties. Such suits may be made by stockholders or by persons outside the corporation. In recognition of this loss exposure, many corporations agree (or may even be required by law) to indemnify their directors and officers for the costs resulting from suits against them.

Directors and officers (D&O) liability policies have traditionally contained two insuring agreements. The first agreement, often referred to as "side A," covers the directors and officers of the insured corporation for their personal liability as directors and officers that results from a "wrongful act." The second agreement, often referred to as "side B," covers the sums that the insured corporation is required or permitted by law to pay to the directors and officers as indemnification. In addition, some D&O liability policies also include so-called entity coverage, which covers the named corporation against suits made directly against the corporation alleging wrongful acts covered by the policy.

Because many insurers use independently developed policies to write directors and officers liability insurance, the names of their policies can vary. For example, the policy reprinted in the *Handbook* is titled "Executive Protection Portfolio."

Employment Practices Liability Insurance

To cover liability resulting from lawsuits made by employees against their employers for various employment-related offenses, many organizations purchase employment practices liability insurance. This insurance covers the insured organization, its directors and officers, and often its employees for liability arising out of various employment-related offenses alleged to have been committed against its employees. Examples of such offenses are wrongful termination, discrimination, and sexual harassment.

Professional Liability Insurance

Insurers provide professional liability insurance for people in many different professions and occupations. Those who purchase professional liability insurance include, but are not limited to, physicians, dentists, veterinarians, nurses, accountants, architects, engineers, lawyers, and insurance agents and brokers.

The coverage provided by a professional liability policy varies with the type of professional activity being insured. For example, a physician's professional liability policy typically covers a patient's injuries resulting from a medical incident, whereas an accountant's professional liability policy typically covers all sums that the insured becomes legally obligated to pay because of errors or omissions in providing accounting services, excluding bodily injury or property damage. Virtually all professional liability policies are on a claims-made basis.

The *Handbook* includes a sample of a physicians' professional liability form.

Environmental Insurance

Insurers have developed various types of environmental insurance, both first-party and third-party, to manage pollution-related loss exposures that are largely excluded by most other commercial insurance policies. The leading insurers in the environmental insurance market use independently developed policies that go by various names. The Pollution and Remediation Legal Liability Policy reprinted in the *Handbook* is an example of a site-specific environmental impairment liability (EIL) policy. Typically, this type of policy covers the insured's liability for bodily injury and property damage resulting from pollution occurring at or emanating from the insured premises, the costs of cleaning up and removing such pollutants, and the costs of defending against claims alleging covered damages.

Commercial Umbrella Liability Insurance

The main purposes of a commercial umbrella liability policy are as follows:

1. To provide an additional amount of insurance when damages for which the insured is held liable exceed the per-occurrence limit in an "underlying" liability policy
2. To pay liability claims that are not covered in full by an underlying policy because the aggregate limit in the underlying policy has been depleted or exhausted
3. To cover claims that are outside the scope of the coverage of underlying policies

A similar coverage is commercial excess liability insurance, which can serve purposes 1 and 2, but not 3. Not all insurers follow the terminology used here. An insurer that provides a true umbrella liability policy might name it "Excess Liability Policy," and an insurer whose form provides only excess liability coverage (as defined here) might call the policy its "Umbrella Excess Liability Policy."

An important condition of umbrella liability policies is that the insured must maintain certain underlying coverages, up to stipulated limits of liability, during the policy period. Thus, virtually every umbrella policy contains a schedule of underlying coverages. Requirements for underlying insurance vary by insurer.

Misc. Commercial

GENERAL PROPERTY FORM

Summary of Significant Changes, December 31, 2000

1. Section III. Property Covered, A. Coverage A - Building Property, 3.

Additions and extensions to buildings that are connected by a rigid exterior wall, a solid load-bearing interior wall, a stairway, an elevated walkway, or a roof may be insured as part of the building. At the option of the insured, these extensions and additions may be insured separately. Additions and extensions that are attached to and in contact with the building by means of a common interior wall that is not a solid load-bearing wall are always considered part of the building and cannot be insured separately.

2. Section III. Property Covered, B. Coverage B - Personal Property, 5. Special Limits

Coverage for fine arts, collectibles, jewelry, and furs, etc., has been increased to $2500.

3. Section III. Property Covered B. Coverage B - Personal Property, 8.

Coverage for condominium unit owners has been extended to apply up to 10 percent of the contents coverage for losses to interior walls, floors, and ceilings not covered by the condominium association's master policy.

4. Section III. Property Covered, C. Coverage C - Other Coverages, 2.a. & b.

Coverage for the two loss avoidance measures (sandbagging and relocation of property to protect it from flood or the imminent danger of flood) has been increased to $1,000 for each.

5. Section III. Property Covered, C. Coverage C - Other Coverages, 3. Pollution Damage

Coverage for damage caused by pollutants to covered property has been limited to $10,000. This does not cover the cost of testing for or monitoring of pollutants unless it is required by law or ordinance.

6. Section IV. Property Not Covered, 5.a. & b.

Coverage has been changed to pay for losses to self-propelled vehicles used to service the described location or designed to assist handicapped persons provided that the vehicles are in a building at the described location.

7. Section IV. Property Not Covered, 7.

Coverage is now specifically excluded for scrip and stored value cards.

8. Section IV. Property Not Covered, 14.

Coverage for swimming pools, hot tubs, and spas (that are not bathroom hot tubs or spas), and their equipment is now excluded.

9. Section V. Exclusions, B.1 & 2.

The explanation of when coverage begins as it relates to a loss in progress has been simplified.

10. Section V. Exclusions, C.

Coverage has been clarified to pay for losses from land subsidence under certain circumstances. Subsidence of land along a lake shore or similar body of water which results from the erosion or undermining of the shoreline caused by waves or currents of water exceeding cyclical levels that result in a flood continues to be covered. All other land subsidence is now excluded.

11. Section V. Exclusions, D.4.b.(3)

Coverage is now excluded for water, moisture, mildew, or mold damage caused by the policyholder's failure to inspect and maintain the insured property after the flood waters recede.

12. Section V. Exclusions, D.6.

Coverage is added for damage from the pressure of water against the insured structure with the requirement that there be a flood in the area and the flood is the proximate cause of damage from the pressure of water against the insured structure.

13. Section VII. General Conditions, G. Reduction and Reformation of Coverage, 2.a.(2)

If it is discovered before a claim occurs that there is incomplete rating information, the policyholder has 60 days to submit missing rating information. Otherwise, the coverage is limited to the amount of coverage that can be purchased for the premium originally received and can only be increased by an endorsement that is subject to the appropriate waiting period (currently 30 days).

FEDERAL EMERGENCY MANAGEMENT AGENCY
NATIONAL FLOOD INSURANCE PROGRAM

STANDARD FLOOD INSURANCE POLICY

GENERAL PROPERTY FORM

PLEASE READ THE POLICY CAREFULLY.   THE FLOOD INSURANCE PROVIDED IS SUBJECT TO LIMITATIONS, RESTRICTIONS, AND EXCLUSIONS.

THIS POLICY PROVIDES NO COVERAGE:

1. IN A REGULAR PROGRAM COMMUNITY, FOR A RESIDENTIAL CONDOMINIUM BUILDING, AS DEFINED IN THIS POLICY; AND

2. EXCEPT FOR PERSONAL PROPERTY COVERAGE, FOR A UNIT IN A CONDOMINIUM BUILDING.

I. AGREEMENT

The Federal Emergency Management Agency (FEMA) provides flood insurance under the terms of the National Flood Insurance Act of 1968 and its amendments, and Title 44 of the Code of Federal Regulations (CFR).

We will pay you for **direct physical loss by or from flood** to your insured property if you:

1. Have paid the correct premium;

2. Comply with all terms and conditions of this **policy**; and

3. Have furnished accurate information and statements.

We have the right to review the information you give us at any time and to revise your **policy** based on our review.

II. DEFINITIONS

A. In this **policy**, "you" and "your" refer to the insured(s) shown on the **Declarations Page** of this **policy**. "Insured(s)" includes: Any mortgagee and loss payee named in the **Application** and **Declarations Page**, as well as any other mortgagee or loss payee determined to exist at the time of loss in the order of precedence. "We," "us," and "our" refer to the insurer.

Some definitions are complex because they are provided as they appear in the law or regulations, or result from court cases. The precise definitions are intended to protect you.

Flood, as used in this flood insurance **policy**, means:

1. A general and temporary condition of partial or complete inundation of two or more acres of normally dry land area or of two or more properties (at least one of which is your property) from:

    a. Overflow of inland or tidal waters;

    b. Unusual and rapid accumulation or runoff of surface waters from any source;

    c. **Mudflow**.

2. Collapse or subsidence of land along the shore of a lake or similar body of water as a result of erosion or undermining caused by waves or currents of water exceeding anticipated cyclical levels that result in a **flood** as defined in **A.1.a.** above.

B. The following are the other key definitions that we use in this **policy**:

1. **Act.** The National Flood Insurance Act of 1968 and any amendments to it.

2. **Actual Cash Value.** The cost to replace an insured item of property at the time of loss, less the value of its physical depreciation.

3. **Application.** The statement made and signed by you or your agent in applying for this **policy**. The **application** gives information we use to determine the eligibility of the risk, the kind of **policy** to be issued, and the correct premium payment. The **application** is part of this flood insurance **policy**. For us to issue you a **policy**, the correct premium payment must accompany the **application**.

4. **Base Flood.** A flood having a one percent chance of being equaled or exceeded in any given year.

Page 1 of 18

5. **Basement.** Any area of the **building**, including any sunken room or sunken portion of a room, having its floor below ground level (subgrade) on all sides.

6. **Building.**

   a. A structure with two or more outside rigid walls and a fully secured roof, that is affixed to a permanent site;

   b. A manufactured home (a "manufactured home," also known as a mobile home, is a structure: built on a permanent chassis, transported to its site in one or more sections, and affixed to a permanent foundation); or

   c. A travel trailer without wheels, built on a chassis and affixed to a permanent foundation, that is regulated under the community's floodplain management and building ordinances or laws.

   Building does not mean a gas or liquid storage tank or a recreational vehicle, park trailer, or other similar vehicle, except as described in **B.6.c.**, above.

7. **Cancellation.** The ending of the insurance coverage provided by this **policy** before the expiration date.

8. **Condominium.** That form of ownership of real property in which each **unit** owner has an undivided interest in common elements.

9. **Condominium Association.** The entity made up of the **unit** owners responsible for the maintenance and operation of:

   a. Common elements owned in undivided shares by **unit** owners; and

   b. Other real property in which the **unit** owners have use rights ;

   where membership in the entity is a required condition of **unit** ownership.

10. **Declarations Page.** A computer-generated summary of information you provided in the **application** for insurance. The **Declarations Page** also describes the term of the **policy**, limits of coverage, and displays the premium and our name. The **Declarations Page** is a part of this flood insurance **policy.**

11. **Described Location.** The location where the insured **building** or personal property are found. The **described location** is shown on the **Declarations Page.**

12. **Direct Physical Loss By or From Flood.** Loss or damage to insured property, directly caused by a **flood**. There must be evidence of physical changes to the property.

13. **Elevated Building.** A **building** that has no **basement** and that has its lowest elevated floor raised above ground level by foundation walls, shear walls, posts, piers, pilings, or columns.

14. **Emergency Program.** The initial phase of a community's participation in the **National Flood Insurance Program.** During this phase, only limited amounts of insurance are available under the **Act.**

15. **Expense Constant.** A flat charge you must pay on each new or renewal **policy** to defray the expenses of the Federal Government related to **flood** insurance.

16. **Federal Policy Fee.** A flat charge you must pay on each new or renewal **policy** to defray certain administrative expenses incurred in carrying out the **National Flood Insurance Program.** This fee covers expenses not covered by the **expense constant.**

17. **Improvements.** Fixtures, alterations, installations, or additions comprising a part of the insured **building.**

18. **Mudflow.** A river of liquid and flowing mud on the surfaces of normally dry land areas, as when earth is carried by a current of water. Other earth movements, such as landslide, slope failure, or a saturated soil mass moving by liquidity down a slope, are not **mudflows.**

19. **National Flood Insurance Program (NFIP).** The program of flood insurance coverage and floodplain management administered under the **Act** and applicable Federal regulations in Title 44 of the Code of Federal Regulations, Subchapter B.

20. **Policy.** The entire written contract between you and us. It includes:

    a. This printed form;

    b. The **application** and **Declarations Page;**

    c. Any endorsement(s) that may be issued; and

    d. Any renewal certificate indicating that coverage has been instituted for a new **policy** and new **policy** term.

    Only one **building,** which you specifically described in the **application,** may be insured under this **policy.**

21. **Pollutants.** Substances that include, but are not limited to, any solid, liquid, gaseous, or thermal irritant or contaminant, including smoke, vapor, soot, fumes, acids, alkalis, chemicals, and waste. "Waste" includes, but is not limited to, materials to be recycled, reconditioned, or reclaimed.

22. **Post-FIRM Building.** A **building** for which construction or substantial improvement occurred

after December 31, 1974, or on or after the effective date of an initial Flood Insurance Rate Map (FIRM), whichever is later.

23. **Probation Premium.** A flat charge you must pay on each new or renewal **policy** issued covering property in a community that the NFIP has placed on probation under the provisions of 44 CFR 59.24.

24. **Regular Program.** The final phase of a community's participation in the **National Flood Insurance Program.** In this phase, a Flood Insurance Rate Map is in effect and full limits of coverage are available under the **Act**.

25. **Residential Condominium Building.** A **building,** owned and administered as a **condominium,** containing one or more family **units** and in which at least 75 percent of the floor area is residential.

26. **Special Flood Hazard Area.** An area having special **flood,** or **mudflow,** and/or **flood**-related erosion hazards, and shown on a Flood Hazard Boundary Map or Flood Insurance Rate Map as Zone A, AO, A1-A30, AE, A99, AH, AR, AR/A, AR/AE, AR/AH, AR/AO, AR/A1-A30, V1-V30, VE, or V.

27. **Stock.** Merchandise held in storage or for sale, raw materials, and in-process or finished goods, including supplies used in their packing or shipping. **Stock** does not include any property not covered under Section **IV.** Property Not Covered, except the following:

    a. Parts and equipment for self-propelled vehicles;

    b. Furnishings and equipment for watercraft;

    c. Spas and hot-tubs, including their equipment; and

    d. Swimming pool equipment.

28. **Unit.** A **unit** in a **condominium building**.

29. **Valued Policy.** A **policy** in which the insured and the insurer agree on the value of the property insured, that value being payable in the event of a total loss. The Standard Flood Insurance Policy is not a **valued policy**.

Misc. Commercial

III. PROPERTY COVERED

A. COVERAGE A - BUILDING PROPERTY

We insure against **direct physical loss by or from flood** to:

1. The **building** described on the **Declarations Page** at the **described location.** If the **building** is a **condominium building** and the named insured is the **condominium association,** Coverage **A** includes all **units** within the **building** and the **improvements** within the **units,** provided the **units** are owned in common by all **unit** owners.

2. We also insure **building** property for a period of 45 days at another location, as set forth in **III.C.2.b.,** Property Removed to Safety.

3. Additions and extensions attached to and in contact with the **building** by means of a rigid exterior wall, a solid load-bearing interior wall, a stairway, an elevated walkway, or a roof. At your option, additions and extensions connected by any of these methods may be separately insured. Additions and extensions attached to and in contact with the **building** by means of a common interior wall that is not a solid load-bearing wall are always considered part of the **building** and cannot be separately insured.

4. The following fixtures, machinery, and equipment, which are covered under Coverage **A** only:

    a. Awnings and canopies;

    b. Blinds;

    c. Carpet permanently installed over unfinished flooring;

    d. Central air conditioners;

    e. Elevator equipment;

    f. Fire extinguishing apparatus;

    g. Fire sprinkler systems;

    h. Walk-in freezers;

    i. Furnaces;

    j. Light fixtures;

    k. Outdoor antennas and aerials attached to **buildings**;

    l. Permanently installed cupboards, bookcases, paneling, and wallpaper;

    m. Pumps and machinery for operating pumps;

    n. Ventilating equipment;

    o. Wall mirrors, permanently installed; and

    p. In the **units** within the **building,** installed:

        (1) Built-in dishwashers;
        (2) Built-in microwave ovens;
        (3) Garbage disposal units;
        (4) Hot water heaters, including solar water heaters;
        (5) Kitchen cabinets;
        (6) Plumbing fixtures;
        (7) Radiators;
        (8) Ranges;
        (9) Refrigerators; and
        (10) Stoves.

5. Materials and supplies to be used for construction, alteration, or repair of the insured **building** while the materials and supplies are stored in a fully enclosed **building** at the **described location** or on an adjacent property.

6. A **building** under construction, alteration, or repair at the **described location**.

   a. If the structure is not yet walled or roofed as described in the definition for **building** (see **II.B. 6.a.**), then coverage applies:

      (1) Only while such work is in progress; or

      (2) If such work is halted, only for a period of up to 90 continuous days thereafter.

   b. However, coverage does not apply until the **building** is walled and roofed if the lowest floor, including the **basement** floor, of a non-**elevated building** or the lowest elevated floor of an **elevated building** is:

      (1) Below the **base flood** elevation in Zones AH, AE, A1-A30, AR, AR/AE, AR/AH, AR/A1-A30, AR/A, AR/AO; or

      (2) Below the **base flood** elevation adjusted to include the effect of wave action in Zones VE or V1-V30.

   The lowest floor levels are based on the bottom of the lowest horizontal structural member of the floor in Zones VE or V1-V30 and the top of the floor in Zones AH, AE, A1-A30, AR, AR/AE, AR/AH, AR/A1-A30, AR/A, AR/AO.

7. A manufactured home or a travel trailer as described in the Definitions section (see **II.B.6.b.**and **II.B.6.c.**).

   If the manufactured home or travel trailer is in a **special flood hazard area**, it must be anchored in the following manner at the time of the loss:

   a. By over-the-top or frame ties to ground anchors; or

   b. In accordance with the manufacturer's specifications; or

   c. In compliance with the community's floodplain management requirements

   unless it has been continuously insured by the **NFIP** at the same **described location** since September 30, 1982.

8. Items of property in a **building** enclosure below the lowest elevated floor of an **elevated post-FIRM building** located in Zones A1-A30, AE, AH, AR,

AR/A, AR/AE, AR/AH, AR/A1-A30, V1-V30, or VE, or in a **basement,** regardless of the zone. Coverage is limited to the following:

a. Any of the following items, if installed in their functioning locations and, if necessary for operation, connected to a power source:

   (1) Central air conditioners;
   (2) Cisterns and the water in them;
   (3) Drywall for walls and ceilings in a **basement** and the cost of labor to nail it, unfinished and unfloated and not taped, to the framing;
   (4) Electrical junction and circuit breaker boxes;
   (5) Electrical outlets and switches;
   (6) Elevators, dumbwaiters, and related equipment, except for related equipment installed below the **base flood** elevation after September 30, 1987;
   (7) Fuel tanks and the fuel in them;
   (8) Furnaces and hot water heaters;
   (9) Heat pumps;
   (10) Nonflammable insulation in a **basement**;
   (11) Pumps and tanks used in solar energy systems;
   (12) Stairways and staircases attached to the **building**, not separated from it by elevated walkways;
   (13) Sump pumps;
   (14) Water softeners and the chemicals in them, water filters, and faucets installed as an integral part of the plumbing system;
   (15) Well water tanks and pumps;
   (16) Required utility connections for any item in this list; and
   (17) Footings, foundations, posts, pilings, piers, or other foundation walls and anchorage systems required to support a **building**.

b. Clean-up.

B. COVERAGE B - PERSONAL PROPERTY

1. If you have purchased personal property coverage, we insure, subject to **B.2.**, **3.**, and **4.** below, against **direct physical loss by or from flood** to personal property inside a fully enclosed insured **building**:

   a. Owned solely by you, or in the case of a **condominium**, owned solely by the **condominium association** and used exclusively in the conduct of the business affairs of the **condominium association**; or

   b. Owned in common by the **unit** owners of the **condominium association**.

   We also insure such personal property for 45 days while stored at a temporary location, as set forth in **III.C.2.b.** Property Removed to Safety.

2. When this **policy** covers personal property, coverage will be either for household personal property or other than household personal property, while within the insured **building**, but not both.

   a. If this policy covers household personal property, it will insure household personal property usual to a living quarters, that:

      (1) Belongs to you, or a member of your household, or at your option:

         (a) Your domestic worker;

         (b) Your guest; or

      (2) You may be legally liable for.

   b. If this policy covers other than household personal property, it will insure your:

      (1) Furniture and fixtures;

      (2) Machinery and equipment;

      (3) **Stock**; and

      (4) Other personal property owned by you and used in your business, subject to **IV. Property Not Covered**.

3. Coverage for personal property includes the following property, subject to **B.1.a.** and **B.1.b.** above, which is covered under Coverage **B** only:

   a. Air conditioning units installed in the **building**;
   b. Carpet, not permanently installed, over unfinished flooring;
   c. Carpets over finished flooring;
   d. Clothes washers and dryers;
   e. "Cook-out" grills;
   f. Food freezers, other than walk-in, and food in any freezer;
   g. Outdoor equipment and furniture stored inside the insured **building**;
   h. Ovens and the like; and
   i. Portable microwave ovens and portable dishwashers.

4. Coverage for items of property in a **building** enclosure below the lowest elevated floor of an **elevated post-FIRM building** located in Zones A1-A30, AE, AH, AR, AR/A, AR/AE, AR/AH, AR/A1-A30, V1-V30, or VE, or in a **basement,** regardless of the zone, is limited to the following items, if installed in their functioning locations and, if necessary for operation, connected to a power source:

   a. Air conditioning units, portable or window type;
   b. Clothes washers and dryers; and
   c. Food freezers, other than walk-in, and food in any freezer.

5. **Special Limits.** We will pay no more than $2,500 for any loss to one or more of the following kinds of personal property:

   a. Artwork, photographs, collectibles, or memorabilia, including but not limited to, porcelain or other figures, and sports cards;

   b. Rare books or autographed items;

   c. Jewelry, watches, precious and semiprecious stones, or articles of gold, silver, or platinum;

   d. Furs or any article containing fur which represents its principal value.

6. We will pay only for the functional value of antiques.

7. If you are a tenant, you may apply up to 10 percent of the Coverage **B** limit to **improvements**:

   a. Made a part of the **building** you occupy; and

   b. You acquired or made at your expense, even though you cannot legally remove them.

   This coverage does not increase the amount of insurance that applies to insured personal property.

8. If you are a **condominium unit** owner, you may apply up to 10 percent of the Coverage **B** limit to cover loss to interior:

   a. Walls;

   b. Floors; and

   c. Ceilings;

   that are not covered under a **policy** issued to the **condominium association** insuring the **condominium building**.

   This coverage does not increase the amount of insurance that applies to insured personal property.

9. If you are a tenant, personal property must be inside the fully enclosed **building**.

C. COVERAGE C - OTHER COVERAGES

1. **Debris Removal**

   a. We will pay the expense to remove non-owned debris on or in insured property and owned debris anywhere.

   b. If you or a member of your household perform the removal work, the value of your work will be based on the Federal minimum wage.

   c. This coverage does not increase the Coverage **A** or Coverage **B** limit of liability.

Misc. Commercial

Page 5 of 18

2. **Loss Avoidance Measures**

    a. **Sandbags, Supplies, and Labor**

        (1) We will pay up to $1,000 for the costs you incur to protect the insured **building** from a **flood** or imminent danger of **flood**, for the following:

            (a) Your reasonable expenses to buy:

                (i)   Sandbags, including sand to fill them;

                (ii) Fill for temporary levees;

                (iii) Pumps; and

                (iv) Plastic sheeting and lumber used in connection with these items; and

            (b) The value of work, at the Federal minimum wage, that you perform.

        (2) This coverage for Sandbags, Supplies, and Labor only applies if damage to insured property by or from **flood** is imminent and the threat of **flood** damage is apparent enough to lead a person of common prudence to anticipate **flood** damage. One of the following must also occur:

            (a) A general and temporary condition of flooding in the area near the **described location** must occur, even if the **flood** does not reach the insured **building**; or

            (b) A legally authorized official must issue an evacuation order or other civil order for the community in which the insured **building** is located calling for measures to preserve life and property from the peril of **flood**.

        This coverage does not increase the Coverage **A** or Coverage **B** limit of liability.

    b. **Property Removed to Safety**

        (1) We will pay up to $1,000 for the reasonable expenses you incur to move insured property to a place other than the **described location** that contains the property in order to protect it from **flood** or the imminent danger of **flood**.

            Reasonable expenses include the value of work, at the Federal minimum wage, that you perform.

        (2) If you move insured property to a location other than the **described location** that contains the property, in order to protect it from **flood** or the imminent danger of **flood**, we will cover such property while at that location for a period of 45 consecutive days from the date you begin to move it there. The personal property that is moved must be placed in a fully enclosed **building** or otherwise reasonably protected from the elements.

        Any property removed, including a moveable home described in **II.B.6.b.** and **c.**, must be placed above ground level or outside of the **special flood hazard area**.

        This coverage does not increase the Coverage **A** or Coverage **B** limit of liability.

3. **Pollution Damage**

    We will pay for damage caused by **pollutants** to covered property if the discharge, seepage, migration, release, or escape of the **pollutants** is caused by or results from **flood**. The most we will pay under this coverage is $10,000. This coverage does not increase the Coverage **A** or Coverage **B** limits of liability. Any payment under this provision when combined with all other payments for the same loss cannot exceed the **replacement cost** or **actual cash value**, as appropriate, of the covered property. This coverage does not include the testing for or the monitoring of **pollutants** unless required by law or ordinance.

D. **COVERAGE D - INCREASED COST OF COMPLIANCE**

1. **General**

    This **policy** pays you to comply with a State or local floodplain management law or ordinance affecting repair or reconstruction of a structure suffering **flood** damage. Compliance activities eligible for payment are: elevation, floodproofing, relocation, or demolition (or any combination of these activities) of your structure. Eligible floodproofing activities are limited to:

    a. Nonresidential structures.

    b. Residential structures with **basements** that satisfy FEMA's standards published in the Code of Federal Regulations [44 CFR 60.6 (b) or (c)].

2. **Limit of Liability**

    We will pay you up to $30,000 under this Coverage **D** - Increased Cost of Compliance, which only applies to **policies** with **building** coverage (Coverage **A**).

Our payment of claims under Coverage **D** is in addition to the amount of coverage which you selected on the **application** and which appears on the **Declarations Page**. But the maximum you can collect under this **policy** for both Coverage **A** - Building Property and Coverage **D** - Increased Cost of Compliance cannot exceed the maximum permitted under the **Act.** We do not charge a separate deductible for a claim under Coverage **D**.

3. **Eligibility**

    a. A structure covered under Coverage **A** - Building Property sustaining a loss caused by a **flood** as defined by this **policy** must:

        (1) Be a "repetitive loss structure." A repetitive loss structure is one that meets the following conditions:

            (a) The structure is covered by a contract of flood insurance issued under the **NFIP**.

            (b) The structure has suffered **flood** damage on two occasions during a 10-year period which ends on the date of the second loss.

            (c) The cost to repair the **flood** damage, on average, equaled or exceeded 25 percent of the market value of the structure at the time of each **flood** loss.

            (d) In addition to the current claim, the **NFIP** must have paid the previous qualifying claim, and the State or community must have a cumulative, substantial damage provision or repetitive loss provision in its floodplain management law or ordinance being enforced against the structure; or

        (2) Be a structure that has had **flood** damage in which the cost to repair equals or exceeds 50 percent of the market value of the structure at the time of the **flood**. The State or community must have a substantial damage provision in its floodplain management law or ordinance being enforced against the structure.

    b. This Coverage **D** pays you to comply with State or local floodplain management laws or ordinances that meet the minimum standards of the **National Flood Insurance Program** found in the Code of Federal Regulations at 44 CFR 60.3. We pay for compliance activities that exceed those standards under these conditions:

        (1) **3.a.(1)** above.

        (2) Elevation or floodproofing in any risk zone to preliminary or advisory **base flood** elevations provided by FEMA which the State or local government has adopted and is enforcing for **flood**-damaged structures in such areas. (This includes compliance activities in B, C, X, or D zones which are being changed to zones with **base flood** elevations. This also includes compliance activities in zones where **base flood** elevations are being increased, and a **flood**-damaged structure must comply with the higher advisory **base flood** elevation.) Increased Cost of Compliance coverage does not apply to situations in B, C, X, or D zones where the community has derived its own elevations and is enforcing elevation or floodproofing requirements for **flood**-damaged structures to elevations derived solely by the community.

        (3) Elevation or floodproofing above the **base flood** elevation to meet State or local "freeboard" requirements, i.e., that a structure must be elevated above the **base flood** elevation.

    c. Under the minimum **NFIP** criteria at 44 CFR 60.3 (b)(4), States and communities must require the elevation or floodproofing of structures in unnumbered A zones to the **base flood** elevation where elevation data is obtained from a Federal, State, or other source. Such compliance activities are also eligible for Coverage **D**.

    d. This coverage will also pay for the incremental cost, after demolition or relocation, of elevating or floodproofing a structure during its rebuilding at the same or another site to meet State or local floodplain management laws or ordinances, subject to Exclusion **D.5.g.** below.

    e. This coverage will also pay to bring a **flood**-damaged structure into compliance with State or local floodplain management laws or ordinances even if the structure had received a variance before the present loss from the applicable floodplain management requirements.

4. **Conditions**

    a. When a structure covered under Coverage **A** - Building Property sustains a loss caused by a **flood,** our payment for the loss under this Coverage D will be for the increased cost to elevate, floodproof, relocate, or demolish (or any combination of these activities) caused by the enforcement of current State or local floodplain management ordinances or laws. Our payment for eligible demolition activities will be for the cost to demolish and clear the site of the **building** debris or a portion thereof caused by the enforcement of current State or local floodplain management ordinances or laws. Eligible activities for the cost of clearing the site will include those necessary to discontinue utility service to the site and ensure proper abandonment of on-site utilities.

b. When the **building** is repaired or rebuilt, it must be intended for the same occupancy as the present **building** unless otherwise required by current floodplain management ordinances or laws.

5. Exclusions

Under this Coverage **D** - Increased Cost of Compliance we will not pay for:

a. The cost to comply with any floodplain management law or ordinance in communities participating in the **Emergency Program**.

b. The cost associated with enforcement of any ordinance or law that requires any insured or others to test for, monitor, clean up, remove, contain, treat, detoxify or neutralize, or in any way respond to, or assess the effects of **pollutants**.

c. The loss in value to any insured **building** or other structure due to the requirements of any ordinance or law.

d. The loss in residual value of the undamaged portion of a **building** demolished as a consequence of enforcement of any State or local floodplain management law or ordinance.

e. Any Increased Cost of Compliance under this Coverage **D**:

(1) Until the **building** is elevated, floodproofed, demolished, or relocated on the same or to another premises; and

(2) Unless the building is elevated, flood-proofed, demolished, or relocated as soon as reasonably possible after the loss, not to exceed 2 years.

f. Any code upgrade requirements, e. g., plumbing or electrical wiring, not specifically related to the State or local floodplain management law or ordinance.

g. Any compliance activities needed to bring additions or **improvements** made after the loss occurred into compliance with State or local floodplain management laws or ordinances.

h. Loss due to any ordinance or law that you were required to comply with before the current loss.

i. Any rebuilding activity to standards that do not meet the **NFIP's** minimum requirements. This includes any situation where the insured has received from the State or community a variance in connection with the current flood loss to rebuild the property to an elevation below the **base flood** elevation.

j. Increased Cost of Compliance for a garage or carport.

k. Any structure insured under an **NFIP** Group Flood Insurance Policy.

l. Assessments made by a **condominium association** on individual **condominium unit** owners to pay increased costs of repairing commonly owned **buildings** after a **flood** in compliance with State or local floodplain management ordinances or laws.

6. Other Provisions

All other conditions and provisions of this **policy** apply.

IV. PROPERTY NOT COVERED

We do not cover any of the following property:

1. Personal property not inside the fully enclosed **building**;

2. A **building,** and personal property in it, located entirely in, on, or over water or seaward of mean high tide, if it was constructed or substantially improved after September 30, 1982;

3. Open structures, including a **building** used as a boathouse or any structure or **building** into which boats are floated, and personal property located in, on, or over water;

4. Recreational vehicles other than travel trailers described in **II.B.6.c.**, whether affixed to a permanent foundation or on wheels;

5. Self-propelled vehicles or machines, including their parts and equipment. However, we do cover self-propelled vehicles or machines not licensed for use on public roads that are:

a. Used mainly to service the **described location**, or

b. Designed and used to assist handicapped persons,

while the vehicles or machines are inside a **building** at the **described location**;

6. Land, land values, lawns, trees, shrubs, plants, growing crops, or animals;

7. Accounts, bills, coins, currency, deeds, evidences of debt, medals, money, scrip, stored value cards, postage stamps, securities, bullion, manuscripts, or other valuable papers;

8. Underground structures and equipment, including wells, septic tanks, and septic systems;

9. Those portions of walks, walkways, decks, driveways, patios, and other surfaces, all whether protected by a roof or not, located outside the perimeter, exterior walls of the insured **building**;

10. Containers, including related equipment, such as, but not limited to, tanks containing gases or liquids;

11. **Buildings** or **units** and all their contents if more than 49 percent of the **actual cash value** of the **building** or **unit** is below ground, unless the lowest level is at or above the **base flood** elevation and is below

ground by reason of earth having been used as insulation material in conjunction with energy efficient building techniques;

12. Fences, retaining walls, seawalls, bulkheads, wharves, piers, bridges, and docks;

13. Aircraft or watercraft, or their furnishings and equipment;

14. Hot tubs and spas that are not bathroom fixtures, and swimming pools, and their equipment such as, but not limited to, heaters, filters, pumps, and pipes, wherever located;

15. Property not eligible for flood insurance pursuant to the provisions of the Coastal Barrier Resources Act and the Coastal Barrier Improvement Act of 1990 and amendments to these acts;

16. Personal property owned by or in the care, custody, or control of a **unit** owner, except for property of the type and under the circumstances set forth under Coverage **B** - Personal Property;

17. A **residential condominium building** located in a **Regular Program** community.

V. EXCLUSIONS

A. We only provide coverage for **direct physical loss by or from flood**, which means that we do not pay you for:

1. Loss of revenue or profits;

2. Loss of access to the insured property or **described location**;

3. Loss of use of the insured property or **described location**;

4. Loss from interruption of business or production;

5. Any additional living expenses incurred while the insured **building** is being repaired or is unable to be occupied for any reason;

6. The cost of complying with any ordinance or law requiring or regulating the construction, demolition, remodeling, renovation, or repair of property, including removal of any resulting debris. This exclusion does not apply to any eligible activities that we describe in Coverage **D** - Increased Cost of Compliance; or

7. Any other economic loss.

B. We do not insure a loss directly or indirectly caused by a **flood** that is already in progress at the date and time:

1. The **policy** term begins; or

2. Coverage is added at your request.

C. We do not insure for loss to property caused directly by earth movement even if the earth movement is caused by **flood**. Some examples of earth movement that we do not cover are:

1. Earthquake;

2. Landslide;

3. Land subsidence;

4. Sinkholes;

5. Destabilization or movement of land that results from accumulation of water in subsurface land areas; or

6. Gradual erosion.

We do, however, pay for losses from **mudflow** and land subsidence as a result of erosion that are specifically covered under our definition of **flood** (see **II.A.1.c.** and **II.A.2.**).

D. We do not insure for direct physical loss caused directly or indirectly by:

1. The pressure or weight of ice;

2. Freezing or thawing;

3. Rain, snow, sleet, hail, or water spray;

4. Water, moisture, mildew, or mold damage that results primarily from any condition:

    a. Substantially confined to the insured **building**; or

    b. That is within your control including, but not limited to:

        (1) Design, structural, or mechanical defects;

        (2) Failure, stoppage, or breakage of water or sewer lines, drains, pumps, fixtures, or equipment; or

        (3) Failure to inspect and maintain the property after a **flood** recedes;

5. Water or waterborne material that:

    a. Backs up through sewers or drains;

    b. Discharges or overflows from a sump, sump pump, or related equipment; or

    c. Seeps or leaks on or through insured property;

unless there is a **flood** in the area and the **flood** is the proximate cause of the sewer or drain backup, sump pump discharge or overflow, or the seepage of water;

6. The pressure or weight of water unless there is a **flood** in the area and the **flood** is the proximate cause of the damage from the pressure or weight of water;

7. Power, heating, or cooling failure unless the failure results from **direct physical loss by or from flood** to power, heating, or cooling equipment situated on the **described location**;

8. Theft, fire, explosion, wind, or windstorm;

9. Anything you or your agent do or conspire to do to cause loss by **flood** deliberately; or

10. Alteration of the insured property that significantly increases the risk of flooding.

E. We do not insure for loss to any **building** or personal property located on land leased from the Federal Government, arising from or incident to the flooding of the land by the Federal Government, where the lease expressly holds the Federal Government harmless under flood insurance issued under any Federal Government program.

VI. DEDUCTIBLES

A. When a loss is covered under this **policy**, we will pay only that part of the loss that exceeds the applicable deductible amount, subject to the limit of liability that applies. The deductible amount is shown on the **Declarations Page**.

However, when a **building** under construction, alteration, or repair does not have at least two rigid exterior walls and a fully secured roof at the time of loss, your deductible amount will be two times the deductible that would otherwise apply to a completed **building**.

B. In each loss from **flood**, separate deductibles apply to the **building** and personal property insured by this **policy**.

C. No deductible applies to:

1. **III.C.2.** Loss Avoidance Measures; or

2. **III.D.** Increased Cost of Compliance.

VII. GENERAL CONDITIONS

A. Pairs and Sets

In case of loss to an article that is part of a pair or set, we will have the option of paying you:

1. An amount equal to the cost of replacing the lost, damaged, or destroyed article, less depreciation; or

2. An amount that represents the fair proportion of the total value of the pair or set that the lost, damaged, or destroyed article bears to the pair or set.

B. Concealment or Fraud and Policy Voidance

1. With respect to all insureds under this **policy**, this **policy:**

   a. Is void;

   b. Has no legal force or effect;

   c. Cannot be renewed; and

   d. Cannot be replaced by a new **NFIP policy;**

   if, before or after a loss, you or any other insured or your agent have at any time:

   (1) Intentionally concealed or misrepresented any material fact or circumstance;

   (2) Engaged in fraudulent conduct; or

   (3) Made false statements;

   relating to this **policy** or any other **NFIP** insurance.

2. This **policy** will be void as of the date the wrongful acts described in **B.1.** above were committed.

3. Fines, civil penalties, and imprisonment under applicable Federal laws may also apply to the acts of fraud or concealment described above.

4. This **policy** is also void for reasons other than fraud, misrepresentation, or wrongful act. This **policy** is void from its inception and has no legal force under the following conditions:

   a. If the property is located in a community that was not participating in the **NFIP** on the **policy's** inception date and did not join or reenter the program during the **policy** term and before the loss occurred; or

   b. If the property listed on the **application** is otherwise not eligible for coverage under the **NFIP**.

C. Other Insurance

1. If a loss covered by this **policy** is also covered by other insurance that includes **flood** coverage not issued under the **Act**, we will not pay more than the amount of insurance that you are entitled to for lost, damaged, or destroyed property insured under this **policy** subject to the following:

   a. We will pay only the proportion of the loss that the amount of insurance that applies under this **policy** bears to the total amount of insurance covering the loss, unless **C.1.b.** or **c.** immediately below applies.

   b. If the other policy has a provision stating that it is excess insurance, this **policy** will be primary.

   c. This **policy** will be primary (but subject to its own deductible) up to the deductible in the other **flood** policy (except another policy as described in **C.1.b.** above). When the other deductible amount is reached, this **policy** will participate in the same proportion that the amount of insurance under this **policy** bears to the total amount of both policies, for the remainder of the loss.

2. If this **policy** covers a **condominium association** and there is a flood insurance **policy** in the name of a **unit** owner that covers the same loss as this **policy**, then this **policy** will be primary.

D. Amendments, Waivers, Assignment

This **policy** cannot be changed nor can any of its provisions be waived without the express written consent of the Federal Insurance Administrator. No action that we take under the terms of this **policy** can constitute a waiver of any of our rights. You may assign this **policy** in writing when you transfer title of your property to someone else, except under these conditions:

1. When this **policy** covers only personal property; or

2. When this **policy** covers a structure during the course of construction.

E. Cancellation of Policy by You

1. You may cancel this **policy** in accordance with the applicable rules and regulations of the **NFIP**.

2. If you cancel this **policy**, you may be entitled to a full or partial refund of premium also under the applicable rules and regulations of the **NFIP**.

F. Nonrenewal of the Policy by Us

Your **policy** will not be renewed:

1. If the community where your covered property is located stops participating in the **NFIP**; or

2. If your **building** has been declared ineligible under Section 1316 of the **Act**.

G. Reduction and Reformation of Coverage

1. If the premium we received from you was not enough to buy the kind and amount of coverage you requested, we will provide only the amount of coverage that can be purchased for the premium payment we received.

2. The **policy** can be reformed to increase the amount of coverage resulting from the reduction described in **G.1.** above to the amount you requested as follows:

a. Discovery of insufficient premium or incomplete rating information before a loss.

(1) If we discover before you have a **flood** loss that your premium payment was not enough to buy the requested amount of coverage, we will send you and any mortgagee or trustee known to us a bill for the required additional premium for the current **policy** term (or that portion of the current **policy** term following any endorsement changing the amount of coverage). If you or the mortgagee or trustee pay the additional premium within 30 days from the date of our bill, we will reform the **policy** to increase the amount of coverage to the originally requested amount effective to the beginning of the current **policy** term (or subsequent date of any endorsement changing the amount of coverage).

(2) If we determine before you have a **flood** loss that the rating information we have is incomplete and prevents us from calculating the additional premium, we will ask you to send the required information. You must submit the information within 60 days of our request. Once we determine the amount of additional premium for the current **policy** term, we will follow the procedure in **G.2.a.(1)** above.

(3) If we do not receive the additional premium (or additional information) by the date it is due, the amount of coverage can only be increased by endorsement subject to any appropriate waiting period.

b. Discovery of insufficient premium or incomplete rating information after a loss.

(1) If we discover after you have a **flood** loss that your premium payment was not enough to buy the requested amount of coverage, we will send you and any mortgagee or trustee known to us a bill for the required additional premium for the current and the prior **policy** terms. If you or the mortgagee or trustee pay the additional premium within 30 days from the date of our bill, we will reform the **policy** to increase the amount of coverage to the originally requested amount effective to the beginning of the prior **policy** term.

(2) If we discover after you have a **flood** loss that the rating information we have is incomplete and prevents us from calculating the additional premium, we will ask you to send the required information. You must

submit the information before your claim can be paid. Once we determine the amount of additional premium for the current and prior **policy** terms, we will follow the procedure in **G.2.b.(1)** above.

(3) If we do not receive the additional premium by the date it is due, your flood insurance claim will be settled based on the reduced amount of coverage. The amount of coverage can only be increased by endorsement subject to any appropriate waiting period.

3. However, if we find that you or your agent intentionally did not tell us, or falsified, any important fact or circumstance or did anything fraudulent relating to this insurance, the provisions of Condition **B.** Concealment or Fraud and Policy Voidance apply.

H. Policy Renewal

1. This **policy** will expire at 12:01 a.m. on the last day of the **policy** term.

2. We must receive the payment of the appropriate renewal premium within 30 days of the expiration date.

3. If we find, however, that we did not place your renewal notice into the U.S. Postal Service, or if we did mail it, we made a mistake, e.g., we used an incorrect, incomplete, or illegible address, which delayed its delivery to you before the due date for the renewal premium, then we will follow these procedures:

a. If you or your agent notified us, not later than one year after the date on which the payment of the renewal premium was due, of nonreceipt of a renewal notice before the due date for the renewal premium, and we determine that the circumstances in the preceding paragraph apply, we will mail a second bill providing a revised due date, which will be 30 days after the date on which the bill is mailed.

b. If we do not receive the premium requested in the second bill by the revised due date, then we will not renew the **policy**. In that case, the **policy** will remain an expired **policy** as of the expiration date shown on the **Declarations Page**.

4. In connection with the renewal of this **policy**, we may ask you during the **policy** term to recertify, on a Recertification Questionnaire that we will provide to you, the rating information used to rate your most recent **application** for or renewal of insurance.

I. Conditions Suspending or Restricting Insurance

We are not liable for loss that occurs while there is a hazard that is increased by any means within your control or knowledge.

J. Requirements in Case of Loss

In case of a **flood** loss to insured property, you must:

1. Give prompt written notice to us;

2. As soon as reasonably possible, separate the damaged and undamaged property, putting it in the best possible order so that we may examine it;

3. Prepare an inventory of damaged property showing the quantity, description, **actual cash value**, and amount of loss. Attach all bills, receipts, and related documents;

4. Within 60 days after the loss, send us a proof of loss, which is your statement of the amount you are claiming under the **policy** signed and sworn to by you, and which furnishes us with the following information:

    a. The date and time of loss;

    b. A brief explanation of how the loss happened;

    c. Your interest (for example, "owner") and the interest, if any, of others in the damaged property;

    d. Details of any other insurance that may cover the loss;

    e. Changes in title or occupancy of the insured property during the term of the **policy**;

    f. Specifications of damaged **buildings** and detailed repair estimates;

    g. Names of mortgagees or anyone else having a lien, charge, or claim against the insured property;

    h. Details about who occupied any insured **building** at the time of loss and for what purpose; and

    i. The inventory of damaged property described in **J.3.** above.

5. In completing the proof of loss, you must use your own judgment concerning the amount of loss and justify that amount.

6. You must cooperate with the adjuster or representative in the investigation of the claim.

7. The insurance adjuster whom we hire to investigate your claim may furnish you with a proof of loss form, and she or he may help you complete it. However, this is a matter of courtesy only, and you must still send us a proof of loss within 60 days after the loss even if the adjuster does not furnish the form or help you complete it.

8. We have not authorized the adjuster to approve or disapprove claims or to tell you whether we will approve your claim.

9. At our option, we may accept the adjuster's report of the loss instead of your proof of loss. The adjuster's report will include information about your loss and the damages you sustained. You must sign the adjuster's report. At our option, we may require you to swear to the report.

K. Our Options After a Loss

Options we may, in our sole discretion, exercise after loss include the following:

1. At such reasonable times and places that we may designate, you must:

    a. Show us or our representative the damaged property;

    b. Submit to examination under oath, while not in the presence of another insured, and sign the same; and

    c. Permit us to examine and make extracts and copies of:

        (1) Any policies of property insurance insuring you against loss and the deed establishing your ownership of the insured real property;

        (2) **Condominium association** documents including the Declarations of the **condominium**, its Articles of Association or Incorporation, Bylaws, and rules and regulations; and

        (3) All books of accounts, bills, invoices and other vouchers, or certified copies pertaining to the damaged property if the originals are lost.

2. We may request, in writing, that you furnish us with a complete inventory of the lost, damaged, or destroyed property, including:

    a. Quantities and costs;

    b. **Actual cash values**;

    c. Amounts of loss claimed;

    d. Any written plans and specifications for repair of the damaged property that you can reasonably make available to us; and

    e. Evidence that prior **flood** damage has been repaired.

3. If we give you written notice within 30 days after we receive your signed, sworn proof of loss, we may:

Page 13 of 18

a. Repair, rebuild, or replace any part of the lost, damaged, or destroyed property with material or property of like kind and quality or its functional equivalent; and

b. Take all or any part of the damaged property at the value we agree upon or its appraised value.

L.   No Benefit to Bailee

No person or organization, other than you, having custody of covered property will benefit from this insurance.

M.   Loss Payment

1. We will adjust all losses with you. We will pay you unless some other person or entity is named in the **policy** or is legally entitled to receive payment. Loss will be payable 60 days after we receive your proof of loss (or within 90 days after the insurance adjuster files an adjuster's report signed and sworn to by you in lieu of a proof of loss) and:

    a. We reach an agreement with you;

    b. There is an entry of a final judgment; or

    c. There is a filing of an appraisal award with us, as provided in **VII.P.**

2. If we reject your proof of loss in whole or in part you may:

    a. Accept such denial of your claim;

    b. Exercise your rights under this **policy**; or

    c. File an amended proof of loss, as long as it is filed within 60 days of the date of the loss.

N.   Abandonment

You may not abandon damaged or undamaged insured property to us.

O.   Salvage

We may permit you to keep damaged insured property after a loss, and we will reduce the amount of the loss proceeds payable to you under the **policy** by the value of the salvage.

P.   Appraisal

If you and we fail to agree on the **actual cash value** of the damaged property so as to determine the amount of loss, either may demand an appraisal of the loss. In this event, you and we will each choose a competent and impartial appraiser within 20 days after receiving a written request from the other. The two appraisers will choose an umpire. If they cannot agree upon an umpire within 15 days, you or we may request that the choice be made by a judge of a court of record in the State where the insured property is

located. The appraisers will separately state the **actual cash value** and the amount of loss to each item. If the appraisers submit a written report of an agreement to us, the amount agreed upon will be the amount of loss. If they fail to agree, they will submit their differences to the umpire. A decision agreed to by any two will set the amount of **actual cash value** and loss.

Each party will:

1. Pay its own appraiser; and

2. Bear the other expenses of the appraisal and umpire equally.

Q.   Mortgage Clause

The word "mortgagee" includes trustee.

Any loss payable under Coverage **A - Building Property** will be paid to any mortgagee of whom we have actual notice as well as any other mortgagee or loss payee determined to exist at the time of loss, and you, as interests appear. If more than one mortgagee is named, the order of payment will be the same as the order of precedence of the mortgages.

If we deny your claim, that denial will not apply to a valid claim of the mortgagee, if the mortgagee:

1. Notifies us of any change in the ownership or occupancy, or substantial change in risk of which the mortgagee is aware;

2. Pays any premium due under this **policy** on demand if you have neglected to pay the premium; and

3. Submits a signed, sworn proof of loss within 60 days after receiving notice from us of your failure to do so.

All of the terms of this **policy** apply to the mortgagee.

The mortgagee has the right to receive loss payment even if the mortgagee has started foreclosure or similar action on the **building**.

If we decide to cancel or not renew this **policy,** it will continue in effect for the benefit of the mortgagee only for 30 days after we notify the mortgagee of the cancellation or nonrenewal.

If we pay the mortgagee for any loss and deny payment to you, we are subrogated to all the rights of the mortgagee granted under the mortgage on the property. Subrogation will not impair the right of the mortgagee to recover the full amount of the mortgagee's claim.

R.   Suit Against Us

You may not sue us to recover money under this **policy** unless you have complied with all the requirements of the **policy**. If you do sue, you must start the suit within one year of the date of the written denial of all or part of the claim, and you must file the suit in the United States District Court of the district in which the insured property was located at the time of loss. This requirement applies to any claim that you may have under this **policy** and to any dispute that you may have arising out of the handling of any claim under the **policy**.

S. Subrogation

Whenever we make a payment for a loss under this **policy**, we are subrogated to your right to recover for that loss from any other person. That means that your right to recover for a loss that was partly or totally caused by someone else is automatically transferred to us, to the extent that we have paid you for the loss. We may require you to acknowledge this transfer in writing. After the loss, you may not give up our right to recover this money or do anything that would prevent us from recovering it. If you make any claim against any person who caused your loss and recover any money, you must pay us back first before you may keep any of that money.

T. Continuous Lake Flooding

1. If your insured **building** has been flooded by rising lake waters continuously for 90 days or more and it appears reasonably certain that a continuation of this flooding will result in a covered loss to the insured **building** equal to or greater than the **building policy** limits plus the deductible or the maximum payable under the **policy** for any one **building** loss, we will pay you the lesser of these two amounts without waiting for the further damage to occur if you sign a release agreeing:

   a. To make no further claim under this **policy**;

   b. Not to seek renewal of this **policy**;

   c. Not to apply for any flood insurance under the **Act** for property at the **described location**; and

   d. Not to seek a premium refund for current or prior terms.

   If the **policy** term ends before the insured **building** has been flooded continuously for 90 days, the provisions of this paragraph **T.1.** will apply when the insured **building** suffers a covered loss before the **policy** term ends.

2. If your insured **building** is subject to continuous lake flooding from a closed basin lake, you may elect to file a claim under either paragraph **T.1.** above or this paragraph **T.2.** (A "closed basin lake" is a natural lake from which water leaves primarily through evaporation and whose surface area now exceeds or has exceeded one square mile at any time in the recorded past. Most of the nation's closed basin lakes are in the western half of the United States, where annual evaporation exceeds annual precipitation and where lake levels and surface areas are subject to considerable fluctuation

due to wide variations in the climate. These lakes may overtop their basins on rare occasions.) Under this paragraph **T.2.** we will pay your claim as if the **building** is a total loss even though it has not been continuously inundated for 90 days, subject to the following conditions:

   a. Lake **flood** waters must damage or imminently threaten to damage your **building**.

   b. Before approval of your claim, you must:

      (1) Agree to a claim payment that reflects your buying back the salvage on a negotiated basis; and

      (2) Grant the conservation easement described in FEMA's "Policy Guidance for Closed Basin Lakes," to be recorded in the office of the local recorder of deeds. FEMA, in consultation with the community in which the property is located, will identify on a map an area or areas of special consideration (ASC) in which there is a potential for **flood** damage from continuous lake flooding. FEMA will give the community the agreed-upon map showing the ASC. This easement will only apply to that portion of the property in the ASC. It will allow certain agricultural and recreational uses of the land. The only structures that it will allow on any portion of the property within the ASC are certain simple agricultural and recreational structures. If any of these allowable structures are insurable **buildings** under the **NFIP** and are insured under the **NFIP**, they will not be eligible for the benefit of this paragraph **T.2.** If a U.S. Army Corps of Engineers certified **flood** control project or otherwise certified **flood** control project later protects the property, FEMA will, upon request, amend the ASC to remove areas protected by those projects. The restrictions of the easement will then no longer apply to any portion of the property removed from the ASC; and

      (3) Comply with paragraphs **T.1.a.** through **T.1.d.** above.

   c. Within 90 days of approval of your claim, you must move your **building** to a new location outside the ASC. FEMA will give you an additional 30 days to move if you show that there is sufficient reason to extend the time.

   d. Before the final payment of your claim, you must acquire an elevation certificate and a floodplain development permit from the local floodplain administrator for the new location of your **building**.

   e. Before the approval of your claim, the community having jurisdiction over your **building** must:

Misc. Commercial

(1) Adopt a permanent land use ordinance, or a temporary moratorium for a period not to exceed 6 months to be followed immediately by a permanent land use ordinance, that is consistent with the provisions specified for the easement required in paragraph **T.2.b.** above;

(2) Agree to declare and report any violations of this ordinance to FEMA so that under Section 1316 of the National Flood Insurance Act of 1968, as amended, flood insurance to the **building** can be denied; and

(3) Agree to maintain as deed-restricted, for purposes compatible with open space or agricultural or recreational use only, any affected property the community acquires an interest in. These deed restrictions must be consistent with the provisions of paragraph **T.2.b.** above, except that, even if a certified project protects the property, the land use restrictions continue to apply if the property was acquired under the Hazard Mitigation Grant Program or the Flood Mitigation Assistance Program. If a nonprofit land trust organization receives the property as a donation, that organization must maintain the property as deed-restricted, consistent with the provisions of paragraph **T.2.b.** above.

f. Before the approval of your claim, the affected State must take all action set forth in FEMA's "Policy Guidance for Closed Basin Lakes."

g. You must have **NFIP** flood insurance coverage continuously in effect from a date established by FEMA until you file a claim under this paragraph **T.2.** If a subsequent owner buys **NFIP** insurance that goes into effect within 60 days of the date of transfer of title, any gap in coverage during that 60-day period will not be a violation of this continuous coverage requirement. For the purpose of honoring a claim under this paragraph **T.2.**, we will not consider to be in effect any increased coverage that became effective after the date established by FEMA. The exception to this is any increased coverage in the amount suggested by your insurer as an inflation adjustment.

h. This paragraph **T.2.** will be in effect for a community when the FEMA Regional Director for the affected region provides to the community, in writing, the following:

(1) Confirmation that the community and the State are in compliance with the conditions in paragraphs **T.2.e.** and **T.2.f.** above; and

(2) The date by which you must have flood insurance in effect.

U.   Duplicate Policies Not Allowed

1. We will not insure your property under more than one **NFIP policy**.

If we find that the duplication was not knowingly created, we will give you written notice. The notice will advise you that you may choose one of several options under the following procedures:

a. If you choose to keep in effect the **policy** with the earlier effective date, you may also choose to add the coverage limits of the later **policy** to the limits of the earlier **policy**. The change will become effective as of the effective date of the later **policy**.

b. If you choose to keep in effect the **policy** with the later effective date, you may also choose to add the coverage limits of the earlier **policy** to the limits of the later **policy**. The change will be effective as of the effective date of the later **policy**.

In either case, you must pay the pro rata premium for the increased coverage limits within 30 days of the written notice. In no event will the resulting coverage limits exceed the permissible limits of coverage under the **Act** or your insurable interest, whichever is less.

We will make a refund to you, according to applicable **NFIP** rules, of the premium for the **policy** not being kept in effect.

2. The insured's option under this Condition **U.** Duplicate Policies Not Allowed to elect which **NFIP policy** to keep in effect does not apply when duplicates have been knowingly created. Losses occurring under such circumstances will be adjusted according to the terms and conditions of the earlier **policy**. The **policy** with the later effective date must be canceled.

V.   Loss Settlement

We will pay the least of the following amounts after application of the deductible:

1. The applicable amount of insurance under this **policy**;

2. The **actual cash value**; or

3. The amount it would cost to repair or replace the property with material of like kind and quality within a reasonable time after the loss.

VIII. LIBERALIZATION CLAUSE

If we make a change that broadens your coverage under this edition of our **policy**, but does not require any additional premium, then that change will automatically apply to your insurance as of the date we implement the change, provided that this implementation date falls within 60 days before, or during, the **policy** term stated on the **Declarations Page**.

IX. WHAT LAW GOVERNS

This **policy** and all disputes arising from the handling of any claim under the **policy** are governed exclusively by the flood insurance regulations issued by FEMA, the National Flood Insurance Act of 1968, as amended (42 U.S.C. 4001, et seq.), and Federal common law.

IN WITNESS WHEREOF, we have signed this **policy** below and hereby enter into this Insurance Agreement.

Edward L. Connor

Edward L. Connor
Acting Administrator, National Flood Insurance Program
Federal Emergency Management Agency

Misc. Commercial

CLAIM GUIDELINES IN CASE OF A FLOOD

For the protection of you and your family, the following claim guidelines are provided by the National Flood Insurance Program (NFIP). If you are ever in doubt as to what action is needed, consult your insurance representative or call the NFIP toll-free at 1-800-638-6620 or on the TDD line at 1-800-447-9487.

Know your insurance representative's name and telephone number. List them here for fast reference:

Insurance Representative _____

Representative's Phone Number _____

- Notify us or your insurance representative, in writing, as soon as possible after the flood.

- If you report to your insurance representative, remind him or her to assign the claim to an NFIP-approved claims adjuster. The NFIP pays for the services of the independent claims adjuster assigned to your claim.

- Determine the independent claims adjuster assigned to your claim and contact him or her if you have not been contacted within 24 hours after you reported the claim to your insurance representative.

- As soon as possible, separate damaged property from undamaged property so that damage can be inspected and evaluated.

- Discuss with the claims adjuster any need you may have for an advance or partial payment for your loss.

- To help the claims adjuster, try to take photographs of the outside of the premises showing the flooding and the damage and photographs of the inside of the premises showing the height of the water and the damaged property.

- Place all account books, financial records, receipts, and other loss verification material in a safe place for examination and evaluation by the claims adjuster.

- Work cooperatively and promptly with the claims adjuster to determine and document all claim items. Be prepared to advise the claims adjuster of the cause and responsible party(ies), if the flooding resulted from other than natural cause.

- Make sure that the claims adjuster fully explains, and that you fully understand, all allowances and procedures for processing claim payments on the basis of your proof of loss. This policy requires you to send us detailed proof of loss within 60 days after the loss.

- Any and all coverage problems and claim allowance restrictions must be communicated directly from the NFIP. Claims adjusters are not authorized to approve or deny claims; their job is to report to the NFIP on the elements of flood cause and damage.

At our option, we may accept an adjuster's report of the loss instead of your proof of loss. The adjuster's report will include information about your loss and the damages to your insured property. You must sign the adjuster's report. At our option, we may require you to swear to the report.

This specimen policy is provided for illustrative purpose only. The precise coverage afforded by any policy is subject to the terms and conditions of the policy as issued.

Chubb Group of Insurance Companies
15 Mountain View Road
Warren, New Jersey 07059

CHUBB

Executive Protection Portfolio ^{SM}

Executive Liability and Entity Securities Liability Coverage Section

DECLARATIONS

FEDERAL INSURANCE COMPANY
A stock insurance company, incorporated under the laws of Indiana, herein called the Company

THIS COVERAGE SECTION PROVIDES CLAIMS MADE COVERAGE, WHICH APPLIES ONLY TO "CLAIMS" FIRST MADE DURING THE "POLICY PERIOD", OR ANY EXTENDED REPORTING PERIOD.   THE LIMIT OF LIABILITY TO PAY   "LOSS" WILL BE REDUCED, AND MAY BE EXHAUSTED, BY "DEFENSE COSTS", AND "DEFENSE COSTS" WILL BE APPLIED AGAINST THE RETENTION.   READ THE ENTIRE POLICY CAREFULLY.

Item 1.   **Parent Organization:**

Item 2.   Limits of Liability:

    (A)   Each **Claim**: $

    (B)   Each **Policy Period**: $

    (C)   Sublimit for all **Securityholder Derivative Demands** under Insuring Clause 4: $

Item 3.   Coinsurance Percentage:

    (A)   **Securities Claims**:   __%

    (B)   **Claims** other than **Securities Claims**:   __%

Item 4.   Retention:

    (A)   Insuring Clauses 1 and 4:   None

    (B)   Insuring Clause 2 (**Claims** other than **Securities Claims**):
    $

    (C)   Insuring Clauses 2 and 3 (**Securities Claims** only): $

Item 5.   **Organization:**

Item 6.   Extended Reporting Period:

    (A)   Additional Period:

    (B)   Additional Premium: __% of Annualized Premium for the Expiring **Policy Period**

Item 7.   Pending or Prior Date:

SPECIMEN

Misc. Commercial

Executive Protection Portfolio ^{SM}
*Executive Liability and Entity Securities
Liability Coverage Section*

In consideration of payment of the premium and subject to the Declarations, the General Terms and Conditions, and the limitations, conditions, provisions and other terms of this coverage section, the Company and the Insureds agree as follows:

Insuring Clauses

Executive Liability Coverage Insuring Clause 1

1. The Company shall pay, on behalf of each of the **Insured Persons**, **Loss** for which the **Insured Person** is not indemnified by the **Organization** and which the **Insured Person** becomes legally obligated to pay on account of any **Claim** first made against the **Insured Person**, individually or otherwise, during the **Policy Period** or, if exercised, during the Extended Reporting Period, for a **Wrongful Act** committed, attempted, or allegedly committed or attempted by such **Insured Person** before or during the **Policy Period**, but only if such **Claim** is reported to the Company in writing in the manner and within the time provided in Subsection 15 of this coverage section.

Executive Indemnification Coverage Insuring Clause 2

2. The Company shall pay, on behalf of the **Organization**, **Loss** for which the **Organization** grants indemnification to an **Insured Person**, as permitted or required by law, and which the **Insured Person** becomes legally obligated to pay on account of any **Claim** first made against the **Insured Person**, individually or otherwise, during the **Policy Period** or, if exercised, during the Extended Reporting Period, for a **Wrongful Act** committed, attempted, or allegedly committed or attempted by such **Insured Person** before or during the **Policy Period**, but only if such **Claim** is reported to the Company in writing in the manner and within the time provided in Subsection 15 of this coverage section.

Entity Securities Coverage Insuring Clause 3

3. The Company shall pay, on behalf of the **Organization**, **Loss** which the **Organization** becomes legally obligated to pay on account of any **Securities Claim** first made against the **Organization** during the **Policy Period** or, if exercised, during the Extended Reporting Period, for a **Wrongful Act** committed, attempted, or allegedly committed or attempted by the **Organization** or the **Insured Persons** before or during the **Policy Period**, but only if such **Securities Claim** is reported to the Company in writing in the manner and within the time provided in Subsection 15 of this coverage section.

Securityholder Derivative Demand Coverage Insuring Clause 4

4. The Company shall pay, on behalf of the **Organization**, **Investigative Costs** resulting from a **Securityholder Derivative Demand** first received by the **Organization** during the **Policy Period** or, if exercised, during the Extended Reporting Period, for a **Wrongful Act** committed, attempted, or allegedly committed or attempted before or during the **Policy Period**, but only if such **Securityholder Derivative Demand** is reported to the Company in writing in the manner and within the time provided in Subsection 15 of this coverage section.

Executive Protection Portfolio ^{SM}
Executive Liability and Entity Securities
Liability Coverage Section

Definitions

5.   When used in this coverage section:

Application means all signed applications, including attachments and other materials submitted therewith or incorporated therein, submitted by the **Insureds** to the Company for this coverage section or for any coverage section or policy of which this coverage section is a direct or indirect renewal or replacement.

Application shall also include, for each **Organization**, all of the following documents whether or not submitted with or attached to any such signed application: (i) the Annual Report (including financial statements) last issued to shareholders before this policy's inception date; (ii) the report last filed with the Securities and Exchange Commission on Form 10-K before this policy's inception date; (iii) the report last filed with the Securities and Exchange Commission on Form 10-Q before this policy's inception date; (iv) the proxy statement and (if different) definitive proxy statement last filed with the Securities and Exchange Commission before this policy's inception date; (v) all reports filed with the Securities and Exchange Commission on Form 8-K during the twelve months preceding this policy's inception date; and (vi) all reports filed with the Securities and Exchange Commission on Schedule 13D, with respect to any equity securities of such **Organization**, during the twelve months preceding this policy's inception date. All such applications, attachments, materials and other documents are deemed attached to, incorporated into and made a part of this coverage section.

Claim means:

(1)   when used in reference to the coverage provided by Insuring Clause 1 or 2:

(a)   a written demand for monetary damages or non-monetary relief;

(b)   a civil proceeding commenced by the service of a complaint or similar pleading; or

(c)   a formal civil administrative or civil regulatory proceeding commenced by the filing of a notice of charges or similar document or by the entry of a formal order of investigation or similar document,

against an **Insured Person** for a **Wrongful Act**, including any appeal therefrom;

(2)   when used in reference to the coverage provided by Insuring Clause 3:

(a)   a written demand for monetary damages or non-monetary relief;

(b)   a civil proceeding commenced by the service of a complaint or similar pleading; or

(c)   a formal civil administrative or civil regulatory proceeding commenced by the filing of a notice of charges or similar document or by the entry of a formal order of investigation or similar document, but only while such proceeding is also pending against an **Insured Person**,

against an **Organization** for a **Wrongful Act**, including any appeal therefrom; or

Executive Protection Portfolio ^{SM}
Executive Liability and Entity Securities
Liability Coverage Section

(3)   when used in reference to the coverage provided by Insuring Clause 4, a **Securityholder Derivative Demand**.

Except as may otherwise be provided in Subsection 12, Subsection 13(g),or Subsection 15(b) of this coverage section, a **Claim** will be deemed to have first been made when such **Claim** is commenced as set forth in this definition (or, in the case of a written demand, including but not limited to any **Securityholder Derivative Demand**, when such demand is first received by an **Insured**).

Defense Costs means that part of **Loss** consisting of reasonable costs, charges, fees (including but not limited to attorneys' fees and experts' fees) and expenses (other than regular or overtime wages, salaries, fees or benefits of the directors, officers or employees of the **Organization**) incurred in defending any **Claim** and the premium for appeal, attachment or similar bonds.

Domestic Partner means any natural person qualifying as a domestic partner under the provisions of any applicable federal, state or local law or under the provisions of any formal program established by the **Organization**.

Financial Impairment means the status of an **Organization** resulting from:

(a)   the appointment by any state or federal official, agency or court of any receiver, conservator, liquidator, trustee, rehabilitator or similar official to take control of, supervise, manage or liquidate such **Organization**; or

(b)   such **Organization** becoming a debtor in possession under the United States bankruptcy law or the equivalent of a debtor in possession under the law of any other country.

Insured means the **Organization** and any **Insured Person**.

Insured Capacity means the position or capacity of an **Insured Person** that causes him or her to meet the definition of **Insured Person** set forth in this coverage section. **Insured Capacity** does not include any position or capacity held by an **Insured Person** in any organization other than the **Organization**, even if the **Organization** directed or requested the **Insured Person** to serve in such position or capacity in such other organization.

Insured Person means any natural person who was, now is or shall become:

(a)   a duly elected or appointed director, officer, **Manager**, or the in-house general counsel of any **Organization** chartered in the United States of America;

(b)   a holder of a position equivalent to any position described in (a) above in an **Organization** that is chartered in any jurisdiction other than the United States of America; or

(c)   solely with respect to **Securities Claims**, any other employee of an **Organization**, provided that such other employees shall not, solely by reason of their status as employees, be **Insured Persons** for purposes of Exclusion 6(c).

Investigative Costs means reasonable costs, charges, fees (including but not limited to attorneys' fees and experts' fees) and expenses (other than regular or overtime wages, salaries, fees, or benefits of the directors, officers or employees of the **Organization**)

incurred by the **Organization** (including its Board of Directors or any committee of its Board of Directors) in investigating or evaluating on behalf of the **Organization** whether it is in the best interest of the **Organization** to prosecute the claims alleged in a **Securityholder Derivative Demand**.

Loss means:

(a) the amount that any **Insured Person** (for purposes of Insuring Clauses 1 and 2) or the **Organization** (for purposes of Insuring Clause 3) becomes legally obligated to pay on account of any covered **Claim**, including but not limited to damages (including punitive or exemplary damages, if and to the extent that such punitive or exemplary damages are insurable under the law of the jurisdiction most favorable to the insurability of such damages provided such jurisdiction has a substantial relationship to the relevant **Insureds**, to the Company, or to the **Claim** giving rise to the damages), judgments, settlements, pre-judgment and post-judgment interest and **Defense Costs**; or

(b) for purposes of Insuring Clause 4, covered **Investigative Costs**.

Loss does not include:

(a) any amount not indemnified by the **Organization** for which an **Insured Person** is absolved from payment by reason of any covenant, agreement or court order;

(b) any costs incurred by the **Organization** to comply with any order for injunctive or other non-monetary relief, or to comply with an agreement to provide such relief;

(c) any amount incurred by an **Insured** in the defense or investigation of any action, proceeding or demand that is not then a **Claim** even if (i) such amount also benefits the defense of a covered **Claim**, or (ii) such action, proceeding or demand subsequently gives rise to a **Claim**;

(d) taxes, fines or penalties, or the multiple portion of any multiplied damage award, except as provided above with respect to punitive or exemplary damages;

(e) any amount not insurable under the law pursuant to which this coverage section is construed, except as provided above with respect to punitive or exemplary damages;

(f) any amount allocated to non-covered loss pursuant to Subsection 17 of this coverage section; or

(g) any amount that represents or is substantially equivalent to an increase in the consideration paid (or proposed to be paid) by an **Organization** in connection with its purchase of any securities or assets.

Manager means any natural person who was, now is or shall become a manager, member of the Board of Managers or equivalent executive of an **Organization** that is a limited liability company.

Organization means, collectively, those organizations designated in Item 5 of the Declarations for this coverage section, including any such organization in its capacity as a debtor in possession under the United States bankruptcy law or in an equivalent status under the law of any other country.

Pollutants means (a) any substance located anywhere in the world exhibiting any hazardous characteristics as defined by, or identified on a list of hazardous substances issued by, the United States Environmental Protection Agency or any state, county, municipality or locality counterpart thereof, including, without limitation, solids, liquids, gaseous or thermal irritants, contaminants or smoke, vapor, soot, fumes, acids, alkalis, chemicals or waste materials, or (b) any other air emission, odor, waste water, oil or oil products, infectious or medical waste, asbestos or asbestos products or any noise.

Related Claims means all **Claims** for **Wrongful Acts** based upon, arising from, or in consequence of the same or related facts, circumstances, situations, transactions or events or the same or related series of facts, circumstances, situations, transactions or events.

Securities Claim means that portion of a **Claim** which:

    (a)   is brought by a securityholder of an **Organization**

        (i)   in his or her capacity as a securityholder of such **Organization**, with respect to his or her interest in securities of such **Organization**, and against such **Organization** or any of its **Insured Persons**; or

        (ii)   derivatively, on behalf of such **Organization**, against an **Insured Person** of such **Organization**; or

    (b)   alleges that an **Organization** or any of its **Insured Persons**

        (i)   violated a federal, state, local or foreign securities law or a rule or regulation promulgated under any such securities law; or

        (ii)   committed a **Wrongful Act** that constitutes or arises from a purchase, sale, or offer to purchase or sell securities of such **Organization**,

provided that **Securities Claim** does not include any **Claim** by or on behalf of a former, current, future or prospective employee of the **Organization** that is based upon, arising from, or in consequence of any offer, grant or issuance, or any plan or agreement relating to the offer, grant or issuance, by the **Organization** to such employee in his or her capacity as such of stock, stock warrants, stock options or other securities of the **Organization**, or any payment or instrument the amount or value of which is derived from the value of securities of the **Organization**; and provided, further, that **Securities Claim** does not include any **Securityholder Derivative Demand**.

Securityholder Derivative Demand means:

    (a)   any written demand, by a securityholder of an **Organization**, upon the Board of Directors or Board of **Managers** of such **Organization** to bring a civil proceeding in a court of law against an **Insured Person** for a **Wrongful Act**; or

    (b)   any lawsuit by a securityholder of an **Organization**, brought derivatively on behalf of such **Organization** against an **Insured Person** for a **Wrongful Act** without first making a demand as described in (a) above,

14-02-7303 (Ed. 11/2002)   Page 6 of 18

Executive Protection Portfolio ^{SM}
*Executive Liability and Entity Securities
Liability Coverage Section*

provided such demand or lawsuit is brought and maintained without any active assistance or participation of, or solicitation by, any **Insured Person**.

Subsidiary, either in the singular or plural, means any organization while more than fifty percent (50%) of the outstanding securities or voting rights representing the present right to vote for election of or to appoint directors or **Managers** of such organization are owned or controlled, directly or indirectly, in any combination, by one or more **Organizations**.

Wrongful Act means:

(a)   any error, misstatement, misleading statement, act, omission, neglect, or breach of duty committed, attempted, or allegedly committed or attempted by an **Insured Person** in his or her **Insured Capacity**, or for purposes of coverage under Insuring Clause 3, by the **Organization**, or

(b)   any other matter claimed against an **Insured Person** solely by reason of his or her serving in an **Insured Capacity**.

Exclusions

Applicable To All Insuring Clauses

6.   The Company shall not be liable for **Loss** on account of any **Claim**:

(a)   based upon, arising from, or in consequence of any fact, circumstance, situation, transaction, event or **Wrongful Act** that, before the inception date set forth in Item 2 of the Declarations of the General Terms and Conditions, was the subject of any notice given under any policy or coverage section of which this coverage section is a direct or indirect renewal or replacement;

(b)   based upon, arising from, or in consequence of any demand, suit or other proceeding pending against, or order, decree or judgment entered for or against any **Insured**, on or prior to the Pending or Prior Date set forth in Item 7 of the Declarations for this coverage section, or the same or substantially the same fact, circumstance or situation underlying or alleged therein;

(c)   brought or maintained by or on behalf of any **Insured** in any capacity; provided that this Exclusion 6(c) shall not apply to:

(i)   a **Claim** brought or maintained derivatively on behalf of the **Organization** by one or more securityholders of the **Organization**, provided such **Claim** is brought and maintained without any active assistance or participation of, or solicitation by, any **Insured Person**;

(ii)   an employment **Claim** brought or maintained by or on behalf of an **Insured Person**;

(iii)   a **Claim** brought or maintained by an **Insured Person** for contribution or indemnity, if such **Claim** directly results from another **Claim** covered under this coverage section; or

(iv)   a **Claim** brought by an **Insured Person** who has not served in an **Insured Capacity** for at least four (4) years prior to the date such **Claim** is first made and who brings and maintains such **Claim** without any active assistance or participation of, or solicitation by, the **Organization** or any other **Insured Person** who is serving or has served in an **Insured Capacity** within such four (4) year period;

(d)   based upon, arising from, or in consequence of:

    (i)   any actual, alleged, or threatened exposure to, or generation, storage, transportation, discharge, emission, release, dispersal, escape, treatment, removal or disposal of any **Pollutants**; or

    (ii)   any regulation, order, direction or request to test for, monitor, clean up, remove, contain, treat, detoxify or neutralize any **Pollutants**, or any action taken in contemplation or anticipation of any such regulation, order, direction or request,

including but not limited to any **Claim** for financial loss to the **Organization**, its securityholders or its creditors based upon, arising from, or in consequence of any matter described in clause (i) or clause (ii) of this Exclusion 6(d);

(e)   for bodily injury, mental anguish, emotional distress, sickness, disease or death of any person or damage to or destruction of any tangible property including loss of use thereof whether or not it is damaged or destroyed; provided that this Exclusion 6(e) shall not apply to mental anguish or emotional distress for which a claimant seeks compensation in an employment **Claim**;

(f)   for an actual or alleged violation of the responsibilities, obligations or duties imposed on fiduciaries by the Employee Retirement Income Security Act of 1974, or any amendments thereto, or any rules or regulations promulgated thereunder, or any similar provisions of any federal, state, or local statutory law or common law anywhere in the world;

(g)   for **Wrongful Acts** of an **Insured Person** in his or her capacity as a director, officer, manager, trustee, regent, governor or employee of any entity other than the **Organization**, even if the **Insured Person's** service in such capacity is with the knowledge or consent or at the request of the **Organization**; or

(h)   made against a **Subsidiary** or an **Insured Person** of such **Subsidiary** for any **Wrongful Act** committed, attempted, or allegedly committed or attempted during any time when such entity was not a **Subsidiary**.

Applicable To Insuring Clauses 1 and 2 Only

7.   The **Company** shall not be liable under Insuring Clause 1 or 2 for **Loss** on account of any **Claim** made against any **Insured Person**:

(a)   for an accounting of profits made from the purchase or sale by such **Insured Person** of securities of the **Organization** within the meaning of Section 16(b) of the Securities Exchange Act of 1934, any amendments thereto, or any similar provision of any federal, state, or local statutory law or common law anywhere in the world; or

14-02-7303 (Ed. 11/2002)   Page 8 of 18

Reprinted with permission from Chubb Group of Insurance Companies.

(b)   based upon, arising from, or in consequence of:

   (i)   the committing in fact of any deliberately fraudulent act or omission or any willful violation of any statute or regulation by such **Insured Person**; or

   (ii)   such **Insured Person** having gained in fact any profit, remuneration or advantage to which such **Insured Person** was not legally entitled,

   as evidenced by (A) any written statement or written document by any **Insured** or (B) any judgment or ruling in any judicial, administrative or alternative dispute resolution proceeding.

Applicable To Insuring Clause 3 Only

8.   The Company shall not be liable under Insuring Clause 3 for **Loss** on account of any **Securities Claim** made against any **Organization**:

(a)   based upon, arising from, or in consequence of:

   (i)   the committing in fact of any deliberately fraudulent act or omission or any willful violation of any statute or regulation by an **Organization** or by any past, present or future chief financial officer, in-house general counsel, president, chief executive officer or chairperson of an **Organization**; or

   (ii)   such **Organization** having gained in fact any profit, remuneration or advantage to which such **Organization** was not legally entitled,

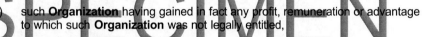

   as evidenced by (A) any written statement or written document by any **Insured** or (B) any judgment or ruling in any judicial, administrative or alternative dispute resolution proceeding; or

(b)   for any actual or alleged liability of an **Organization** under any contract or agreement that relates to the purchase, sale, or offer to purchase or sell any securities; provided that this Exclusion 8(b) shall not apply to liability that would have attached to such **Organization** in the absence of such contract or agreement.

Severability of Exclusions

9.   (a)   No fact pertaining to or knowledge possessed by any **Insured Person** shall be imputed to any other **Insured Person** for the purpose of applying the exclusions in Subsection 7 of this coverage section.

   (b)   Only facts pertaining to and knowledge possessed by any past, present, or future chief financial officer, in-house general counsel, president, chief executive officer or chairperson of an **Organization** shall be imputed to such **Organization** for the purpose of applying the exclusions in Subsection 8 of this coverage section.

14-02-7303 (Ed. 11/2002)   Page 9 of 18

Spouses, Estates and Legal Representatives

10.   Subject otherwise to the General Terms and Conditions and the limitations, conditions, provisions and other terms of this coverage section, coverage shall extend to **Claims** for the **Wrongful Acts** of an **Insured Person** made against:

   (a)   the estate, heirs, legal representatives or assigns of such **Insured Person** if such **Insured Person** is deceased or the legal representatives or assigns of such **Insured Person** if such **Insured Person** is incompetent, insolvent or bankrupt; or

   (b)   the lawful spouse or **Domestic Partner** of such **Insured Person** solely by reason of such spouse or **Domestic Partner's** status as a spouse or **Domestic Partner**, or such spouse or **Domestic Partner's** ownership interest in property which the claimant seeks as recovery for an alleged **Wrongful Act** of such **Insured Person**.

   All terms and conditions of this coverage section, including without limitation the Retention, applicable to **Loss** incurred by the **Insured Persons**, shall also apply to loss incurred by the estates, heirs, legal representatives, assigns, spouses and **Domestic Partners** of such **Insured Persons**. The coverage provided by this Subsection 10 shall not apply with respect to any loss arising from an act or omission by an **Insured Person's** estate, heirs, legal representatives, assigns, spouse or **Domestic Partner**.

Coordination With Employment Practices Liability Coverage Section

11.   Any **Loss** otherwise covered by both (i) this coverage section and (ii) any employment practices liability coverage section or policy issued by the Company or by any affiliate of the Company (an "Employment Practices Liability Coverage") first shall be covered as provided in, and shall be subject to the limit of liability, retention and coinsurance percentage applicable to such Employment Practices Liability Coverage. Any remaining **Loss** otherwise covered by this coverage section which is not paid under such Employment Practices Liability Coverage shall be covered as provided in, and shall be subject to the Limit of Liability, Retention and Coinsurance Percentage applicable to this coverage section; provided the Retention applicable to such **Loss** under this coverage section shall be reduced by the amount of **Loss** otherwise covered by this coverage section which is paid by the **Insureds** as the retention under such Employment Practices Liability Coverage.

Extended Reporting Period

12.   If the Company or the **Parent Organization** terminates or does not renew this coverage section, other than termination by the Company for nonpayment of premium, the **Parent Organization** and the **Insured Persons** shall have the right, upon payment of the additional premium set forth in Item 6(B) of the Declarations for this coverage section, to an extension of the coverage granted by this coverage section for **Claims** that are (i) first made during the period set forth in Item 6(A) of the Declarations for this coverage section (the "Extended Reporting Period") following the effective date of termination or nonrenewal, and (ii) reported to the Company in writing within the time provided in Subsection 15(a) of this coverage section, but only to the extent such **Claims** are for **Wrongful Acts** committed, attempted, or allegedly committed or attempted before the earlier of the effective date of termination or nonrenewal or the date of the first merger, consolidation or acquisition event described in Subsection 21 below. The offer of renewal terms and conditions or premiums different from those in effect prior to renewal shall not constitute

refusal to renew. The right to purchase an extension of coverage as described in this Subsection shall lapse unless written notice of election to purchase the extension, together with payment of the additional premium due, is received by the Company within thirty (30) days after the effective date of termination or nonrenewal. Any **Claim** made during the Extended Reporting Period shall be deemed to have been made during the immediately preceding **Policy Period**. The entire additional premium for the Extended Reporting Period shall be deemed fully earned at the inception of such Extended Reporting Period.

Limit of Liability, Retention and Coinsurance

13. (a) The Company's maximum liability for all **Loss** on account of each **Claim**, whether covered under one or more Insuring Clauses, shall be the Limit of Liability set forth in Item 2(A) of the Declarations for this coverage section. The Company's maximum aggregate liability for all **Loss** on account of all **Claims** first made during the **Policy Period**, whether covered under one or more Insuring Clauses, shall be the Limit of Liability for each **Policy Period** set forth in Item 2(B) of the Declarations for this coverage section.

(b) The Company's maximum aggregate liability under Insuring Clause 4 for all **Investigative Costs** on account of all **Securityholder Derivative Demands** shall be the Sublimit set forth in Item 2(C) of the Declarations for this coverage section. Such Sublimit is part of, and not in addition to, the Limits of Liability set forth in Items 2(A) and 2(B) of the Declarations.

(c) **Defense Costs** are part of, and not in addition to, the Limits of Liability set forth in Item 2 of the Declarations for this coverage section, and the payment by the Company of **Defense Costs** shall reduce and may exhaust such applicable Limits of Liability.

(d) The Company's liability under Insuring Clause 2 or 3 shall apply only to that part of covered **Loss** (as determined by any applicable provision in Subsection 17 of this coverage section) on account of each **Claim** which is excess of the applicable Retention set forth in Item 4 of the Declarations for this coverage section. Such Retention shall be depleted only by **Loss** otherwise covered under this coverage section and shall be borne by the **Insureds** uninsured and at their own risk. Except as otherwise provided in Subsection 14, no Retention shall apply to any **Loss** under Insuring Clause 1 or 4.

(e) If different parts of a single **Claim** are subject to different Retentions, the applicable Retentions will be applied separately to each part of such **Claim**, but the sum of such Retentions shall not exceed the largest applicable Retention.

(f) To the extent that **Loss** resulting from a **Securities Claim** is covered under Insuring Clause 2 or 3 (as determined by Subsection 17(a) of this coverage section) and is in excess of the applicable Retention, the **Insureds** shall bear uninsured and at their own risk that percentage of such **Loss** specified as the Coinsurance Percentage in Item 3(A) of the Declarations for this coverage section, and the Company's liability shall apply only to the remaining percentage of such **Loss**. To the extent that **Loss** resulting from a **Claim** other than a **Securities Claim** is covered under Insuring Clause 2 or 3 (as determined by Subsection 17(b) of this coverage section) and is in excess of the applicable Retention, the **Insureds** shall bear uninsured and at their own risk that percentage of such **Loss** specified as the Coinsurance Percentage in

Item 3(B) of the Declarations for this coverage section, and the Company's liability shall apply only to the remaining percentage of such **Loss**.

(g)   All **Related Claims** shall be treated as a single **Claim** first made on the date the earliest of such **Related Claims** was first made, or on the date the earliest of such **Related Claims** is treated as having been made in accordance with Subsection 15(b) below, regardless of whether such date is before or during the **Policy Period**.

(h)   The limit of liability available during the Extended Reporting Period (if exercised) shall be part of, and not in addition to, the Company's maximum aggregate limit of liability for all **Loss** on account of all **Claims** first made during the immediately preceding **Policy Period**.

Presumptive Indemnification

14.   If the **Organization** fails or refuses, other than for reason of **Financial Impairment**, to indemnify an **Insured Person** for **Loss**, or to advance **Defense Costs** on behalf of an **Insured Person**, to the fullest extent permitted by statutory or common law, then, notwithstanding any other conditions, provisions or terms of this coverage section to the contrary, any payment by the Company of such **Defense Costs** or other **Loss** shall be subject to:

(i)   the applicable Insuring Clause 2 Retention set forth in Item 4 of the Declarations for this coverage section; and

(ii)   the applicable Coinsurance Percentage set forth in Item 3 of the Declarations for this coverage section.

Reporting and Notice

15.   (a)   The **Insureds** shall, as a condition precedent to exercising any right to coverage under this coverage section, give to the Company written notice of any **Claim** as soon as practicable, but in no event later than the earliest of the following dates:

(i)   sixty (60) days after the date on which any **Organization's** chief financial officer, in-house general counsel, risk manager, president, chief executive officer or chairperson first becomes aware that the **Claim** has been made;

(ii)   if this coverage section expires (or is otherwise terminated) without being renewed and if no Extended Reporting Period is purchased, sixty (60) days after the effective date of such expiration or termination; or

(iii)   the expiration date of the Extended Reporting Period, if purchased;

provided that if the Company sends written notice to the **Parent Organization**, at any time before the date set forth in (i) above with respect to any **Claim**, stating that this coverage section is being terminated for nonpayment of premium, the **Insureds** shall give to the Company written notice of such **Claim** prior to the effective date of such termination.

Executive Protection Portfolio *SM*
Executive Liability and Entity Securities
Liability Coverage Section

(b)   If during the **Policy Period** an **Insured**:

(i)   becomes aware of circumstances which could give rise to a **Claim** and gives written notice of such circumstances to the Company;

(ii)   receives a written request to toll or waive a statute of limitations applicable to **Wrongful Acts** committed, attempted, or allegedly committed or attempted before or during the **Policy Period** and gives written notice of such request and of such alleged **Wrongful Acts** to the Company; or

(iii)   gives written notice to the Company of a **Securityholder Derivative Demand**,

then any **Claim** subsequently arising from the circumstances referred to in (i) above, from the **Wrongful Acts** referred to in (ii) above, or from the **Securityholder Derivative Demand** referred to in (iii) above, shall be deemed to have been first made during the **Policy Period** in which the written notice described in (i), (ii) or (iii) above was first given by an **Insured** to the Company, provided any such subsequent **Claim** is reported to the Company as set forth in Subsection 15(a) above. With respect to any such subsequent **Claim**, no coverage under this coverage section shall apply to loss incurred prior to the date such subsequent **Claim** is actually made.

(c)   The **Insureds** shall, as a condition precedent to exercising any right to coverage under this coverage section, give to the Company such information, assistance, and cooperation as the Company may reasonably require, and shall include in any notice under Subsection 15(a) or (b) a description of the **Claim**, circumstances, or **Securityholder Derivative Demand**, the nature of any alleged **Wrongful Acts**, the nature of the alleged or potential damage, the names of all actual or potential claimants, the names of all actual or potential defendants, and the manner in which such **Insured** first became aware of the **Claim**, circumstances, or **Securityholder Derivative Demand**.

Defense and Settlement

16.   (a)   It shall be the duty of the **Insureds** and not the duty of the Company to defend **Claims** made against the **Insureds**.

(b)   The **Insureds** agree not to settle or offer to settle any **Claim**, incur any **Defense Costs** or otherwise assume any contractual obligation or admit any liability with respect to any **Claim** without the Company's prior written consent. The Company shall not be liable for any element of **Loss** incurred, for any obligation assumed, or for any admission made, by any **Insured** without the Company's prior written consent. Provided the **Insureds** comply with Subsections 16(c) and (d) below, the Company shall not unreasonably withhold any such consent.

(c)   With respect to any **Claim** that appears reasonably likely to be covered in whole or in part under this coverage section, the Company shall have the right and shall be given the opportunity to effectively associate with the **Insureds**, and shall be consulted in advance by the **Insureds**, regarding the investigation, defense and settlement of such **Claim**, including but not limited to selecting appropriate defense counsel and negotiating any settlement.

Executive Protection Portfolio ^{SM}
*Executive Liability and Entity Securities
Liability Coverage Section*

(d) The **Insureds** agree to provide the Company with all information, assistance and cooperation which the Company may reasonably require and agree that in the event of a **Claim** the **Insureds** will do nothing that could prejudice the Company's position or its potential or actual rights of recovery.

(e) Any advancement of **Defense Costs** shall be repaid to the Company by the **Insureds**, severally according to their respective interests, if and to the extent it is determined that such **Defense Costs** are not insured under this coverage section.

Allocation

17. (a) If in any **Securities Claim** the **Insureds** incur both **Loss** that is covered under this coverage section and loss that is not covered under this coverage section, the **Insureds** and the Company shall allocate such amount between covered **Loss** and non-covered loss as follows:

    (i) The portion, if any, of such amount that is in part covered and in part not covered under Insuring Clause 2 shall be allocated in its entirety to covered **Loss**, subject, however, to the applicable Retention and Coinsurance Percentage set forth in Items 4(C) and 3(A) of the Declarations for this coverage section, respectively; and

    (ii) The portion, if any, of such amount that is in part covered and in part not covered under Insuring Clause 1 or 3 shall be allocated between covered **Loss** and non-covered loss based on the relative legal and financial exposures of the **Insureds** to covered and non-covered matters and, in the event of a settlement in such **Securities Claim**, based also on the relative benefits to the **Insureds** from settlement of the covered matters and from settlement of the non-covered matters; provided that the amount so allocated to covered **Loss** under Insuring Clause 3 shall be subject to the Retention and Coinsurance Percentage set forth in Items 4(C) and 3(A) of the Declarations for this coverage section, respectively.

    The Company shall not be liable under this coverage section for the portion of such amount allocated to non-covered loss. The allocation described in (i) above shall be final and binding on the Company and the **Insureds** under Insuring Clause 2, but shall not apply to any allocation under Insuring Clauses 1 and 3.

    (b) If in any **Claim** other than a **Securities Claim** the **Insured Persons** incur both **Loss** that is covered under this coverage section and loss that is not covered under this coverage section, either because such **Claim** includes both covered and non-covered matters or because such **Claim** is made against both **Insured Persons** and others (including the **Organization**), the **Insureds** and the Company shall allocate such amount between covered **Loss** and non-covered loss based on the relative legal and financial exposures of the parties to covered and non-covered matters and, in the event of a settlement in such **Claim**, based also on the relative benefits to the parties from such settlement. The Company shall not be liable under this coverage section for the portion of such amount allocated to non-covered loss.

    (c) If the **Insureds** and the Company agree on an allocation of **Defense Costs**, the Company shall advance on a current basis **Defense Costs** allocated to the covered **Loss**. If the **Insureds** and the Company cannot agree on an allocation:

(i)   no presumption as to allocation shall exist in any arbitration, suit or other proceeding;

(ii)   the Company shall advance on a current basis **Defense Costs** which the Company believes to be covered under this coverage section until a different allocation is negotiated, arbitrated or judicially determined; and

(iii)   the Company, if requested by the **Insureds**, shall submit the dispute to binding arbitration. The rules of the American Arbitration Association shall apply except with respect to the selection of the arbitration panel, which shall consist of one arbitrator selected by the **Insureds**, one arbitrator selected by the Company, and a third independent arbitrator selected by the first two arbitrators.

(d)   Any negotiated, arbitrated or judicially determined allocation of **Defense Costs** on account of a **Claim** shall be applied retroactively to all **Defense Costs** on account of such **Claim**, notwithstanding any prior advancement to the contrary. Any allocation or advancement of **Defense Costs** on account of a **Claim** shall not apply to or create any presumption with respect to the allocation of other **Loss** on account of such **Claim**.

Other Insurance

18.   If any **Loss** under this coverage section is insured under any other valid insurance policy(ies), then this coverage section shall cover such **Loss**, subject to its limitations, conditions, provisions and other terms, only to the extent that the amount of such **Loss** is in excess of the applicable retention (or deductible) and limit of liability under such other insurance, whether such other insurance is stated to be primary, contributory, excess, contingent or otherwise, unless such other insurance is written only as specific excess insurance over the Limits of Liability provided in this coverage section. Any payment by **Insureds** of a retention or deductible under such other insurance shall reduce, by the amount of such payment which would otherwise have been covered under this coverage section, the applicable Retention under this coverage section.

Payment of Loss

19.   In the event payment of **Loss** is due under this coverage section but the amount of such **Loss** in the aggregate exceeds the remaining available Limit of Liability for this coverage section, the Company shall:

(a)   first pay such **Loss** for which coverage is provided under Insuring Clause 1 of this coverage section; then

(b)   to the extent of any remaining amount of the Limit of Liability available after payment under (a) above, pay such **Loss** for which coverage is provided under any other Insuring Clause of this coverage section.

Except as otherwise provided in this Subsection 19, the Company may pay covered **Loss** as it becomes due under this coverage section without regard to the potential for other future payment obligations under this coverage section.

Changes in Exposure

Acquisition /Creation of Another Organization

20.   If before or during the **Policy Period** any **Organization**:

(a)   acquires securities or voting rights in another organization or creates another organization, which as a result of such acquisition or creation becomes a **Subsidiary**; or

(b)   acquires another organization by merger into or consolidation with an **Organization** such that the **Organization** is the surviving entity,

such other organization and its **Insured Persons** shall be **Insureds** under this coverage section, but only with respect to **Wrongful Acts** committed, attempted, or allegedly committed or attempted after such acquisition or creation unless the Company agrees, after presentation of a complete application and all other appropriate information, to provide coverage by endorsement for **Wrongful Acts** committed, attempted, or allegedly committed or attempted by such **Insureds** before such acquisition or creation.

If the total assets of any such acquired organization or new **Subsidiary** exceed ten percent (10%) of the total assets of the **Parent Organization** (as reflected in the most recent audited consolidated financial statements of such organization and the **Parent Organization**, respectively, as of the date of such acquisition or creation), the **Parent Organization** shall give written notice of such acquisition or creation to the Company as soon as practicable, but in no event later than sixty (60) days after the date of such acquisition or creation, together with such other information as the Company may require and shall pay any reasonable additional premium required by the Company. If the **Parent Organization** fails to give such notice within the time specified in the preceding sentence, or fails to pay the additional premium required by the Company, coverage for such acquired or created organization and its **Insured Persons** shall terminate with respect to **Claims** first made more than sixty (60) days after such acquisition or creation. Coverage for any acquired or created organization described in this paragraph, and for the **Insured Persons** of such organization, shall be subject to such additional or different terms, conditions and limitations of coverage as the Company in its sole discretion may require.

Acquisition by Another Organization

21.   If:

(a)   the **Parent Organization** merges into or consolidates with another organization and the **Parent Organization** is not the surviving entity; or

(b)   another organization or person or group of organizations and/or persons acting in concert acquires securities or voting rights which result in ownership or voting control by the other organization(s) or person(s) of more than fifty percent (50%) of the outstanding securities or voting rights representing the present right to vote for the election of or to appoint directors or **Managers** of the **Parent Organization**,

coverage under this coverage section shall continue until termination of this coverage section, but only with respect to **Claims** for **Wrongful Acts** committed, attempted, or allegedly committed or attempted by **Insureds** before such merger, consolidation or acquisition. Upon the occurrence of any event described in (a) or (b) of this Subsection 21, the entire premium for this coverage section shall be deemed fully earned.

The **Parent Organization** shall give written notice of such merger, consolidation or acquisition to the Company as soon as practicable, but in no event later than sixty (60) days after the date of such merger, consolidation or acquisition, together with such other information as the Company may require. Upon receipt of such notice and information and at the request of the **Parent Organization**, the Company shall provide to the **Parent Organization** a quotation for an extension of coverage (for such period as may be negotiated between the Company and the **Parent Organization**) with respect to **Claims** for **Wrongful Acts** committed, attempted, or allegedly committed or attempted by **Insureds** before such merger, consolidation or acquisition. Any coverage extension pursuant to such quotation shall be subject to such additional or different terms, conditions and limitations of coverage, and payment of such additional premium, as the Company in its sole discretion may require.

Cessation of Subsidiary

22. In the event an organization ceases to be a **Subsidiary** before or during the **Policy Period**, coverage with respect to such **Subsidiary** and its **Insured Persons** shall continue until termination of this coverage section, but only with respect to **Claims** for **Wrongful Acts** committed, attempted, or allegedly committed or attempted while such organization was a **Subsidiary**.

Related Entity Public Offering

23. If any **Organization** files or causes to be filed, with the United States Securities and Exchange Commission or an equivalent agency or government department in any country other than the United States of America, any registration statement in contemplation of a public offering of equity securities by any entity other than the **Parent Organization** (irrespective of whether such public offering is an initial public offering or a secondary or other offering subsequent to an initial public offering), then the Company shall not be liable for **Loss** on account of any **Claim** based upon, arising from, or in consequence of such registration statement or the sale, offer to sell, distribution or issuance of any securities pursuant to such registration statement, unless (i) the Company receives written notice at least thirty (30) days prior to the effective date of such registration statement providing full details of the contemplated offering, and (ii) the Company, in its sole discretion, agrees by written endorsement to this coverage section to provide coverage for such **Claims** upon such terms and conditions, subject to such limitations and other provisions, and for such additional premium as the Company may require. If the Company in its sole discretion agrees to provide coverage for such **Claims**, the additional premium specified by the Company shall be payable to the Company in full not later than the date on which such registration statement becomes effective.

Representations and Severability

24. In issuing this coverage section the Company has relied upon the statements, representations and information in the **Application**. All of the **Insureds** acknowledge and agree that all such statements, representations and information (i) are true and accurate, (ii) were made or provided in order to induce the Company to issue this coverage section,

14-02-7303 (Ed. 11/2002)   Page 17 of 18

and (iii) are material to the Company's acceptance of the risk to which this coverage section applies.

In the event that any of the statements, representations or information in the **Application** are not true and accurate, this coverage section shall be void with respect to (i) any **Insured** who knew as of the effective date of the **Application** the facts that were not truthfully and accurately disclosed (whether or not the **Insured** knew of such untruthful disclosure in the **Application**) or to whom knowledge of such facts is imputed, and (ii) the **Organization** under Insuring Clause 2 to the extent it indemnifies an **Insured Person** who had such actual or imputed knowledge. For purposes of the preceding sentence:

(a)   the knowledge of any **Insured Person** who is a past, present or future chief financial officer, in-house general counsel, chief executive officer, president or chairperson of an **Organization** shall be imputed to such **Organization** and its **Subsidiaries**;

(b)   the knowledge of the person(s) who signed the **Application** for this coverage section shall be imputed to all of the **Insureds**; and

(c)   except as provided in (a) above, the knowledge of an **Insured Person** who did not sign the **Application** shall not be imputed to any other **Insured**.

SPECIMEN

EMPLOYMENT-RELATED PRACTICES LIABILITY
EP 00 01 11 09

EMPLOYMENT-RELATED PRACTICES LIABILITY COVERAGE FORM

THIS FORM PROVIDES CLAIMS-MADE AND REPORTED COVERAGE.
PLEASE READ THE ENTIRE FORM CAREFULLY.

Various provisions in this policy restrict coverage. Read the entire policy carefully to determine rights, duties and what is and is not covered.

Throughout this policy the words "you" and "your" refer to the Named Insured shown in the Declarations, and any other person or organization qualifying as a Named Insured under this policy. The words "we", "us" and "our" refer to the company providing this insurance.

The word "insured" means any person or organization qualifying as such under Section **II** – Who Is An Insured.

Other words and phrases that appear in quotation marks have special meaning. Refer to Section **VII** – Definitions.

SECTION I – EMPLOYMENT-RELATED PRACTICES LIABILITY COVERAGE

A. Insuring Agreement

1. We will pay those sums the insured becomes legally obligated to pay as damages resulting from a "wrongful act" to which this insurance applies. We will have the right and duty to defend the insured against any "suit" seeking those damages. However, we will have no duty to defend the insured against any "suit" seeking damages because of a "wrongful act" to which this insurance does not apply. We may, at our discretion, investigate any incident that may result from a "wrongful act". We may, with your written consent, settle any "claim" that may result. But:

   a. The amount we will pay for damages and "defense expenses" is limited as described in Section **III** – Limit Of Insurance and in Section **IV** – Deductible; and

   b. The coverage and duty to defend provided by this policy will end when we have used up the applicable limit of insurance for "defense expenses" or the payment of judgments or settlements.

   No other obligation or liability to pay sums, such as civil or criminal fines, imposed on you or any other insured, or to perform acts or services is covered unless explicitly provided for under Supplementary Payments.

2. This insurance applies to "wrongful acts" only if:

   a. The "wrongful act" takes place in the "coverage territory";

   b. The "wrongful act" did not commence before the Retroactive Date, if any, shown in the Declarations or after the end of the policy period; and

   c. A "claim" against any insured for damages because of the "wrongful act" is first made during the policy period or the Section **VI** – Extended Reporting Period, if provided, in accordance with Paragraphs **3.** and **4.** below.

3. A "claim" will be deemed to have been made at the earlier of the following times:

   a. When notice of such "claim", after being received by any insured, is reported to us in writing; or

   b. When a claim against an insured is made directly to us in writing.

   A "claim" received by the insured during the policy period and reported to us within 30 days after the end of the policy period will be considered to have been reported within the policy period. However, this 30-day grace period does not apply to "claims" that are covered under any subsequent insurance you purchase, or that would be covered but for exhaustion of the amount of insurance applicable to such "claims".

4. If during the policy period you become aware of a "wrongful act" that may reasonably be expected to give rise to a "claim" against any insured, you must provide notice to us in accordance with the provisions of Section **V**, Condition **C.** Duties In The Event Of A Claim Or Wrongful Act That May Result In A Claim. If such notice is provided, then any "claim" subsequently made against any insured arising out of that "wrongful act" shall be deemed under this policy to be a "claim" made during the policy period in which the "wrongful act" was first reported to us.

Misc. Commercial

5. All "claims" for damages because of a "wrongful act" committed against the same person, including damages claimed by any person for care, loss of services or death resulting at any time from the "wrongful act", will be deemed to have been made at the time the first of such "claims" is made, regardless of the number of "claims" subsequently made.

B. Exclusions

This insurance does not apply to:

1. Criminal, Fraudulent Or Malicious Acts

An insured's liability arising out of criminal, fraudulent or malicious acts or omissions by that insured.

This exclusion does not affect our duty to defend, in accordance with Paragraph **A.1.** above, an insured prior to determining, through the appropriate legal processes, that that insured is responsible for a criminal, fraudulent or malicious act or omission.

2. Contractual Liability

Any "wrongful act" for which the insured is obligated to pay damages by reason of the assumption of liability in a contract or agreement. This exclusion does not apply to liability for damages that the insured would have in the absence of the contract or agreement.

3. Workers' Compensation And Similar Laws

Any obligation of the insured under a workers' compensation, disability benefits or unemployment compensation law or any similar law.

4. Violation Of Laws Applicable To Employers

A violation of your responsibilities or duties required by any other federal, state or local statutes, rules or regulations, and any rules or regulations promulgated therefor or amendments thereto, except for the following, and including amendments thereto: Title VII of the Civil Rights Act of 1964, the Americans With Disabilities Act, the Age Discrimination in Employment Act, the Equal Pay Act, the Pregnancy Discrimination Act of 1978, the Immigration Reform and Control Act of 1986, the Family and Medical Leave Act of 1993 and the Genetic Information Nondiscrimination Act of 2008 or any other similar state or local statutes, rules or regulations to the extent that they prescribe responsibilities or duties concerning the same acts or omissions.

However, this insurance does not apply to a "wrongful act" arising out of your failure to comply with any of the accommodations for the disabled required of you by, or any expenses incurred as the result of physical modifications made to accommodate any person pursuant to, the Americans With Disabilities Act, or any amendments thereto, or any similar state or local statutes, rules or regulations to the extent that they prescribe responsibilities or duties concerning the same acts or omissions.

This Exclusion **4.** does not apply to any "claim" for retaliatory treatment by an insured against any person making a "claim" pursuant to such person's rights under any statutes, rules or regulations.

5. Strikes And Lockouts

Any "wrongful act" committed against any striking or locked-out "employee", or to an "employee" who has been temporarily or permanently replaced due to any labor dispute.

6. Prior Or Pending Litigation

Any "claim" or "suit" against any insured which was pending on, or existed prior to, the applicable Pending or Prior Litigation Date shown in the Declarations, or any "claim" or "suit" arising out of the same or substantially the same facts, circumstances or allegations which are the subject of, or the basis for, such "claim" or "suit".

7. Prior Notice

Any "wrongful act" alleged or contained in any "claim" which has been reported, or for which, in any circumstance, notice has been given, under any other prior insurance policy providing essentially the same type of coverage.

C. Supplementary Payments

We will pay, with respect to any "claim" we investigate or settle, or any "suit" against an insured we defend:

1. Prejudgment interest awarded against the insured on that part of the judgment we pay. If we make an offer to pay the applicable limit of insurance, we will not pay any prejudgment interest based on that period of time after the offer.

2. All interest on the full amount of any judgment that accrues after entry of the judgment and before we have paid, offered to pay, or deposited in court the part of the judgment that is within the applicable limit of insurance.

These payments will not reduce the limit of insurance nor be subject to Section **IV** – Deductible.

SECTION II – WHO IS AN INSURED

A. If you are designated in the Declarations as:

1. An individual, you and your spouse are insureds.

2. A partnership or joint venture, you are an insured. Your partners or members are also insureds.

3. A limited liability company, you are an insured. Your members and managers are also insureds.

4. An organization other than a partnership, joint venture or limited liability company, you are an insured. Your "executive officers" and directors are also insureds.

B. Your "employees" are also insureds, unless otherwise excluded in this policy.

C. Your former "employees" are also insureds, unless otherwise excluded in this policy, but only with respect to "wrongful acts" committed while in your employ.

D. Any organization you newly acquire or form, other than a partnership, joint venture or limited liability company, and over which you maintain ownership or majority interest, will qualify as a Named Insured if no other similar insurance applies to that organization. You must notify us of such acquisition or formation as soon as practicable. However, coverage under this provision:

1. Is afforded only until the 90th day after you acquire or form the organization, or until the end of the policy period, whichever is earlier; and

2. Does not apply to a "wrongful act" committed before you acquired or formed the organization.

No person or organization is an insured with respect to the conduct of any current or past partnership, joint venture or limited liability company that is not shown as a Named Insured in the Declarations.

SECTION III – LIMIT OF INSURANCE

A. The Limit of Insurance shown in the Declarations and the rules below fix the most we will pay regardless of the number of:

1. Insureds;

2. "Claims" made or "suits" brought; or

3. Persons, organizations or government agencies making "claims" or bringing "suits".

B. The Limit of Insurance is the most we will pay for the sum of:

1. All damages; and

2. All "defense expenses"

because of all "wrongful acts" to which this insurance applies.

The Limit of Insurance of this Coverage Part applies separately to each consecutive annual period and to any remaining period of less than 12 months, starting with the beginning of the policy period shown in the Declarations, unless the policy period is extended after issuance for an additional period of less than 12 months. In that case, the additional period will be deemed part of the last preceding period for purposes of determining the Limit of Insurance.

SECTION IV – DEDUCTIBLE

A. We will not pay for our share of damages and "defense expenses" until the amount of damages and "defense expenses" exceeds the Deductible shown in the Declarations. We will then pay the amount of damages and "defense expenses" in excess of the Deductible, up to the limit of insurance.

Example No. 1

Deductible: $5,000

Limit of Insurance: $100,000

Damages and "Defense Expenses": $75,000

The Deductible will be subtracted from the amount of damages and "defense expenses" in calculating the amount payable:

$75,000 - $5,000 = $70,000 Amount Payable

Example No. 2

Deductible: $5,000

Limit of Insurance: $100,000

Damages and "Defense Expenses": $120,000

The Deductible will be subtracted from the amount of damages and "defense expenses" ($120,000 - $5,000 = $115,000). Since the amount of the damages and "defense expenses" minus the Deductible exceeds the Limit of Insurance, the policy will pay the full Limit of Insurance ($100,000).

B. The Deductible amount shown in the Declarations applies to all "claims" arising out of:

1. The same "wrongful acts"; or

2. A series of incidents, circumstances or behaviors which arise from a common cause

regardless of the number of persons, organizations or government agencies making such "claims".

C. We may pay any part or all of the Deductible amount to effect settlement of any "claim" and, upon notification of the action taken, you shall promptly reimburse us for such part of the Deductible amount as has been paid by us.

Misc. Commercial

SECTION V – CONDITIONS

A. Bankruptcy

Bankruptcy or insolvency of the insured or of the insured's estate will not relieve us of our obligations under this policy.

B. Consent To Settle

If we recommend a settlement to you which is acceptable to the claimant, but to which you do not consent, the most we will pay as damages in the event of any later settlement or judgment is the amount for which the "claim" could have been settled, to which you did not give consent, less any deductible.

C. Duties In The Event Of A Claim Or Wrongful Act That May Result In A Claim

1. If a "claim" is received by any insured, you must:

   a. Immediately record the specifics of the "claim" and the date received; and

   b. Notify us, in writing, as soon as practicable.

2. You and any other involved insured must:

   a. Immediately send us copies of any demands, notices, summonses or legal papers received in connection with the "claim";

   b. Authorize us to obtain records and other information;

   c. Cooperate with us in the investigation or settlement of the "claim" or defense against the "suit"; and

   d. Assist us, upon our request, in the enforcement of any right against any person or organization which may be liable to the insured because of a "wrongful act" to which this insurance may also apply.

3. No insured will, except at that insured's own cost, voluntarily make a payment, assume any obligation, or incur any expense without our written consent.

4. If you become aware of a "wrongful act" that may reasonably be expected to give rise to a "claim" and for which a "claim" has not yet been received, you must notify us, in writing, as soon as practicable. Such notice must provide:

   a. A description of the "wrongful act", including all relevant dates;

   b. The names of the persons involved in the "wrongful act", including names of the potential claimants;

   c. Particulars as to the reasons why you became aware of and reasonably expect a "claim" which may result from such "wrongful act";

   d. The nature of the alleged or potential damages arising from such "wrongful act"; and

   e. The circumstances by which the insured first became aware of the "wrongful act".

D. Legal Action Against Us

No person or organization has a right under this policy:

1. To join us as a party or otherwise bring us into a "suit" asking for damages from an insured; or

2. To sue us on this policy unless all of its terms have been fully complied with.

A person or organization may sue us to recover on an agreed settlement or on a final judgment against an insured obtained after an actual trial; but we will not be liable for damages that are not payable under the terms of this policy or that are in excess of the applicable limit of insurance. An agreed settlement means a settlement and release of liability signed by us, the insured and the claimant or the claimant's legal representative.

We will also not be liable for the insured's share of any payment due because of a settlement or judgment for which the insured is responsible under Section **IV** – Deductible.

E. Other Insurance

If other valid and collectible insurance is available to the insured, our obligations are limited as follows:

1. **Primary Insurance**

   This insurance is primary. We will not seek contribution from any other insurance available to you or the involved insured unless the other insurance is specifically designed to provide coverage because of liability arising out of a "wrongful act". Then we will share with that other insurance by the method described below.

2. **Method Of Sharing**

   If all of the other insurance permits contribution by equal shares, we will follow this method also. Under this approach each insurer contributes equal amounts until it has paid its applicable limit of insurance or none of the liability remains, whichever comes first.

If any of the other insurance does not permit contribution by equal shares, we will contribute by limits. Under this method, each insurer's share is based on the ratio of its applicable limit of insurance to the total applicable limits of insurance of all insurers.

The method chosen for the handling of other valid insurance will not affect your responsibility to share with us as specified under Section **IV** – Deductible.

F. Premium Audit

1. We will compute all premiums for this policy in accordance with our rules and rates.

2. Premium shown in this policy as advance premium is a deposit premium only. At the close of each audit period we will compute the earned premium for that period and send notice to the first Named Insured. The due date for audit premiums is the date shown as the due date on the bill. If the sum of the advance and audit premiums paid for the policy period is greater than the earned premium, we will return the excess to the first Named Insured.

3. The first Named Insured must keep records of the information we need for premium computation and send us copies at such times as we may request.

4. We will waive the premium audit only with your consent.

G. Representations

By accepting this policy, you agree that:

1. The statements in the Declarations are accurate and complete;

2. Those statements are based upon representations you made to us; and

3. We have issued this policy in reliance upon your representations.

H. Separation Of Insureds

Except with respect to the Limit of Insurance, and any rights or duties specifically assigned in this policy to the first Named Insured, this insurance applies:

1. As if each Named Insured were the only Named Insured; and

2. Separately to each insured against whom "claim" is made.

I. Transfer Of Rights Of Recovery Against Others To Us

If the insured has rights to recover all or part of any payment we have made under this policy, those rights are transferred to us. The insured must do nothing to impair those rights. At our request, the insured will bring "suit" or transfer those rights to us and help us enforce them.

J. If You Are Permitted To Select Defense Counsel

If, by mutual agreement or court order, the insured is given the right to select defense counsel and the Limit of Insurance has not been used up, the following provisions apply:

1. We retain the right, at our discretion, to:

   a. Settle, approve or disapprove the settlement of any "claim"; and

   b. Appeal any judgment, award or ruling at our expense.

2. You and any other involved insured must:

   a. Continue to comply with Section **V** – Paragraph **C.** Duties In The Event Of A Claim Or Wrongful Act That May Result In A Claim Condition as well as the other provisions of this policy; and

   b. Direct defense counsel of the insured to:

      (1) Furnish us with the information we may request to evaluate those "suits" for coverage under this policy; and

      (2) Cooperate with any counsel we may select to monitor or associate in the defense of those "suits".

3. If we defend you under a reservation of rights, both your and our counsel will be required to maintain records pertinent to your "defense expenses". These records will be used to determine the allocation of any "defense expenses" for which you may be solely responsible, including defense of an allegation not covered by this insurance.

K. Transfer Of Duties When Limit Of Insurance Is Used Up

1. If we conclude that, based on "claims" which have been reported to us and to which this insurance may apply, the Limit of Insurance is likely to be used up in the payment of judgments or settlements for damages or the payment of "defense expenses", we will notify the first Named Insured, in writing, to that effect.

2. When the Limit of Insurance has actually been used up in the payment of judgments or settlements for damages or the payment of "defense expenses", we will:

   a. Notify the first Named Insured in writing, as soon as practicable, that such a limit has actually been used up, and that our duty to defend the insured against "suits" seeking damages subject to that limit has also ended;

   b. Initiate, and cooperate in, the transfer of control, to any appropriate insured, of all "suits" for which the duty to defend has ended for the reason described in Paragraph **2.a.** above and which are reported to us before that duty to defend ended; and

   c. Take such steps, as we deem appropriate, to avoid a default in, or continue the defense of, such "suits" until such transfer is completed, provided the appropriate insured is cooperating in completing such transfer.

3. When **2.a.** above has occurred, the first Named Insured, and any other insured involved in a "suit" seeking damages subject to that limit, must:

   a. Cooperate in the transfer of control of "suits"; and

   b. Arrange for the defense of such "suit" within such time period as agreed to between the appropriate insured and us. Absent any such agreement, arrangements for the defense of such "suit" must be made as soon as practicable.

4. We will take no action with respect to defense for any "claim" if such "claim" is reported to us after the applicable limit of insurance has been used up. It becomes the responsibility of the first Named Insured, and any other insured involved in such a "claim", to arrange defense for such "claim".

5. The first Named Insured will reimburse us as soon as practicable for expenses we incur in taking those steps we deem appropriate in accordance with Paragraph **2.** above.

6. The exhaustion of the applicable limit of insurance and the resulting end of our duty to defend will not be affected by our failure to comply with any of the provisions of this Condition.

L. When We Do Not Renew

If we decide not to renew this policy, we will mail or deliver to the first Named Insured shown in the Declarations written notice of the nonrenewal at least 30 days before the end of the policy period, or earlier if required by the state law or regulation controlling the application of this Coverage Part.

If notice is mailed, proof of mailing will be sufficient proof of notice.

SECTION VI – EXTENDED REPORTING PERIOD

A. You will have the right to purchase an Extended Reporting Period from us if:

   1. This Coverage Part is cancelled or not renewed for any reason; or

   2. We renew or replace this Coverage Part with insurance that:

      a. Has a Retroactive Date later than the date shown in the Declarations of this Coverage Part; or

      b. Does not apply to "wrongful acts" on a claims-made basis.

B. An Extended Reporting Period, as specified in Paragraph **A.** above, lasts three years and is available only by endorsement and for an additional charge.

C. The Extended Reporting Period starts with the end of the policy period. It does not extend the policy period or change the scope of coverage provided. It applies only to "claims" to which the following applies:

   1. The "claim" is first made during the Extended Reporting Period;

   2. The "wrongful act" occurs before the end of the policy period; and

   3. The "wrongful act" did not commence before the Retroactive Date, if any.

D. You must give us a written request for the Extended Reporting Period Endorsement within 30 days after the end of the policy period or the effective date of cancellation, whichever comes first.

E. The Extended Reporting Period will not go into effect unless you pay the additional premium promptly when due and any premium or deductible you owe us for coverage provided under this policy. Once in effect, the Extended Reporting Period may not be cancelled.

F. We will determine the additional premium in accordance with our rules and rates. In doing so, we may take into account the following:

1. The exposures insured;

2. Previous types and amounts of insurance;

3. Limit of Insurance available under this policy for future payment of damages; and

4. Other related factors.

The additional premium will not exceed 200% of the annual premium for this policy.

G. When the Extended Reporting Period Endorsement is in effect, we will provide a Supplemental Limit of Insurance for any "claim" first made during the Extended Reporting Period.

The Supplemental Limit of Insurance will be equal to the dollar amount shown in the Declarations in effect at the end of the policy period.

Paragraph **B.** of Section **III** – Limit Of Insurance will be amended accordingly.

SECTION VII – DEFINITIONS

A. "Claim" means a "suit" or demand made by or for a current, former or prospective "employee" for damages because of an alleged "wrongful act".

B. "Coverage territory" means:

1. The United States of America (including its territories or possessions) and Puerto Rico; or

2. All parts of the world if the insured's responsibility to pay damages is determined in a "suit" on the merits brought in the territory described in Paragraph **1.** above or in a settlement we agree to.

C. "Defense expenses" means payments allocated to a specific "claim" we investigate, settle or defend, for its investigation, settlement or defense, including:

1. Fees and salaries of attorneys and paralegals we retain, including attorneys and paralegals who are our "employees".

2. Fees of attorneys the insured retains when, by our mutual agreement or court order (or when required by administrative hearing or proceeding), the insured is given the right to retain defense counsel to defend against a "claim".

3. All other litigation or administrative hearing expenses, including fees or expenses of expert witnesses hired either by us or by the defense attorney retained by an insured.

4. Reasonable expenses incurred by the insured at our request to assist us in the investigation or defense of the "claim", including actual loss of earnings up to $250 a day because of time off from work.

5. Costs taxed against the insured in the "suit".

"Defense expenses" does not include salaries and expenses of our "employees" or the insured's "employees" (other than those described in Paragraphs **1.** and **4.** above).

D. "Discrimination" means violation of a person's civil rights with respect to such person's race, color, national origin, religion, gender, marital status, age, sexual orientation or preference, physical or mental condition, or any other protected class or characteristic established by any federal, state or local statutes, rules or regulations.

E. "Employee" includes a "leased worker" and a "temporary worker" but does not include an independent contractor.

F. "Executive officer" means a person holding any of the officer positions created by your charter, constitution, by-laws or any other similar governing document.

G. "Leased worker" means a person leased to you by a labor leasing firm under an agreement between you and the labor leasing firm to perform duties related to the conduct of your business. "Leased worker" does not include a "temporary worker".

H. "Suit" means a civil proceeding in which damages because of a "wrongful act" to which this insurance applies are alleged, including:

1. An arbitration proceeding in which such damages are claimed and to which the insured must submit or does submit with our consent;

2. Any other alternative dispute resolution proceeding in which such damages are claimed and to which the insured submits with our consent; or

3. Any administrative proceeding or hearing conducted by a governmental agency (federal, state or local) having the proper legal authority over the matter in which such damages are claimed.

I. "Temporary worker" means a person who is furnished to you to substitute for a permanent "employee" on leave or to meet seasonal or short-term workload conditions.

J. "Wrongful act" means one or more of the following offenses, but only when they are employment-related:

1. Wrongful demotion or failure to promote, negative evaluation, reassignment or discipline of your current "employee" or wrongful refusal to employ;

2. Wrongful termination, meaning the actual or constructive termination of an "employee":

a. In violation or breach of applicable law or public policy; or

    b. Which is determined to be in violation of a contract or agreement, other than any employment contract or agreement, whether written, oral or implied, which stipulates financial consideration if such financial consideration is due as the result of a breach of the contract;

3. Wrongful denial of training, wrongful deprivation of career opportunity or breach of employment contract;

4. Negligent hiring or supervision which results in any of the other offenses listed in this definition;

5. Retaliatory action against an "employee" because the "employee" has:

    a. Declined to perform an illegal or unethical act;

    b. Filed a complaint with a governmental authority or a "suit" against you or any other insured in which damages are claimed;

    c. Testified against you or any other insured at a legal proceeding; or

    d. Notified a proper authority of any aspect of your business operation which is illegal;

6. Coercing an "employee" to commit an unlawful act or omission within the scope of that person's employment;

7. Harassment;

8. Libel, slander, invasion of privacy, defamation or humiliation; or

9. Verbal, physical, mental or emotional abuse arising from "discrimination".

EP 00 01 11 09   □

EVANSTON INSURANCE COMPANY

Policy No.
Prev. No.
Prod. No.

DECLARATIONS - PHYSICIANS, SURGEONS, DENTISTS AND PODIATRISTS PROFESSIONAL LIABILITY INSURANCE

Claims Made Policy: This policy is limited to liability for only those CLAIMS THAT ARE FIRST MADE AGAINST THE INSURED DURING THE POLICY PERIOD OR THE EXTENDED REPORTING PERIOD, if exercised. Please review the policy carefully.

1.   **NAMED INSURED:**

(a) Coverage A.: Individual Liability Coverage:

(b) Coverage B.: Association, Corporation or Partnership Liability Coverage:

2.   **BUSINESS ADDRESS OF THE INSURED:**

3.   **PROFESSIONAL SPECIALTY OF THE INSURED:**

4.   **POLICY PERIOD:**   From   to
                             12:01 A.M. Standard Time at address of Insured stated above.

5.   **RETROACTIVE DATE:**

6.   **COVERAGE AND LIMITS OF LIABILITY:**

COVERAGE A.:   (a) Each Claim, Each Insured: $

                  (b) Aggregate For All Claims, Each Insured: $

COVERAGE B.:   (c) Each Claim, Each Insured: $

                  (d) Aggregate For All Claims, Each Insured: $

COVERAGE A. OR COVERAGE B. OR BOTH COMBINED:
                  (e) Single Per Patient Claim, All Insureds: $

COVERAGE A. AND COVERAGE B. POLICY LIMIT:
                  (f)   Subject to the limits above, the Total Aggregate Limit
                        of Liability for the Policy Period, including the Extended
                        Reporting Period, for All Claims, All Insureds: $

SUPPLEMENTARY PAYMENTS:
                  (g) Trial Attendance Supplementary Payments: $ per diem

7.   **DEDUCTIBLE:**

COVERAGE A. and B.:
                  (a) Applicable to each claim, including claim expenses: $

SUPPLEMENTARY PAYMENTS:
                  (b) $

8.   **PREMIUM FOR POLICY PERIOD:** $

Page 1

Policy No. XX-000000

9. **EXTENDED REPORTING PERIOD:**

    12 months at 150% of the full annual premium; 24 months for 200% of the full annual premium; or 36 months at 250% of the full annual premium

10. The Insured is not a proprietor, superintendent, executive officer, director, partner, or trustee of any hospital, sanitarium, clinic with bed-and-board facilities, laboratory, or any business enterprise and not named in Item 1 hereinabove, except as follows:

    None

11. **ENDORSEMENTS ATTACHED AT POLICY INCEPTION:**

12. **NOTICES:**

    Notices required to be provided to the Company under this policy shall be addressed to:

    CLAIM OR DISCOVERY CLAUSE NOTICES:

    Claims Service Center
    MARKEL SERVICE, INCORPORATED
    Ten Parkway North
    Deerfield, Illinois 60015

    Fax: (847) 572-6338
    E-mail: newclaims@markelcorp.com
    Phone: (847) 572-6000; (888) 502-3200

    ALL OTHER NOTICES:

    MARKEL MIDWEST
    Ten Parkway North
    Deerfield, IL 60015

    Fax: (866) 730-2526
    Phone: (847) 572-6000

Policy Form: SPECIMEN
Dec: MM-10003 08/09
Date Printed: December 2, 2010

SPECIMEN
(Authorized Representative)

Physicians, Surgeons, Dentists and Podiatrists Professional Liability Insurance Policy

THIS IS A CLAIMS MADE POLICY. PLEASE READ IT CAREFULLY.

In consideration of the payment of the premium, the undertaking of the Coverage A. Named Insured authorized to act on behalf of all Insureds to pay the deductible as described herein and in the amount stated in the Declarations, in reliance upon the statements in the application attached hereto and made a part hereof, and subject to the limits of liability shown in the Declarations, and subject to all the terms of this insurance, the Company agrees with the Coverage A. Named Insured and the Coverage B. Named Insured as follows:

THE INSURED

The unqualified word "Insured," either in the singular or plural, means:

A.   under Coverage A. Individual Professional Liability, the Coverage A. Insured which means:

    1.   the Coverage A. Named Insured which is herein defined as each individual stated in Item 1.(a) of the Declarations;

    2.   any Locum Tenens physician, surgeon, dentist or podiatrist utilized by the Coverage A. Named Insured but only to continue the practice on behalf of the Coverage A. Named Insured in his absence;

    3.   any Employee or Volunteer Worker of the Coverage A. Named Insured, but only while acting within the scope of that person's duties on behalf of the Coverage A. Named Insured;

    4.   the heirs, executors, administrators, assigns and legal representatives of each Insured in Items A.1.-3. above in the event of his death, incapacity or bankruptcy.

B.   under Coverage B. Association, Corporation or Partnership Liability, the Coverage B. Insured which means:

    1.   the Coverage B. Named Insured which is herein defined as the association, corporation or partnership if any is stated in Item 1.(b) of the Declarations;

    2.   any member, stockholder or partner of the Coverage B. Named Insured with respect to Malpractice of others, provided that no member, stockholder or partner shall be an Insured under this paragraph B. with respect to liability for his personal acts of a professional nature;

    3.   any Employee or Volunteer Worker of the Coverage B. Named Insured, but only while acting within the scope of that person's duties on behalf of the Coverage B. Named Insured;

    4.   the heirs, executors, administrators, assigns and legal representatives of each Insured in Items B.1.-3. above in the event of his death, incapacity or bankruptcy.

INSURING AGREEMENTS

A.   **Professional Liability and Claims Made Clause:** The Company shall pay on behalf of the Insured all sums in excess of the Deductible amount stated in Item 7. of the Declarations, which the Insured shall become legally obligated to pay as Damages as a result of Claims first made against the Insured during the Policy Period or during the Extended Reporting Period, if exercised, and reported to the Company pursuant to Section Claims A., Claim Reporting Provision:

    1.   under Coverage A. Individual Professional Liability: because of Malpractice or Personal Injury, sustained by a patient and committed by the Coverage A. Named Insured, or by any person for whose Malpractice or Personal Injury the Coverage A. Named Insured is legally responsible, except as a member, stockholder or partner of an association, corporation, or partnership, arising out of the professional activities of the Insured as a medical, podiatric, or dental practitioner;

    2.   under Coverage B. Association, Corporation or Partnership Liability: because of Malpractice or Personal Injury, sustained by a patient and committed by any person for whom the

Reprinted with permission from Markel Corporation

Coverage B. Named Insured is legally responsible, arising out of the practice of medicine, podiatry or dentistry;

Provided:

a.   that such Malpractice or Personal Injury happens during the Policy Period or on or after the Retroactive Date stated in Item 5. of the Declarations and before the end of the Policy Period.

b.   prior to the effective date of this policy the Insured had no knowledge of such Malpractice or Personal Injury or any fact, circumstance, situation or incident which may lead a reasonable person in that Insured's position to conclude that a Claim was likely.

SUPPLEMENTARY PAYMENTS

A.   **Trial Attendance Supplementary Payments:** The Company shall pay a per diem trial attendance allowance to any Coverage A. Named Insured physician, surgeon, dentist or podiatrist who attends the trial, mediation or arbitration of a Claim; but only if (a) the Claim is against the Coverage A. Named Insured physician, surgeon, dentist or podiatrist; and (b) the Claim is covered by this policy; and (c) the Coverage A. Named Insured physician, surgeon, dentist or podiatrist attends the trial, mediation or arbitration at the written request of the Company.

Payments to the Coverage A. Named Insured pursuant to this Section shall be in addition to the Limits of Liability applicable to Coverages A. and B. and shall not be subject to the Deductible.

DEFINITIONS

A.   **Claim** means a demand received by the Insured for monetary damages or services and shall include the service of suit or institution of arbitration proceedings against the Insured.

B.   **Claim Expenses** means reasonable and necessary amounts incurred by the Company or by the Insured with the prior written consent of the Company in the defense of that portion of any Claim for which coverage is afforded under this policy, including costs of investigation, court costs, costs of bonds to release attachments and similar bonds, but without any obligation of the Company to apply for or furnish any such bonds, and costs of appeals; provided, however, Claim Expenses shall not include: (1) salary, wages, overhead, or benefit expenses of or associated with employees or officials of the Coverage A. Named Insured or the Coverage B. Named Insured or employees or officials of the Company; or (2) salary, wages, administration, overhead, benefit expenses, or charges of any kind attributable to any in-house counsel or captive out-of-house counsel for the Coverage A. Named Insured or the Coverage B. Named Insured or the Company.

C.   **Damages** means the monetary portion of any judgment, award or settlement; provided, however, Damages shall not include: (1) punitive or exemplary damages or any multiplied portions of damages in excess of actual damages, including trebling of damages; (2) taxes, criminal or civil fines, or attorneys' fees of a party other than an Insured or other penalties imposed by law; (3) sanctions; (4) matters which are uninsurable under the law pursuant to which this policy shall be construed; or (5) the return, withdrawal, reduction or restitution or payment of fees, profits or charges for services or consideration and/or any expenses paid to the Insured.

D.   **Employee** means any natural person other than (1) an insured physician, Locum Tenens, dentist, podiatrist, psychologist, nurse midwife, nurse anesthetist, anesthesiologist assistant, nurse practitioner, physician's assistant, surgeon's assistant, perfusionist, optometrist; or (2) any person licensed, certified or otherwise authorized to deliver advanced level health care in the absence of direct supervision by a licensed physician, surgeon, dentist or podiatrist; but only while acting within the scope of that person's duties on behalf of the Coverage A. Named Insured or the Coverage B. Named Insured.

E.   **Good Samaritan Act** means emergency health care, emergency medical care, or emergency treatment provided to a patient without compensation or expectation of compensation at the scene of any emergency; and only if provided by a Coverage A. Named Insured other than a Locum Tenens.

F.   **Locum Tenens** means a temporary, substitute physician, surgeon, dentist or podiatrist who has been designated to provide professional services as a replacement of a Coverage A. Named Insured.

G.   **Malpractice** means an act, error or omission: (1) in professional services rendered or that should have been rendered; (2) in rendering a Good Samaritan Act; or (3) in services rendered by a Coverage A. Named Insured as a member of a formal accreditation or similar professional board or committee of a hospital at which he/she is a staff member.

H.   **Personal Injury** means, whenever used in this policy:

1.   any physical or mental injury to or death of any patient;

2.   false arrest, detention, or imprisonment, and malicious prosecution or humiliation except when inflicted by, at the direction of, or with the consent or acquiescence of the Insured who has predetermined to commit such act, or allowed such act to have been committed, without legal justification;

3.   the publication or utterance of a libel or slander or a publication or an utterance in violation of a patient's right to professional confidence, except when published or uttered by, at the direction of, or with the consent or acquiescence of the Insured who has predetermined to commit such act, or allowed such act to have been committed, without legal justification.

I.   **Policy Period** means the period from the inception date of this policy to the policy expiration date as stated in Item 4. of the Declarations, or the effective date of any earlier cancellation or termination.

J.   **Volunteer Worker** means any person who is not an Employee of the Coverage A. Named Insured or the Coverage B. Named Insured and who donates his/her work at the direction of and within the scope of duties determined by the Coverage A. Named Insured or the Coverage B. Named Insured and is not paid a fee, salary or other compensation by the Coverage A. Named Insured or the Coverage B. Named Insured or by anyone else for such work performed for the Coverage A. Named Insured or the Coverage B. Named Insured.

THE EXCLUSIONS

This policy does not apply to:

A.   any Malpractice or Personal Injury committed in violation of any law or ordinance; to any Claim based upon or arising out of any dishonest, fraudulent, criminal, malicious, knowingly, wrongful, deliberate, or intentional acts, errors or omissions committed by or at the direction of the Insured;

B.   any Malpractice or Personal Injury that happens while the Insured's license or certificate to practice the Insured's profession is suspended, surrendered, revoked, expired, terminated, or otherwise not in effect;

C.   any Malpractice or Personal Injury that involves professional services that are outside the scope of the Insured's practice as stated in Item 3. of the Declarations; however, this exclusion will not apply to a Good Samaritan Act that is otherwise covered by this policy;

D.   any Claim based upon or arising out of the invasion of privacy, or the infringement or interference with the right of privacy resulting from the use, visitation of, posting or browsing of any bulletin board services, website or URL location;

E.   any Claim based upon or arising out of the gathering, use or dissemination of personal information in any form including but not limited to any violation of the Health Insurance Portability and Accountability Act of 1996 (HIPAA);

F.   any Claim based upon or arising out of discrimination by the Insured on the basis of race, creed, age, sex, sexual preference, physical handicap or national origin;

G.   any Claim based upon or arising out of any act, error or omission committed or alleged to have been committed by the Insured that in any manner relates to or arises out of the actual, alleged or threatened discharge, dispersal, release, escape or existence of pollutants, hazardous substances, toxic substances or substances which in any manner impair or allegedly impair the environment or which result in bodily injury or property damage;

H.   any liability arising out of the Insured's activities in his capacity as proprietor, superintendent, executive officer, director, partner or trustee of any hospital, sanitarium, clinic with bed-and-board

MM-20000 08/09   Page 3

facilities, laboratory or any business enterprise not named as an Insured under this policy unless such activities are disclosed in the application and listed in Item 10. of the Declarations;

I. any liability of others assumed by the Insured under any contract or agreement, unless such liability would have attached to the Insured even in the absence of such contract or agreement;

J. any Claim arising out of general liability, or goods or products manufactured, sold, handled or distributed by the Insured or by others trading under an Insured's name;

K. any liability arising out of the ownership, maintenance, operation, use, loading or unloading of any vehicle, watercraft or aircraft;

L. any Claim based upon or arising out of: (1) the use of excessive influence or power on any patient; or (2) any actions intended to lead to or culminate in any sexual acts. However, the Company does agree to defend any such Claim, subject to the applicable limits of liability, until a final judgment has been determined; however, if judgment is rendered against the Coverage A. Named Insured, the Coverage A. Named Insured, upon written demand by the Company, agrees to reimburse the Company for all Claim Expenses incurred in the defense of such Claim, within ten (10) days;

M. any Claim which is based upon or arises out of professional services rendered while an Insured was under the influence of alcohol, narcotics, hallucinogenic agents or which involves any other allegation of substance abuse; however, the Company does agree to defend any such Claim, subject to the applicable limits of liability, until a final judgment has been determined; however, if judgment is rendered against the Coverage A. Named Insured, the Coverage A. Named Insured, upon written demand by the Company, agrees to reimburse the Company for all Claim Expenses incurred in the defense of such Claim, within ten (10) days;

N. any obligation for which the Insured or any carrier as his insurer may be held liable under any workers' compensation, unemployment compensation or disability benefits law, or under any similar law;

O. any Claim based upon or arising out of any employment dispute, or to Personal Injury to, or sickness, disease or death of any employee of the Insured arising out of, and in the course of his employment by the Insured;

P. use, administration or prescription of any drug, pharmaceutical, medical device or procedure which has not received final approval by the U. S. Food and Drug Administration (FDA) for treatment of human beings or which is not used, administered or prescribed as part of an FDA approved study;

Q. any Claim based upon or arising out of a warranty or guarantee of cure or success of treatment which is alleged to have arisen out of advertisement;

R. any Claim based upon or arising out of any actual or alleged violation of the Employee Retirement Income Security Act of 1974 (ERISA) and its amendments or any regulation or order issued pursuant thereto or any similar federal, state or local law; or

S. any Claim based upon or arising out of the Racketeer Influenced and Corrupt Organizations Act, 18 U.S.C., Section 1961, et seq.

TERRITORY

The insurance afforded by this policy applies worldwide, provided the Claim is made in the United States of America, its territories or possessions or Puerto Rico.

LIMITS OF LIABILITY

A. **Coverage A. Limit of Liability-Each Claim:** The total liability of the Company under Coverage A. for the combined total of Damages and Claim Expenses for each Claim first made against each Coverage A. Insured during the Policy Period or the Extended Reporting Period, if exercised, shall not exceed the Coverage A. Limit of Liability stated in Item 6.(a) of the Declarations.

B. **Coverage A. Limit of Liability-Aggregate:** Subject to the above Limits of Liability A., the total liability of the Company under Coverage A. shall not exceed the Coverage A. Aggregate Limit of Liability stated in Item 6.(b) of the Declarations for the combined total of Damages and Claim

Expenses arising out of all Claims first made against each Coverage A. Insured during the Policy Period and the Extended Reporting Period, if exercised.

C. **Coverage B. Limit of Liability-Each Claim:** The liability of the Company under Coverage B. for the combined total of Damages and Claim Expenses for each Claim first made against each Coverage B. Insured during the Policy Period or the Extended Reporting Period, if exercised, shall not exceed the amount stated in Item 6.(c) of the Declarations.

D. **Coverage B. Limit of Liability-Aggregate:** Subject to the liability of the Company for each Claim against each Coverage B. Insured, the total liability of the Company under Coverage B. shall not exceed the Coverage B. Aggregate Limit of Liability stated in Item 6(d) of the Declarations for the combined total of Damages and Claim Expenses arising out of all Claims first made against each Coverage B. Insured during the Policy Period and the Extended Reporting Period, if exercised.

E. **Coverage A., Coverage B. & Both Combined:** Subject to A., B., C., and D. above, one or more Claims made against two or more Insureds under Coverage A. or Coverage B. or both combined arising out of Malpractice or Personal Injury sustained by one patient shall be a single patient Claim to which the limit of liability for "Single Per Patient Claim" shall apply to all Insureds. The total liability of the Company shall not exceed the limit applicable to "Single Per Patient Claim" as stated in Item 6.(e) of the Declarations regardless of the number of Insureds against whom Claim is made by or on behalf of one patient. All such Claims, whenever made, shall be deemed to be first made on the date on which the earliest Claim arising out of such Malpractice or Personal Injury is made or with regard to notice given to and accepted by the Company pursuant to Section Claims B., Discovery Clause, on the date within the Policy Period on which such notice of potential Claim is first received by the Company and all such Claims shall be subject to the same "Single Per Patient Claim" limit of liability.

F. **Policy Limit:** Subject to A., B., C., D. and E. above, the total liability of the Company under Coverage A. and Coverage B. shall not exceed the Coverage A. and Coverage B. Policy Limit stated in Item 6.(f) of the Declarations for the combined total of Damages and Claim Expenses for all Claims first made against all Insureds during the Policy Period and the Extended Reporting Period, if exercised.

G. **Trial Attendance Supplementary Payments:** The Company will pay a per diem trial allowance of two hundred fifty dollars ($250) per day to any Coverage A. Named Insured pursuant to the terms stated in Section Supplementary Payments A.

H. **Deductible:**

1. **Coverages A. and B.:** The deductible amount stated in Item 7. of the Declarations shall be paid by the Coverage A. Named Insured and shall be applicable to each Claim and shall include Damages and Claim Expenses, whether or not Damages payments are made.

   Such amounts shall, upon written demand by the Company, be paid by the Coverage A. Named Insured within thirty (30) days. The total payments requested from the Coverage A. Named Insured in respect of each Claim shall not exceed the deductible amount stated in Item 7. of the Declarations.

   The determination of the Company as to the reasonableness of the Claim Expenses shall be conclusive on the Insured.

2. **Supplementary Payments:** No deductible will apply to the coverage afforded under Section Supplementary Payments A.

I. **Apportionment of Losses Against Aggregate Limits:** All sums which the Company pays on behalf of a Coverage B. Insured and one or more Coverage A. Insureds as the result of a Claim or as the result of a notice given to the Company pursuant to Section Claims B., Discovery Clause, shall be apportioned against the Coverage B. Limit of Liability and the Coverage A. Limit of Liability and the respective apportioned amounts shall thereby reduce (1) each aggregate limit of liability applicable under Coverage B. and (2) each aggregate limit of liability applicable under Coverage A. Nothing stated herein shall operate to increase any limit of liability of the Company as stated in Item 6. of the Declarations. Such sums shall be apportioned among the Insureds under this policy as follows:

1. In the event notice is given to the Company pursuant to the Section Claims B., Discovery Clause, or if a Claim is settled or withdrawn prior to judgment, award or verdict, or if a judgment, award or verdict is rendered generally and without regard to the relative culpability of those against whom it is rendered, the Damages and Claim Expenses shall be apportioned, in equal shares against (a) the remaining aggregate limits of liability available under Coverage B. and (b) the remaining aggregate limits of liability available under Coverage A. to each Coverage A. Insured against whom such Claim has been made individually, until each applicable aggregate limit of liability has been exhausted.

2. In the event that subparagraph 1. does not apply and judgment, award or verdict is rendered, the Damages and Claim Expenses shall be apportioned, in such shares as those shares relate to the judgment, award or verdict in the manner of its rendition against each Insured against (a) the remaining aggregate limits of liability available under Coverage B. and (b) the remaining aggregate limits of liability available under Coverage A. to each Coverage A. Insured against whom such judgment, award or verdict has been rendered individually, until each applicable aggregate limit of liability has been exhausted.

J. **Multiple Insureds, Claims and Claimants:**

1. The inclusion herein of more than one Insured or one Insured in multiple capacities or the making of Claims or the bringing of suits by more than one person or organization shall not operate to increase any liability of the Company. Two or more Claims arising out of a single Malpractice or Personal Injury or a series of related Malpractices or Personal Injuries shall be considered a single Claim. All such Claims, whenever made, shall be deemed to be first made on the date on which the earliest Claim arising out of such Malpractice or Personal Injury is made or with regard to notice given to and accepted by the Company pursuant to Section Claims B., Discovery Clause, on the date within the Policy Period on which such notice of potential Claim is first received by the Company.

2. Subject to Sections Limits of Liability A., B., C., D., E. and F. above, and regardless of the number of Claims made, or the number of claimants or the number of Insureds hereunder, two or more Claims made during the Policy Period including any Extended Reporting Period, if exercised, against any one Insured arising out of injuries sustained by any one patient or person as a result of Malpractice or Personal Injury shall constitute a single Claim and the liability of the Company shall not exceed the amount stated in Item 6.(e) of the Declarations.

3. Subject to sections Limits of Liability A., B., C., D., E. and F. above, and regardless of the number of Claims made, or the number of claimants or the number of Insureds hereunder, if one or more Claims are first made during the Policy Period, including any Extended Reporting Period, if exercised, against two or more Insureds arising out of injuries sustained by one patient or person as a result of Malpractice or Personal Injury shall constitute a single Claim and the liability of the Company shall not exceed the amount stated in Item 6.(e) of the Declarations.

4. In the event that a Claim is first made during the Policy Period, including any Extended Reporting Period, if exercised, against an individual in both capacities as described in Coverage A. and Coverage B., a single limit of liability shall apply and, in the event that the Coverage A. and Coverage B. Each Claim, Each Insured limits are not of equal amounts, that limit shall be the greater of the amount stated in Item 6.(a) or 6.(c) of the Declarations.

DEFENSE, SETTLEMENTS AND CLAIM EXPENSES

A. **Defense and Investigation:** The Company shall have the right and duty to defend and investigate any Claim to which coverage under this policy applies pursuant to the following provisions:

1. Claim Expenses incurred in defending and investigating such Claim shall be a part of and shall not be in addition to the applicable Limits of Liability stated in Item 6. of the Declarations. Such Claim Expenses shall reduce the Limits of Liability and shall be applied against the Deductible. The Company shall have no obligation to pay any Damages or to defend or continue to defend any Claim or to pay Claim Expenses after the applicable Limits of Liability stated in Item 6. of the Declarations have been exhausted by payment(s) of Damages and/or Claim Expenses.

MM-20000 08/09   Page 6

2. The Company shall select defense counsel; provided, however, that if the law of the state of the Insured's domicile, stated in Item 2. of the Declarations, allows the Insured to control the selection of defense counsel where a conflict of interest has arisen between the Insured and the Company, the Company will provide a list of attorneys or law firms from which the Insured may designate defense counsel who shall act solely in the interest of the Insured, and the Insured shall direct such defense counsel to cooperate with the Company. Such cooperation shall include:

    (a) providing on a regular basis, but not less frequently than every three (3) months, written reports on claimed Damages, potential liability, progress of any litigation, any settlement demands, or any investigation developments that materially affect the Claim;

    (b) providing any other reasonable information requested;

    (c) fully itemized billing on a periodic basis; and

    (d) cooperating with the Company and the Insured in resolving any discrepancies;

and the fees and costs incurred by such defense counsel, including those fees and costs generated by cooperation with the Company, as set forth above, shall be included in Claim Expenses. Such Claim Expenses shall be a part of and shall not be in addition to the applicable Limits of Liability stated in Item 6. of the Declarations. Such Claim Expenses shall reduce the Limits of Liability and shall be applied against the Deductible.

B. **Consent to Settlement:** The Company shall not settle any Claim without the consent of the applicable Coverage A. Named Insured(s). If the Insured is an association, corporation or partnership, the written consent of an Insured who was formerly but is no longer a member, stockholder, or partner of the Coverage B. Named Insured will not be required, provided the written consent of the first Coverage A Named Insured named in Item 1. of the Declarations has been obtained. If, however, the Insured shall refuse to consent to any settlement recommended by the Company and shall elect to contest the Claim or continue any legal proceedings in connection with such Claim, then the Company's liability for the Claim shall not exceed the amount for which the Claim could have been so settled including Claim Expenses incurred up to the date of such refusal. Such amounts are subject to the provisions of Section Limits of Liability.

CLAIMS

A. **Claim Reporting Provision:** The Insured shall give to the Company written notice as stated in Item 12. of the Declarations as soon as practicable of any Claim first made against the Insured during the Policy Period or the Extended Reporting Period, if exercised.

In the event suit is brought against the Insured, the Insured shall immediately forward to Markel Service, Incorporated, on behalf of the Company, every demand, notice, summons or other process received by him/her or by his/her representatives.

B. **Discovery Clause:** If during the Policy Period, the Insured first becomes aware of a specific act, error or omission in Professional Services which may result in a Claim within the scope of coverage of this policy, then the Insured may provide written notice as stated in Item 12. of the Declarations to the Company containing the information listed below. If such written notice is received by the Company during the Policy Period, then any Claim subsequently made against the Insured arising out of such act, error or omission in Professional Services shall be deemed for the purpose of this insurance to have been made on the date on which such written notice is received by the Company.

It is a condition precedent to the coverage afforded by this Discovery Clause that written notice be given to the Company containing the following information:

1. the description of the specific act, error or omission;

2. the date on which such act, error or omission took place;

3. the injury or damage which has or may result from such act, error or omission;

4. the identity of any injured persons; and

5. the circumstances by which the Insured first became aware of such act, error or omission.

MM-20000 08/09   Page 7

Subject to the paragraphs hereinabove, if during the Policy Period the Insured provides such written notice of a specific act, error or omission which is reasonably expected to result in a Claim within the scope of coverage of this policy, the Company at its sole option, may investigate such specific act, error or omission. Such matter shall be subject to all terms, conditions and provisions in this policy as applicable to a Claim.

C.   **Assistance and Cooperation of the Insured:** The Insured shall cooperate with the Company and upon the Company's request, the Insured shall: (1) submit to examination and interview by a representative of the Company, under oath if required; (2) attend hearings, depositions and trials; (3) assist in effecting settlement, securing and giving evidence, obtaining the attendance of witnesses in the conduct of suits; (4) give a written statement or statements to the Company's representatives and meet with such representatives for the purpose of determining coverage and investigating and/or defending any Claim; (5) provide any information required to comply with federal or state reporting regulations; all without cost to the Company. The Insured shall further cooperate with the Company and do whatever is necessary to secure and effect any right of indemnity, contribution or apportionment which the Insured may have. The Insured shall not, except at his/her own cost, make any payment, admit any liability, settle any Claims, assume any obligation or incur any expense without the written consent of the Company.

D.   **False or Fraudulent Claims:**   If any Insured shall commit fraud in proffering any Claim, this insurance shall become void as to such Insured from the date such fraudulent Claim is proffered.

EXTENDED REPORTING PERIOD

A.   In the event of the termination of this insurance by reason of nonrenewal or cancellation by the Coverage A. Named Insured authorized to act on behalf of all Insureds or if the Company shall cancel coverage or terminate it by refusing to renew, for reasons other than the nonpayment of premium and/or deductible or non-compliance with the terms and conditions of this policy, then the Coverage A. Named Insured authorized to act on behalf of all Insureds shall have the right upon payment of an additional premium calculated at the percentage stated in Item 9. of the Declarations of the annual premium for the Policy Period to extend the coverage granted under this policy for the period of months stated in Item 9. of the Declarations, as elected by the Coverage A. Named Insured, to apply to Claims first made against the Insured during the period of months as elected, and reported to the Company pursuant to Section Claims A., Claim Reporting Provision, following immediately upon the effective date of such cancellation or nonrenewal, for any Malpractice or Personal Injury committed on or after the Retroactive Date stated in Item 5. of the Declarations and prior to the effective date of such cancellation or nonrenewal and which is otherwise covered by this policy. This extended period of coverage as elected by the Coverage A. Named Insured and described in this paragraph shall be referred to in this policy as the Extended Reporting Period.

If however, this insurance is succeeded within thirty (30) days by CLAIMS MADE insurance coverage on which the Retroactive Date is the same as or earlier than that shown in Item 5. of the Declarations of this policy, the succeeding insurance shall be deemed to be a renewal hereof, and in consequence the Coverage A. Named Insured authorized to act on behalf of all Insureds shall have no right to secure an Extended Reporting Period.

The quotation of a different premium and/or deductible and/or limit of liability for renewal does not constitute a cancellation or refusal to renew for the purpose of this provision.

This Extended Reporting Period shall not be available when any Insured's license or right to practice his/her profession is revoked, suspended or surrendered.

B.   As a condition precedent to the Coverage A. Named Insured's right to purchase the Extended Reporting Period, the Coverage A. Named Insured authorized to act on behalf of all Insureds must have paid: (1) all Deductibles when due; (2) all premiums due for the Policy Period; and (3) all premium and deductible(s), if any, due on any other policy(ies) issued by the Company or any of its affiliated companies in an uninterrupted series of policies for which this policy is a renewal or replacement. The right to purchase the Extended Reporting Period shall terminate unless a written request for the Extended Reporting Period is received by the Company within thirty (30) days after the effective date of cancellation or nonrenewal together with full payment for the Extended Reporting Period. If such written request and premium payment for the Extended Reporting Period are not so received by the Company, there shall be no right to purchase the Extended Reporting Period at a later date.

C.   In the event of the purchase of the Extended Reporting Period the entire premium therefor shall be fully earned at its commencement.

D.   The Extended Reporting Period shall not in any way increase the Limits of Liability stated in Item 6. of the Declarations.

OTHER CONDITIONS

A.   **Cancellation:** This policy may be cancelled by the Coverage A. Named Insured authorized to act on behalf of all Insureds by surrender thereof to the Company or to its underwriting manager, on behalf of the Company, at Ten Parkway North, Deerfield, Illinois 60015 or by mailing to the aforementioned written notice stating when thereafter such cancellation shall be effective. If cancelled by the Coverage A. Named Insured, the Company shall retain the customary short rate proportion of the premium.

This policy may be cancelled by the Company or by its underwriting manager, by mailing to the Coverage A. Named Insured authorized to act on behalf of all Insureds at the address stated in the Declarations written notice stating when, not less than thirty (30) days thereafter, such cancellation shall be effective. However, if the Company cancels the policy because the Coverage A. Named Insured authorized to act on behalf of all Insureds has failed to pay a premium or deductible when due, including premium and deductible(s) due on any other policy(ies) issued by the Company or any of its affiliated companies in an uninterrupted series of policies for which this policy is a renewal or replacement, this policy may be cancelled by the Company by mailing a written notice of cancellation to the Coverage A. Named Insured stating when, not less than ten (10) days thereafter, such cancellation shall be effective. The mailing of notice as aforementioned shall be sufficient notice and the effective date of cancellation stated in the notice shall become the end of the Policy Period. Delivery of such written notice by the Coverage A. Named Insured, the Company, or its underwriting manager shall be equivalent to mailing. If cancelled by the Company or its underwriting manager, earned premium shall be computed pro rata. Premium adjustment may be made at the time cancellation is effected or as soon as practicable thereafter.

B.   **Representations:** By acceptance of this policy, the Insureds agree as follows:

1.   that the information and statements contained in the application(s) are the basis of this policy and are to be considered as incorporated into and constituting a part of this policy; and

2.   that the information and statements contained in the application(s) are their representations, that they shall be deemed material to the acceptance of the risk or hazard assumed by the Company under this policy, and that this policy is issued in reliance upon the truth of such representations.

C.   **Entire Agreement:** This policy, the Declarations, the application(s) and any written endorsements attached hereto shall be deemed to be a single unitary contract.

D.   **Other Insurance:** This insurance shall be in excess of the Deductible stated in Item 7. of the Declarations and any other valid and collectible insurance available to the Insured whether such other insurance is stated to be primary, contributory, excess, contingent or otherwise, unless such other insurance is written only as a specific excess insurance over the Limits of Liability provided in this policy.

E.   **Changes:** Notice to any agent or knowledge possessed by any agent or other person acting on behalf of the Company shall not effect a waiver or a change in any part of this policy and shall not estop the Company from asserting any right under the terms of the policy. The terms of this policy shall not be waived or changed, except by written endorsement issued to form a part of this policy, and this policy embodies all agreements existing between the Insureds and the Company or any of its agents relating to this insurance.

F.   **Assignment of Interest:** Assignment of interest under this policy shall not bind the Company unless its consent is endorsed hereon.

G.   **Subrogation:** In the event of any payment under this policy, the Company shall be subrogated to the right of recovery of all Insureds to the extent of such payment. The Insured shall execute and deliver instruments and papers and do whatever else is necessary to secure such rights. The Insured shall do nothing after the Claim to prejudice such rights.

The Company shall not exercise any such rights against any person or organization included in the definition of Insured. Notwithstanding the foregoing, however, the Company reserves the right to exercise any rights of subrogation against an Insured in respect of any Claim brought about or contributed to by an intentional, willful, dishonest, fraudulent act or omission of such Insured or by an act or omission of such Insured that constitutes a willful violation of any statute or regulation.

Any amount so recovered, whether effected by the Company or by the Insured, shall first be used for the repayment of expenses incurred toward subrogation; second, for any Damages and Claim Expenses payment by the Insured which is in excess of the amount of the Limit of Liability under this policy and which is excess of any amount paid by any insurer under any other policy; third, for any damages and claims expenses payment by any excess carrier on behalf of the Insured; fourth, for any damages and claim expenses payment by any primary carrier on behalf of the Insured; and, last, for repayment of the Insured's Deductible.

H. **Inspection and Audit:** The Company shall be permitted but not obligated to inspect the Insured's operations at any time. Neither the Company's right to make inspections, nor the making thereof, nor any report thereon shall constitute an undertaking on behalf of or for the benefit of the Insured or others, to determine or warrant that such operations are safe or healthful, or are in compliance with any law, rule or regulation.

The Company may examine and audit the Insured's books and records at any time during the Policy Period and within three years after the final termination of this policy, as far as they relate to the subject matter of this policy.

I. **Action Against the Company:** No action shall lie against the Company unless, as a condition precedent thereto, the Insured shall have fully complied with all of the terms and conditions of this policy, nor until the amount of the Insured's obligation to pay shall have been fully and finally determined either by judgment against the Insured after actual trial or by written agreement of the Insured, the claimant and the Company.

Nothing contained in this policy shall give any person or organization any right to join the Company as a co-defendant in any action against the Insured to determine the Insured's liability. Bankruptcy or insolvency of the Insured or of the Insured's estate shall not relieve the Company of any of its obligations hereunder.

J. **Authorization:** By acceptance of this policy, the first Coverage A. Named Insured named in Item 1. of the Declarations shall act on behalf of all Insureds with respect to the giving and receiving of all notices to and from the Company as provided herein: the exercising of the Extended Reporting Period; the consent to settlement of a Claim brought exclusively under Coverage B., if purchased; the cancellation of this policy in whole or part; the payment of premiums and Deductibles when due; the receiving of any return premiums that may become due under this policy; and the Insureds agree that such person or organization shall act on their behalf.

K. **Service of Suit:** Except with respect to any policy issued in any state in which the Company is licensed as an admitted insurer to transact business, it is agreed that in the event of the failure of the Company to pay any amount claimed to be due hereunder, the Company, at the request of the Coverage A. Named Insured authorized to act on behalf of all Insureds, will submit to the jurisdiction of a court of competent jurisdiction within the United States and will comply with all requirements necessary to give such court jurisdiction and all matters arising hereunder shall be determined in accordance with the law and practice of such court. Nothing in this clause constitutes or should be understood to constitute a waiver of the Company's rights to commence an action in any court of competent jurisdiction in the United States, to remove an action to a United States District Court, or to seek a transfer of a case to another court as permitted by the laws of the United States or of any state in the United States. It is further agreed that service of process in such suit may be made upon Secretary, Legal Department, Markel Midwest, Ten Parkway North, Deerfield, Illinois 60015 and that in any suit instituted against the Company upon this policy, the Company will abide by the final decision of such court or of any appellate court in the event of an appeal.

Further, pursuant to any statute of any state, territory, or district of the United States which makes provision therefor, the Company hereby designates the Superintendent, Commissioner, or Director of Insurance or other official specified for that purpose in the statute, or his/her successor or successors in office, as its true and lawful attorney upon whom may be served any lawful process in any action, suit or proceeding instituted by or on behalf of the Coverage A. Named Insured or the Coverage B. Named Insured or any beneficiary hereunder arising out of this policy, and hereby designates the above-named as the person to whom the said officer is authorized to mail such process or a true copy thereof.

IN WITNESS WHEREOF, the Company has caused this policy to be signed by its President and Secretary, but this policy shall not be valid unless countersigned on the Declarations page by a duly authorized representative of the Company.

SPECIMEN
_____
Secretary

SPECIMEN
_____
President

Misc. Commercial

NUCLEAR ENERGY LIABILITY
EXCLUSION ENDORSEMENT (BROAD FORM)

This endorsement modifies the provisions of this policy.

It is agreed that:

1.   **This policy does not apply:**

A.   Under any Liability Coverage, to bodily injury or property damage

   (1)   with respect to which an Insured under this policy is also an Insured under a nuclear energy liability policy issued by Nuclear Energy Liability Insurance Association, Mutual Atomic Energy Liability Underwriters or Nuclear Insurance Association of Canada, or would be an Insured under any such policy but for its termination upon exhaustion of its limit of liability; or

   (2)   resulting from the hazardous properties of nuclear material and with respect to which (a) any person or organization is required to maintain financial protection pursuant to the Atomic Energy Act of 1954, or any law amendatory thereof, or (b) the Insured is, or had this policy not been issued would be, entitled to indemnity from the United States of America, or any agency thereof, under any agreement entered into by the United States of America, or any agency thereof, with any person or organization.

B.   Under any Medical Payments Coverage, or any Supplementary Payments provision relating to first aid, to expenses incurred with respect to bodily injury resulting from the hazardous properties of nuclear material and arising out of the operation of a nuclear facility by any person or organization.

C.   Under any Liability Coverage, to bodily injury or property damage resulting from the hazardous properties of nuclear material, if

   (1)   the nuclear material (a) is at any nuclear facility owned by, or operated by or on behalf of, an Insured or (b) has been discharged or dispersed therefrom;

   (2)   the nuclear material is contained in spent fuel or waste at any time possessed, handled, used, processed, stored, transported or disposed of by or on behalf of an Insured; or

   (3)   the bodily injury or property damage arises out of the furnishing by an Insured of services, materials, parts or equipment in connection with the planning, construction, maintenance, operation or use of any nuclear facility, but if such facility is located within the United States of America, its territories or possessions or Canada, this exclusion (3) applies only to property damage to such nuclear facility and any property thereat.

2.   **As used in this endorsement:**

"hazardous properties" include radioactive, toxic or explosive properties;

"nuclear material" means source material, special nuclear material or by-product material;

"source material", "special nuclear material", and "by-product material" have the meanings given them in the Atomic Energy Act of 1954 or in any law amendatory thereof;

"spent fuel" means any fuel element or fuel component, solid or liquid, which has been used or exposed to radiation in a nuclear reactor;

"waste" means any waste material (1) containing by-product material and (2) resulting from the operation by any person or organization of any nuclear facility within the definition of nuclear facility under paragraph (a) or (b) thereof;

"nuclear facility" means

   (a)   any nuclear reactor,

(b)   any equipment or device designed or used for (1) separating the isotopes of uranium or plutonium, (2) processing or utilizing spent fuel, or (3) handling, processing or packaging waste,

(c)   any equipment or device used for the processing, fabricating or alloying of special nuclear material if at any time the total amount of such material in the custody of the Insured at the premises where such equipment or device is located consists of or contains more than 25 grams of plutonium or uranium 233 or any combination thereof, or more than 250 grams of uranium 235.

(d)   any structure, basin, excavation, premises or place prepared or used for the storage or disposal of waste.

and includes the site on which any of the foregoing is located, all operations conducted on such site and all premises used for such operations;

"nuclear reactor" means any apparatus designed or used to sustain nuclear fission in a self-supporting chain reaction or to contain a critical mass of fissionable material;

"property damage" includes all forms of radioactive contamination of property.

MM-20000 08/09   Page 13

Misc. Commercial

XL Insurance America, Inc.
STAMFORD, CONNECTICUT
(A Stock Insurance Company Herein Called the Company)

POLLUTION AND REMEDIATION LEGAL LIABILITY POLICY

THIS IS A "CLAIMS-MADE AND REPORTED" POLICY. THIS POLICY REQUIRES THAT A CLAIM BE MADE AGAINST THE INSURED DURING THE POLICY PERIOD AND REPORTED TO THE COMPANY DURING THE POLICY PERIOD OR, WHERE APPLICABLE, THE EXTENDED REPORTING PERIOD. IN ADDITION, THIS POLICY MAY HAVE PROVISIONS OR REQUIREMENTS DIFFERENT FROM OTHER POLICIES YOU MAY HAVE PURCHASED. PLEASE READ CAREFULLY.

THIS POLICY CONTAINS PROVISIONS WHICH LIMIT THE AMOUNT OF LEGAL EXPENSE THE COMPANY IS RESPONSIBLE TO PAY. LEGAL EXPENSE SHALL BE APPLIED AGAINST THE SELF-INSURED RETENTION AMOUNT STATED IN ITEM 4. OF THE DECLARATIONS AND IS SUBJECT TO THE LIMITS OF LIABILITY STATED IN ITEM 3. OF THE DECLARATIONS.

In consideration of the payment of the Policy Premium stated in Item 7. of the Declarations and in reliance upon the statements contained in the Application and any other supplemental materials and information submitted herewith, and subject to all the terms and conditions of this Policy, and the Limits of Liability, and Self-Insured Retention Amount stated in the Declarations, the Company agrees with the INSURED as follows:

I. INSURING AGREEMENT

A. **Coverage A - POLLUTION LEGAL LIABILITY**

The Company will pay on behalf of the INSURED for LOSS and related LEGAL EXPENSE resulting from any POLLUTION CONDITION on, at, under or migrating from any COVERED LOCATION, which the INSURED has or will become legally obligated to pay as a result of a CLAIM first made against the INSURED during the POLICY PERIOD and reported to the Company, in writing, by the INSURED, during the POLICY PERIOD or, where applicable, the EXTENDED REPORTING PERIOD.

B. **Coverage B - REMEDIATION LEGAL LIABILITY**

The Company will pay on behalf of the INSURED for REMEDIATION EXPENSE and related LEGAL EXPENSE resulting from any POLLUTION CONDITION on, at, under or migrating from any COVERED LOCATION:

1. for a CLAIM first made against the INSURED during the POLICY PERIOD which the INSURED has or will become legally obligated to pay; or

2. that is first discovered during the POLICY PERIOD,

provided that the INSURED reports such CLAIM or POLLUTION CONDITION to the Company, in writing, during the POLICY PERIOD or, where applicable, the EXTENDED REPORTING PERIOD.

C.   Coverage C - CONTINGENT TRANSPORTATION COVERAGE

The Company will pay on behalf of the INSURED for LOSS, REMEDIATION EXPENSE and related LEGAL EXPENSE resulting from any POLLUTION CONDITION that arises solely during the course of TRANSPORTATION by any CARRIER, which the INSURED has or will become legally obligated to pay as a result of a CLAIM first made against the INSURED during the POLICY PERIOD and reported to the Company, in writing, by the INSURED, during the POLICY PERIOD or, where applicable, the EXTENDED REPORTING PERIOD.

II. DEFINITIONS

A.   ADDITIONAL NAMED INSURED means any person(s) or entity(ies) endorsed onto this Policy as an ADDITIONAL NAMED INSURED, but solely to the extent such person(s) or entity(ies) is liable as a result of the ownership, occupation, development, operation, maintenance, financing or use of any COVERED LOCATION.

B.   BODILY INJURY means:

1.   physical injury, sickness, disease or building related illness, including death resulting therefrom, and any accompanying medical or environmental monitoring; and/or

2.   mental anguish, emotional distress, or shock,

caused by any POLLUTION CONDITION.

C.   CARRIER means any person(s) or entity(ies), other than the INSURED or any subsidiary or affiliate company of the INSURED, engaged by or on behalf of the INSURED, licensed and in the business of transporting property for hire by land motor vehicle or watercraft.

D.   CLAIM means any demand(s), notice(s) or assertion(s) of a legal right alleging liability or responsibility on the part of the INSURED and shall include but not be limited to lawsuit(s), petition(s), order(s) or government and/or regulatory action(s), filed against the INSURED.

E.   COVERED LOCATION means any location(s) listed in the Covered Location Schedule endorsed onto this Policy.

F.   EXTENDED REPORTING PERIOD means the Automatic Extended Reporting Period or, if applicable, the Optional Extended Reporting Period, as described in Section V. EXTENDED REPORTING PERIOD of this Policy.

G.   FIRST NAMED INSURED means the person or entity stated in Item 1. of the Declarations.

H.   INSURED means the FIRST NAMED INSURED, any ADDITIONAL NAMED INSURED endorsed onto this Policy, and any present or former director, officer, partner, employee, leased worker or temporary worker thereof while acting within the course and scope of his/her duties as such.

I.   LEGAL EXPENSE means legal costs, charges and expenses incurred in the investigation, adjustment or defense of any CLAIM for LOSS or REMEDIATION EXPENSE, or in connection with the payment of any REMEDIATION EXPENSE as applicable, and shall include any necessary expert fees paid to experts retained by defense counsel.

LEGAL EXPENSE does not include the time and expense incurred by the INSURED in assisting in the investigation or resolution of a CLAIM or in connection with REMEDIATION EXPENSE, including but not limited to the costs of the INSURED'S in-house counsel, salary charges of regular employees or officials of the INSURED, and fees and expenses of supervisory counsel retained by the INSURED.

J.   **LOSS** means monetary judgment, award or settlement of compensatory damages as well as related punitive, exemplary or multiplied damages where insurance coverage is allowable by law arising from:

    1.   BODILY INJURY; and/or

    2.   PROPERTY DAMAGE.

K.   **LOW-LEVEL RADIOACTIVE WASTE AND MATERIAL** means:

    1.   Waste as defined in Title 10 Code of Federal Regulations, Part 61.2; and/or

    2.   material regulated by the United States Nuclear Regulatory Commission or an Agreement State under a Type A, B or C Specific License of Broad Scope as defined in Title 10 Code of Federal Regulations, Part 33.11.

L.   **MOLD MATTER** means mold, mildew or any type or form of fungus; including any mycotoxins, spores, or byproducts produced or released by fungi.

M.   **MOLD MATTER REMEDIATION STANDARD** means standards for the investigation and abatement of MOLD MATTER imposed by a Federal, State, Local or Provincial governmental authority pursuant to a law or regulation governing the investigation and abatement of MOLD MATTER. If no standards have been imposed by such authority, then the standards for investigation and abatement shall be those necessary to protect human health at the COVERED LOCATION, as determined in consultation with a MOLD MATTER PROFESSIONAL, and shall be no less than those remediation activities recommended by the New York City Department of Health & Mental Hygiene Guidelines on Assessment and Remediation of Fungi in Indoor Environments ("NYC Guidelines"), or any subsequent amendments thereof. All of these standards shall take into consideration the use of the COVERED LOCATION on the date the COVERED LOCATION was endorsed onto this Policy.

N.   **MOLD MATTER PROFESSIONAL** means a Certified Industrial Hygienist, or similarly qualified health and safety professional experienced in performing mold investigation and remediation, retained by or with the prior written consent of the Company.

O.   **NATURAL RESOURCE DAMAGE** means physical injury to or destruction of, as well as the assessment of such injury or destruction, including the resulting loss of value of land, fish, wildlife, biota, air, water, groundwater, drinking water supplies, and other such resources belonging to, managed by, held in trust by, appertaining to, or otherwise controlled by the United States (including the resources of the fishery conservation zone established by the Magnuson-Stevens Fishery Conservation and Management Act 16 U.S.C. 1801 et. seq.), any State, Local or Provincial government, any foreign government, any Native American tribe or, if such resources are subject to a trust restriction on alienation, any member of a Native American tribe.

P.   **POLICY PERIOD** means the period stated in Item 2. of the Declarations, or any shorter period arising as a result of cancellation.

Q.   **POLLUTANTS** means any solid, liquid, gaseous or thermal pollutant, irritant or contaminant including but not limited to smoke, vapors, odors, soot, fumes, acids, alkalis, toxic chemicals, hazardous substances, waste materials, including medical, infectious and pathological wastes, electromagnetic fields, LOW-LEVEL RADIOACTIVE WASTE AND MATERIAL, and MOLD MATTER.

R.   **POLLUTION CONDITION** means:

1.   the discharge, dispersal, release, seepage, migration, or escape of POLLUTANTS into or upon land, or structures thereupon, the atmosphere, or any watercourse or body of water including groundwater;

2.   the presence of any uncontrolled or uncontained POLLUTANTS into land, the atmosphere, or any watercourse or body of water including groundwater; or

3.   the presence of MOLD MATTER on buildings or structures.

S.   PROPERTY DAMAGE means:

1.   physical injury to or destruction of tangible property, including the resulting loss of use thereof, and including the personal property of third parties;

2.   loss of use of such property that has not been physically injured or destroyed;

3.   diminished third party property value; and/or

4.   NATURAL RESOURCE DAMAGE,

caused by any POLLUTION CONDITION.

PROPERTY DAMAGE does not include REMEDIATION EXPENSE.

T.   REMEDIATION EXPENSE means expenses caused by a POLLUTION CONDITION and incurred to investigate, assess, remove, dispose of, abate, contain, treat or neutralize a POLLUTION CONDITION, to the extent required by:

1.   Federal, State, Local or Provincial Laws, Regulations or Statutes, or any subsequent amendments thereof, or MOLD MATTER REMEDIATION STANDARDS, enacted to address a POLLUTION CONDITION, including any individual or entity acting under the authority thereof; and/or

2.   a legally executed state voluntary program governing the cleanup of a POLLUTION CONDITION.

REMEDIATION EXPENSE shall also include any associated (i) monitoring and testing costs, or (ii) punitive, exemplary or multiplied damages, where insurable by law. REMEDIATION EXPENSE shall also include RESTORATION COSTS.

U.   RESTORATION COSTS means reasonable and necessary costs incurred by the INSURED to restore, repair or replace real or personal property to substantially the same condition it was in prior to being damaged during work performed in the course of incurring REMEDIATION EXPENSE.

However, these costs shall not exceed the actual cash value of such real or personal property immediately prior to incurring the REMEDIATION EXPENSE or include costs associated with improvements or betterments. Actual cash value is defined as the cost to replace such real or personal property, immediately prior to incurring the REMEDIATION EXPENSE, minus the accumulated depreciation of the real or personal property.

V.   RESPONSIBLE INSURED means:

1.   any officer, director, or partner of the INSURED;

2.   any person(s) or entity(ies) authorized by the INSURED to act for or in place of the INSURED; and/or

3.   any employee of the INSURED responsible for the environmental or health and safety affairs of the INSURED.

W.   **TRANSPORTATION** means:

1.   **Out-Bound** - the movement by a CARRIER of the INSURED'S product or waste generated by the INSURED, after a CARRIER crosses the legal boundary of a COVERED LOCATION until the INSURED'S waste or product is delivered or unloaded by the CARRIER; and/or

2.   **In-Bound** - the loading and movement by a CARRIER of material, from a location other than a COVERED LOCATION, until the CARRIER crosses the legal boundary of a COVERED LOCATION.

X.   **UNDERGROUND STORAGE TANK(S)** means any stationary container or vessel, including the associated piping connected thereto, which is ten percent (10%) or more beneath the surface of the ground and is: (i) constructed primarily of non-earthen materials; and (ii) designed to contain any substance.

III. TERRITORY

A CLAIM must be made or brought in the United States, its territories or possessions or in Canada.

This Policy shall not apply to any risk which would be in violation of the laws of the United States or Canada, as applicable, including, but not limited to, United States economic or trade sanction laws or export control laws administered by the United States Treasury, State, and Commerce Departments (e.g. the economic and trade sanctions administered by the United States Treasury Office of Foreign Assets Control).

IV. EXCLUSIONS

This Policy does not apply to LOSS, REMEDIATION EXPENSE, LEGAL EXPENSE or any other coverages afforded by endorsement attached to this Policy:

1.   **Non-Disclosed Conditions**
arising from any POLLUTION CONDITION existing prior to the inception date of this Policy, and reported to or known by a RESPONSIBLE INSURED, which was not disclosed in writing to the Company in the Application or related materials prior to the inception date of this Policy or prior to the COVERED LOCATION being endorsed onto this Policy. Any POLLUTION CONDITION disclosed in writing to the Company and not otherwise excluded under this Policy is deemed to be first discovered on the date a COVERED LOCATION is endorsed onto this Policy.

2.   **Fines/Penalties/Assessments**
based upon or arising out of any fines, penalties or assessments.

This exclusion does not apply to punitive, exemplary or multiplied damages.

3.   **Employer's Liability/Workers' Compensation**
based upon or arising out of injury to:

a.   any employee, director, officer, partner, leased worker or temporary worker of the INSURED if such injury occurs during and in the course of said employment, or during the performance of duties related to the conduct of the INSURED'S business, or arising out of any Workers' Compensation, unemployment compensation or disability benefits law or similar law; and

b.   the spouse, child, parent, brother or sister of such employee, director, officer, partner, leased worker or temporary worker of the INSURED as a consequence of Item a. above.

4. Contractual Liability

based upon or arising as a result of liability of others assumed by the INSURED in any contract or agreement unless the liability would exist in the absence of a contract or agreement.

Only as it applies to coverages offered under this Policy, this exclusion does not apply to liability of others assumed by the INSURED in contracts listed in the Insured Contract(s) Schedule endorsed onto this Policy.

5. Insured's Property/Bailee Liability

with respect to PROPERTY DAMAGE only, to property owned, leased or operated by, or in the care, custody or control of the INSURED, even if such PROPERTY DAMAGE is incurred to avoid or mitigate LOSS or REMEDIATION EXPENSE which may be covered under this Policy.

This exclusion does not apply to RESTORATION COSTS or NATURAL RESOURCE DAMAGE.

6. New Pollution Conditions at Divested Property

based upon or arising from any POLLUTION CONDITION on, at, under or migrating from any COVERED LOCATION, where the actual discharge, dispersal, release, seepage, migration or escape of POLLUTANTS commenced subsequent to the time such COVERED LOCATION was sold, given away, or abandoned by the INSURED, or condemned.

7. Radioactive / Nuclear Material

based upon or arising out of:

a.   ionizing radiations or contamination by radioactivity from any nuclear fuel or from any nuclear waste from the processing or reaction of nuclear fuel;

b.   the radioactive, toxic, explosive or other hazardous properties of any explosive nuclear assembly or nuclear component thereof;

c.   the existence, required removal or abatement of Naturally Occurring Radioactive Material, including but not limited to radon;

d.   high-level radioactive waste (spent nuclear fuel or the highly radioactive waste produced if spent fuel is reprocessed), uranium milling residues and waste with greater than specified quantities of elements heavier than uranium; or

e.   mixed Waste as defined in Title 40 Code of Federal Regulations, Part 266.210; however, this clause e. does not apply to Mixed Waste that contains Waste as defined in Title 10 Code of Federal Regulations, Part 61.2,

including, but not limited to the actual, alleged or threatened exposure of any person(s) or property to any such matter.

8. Products Liability

based upon or arising out of goods or products manufactured, sold, handled, distributed, altered or repaired by the INSURED or by others trading under the INSURED's name including any container thereof, any failure to warn, or any reliance upon a representation or warranty made at any time with respect thereto, but only if the POLLUTION CONDITION took place away from a COVERED LOCATION and after physical possession of such goods or products has been relinquished to others.

This exclusion does not apply to <u>Coverage C – CONTINGENT TRANSPORTATION COVERAGE</u>, as stated in Section I. INSURING AGREEMENT of this Policy.

9. Non-Compliance

PARL6CP 0909

Misc. Commercial

arising from any POLLUTION CONDITION that results from the intentional disregard of, or the deliberate, willful or dishonest non-compliance by a RESPONSIBLE INSURED with any statute, regulation, ordinance, order, notice letter or instruction from, by or on behalf of any governmental body or entity.

10.   Hostile Acts
based upon or arising out of any consequence, whether direct or indirect, of war, invasion, act of foreign enemy, hostilities (whether war be declared or not), civil war, rebellion, revolution, insurrection or military or usurped power.

11.   Lead-Based Paint and Asbestos
based upon or arising out of the existence, required removal or abatement of lead-based paint or asbestos, in any form, in any building or structure, including but not limited to products containing asbestos, asbestos fibers, asbestos dust, and asbestos containing materials.

12.   Underground Storage Tank(s)
based upon or arising out of the existence of any UNDERGROUND STORAGE TANK(S) on, at or under a COVERED LOCATION. This exclusion does not apply to UNDERGROUND STORAGE TANK(S):

a.   which are closed, abandoned-in-place or removed prior to the inception date of this Policy, in accordance with all applicable Federal, State, Local or Provincial Regulations in effect at the time of closure, abandonment or removal;

b.   listed in the Underground Storage Tank(s) Schedule endorsed onto this Policy, if any;

c.   the existence of which is unknown by a RESPONSIBLE INSURED as of the inception date of this Policy;

d.   flow-through process tanks, including oil/water separators; or

e.   storage tank(s) situated in an underground area (such as a basement, cellar, mine shaft or tunnel) if the storage tank is situated upon or above the surface of the floor.

13.   Insured vs. Insured
based upon or arising from a CLAIM by one INSURED against another INSURED.

14.   Material Change in Use or Operations
based upon or arising out of a material change in the use of, or a material change in the operations at, any COVERED LOCATION from those set forth by the INSURED in the Application or related materials as of the inception date of this Policy.

15.   Retroactive Date
based upon or arising out of any POLLUTION CONDITION that commenced prior to the Retroactive Date stated in Item 5. of the Declarations which includes any dispersal, migration or further movement of the aforementioned POLLUTION CONDITION on or after the Retroactive Date stated in Item 5. of the Declarations.

16.   Reverse Retroactive Date
based upon or arising out of any POLLUTION CONDITION that commenced subsequent to the Reverse Retroactive Date stated in Item 6. of the Declarations.

17.   Communicable Diseases
based upon or arising out of the exposure to infected individuals or animals, or contact with bodily fluids of infected individuals or animals.

PARL6CP 0909   Page 7

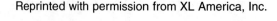

V. EXTENDED REPORTING PERIOD

A.   Automatic Extended Reporting Period:

The INSURED shall be entitled to a ninety (90) day Automatic Extended Reporting Period for no additional premium, commencing on the last day of the POLICY PERIOD, subject to the following terms and conditions:

1.   The Automatic Extended Reporting Period shall apply to a CLAIM first made against the INSURED during the POLICY PERIOD and reported to the Company, in writing, by the INSURED during the Automatic Extended Reporting Period and otherwise covered by this Policy.

2.   The Automatic Extended Reporting Period shall also apply to a CLAIM first made against the INSURED during the Automatic Extended Reporting Period, resulting from any POLLUTION CONDITION first discovered and reported to the Company, in writing, by the INSURED during the POLICY PERIOD and otherwise covered by this Policy. In this case, the CLAIM shall be deemed to have been made against the INSURED on the last day of the POLICY PERIOD.

3.   The Automatic Extended Reporting Period shall also apply to any POLLUTION CONDITION first discovered by the INSURED during the POLICY PERIOD and reported to the Company, in writing, by the INSURED within the Automatic Extended Reporting Period and otherwise covered under this Policy.

The ninety (90) day Automatic Extended Reporting Period does not apply where:

1.   this Policy is terminated for fraud, misrepresentation or non-payment of premium as described in Section IX. CONDITIONS, B. Cancellation, Items 2.a. and 2.b.; or

2.   the INSURED has purchased other insurance to replace this Policy, which provides coverage for a CLAIM and/or POLLUTION CONDITION.

B.   Optional Extended Reporting Period:

The FIRST NAMED INSURED shall be entitled to purchase an Optional Extended Reporting Period in the event this Policy is non-renewed, subject to the following terms and conditions:

1.   The Optional Extended Reporting Period shall become effective upon payment of an additional premium of not more than one hundred percent (100%) of the full Policy Premium. The Optional Extended Reporting Period shall be effective for three (3) consecutive three-hundred and sixty-five (365) day periods commencing on the last day of the POLICY PERIOD. The FIRST NAMED INSURED must indicate its intention, in writing, to purchase this Optional Extended Reporting Period within thirty (30) days from the last day of the POLICY PERIOD. The Automatic Extended Reporting Period of ninety (90) days will be merged into this period and is not in addition to this period.

2.   The Optional Extended Reporting Period shall only apply to a CLAIM first made against the INSURED during the Optional Extended Reporting Period, resulting from any POLLUTION CONDITION first discovered and reported to the Company, in writing, by the INSURED, during the POLICY PERIOD and otherwise covered by this Policy.

The Optional Extended Reporting Period does not apply where:

1.   this Policy is terminated for fraud, misrepresentation or non-payment of premium as described in Section IX. CONDITIONS, B. Cancellation, Items 2.a. and 2.b.; or

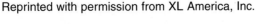

2.   the INSURED has purchased other insurance to replace this Policy, which provides coverage for a CLAIM and/or POLLUTION CONDITION.

It is a condition precedent to the operation of the rights granted under Item B. above that payment of the appropriate premium shall be made not later than thirty (30) days after expiration of this Policy in the case of non-renewal.

For purposes of Item B. Optional Extended Reporting Period as referenced above, the quotation of different terms and conditions by the Company shall not be construed as a non-renewal of this Policy.

VI. LIMITS OF LIABILITY AND SELF-INSURED RETENTION

A.   The Company will pay one hundred percent (100%) of all covered LOSS, REMEDIATION EXPENSE, LEGAL EXPENSE and any other coverages afforded by endorsement attached to this Policy in excess of the applicable Self-Insured Retention Amount stated in Item 4. of the Declarations and subject to the Limits of Liability stated in Item 3. of the Declarations and the other terms and conditions of this Policy.

B.   The Self-Insured Retention Amount is borne by the INSURED and is not to be insured unless the Company has expressed its prior consent in writing to the FIRST NAMED INSURED. The applicable Self-Insured Retention Amount stated Item 4. of the Declarations shall apply.

C.   All LOSS, REMEDIATION EXPENSE, LEGAL EXPENSE and any other coverages afforded by endorsement attached to this Policy arising out of the same or related POLLUTION CONDITION at any one COVERED LOCATION shall be considered a single POLLUTION CONDITION and shall be subject to the applicable Limits of Liability stated in Item 3a. of the Declarations and the Self-Insured Retention Amount stated in Item 4. of the Declarations.

D.   All LOSS, REMEDIATION EXPENSE, LEGAL EXPENSE or any other coverages afforded by endorsement attached to this Policy during the POLICY PERIOD or, where applicable, the EXTENDED REPORTING PERIOD shall not exceed the Limits of Liability stated in Item 3b. of the Declarations.

E.   Any LOSS, REMEDIATION EXPENSE, LEGAL EXPENSE and any other coverages afforded by endorsement incurred and reported to the Company, in writing, over more than one policy period, and resulting from the same or related POLLUTION CONDITION, shall be considered a single POLLUTION CONDITION. The LOSS, REMEDIATION EXPENSE, LEGAL EXPENSE and any other coverages afforded by endorsement attached to this Policy will be subject to the same Limits of Liability and the Self-Insured Retention Amount in effect at the time the POLLUTION CONDITION was first reported to the Company, in writing, by the INSURED, during the POLICY PERIOD or, where applicable, the EXTENDED REPORTING PERIOD.

VII. REPORTING, DEFENSE, SETTLEMENT AND COOPERATION

A.   As a condition precedent to the coverage hereunder, in the event any CLAIM is made against the INSURED for LOSS or REMEDIATION EXPENSE, or any POLLUTION CONDITION is first discovered by the INSURED that results in a LOSS or REMEDIATION EXPENSE:

1.   The INSURED shall forward to the Company or to any of its authorized agents every demand, notice, summons, order or other process received by the INSURED or the INSURED's representative as soon as practicable; and

2.   The INSURED shall provide to the Company, whether orally or in writing, notice of the particulars with respect to the time, place and circumstances thereof, along with the names

and addresses of the injured and of available witnesses. In the event of oral notice, the INSURED agrees to furnish to the Company a written report as soon as practicable.

It is further agreed, that the INSURED shall cooperate with the Company and upon the Company's request shall submit to examination by a representative of the Company, under oath if required, and shall attend hearings, depositions and trials and shall assist in effecting settlement, securing and giving evidence, obtaining the attendance of witnesses and in the conduct of suits, as well as in the investigation and/or defense thereof, all without charge to the Company. The INSURED shall further cooperate with the Company and do whatever is necessary to secure and effect any rights of indemnity, contribution or apportionment which the INSURED may have.

B. No costs, charges or expenses shall be incurred, nor payments made, obligations assumed or remediation commenced without the Company's written consent which shall not be unreasonably withheld. This provision does not apply to costs incurred by the INSURED on an emergency basis, where any delay on the part of the INSURED would cause injury to persons or damage to property, or increase significantly the cost of responding to any POLLUTION CONDITION. If such emergency occurs, the INSURED shall notify the Company immediately thereafter.

C. The Company shall have the right and the duty to defend an INSURED against any CLAIM seeking damages for a LOSS or for REMEDIATION EXPENSE. The Company will have no duty to defend the INSURED against any CLAIM for LOSS or for REMEDIATION EXPENSE to which this Policy does not apply.

D. The Company shall have the right and the duty to assume the investigation, adjustment or defense of any CLAIM. In case of the exercise of this right, the INSURED, on demand of the Company, shall promptly reimburse the Company for any element of LOSS, REMEDIATION EXPENSE, LEGAL EXPENSE or any other coverages afforded by endorsement falling within the Self-Insured Retention Amount stated in Item 4. of the Declarations.

The INSURED shall not admit liability or settle any CLAIM without the Company's consent. If the Company recommends a settlement of any CLAIM:

1. for an amount within the Self-Insured Retention Amount and the INSURED refuses such settlement, the Company shall not be liable for any LOSS, REMEDIATION EXPENSE, LEGAL EXPENSE and any other coverages afforded by endorsement in excess of the Self-Insured Retention Amount; or

2. for a total amount in excess of the Self-Insured Retention Amount and the INSURED refuses such settlement, the Company's liability for LOSS, REMEDIATION EXPENSE, LEGAL EXPENSE and any other coverages afforded by endorsement shall be limited to that portion of the recommended settlement and the costs, charges and expenses as of the date of the INSURED's refusal which exceed the Self-Insured Retention Amount but fall within the Limits of Liability.

E. If a POLLUTION CONDITION is first discovered by the INSURED during the POLICY PERIOD and reported in writing to the Company during the POLICY PERIOD or, where applicable, the EXTENDED REPORTING PERIOD, and a CLAIM associated with such POLLUTION CONDITION is made against the INSURED and reported to the Company after the expiration of this Policy, such CLAIM shall be deemed to have been first made and reported on the last day of the POLICY PERIOD in which the POLLUTION CONDITION is first discovered, provided that the INSURED has maintained an equivalent policy with the Company on a continuous uninterrupted basis and the CLAIM is made against the INSURED and reported to the Company prior to the cancellation or expiration of such subsequent policy. It is further agreed that coverage for such CLAIM will not be provided under any subsequent policy issued by the Company.

PARL6CP 0909

F.   The Company shall have the right to designate legal counsel for the investigation, adjustment and defense of a CLAIM. The Company shall consult with the INSURED in conjunction with the selection of counsel.

VIII. TRANSFER OF LEGAL DEFENSE DUTIES

A.   If the Company believes that the Limits of Liability stated in Item 3. of the Declarations has been or soon will be exhausted in defending a CLAIM or that the Company has paid out or will soon pay out the Aggregate Liability stated in Item 3.b. of the Declarations, the Company will so notify the FIRST NAMED INSURED in writing as soon as possible. The Company will advise that its duty to defend a CLAIM seeking damages within those Limits of Liability has terminated, subject to payment of the Limits of Liability, and that it will have no duty to defend or indemnify the INSURED for any CLAIM for which notice is given after the date it sends out such notice. The Company will take immediate and appropriate steps to transfer control of any existing defense prior to exhaustion of the limits to the FIRST NAMED INSURED. The FIRST NAMED INSURED agrees to reimburse the Company for any costs which the Company bears in connection with the transfer of the defense.

B.   The Company will take appropriate steps necessary to defend the CLAIM during the transfer of the defense and avoid any unfavorable legal action provided that the FIRST NAMED INSURED cooperates in the transfer of the duties of the defense.

C.   The exhaustion of the applicable Limits of Liability by the payment of LOSS, REMEDIATION EXPENSE, LEGAL EXPENSE and any other coverages afforded by endorsement will not be affected by the Company's failure to comply with any of the provisions of this section.

IX. CONDITIONS

A.   **Inspection and Audit --** The Company shall be permitted but not obligated to inspect and monitor on a continuing basis the INSURED'S property or operations at any COVERED LOCATION, at any time. Neither the Company's right to make inspections and monitor nor the actual undertaking thereof nor any report thereon shall constitute an undertaking, on behalf of the INSURED or others, to determine or warrant that property or operations are safe, healthful or conform to acceptable engineering practice or are in compliance with any law, rule or regulation. Access for the inspection and audit may be coordinated through the broker or agent of the FIRST NAMED INSURED.

B.   **Cancellation --** The INSURED and the Company agree to the following with regard to cancellation:

1.   **Cancellation by the FIRST NAMED INSURED --** This Policy may be canceled by the FIRST NAMED INSURED by surrender thereof to the Company or any of its authorized agents or by mailing to the Company written notice stating when thereafter the cancellation shall be effective. The mailing of notice as aforesaid shall be sufficient proof of notice of cancellation. The time of surrender or the effective date and hour of cancellation stated in the notice shall become the end of the POLICY PERIOD. Confirmed delivery of such written notice by the FIRST NAMED INSURED shall be equivalent to mailing.

The Minimum Earned Premium for this Policy will be the percentage stated in Item 8. of the Declarations of the total premium for this Policy. The FIRST NAMED INSURED is not entitled to any return of the Minimum Earned Premium upon cancellation by the FIRST NAMED INSURED.

If the Minimum Earned Premium is less than one hundred percent (100%), and the FIRST NAMED INSURED cancels this Policy, then the amount of premium returnable after the minimum premium earned is retained by the Company shall be computed in accordance with the customary short rate table and procedure.

2.   **Cancellation by the Company** -- This Policy may be canceled by the Company by mailing to the FIRST NAMED INSURED at the address shown in Item 1. of the Declarations, written notice stating when not less than sixty (60) days [ten (10) days for non-payment of premium] thereafter such cancellation shall be effective. The mailing of notice as aforesaid shall be sufficient proof of notice of cancellation. The effective date and hour of cancellation stated in the notice shall become the end of the POLICY PERIOD.

The Company may cancel this Policy at any time, but only for the following reasons:

a.   the INSURED has made a material misrepresentation which affects the Company's assessment of the risk of insuring any COVERED LOCATION; or

b.   the INSURED breaches or fails to comply with Policy terms, conditions, contractual duties, or any of its obligations under this Policy or at law; or

c.   the INSURED fails to pay the premium or fails to pay any Deductible or the Self-Insured Retention Amount for this Policy.

If the Company cancels this Policy, then the amount of premium returnable to the INSURED shall be computed pro rata and no minimum earned premium shall apply.

In the event of cancellation of this Policy by the Company from Item b. above, the INSURED shall have sixty (60) days from the date of notice to remedy such breach or failure to comply that is the cause for cancellation. If such remedy is satisfactory to the Company, in its sole discretion, during the applicable notice period, the Company will rescind the Notice of Cancellation with a written confirmation to the FIRST NAMED INSURED that the Policy shall remain in place.

With regard to both Items 1. and 2. above:

1.   The premium adjustment may be made either at the time cancellation is affected or as soon as practicable after cancellation becomes effective, but payment or tender of unearned premium is not a condition of cancellation; and

2.   If a CLAIM is made against the INSURED, and the POLLUTION CONDITION related to such CLAIM is discovered or coverage is requested from the Company by the INSURED during the POLICY PERIOD or, where applicable, the EXTENDED REPORTING PERIOD, then the total premium shall be considered one hundred percent (100%) earned, and the INSURED is not entitled to any return of premium upon cancellation.

C.   **Declarations and Representations** -- By acceptance of this Policy, the INSURED agrees that the statements contained in the Application and any other supplemental materials and information submitted herewith are the INSURED's agreements and representations, that they shall be deemed material, that this Policy is issued in reliance upon the truth of such representations and that this Policy embodies all agreements existing between the INSURED and the Company or any of its agents relating to this insurance.

D.   **Action Against Company** -- No action shall lie against the Company unless, as a condition precedent thereto:

1.   the INSURED has fully complied with all of the terms of this Policy; and

2.   the amount the INSURED is obligated to pay has been finally determined either by judgment against the INSURED after actual trial or by written agreement of the INSURED, the claimant and the Company.

PARL6CP 0909   Page 12

Any person or organization or the legal representative thereof who has secured such judgment or written agreement shall thereafter be entitled to recover under this Policy to the extent of the insurance afforded by this Policy. No person or organization shall have any right under this Policy to join the Company as a party to any action against the INSURED to determine the INSURED's liability, nor shall the Company be impleaded by the INSURED or its legal representative. Bankruptcy or insolvency of the INSURED or of the INSURED's estate shall not relieve the Company of any of its obligations hereunder.

E. **Assignment** -- This Policy shall be void as to the assignee or transferee, if assigned or transferred without written consent of the Company. Such consent shall not be unreasonably withheld or delayed by the Company.

F. **Subrogation** -- In the event of any payment under this Policy, the Company shall be subrogated to all the INSURED'S rights of recovery against any person or organization and the INSURED shall execute and deliver instruments and papers and do whatever else is necessary to secure such rights. The INSURED shall do nothing to prejudice such rights.

G. **Changes** -- Notice to any agent or knowledge possessed by any agent or by any other person shall not effect a waiver or a change in any part of this Policy or estop the Company from asserting any right under the terms of this Policy; nor shall the terms of this Policy be waived or changed, except by endorsement issued to form a part of this Policy.

H. **Sole Agent** -- The FIRST NAMED INSURED stated in Item 1. of the Declarations shall act on behalf of all INSUREDS for the payment or return of premium, receipt and acceptance of any endorsement issued to form a part of this Policy, giving and receiving notice of cancellation or non-renewal and the exercise of the rights provided in Section V. EXTENDED REPORTING PERIOD, Item B. Optional Extended Reporting Period.

I. **Other Insurance** -- Subject to Section VI. LIMITS OF LIABILITY AND SELF-INSURED RETENTION, this insurance shall be in excess of the Self-Insured Retention Amount stated in Item 4. of the Declarations and any other valid and collectible insurance available to the INSURED, whether such other insurance is stated to be primary, pro rata, contributory, excess, contingent or otherwise, unless such other insurance is written only as specific excess insurance over the Limits of Liability provided in this Policy.

J. **Headings** -- The descriptions in the headings of this Policy are solely for convenience and form no part of this Policy terms and conditions.

K. **Jurisdiction and Venue** -- It is agreed that in the event of the failure of the Company to pay any amount claimed to be due hereunder, the Company and the INSURED will submit to the jurisdiction of the State of New York and will comply with all the requirements necessary to give such court jurisdiction. Nothing in this clause constitutes or should be understood to constitute a waiver of the Company's right to remove an action to a United States District Court.

L. **Choice of Law** -- All matters arising hereunder including questions related to the validity interpretation, performance and enforcement of this Policy shall be determined in accordance with the law and practice of the State of New York (notwithstanding New York's conflicts of law rules).

M. **Severability** -- Except with respect to Limits of Liability and any rights and duties assigned in this Policy to the FIRST NAMED INSURED, this insurance applies as if each INSURED were the only INSURED and separately to each INSURED against whom a CLAIM is made.

Any misrepresentation, act or omission that is in violation of a term, duty or condition under this Policy by one INSURED shall not by itself affect coverage for another INSURED under this Policy.

However, this condition shall not apply to the INSURED who is a parent, subsidiary or affiliate of the INSURED which committed the misrepresentation, act or omission referenced above.

Misc. Commercial

Page 14

COMMERCIAL LIABILITY UMBRELLA COVERAGE FORM

Various provisions in this policy restrict coverage. Read the entire policy carefully to determine rights, duties and what is and is not covered.

Throughout this policy the words "you" and "your" refer to the Named Insured shown in the Declarations, and any other person or organization qualifying as a Named Insured under this policy. The words "we", "us" and "our" refer to the company providing this insurance.

The word "insured" means any person or organization qualifying as such under Section **II** – Who Is An Insured.

Other words and phrases that appear in quotation marks have special meaning. Refer to Section **V** – Definitions.

SECTION I – COVERAGES

COVERAGE A – BODILY INJURY AND PROPERTY DAMAGE LIABILITY

1. Insuring Agreement

   a. We will pay on behalf of the insured the "ultimate net loss" in excess of the "retained limit" because of "bodily injury" or "property damage" to which this insurance applies. We will have the right and duty to defend the insured against any "suit" seeking damages for such "bodily injury" or "property damage" when the "underlying insurance" does not provide coverage or the limits of "underlying insurance" have been exhausted. When we have no duty to defend, we will have the right to defend, or to participate in the defense of, the insured against any other "suit" seeking damages to which this insurance may apply. However, we will have no duty to defend the insured against any "suit" seeking damages for "bodily injury" or "property damage" to which this insurance does not apply. At our discretion, we may investigate any "occurrence" that may involve this insurance and settle any resultant claim or "suit", for which we have the duty to defend. But:

      (1) The amount we will pay for the "ultimate net loss" is limited as described in Section **III** – Limits Of Insurance; and

      (2) Our right and duty to defend ends when we have used up the applicable limit of insurance in the payment of judgments or settlements under Coverages **A** or **B**.

No other obligation or liability to pay sums or perform acts or services is covered unless explicitly provided for under Supplementary Payments – Coverages **A** and **B**.

   b. This insurance applies to "bodily injury" and "property damage" only if:

      (1) The "bodily injury" or "property damage" is caused by an "occurrence" that takes place in the "coverage territory";

      (2) The "bodily injury" or "property damage" occurs during the policy period; and

      (3) Prior to the policy period, no insured listed under Paragraph **1.a.** of Section **II** – Who Is An Insured and no "employee" authorized by you to give or receive notice of an "occurrence" or claim, knew that the "bodily injury" or "property damage" had occurred, in whole or in part. If such a listed insured or authorized "employee" knew, prior to the policy period, that the "bodily injury" or "property damage" occurred, then any continuation, change or resumption of such "bodily injury" or "property damage" during or after the policy period will be deemed to have been known prior to the policy period.

   c. "Bodily injury" or "property damage" which occurs during the policy period and was not, prior to the policy period, known to have occurred by any insured listed under Paragraph **1.a.** of Section **II** – Who Is An Insured or any "employee" authorized by you to give or receive notice of an "occurrence" or claim, includes any continuation, change or resumption of that "bodily injury" or "property damage" after the end of the policy period.

   d. "Bodily injury" or "property damage" will be deemed to have been known to have occurred at the earliest time when any insured listed under Paragraph **1.a.** of Section **II** – Who Is An Insured or any "employee" authorized by you to give or receive notice of an "occurrence" or claim:

      (1) Reports all, or any part, of the "bodily injury" or "property damage" to us or any other insurer;

      (2) Receives a written or verbal demand or claim for damages because of the "bodily injury" or "property damage"; or

(3) Becomes aware by any other means that "bodily injury" or "property damage" has occurred or has begun to occur.

e. Damages because of "bodily injury" include damages claimed by any person or organization for care, loss of services or death resulting at any time from the "bodily injury".

2. Exclusions

This insurance does not apply to:

a. Expected Or Intended Injury

"Bodily injury" or "property damage" expected or intended from the standpoint of the insured. This exclusion does not apply to "bodily injury" resulting from the use of reasonable force to protect persons or property.

b. Contractual Liability

"Bodily injury" or "property damage" for which the insured is obligated to pay damages by reason of the assumption of liability in a contract or agreement. This exclusion does not apply to liability for damages:

(1) That the insured would have in the absence of the contract or agreement; or

(2) Assumed in a contract or agreement that is an "insured contract", provided the "bodily injury" or "property damage" occurs subsequent to the execution of the contract or agreement. Solely for the purposes of liability assumed in an "insured contract", reasonable attorney fees and necessary litigation expenses incurred by or for a party other than an insured are deemed to be damages because of "bodily injury" or "property damage", provided:

(a) Liability to such party for, or for the cost of, that party's defense has also been assumed in the same "insured contract"; and

(b) Such attorney fees and litigation expenses are for defense of that party against a civil or alternative dispute resolution proceeding in which damages to which this insurance applies are alleged.

c. Liquor Liability

"Bodily injury" or "property damage" for which any insured may be held liable by reason of:

(1) Causing or contributing to the intoxication of any person;

(2) The furnishing of alcoholic beverages to a person under the legal drinking age or under the influence of alcohol; or

(3) Any statute, ordinance or regulation relating to the sale, gift, distribution or use of alcoholic beverages.

This exclusion applies only if you are in the business of manufacturing, distributing, selling, serving or furnishing alcoholic beverages.

This exclusion does not apply to the extent that valid "underlying insurance" for the liquor liability risks described above exists or would have existed but for the exhaustion of underlying limits for "bodily injury" and "property damage". Coverage provided will follow the provisions, exclusions and limitations of the "underlying insurance" unless otherwise directed by this insurance.

d. Workers' Compensation And Similar Laws

Any obligation of the insured under a workers' compensation, disability benefits or unemployment compensation law or any similar law.

e. E.R.I.S.A.

Any obligation of the insured under the Employees' Retirement Income Security Act (E.R.I.S.A.), and any amendments thereto or any similar federal, state or local statute.

f. Auto Coverages

(1) "Bodily injury" or "property damage" arising out of the ownership, maintenance or use of any "auto" which is not a "covered auto"; or

(2) Any loss, cost or expense payable under or resulting from any first party physical damage coverage; no-fault law; personal injury protection or auto medical payments coverage; or uninsured or underinsured motorist law.

g. Employer's Liability

"Bodily injury" to:

(1) An "employee" of the insured arising out of and in the course of:

(a) Employment by the insured; or

(b) Performing duties related to the conduct of the insured's business; or

(2) The spouse, child, parent, brother or sister of that "employee" as a consequence of Paragraph **(1)** above.

This exclusion applies whether the insured may be liable as an employer or in any other capacity, and to any obligation to share damages with or repay someone else who must pay damages because of the injury.

This exclusion does not apply to liability assumed by the insured under an "insured contract".

With respect to injury arising out of a "covered auto", this exclusion does not apply to "bodily injury" to domestic "employees" not entitled to workers' compensation benefits. For the purposes of this insurance, a domestic "employee" is a person engaged in household or domestic work performed principally in connection with a residence premises.

This exclusion does not apply to the extent that valid "underlying insurance" for the employer's liability risks described above exists or would have existed but for the exhaustion of underlying limits for "bodily injury". Coverage provided will follow the provisions, exclusions and limitations of the "underlying insurance" unless otherwise directed by this insurance.

h. Employment-Related Practices

"Bodily injury" to:

(1) A person arising out of any:

   (a) Refusal to employ that person;

   (b) Termination of that person's employment; or

   (c) Employment-related practices, policies, acts or omissions, such as coercion, demotion, evaluation, reassignment, discipline, defamation, harassment, humiliation, discrimination or malicious prosecution directed at that person; or

(2) The spouse, child, parent, brother or sister of that person as a consequence of "bodily injury" to that person at whom any of the employment-related practices described in Paragraphs **(a)**, **(b)**, or **(c)** above is directed.

This exclusion applies whether the injury-causing event described in Paragraphs **(a)**, **(b)** or **(c)** above occurs before employment, during employment or after employment of that person.

This exclusion applies whether the insured may be liable as an employer or in any other capacity, and to any obligation to share damages with or repay someone else who must pay damages because of the injury.

i. Pollution

(1) "Bodily injury" or "property damage" which would not have occurred in whole or part but for the actual, alleged or threatened discharge, dispersal, seepage, migration, release or escape of "pollutants" at any time; or

(2) "Pollution cost or expense".

This exclusion does not apply if valid "underlying insurance" for the pollution liability risks described above exists or would have existed but for the exhaustion of underlying limits for "bodily injury" and "property damage". Coverage provided will follow the provisions, exclusions and limitations of the "underlying insurance".

j. Aircraft Or Watercraft

"Bodily injury" or "property damage" arising out of the ownership, maintenance, use or entrustment to others of any aircraft or watercraft owned or operated by or rented or loaned to any insured. Use includes operation and "loading or unloading".

This exclusion applies even if the claims against any insured allege negligence or other wrongdoing in the supervision, hiring, employment, training or monitoring of others by that insured, if the "occurrence" which caused the "bodily injury" or "property damage" involved the ownership, maintenance, use or entrustment to others of any aircraft or watercraft that is owned or operated by or rented or loaned to any insured.

This exclusion does not apply to:

(1) A watercraft while ashore on premises you own or rent;

(2) A watercraft you do not own that is:

   (a) Less than 50 feet long; and

   (b) Not being used to carry persons or property for a charge;

(3) Liability assumed under any "insured contract" for the ownership, maintenance or use of aircraft or watercraft.

(4) The extent that valid "underlying insurance" for the aircraft or watercraft liability risks described above exists or would have existed but for the exhaustion of underlying limits for "bodily injury" or "property damage". Coverage provided will follow the provisions, exclusions and limitations of the "underlying insurance" unless otherwise directed by this insurance; or

(5) Aircraft that is:

    (a) Chartered by, loaned to, or hired by you with a paid crew; and

    (b) Not owned by any insured.

k. Racing Activities

"Bodily injury" or "property damage" arising out of the use of "mobile equipment" or "autos" in, or while in practice for, or while being prepared for, any prearranged professional or organized racing, speed, demolition, or stunting activity or contest.

l. War

"Bodily injury" or "property damage", however caused, arising, directly or indirectly, out of:

(1) War, including undeclared or civil war;

(2) Warlike action by a military force, including action in hindering or defending against an actual or expected attack, by any government, sovereign or other authority using military personnel or other agents; or

(3) Insurrection, rebellion, revolution, usurped power, or action taken by governmental authority in hindering or defending against any of these.

m. Damage To Property

"Property damage" to:

(1) Property:

    (a) You own, rent, or occupy including any costs or expenses incurred by you, or any other person, organization or entity, for repair, replacement, enhancement, restoration or maintenance of such property for any reason, including prevention of injury to a person or damage to another's property; or

    (b) Owned or transported by the insured and arising out of the ownership, maintenance or use of a "covered auto".

(2) Premises you sell, give away or abandon, if the "property damage" arises out of any part of those premises;

(3) Property loaned to you;

(4) Personal property in the care, custody or control of the insured;

(5) That particular part of real property on which you or any contractors or subcontractors working directly or indirectly on your behalf are performing operations, if the "property damage" arises out of those operations; or

(6) That particular part of any property that must be restored, repaired or replaced because "your work" was incorrectly performed on it.

Paragraph **(2)** of this exclusion does not apply if the premises are "your work" and were never occupied, rented or held for rental by you.

Paragraphs **(1)(b)**, **(3)**, **(4)**, **(5)** and **(6)** of this exclusion do not apply to liability assumed under a sidetrack agreement.

Paragraphs **(3)** and **(4)** of this exclusion do not apply to liability assumed under a written Trailer Interchange agreement.

Paragraph **(6)** of this exclusion does not apply to "property damage" included in the "products-completed operations hazard".

n. Damage To Your Product

"Property damage" to "your product" arising out of it or any part of it.

o. Damage To Your Work

"Property damage" to "your work" arising out of it or any part of it and included in the "products-completed operations hazard".

This exclusion does not apply if the damaged work or the work out of which the damage arises was performed on your behalf by a subcontractor.

p. Damage To Impaired Property Or Property Not Physically Injured

"Property damage" to "impaired property" or property that has not been physically injured, arising out of:

(1) A defect, deficiency, inadequacy or dangerous condition in "your product" or "your work"; or

(2) A delay or failure by you or anyone acting on your behalf to perform a contract or agreement in accordance with its terms.

This exclusion does not apply to the loss of use of other property arising out of sudden and accidental physical injury to "your product" or "your work" after it has been put to its intended use.

q. Recall Of Products, Work Or Impaired Property

Damages claimed for any loss, cost or expense incurred by you or others for the loss of use, withdrawal, recall, inspection, repair, replacement, adjustment, removal or disposal of:

(1) "Your product";

(2) "Your work"; or

(3) "Impaired property";

if such product, work, or property is withdrawn or recalled from the market or from use by any person or organization because of a known or suspected defect, deficiency, inadequacy or dangerous condition in it.

r. Personal And Advertising Injury

"Bodily injury" arising out of "personal and advertising injury".

s. Professional Services

"Bodily injury" or "property damage" due to rendering or failure to render any professional service. This includes but is not limited to:

(1) Legal, accounting or advertising services;

(2) Preparing, approving, or failing to prepare or approve, maps, shop drawings, opinions, reports, surveys, field orders, change orders or drawings and specifications by any architect, engineer or surveyor performing services on a project on which you serve as construction manager;

(3) Inspection, supervision, quality control, architectural or engineering activities done by or for you on a project on which you serve as construction manager;

(4) Engineering services, including related supervisory or inspection services;

(5) Medical, surgical, dental, x-ray or nursing services treatment, advice or instruction;

(6) Any health or therapeutic service treatment, advice or instruction;

(7) Any service, treatment, advice or instruction for the purpose of appearance or skin enhancement, hair removal or replacement, or personal grooming or therapy;

(8) Any service, treatment, advice or instruction relating to physical fitness, including service, treatment, advice or instruction in connection with diet, cardio-vascular fitness, body building or physical training programs;

(9) Optometry or optical or hearing aid services including the prescribing, preparation, fitting, demonstration or distribution of ophthalmic lenses and similar products or hearing aid devices;

(10) Body piercing services;

(11) Services in the practice of pharmacy; but this exclusion does not apply if you are a retail druggist or your operations are those of a retail drugstore;

(12) Law enforcement or firefighting services; and

(13) Handling, embalming, disposal, burial, cremation or disinterment of dead bodies.

t. Electronic Data

Damages arising out of the loss of, loss of use of, damage to, corruption of, inability to access or inability to manipulate electronic data.

As used in this exclusion, electronic data means information, facts or programs stored as or on, created or used on, or transmitted to or from computer software, including systems and applications software, hard or floppy disks, CD-ROMS, tapes, drives, cells, data processing devices or any other media which are used with electronically controlled equipment.

This exclusion does not apply if valid "underlying insurance" for the electronic data risks described above exists or would have existed but for the exhaustion of underlying limits for "bodily injury" and "property damage". Coverage provided will follow the provisions, exclusions and limitations of the "underlying insurance", unless otherwise directed by this insurance.

u. Distribution Of Material In Violation Of Statutes

"Bodily injury" or "property damage" arising directly or indirectly out of any action or omission that violates or is alleged to violate:

(1) The Telephone Consumer Protection Act (TCPA), including any amendment of or addition to such law; or

(2) The CAN-SPAM Act of 2003, including any amendment of or addition to such law; or

(3) Any statute, ordinance or regulation, other than the TCPA or CAN-SPAM Act of 2003, that prohibits or limits the sending, transmitting, communicating or distribution of material or information.

COVERAGE B – PERSONAL AND ADVERTISING INJURY LIABILITY

1. Insuring Agreement

a. We will pay on behalf of the insured the "ultimate net loss" in excess of the "retained limit" because of "personal and advertising injury" to which this insurance applies. We will have the right and duty to defend the insured against any "suit" seeking damages for such "personal and advertising injury" when the "underlying insurance" does not provide coverage or the limits of "underlying insurance" have been exhausted. When we have no duty to defend, we will have the right to defend, or to participate in the defense of, the insured against any other "suit" seeking damages to which this insurance may apply. However, we will have no duty to defend the insured against any "suit" seeking damages for "personal and advertising injury" to which this insurance does not apply. At our discretion, we may investigate any offense that may involve this insurance and settle any resultant claim or "suit", for which we have the duty to defend. But:

(1) The amount we will pay for the "ultimate net loss" is limited as described in Section **III** – Limits Of Insurance; and

(2) Our right and duty to defend end when we have used up the applicable limit of insurance in the payment of judgments or settlements under Coverages **A** or **B**.

No other obligation or liability to pay sums or perform acts or services is covered unless explicitly provided for under Supplementary Payments – Coverages **A** and **B**.

b. This insurance applies to "personal and advertising injury" caused by an offense arising out of your business but only if the offense was committed in the "coverage territory" during the policy period.

2. Exclusions

This insurance does not apply to:

a. "Personal and advertising injury":

(1) Knowing Violation Of Rights Of Another

Caused by or at the direction of the insured with the knowledge that the act would violate the rights of another and would inflict "personal and advertising injury".

(2) Material Published With Knowledge Of Falsity

Arising out of oral or written publication of material, if done by or at the direction of the insured with knowledge of its falsity.

(3) Material Published Prior To Policy Period

Arising out of oral or written publication of material whose first publication took place before the beginning of the policy period.

(4) Criminal Acts

Arising out of a criminal act committed by or at the direction of the insured.

(5) Contractual Liability

For which the insured has assumed liability in a contract or agreement. This exclusion does not apply to:

(a) Liability for damages that the insured would have in the absence of the contract or agreement.

(b) Liability for false arrest, detention or imprisonment assumed in a contract or agreement.

(6) Breach Of Contract

Arising out of a breach of contract, except an implied contract to use another's advertising idea in your "advertisement".

(7) Quality Or Performance Of Goods – Failure To Conform To Statements

Arising out of the failure of goods, products or services to conform with any statement of quality or performance made in your "advertisement".

(8) Wrong Description Of Prices

Arising out of the wrong description of the price of goods, products or services stated in your "advertisement".

(9) Infringement Of Copyright, Patent, Trademark Or Trade Secret

Arising out of the infringement of copyright, patent, trademark, trade secret or other intellectual property rights. Under this exclusion, such other intellectual property rights do not include the use of another's advertising idea in your "advertisement".

However, this exclusion does not apply to infringement, in your "advertisement", of copyright, trade dress or slogan.

(10) Insureds In Media And Internet Type Businesses

Committed by an insured whose business is:

(a) Advertising, broadcasting, publishing or telecasting;

(b) Designing or determining content of websites for others; or

(c) An Internet search, access, content or service provider.

However, this exclusion does not apply to Paragraphs **14.a., b.** and **c.** of "personal and advertising injury" under the Definitions Section.

For the purposes of this exclusion, the placing of frames, borders or links, or advertising, for you or others anywhere on the Internet, is not by itself, considered the business of advertising, broadcasting, publishing or telecasting.

(11) Electronic Chatrooms Or Bulletin Boards

Arising out of an electronic chatroom or bulletin board the insured hosts, owns, or over which the insured exercises control.

(12) Unauthorized Use Of Another's Name Or Product

Arising out of the unauthorized use of another's name or product in your e-mail address, domain name or metatag, or any other similar tactics to mislead another's potential customers.

(13) Pollution

Arising out of the actual, alleged or threatened discharge, dispersal, seepage, migration, release or escape of "pollutants" at any time.

(14) Employment-Related Practices

To:

(a) A person arising out of any:

  (i) Refusal to employ that person;

  (ii) Termination of that person's employment; or

  (iii) Employment-related practices, policies, acts or omissions, such as coercion, demotion, evaluation, reassignment, discipline, defamation, harassment, humiliation, discrimination or malicious prosecution directed at that person; or

(b) The spouse, child, parent, brother or sister of that person as a consequence of "personal and advertising injury" to that person at whom any of the employment-related practices described in Paragraphs **(i)**, **(ii)** or **(iii)** above is directed.

This exclusion applies whether the injury-causing event described in Paragraphs **(i)**, **(ii)** or **(iii)** above occurs before employment, during employment or after employment of that person.

This exclusion applies whether the insured may be liable as an employer or in any other capacity, and to any obligation to share damages with or repay someone else who must pay damages because of the injury.

(15) Professional Services

Arising out of the rendering or failure to render any professional service. This includes but is not limited to:

(a) Legal, accounting or advertising services;

(b) Preparing, approving, or failing to prepare or approve, maps, shop drawings, opinions, reports, surveys, field orders, change orders or drawings and specifications by any architect, engineer or surveyor performing services on a project on which you serve as construction manager;

(c) Inspection, supervision, quality control, architectural or engineering activities done by or for you on a project on which you serve as construction manager.

(d) Engineering services, including related supervisory or inspection services;

(e) Medical, surgical, dental, x-ray or nursing services treatment, advice or instruction;

(f) Any health or therapeutic service treatment, advice or instruction;

(g) Any service, treatment, advice or instruction for the purpose of appearance or skin enhancement, hair removal or replacement, or personal grooming or therapy;

(h) Any service, treatment, advice or instruction relating to physical fitness, including service, treatment, advice or instruction in connection with diet, cardiovascular fitness, body building or physical training programs;

 i) Optometry or optical or hearing aid services including the prescribing, preparation, fitting, demonstration or distribution of ophthalmic lenses and similar products or hearing aid devices;

(j) Body piercing services;

(k) Services in the practice of pharmacy; but this exclusion does not apply if you are a retail druggist or your operations are those of a retail drugstore;

(l) Law enforcement or firefighting services; and

(m) Handling, embalming, disposal, burial, cremation or disinterment of dead bodies.

(16) War

"Personal and advertising injury", however caused, arising, directly or indirectly, out of:

(a) War, including undeclared or civil war;

(b) Warlike action by a military force, including action in hindering or defending against an actual or expected attack, by any government, sovereign or other authority using military personnel or other agents; or

(c) Insurrection, rebellion, revolution, usurped power, or action taken by governmental authority in hindering or defending against any of these.

(17) Distribution Of Material In Violation Of Statutes

"Personal and advertising injury" arising directly or indirectly out of any action or omission that violates or is alleged to violate:

(a) The Telephone Consumer Protection Act (TCPA), including any amendment of or addition to such law; or

(b) The CAN-SPAM Act of 2003, including any amendment of or addition to such law; or

(c) Any statute, ordinance or regulation, other than the TCPA or CAN-SPAM Act of 2003, that prohibits or limits the sending, transmitting, communicating or distribution of material or information.

b. "Pollution cost or expense".

SUPPLEMENTARY PAYMENTS – COVERAGES A AND B

1. We will pay, with respect to any claim we investigate or settle, or any "suit" against an insured we defend, when the duty to defend exists:

a. All expenses we incur.

b. Up to $2000 for cost of bail bonds (including bonds for related traffic law violations) required because of an "occurrence" we cover. We do not have to furnish these bonds.

c. The cost of bonds to release attachments, but only for bond amounts within the applicable limit of insurance. We do not have to furnish these bonds.

d. All reasonable expenses incurred by the insured at our request to assist us in the investigation or defense of the claim or "suit", including actual loss of earnings up to $250 a day because of time off from work.

e. All court costs taxed against the insured in the "suit". However, these payments do not include attorneys' fees or attorneys' expenses taxed against the insured.

f. Prejudgment interest awarded against the insured on that part of the judgment we pay. If we make an offer to pay the applicable limit of insurance, we will not pay any prejudgment interest based on that period of time after the offer.

g. All interest on the full amount of any judgment that accrues after entry of the judgment and before we have paid, offered to pay, or deposited in court the part of the judgment that is within the applicable limit of insurance.

These payments will not reduce the limits of insurance.

2. When we have the right but not the duty to defend the insured and elect to participate in the defense, we will pay our own expenses but will not contribute to the expenses of the insured or the "underlying insurer".

3. If we defend an insured against a "suit" and an indemnitee of the insured is also named as a party to the "suit", we will defend that indemnitee if all of the following conditions are met:

a. The "suit" against the indemnitee seeks damages for which the insured has assumed the liability of the indemnitee in a contract or agreement that is an "insured contract";

b. This insurance applies to such liability assumed by the insured;

c. The obligation to defend, or the cost of the defense of, that indemnitee, has also been assumed by the insured in the same "insured contract";

d. The allegations in the "suit" and the information we know about the "occurrence" are such that no conflict appears to exist between the interests of the insured and the interests of the indemnitee;

e. The indemnitee and the insured ask us to conduct and control the defense of that indemnitee against such "suit" and agree that we can assign the same counsel to defend the insured and the indemnitee; and

f. The indemnitee:

(1) Agrees in writing to:

(a) Cooperate with us in the investigation, settlement or defense of the "suit";

(b) Immediately send us copies of any demands, notices, summonses or legal papers received in connection with the "suit";

(c) Notify any other insurer whose coverage is available to the indemnitee; and

(d) Cooperate with us with respect to coordinating other applicable insurance available to the indemnitee; and

(2) Provides us with written authorization to:

(a) Obtain records and other information related to the "suit"; and

(b) Conduct and control the defense of the indemnitee in such "suit".

So long as the above conditions are met, attorneys' fees incurred by us in the defense of that indemnitee, necessary litigation expenses incurred by us and necessary litigation expenses incurred by the indemnitee at our request will be paid as Supplementary Payments. Notwithstanding the provisions of Paragraph **2.b.(2)** of Section **I** – Coverage **A** – Bodily Injury And Property Damage Liability, such payments will not be deemed to be damages for "bodily injury" and "property damage" and will not reduce the limits of insurance.

Our obligation to defend an insured's indemnitee and to pay for attorneys' fees and necessary litigation expenses as Supplementary Payments ends when we have used up the applicable limit of insurance in the payment of judgments or settlements or the conditions set forth above, or the terms of the agreement described in Paragraph **f.** above, are no longer met.

SECTION II – WHO IS AN INSURED

1. Except for liability arising out of the ownership, maintenance or use of "covered autos":

a. If you are designated in the Declarations as:

(1) An individual, you and your spouse are insureds, but only with respect to the conduct of a business of which you are the sole owner.

(2) A partnership or joint venture, you are an insured. Your members, your partners, and their spouses are also insureds, but only with respect to the conduct of your business.

(3) A limited liability company, you are an insured. Your members are also insureds, but only with respect to the conduct of your business. Your managers are insureds, but only with respect to their duties as your managers.

(4) An organization other than a partnership, joint venture or limited liability company, you are an insured. Your "executive officers" and directors are insureds, but only with respect to their duties as your officers or directors. Your stockholders are also insureds, but only with respect to their liability as stockholders.

(5) A trust, you are an insured. Your trustees are also insureds, but only with respect to their duties as trustees.

b. Each of the following is also an insured:

(1) Your "volunteer workers" only while performing duties related to the conduct of your business, or your "employees", other than either your "executive officers" (if you are an organization other than a partnership, joint venture or limited liability company) or your managers (if you are a limited liability company), but only for acts within the scope of their employment by you or while performing duties related to the conduct of your business. However, none of these "employees" or "volunteer workers" are insureds for:

(a) "Bodily injury" or "personal and advertising injury":

(i) To you, to your partners or members (if you are a partnership or joint venture), to your members (if you are a limited liability company), to a co-"employee" in the course of his or her employment or performing duties related to the conduct of your business or to your other "volunteer workers" while performing duties related to the conduct of your business;

(ii) To the spouse, child, parent, brother or sister of that co-"employee" or "volunteer worker" as a consequence of Paragraph **(a)(i)** above; or

(iii) For which there is any obligation to share damages with or repay someone else who must pay damages because of the injury described in Paragraphs **(a)(i)** or **(ii)** above.

(b) "Property damage" to property:

(i) Owned, occupied or used by,

(ii) Rented to, in the care, custody or control of, or over which physical control is being exercised for any purpose by

you, any of your "employees", "volunteer workers", any partner or member (if you are a partnership or joint venture), or any member (if you are a limited liability company).

(2) Any person (other than your "employee" or "volunteer worker"), or any organization while acting as your real estate manager.

(3) Any person or organization having proper temporary custody of your property if you die, but only:

(a) With respect to liability arising out of the maintenance or use of that property; and

(b) Until your legal representative has been appointed.

(4) Your legal representative if you die, but only with respect to duties as such. That representative will have all your rights and duties under this Coverage Part.

c. Any organization you newly acquire or form, other than a partnership, joint venture or limited liability company, and over which you maintain ownership or majority interest, will qualify as a Named Insured if there is no other similar insurance available to that organization. However:

(1) Coverage under this provision is afforded only until the 90th day after you acquire or form the organization or the end of the policy period, whichever is earlier;

(2) Coverage **A** does not apply to "bodily injury" or "property damage" that occurred before you acquired or formed the organization; and

(3) Coverage **B** does not apply to "personal and advertising injury" arising out of an offense committed before you acquired or formed the organization.

2. Only with respect to liability arising out of the ownership, maintenance or use of "covered autos":

a. You are an insured.

b. Anyone else while using with your permission a "covered auto" you own, hire or borrow is also an insured except:

(1) The owner or anyone else from whom you hire or borrow a "covered auto". This exception does not apply if the "covered auto" is a trailer or semitrailer connected to a "covered auto" you own.

(2) Your "employee" if the "covered auto" is owned by that "employee" or a member of his or her household.

(3) Someone using a "covered auto" while he or she is working in a business of selling, servicing, repairing, parking or storing "autos" unless that business is yours.

(4) Anyone other than your "employees", partners (if you are a partnership), members (if you are a limited liability company), or a lessee or borrower or any of their "employees", while moving property to or from a "covered auto".

(5) A partner (if you are a partnership), or a member (if you are a limited liability company) for a "covered auto" owned by him or her or a member of his or her household.

(6) "Employees" with respect to "bodily injury" to any fellow "employee" of the insured arising out of and in the course of the fellow "employee's" employment or while performing duties related to the conduct of your business.

c. Anyone liable for the conduct of an insured described above is also an insured, but only to the extent of that liability.

3. Any additional insured under any policy of "underlying insurance" will automatically be an insured under this insurance.

If coverage provided to the additional insured is required by a contract or agreement, the most we will pay on behalf of the additional insured is the amount of insurance required by the contract, less any amounts payable by any "underlying insurance".

Additional insured coverage provided by this insurance will not be broader than coverage provided by the "underlying insurance".

No person or organization is an insured with respect to the conduct of any current or past partnership, joint venture or limited liability company that is not shown as a Named Insured in the Declarations.

SECTION III – LIMITS OF INSURANCE

1. The Limits of Insurance shown in the Declarations and the rules below fix the most we will pay regardless of the number of:

   a. Insureds;

   b. Claims made, "suits" brought, or number of vehicles involved; or

   c. Persons or organizations making claims or bringing "suits".

2. The Aggregate Limit is the most we will pay for the sum of all "ultimate net loss" under:

   a. Coverage **A,** except "ultimate net loss" because of "bodily injury" or "property damage" arising out of the ownership, maintenance or use of a "covered auto"; and

   b. Coverage **B.**

3. Subject to Paragraph **2.** above, the Each Occurrence Limit is the most we will pay for the sum of all "ultimate net loss" under Coverage **A** because of all "bodily injury" and "property damage" arising out of any one "occurrence".

4. Subject to Paragraph **2.** above, the Personal and Advertising Injury Limit is the most we will pay under Coverage **B** for the sum of all "ultimate net loss" because of all "personal and advertising injury" sustained by any one person or organization.

5. If there is "underlying insurance" with a policy period that is non-concurrent with the policy period of this Commercial Liability Umbrella Coverage Part, the "retained limit(s)" will only be reduced or exhausted by payments for:

   a. "Bodily injury" or "property damage" which occurs during the policy period of this Coverage Part; or

   b. "Personal and advertising injury" for offenses that are committed during the policy period of this Coverage Part.

   However, if any "underlying insurance" is written on a claims-made basis, the "retained limit(s)" will only be reduced or exhausted by claims for that insurance that are made during the policy period, or any Extended Reporting Period, of this Coverage Part.

The Aggregate Limit, as described in Paragraph **2.** above, applies separately to each consecutive annual period and to any remaining period of less than 12 months, starting with the beginning of the policy period shown in the Declarations, unless the policy period is extended after issuance for an additional period of less than 12 months. In that case, the additional period will be deemed part of the last preceding period for purposes of determining the Limits of Insurance.

SECTION IV – CONDITIONS

1. **Appeals**

   If the "underlying insurer" or insured elects not to appeal a judgment in excess of the "retained limit", we may do so at our own expense. We will be liable for taxable costs, pre- and postjudgment interest and disbursements.

2. **Bankruptcy**

   a. **Bankruptcy Of Insured**

   Bankruptcy or insolvency of the insured or of the insured's estate will not relieve us of our obligations under this Coverage Part.

   b. **Bankruptcy Of Underlying Insurer**

   Bankruptcy of the "underlying insurer" will not relieve us of our obligations under this Coverage Part.

   However, this insurance will not replace the "underlying insurance" in the event of bankruptcy or insolvency of the "underlying insurer". This insurance will apply as if the "underlying insurance" were in full effect.

3. **Duties In The Event Of Occurrence, Offense, Claim Or Suit**

   a. You must see to it that we are notified as soon as practicable of an "occurrence" or an offense, regardless of the amount, which may result in a claim. To the extent possible, notice should include:

      (1) How, when and where the "occurrence" or offense took place;

      (2) The names and addresses of any injured persons and witnesses; and

      (3) The nature and location of any injury or damage arising out of the "occurrence" or offense.

   b. If a claim is made or "suit" is brought against any insured, you must:

      (1) Immediately record the specifics of the claim or "suit" and the date received; and

      (2) Notify us as soon as practicable.

      You must see to it that we receive written notice of the claim or "suit" as soon as practicable.

   c. You and any other involved insured must:

      (1) Immediately send us copies of any demands, notices, summonses or legal papers received in connection with the claim or "suit";

      (2) Authorize us to obtain records and other information;

(3) Cooperate with us in the investigation or settlement of the claim or defense against the "suit"; and

(4) Assist us, upon our request, in the enforcement of any right against any person or organization which may be liable to the insured because of injury or damage to which this insurance may also apply.

d. No insured will, except at that insured's own cost, voluntarily make a payment, assume any obligation, or incur any expense, other than for first aid, without our consent.

4. Legal Action Against Us

No person or organization has a right under this Coverage Part:

a. To join us as a party or otherwise bring us into a "suit" asking for damages from an insured; or

b. To sue us on this Coverage Part unless all of its terms have been fully complied with.

A person or organization may sue us to recover on an agreed settlement or on a final judgment against an insured; but we will not be liable for damages that are not payable under the terms of this Coverage Part or that are in excess of the applicable limit of insurance. An agreed settlement means a settlement and release of liability signed by us, the insured and the claimant or the claimant's legal representative.

5. Other Insurance

a. This insurance is excess over, and shall not contribute with any of the other insurance, whether primary, excess, contingent or on any other basis. This condition will not apply to insurance specifically written as excess over this Coverage Part.

When this insurance is excess, we will have no duty under Coverages **A** or **B** to defend the insured against any "suit" if any other insurer has a duty to defend the insured against that "suit". If no other insurer defends, we will undertake to do so, but we will be entitled to the insured's rights against all those other insurers.

b. When this insurance is excess over other insurance, we will pay only our share of the "ultimate net loss" that exceeds the sum of:

(1) The total amount that all such other insurance would pay for the loss in the absence of this insurance; and

(2) The total of all deductible and self-insured amounts under all that other insurance.

6. Premium Audit

a. We will compute all premiums for this Coverage Part in accordance with our rules and rates.

b. Premium shown in this Coverage Part as advance premium is a deposit premium only. At the close of each audit period we will compute the earned premium for that period and send notice to the first Named Insured. The due date for audit and retrospective premiums is the date shown as the due date on the bill. If the sum of the advance and audit premiums paid for the policy period is greater than the earned premium, we will return the excess to the first Named Insured.

c. The first Named Insured must keep records of the information we need for premium computation, and send us copies at such times as we may request.

7. Representations Or Fraud

By accepting this policy, you agree:

a. The statements in the Declarations are accurate and complete;

b. Those statements are based upon representations you made to us;

c. We have issued this policy in reliance upon your representations; and

d. This policy is void in any case of fraud by you as it relates to this policy or any claim under this policy.

8. Separation Of Insureds

Except with respect to the Limits of Insurance, and any rights or duties specifically assigned in this Coverage Part to the first Named Insured, this insurance applies:

a. As if each Named Insured were the only Named Insured; and

b. Separately to each insured against whom claim is made or "suit" is brought.

9. Transfer Of Rights Of Recovery Against Others To Us

If the insured has rights to recover all or part of any payment we have made under this Coverage Part, those rights are transferred to us. The insured must do nothing after loss to impair them. At our request, the insured will bring "suit" or transfer those rights to us and help us enforce them.

10. When We Do Not Renew

If we decide not to renew this Coverage Part, we will mail or deliver to the first Named Insured shown in the Declarations written notice of the nonrenewal not less than 30 days before the expiration date.

If notice is mailed, proof of mailing will be sufficient proof of notice.

11. Loss Payable

Liability under this Coverage Part shall not apply unless and until the insured or insured's "underlying insurer" has become obligated to pay the "retained limit". Such obligation by the insured to pay part of the "ultimate net loss" shall have been previously determined by a final settlement or judgment after an actual trial or written agreement between the insured, claimant, and us.

12. Transfer Of Defense

When the underlying limits of insurance have been used up in the payment of judgments or settlements, the duty to defend will be transferred to us. We will cooperate in the transfer of control to us of any outstanding claims or "suits" seeking damages to which this insurance applies which would have been covered by the "underlying insurance" had the applicable limit not been used up.

13. Maintenance Of/Changes To Underlying Insurance

The "underlying insurance" listed in the Schedule of "underlying insurance" in the Declarations shall remain in full effect throughout the policy period except for reduction of the aggregate limit due to payment of claims, settlement or judgments.

Failure to maintain "underlying insurance" will not invalidate this insurance. However, this insurance will apply as if the "underlying insurance" were in full effect.

If there is an increase in the scope of coverage of any "underlying insurance" during the term of this policy, our liability will be no more than it would have been if there had been no such increase.

You must notify us as soon as practicable when any "underlying insurance" is no longer in effect or if the limits or scope of coverage of any "underlying insurance" is changed.

14. Expanded Coverage Territory

a. If a "suit" is brought in a part of the "coverage territory" that is outside the United States of America (including its territories and possessions), Puerto Rico or Canada, and we are prevented by law, or otherwise, from defending the insured, the insured will initiate a defense of the "suit". We will reimburse the insured, under Supplementary Payments, for any reasonable and necessary expenses incurred for the defense of a "suit" seeking damages to which this insurance applies, that we would have paid had we been able to exercise our right and duty to defend.

If the insured becomes legally obligated to pay sums because of damages to which this insurance applies in a part of the "coverage territory" that is outside the United States of America (including its territories and possessions), Puerto Rico or Canada, and we are prevented by law, or otherwise, from paying such sums on the insured's behalf, we will reimburse the insured for such sums.

b. All payments or reimbursements we make for damages because of judgments or settlements will be made in U.S. currency at the prevailing exchange rate at the time the insured became legally obligated to pay such sums. All payments or reimbursements we make for expenses under Supplementary Payments will be made in U.S. currency at the prevailing exchange rate at the time the expenses were incurred.

c. Any disputes between you and us as to whether there is coverage under this policy must be filed in the courts of the United States of America (including its territories and possessions), Canada or Puerto Rico.

d. The insured must fully maintain any coverage required by law, regulation or other governmental authority during the policy period, except for reduction of the aggregate limits due to payments of claims, judgments or settlements.

Failure to maintain such coverage required by law, regulation or other governmental authority will not invalidate this insurance. However, this insurance will apply as if the required coverage by law, regulation or other governmental authority was in full effect.

SECTION V – DEFINITIONS

1. "Advertisement" means a notice that is broadcast or published to the general public or specific market segments about your goods, products or services for the purpose of attracting customers or supporters. For the purposes of this definition:

    a. Notices that are published include material placed on the Internet or on similar electronic means of communication; and

    b. Regarding websites, only that part of a website that is about your goods, products or services for the purposes of attracting customers or supporters is considered an advertisement.

2. "Auto" means:

    a. A land motor vehicle, trailer or semitrailer designed for travel on public roads, including any attached machinery or equipment; or

    b. Any other land vehicle that is subject to a compulsory or financial responsibility law or other motor vehicle insurance law where it is licensed or principally garaged.

    However, "auto" does not include "mobile equipment".

3. "Bodily injury" means bodily injury, disability, sickness, or disease sustained by a person, including death resulting from any of these at any time. "Bodily injury" includes mental anguish or other mental injury resulting from "bodily injury".

4. "Coverage territory" means anywhere in the world with the exception of any country or jurisdiction which is subject to trade or other economic sanction or embargo by the United States of America.

5. "Covered auto" means only those "autos" to which "underlying insurance" applies.

6. "Employee" includes a "leased worker". "Employee" does not include a "temporary worker".

7. "Executive officer" means a person holding any of the officer positions created by your charter, constitution, by-laws or any other similar governing document.

8. "Impaired property" means tangible property, other than "your product" or "your work", that cannot be used or is less useful because:

    a. It incorporates "your product" or "your work" that is known or thought to be defective, deficient, inadequate or dangerous; or

    b. You have failed to fulfill the terms of a contract or agreement;

    if such property can be restored to use by the repair, replacement, adjustment or removal of "your product" or "your work", or your fulfilling the terms of the contract or agreement.

9. "Insured contract" means:

    a. A contract for a lease of premises. However, that portion of the contract for a lease of premises that indemnifies any person or organization for damage by fire to premises while rented to you or temporarily occupied by you with permission of the owner is not an "insured contract";

    b. A sidetrack agreement;

    c. Any easement or license agreement, except in connection with construction or demolition operations on or within 50 feet of a railroad;

    d. An obligation, as required by ordinance, to indemnify a municipality, except in connection with work for a municipality;

    e. An elevator maintenance agreement;

    f. That part of any contract or agreement entered into, as part of your business, pertaining to the rental or lease, by you or any of your "employees", of any "auto". However, such contract or agreement shall not be considered an "insured contract" to the extent that it obligates you or any of your "employees" to pay for "property damage" to any "auto" rented or leased by you or any of your "employees".

    g. That part of any other contract or agreement pertaining to your business (including an indemnification of a municipality in connection with work performed for a municipality) under which you assume the tort liability of another party to pay for "bodily injury" or "property damage" to a third person or organization. Tort liability means a liability that would be imposed by law in the absence of any contract or agreement.

    Paragraphs **f.** and **g.** do not include that part of any contract or agreement:

    (1) That indemnifies a railroad for "bodily injury" or "property damage" arising out of construction or demolition operations, within 50 feet of any railroad property and affecting any railroad bridge or trestle, tracks, roadbeds, tunnel, underpass or crossing;

    (2) That pertains to the loan, lease or rental of an "auto" to you or any of your "employees", if the "auto" is loaned, leased or rented with a driver; or

    (3) That holds a person or organization engaged in the business of transporting property by "auto" for hire harmless for your use of a "covered auto" over a route or territory that person or organization is authorized to serve by public authority.

© ISO Properties, Inc., 2007

10. "Leased worker" means a person leased to you by a labor leasing firm under an agreement between you and the labor leasing firm, to perform duties related to the conduct of your business. "Leased worker" does not include a "temporary worker".

11. "Loading or unloading" means the handling of property:

   a. After it is moved from the place where it is accepted for movement into or onto an aircraft, watercraft or "auto";

   b. While it is in or on an aircraft, watercraft or "auto"; or

   c. While it is being moved from an aircraft, watercraft or "auto" to the place where it is finally delivered;

   but "loading or unloading" does not include the movement of property by means of a mechanical device, other than a hand truck, that is not attached to the aircraft, watercraft or "auto".

12. "Mobile equipment" means any of the following types of land vehicles, including any attached machinery or equipment:

   a. Bulldozers, farm machinery, forklifts and other vehicles designed for use principally off public roads;

   b. Vehicles maintained for use solely on or next to premises you own or rent;

   c. Vehicles that travel on crawler treads;

   d. Vehicles, whether self-propelled or not, maintained primarily to provide mobility to permanently mounted:

      (1) Power cranes, shovels, loaders, diggers or drills; or

      (2) Road construction or resurfacing equipment such as graders, scrapers or rollers;

   e. Vehicles not described in Paragraph a., b., c. or d. above that are not self-propelled and are maintained primarily to provide mobility to permanently attached equipment of the following types:

      (1) Air compressors, pumps and generators, including spraying, welding, building cleaning, geophysical exploration, lighting and well servicing equipment; or

      (2) Cherry pickers and similar devices used to raise or lower workers;

   f. Vehicles not described in Paragraph a., b., c. or d. above maintained primarily for purposes other than the transportation of persons or cargo.

However, self-propelled vehicles with the following types of permanently attached equipment are not "mobile equipment" but will be considered "autos":

   (1) Equipment designed primarily for:

      (a) Snow removal;

      (b) Road maintenance, but not construction or resurfacing; or

      (c) Street cleaning;

   (2) Cherry pickers and similar devices mounted on automobile or truck chassis and used to raise or lower workers; and

   (3) Air compressors, pumps and generators, including spraying, welding, building cleaning, geophysical exploration, lighting and well servicing equipment.

However, "mobile equipment" does not include land vehicles that are subject to a compulsory or financial responsibility law or other motor vehicle insurance law where it is licensed or principally garaged. Land vehicles subject to a compulsory or financial responsibility law or other motor vehicle insurance law are considered "autos".

13. "Occurrence" means an accident, including continuous or repeated exposure to substantially the same general harmful conditions.

14. "Personal and advertising injury" means injury, including consequential "bodily injury", arising out of one or more of the following offenses:

   a. False arrest, detention or imprisonment;

   b. Malicious prosecution;

   c. The wrongful eviction from, wrongful entry into, or invasion of the right of private occupancy of a room, dwelling or premises that a person occupies, committed by or on behalf of its owner, landlord or lessor;

   d. Oral or written publication, in any manner, of material that slanders or libels a person or organization or disparages a person's or organization's goods, products or services;

   e. Oral or written publication, in any manner, of material that violates a person's right of privacy;

   f. The use of another's advertising idea in your "advertisement"; or

   g. Infringing upon another's copyright, trade dress or slogan in your "advertisement".

15. "Pollutants" mean any solid, liquid, gaseous or thermal irritant or contaminant, including smoke, vapor, soot, fumes, acids, alkalis, chemicals and waste. Waste includes materials to be recycled, reconditioned or reclaimed.

16. "Pollution cost or expense" means any loss, cost or expense arising out of any:

a. Request, demand, order or statutory or regulatory requirement that any insured or others test for, monitor, clean up, remove, contain, treat, detoxify or neutralize, or in any way respond to, or assess the effects of, "pollutants"; or

b. Claim or suit by or on behalf of a governmental authority for damages because of testing for, monitoring, cleaning up, removing, containing, treating, detoxifying or neutralizing, or in any way responding to, or assessing the effects of, "pollutants".

17. "Products-completed operations hazard":

a. Includes all "bodily injury" and "property damage" occurring away from premises you own or rent and arising out of "your product" or "your work" except:

(1) Products that are still in your physical possession; or

(2) Work that has not yet been completed or abandoned. However, "your work" will be deemed completed at the earliest of the following times:

(a) When all of the work called for in your contract has been completed.

(b) When all of the work to be done at the job site has been completed if your contract calls for work at more than one job site.

(c) When that part of the work done at a job site has been put to its intended use by any person or organization other than another contractor or subcontractor working on the same project.

Work that may need service, maintenance, correction, repair or replacement, but which is otherwise complete, will be treated as completed.

b. Does not include "bodily injury" or "property damage" arising out of:

(1) The transportation of property, unless the injury or damage arises out of a condition in or on a vehicle not owned or operated by you, and that condition was created by the "loading or unloading" of that vehicle by any insured; or

(2) The existence of tools, uninstalled equipment or abandoned or unused materials.

18. "Property damage" means:

a. Physical injury to tangible property, including all resulting loss of use of that property. All such loss of use shall be deemed to occur at the time of the physical injury that caused it; or

b. Loss of use of tangible property that is not physically injured. All such loss of use shall be deemed to occur at the time of the "occurrence" that caused it.

With respect to the ownership, maintenance or use of "covered autos", property damage also includes "pollution cost or expense", but only to the extent that coverage exists under the "underlying insurance" or would have existed but for the exhaustion of the underlying limits.

For the purposes of this insurance, with respect to other than the ownership, maintenance or use of "covered autos", electronic data is not tangible property.

As used in this definition, electronic data means information, facts or programs stored as or on, created or used on, or transmitted to or from computer software (including systems and applications software), hard or floppy disks, CD-ROMS, tapes, drives, cells, data processing devices or any other media which are used with electronically controlled equipment.

19. "Retained limit" means the available limits of "underlying insurance" scheduled in the Declarations or the "self-insured retention", whichever applies.

20. "Self-insured retention" means the dollar amount listed in the Declarations that will be paid by the insured before this insurance becomes applicable only with respect to "occurrences" or offenses not covered by the "underlying insurance". The "self-insured retention" does not apply to "occurrences" or offenses which would have been covered by "underlying insurance" but for the exhaustion of applicable limits.

21. "Suit" means a civil proceeding in which damages because of "bodily injury", "property damage" or "personal and advertising injury" to which this insurance applies are alleged. "Suit" includes:

a. An arbitration proceeding in which such damages are claimed and to which the insured must submit or does submit with our consent; or

b. Any other alternative dispute resolution proceeding in which such damages are claimed and to which the insured submits with our consent or the "underlying insurer's" consent.

22. "Temporary worker" means a person who is furnished to you to substitute for a permanent "employee" on leave or to meet seasonal or short-term workload conditions.

23. "Ultimate net loss" means the total sum, after reduction for recoveries or salvages collectible, that the insured becomes legally obligated to pay as damages by reason of settlement or judgments or any arbitration or other alternate dispute method entered into with our consent or the "underlying insurer's" consent.

24. "Underlying insurance" means any policies of insurance listed in the Declarations under the Schedule of "underlying insurance".

25. "Underlying insurer" means any insurer who provides any policy of insurance listed in the Schedule of "underlying insurance".

26. "Volunteer worker" means a person who is not your "employee", and who donates his or her work and acts at the direction of and within the scope of duties determined by you, and is not paid a fee, salary or other compensation by you or anyone else for their work performed for you.

27. "Your product":

  a. Means:

    (1) Any goods or products, other than real property, manufactured, sold, handled, distributed or disposed of by:

      (a) You;

      (b) Others trading under your name; or

      (c) A person or organization whose business or assets you have acquired; and

    (2) Containers (other than vehicles), materials, parts or equipment furnished in connection with such goods or products.

  b. Includes:

    (1) Warranties or representations made at any time with respect to the fitness, quality, durability, performance or use of "your product"; and

    (2) The providing of or failure to provide warnings or instructions.

  c. Does not include vending machines or other property rented to or located for the use of others but not sold.

28. "Your work":

  a. Means:

    (1) Work or operations performed by you or on your behalf; and

    (2) Materials, parts or equipment furnished in connection with such work or operations.

  b. Includes:

    (1) Warranties or representations made at any time with respect to the fitness, quality, durability, performance or use of "your work", and

    (2) The providing of or failure to provide warnings or instructions.

Surety Bonds

A surety bond involves three parties: the principal, the obligee, and the surety. The principal is obligated to perform in some way for the benefit of the obligee. The surety guarantees to the obligee that the principal will fulfill the underlying obligations. In most cases, the party making the guarantee—the surety—is an insurer that also writes property and liability insurance.

Many types of surety bonds are used in a variety of circumstances. Common categories of surety bonds are as follows.

Contract bonds guarantee the performance of public or private contracts. The three bonds reproduced in this section of the *Handbook*—a bid bond, a performance bond, and a payment bond—are common examples of contract bonds.

License and permit bonds are required by federal, state, or municipal governments as prerequisites to engaging in certain business activities. Among those parties that may need such bonds are contractors who work on public streets, plumbers, electricians, and automobile dealers.

Public official bonds guarantee the honesty and faithful performance of people who are elected or appointed to positions in government.

Court bonds are a classification that includes judicial bonds and fiduciary bonds. Judicial bonds arise out of litigation and are posted by parties seeking court remedies or defending against legal actions seeking court remedies. Fiduciary bonds are filed in probate courts and courts that exercise equitable jurisdiction; they guarantee that persons entrusted with the care of others' property will perform their specified duties faithfully.

Miscellaneous bonds are those that do not fit well under other commercial surety bond classifications. They often support private relationships and unique business needs. Some significant miscellaneous bonds include lost securities bonds, hazardous waste bonds, and financial guaranty bonds.

BID BOND
(See instruction on reverse)

| DATE BOND EXECUTED *(Must not be later than bid opening date)* | OMB NO.: **9000-0045** |

Public reporting burden for this collection of information is estimated to average 25 minutes per response, including the time for reviewing instructions, searching existing data sources, gathering and maintaining the data needed, and completing and reviewing the collection of information. Send comments regarding this burden estimate or any other aspect of this collection of information, including suggestions for reducing this burden, to the FAR Secretariat (MVR), Federal Acquisition Policy Division, GSA, Washington, DC 20405.

PRINCIPAL *(Legal name and business address)*

TYPE OF ORGANIZATION *("X" one)*

☐ INDIVIDUAL   ☐ PARTNERSHIP

☐ JOINT VENTURE   ☐ CORPORATION

STATE OF INCORPORATION

SURETY(IES) *(Name and business address)*

PENAL SUM OF BOND					BID IDENTIFICATION	
PERCENT OF BID PRICE	AMOUNT NOT TO EXCEED				BID DATE	INVITATION NO.
	MILLION(S)	THOUSAND(S)	HUNDRED(S)	CENTS		
					FOR *(Construction, Supplies, or Services)*	

OBLIGATION:

We, the Principal and Surety(ies) are firmly bound to the United States of America (hereinafter called the Government) in the above penal sum. For payment of the penal sum, we bind ourselves, our heirs, executors, administrators, and successors, jointly and severally. However, where the Sureties are corporations acting as co-sureties, we, the Sureties, bind ourselves in such sum "jointly and severally" as well as "severally" only for the purpose of allowing a joint action or actions against any or all of us. For all other purposes, each Surety binds itself, jointly and severally with the Principal, for the payment of the sum shown opposite the name of the Surety. If no limit of liability is indicated, the limit of liability is the full amount of the penal sum.

CONDITIONS:

The Principal has submitted the bid identified above.

THEREFORE:

The above obligation is void if the Principal - (a) upon acceptance by the Government of the bid identified above, within the period specified therein for acceptance (sixty (60) days if no period is specified), executes the further contractual documents and gives the bond(s) required by the terms of the bid as accepted within the time specified (ten (10) days if no period is specified) after receipt of the forms by the principal; or (b) in the event of failure to execute such further contractual documents and give such bonds, pays the Government for any cost of procuring the work which exceeds the amount of the bid.

Each Surety executing this instrument agrees that its obligation is not impaired by any extension(s) of the time for acceptance of the bid that the Principal may grant to the Government. Notice to the surety(ies) of extension(s) are waived. However, waiver of the notice applies only to extensions aggregating not more than sixty (60) calendar days in addition to the period originally allowed for acceptance of the bid.

WITNESS:

The Principal and Surety(ies) executed this bid bond and affixed their seals on the above date.

PRINCIPAL

	1.	2.	3.	Corporate Seal
SIGNATURE(S)	*(Seal)*	*(Seal)*	*(Seal)*	
NAME(S) & TITLE(S) *(Typed)*	1.	2.	3.	

INDIVIDUAL SURETY(IES)

	1.	2.	
SIGNATURE(S)	*(Seal)*	*(Seal)*	
NAME(S) *(Typed)*	1.	2.	

CORPORATE SURETY(IES)

SURETY A	NAME & ADDRESS		STATE OF INC.	LIABILITY LIMIT ($)	Corporate Seal
	SIGNATURE(S)	1.	2.		
	NAME(S) & TITLE(S) *(Typed)*	1.	2.		

AUTHORIZED FOR LOCAL REPRODUCTION
Previous edition is usable

STANDARD FORM 24 (REV. 10-98)
Prescribed by GSA - FAR (48 CFR) 53.228(a)

SURETY B	NAME & ADDRESS		STATE OF INC.	LIABILITY LIMIT ($)	*Corporate Seal*
	SIGNATURE(S)	1.	2.		
	NAME(S) & TITLE(S) *(Typed)*	1.	2.		
SURETY C	NAME & ADDRESS		STATE OF INC.	LIABILITY LIMIT ($)	*Corporate Seal*
	SIGNATURE(S)	1.	2.		
	NAME(S) & TITLE(S) *(Typed)*	1.	2.		
SURETY D	NAME & ADDRESS		STATE OF INC.	LIABILITY LIMIT ($)	*Corporate Seal*
	SIGNATURE(S)	1.	2.		
	NAME(S) & TITLE(S) *(Typed)*	1.	2.		
SURETY E	NAME & ADDRESS		STATE OF INC.	LIABILITY LIMIT ($)	*Corporate Seal*
	SIGNATURE(S)	1.	2.		
	NAME(S) & TITLE(S) *(Typed)*	1.	2.		
SURETY F	NAME & ADDRESS		STATE OF INC.	LIABILITY LIMIT ($)	*Corporate Seal*
	SIGNATURE(S)	1.	2.		
	NAME(S) & TITLE(S) *(Typed)*	1.	2.		
SURETY G	NAME & ADDRESS		STATE OF INC.	LIABILITY LIMIT ($)	*Corporate Seal*
	SIGNATURE(S)	1.	2.		
	NAME(S) & TITLE(S) *(Typed)*	1.	2.		

INSTRUCTIONS

1. This form is authorized for use when a bid guaranty is required. Any deviation from this form will require the written approval of the Administrator of General Services.

2. Insert the full legal name and business address of the Principal in the space designated "Principal" on the face of the form. An authorized person shall sign the bond. Any person signing in a representative capacity (e.g., an attorney-in-fact) must furnish evidence of authority if that representative is not a member of the firm, partnership, or joint venture, or an officer of the corporation involved.

3. The bond may express penal sum as a percentage of the bid price. In these cases, the bond may state a maximum dollar limitation (e.g., (e.g., 20% of the bid price but the amount not to exceed_____ dollars).

4. (a) Corporations executing the bond as sureties must appear on the Department of the Treasury's list of approved sureties and must act within the limitation listed therein. where more than one corporate surety is involved, their names and addresses shall appear in the spaces (Surety A, Surety B, etc.) headed "CORPORATE SURETY(IES)." In the space designed "SURETY(IES)" on the face of the form, insert only the letter identification of the sureties.

(b) Where individual sureties are involved, a completed Affidavit of Individual surety (Standard Form 28), for each individual surety, shall accompany the bond. The Government may require the surety to furnish additional substantiating information concerning its financial capability.

5. Corporations executing the bond shall affix their corporate seals. Individuals shall execute the bond opposite the word "Corporate Seal"; and shall affix an adhesive seal if executed in Maine, New Hampshire, or any other jurisdiction requiring adhesive seals.

6. Type the name and title of each person signing this bond in the space provided.

7. In its application to negotiated contracts, the terms "bid" and "bidder" shall include "proposal" and "offeror."

STANDARD FORM 24 (REV. 10-98) **BACK**

PERFORMANCE BOND *(See instructions on reverse)*	DATE BOND EXECUTED *(Must be same or later than date of contract)*	OMB No.: **9000-0045**

Public reporting burden for this collection of information is estimated to average 25 minutes per response, including the time for reviewing instructions, searching existing data sources, gathering and maintaining the data needed, and completing and reviewing the collection of information. Send comments regarding this burden estimate or any other aspect of this collection of information, including suggestions for reducing this burden, to the FAR Secretariat (MVR), Federal Acquisition Policy Division, GSA, Washington, DC 20405

PRINCIPAL *(Legal name and business address)*

TYPE OF ORGANIZATION *("X" one)*

☐ INDIVIDUAL   ☐ PARTNERSHIP

☐ JOINT VENTURE   ☐ CORPORATION

STATE OF INCORPORATION

SURETY(IES) *(Name(s) and business address(es))*

PENAL SUM OF BOND

MILLION(S)	THOUSAND(S)	HUNDRED(S)	CENTS

CONTRACT DATE	CONTRACT NO.

OBLIGATION:

We, the Principal and Surety(ies), are firmly bound to the United States of America (hereinafter called the Government) in the above penal sum. For payment of the penal sum, we bind ourselves, our heirs, executors, administrators, and successors, jointly and severally. However, where the Sureties are corporations acting as co-sureties, we, the Sureties, bind ourselves in such sum "jointly and severally" as well as "severally" only for the purpose of allowing a joint action or actions against any or all of us. For all other purposes, each Surety binds itself, jointly and severally with the Principal, for the payment of the sum shown opposite the name of the Surety. If no limit of liability is indicated, the limit of liability is the full amount of the penal sum.

CONDITIONS:

The Principal has entered into the contract identified above.

THEREFORE:

The above obligation is void if the Principal -

  (a)(1) Performs and fulfills all the undertakings, covenants, terms, conditions, and agreements of the contract during the original term of the contract and any extensions thereof that are granted by the Government, with or without notice to the Surety(ies), and during the life of any guaranty required under the contract, and (2) performs and fulfills all the undertakings, covenants, terms conditions, and agreements of any and all duly authorized modifications of the contract that hereafter are made. Notice of those modifications to the Surety(ies) are waived.

  (b)   Pays to the Government the full amount of the taxes imposed by the Government, if the said contract is subject to the Miller Act, (40 U.S.C. 270a-270e), which are collected, deducted, or withheld from wages paid by the Principal in carrying out the construction contract with respect to which this bond is furnished.

WITNESS:

The Principal and Surety(ies) executed this performance bond and affixed their seals on the above date.

PRINCIPAL

SIGNATURE(S)	1. (Seal)	2. (Seal)	3. (Seal)	Corporate Seal
NAME(S) & TITLE(S) *(Typed)*	1.	2.	3.	

INDIVIDUAL SURETY(IES)

SIGNATURE(S)	1. (Seal)	2. (Seal)	
NAME(S) *(Typed)*	1.	2.	

CORPORATE SURETY(IES)

SURETY A	NAME & ADDRESS		STATE OF INC.	LIABILITY LIMIT $	Corporate Seal
	SIGNATURE(S)	1.		2.	
	NAME(S) & TITLE(S) *(Typed)*	1.		2.	

AUTHORIZED FOR LOCAL REPRODUCTION
Previous edition not usable

STANDARD FORM 25 (REV. 5-96)
Prescribed by GSA-FAR (48 CFR) 53.228(b)

CORPORATE SURETY(IES) *(Continued)*

			STATE OF INC.	LIABILITY LIMIT	
SURETY B	NAME & ADDRESS			$	Corporate Seal
	SIGNATURE(S)	1.	2.		
	NAME(S) & TITLE(S) *(Typed)*	1.	2.		
SURETY C	NAME & ADDRESS		STATE OF INC.	LIABILITY LIMIT $	Corporate Seal
	SIGNATURE(S)	1.	2.		
	NAME(S) & TITLE(S) *(Typed)*	1.	2.		
SURETY D	NAME & ADDRESS		STATE OF INC.	LIABILITY LIMIT $	Corporate Seal
	SIGNATURE(S)	1.	2.		
	NAME(S) & TITLE(S) *(Typed)*	1.	2.		
SURETY E	NAME & ADDRESS		STATE OF INC.	LIABILITY LIMIT $	Corporate Seal
	SIGNATURE(S)	1.	2.		
	NAME(S) & TITLE(S) *(Typed)*	1.	2.		
SURETY F	NAME & ADDRESS		STATE OF INC.	LIABILITY LIMIT $	Corporate Seal
	SIGNATURE(S)	1.	2.		
	NAME(S) & TITLE(S) *(Typed)*	1.	2.		
SURETY G	NAME & ADDRESS		STATE OF INC.	LIABILITY LIMIT $	Corporate Seal
	SIGNATURE(S)	1.	2.		
	NAME(S) & TITLE(S) *(Typed)*	1.	2.		

BOND PREMIUM ▶	RATE PER THOUSAND ($)	TOTAL ($)

INSTRUCTIONS

1. This form is authorized for use in connection with Government contracts. Any deviation from this form will require the written approval of the Administrator of General Services.

2. Insert the full legal name and business address of the Principal in the space designated "Principal" on the face of the form. An authorized person shall sign the bond. Any person signing in a representative capacity (e.g., an attorney-in-fact) must furnish evidence of authority if that representative is not a member of the firm, partnership, or joint venture, or an officer of the corporation involved.

3. (a) Corporations executing the bond as sureties must appear on the Department of the Treasury's list of approved sureties and must act within the limitation listed therein. Where more than one corporate surety is involved, their names and addresses shall appear in the spaces (Surety A, Surety B, etc.) headed "CORPORATE SURETY(IES)." In the space designated "SURETY(IES)" on the face of the form, insert only the letter identification of the sureties.

(b) Where individual sureties are involved, a completed Affidavit of Individual Surety (Standard Form 28) for each individual surety, shall accompany the bond. The Government may require the surety to furnish additional substantiating information concerning their financial capability.

4. Corporations executing the bond shall affix their corporate seals. Individuals shall execute the bond opposite the word "Corporate Seal", and shall affix an adhesive seal if executed in Maine, New Hampshire, or any other jurisdiction requiring adhesive seals.

5. Type the name and title of each person signing this bond in the space provided.

PAYMENT BOND *(See instructions on reverse)*	DATE BOND EXECUTED *(Must be same or later than date of contract)*	OMB No.:9000-0045

Public reporting burden for this collection of information is estimate to average 25 minutes per response, including the time for reviewing instructions, searching existing data sources, gathering and maintaining the data needed, and completing and reviewing the collection of information. Send comments regarding this burden estimate or any other aspect of this collection of information, including suggestions for reducing this burden, to the FAR Secretariat (MVR), Federal Acquisition Policy Division, GSA, Washington, DC 20405

PRINCIPAL *(Legal name and business address)*

TYPE OF ORGANIZATION *("X" one)*

☐ INDIVIDUAL   ☐ PARTNERSHIP

☐ JOINT VENTURE   ☐ CORPORATION

STATE OF INCORPORATION

SURETY(IES) *(Name(s) and business address(es)*

PENAL SUM OF BOND

MILLION(S)	THOUSAND(S)	HUNDRED(S)	CENTS
CONTRACT DATE		CONTRACT NO.	

OBLIGATION:

We, the Principal and Surety(ies), are firmly bound to the United States of America (hereinafter called the Government) in the above penal sum. For payment of the penal sum, we bind ourselves, our heirs, executors, administrators, and successors, jointly and severally. However, where the Sureties are corporations acting as co-sureties, we, the Sureties, bind ourselves in such sum "jointly and severally" as well as "severally" only for the purpose of allowing a joint action or actions against any or all of us. For all other purposes, each Surety binds itself, jointly and severally with the Principal, for the payment of the sum shown opposite the name of the Surety. If no limit of liability is indicated, the limit of liability is the full amount of the penal sum.

CONDITIONS:

The above obligation is void if the Principal promptly makes payment to all persons having a direct relationship with the Principal or a subcontractor of the Principal for furnishing labor, material or both in the prosecution of the work provided for in the contract identified above, and any authorized modifications of the contract that subsequently are made. Notice of those modifications to the Surety(ies) are waived.

WITNESS:

The Principal and Surety(ies) executed this payment bond and affixed their seals on the above date.

PRINCIPAL

SIGNATURE(S)	1. (Seal)	2. (Seal)	3. (Seal)	Corporate Seal
NAME(S) & TITLE(S) *(Typed)*	1.	2.	3.	

INDIVIDUAL SURETY(IES)

SIGNATURE(S)	1. (Seal)	2. (Seal)
NAME(S) *(Typed)*	1.	2.

CORPORATE SURETY(IES)

SURETY A	NAME & ADDRESS		STATE OF INC.	LIABILITY LIMIT $	Corporate Seal
	SIGNATURE(S)	1.	2.		
	NAME(S) & TITLE(S) *(Typed)*	1.	2.		

AUTHORIZED FOR LOCAL REPRODUCTION
Previous edition is usable

STANDARD FORM 25A (REV. 10-98)
Prescribed by GSA-FAR (48 CFR) 53.2228(c)

CORPORATE SURETY(IES) *(Continued)*

SURETY B	NAME & ADDRESS		STATE OF INC.	LIABILITY LIMIT $	Corporate Seal
	SIGNATURE(S)	1.	2.		
	NAME(S) & TITLE(S) *(Typed)*	1.	2.		

SURETY C	NAME & ADDRESS		STATE OF INC.	LIABILITY LIMIT $	Corporate Seal
	SIGNATURE(S)	1.	2.		
	NAME(S) & TITLE(S) *(Typed)*	1.	2.		

SURETY D	NAME & ADDRESS		STATE OF INC.	LIABILITY LIMIT $	Corporate Seal
	SIGNATURE(S)	1.	2.		
	NAME(S) & TITLE(S) *(Typed)*	1.	2.		

SURETY E	NAME & ADDRESS		STATE OF INC.	LIABILITY LIMIT $	Corporate Seal
	SIGNATURE(S)	1.	2.		
	NAME(S) & TITLE(S) *(Typed)*	1.	2.		

SURETY F	NAME & ADDRESS		STATE OF INC.	LIABILITY LIMIT $	Corporate Seal
	SIGNATURE(S)	1.	2.		
	NAME(S) & TITLE(S) *(Typed)*	1.	2.		

SURETY G	NAME & ADDRESS		STATE OF INC.	LIABILITY LIMIT $	Corporate Seal
	SIGNATURE(S)	1.	2.		
	NAME(S) & TITLE(S) *(Typed)*	1.	2.		

INSTRUCTIONS

1. This form, for the protection of persons supplying labor and material, is used when a payment bond is required under the Act of August 24, 1935, 49 Stat. 793 (40 U.S.C. 270a-270e). Any deviation from this form will require the written approval of the Administrator of General Services.

2. Insert the full legal name and business address of the Principal in the space designated "Principal" on the face of the form. An authorized person shall sign the bond. Any person signing in a representative capacity (e.g., an attorney-in-fact) must furnish evidence of authority if that representative is not a member of the firm, partnership, or joint venture, or an officer of the corporation involved.

3. (a) Corporations executing the bond as sureties must appear on the Department of the Treasury's list of approved sureties and must act within the limitation listed therein. Where more than one corporate surety is involved, their names and addresses shall appear in the spaces (Surety A, Surety B, etc.) headed "CORPORATE SURETY(IES)." In the space

designated "SURETY(IES)" on the face of the form, insert only the letter identification of the sureties.

(b) Where individual sureties are involved, a completed Affidavit of Individual Surety (Standard Form 28) for each individual surety, shall accompany the bond. The Government may require the surety to furnish additional substantiating information concerning their financial capability.

4. Corporations executing the bond shall affix their corporate seals. Individuals shall execute the bond opposite the word "Corporate Seal", and shall affix an adhesive seal if executed in Maine, New Hampshire, or any other jurisdiction requiring adhesive seals.

5. Type the name and title of each person signing this bond in the space provided.